HISTORY OF MY LIFE

GIACOMO CASANOVA

Chevalier de Seingalt

HISTORY OF MY LIFE

FIRST TRANSLATED INTO ENGLISH IN ACCORDANCE
WITH THE ORIGINAL FRENCH MANUSCRIPT

by Willard R. Trask

VOLUMES 7 AND 8

———————

THE JOHNS HOPKINS UNIVERSITY PRESS
Baltimore and London

Originally published as *Histoire de Ma Vie,* Edition intégrale, by
Jacques Casanova de Seingalt, Vénitien, by F. A. Brockhaus,
Wiesbaden, Librairie Plon, Paris, 1960. © F. A. Brockhaus,
Wiesbaden, 1960.

This edition originally published in the United States as a Helen and
Kurt Wolff book by Harcourt, Brace & World, Inc.
Johns Hopkins Paperbacks edition, 1997
9 8 7 6 5 4 3 2

The Johns Hopkins University Press
2715 North Charles Street
Baltimore, Maryland 21218-4363
The Johns Hopkins Press Ltd., London

Library of Congress Catalog Card Number 97-70304

A catalog record for this book is available from the British Library.

ISBN 0-8018-5665-5 (pbk.: Vols. 7 and 8)

HISTORY OF MY LIFE

Volume 7

CONTENTS

Volume 7

LIST OF PLATES

Volume 7

VOLUME 7

VOLUME I

CHAPTER I

Conclusion of my adventure with the nun
from Chambéry. My flight from Aix.

"YESTERDAY," SHE said, "you left with me two portraits of my Venetian sister M. M. I beg you to make me a present of them."

"They are yours."

"I thank you. So much for that. The second favor I ask of you is to accept my portrait; such as it is, I will give it to you tomorrow."

"It will be, my dear friend, the most cherished of all my jewels; but I am surprised that you ask it of me as a favor, when in fact you are doing me one which I should never have dared ask of you. What can I possibly do to deserve your wanting my portrait?"

"Ah, my dear friend! It would be very precious to me; but God preserve me from having it at the convent."

"I will have myself painted in the dress of St. Aloysius Gonzaga,[1] or of St. Anthony of Padua."[2]

"It would damn me."

To my surprise she was wearing a dimity corset with

pink ribbons and a cambric shift, on which, though politeness did not permit me to ask where they came from, I kept my eyes; but easily guessing my thought, she laughed and said they were a present the peasant woman had given her because she was fond of lying in bed.

"Finding herself rich," she said, "she tries to think of every way to convince her benefactor that she is grateful to him. Look at this great bed; she was certainly thinking of you; look at the fine sheets. This very fine shift, I must admit, pleases me. I shall sleep the better tonight, provided I can defend myself against the seductive dreams which set my soul on fire last night."

"Do you think this bed, these sheets, and such a shift can deliver your soul from the dreams which you fear?"

"On the contrary. Softness excites the senses to voluptuousness. I will leave her all these things, for what would they say at the convent if they saw me bedded in this fashion? But you seem sad. You were so gay last night."

"How could I be gay when I see myself constrained not to fondle you again because I am sure to give you pain?"

"Say instead 'sure to give me too much pleasure.'"

"Then consent to feel pleasure for the sake of the pleasure it lies with you to give me."

"But your pleasure is innocent, and mine is sinful."

"What would you do if mine were as sinful as yours?"

"You would have made me unhappy last evening, for I could have refused you nothing."

"Unhappy? Consider that you would not have had to fight against dreams and would have slept perfectly well. In short, by giving you this corset the peasant woman has given you a present which will make me unhappy all my life; for I should at least have seen my infants without fearing bad dreams."

"But you cannot be angry with the peasant woman

on that account, for if she believes we love each other
she must also know that nothing is easier than to unlace
a corset. My dear friend, I do not want to see you sad.
That is all that matters.''

As she uttered these words her beautiful face became
red as fire, and she let me cover it with kisses. The peasant woman came up to set a pretty, brand-new table, just
as I was about to unlace her without seeing even a
shadow of resistance on her face.

This favorable omen put me in a good humor; but, for
her part, I saw M. M. become pensive. I took good care
not to ask the reason, for I knew it, and I did not want
to come to conditions which religion and honor would
have made inviolable. I stimulated her appetite by setting
her the example of mine, and she drank claret with as
much relish as I did, untroubled by any apprehension
that, not being accustomed to it, she might find it rous-
ing her to a gaiety which is the inveterate enemy of
continence, though favorable to the other virtues. She
could not be aware of this, for her gaiety itself, by
increasing the brilliance of her reason, made her think
it all the more admirable and more firmly attached to
pure sentiment than before supper.

As soon as we were alone I congratulated her on her
high spirits, assuring her that it was all I needed to rid
me of gloom and to make me pass whole hours with her
as if they were minutes.

''Only be generous, my dear friend, of the same gifts
you gave me last evening.''

''I would rather damn myself, my dear friend, and
die a hundred times, than risk seeming ungrateful to
you. There.''

With that, she pulled off her cap, let her hair fall, took
off her corset, and, drawing her arms out of her shift,
displayed herself to my amorous eyes even as we see the
sirens in Correggio's[3] most beautiful canvas. But when

I saw her move over to make room for me, I understood
that it was time to reason no more and that love demanded I should seize the moment.

I flung myself beside her rather than on her, and,
clasping her in my arms, I pressed my lips to hers. A
moment later she turned her head aside, and, since she
closed her eyes, I thought she was going to sleep, so I
moved a little away from her to contemplate the incal-
culable riches which fortune and love were offering me
and of which I was to take possession. M. M. was asleep;
she could not be pretending, she was asleep. But even if
she had been pretending, could I hold her ruse against
her? Be it real or feigned, her sleep tells the intelligent
lover of an adored object that he is unworthy to enjoy
her the moment he begins to wonder if he may or may
not take advantage of it. If it is real, he risks nothing;
if it is feigned, can he accord her a more inadequate or
more dishonorable return than to doubt of her consent?
But M. M. was incapable of feigning. The poppies of
Morpheus made her face radiant. She muttered words
which I could not understand; she was dreaming.

I decide to undress, though whether to court a sleep
like hers, or to calm my ardor by taking possession of
her, I do not know.

Having lain down beside her, I do not fear to wake
her by clasping her in my arms; the movement she made
to meet mine convinced me that she was continuing her
dream, and that whatever I might do could only help
to make it real. I finish drawing off her delicate shift,
and she stirs like an infant which, feeling itself un-
swaddled, takes a deep breath. I consummated the sweet
crime in her and with her; but before the climax she
opened her beautiful eyes.

"Oh, God," she cried in a dying voice, "so it is true!"

After uttering these words she put her mouth against
mine to receive my soul, giving me hers. But for that
happy exchange we should both have perished. Four or

five hours later, waking in the same position and seeing
the faint light of dawn mingling with the pale light
from the unsnuffed candles, we tranquilly and content-
edly learned from each other all the links in our sweet
story.

"But we will talk about it more this evening," she
said; "let us dress quickly. We love each other, and we
have crowned our love. I am freed at last from all my
anxieties. We have followed our destiny, obeying the
commands of imperious nature. Do you still love me?"

"Can you doubt it? I will answer you this evening."

I dressed again very quickly, and I left her in bed. I
saw her laugh when she went to look for her shift, which
she did not remember having taken off.

I reached my lodging in broad daylight. Leduc, who
had not gone to bed, gave me a letter from Madame Z^4
which he had received at eleven o'clock. I had missed
her supper and the honor of escorting her to Chambéry;
but I had not even remembered either engagement. I
was sorry, but I did not know what to do about it. I
open her letter and see only six lines; but they said a
great deal. She advised me never to go to Turin, for
there she would find means to avenge herself for the
cutting affront I had put on her. She reproached me for
having publicly shown contempt for her by not going
to her supper, saying that it dishonored her.

There was no possibility of my going there. I tore up
her letter, I had my hair dressed, and I went to the fountain.

Everyone begins by chiding me for not having appeared at Madame Z's supper; in my defense I allege
my regimen, which did not allow me to sup; but they
laugh at me and say that all is known, and the Marquis's[5]
mistress, taking my arm, tells me in so many words that
I have the reputation of being fickle; politeness demands
my replying that I do not have that base fault, but that
in any case no one could reproach me with it if I had

the honor of serving a lady like herself; my compliment
flatters her; and I at once repent of having paid it
when, in the most gracious way, she asks me why I do not
come to breakfast at the Marquis's sometimes. I reply
that I supposed he had things to do; she answers that
he has not and that he would consider it a pleasure, and
she ends by making me promise to go there the next
morning, saying, as if in passing, that he always breakfasted in her room.

The woman was the widow of a man of rank, fairly
young, indubitably pretty, and perfectly versed in all
the chatter of the wits; but she did not appeal to me.
Having just had Madame *Z*, and having crowned my
desires with the nun, I was not able at the time to think
even passingly of a new object. Yet I had to pretend I
considered myself very fortunate in the lady's giving me
the preference over anyone else. She asked the Marquis
if she might go back to the inn, and he answered that
he had business to finish with the person with whom he
was talking, and that I might escort her. On the way she
said that if Madame *Z* had not left she would not have
dared to take my arm. I could answer only equivocally,
for I had absolutely no wish to enter into a relationship
with her. Nevertheless I had to see her upstairs to her
room, where I had to sit down and where, since I had
slept very little during the previous night, I found myself yawning. I asked her a thousand pardons, swearing
that I was ill; and she believed it. Indeed, I should have
gone to sleep if I had not put a little errhine under my
nose; by making me sneeze it forced me to stay awake.

The Marquis arrived and, saying that he was pleased
to find me still with her, proposed a game of quinze. I
asked him to excuse me, and Madame said with a laugh
that if I went on sneezing so hard I really could not play.
We went down to dinner, and I let them persuade me
to make the bank, all the more easily because my losses
of the night before still rankled.

I made it, as always, of five hundred louis, and about seven o'clock I announced the last deal to the company, despite the fact that my bank was diminished by two thirds. But the Marquis and two other heavy players having undertaken to break me, Fortune favored me to such effect that in the end I had recouped and was the winner by two or three hundred louis. I left, promising the company that I would make the same bank the next day. All the ladies had won, because Desarmoises[6] had orders to let them play as they pleased so long as he saw that their stakes were not high. After going to put my money away in my room and telling Leduc that I would spend the night elsewhere, I arrived at my new idol's lodging, soaked to the skin by a heavy rain which caught me halfway there.

I found my love dressed as a nun and lying on the Roman couch. When the peasant woman had left, after drying me as well as she could, I asked M. M. why she had not waited for me in bed.

"I never felt better, my dear friend, except for a slight discomfort which, according to what my midwife says, will remain with me for another five weeks. So I got up to have supper at the table. If you wish, we will go to bed afterward."

"But I hope you will wish it too."

"Alas, I am lost! I believe I shall die when the time arrives for me to leave you."

"Come with me to Rome, and leave everything to me. You will become my wife. We will make each other happy until death."

"I could never bring myself to that, and I beg you not to speak of it again."

Since I was certain that I should spend the night with her, we passed an hour in pleasant talk. At the end of our supper the peasant woman brought her a package and wished us good night. I asked her what the package contained, and she said that it was the present she had promised me, her portrait to the life, but that I was not to see it until she had gone to bed. Being both curious and impatient to see it, I said that it was a foolish whim, and she said that I would approve of it.

I insisted on undressing her myself and taking off her cap; and when she was in bed she opened the package and handed me a piece of parchment, on which I saw a very good likeness of her, stark naked and in the same pose as M. M. in the portrait which I had given her earlier. I praised the skillful painter who had made so good a copy, only changing the color of the eyes and the hair.

"It is not a copy at all," she said, "for he would not have had time. He only made her eyes black, her hair like mine, and her fleece thicker. So you can now say that you have in one portrait the image of the first M. M. and the second, who ought by rights to make you forget the first, who disappeared in the decent portrait too, for there I am dressed as a nun and with black eyes. In such a portrait I can let everyone see me."

"You cannot conceive how dear this gift is to me. Tell me, my angel, how you got your plan so well carried out."

"I told it yesterday to the peasant woman, who said she had a foster son at Annecy who was learning to paint miniatures, but that she would only commission him to take the two miniatures to the most skillful miniature painter in Geneva, who for four or five louis would make the metamorphosis on the spot in two or three hours. I entrusted the two portraits to her, and here they are, executed to perfection. It seems she did not receive them until you saw her bring them to me. Tomorrow morning you can learn more of our little story from her."

"Your peasant is a woman among women, and I must reimburse her. But tell me why you did not want to give me your portrait before you undressed. May I guess the reason?''

''Guess.''

''So that I can at once put you in the same pose as that in which you are painted.''

''Exactly.''

''That charming idea comes from love, but now you must wait for me to undress too.''

Both of us thus being in the divine costume of innocence, I placed M. M. as she appeared on the parchment, and she submitted. Divining what I was about to do, she opened her arms; but I told her to wait a moment, for I, too, had something in a package which should be precious to her.

I then take from my portfolio a little jacket of very fine, transparent skin, eight inches long and closed at one end, and which by way of a pouch string at its open end had a narrow pink ribbon. I display it to her, she looks at it, laughs, and says I had used just such jackets with her Venetian sister, and that she was curious about it.

''I will put it on you myself,'' she said, ''and you cannot imagine how glad I am. Tell me why you did not use it last night? I think it impossible that I did not conceive. Alas for me! What shall I do four or five months from now when I can have no doubt of my second pregnancy?''

''My dear friend, we must make up our minds not to think about it, for if the harm is done there is no remedy. But what I can tell you is that experience and deductions from the known laws of nature can lead us to hope that what we did yesterday in the intoxication of our senses will not have the result we fear. It has been said, and indeed written, that one cannot fear it before a certain thing appears which I believe you have not yet seen.''

"You are right, it has not."

"So let us dismiss this panic terror, which at the moment can only be fatal to us."

"You console me completely. But, arguing from what you have just said, I do not see why you fear today what did not need to be feared yesterday. I am in the same condition."

"The event, my angel, has often proved the wisest natural scientists wrong, despite their so-called experiential proofs. Nature is wiser than they; let us beware of defying her, and forgive ourselves if we defied her yesterday."

"I love to hear you talk so wisely. So be it. Let us be prudent. There you are, caparisoned by my hands. It is nearly the same thing; but despite the fineness and transparency of the skin, the little fellow pleases me less well in costume. It seems that this covering degrades him, or degrades me—one or the other."

"Both, my angel; but let us at this juncture turn a blind eye to certain speculative ideas which can only spoil our pleasure."

"We will very soon recover it in all its purity; for the moment let me enjoy my reason, to which I have never before in all my life dared to give the reins on this subject; it was Love who invented these little jackets, but he had to ally himself with Precaution; and it seems to me that the alliance must have been displeasing to him, for it belongs only to the dark realm of Policy."

"Alas, that is true! You astonish me. But, my dear friend, we will philosophize afterward."

"Wait another minute; for I have never seen a man, and I have never been so curious to see one as I am now. Ten months ago I should have said that it was the devil who invented these pouches, and today I say that their inventor was not so devilish, for if the hunchback Cou . . . had used one he would not have exposed me to losing my honor and my life. But tell me, I beg you,

how the shameless artisans who make these pouches are
allowed to live in peace, for they must be known and
should be excommunicated a hundred times, or subjected
to large fines and corporal punishment if they are Jews,
as I believe. Look. The one who made this one for you
measured you badly. Here it is too narrow, there too
wide; it is almost an arc; it is made for a curved body.
What a fool, ignorant of his trade! But what do I see!''

"You make me laugh. It is your fault. Feel, feel. It
was bound to happen. I foresaw it.''

"You couldn't wait another minute? And you're still
at it; I'm sorry, my dear friend; but you are right.
O God, what a pity!''

"Oh, there's no great harm done.''

"No great harm done? Alas for me! He is dead? You
laugh?''

"Let me laugh; for your fear delights me. In a minute
you will see the little fellow revived, and so full of life
that next time he will not die so easily.''

"It is unbelievable.''

I take it off, I put it aside, and I offer her another one,
which pleases her better for she thinks it will fit me
better, and she bursts out laughing when she sees that
she can put it on me. M. M. was ignorant of these miracles of nature. Before she knew me, her mind, under
strict restraint, had been unable to find its way to truth;
no sooner was it free than its own inner elasticity had
carried it beyond its barriers with all the swiftness which
was its natural endowment, after which it proceeded
more slowly. She said that if the jacket should break at
its end during the act, the precaution would be useless.
I convinced her of the difficulty of such an accident; I
informed her that these little pouches were made in England,[7] that one bought them in whatever sizes they happened to come, and I told her where such skins were to
be obtained. After all this talk we surrendered to love,
then to sleep, then again to love, until it was time for

me to go back to my lodging. The peasant woman told me that her foster son had spent only four louis and that she had made him a present of two. I gave her twelve.

I slept until noon, not appearing for breakfast at the Marquis de Prié's, but I sent him word. His mistress was sulky with me all through dinner, but she softened when I let her persuade me to make the bank; however, seeing that she was playing for high stakes, I did not let her go on; after being stopped two or three times she retired to her room; but her lover was winning, and I losing, when the taciturn Duke of Roxburghe arrived from Geneva with Schmit,[8] his tutor, and two other Englishmen. He came to the bank, saying nothing to me except "How do you do, Sir,"[9] and played, urging his two friends to do likewise. After the deal, seeing my bank on its last legs, I sent Leduc to my room to bring me my strongbox, from which I took five rolls of a hundred louis. The Marquis de Prié said coolly that he would be my partner on half shares, and I no less coolly asked him to give me leave not to accept his offer. He continued to punt, taking no offense at my refusal, and when I laid down the cards to end the game, he was ahead by nearly two hundred louis; but most of the others having lost, and especially one of the two Englishmen, I was left with over a thousand louis. The Marquis having asked me to invite him for chocolate in my room the next morning, I replied that it would be an honor. After taking Leduc back to my quarters with my strongbox, I went to my cottage, rather well satisfied with my day's work.

I found my new angel with a look of sadness on her pretty face.

"A nephew of my hostess," she said, "a peasant lad who she assures me is very discreet and who knows a lay sister at my convent, arrived from Chambéry an hour ago and said that the lay sister had told him that day after tomorrow two lay sisters would leave at day-

break to come here and take me back to the convent. That
is the whole reason for my sadness and my tears.''

''She was not to send them until a week or ten days
hence.''

''She acted sooner.''

''We are unhappy even in our happiness. Make up
your mind. Let us go to Rome.''

''No. I have lived enough. Let me return to my tomb.''

After our supper I told the peasant woman that she
must send her nephew to Chambéry with orders to leave
there and come back to her the moment the lay sisters
set out; traveling quickly, he would reach us at least
two hours before they did; I promised my angel I would
stay with her until they arrived. I thus dispelled her
sorrow; but I left her at midnight in order to be at my
lodging in the morning, having promised to give the
Marquis breakfast; he came, accompanied by his mistress and by two other ladies with their lovers.

Besides chocolate I gave them everything I could think
of which might be supposed appropriate to a so-called
breakfast; and after it I ordered Leduc to lock my door
and tell everyone I was ill and busy writing in bed, so
that I could see no one. I told him that I would be out
all day, all night, and all the next day. In conclusion,
I ordered him to wait for me until I returned, never
leaving my room except when he could not help it. I
went to dine with my passion, determined not to leave
her until a half hour before the arrival of the lay sisters.
When she saw me and heard that I would not leave her
until half an hour before the two women the Abbess
was sending for her arrived, she trembled with joy. We
conceived the idea of not having dinner, supping choicely,
and going to bed afterward, not to get up again until
the peasant lad came to announce the arrival of the two
nuns. We immediately informed the peasant woman,
who declared our plan sublime.

We did not find the hours long. Two lovers are never

at a loss for things to talk about, since they are themselves the subjects of their discourse. After a very choice
supper we spent twelve hours in bed, now making love,
now sleeping. The next day after dining we went back
to bed, and at four o'clock the peasant woman came up
to tell us that the lay sisters would arrive at six. We then
took leave of each other in every way of which we were
capable, and I sealed our last farewell with my blood. If
the first M. M. had seen it, the second was entitled to
see it too, and she was terrified, but I easily calmed her.
I begged her to keep fifty louis for me, assuring her that
I would come for them to her grating before two years
had passed, and she was well aware of the reason which
prevented her from refusing me the favor. She spent
the last quarter of an hour shedding tears, and I held
mine back only that they might not increase her grief.
After promising the peasant woman that I would see her
again the next evening, I returned to my lodging, where
I went to bed, only to rise at daybreak and start out
on the road to Chambéry. A quarter of a league from
Aix I saw my angel, walking slowly, and the two lay
sisters, who asked me for alms in God's name. I gave
them a louis and wished them a good journey. M. M.
did not look at me.

Retracing my steps, I went to the peasant woman's,
who told me that M. M. had set out at daybreak, charging her only to tell me that she would expect me at the
grating. After giving her nephew all the silver money
I had, I went and ordered all my luggage tied onto my
coach, and I should have left at once if I had had horses.
I return to the inn and go upstairs to the Marquis's room
to take my leave. I find his mistress alone. I tell her that
I am to leave at two o'clock; she replies that I shall
not leave, that I will do her the favor of staying on for
two more days. I say that I am greatly flattered by her
urgency, but that business of the utmost importance
obliges me to leave. Still saying that I must stay, she

rises, goes to a large mirror, and unlaces her corset, ostensibly in order to lace it better after readjusting her shift. In the course of the maneuver she shows me two globes capable of making all resistance vain, but I pretend not to see them. I saw a calculated plan, but I was determined to foil it. She puts one foot on the edge of the sofa on which I was sitting, and, on the pretext of fastening a garter below her knee, she lets me see a perfectly turned leg, then, shifting to the other, she gives me a glimpse of beauties which would have conquered me if the Marquis had not arrived. He proposes a game of quinze at small stakes, the lady wants to go halves with me, I feel ashamed to refuse her; she sits down beside me and deals to him. When dinner was announced I stopped, losing forty louis. Madame said she owed me twenty of them. At dessert Leduc announces that my carriage is at the door. I rise, Madame says she owes me twenty louis, she insists on paying them, and she makes me accompany her to her room.

No sooner are we there than she tells me earnestly that if I leave I will dishonor her, for the whole company knows she has undertaken to make me stay. She says she does not think herself a woman to be scorned, she pushes me down on the sofa, and she returns to the charge, again fastening her accursed garters in my sight. Unable to deny seeing what she sees that I see, I praise everything, I touch, I kiss, she lets herself fall on me, and she triumphs when she finds the inevitable sign of my sensibility; kissing me mouth to mouth, she promises to be wholly mine the next day. Not knowing how else to get rid of her, I signify that I will hold her to her promise; and I am just saying that I will have the horses unharnessed when the Marquis comes in. I go downstairs as if intending to come back, hearing him tell me that he will give me my revenge. I do not answer. I walk out of the inn, I get into my carriage, and I leave.

CHAPTER II

The caretaker's daughters. The horoscopes.
Mademoiselle Roman.

I STOPPED at Chambéry only to change horses and arrived at Grenoble, where, intending to stay for a week but being poorly lodged, I did not have my trunks untied. At the post I found all the letters I expected, among them one from Madame d'Urfé, containing another addressed to a Lorrainese officer, the Baron de Valenglart.[1] She said that he was a man of learning and that he would introduce me at all the good houses in the town.

I at once go to this officer, who, after reading the letter, offers to do anything for me which lies in his power. He was a pleasant, rather elderly man who fifteen years earlier had been a friend of Madame d'Urfé and, much more intimately, of her daughter the Princess of Estouteville.[2] I begged him to find me a good lodging, for I was very uncomfortable at the inn. After thinking for a little he said that he could arrange for me to lodge in a splendid house outside of the city,[3] from which I should see the Isère.[4] The caretaker was a cook, and for the sake of serving me in that capacity he would lodge me gratis, for, the house being for sale, he was hoping to find someone who would fall in love with it and buy it. It belonged to the widow of some judge whose name I have forgotten. We go to see it; I take an apartment of three rooms, I order him to prepare supper for two, impressing it upon him that I am an epicure, a hearty eater, and not at all stingy. At the same time I ask Monsieur de Valenglart to be so good as to sup with me. The caretaker says that if I am not satisfied I must tell him so; he at once sent a man to the inn with a note from me in which I ordered Leduc to come to my new quarters with all my luggage; and so I am well lodged. On the ground floor I see three charming girls and the caretaker's wife, who curtsy to me. Monsieur de Valenglart takes me to the concert,[5] saying that he will introduce me to everyone. I begged him to introduce me to no one, on the understanding that, when I had seen the ladies, I would tell him which of them had inspired me with a wish to make their acquaintance.

The only one who struck me in the whole large company was a tall young lady of modest demeanor, dark haired, very well built, and dressed very simply. This extremely interesting girl, after giving me a single glance from her beautiful eyes, stubbornly refused to look at me again. My vanity at once made me think that it was only so that I should be at full liberty to study her impeccable beauty. It was on this girl that I instantly set my sights, as if all Europe were only a seraglio provided for my pleasures. I told Valenglart that I wanted to make her acquaintance; he replied that she was discreet, received no one, and was extremely poor.

"Those three qualities increase my interest."

"I assure you there is nothing to be done there."

"That is what I want."

"When we leave the concert I will introduce you to her aunt—there she is."

After doing me that honor he came to supper with me. I thought the caretaker-cook a man of exactly the same pattern as Lebel.[6] He had me served at table by his two daughters, who were as pretty as sweethearts, and I saw Valenglart delighted to see me satisfied; but I saw him put out when he saw fifteen dishes in five courses.

"This fellow," he said, "is making fools of you and me."

"The fellow," I said, "has divined my taste. Did you not find everything excellent?"

"True. But—"

"Fear nothing. I love to spend."

"Then excuse me. I want you to be satisfied."

He gave us exquisite wines and at dessert a ratafia[7] superior to the Turkish visnat[8] which I had drunk in Yusuf Ali's[9] house seventeen years earlier. When he came upstairs at the end of supper I told him in the presence of his daughters that he deserved to be first cook to Louis XV.

"Do as well every day, and even better if you can; but always let me have the account the next morning."

"You are right."

"Please always give me ices too, and put two more lights on the table. What I see there are tallow candles, if I am not mistaken; I do not want to see any more of them. I am a Venetian."[10]

"It is your valet's fault, Monsieur, because he said he was sick and went to bed, but after eating a hearty supper."

"He is an imaginary invalid."

"He asked my wife to make you the chocolate he gave her for tomorrow morning; but I will whip it myself."

Surprised and very pleased, Valenglart said that apparently Madame d'Urfé had been making fun of him when she had instructed him to keep my expenditures in check. We remained at table until eleven o'clock, talking and emptying a bottle of the divine liqueur of Grenoble. It is composed of brandy, sugar, cherries, and cinnamon. I thanked him as I saw him to my carriage, which took him home; I asked him to share my table with me night and morning, and he promised to do so except on the days he would be on guard duty. During supper I gave him my bill of exchange on Zappata,[11] which I endorsed in his presence with the name Seingalt, by which Madame d'Urfé had announced me. He assured me that he would have it negotiated the next day, and he kept his word. At nine o'clock a banker brought me four hundred louis. I had thirteen hundred in my strongbox. I always dreaded being a pinchpenny. I took the greatest pleasure in the thought that Valenglart would write all that he had seen and heard to the avaricious Madame d'Urfé, who had a mania for preaching economy to me. I laughed when, returning to my apartment, I saw the caretaker's two daughters.

Leduc did not wait for me to tell him that he must trump up some excuse for not serving me. He knew that when there were pretty girls in the houses in which I stayed I did not like to see him about.

Seeing the two girls, who appeared to be perfectly virtuous, eagerly serving me with an air of the greatest confidence, I took it into my head to convince them that I deserved it. They removed my shoes and stockings, arranged my hair for the night, and put me into my nightshirt with the greatest decency. When I was in bed I told them to lock my door and to bring me my chocolate at eight o'clock.

I could not refrain from examining myself and finding that I was happy. In perfect health and in the prime of life, with no duties, with no need to look ahead, amply provided with money, dependent upon no one, lucky at cards, and favorably received by the women who inter-

ested me, I had every justification for saying to myself:
"*Saute, Marquis!*" [12]

I fell asleep thinking of the young lady who had made
so strong an impression on me at the concert. Certain
that I would make her acquaintance, I was curious to
see what would come of it. She was discreet and poor,
and I discreet and rich; so she should not scorn my
friendship.

The next morning at eight o'clock I see my door open
and one of the caretaker's two daughters bringing me
my chocolate, saying that Leduc had been feverish and
that her cousin would take him a bowl of broth in bed.
I say that my chocolate is very well prepared, I ask her
her name, she replies that she is named Rose and her
sister Manon, whereupon Manon herself appears with
my shirt, which she had ironed. I thank her and tell
her she must not go to so much trouble except for shirts
with lace. The charming Manon says, blushing, that she
dresses her father's hair; and Rose laughs and says she
shaves him.

"In that case," I replied, "you will both be so kind
as to do the same for me until Leduc recovers."

Curious to see how the girl would shave me, I quickly
get up, while she goes to fetch hot water. Manon sets
out powder, pomade, and everything she needed on my
toilet table. Rose comes back, and acquits herself most
skillfully, whereupon I offer her my freshly washed and
shaven face for the first salutation of the day—it could
not have been cleaner. She does not understand me; I
tell her seriously but gently that she will mortify me if
she refuses me a kiss. She excuses herself with a sly
smile, saying that it is not the custom in Grenoble; I
insist, I say she shall not shave me again; her father
comes in with the account, he hears the dispute, he says
that it is the custom in Paris, that she kissed *him* after
shaving him, and that she should be as polite to me. She

thereupon kissed me with an air of sweet submission which made Manon laugh.

"Your turn will come," he told her, "when you have dressed his hair."

It was the best way to keep me from reducing his bill; but he need not have used it, for I found him honest and, when I deducted nothing, I saw him leave well content. I established a fixed price for the future, as I did not want to be bothered with going over an account every day.

Manon dressed my hair as skillfully as my late housekeeper, whom I always remembered with pleasure, and kissed me afterward, showing less hesitation than her sister. I foresaw the best from them both. They went downstairs when they saw the banker, who announced himself by saying that he had brought me four hundred louis.

The banker, who was a young man, said after paying me over the amount that, being lodged in this house, I must be happy.

"Certainly," I said, "for the two sisters are charming."

"And their cousin is even prettier. They are virtuous."

"And I think they are well off, too."

"Their father has an income of two thousand livres; they will marry merchants, and they will be free to choose."

After he leaves, I go downstairs, curious to see the cousin. I see the caretaker, I ask him where Leduc's room is, and he shows me the door. I enter, and I see him in bed in a dressing gown, with a book in his hand and a countenance which did not look like an invalid's.

"What is the matter with you?"

"I'm having a good time. I fell sick yesterday the minute I saw those three princesses, who are quite the equals of the housekeeper at Soleure who would not let

me kiss her. However, I am kept waiting a little too long
for my broth.''

"Monsieur Leduc, you are a scoundrel.''

"Do you want me to recover?''

"I want to see the end of this comedy, for it bores
me.''

I see the broth arrive, brought by the cousin. I decide
that the banker was right. I notice that, waiting on
Leduc, she looked the mistress of the house, while my
Spaniard looked nothing but what he was.

"I will dine in bed,'' he said to her.

"You shall be attended to.''

She leaves.

"She puts on great airs,'' he said, "but I know better.
You think her pretty, don't you?''

"I think you are insolent. You are up to your monkey
tricks, and you disgust me. Get up and serve me at table.
Afterward you will eat by yourself; you will be shown
respect, but you will no longer lodge in this room. The
caretaker will tell you where you will find your bed.''

Meeting the cousin as I go out, I tell her I am jealous
of the honor she has done my valet, so I beg her to spare
herself the trouble in the future. After that I told the
caretaker to lodge him in a closet where I could ring
for him at night if I needed him. Then I went to write
until Valenglart arrived.

I received him, embracing him and thanking him for
having found me a lodging such as I wanted. He said
that he had just called on the lady to whom he had introduced me. She was the wife of an advocate named
Morin[13] and the aunt of the young lady who had interested me; he had told her so, and she had promised to
send for her and keep her with her all day.

After eating very well we went to call on Madame
Morin, who received me with Parisian ease. She was the
mother of seven children, whom she introduced to me.
Her eldest daughter, who was neither pretty nor ugly,

was twelve years old; I took her for fourteen and said so. At that she fetched a little book in which she showed me the year, day, hour, and minute of her birth. Seeing such precision, I ask if her horoscope has been cast; she replies that she has found no one able to do her the favor. I answer that there is still time; and *God* made me add that it would be I who would cast it for her.

Just then Monsieur Morin comes in, she introduces him to me, and after the customary compliments she returns to the subject of the horoscope. The gentleman says, very sensibly, that judicial astrology[14] is a science which, if not false, is at least highly suspect, that he had dabbled in it for a time, but that he had finally given it up, contenting himself with the truths he learned from astronomy. Valenglart, who believed in astrology, argues with him; in the meanwhile I copy down the moment of Mademoiselle Morin's birth. Her father smiles and bows his head, and I see what he is thinking; but I have no idea of backing out. I made up my mind that day to become an astrologer.

But in comes the beautiful young lady, and her aunt introduces her to me by the name of Roman-Coupier,[15] daughter of her sister. She at once tells her of the ardent desire to make her acquaintance which she had inspired in me at the concert. She replies only by blushing, dropping me a pretty curtsy, and lowering two black eyes than which I did not remember having seen any more beautiful. She was seventeen years of age[16] and had very fair skin, black hair with very little powder, an excellent figure, splendid teeth, and on her lips the charming smile of modesty coupled with obligingness.

After a little polite conversation among the company, Monsieur Morin having gone about his business, I was invited to play quadrille,[17] at which I was considered incredibly unlucky when I had lost a louis. In Mademoiselle Roman I found a sound mind without artificiality or glitter or pretension; unfailing good spirits, an

admirable skill in pretending not to hear a too flattering
compliment or a jest to which she could not have responded without showing that she knew what she was
supposed not to know. Dressed very neatly, she had
about her none of those superfluities which indicate a
certain wealth, no earrings, no ring, no watch; around
her neck she had only a black ribbon from which hung
a small black cross. Except for that, I should not have
allowed myself to look at her beautiful bosom, which
was faultlessly proportioned and of which fashion and
education had accustomed her to display a third as innocently and openly as she displayed her cheeks, in which
lilies were mingled with roses. Examining her bearing to
see if I might hope, I could make nothing of it; she did
not indulge in a gesture; she made no response which
could give me the slightest hope; but neither did she give
me the slightest reason to despair. One small incident,
however, led me to hope a little. During supper, on the
pretext of arranging her napkin I squeezed her thigh
without seeing anything in her face to indicate that she
disapproved of the liberty I had taken. I invited the
whole company to dine and sup with me the next day,
telling Madame Morin that I should not go out, and so
she could have the use of my carriage, which would be
at her door awaiting her convenience. After dropping
Valenglart at his house, I went to my lodging, building
castles in Spain concerning my conquest of Mademoiselle
Roman.

I at once informed the caretaker that we would be
six for dinner and supper the next day. Leduc put me
to bed, saying that to punish him I had punished myself,
and asking if he should dress my hair. I told him he
might take a walk about Grenoble, coming back only in
time to serve at table.

"I will go and catch the pox."

"I will have you cured in the hospital."

Impudent, insolent, sly, lecherous, but obedient, dis-

creet, and loyal—I had to put up with him. The next
morning Rose, coming to bring me my chocolate, said
with a laugh that my valet had sent for a carriage and
a hire manservant and, after dressing like a lord, with
a sword at his side, had gone—or so he had told her—
to pay visits. We laughed. A moment later in came
Manon. I at once saw that the girls had made a com-
pact never to be alone with me separately. I did not like
it. Two or three minutes after I got up I see their cousin
come in with a package under her arm.

"I am delighted to see you, my beautiful young lady,
and to see you laughing, for yesterday I thought you too
serious."

"That is because Monsieur Leduc is apparently a
greater gentleman than you are, and you can imagine
that I did not dare to laugh; but you would have seen
me laugh half an hour ago when I saw him get into his
carriage all dressed up."

"Did he see you laugh?"

"If he wasn't blind."

"He will be mortified."

"I'm glad to hear it."

"You are charming. What have you in that package?"

"Some samples of our handiwork. They are gloves[18]
for men and women, made and embroidered by us."

"They look very fine. How much is the whole lot
worth?"

"Do you haggle?"

"Always."

"It is well to know."

After talking with the other girls for a little the cousin
takes pen in hand, counts the dozens, writes down the
various prices, then adds and says that the lot would
cost me two hundred and ten livres. I hand her nine
louis[19] and tell her to give me back four livres.

"You told me you haggle."

"You shouldn't have believed me."

She blushed and gave me the four livres. After I had Rose shave me they accepted my first salutations of the day as a matter of course, and the cousin, who came last, let me feel a tongue dipped in nectar. I saw that she would be kind at the first opportunity. Rose asked me if they might make bold to serve me at table.

"Please do."

"But we should like to know whom you are having to dine, for if it is officers from the garrison they are almost all such libertines that we wouldn't dare."

Thereupon I told them that I had invited Madame Morin and Mademoiselle Roman, and they were delighted. The cousin told me that in all Grenoble there was not a prettier or more discreet girl than Mademoiselle Roman, but that she would have difficulty finding a husband because she had nothing; I replied that she would find a rich man who would value her beauty and discretion at a million. After dressing my hair Manon left with her cousin, and, Rose remaining behind to dress me, I attacked her a little; but when she defended herself only too well I begged her pardon, assuring her that it would not happen again. When I was dressed I shut myself up to cast the horoscope I had promised Madame Morin. I easily filled eight pages with pedantic charlatanry. Since I made a particular point of saying what must have happened to her daughter up to the age she had then reached, and since I hit on the truth, my predictions concerning the future raised no doubt. I risked nothing, for they were all buttressed with "ifs." The "ifs" always constituted the whole science of astrologers, who have all been fools or knaves. Reading over the horoscope and finding it brilliant, I was not surprised. Being an accomplished cabalist, I must also be an accomplished astrologer.

At half past twelve the whole company arrived, and at one o'clock we sat down at table. I found that the caretaker was a man who needed rather to be discour-

aged than encouraged in his endeavors. Madame Morin
was very gracious to the three girls, whom she knew very
well, and Leduc stood behind her chair, waiting on her
very attentively and wearing a coat finer than mine.
When, at the end of the dinner, Mademoiselle Roman
congratulated me on the three beauties who were at my
service in this charming house, I spoke of their talent,
and, after going for the gloves I had bought, when I saw
them admired I managed to make her accept a dozen
pairs, urged on by her aunt and her cousin, who did me
the same honor. After that I gave Madame Morin her
daughter's horoscope, which her husband read. Though
he did not believe in it he could not help praising it, for
everything was in accordance with the influence of the
planets which together made up the astrological condition of the sky at the minute of his daughter's birth.
After spending two hours discussing astrology and two
more playing quadrille we went for a walk in the garden,
where the company were polite enough to let me talk
alone with the beautiful Mademoiselle Roman. Everything I said to her turned only on the passion she had
inspired in me, her beauty, her discretion, the purity of
my intentions, and my need to be loved if I was not to
remain unhappy all the rest of my life. She replied that
if it was God's will that she should marry, she would
consider herself happy if her husband should be like me;
I pressed my lips to her hand and, all on fire, I said that
I hoped she would not make me wait in vain. She then
turned, looking for her aunt. The day darkening, she
feared what might very well happen to her.

We returned to the apartment, where I made a little
bank at faro to amuse them. Madame Morin gave some
money to the two young ladies, who did not have a
copper, and Valenglart played for them so well that
when I stopped dealing to go to supper I had the pleasure of seeing that everyone had won.

We remained at table until midnight. The wind, which

was coming from the Alps, being too strong, I did not dare to insist on a walk in the garden. Madame Morin left, showering me with compliments, and I kissed, but with all due restraint.

Hearing someone singing in the kitchen, I go in, and I see that it is Leduc, so drunk that he could not stand. When he sees me he starts forward to beg my pardon; he falls, then vomits. He was carried off to bed. I thought the incident might prepare the way for the amusement which I very much wanted; and it might have done so if all the girls had not come in together. What is useful on one occasion is useless on another. The girls' character was such that I could never have had them except one at a time, without the knowledge of the two others. I must not risk failing in an attack which would later have denied me all hope of having them one by one. I saw Rose, openly jealous of her cousin, watching to see at which of them I looked. When I was in bed I dismissed them, and they left.

The next morning Rose came in alone, asking me for a stick of chocolate and saying that Leduc was ill in good earnest. She brings me my strongbox, and, giving her the stick of chocolate, I take her hand and make her feel that I love her, she pretends to be offended and leaves. Manon comes to my bed, showing me a cuff I had torn and asking if I wanted her to mend it. I take her hand, pretending to consider, and when she sees that I want to kiss it she bends down and lets me take the kiss which I see on her parted lips; I quickly take her hand again, and the thing was already begun when her cousin comes in. Manon draws away her hand and, holding the torn cuff, appears to be waiting for my answer. I say absently, and pretending not to see her cousin, that she will do me a favor if she will mend it when she has time, and she leaves.

Exasperated by these two disappointments, I think that her cousin will not leave me in the lurch, for she had given me an earnest the day before. I ask her for a handkerchief, she gives it to me, she does not resist my kiss, she lets me take her hand, and the thing would have been done if Rose had not come in with my chocolate. Both her cousin and I were easily able to regain our outward composure on the instant; but this third disappointment made me furious. I would gladly have killed Rose; however, I had to hide it, I sulked, but I had a right to do that because of the way she had repulsed me a quarter of an hour earlier. I declared the chocolate badly made; it was not true, but I said it. I got up, I would not let her shave me; but I let Manon dress my hair; the two others left, pretending to share a common indignation; but Rose was even more angry with her cousin than she was with Manon. Just then in comes Valenglart.

A man of punctilious honor and, despite his dabbling in the abstruse sciences, of great common sense, he said as we dined that he thought me a little melancholy and that if it sprang from some idea I might have conceived in regard to Mademoiselle Roman he advised me to think of it no more, unless I made up my mind to ask for her hand. I replied that I would be leaving in a few days. We found her at her aunt's.

She receives me in a friendly fashion which flatters me and encourages me to kiss her, making her sit down on my knee. Her aunt laughs, she blushes slightly, she hands me a slip of paper, and runs off. On it I read the year, day, hour, and minute of her birth; I understand perfectly. Her flight from my arms meant that I could expect no favors from her unless I cast her horoscope. Considering how to make the best use of the circumstance, I say that I will tell her if I can or cannot do her the favor at my apartment the next day if she will come there and stay for a ball I am giving. She looks at her aunt, and my proposal is accepted.

"The Russian" is announced. I see a man of my age,

very well built but rather slight, and dressed in traveling clothes. He makes a good appearance, Madame Morin receives him graciously, he speaks well, he is gay with a tinge of melancholy, he scarcely looks at me, and he never says a word to Mademoiselle Roman. Toward nightfall Monsieur Morin arrives, and the Russian gives him a flask full of a white liquid; then he makes to leave, but he is asked to stay for supper.

At table the talk is of his miraculous liquid. Monsieur Morin tells me that in three minutes he had removed every trace of a contusion on the forehead of a young man who had been struck by a misdirected billiard ball which everyone thought had cracked his skull. The Russian gentleman had only rubbed it with his liquid. He said modestly that it was a trifle of his own invention, and he talked chemistry with Valenglart at great length. I had no thought for anything but my beauty, the hope of possessing her the next day having taken away my appetite. I saw Valenglart home to his barracks, he said that no one knew the Russian, yet he was received everywhere.

"Has he a carriage?"

"Nothing—no servants and no money; he has been here for two weeks, but he asks nothing of anyone. The innkeeper allows him credit; he is supposed to be waiting for his servants and carriage to arrive from somewhere."

"It would be simpler to suppose him a vagabond."

"He does not appear to be one, as you saw yourself; and he has buckles set with excellent stones. Anyone can see them."

"Anyone can be deceived. He would sell them."

Back at my apartment, it was Rose who came alone to dress my hair for the night, but she was still sulking. I urged her to be gay; but finding her recalcitrant I told her to let me sleep and to inform her father that I wanted to give a ball the next night, in the room on the ground floor giving on the garden, and a supper for eighteen or twenty. The next morning I confirmed the order to him, saying that I wanted his daughters to dance.

Just as he was going downstairs with Rose, Manon entered and came to my bedside to ask me what laces I wanted; but it was only an excuse: I found her gentle as a lamb and amorous as a pigeon, and we had it over with; but a moment later Rose would have caught us in the act. She came in with Leduc, who asked me for permission to dance, promising that he would behave himself properly and Rose vouching for him. I consented, telling him that he had Mademoiselle Rose to thank for it.

I received a note from Madame Morin asking me if she might invite two ladies of her acquaintance and their daughters to my ball, and I replied that she would be doing me a favor if she would also invite some men, since I had ordered supper for twenty.

She came to dinner with her niece and Valenglart, her daughter having to make a lengthy toilet and her husband being busy until evening; so we were only four at dinner; but she assured me that I would have a numerous company for supper.

Mademoiselle Roman had on the same dress and was wearing her hair as she did every day; but nothing could have made her look more beautiful to me. Standing before me where I sat and pressing her knees against mine, she asked me if I had thought about her horoscope. I replied, taking her by the hand and drawing her down to the seat beside me, that she should have it on the next day but one. In this position I repeatedly kissed the charming mouth of the heavenly being whose destiny I was born to determine. She was more surprised than frightened to see me shaking, but in defending herself against me she never altered the serenity of her countenance, she never turned her face away, she never took her eyes from mine. Yielding to her urgent request, I became calm, and she did not stir. I saw in her eyes the look of satisfaction which betokens a victory won by a generous enemy who returns his arms to his vanquished foe, saying, "Use them against me again if you have the courage." My silence applauded the noble Mademoiselle Roman's virtue.

Madame Morin came and sat down on my other knee to ask me to explain something in her daughter's horoscope. She said that to secure the attendance of four beauties at my ball she had had to write only two notes.

"I will have but one beauty," I exclaimed, looking at her niece.

"God knows," said Valenglart, "what all Grenoble will be finding to say about your ball tomorrow."

"They will say," Madame Morin said to her niece, "that they have been to your wedding ball."

"Yes. They will talk of my splendid dress, my laces and diamonds."

"Of your beauty," I said gravely, "of your intelligence, your discretion, which will make the man who possesses you happy."

There was a silence, for they all thought I meant myself. If I had known how to go about it I would certainly have offered her five hundred louis; but the difficulty would have lain in drawing up the contract, for I should not have wanted to spend them for nothing.

We went into my bedroom, and while Mademoiselle Roman amused herself examining the fine jewels I had on my toilet table, her aunt and Valenglart looked at the books on my bedside stand. I see the lady go to the window, absorbed in examining something she had in her hands. I remember that I had left M. M.'s portrait there. I hurry to her and beg her to give me back the indecent portrait. She replies that the indecency is of no consequence, but that what has surprised her is a resemblance.

I see it all, and I tremble at my involuntary indiscretion.

"Madame," I say, "it is the portrait of a Venetian lady whom I loved seven years ago."

"I believe you, but it is very strange. The two M.'s, these religious robes stripped off and sacrificed to love, it all conspires to increase my surprise."

"She is a nun, and her name is M. M."

"And a distant cousin of mine in Chambéry is also named M. M. and is a nun of the same order as yours. I will tell you more. She was at Aix, whence you have come, to cure an illness."

"I know nothing of all that."

"If you go back to Chambéry, call on her, saying I sent you, and you will be as surprised as I am."

"Madame, I promise I will go there when I return from Italy; but I will not show her this portrait, which I will now lock up."

"Show it to no one, I beg you."

At eight o'clock all the guests arrived, and I saw in my apartment all the prettiest women and the most eligible men to be found in Grenoble. The only thing which annoyed me a little was the fulsome compliments, of which all the French provinces are inclined to be lavish.

I opened the ball with the lady whom Valenglart pointed out to me; then, each in her turn, I danced with them all; but the contradances only with Mademoiselle Roman, who shone more brightly than all the other ladies precisely because she was so simply dressed.

After an energetic contradance I go up to my room to put on a lighter coat, and a minute later I see the cousin, who asks me if I need anything.

"Were you seen coming in here?"

"No, because I came from upstairs. My cousins are in the ballroom."

"My dear, you are beautiful as a star, and the moment has come for me to prove that I adore you."

"What are you doing? No, no! Someone might come in. Put out the candle."

I put it out, and, since I am full of Mademoiselle Roman, she finds me such as I should have been with her; but I needed no illusion, for she was charming. I might not have found Mademoiselle Roman so eager. She begged me to spare her, and just at the moment when it needed to be said; I wanted to begin over again, but she was afraid, and she left. I relit the candle and, after dressing, went downstairs.

We danced until the king of caretakers came to tell me that supper was served.

I saw a cold collation made up of the choicest dishes and covering the entire table; but what especially pleased the ladies was the great number of wax candles. My guests being thirty, I did not sit with them but at a smaller table, where the hardened trenchermen joined me with pleasure. They all urged me most cordially to spend the autumn in their city, and I am sure that they would have entertained me properly, for the nobility of Grenoble has every accomplishment. I said that if I could stay I should be delighted to make the acquaintance of the family of an illustrious man who had been a great friend of my father's.

"What family is that?" they all asked together.

"Bourchenu de Valbonnais." [20]

"He was my uncle. Alas, Monsieur! Come to our house. You danced with my daughter.[21] Be so good as to tell me what your father's name was."

This tale, which I invented on the spur of the moment, seemed to have the effect of a thunderbolt and made me an object of wonder. We all rose together and went to dance again.

After a contradance, seeing Madame Morin, her niece, and Valenglart go outside for a breath of air, I went out too, and, strolling in the moonlight, I took Mademoiselle Roman into a covered walk; but the seductive speeches

with which I assailed her were all in vain. I held her in
my arms in transports of the most ardent love, she could
not escape the violence of my kisses, but her beautiful
mouth did not return me one, and her beautiful hands,
stronger than mine, always obstructed my attempts.
When, a last effort taking her by surprise, I came within
two or three inches of what I desired, she turned me to
stone by saying in an angelic voice:

"Ah, Monsieur, be my friend and do not ruin me."

I begged her pardon on my knees, we rejoined her
aunt; and we returned to the ballroom, but I was in a
frenzy.

I go and sit in a corner, I see Rose, I ask her to bring
me a lemonade. After bringing it she reproaches me for
not having danced either with her or her sister or with
their cousin. I reply that I am tired, but that if she will
promise to be kind I will dance one more minuet, and
with her.

"What must I do?" she replied.

"You must go and wait for me in my bedroom without a light, when your sister and your cousin are busy
dancing a contradance."

"And afterwards you won't dance with anyone but
me?"

"I give you my word."

"I will wait for you."

I went; I found her amorous, and my need was satisfied. I put off dancing the minuet with her until I was
sure that it would be the last, for in common decency
I could not have avoided dancing with the two others as
well.

At daybreak the ladies began leaving without ceremony. Handing Madame Morin and her niece into my
carriage, I said I would not see them that day, but that
if they would visit me for the whole of the next I would
give them the horoscope which they were so eager to
have.

I went to the pantry to thank the excellent caretaker for having cast luster on me, and there I saw his three girls filling their pockets with sweetmeats; he said to them jokingly that in their master's presence they could steal with clear consciences. I told him I would dine at six o'clock, and I went off to bed.

But having slept only until noon, I worked on the horoscope in bed. I decided to predict that fortune awaited her in Paris, where she would become the mistress of her master; but that she must go there without losing any time, for if she let her eighteenth year end without going where the monarch could see her, her destiny would take another course. To give my prediction all the authority it needed, I said astonishing things about what had happened to her until she was seventeen, which was her age at the time. I had learned them in one way or another from herself or her aunt, pretending not to notice what they were saying. With the help of an ephemeris I had and a book on astrology, in six hours I cast and copied out the girl's horoscope, which was of a nature to astonish Morin and Valenglart and awaken fanatical belief in the women. I hoped I should myself be asked to escort the fair jewel to Paris; and I felt more than ready to undertake it; I flattered myself that I should be found indispensable to the maneuver, and that, if not love, at least gratitude would grant me all that I desired; I even thought I saw a prosperous issue for myself, for my enterprise might indirectly make my fortune. The monarch could not but fall in love with her as soon as he saw her; I had no doubt of that. Besides, what man in love does not imagine that the object he loves must delight all mankind? At the moment I was jealous of her; but, knowing myself, I knew that I should cease to be so very soon after I had enjoyed my treasure. I knew that Louis XV's attitude in such matters was not exactly that of a Turk. What gave my prophetic tirade an aura of divinity was the prediction of a son who was destined to be a blessing to France and who

could come only from the blood royal and a predestined
vessel, which, however, would produce nothing if the
chances of human life did not send it to the capital.

The idea of becoming a famous astrologer in my century, in which reason had so thoroughly discredited astrology,[22] filled me with delight. I rejoiced in anticipa-
tion, seeing myself sought out by monarchs and wrapped
in aloofness in my old age. If Mademoiselle Roman
should have borne a daughter, I would simply have
laughed. My horoscope would certainly be known only
to her and her family, who could not but jealously keep
the secret. After finishing, reading, and rereading my
little masterpiece, I dined excellently with my three
young ladies, though I refused to get out of bed. Being
equally gracious to them severally, I could not but please
them all, and in any case I needed an interval. I was
sure that they must all be equally pleased, and not jealous, for each must have thought herself the favorite.

The next morning at nine o'clock I saw Valenglart,
who said that everyone thought I was in love, not with
Mademoiselle Roman, but with my caretaker's three
girls. He asked me if he might write the whole story to
Madame d'Urfé; and I answered that he would be doing
me a favor.

The aunt and the niece came at noon with Monsieur
Morin, and we spent the hour before dinner reading the
horoscope. I find it hard to describe four different kinds
of surprise. Mademoiselle Roman listening very seriously
and, having no idea that she had a will of her own, not
knowing what to say. Monsieur Morin, looking at me
from time to time and, seeing me serious, not daring to
laugh. Valenglart, with his countenance the mirror of his
fanaticism; and Madame Morin, who, the reading finished, at once began drawing conclusions. Not letting the
prediction surprise her in the least, she announced that
her niece had more right than Madame de Maintenon[23]
to become the King's wife or mistress.

"That woman," she said, "would never have been any-

thing if she had not left America[24] and come to France;
and if my niece does not go to Paris the horoscope cannot be proved wrong. So she must go. But how? Such a
journey is next to impossible. The prediction of the birth
of a boy is divine, and I know nothing about it; but she
has better cause to become dear to the King than La
Maintenon; my niece is young and virtuous, the other
had passed her prime and had had lovers.[25] But the
journey will never take place."

Valenglart said gravely that the journey would be
made, because destiny must be fulfilled, and Monsieur
Morin said that *Astra influunt non cogunt* ("The stars
influence, they do not determine").[26] The young lady
was lost in amazement, and I let them talk. We sat down
to dinner.

At dessert we returned to the subject.

"According to the horoscope," Madame Morin resumed, "the King will fall in love with my niece during
her eighteenth year:[27] she is in it now. What is to be
done? Where find a hundred louis, the least that is necessary for such a journey? And when she gets to Paris
is she to go and tell the King, 'Here I am, Sire'? And
with whom shall she go? Not with me."

"With my aunt Roman," said the young lady, blushing to the ears at the indiscreet laughter which no one
could restrain.

"Come to think of it," Madame Morin went on, "it
could happen quite naturally, for Madame Varnier,[28]
who lives in Rue de Richelieu above the Café de Foy,[29]
is your aunt.[30] She maintains a good establishment and
knows everyone in Paris."

"Do you see," said Valenglart, "the ways of destiny?
You talk of a hundred louis. You need only twelve for
a visit to Madame Varnier, who will put Mademoiselle
up; and when she is there, leave it to chance to bring
about the rest."

"If you go to Paris," I said to Mademoiselle Roman,

"you must say nothing about the horoscope either to your aunt here in Grenoble or to Madame Varnier."

"I will say nothing about it to anyone; but, believe me, all this is only a rosy dream. I shall never see Paris, still less Louis XV."

"Wait a moment."

I go for a sealed roll in which I had fifty doblones de a ocho,[31] which amounted to more than a hundred and fifty louis, and I take it to Mademoiselle Roman, saying that it was sweetmeats. She finds the roll too heavy, she unseals it, and she sees the fifty coins, which she takes to be medals. Valenglart tells her they are gold, and Monsieur Morin adds that the goldsmith would give her a hundred and fifty louis for them. I ask her to keep them and to give me a note for that amount, payable at Paris when she becomes rich. She handed the roll back to me, expressing her gratitude. I was sure that she would refuse it; but I admired the strength of mind with which she managed to hold back her tears while never ceasing to smile.

We went to the garden, where, the subject of the horoscope being resumed by Madame Morin and Valenglart, I took the young lady by the hand and left them.

"Tell me, I beg you," she said, "if all this is only a joke."

"It is serious; but it all depends on an 'if'; if you do not go to Paris, it will all come to nothing."

"You must believe that, or you would not have tried to give me the fifty medals."

"You have drawn the wrong conclusion. Accept them secretly this moment."

"I thank you; but why should you give me such a large sum?"

"Hoping that you will allow me to love you."

"If you love me, why should I object? You do not need to buy my consent. Indeed, I am grateful to you. Reflection tells me that, to be happy, I do not need a

King of France. If you knew to what my desires are limited!"

"Speak. To what?"

"To having a kind husband well enough off for me not to go without anything I need."

"And if you did not love him?"

"If he is honorable and kind, how could I help loving him?"

"I see that you do not know love."

"That is true. I do not know the love which makes people lose their heads, and I thank God that I do not."

"You are right. God preserve you from it."

"You insist that at the mere sight of me the King will lose his head; and, to tell you the truth, that is what seems to me sheer fantasy, for he may well find me not ugly, but I do not believe he will be carried away."

"You do not believe it? Let us sit down. Imagine that the King is as much impressed by your merits as I am. The thing will be done."

"What do you find in me that you would not find in many girls of my age? Yet it is true that I may have made a strong impression on you; but that only proves that I was born to affect *you* in such a way, and not the King. Why bring in the King, if you love me yourself?"

"I cannot give you what you deserve."

"From all appearances, that is not true."

"You do not love me."

"As your wife, I should love you alone. Then I would return the kiss you have just given me, which my duty forbids my returning now."

"How grateful I am to you for not being offended by the pleasure I feel when I am with you!"

"On the contrary, I am very glad if I please you."

"Permit me to come to see you very early tomorrow and take coffee with you sitting close beside you on your bed."

"Oh, please do not think of it! I sleep with my aunt,

and I always get up first. Oh, please withdraw that hand.
Please, please! In God's name, end this!"

Alas! I ended only by obeying. But what made me
happy in imagination was that my lapse from propriety
had not brought any change in her sweetness of manner
or in the smile which her face always wore. I looked
like a man who begged to be forgiven and deserved it;
her expression told me she was sorry she could not grant
me what I wanted. I went to my bedroom, where I found
Manon unbasting cuffs, and in no more than a minute
she quenched my thirst, then ran away. I reflected that
Mademoiselle Roman would never grant me more than
I had obtained from her, and that it was useless to try
to obtain more unless I was willing to enter into negotiations which were contrary to her horoscope.

Having gone back to the garden, I asked Madame
Morin to take a stroll with me. What I said to the worthy
lady to persuade her to accept a hundred louis from me
so that she could send her niece to Paris is unbelievable.
I swore that no one should ever know of it; but all my
eloquence was wasted. She said that if it depended on
nothing but the journey, her niece's destiny could be fulfilled, for she had already thought of a way to send her,
if her husband consented. In any case, she thanked me
most sincerely, and she said that her niece was fortunate
to have pleased me so well. I replied that she pleased me
so well that I would leave the next day, for the proposal
I was tempted to make her would destroy the high fortune which destiny promised her.

"Otherwise I should believe that my happiness would
lie in my asking you for her hand in marriage."

"Her happiness would perhaps have a more solid
foundation. Explain yourself."

"I do not dare to oppose destiny."

"But you will not set off tomorrow?"

"Yes, Madame. I shall call on you at two o'clock to
take my leave."

The announcement of my departure made our supper somewhat melancholy. Madame Morin, who may still be alive, was a woman of excellent character. At table she announced that, since my departure was certain and I would not be going out except to call on her, the honor I wished to do her would become an irksome ceremony, and so my farewells should be made then and there. I said that I would at least have the honor of conveying her to her door after supper. And so it turned out. Valenglart walked, and Mademoiselle Roman sat on my lap. I was bold; she was kind to such a degree that I regretted having taken my leave; but it was done. An overturned carriage at the door of an inn obliged my coachman to stop for some minutes. I was far from cursing the accident as he did. Wanting to see if I could read some reflection of my happiness in the expression on my angel's face, I escorted them as far as their apartment, and, all conceit on my part aside, I saw the grief of love. I gave Madame Morin the embrace which was her due as a member of the sister order of "Mops," [32] and she was kind enough immediately to initiate her niece, who at last very voluptuously gave me the kiss which she had always held she must refuse me. I returned to my apartment full of love but in despair, and I was annoyed when I saw the three girls in my bedroom. I needed only one of them.

Putting on my nightcap, Rose heard my whispered request; but she said that since they all slept together in the same room she could not possibly slip away. I then decide to tell them that I shall leave the next day and that I will give them a present of six louis apiece if they will all three sleep in my room. After laughing heartily over my proposal they said very calmly that the thing was impossible. This convinced me that none of them knew anything about the other two, but that they were bitterly jealous of one another. I spent the night alone, holding the adorable Mademoiselle Roman in the embrace of my soul until I woke.

I rang rather late. It was the cousin who entered, saying that Rose was coming with my chocolate and at the same time announcing a Monsieur Charles Ivanov,[33] who wanted to speak to me. I at once guessed that it was "the Russian"; but since no one had introduced him to me I saw that I need not receive him.

"Tell the gentleman that the name is unknown to me."

She goes, and a moment later comes back to say that I knew him from having supped with him at Madame Morin's. Finding myself thus obliged to receive him, I have him shown in.

"I should be glad to have the honor," he said, "of a word in private with you."

"I cannot, Monsieur, order these young ladies to leave my room. So be good enough to wait outside while I get up, and I will come and place myself at your disposition."

"If I am inconveniencing you I will come back tomorrow."

"I leave this evening."

"In that case I will wait for you."

I hastily slip on my dressing gown and go to hear what he wants. He says that he must leave and that, having no money to pay the innkeeper, he has come to beg my help and that he does not dare turn to anyone in the city because his rank does not permit him to risk the insult of a refusal.

"Yet you are risking a refusal at this moment, and certainly I am incapable of insulting you."

"If you knew who I am, I am certain you would not refuse me some small assistance."

"If you are certain of it, tell me who you are, and be confident of my silence."

"I am Charles, second son of Ivan, Duke of Kurland,[34] who is living in exile in Siberia. I escaped."

"In Genoa," I replied, "you will no longer be in want; for the brother of your mother the Duchess cannot abandon you."

"He died in Silesia."

"When?"

"Two years ago, I believe."

"You have been misinformed. I saw him in Stuttgart six months ago. He is Baron Breyden."

I see beyond doubt that the fellow is an impostor, and I feel angry that he has chosen me to trick; I am determined not to become his dupe; otherwise I should have given him six louis, since it was not for me to be the avowed enemy of adventurers, who are all impostors in one degree or another.

I glance at his buckles, which people believed were genuine, and I see beyond doubt that they are of the artificial stones made in Venice which marvelously counterfeited rose-cut diamonds.

"I have been told that your buckles are of diamonds."

"So they are."

"Why do you not sell them?"

"I promised my mother I would never part with them."

"Your buckles, Monsieur, are damaging to you; you should carry them in your pocket. I will tell you that I do not believe they are genuine and that lies offend me."

"Monsieur, I am not lying."

"Very well. Show me that they are genuine, and I will make you a present of six louis. You will also have the pleasure of proving me wrong. Good-by, Monsieur."

He saw Valenglart coming up the stairs and he begged me to say nothing to him about our conversation. I promised that I would not mention it to anyone.

Valenglart had come to wish me a good journey before leaving to see Mademoiselle Roman[35] with Monsieur de Monteynard.[36] He urged me to correspond with him, and I promised that I would do so and indeed thanked him, for Mademoiselle Roman's fate was of the highest interest to me. He embraced me with tears.

CHAPTER III

I leave Grenoble. Avignon. The fountain of Vaucluse. The pretended Astrodi and the hunchback. Gaetano Costa. My arrival in Marseilles.

WHILE THE three girls were helping Leduc pack my valises, the caretaker comes in with the bill. I am satisfied, so is he; wishing to have the pleasure of dining on this last day with his girls, I order dinner for four and post horses at nightfall. Leduc tells him also to order a saddle horse for him to ride, he being above getting up behind the carriage. The cousin laughs at his boasting, and the coxcomb, offended, tells her he is better than she is.

"But you serve her at table," I say.

And he answers:

"As she serves you in bed."

At this piece of insolence I run for my cane; but he scrambles agilely onto the window sill and jumps out.

The girls and their father give a cry of terror, I run to the window, and we see him in the courtyard, jumping about like a monkey. Delighted that he is not injured, I tell him that I pardon him, he comes up again, and I give him a watch. Such was my Spaniard, whom I had to dismiss two years later and whom I have often regretted.

In the company of the three girls, whom I vainly did my best to make tipsy, I found the hours passing so quickly that I decided to put off leaving until the next day. Tired of subterfuge, I wanted to have them all together, and I saw that I might manage it during the course of the night. I told them that if they would spend the whole night in my room I would not leave until morning. While they were conjuring up objections the caretaker came up to tell me that I would be well advised to travel to Avignon by water,[1] in a comfortable boat on which I could also put my carriage and which would cost me much less. I said that I would agree if all three young ladies would spend the night in my room, and he replied with a laugh that it was for them to choose. At this dictum they made up their minds, and the caretaker sent to order the boat and a choice supper for midnight.

It was not until after the supper that, in the truth of the bottle, I made them admit that their scruples were ridiculous after they had all three granted me their favors. At this news they looked at one another with the indignation and surprise which my brazen declaration could not but cause them, but I did not leave them time to summon up the courage to say that it was a calumny. Manon was the first to admit the truth and surrender to my ardor, and the two others sensibly took the same course when their turns came. After four or five extremely lively hours nature was obliged to yield to sleep. In the morning I wanted to give them presents of jewels, but they said they would rather I ordered gloves from them, giving them the money in advance. I ordered thirty louis' worth of gloves, which I never went back to get. I left at seven o'clock, seeing the whole household crying and laughing. I went to sleep on the boat and was not waked until Avignon, where I was taken to the "Saint-

Omer" inn[2] and where I chose to eat supper in my room, despite Leduc's glowing accounts of a beauty who was eating at the public table.

The next day I feel inclined to go to it. My Spaniard tells me that the charming beauty is lodging with her husband in the room next to ours. At the same time he hands me a playbill announcing an Italian comedy, played by some members of the Paris company, in which Mademoiselle Astrodi[3] is to sing and dance; I cry out in amazement. "How can the charming Astrodi, famous for her villainies, be in Avignon? When she sees me she will be very much surprised!"

At the public table I find eighteen or twenty people, all genteel, and such an array of dishes that it seems impossible the charge is only forty sous[4] a head. But the beautiful foreign lady, who absorbed all the attention of the table, completely holds mine too. Foreign, very young, a perfect beauty, never speaking, looking only at her plate, how could she leave any of the guests indifferent? When she was addressed she answered only in monosyllables, just letting her large blue eyes glance for an instant at the face of the person who had spoken to her. She had a husband seated at the other end of the table, who talked and laughed immediately; fairly young, with an ignoble countenance, greedy, pock-marked, his manners were not above those of a servant. Sure that such a man had not learned to refuse, I send him a glass of champagne, and he empties it to my health. I ask him if I may make bold to offer one to Madame, and, with a loud laugh, he tells me to apply to her. She says, after a slight bow, that she never drinks champagne. At dessert she went back to her room and her husband followed her.

A foreigner, who, like myself, was there for the first time, asked who she was; a man dressed in black told him that her husband called himself the Chevalier Stuard,[5] that he had come from Lyons and was on his

way to Marseilles, and that he had been in Avignon for
a week without a servant and with very little luggage.

Having intended to stop in Avignon only long enough
to see Vaucluse and the celebrated fountain, which is
known as the "Cascade," [6] I had not furnished myself
with letters. An Italian who has read, understood, and
enjoyed Petrarch cannot but be curious to see the place
where that great man fell in love with Laura de Sade.[7]

I went to the theater,[8] where I saw the Vice-Legate,[9]
Salviati,[10] women of fashion who were neither beautiful
nor ugly, and a bad comic opera, in which I saw neither
L'Astrodi nor any member of the Comédie Italienne in
Paris.

"But where is L'Astrodi?" I said at the end of the
performance to a man who was there. "I did not see
her."

"I beg your pardon. She sang and danced."

"By God, I know her, and if she has become unrecognizable it is no longer she."

I leave, and two minutes later I am overtaken by the
same man, who asks me to come back to Mademoiselle
Astrodi's dressing room, for she had recognized me. I go,
and I see an ugly wench who comes running to embrace
me, who calls me by my name, and whom I could swear
I have never seen; but she does not let me speak. I
recognize a man who is there as the father of the
beautiful Astrodi whom all Paris knew.[11] She had been
the cause of the death of Count Egmont,[12] one of
the most agreeable noblemen at the court of Louis XV.
I imagine at first that the ugly wench might be her
sister, I accept a chair, and I compliment her on her
talents. She asks my permission to take off her costume,
and she does so chatting, laughing, and removing her
nether garments with a generosity in which she might
not have indulged if what she showed me had been worth
seeing. I was so fresh from Grenoble that she would have

found it hard to tempt me even if she were pretty; she
was thin, dark-skinned, and almost repulsive. I laughed
to myself at her confidence in her poor little stock; she
must have supposed I had the appetite of a devil; but
wenches of her kind very often have recourse to lewd-
ness for what they cannot hope from delicacy. She asked
me, she implored me, to go to supper with her, but I
finally put an end to that with a peremptory refusal.
She then begs me to take four tickets from her for the
next day's performance, which is for her benefit; and I
breathe again. It was only a matter of four petits écus,[13]
I quickly take sixteen, and I think I shall see her die
with gratitude when I give her the two louis. I return
to my inn, where I sup very well in my room.

Putting me to bed, Leduc tells me that before supper
the innkeeper had gone to see the beautiful foreigner,
her husband being present, and had told him very clearly
that he insisted on having his money the next morning,
otherwise they would find no places set for them at his
table; he had added that their effects would not leave
his inn.

"Who told you this?"

"I heard it myself, from in here. The two rooms are
separated by a partition one board thick. I am sure that
if they were there now they would hear everything we
are saying."

"Where are they?"

"At table, where they are eating for tomorrow, but
the lady is crying. You are in luck."

"Hold your tongue. I will have nothing to do with it.
It's a trap. A decent woman would rather die of hunger
than go and cry in public like that."

"Ah! if you knew how much prettier she is when she
cries! I'm a poor man, but the devil take me if I won't
give her two louis if she's willing to earn them."

"Go and offer them to her."

A moment later the couple enter their room and lock the door, and I begin to hear the lady's sobs and the voice of the man talking to her angrily in some patois I do not know. It was the Walloon dialect, which is spoken in the environs of Liège. I sent Leduc off to bed, ordering him to tell the innkeeper that I insisted on having another room the next day, for the partition could easily be forced and the unfortunate couple could even more easily turn thieves. The tears and the husband's harangues ended at midnight.

The next morning I was shaving when Leduc told me that the Chevalier Stuard wished to speak with me.

"Tell him that I do not know any Stuard."

A moment later he comes back and says that, on being thus refused, he had looked at the ceiling and stamped on the floor. He had gone back to his room, from which, coming out a moment later wearing his sword, he had gone downstairs.

"I'm going to see," he added, "if there is powder in the pans of your pistols."

My valet made me laugh; but a desperate man often does more than that. I again order him to ask the innkeeper for another room; and he comes to tell me he cannot give me one until the next day.

"Then I shall leave your house instantly and find lodging elsewhere, for I cannot bear these sobs. Do you hear them? Are they amusing? The woman will kill herself, and you will be to blame."

"I? I only asked her husband for my money."

"There—listen to him, I'm sure he is saying in his patois that you are a monster."

"He may say what he likes provided he pays me."

"You've condemned them to die of starvation. How much do they owe you?"

"Fifty francs, for I lent him six."

"And you're not ashamed to make such a fuss over so little? Here's your money. Go at once and tell them you have been paid and they can eat downstairs, but don't tell them it was I who paid you.''

He hurries out with the money, and I hear him tell them that he has been paid, but that they should never know by whom, and that they were free to go down for dinner and supper; of course in future they must pay him day by day. No sooner had he said all this than he comes back to my room; but I turn him out, calling him a damned fool, for he had led them to guess the truth.

Leduc stood there gaping.

"What's the matter, idiot?"

"Fine doings. I'm learning. I shall turn author. You're a sly one.''

"You're a fool. I'm going for a walk; take care you don't leave this room.''

"Very well.''

But I have scarcely started off before the Chevalier accosts me and overwhelms me with elaborate thanks. I reply that I do not know what he is thanking me for, and he leaves me. Being on the bank of the Rhone, I amuse myself examining the ancient bridge[14] and the river itself, which geographers say is the swiftest in Europe; and at dinnertime I return to my inn, where the innkeeper, informed that I would pay six francs without wine, gives me an excellent repast. While I was there I drank only white Hermitage,[15] a wine of the utmost excellence. I asked him to find me a guide for the next day, as I wanted to see Vaucluse and the fountain. I dress to go to the little Astrodi's benefit performance.

I find her at the theater door, I give her the sixteen tickets and take a place next to the box of the Vice-Legate, Prince Salviati, who arrived with a numerous suite of ladies and men wearing decorations. L'Astrodi's father comes up behind me to whisper that his daughter begged me to say that she was the same famous Astrodi I had known in Paris. I answer, also in a whisper, that I will not risk having my veracity impugned. The ease

with which a scoundrel invites a man of honor to join
in a piece of knavery is unbelievable, but he thinks he is
paying him a compliment.

At the end of the first act a score of servants in Mon-
seigneur's livery distributed ices among the first-tier
boxes. I thought it my part to refuse. A young man as
beautiful as the God of Love politely approaches me
and asks why I have not accepted an ice.

"Because, not having the honor of being known to
anyone, I do not wish to give anyone grounds for saying
that he has done me a courtesy when he does not know
me."

"You are staying at the 'Saint-Omer,' Monsieur?"

"Yes, Monsieur. I have stopped here only to see Vaucluse, and I shall have that pleasure tomorrow if I can
obtain a guide."

"I will come to serve you in that capacity myself, if
you will grant me the honor. I am Dolci,[16] son of the
captain of the Vice-Legate's guard."

"Feeling the honor you are so kind as to do me, I will
put off leaving until you arrive."

"You will see me at seven o'clock."

I am surprised by the dignified courtesy of this Adonis,
whom one might suspect to be a girl. I laughed at the
supposititious Astrodi, who was as bad an actress as
she was ugly and who through the whole performance
never took her pale eyes from my swarthy face. When
she sang she looked at me and smiled, treating me to
little signals which indicated an understanding between
us and which must have made me a marked man to the
entire nobility, who, in turn, must have deplored my
bad taste. An actress whose voice and eyes did not displease me was a big hunchbacked girl, but a hunchback
such as I had never seen; for, though she had enormous
hunches both in front and behind, she was extremely
tall, so that but for the rickets which had made her
hunchbacked she would certainly have measured six

The Concert

Music for the Contradance "La Société"

feet. In addition I imagined that she must be intelligent, as all hunchbacks are.

At the end of the play the hunchbacked girl was at the door of the theater with my favorite Astrodi. The latter was there to thank people, and the former to sell tickets for her own benefit performance, which was to take place three days later.

After receiving L'Astrodi's thanks, I hear the hunchback saying, with a smile which stretched from ear to ear and showed at least twenty-four fine teeth, that she hoped I would honor her benefit too.

"Provided," I replied, "that I do not leave day after tomorrow."

The other began laughing and, in the presence of the ladies who were waiting for their carriages, said that I would stay, that she would not let me go.

"Give him sixteen tickets," she said to the hunchback.

She gives them to me, and, ashamed to refuse them, I give her two louis.

"Day after tomorrow," says L'Astrodi, "we shall come to supper with you, provided you will be alone, for we want to get drunk."

As I returned to my inn the supper struck me as so comical a prospect that I decided to stay.

I was at table alone in my room when the Chevalier and his wife entered theirs, and I heard neither sobs nor tirades; but I was very much surprised when, with the first rays of dawn, I saw Monsieur Stuard, who said that, having heard that I was going to visit Vaucluse alone in a four-seated carriage, he had come to ask if I would permit him to accompany me with his wife, who was very curious to see the cascade. I replied that he would be honoring me, and he hurried off to get ready.

Leduc, who was dressing my hair, asked my permission to come on horseback, adding that he had been a true prophet. It was obvious that Madame Stuard was to be mine, and I was not averse to the prospect, for the adventure was entirely to my advantage. The innkeeper comes up with a guide, whom I dismiss, giving him six francs. Dolci arrives, beautiful as an angel; the lady is ready with her lord and master; the carriage is there, laden with everything we needed to eat well and drink still better, and we set off, Madame and Dolci on the back seat and Stuard and I on the front.

I had felt certain that during the course of the journey the young woman would relax and her gloom would vanish—but not a bit of it. In response to all my remarks to her I received only such very brief replies as, not being a peasant, she could not avoid giving me. Poor Dolci, who was intelligent, was in despair. Reasoning soundly, he thought himself the cause of all the gloom of the expedition; but I quickly put him at his ease by telling him that when he had offered me his company I did not know that I was to have the honor of escorting this beautiful lady, and that when I had learned it at six o'clock that morning I had been delighted to think that chance was putting such a charming companion beside him. To this account the lady made no response. Maintaining her silence, she did nothing but look into the distance and down at the ground to left and right.

Dolci, feeling less awkward after my explanation, began making various remarks designed to touch the springs of speech in her, but all to no purpose. He entered into a long conversation with her husband on a quantity of subjects, giving them all some oblique reference to the lady; but her beautiful mouth never opened.

The beauty of her face was perfect; her blue eyes were wonderfully large, her complexion a pure white enlivened by a rosy bloom, her arms were extremely beautiful, her hands well-fleshed and delicate, her figure showed that her bosom must be superb, and the light chestnut of her unpowdered hair inclined me to pass a most favorable judgment on all her invisible beauties. Nevertheless I sighed as I sadly reflected that, with her gloom, she

might well inspire love, but that it could not last. I
arrived at L'Isle[17] determined never again to be in her
company anywhere; for she might well be insane, or in a
state of desperation, forced as she was to live with a man
whom she could not bear, and in that case I felt sorry
for her; but I could not forgive her when I thought that,
having been genteelly brought up, she should never have
consented to join my outing that day when she knew that,
with her gloom, she could not but arouse aversion.

As for the self-styled Stuard who was with her,
whether as her husband or her lover, I did not need any
profound reflection to know just what kind of man he
was. He was young, neither handsome nor ugly, his
manner promised nothing, and his talk showed him to
be ignorant and stupid. A vagabond, as lacking in money
as in talent, what was he doing traveling about Europe
with this beauty who, since she was not accommodating,
could find nothing to live on except in the purses of fools?
Perhaps he knew that the world was full of them; yet
experience constantly taught him that he could not count
on them. The contemptible fellow became even more contemptible if he did not know that he was so.

Arrived at Vaucluse, I put myself entirely in the
hands of Dolci, who had been there countless times and
who loved Petrarch. We left our carriage in Apt[18] and
went to the celebrated fountain, which was in fullest
flow that day. Nature was the architect of the immense
cave from which it comes. The fountain is at the foot of
a cliff as sheer as a wall, a hundred feet high and of the
same width. The cave itself, under the arch which forms
the entrance to it, is only half as high, and from it the
fountain flows with such an abundance of water that
even at its birth it deserves the name of river. It is the
Sorgue, which mingles with the Rhone near Avignon.
There is no purer water in the world than that of this
fountain, since in all the centuries it has been flowing
the rocks have not received the slightest stain from it.

Those who are repelled by the water because it is black do not reflect that the cave itself, where the darkness is very dense, is what must make it look so.

> *Chiare, fresche, e dolci acque*
> *Ove le belle membra*
> *Pose colei che sola a me par donna.*
>
> ("Clear, fresh, sweet waters, in which
> she who to me is alone a woman
> dipped her beautiful limbs.")[19]

I insist on going to the top of the rock on which Petrarch had his house, the ruins of which I saw, shedding tears, as Leo Allatius[20] shed them when he saw Homer's tomb; and I wept again sixteen years later at Arquà,[21] where Petrarch died and where the house which he occupied still exists. The resemblance between the two places is striking, for from the room in which Petrarch wrote at Arquà one sees the summit of a rock very much like the one which I saw at Vaucluse and which, Dolci told me, was where Madonna Laura lived.

"Let us go there," I said, "it is not far."

What pleasure I felt when I saw the still existing remains of the house of the woman whom the amorous Petrarch immortalized in this one verse, which would melt a heart of stone:

> *Morte bella parea nel suo bel viso.*
>
> ("Death looked beautiful in her beautiful face.")[22]

I flung myself on its ruins with outstretched arms, kissing them and anointing them with my tears, asking Madame Stuard to forgive me if I had abandoned her arm to do homage to the departed spirit of a woman whose lover had been the most profound intellect which it was possible for Nature to produce. I said "intellect," for, whatever people may say, the body had nothing to do with it.

"Madame," I said to the astonished woman, who stood staring at me in her amazement, "four hundred and fifty years have passed since the place where you now are was trodden by the feet of Laura de Sade, who was perhaps not as beautiful as you are, but who was gay, polished, gentle, cheerful, and wise. May the same air which you are breathing at this moment, and which she breathed, make you resemble her, and you will inspire the flame of love in all who approach you; you will see the universe at your feet, and there will not be a mortal in the world who will dare to cause you the slightest pain. Gaiety, Madame, is the portion of the blessed, and gloom is the terrible image of souls condemned to eternal torments. Be gay, then, and deserve to be beautiful."

My enthusiasm impelled Dolci to come and embrace me. Stuard laughed, and the lady, who perhaps thought me mad, showed not the slightest sign of life in response. She took my arm again, and we slowly returned to the house of "Messer Francesco d'Arezzo,"²³ where I spent a quarter of an hour carving my name. *E sciolsi il voto* ("And I fulfilled my vow"). From there we went to dinner.

Dolci showed this extraordinary woman even more attention than I did. Stuard did nothing but eat and drink, refusing the water of the Sorgue, which, according to him, could only spoil the Hermitage wine; and it is possible that Petrarch himself would have been of the same opinion; we emptied eight bottles without our reason suffering from it; but the lady was abstemious. Back in Avignon, we bowed to her at the door of her room, declining the stupid Stuard's pressing invitation to sit down. I went to pass the last hour of the day on the bank of the Rhone with Dolci. Speaking of this strange woman, the young man pronounced judgment, and he hit the mark.

"She is," he said, "a whore²⁴ utterly infatuated with her own merits, who has left her country because, having

lavished her favors too freely too soon, she found no
one any longer interested in her. Sure of making her
fortune wherever she was still a novelty, she set out with
this scoundrel, maintaining her air of melancholy on
principle, for she considers it the one sure means of
making some man who undertakes her conquest fall
madly in love with her. She has not yet found him. He
must be a rich man whom she can set about ruining.
She may have designs on you."

Men who reason so well at Dolci's age are those who
become great masters. I left him, thanking him warmly
and very glad to have made his acquaintance.

On my way to my room I saw at the door of his an
elderly man of prepossessing appearance, who, bowing
and calling me by my name, courteously asked me if I
had found Vaucluse worthy of my interest. With great
pleasure I recognize the Marchese Grimaldi,[25] of Genoa,
a man of intelligence who was both likable and rich and
who lived the greater part of the time in Venice because
he enjoyed the pleasures of life more freely there than
in his native city. My reply demanding a reasoned statement, I go in, thanking him for having done me the
honor to remember me. I have no sooner finished my remarks on the fountain than he asks me if I enjoyed the
promising company of my guests. I reply that I could
not but have enjoyed it. Noticing my reserve, he sets
about overcoming it by the following discourse:

"In Genoa we have very beautiful women; but we
have not one who can match the beauty whom you took
to L'Isle today. Last evening at table she struck me.
Having given her my arm going upstairs, I said that if
she thought I could dispel her melancholy she had only
to speak. Note that I knew she had no money. It was her
husband who thanked me for my offer, and I wished
them good night.

"When, an hour ago, you saw her back to her room
and left her there, I took the liberty of making her a

visit. She received me with a graceful curtsy, and, her husband having asked me to keep her company until he returned, she did not hesitate to sit down on a sofa with me. I tried to take her hand, but she withdrew it. I then told her in a few words that her beauty had struck me, and that if she needed a hundred louis they were at her service, provided she would drop her serious manner in my company and assume a gaiety which would encourage the sentiments of friendship she had inspired in me. She replied only by a motion of the head which expressed gratitude but at the same time an absolute refusal of my proposal. I say that I am leaving tomorrow, and she does not answer. I take her hand again, and she haughtily withdraws it. At that I rise, beg her to excuse me, and leave. This is what happened to me half an hour ago. I have not fallen in love with her, for you see that I am amused; but in the light of her poverty her tactics astonish me. It is possible that you today put her in a position to scorn my offer, and in that case I understand to some extent; short of that, it is a phenomenon which I cannot explain. May I make bold to ask you outright if you fared better than I did?''

Delighted by the worthy gentleman's openness, I was as frank as he. I told him the whole story in detail; and we ended by laughing at it. I promised to call on him in Genoa and give him an account of what happened during the two days I planned to spend in Avignon after he left. He begged me to do so. He invited me to go down to supper with him to admire the recalcitrant's countenance; I said that, having dined very well, she would not be there; but he laughed and said he would wager she would go down; and he was right. When I saw her at table I decided that the role she was playing was assumed. The place beside her had been given to a Count Bussy,[26] who had just arrived, a young, handsome, conceited coxcomb, as anyone could see at a glance. Here is the scene with which we were entertained.

The Count, who was a wag by nature, playing the amiable fool with the fair sex yet at the same time bold and insolent, and who intended to leave at midnight, instantly set himself to cajoling and pestering his beautiful neighbor in a hundred ways. Finding her of a taciturnity which he had never before encountered, he did all the talking, he laughed, and, if the thought occurred to him that she was mocking him, he refused to consider it possible. I looked at Signor Grimaldi, who, like myself, could scarcely keep from laughing. Though nettled, the young roué went on; he gave her a choice bit to eat which he had first tasted himself, he even held it to her mouth; red with rage, she refused it, and he changed her plate, storming because she would not grant him a look. Seeing that no one present showed any decided inclination to defend the fortress, he remains unabashed; he laughs and decides to attack. He forcibly takes her hand and kisses it; she tries to pull it away, she rises, whereupon, still laughing, he catches her by the waist. But at that moment her husband rises, comes and takes her arm, and leaves the room with her. Somewhat disconcerted, the attacker follows her with his eyes, then resumes his place at the table, laughing again, though everyone else remains silent. He turns to ask his courier if his sword is upstairs; he answers no. He asks an abbé who is sitting beside him who the man who left with the lady is, and he replies that he is her husband; at that he laughs and says that husbands never fight.

"However," he added, "I shall offer him my apologies."

He rises, he goes upstairs, and the whole table begins commenting on the scene. A minute later he comes down, angry with the husband, who, shutting the door in his face, had told him he could go to the bordello. Declaring himself sorry that he must leave without finishing the affair, he orders champagne, offers it to everyone, no one accepts, he drinks, he gives the rest to his courier, and he leaves.

Seeing me to my room, Signor Grimaldi asks me what impression the scene had made on me. I said that I would not have stirred even if he had turned up her skirts.

"No more would I," he said; "but not if she had accepted my purse. I am curious to know how she will manage to leave here."

I told him again that I would bring him news of her in Genoa. He would not let me see him off, and he left at daybreak.

The next morning I received a note from L'Astrodi, asking me if I expected her for supper with her companion, and I answered in the affirmative. A moment later I see before me the Russian, the Duke of Kurland, whom I had left in Grenoble. I was alone. He tells me humbly that he is the son of a clockmaker in Narva, that his buckles are worthless, and that he has come to ask me for charity. I give him four louis.

"May I beg you," he says, "to keep my secret?"

"If anyone asks me about you I will say that I do not know who you are."

"In that case I will leave for Marseilles at once."

When the time comes I will recount in what condition I found him at Genoa. I sent for the innkeeper and told him privately that I wanted a choice supper for three people in my room and good wines. After replying that I would be satisfied, he said that he had just been raising a row in the Chevalier Stuard's room because he did not have money to pay for his day's board as they had agreed, and hence he was going to turn him out of the house at once, despite the fact that the lady was in bed with convulsions which were choking her.

"But that," he said, "does not pay me, and the scene yesterday evening brought discredit on my house."

"Go at once and tell her that in future she shall eat

in her room with her husband morning and evening, and
that I will pay for it as long as I remain here.''

''You know that meals in the room are charged
double.''

''I know it.''

''Very well. I'm off.'' [27]

The idea of this beautiful woman turned out into the
street appalled me; but innkeepers do not practice gallantry. A moment later Stuard came to thank me and
ask me to stop in at his room to persuade his wife to
behave differently.

''She will not answer me, and you know I dislike
that.''

''Come, she knows what you have just done, and she
will speak, for after all, right feeling—''

''Who are you to talk to me of right feeling after what
I saw last evening?''

''That gentleman left at midnight; and well for him
that he did, otherwise I would have killed him this
morning.''

''You make me laugh. It was last evening that you
should have thrown your plate in his face.''

I go with him. I see her in her bed, with her back
turned and the covers drawn up to her neck, and I hear
her sobbing. I talk sense to her; but, as always, she does
not answer me. Her husband makes to leave; but I tell
him I will leave too, because no one could do anything
for her and he should be convinced of it after the hundred louis she had refused from the Marchese Grimaldi,
who had only wanted to kiss her hand and see her smiling.

''A hundred louis! By . . . , what behavior! We
would have left at once for Liège, where our house is.
A princess lets her hand be kissed for nothing; even an
abbess. A hundred louis! By . . . , what behavior!''

He made me want to laugh, he cursed, he swore, and
I was about to leave when convulsions, whether real or

feigned, seize the poor woman. They begin by putting out an arm and hurling a bottle of water which was on the night table into the middle of the room. Stuard runs to her, holds her arm, she trembles, extends the other, she writhes with her eyes closed, she gradually arches her back, and the convulsions, seizing her thighs and legs, so disarrange the covers that I see things which I have never in my life been able to resist. The ignoble husband goes for water and leaves me there in motionless contemplation of a woman who lay as if dead in a posture than which voluptuousness could invent nothing more seductive. I feel trapped, and I rebel. I feel certain that it is only play-acting, a device by which, in her insane pride, the woman means to let me do whatever I wish and have the pleasure of denying it afterward. If it should kill me, I make up my mind to foil her. I take the cover and put it back over her. It was a hard task. I condemned to darkness dazzling charms which the monster was bent on using only to degrade me.

Stuard comes back with a bottle of water, he bathes her temples, he talks to her in the patois of Liège, he puts his hands under the cover to straighten her arched back; she pretends to feel nothing. A quarter of an hour later I pull myself together, my inertia vanishes, I leave them, and I go to walk beside the Rhone.

I strode along, angry with myself, for the slut had really bewitched me. I felt that, however brutally, enjoying all that I had seen was necessary to bring me back to reason. I saw that I must buy her, not by my attentions but with money, and, beyond that, by pretending to be taken in by all her artifices. I regretted that I had refrained from defiling her, even if her husband should have caught me in the act. I should have been satisfied, and have had every right to despise her afterward and make her aware of it. In my perplexity I see that it is still not too late, and I decide to tell her husband that I will give him twenty-five louis after he has arranged another interview for me under circumstances which will permit me to end the business.

I return to my inn with this idea in mind, and, not going to see how she is, I dine alone in my room. Leduc tells me that she is dining in her room too, and that the innkeeper has said she would not come down to the table again. I already knew it.

After dining I returned Monsieur Dolci's visit; he introduced me to his father, who was extremely good-hearted but not rich enough to satisfy his son's wish to travel. The young man himself was as agile as a monkey; he showed me his great skill in conjuring tricks. He was sweet-tempered, and, finding me curious to know if he was fortunate in love, he told me some tales from which I saw that he was in the propitious time of life which only inexperience renders unpropitious. He would have nothing to do with a certain rich woman because she demanded from him what he thought it ignoble to give when he did not love her, and he was sighing in vain for a young one because she demanded that he show her respect. I said that a gallant young man like himself ought to accommodate the generous rich woman with his person and very politely fail in respect to the younger one, who, after scolding him, would always be ready to forgive him. He was not a libertine, and he rather leaned toward Non-Conformity;[28] he amused himself innocently with friends of his own age in a garden near Avignon, where a sister of the gardener's wife entertained him when his friends were not there.

Toward nightfall I went back to my inn, and L'Astrodi and the hunchbacked Lepi[29] (for such was her name) did not keep me waiting. When I saw their two figures before me I felt a kind of consternation. I thought it impossible that what I knew was bound to happen would happen. L'Astrodi, ugly and knowing it, was sure she could make up for all her deficiencies by extreme licentiousness. La Lepi, indubitably a hunchback, but remarkably talented in her profession, was sure of arousing desire with her beautiful eyes and her teeth, which seemed to project from her mouth only to show their beauty. L'Astrodi at once came and gave me a Florentine kiss,[30] to which I had to submit willy-nilly; La Lepi timidly offered me only her imaginary cheeks, which I pretended to kiss. When I saw L'Astrodi begin cutting loose, I asked her to go slowly, for being a novice at entertainments of this kind I had to be initiated little by little. She promised to behave.

Before supper, not knowing what to say, I asked her if she had a lover in Avignon, and she answered that she had only the Vice-Legate's Auditor,[31] who, though a pervert, was pleasant and generous.

"I adapted myself to his taste very easily," she said, "though last year in Paris I would have thought it impossible, for I imagined it must hurt, but I was wrong."

"What! The Auditor treats you like a boy?"

"Yes. My sister would have adored him, for it is her passion."

"But your sister was abundantly endowed in the way of hips."

"What about me? Here—look, feel."

"You pass muster very well; but wait, it's too early. We'll be gay after supper."

"Do you know," La Lepi said to her, "that you are a wanton?"

"A wanton?"

"Shame on you! Who ever heard of a woman pulling up her skirts like that!"

"My dear, you'll do the same. Being in good company is being in the Golden Age."[32]

"I am amazed," I said to L'Astrodi, "that you tell everyone what sort of dealings you have with the Auditor."

"It's not I who tell everybody, it's everybody who tells me, and I'm congratulated on it, for he has never

liked girls. I'd be ridiculous if I tried to deny it. I was
surprised at my sister, but in this world one mustn't be
surprised at anything. How about you—don't you like
that?"

"No, I like *this* better."

And so saying, I put my hand out toward La Lepi,
who was standing in front of me, and touched the place
on her dress which ought to correspond to her *this*, and,
my hand having found nothing, L'Astrodi burst out
laughing. She rose, took my hand, and, to place it opposite her friend's *this*, she guided it to no more than six
inches below her hump. It was there that, to my vast
astonishment, my fingers felt the upper end of the
work bench. La Lepi, who was ashamed to play the prude
by moving away, began to laugh; but I was left rather
nonplussed, for instead of having it in the middle of
her person she had it a quarter of the way; the other
three quarters were all thighs and legs. I became animated, thinking of the pleasure which this entirely new
sight would afford me after supper.

"Haven't you a lover, my dear Lepi?"

"So," said L'Astrodi, "she is a virgin."

"That's not true," said the other, "for I had a lover
in Bordeaux and another in Montpellier."

"Nevertheless," L'Astrodi rejoined, "you can say you
are a virgin, for you have never been different from
what you are now."

"That is true, too."

"What!" I said. "Then you were never a virgin?
Tell me about it please, for it's something entirely new."

"Never, for it's a fact that before my first lover
touched me I was just as I was after he had me. I was
twelve years old."

"What did he say when he found you weren't a
virgin?"

"When I swore to him that I was, he believed me,
and he attributed the thing to rickets."

"Then he didn't hurt you?"

"No, for I asked him to be gentle."

"You must try it," L'Astrodi said to me; "we'll do it after supper."

"Oh, no, no!" La Lepi answered. "Monsieur is so big."

"What a reason! Are you afraid he'll put his whole self inside you? Look—I'll show it to you."

"There you are," said La Lepi, "it's just what I supposed. It will never go in."

"You're right," said L'Astrodi, "it's a bit unfair; you shall strike a bargain with him. Monsieur will be satisfied if you take in half of it."

"It's not the length, my dear. The door is too narrow."

"In that case you're lucky. You can sell your virginity after having had two lovers. But that would be nothing new."

The dialogue between the girls made me laugh, and the hunchback's ingenuous talk, which had every appearance of truth, had already decided me to try her after supper.

At table I had the pleasure of seeing the two girls eat as if they were starving and drink relentlessly. The wine having produced its effect, it was L'Astrodi who proposed that we put ourselves in the state of nature, and I agreed, getting into bed first and turning my back. I did not turn toward them again until L'Astrodi called to me; and La Lepi drew all my attention. She was bashful, but by dint of praising everything I saw in detail I put her at ease, and I persuaded her to get into bed beside me; but without L'Astrodi she could never have lain on her back, for she had none; she was all hump. But L'Astrodi doubled up a bolster and fitted it to her so well that she made all her parts parallel, and the task was finally accomplished to perfection. It was she who took charge of the insertion and managed it so successfully that La Lepi, to encourage me, said I had

nothing more to fear. And so we brought the first act
to its conclusion with great pleasure.

During the intermission she gave me the kisses which
she could not give me in her ecstasy, for her head was
actually buried in her chest.

"It's my turn now," said L'Astrodi; "but since I
don't want to cuckold my Auditor, come and look the
land over first. I insist, because afterward you'll make
the journey with more courage. There!"

"What am I supposed to do with this half a lemon?"

"Squeeze the juice of it into the place. I want to see
with my own eyes that you are sure you're taking no
risk. Don't you know that if I were ill I couldn't stand
the smart of it?"

"I've done it. Are you satisfied?"

"Yes. But, above all, don't cheat me, because if I become pregnant my reputation is made. And you, Lepi,
lend our friend a hand." [33]

"What's 'lending a hand'?"

I had to interrupt the proceedings, for I was dying
with laughter. She insisted on teaching her how, and I
had to consent if I wanted her to let me do the same
thing to her. Since I had undertaken not to cheat her,
the business took a long time, but that was what she
wanted. She upbraided La Lepi, who, tired of lending
me a hand, told me to hurry up; and she showed her
so effectively that she had no need of her that we ended
simultaneously.

Thinking, after laughing so hard and doing so much,
that I was incapable of more, I told them to go; but
L'Astrodi objected and demanded punch. I was willing
to make it; but wanting no more of them, I dressed again.

The punch, which I made for them with champagne,
made them so wanton that they made me wanton again
with them. L'Astrodi put the other in such a position
that, seeing neither of her humps, I was pleased to imagine I was going to violate Jupiter's tall daughter. La

Lepi swore to me afterward that she had been the gainer by it; and I did not doubt her; but L'Astrodi, seeing me dead, would not listen to reason. She was determined to perform a miracle; but I would not let her kill me in order to resuscitate me. I promised them another supper of the same sort, intending not to keep my word. When, as they left, they saw ten louis, I thought they would eat me up. They got into my carriage, which was waiting for them at the door, giving me a thousand blessings. After eight hours' sleep I did not find myself in a state to complain of the more than lively entertainment; I quickly dressed to go for a walk.

But up comes Stuard, saying in what appeared to be great distress that if I did not arrange for him to leave before I did he would throw himself into the Rhone.

"I can afford twenty-five louis, Monsieur; but it is only to a lady gentle as a lamb that I will pay them over, and in private."

"Monsieur, it is exactly the amount we need; she is ready, go and talk to her. I shall not return until noon."

I put twenty-five louis into a pretty little purse and I hasten to my triumph. I enter her room in a respectful manner, and I see her in bed. As I approach she sits up, not troubling to pull up her shift, which left one of her breasts uncovered; and, before I open my mouth, here are the words which hers utters:

"I am here, Monsieur, prepared to pay you with my body for the paltry twenty-five louis my husband needs. Do whatever you will with me; you will meet no resistance; but remember that, in taking advantage of my need to assuage your brutality, you ought to feel far more deeply humiliated than I, who sell myself so cheaply only because necessity compels me. Your baseness is more shameful than mine. Come. Do your will."

With that she pushes the coverlet to the foot of the bed, displaying beauties with which I was already acquainted and which so ferocious a soul was unworthy to possess.

I gather up the coverlet, and I throw it over her in the greatest indignation.

"No, Madame," I reply; "it shall not be true that I leave this room humiliated by what you have said to me; it is you whom I will put to shame by telling you truths of which, if you were a decent woman, you could not be ignorant. I am no brute, and to convince you of it I leave without having enjoyed your charms, which I scorn and for which I had no idea of paying by giving you twenty-five paltry louis. There they are; but be sure that I give them to you only from a feeling of pity which I regret that I cannot overcome. Be sure, too, that, as soon as you give yourself to a man for money, even though it is for a hundred million, you are a prostitute if you do not at least pretend to love him; for then the man, unable to guess that you are feigning, will still think you are a decent woman. Farewell."

After that I returned to my room; and when her husband came to thank me, I at once asked him to say no more to me about his wife. The next morning he left with her for Lyons. The reader will learn at the proper time how I met them both again at Liège.

Dolci came during the afternoon to take me to his garden to see the gardener's sister-in-law. He was better looking than she. Put in a good humor, she only momentarily resisted his request to be kind to him in my presence; it was on this occasion that, having seen that nature had endowed him wonderfully well, I assured him that he did not need money from his father to travel, and he profited by my advice. He was a Ganymede[34] who, during his encounter with the girl in the garden, could easily have turned me into Jupiter.

On my way back to my inn, I saw getting out of a boat a young man some twenty-four or twenty-six years of age whose honest countenance was the picture of melancholy. He comes up to me and asks me for charity, displaying a bill authorizing him to ask it and a passport which showed me that he had left Madrid six weeks before. He was from Parma and his name was Gaetano Costa.[35] When I see "Parma," prepossession enters in; he interests me. I ask him what misfortune has reduced him to begging.

"The misfortune of not having money enough to return to my native country."

"What were you doing in Madrid, and why did you go there?"

"I went there four years ago as valet to Doctor Pistoria,[36] physician to the King of Spain; but not satisfied with my position, I asked him for permission to leave his service. This certificate shows you that he did not dismiss me."

"What can you do?"

"I write a good hand; I can serve as a secretary; in my own country I can follow the trade of scribe. Here are some French verses which I copied yesterday, and here are some Italian ones."

"Your handwriting is excellent; but can you write correctly by yourself?"

"From dictation I can write Latin and Spanish too."

"Correctly?"

"Yes, Monsieur, from dictation; for it is the person who dictates who must answer for the correctness."

I at once saw that the young man was an ignoramus; nevertheless, I take him to my room; I tell Leduc to speak to him in Spanish, and he answers reasonably well; but when I dictate to him in Italian and French I find that he does not know the first rules of orthography. I tell him that he does not know how to write, and, seeing him mortified, I console him by saying that I will take him to Genoa at my expense. He kisses my hand and assures me that I will find him a faithful servant.

I took a liking to him because he had a method of reasoning which was all his own and which he used in the belief that it gave him distinction; it was apparently

what had won him the good opinon of the ignoramuses
with whom he had associated until then, and he ingenu-
ously used it with everyone. I laughed in his face when,
by way of beginning, he modestly told me that the art
of writing consisted in having a legible hand, so it followed that the person with a more legible hand than
another was also the wiser. Since he said this with his
eyes fixed on something in my handwriting, he claimed,
without saying so, that I must be inferior to him. He
thought that because of this superiority in him I ought
to grant him a certain consideration. I laughed, I thought
he was not beyond learning, and I kept him. But for
these wild notions of his I should have given him charity,
and the whim of taking him with me would not have
entered my head. He made me laugh. He told me that
correct spelling was unnecessary, since those who read
and know a language do not need it in order to understand what the writing means, and those who do not
know a language cannot see the mistakes in it. Seeing
that I did not contradict him, he thought he had driven
me to the wall and he took my laughter for applause.
Having dictated something to him in French on the subject of the Council of Trent,[37] I exploded when I saw
"Trente" written with a three and a zero;[38] and when
I told him why I was laughing he said that it all came to
the same thing, since the reader could not fail to read
"Trente" if he had any knowledge of arithmetic. In
short, he had some intelligence, which was why he was
stupid; I thought it out of the ordinary, and I kept him.
I was more stupid than he. Then, too, he was a good
sort; he had no vices; he was addicted neither to women
nor to wine nor to gambling nor to bad company, he
seldom went out, and always alone. Leduc disliked him
because he put on airs as if he were my secretary, and
because he told him one day that every Spaniard with
bowlegs was descended from a Moor. Leduc was bow-

legged and, priding himself on old Christian descent, conceived an implacable hatred for Costa, who, after all, was right. It was for this reason that they had a fist fight two weeks later at Nice in Provence. Costa came whining to me with his nose swollen. I laughed. From that day on he respected Leduc, who because he had been longer in my service thought himself his superior. I have dilated on this Costa so that my reader may have an accurate idea of him, for unfortunately I shall have more to say about him in the course of these memoirs.

I left the next morning and went on to Marseilles without troubling to stop at Aix, where the Parlement[39] sits. I put up at the "Thirteen Cantons," [40] being of a mind to spend at least a week in that ancient city, with which I had a great wish to become acquainted and at the same time to be completely free there; for that reason I had furnished myself with no letters of introduction; well supplied with cash, I did not need to be known to anyone. I at once informed the innkeeper that I would always eat in my room alone, and always fish; I knew that the fish to be had in that city were more delicate than those of the Atlantic and the Adriatic.

I went out the next morning, followed by a hire servant to show me the way back to my inn when I should tire of walking about. Strolling at random, I found myself on a remarkably wide and very long quay, where I thought I was in Venice. I see shops in which wines from the Levant and Spain were sold at retail, and where a number of people who preferred them to coffee and chocolate were breakfasting. I see the preoccupied haste of those who are coming and going, bumping into each other and wasting no time begging pardon. I see shopkeepers and hucksters offering all kinds of merchandise, and pretty girls, some dressed well, others poorly, side by side with women whose brazen manner seemed to say to those who looked at them, "You have only to follow me." I also see others who, though well dressed, walk modestly on, looking at no one in order to arouse more interest.

Everywhere I seem to see the freedom of my native country in the mixture of all nations which I observe and in the different costumes. It was a hodgepodge of Greeks, Turks, Africans, pirates (at least to judge from their looks), Jews, monks, charlatans, and from time to time I see Englishmen, who say nothing or talk to each other in low tones without taking much notice of anyone.

I stop at a street corner only long enough to read the announcement of the play[41] which was being performed that day, then I go to dinner very well pleased, and even better pleased after dinner because of the excellent fish I had been served. The red mullet eaten there, which we call *barboni* in Venice and the Tuscans *triglie,* are incomparable. The French call them *rougets,* presumably because their heads and fins are red.

I dressed to go to the play, and took a place in the amphitheater.[42]

CHAPTER IV

Rosalie. Toulon. Nice. My arrival in Genoa.
Signor Grimaldi. Veronica and her sister.

I SEE that the four boxes to my right, like those to
my left, are occupied by pretty women, all prepossessing
and elegantly attired, and I see no men with them. During the first intermission I see young gentlemen wearing
swords, and others without them, approach the boxes and
converse familiarly with these ladies, or light women,
and I hear a young Knight of Malta[1] say to the one
who was alone in the box beside me:

"I will come to breakfast with you tomorrow."

It was all I needed. I examine her more carefully, and,
finding her appetizing, I do not hesitate, as soon as I
see the Knight make off, to ask her if she would let me
come to supper.

"With pleasure, my friend; but I've been caught so
many times that if you don't 'earnest' me, I shan't expect you."

"How am I to 'earnest' you, I don't understand."

"Apparently you have just arrived."

She laughs and summons the Knight with her fan.

"Explain to this foreigner, please, who asks me to let him come to supper tonight, what 'to earnest' means."

He says with a smile that Mademoiselle, to make sure I would not fail to do her the honor, wishes me to pay for the supper in advance. I thank him, and I ask the young lady if a louis is enough. She says it will do, and, giving it to her, I ask for her address. She hadn't a card in her pocket; but she asks the Knight to tell me the way to her house. He very politely says that when we leave the theater he will take me there himself; and he adds that she is the greatest wanton in Marseilles. He asks me if I have been in Marseilles before, I say I have not and that I have just arrived; and he congratulates himself on having made my acquaintance. We go to the center of the amphitheater, and, talking on, he names each of the fourteen or sixteen girls whom we see there, all of them ready to furnish the first comer with supper. He says that they all have free entrance to the theater and that the manager finds it to his advantage, for since decent women would not occupy those boxes they would be empty and the house would be dull. I scrutinize them, and I find five or six who are prettier than the one I had honored with my choice; but I count on the following days. I ask the Knight if he has a favorite among these beauties, and he answers no. He says he is in love with a dancer, whom he supports, but that, not being jealous of her, he will take me to her house. I assure him that it will be a pleasure; the ballet comes on; he points her out to me, and I congratulate him. At the end of the play he takes me to the door of my new conquest, and, after saying that we will meet again, he leaves me there.

I go upstairs, I find her in dishabille, and she no longer attracts me; but she makes some wanton sallies at which I laugh, and I sup reasonably well. After supper she goes to bed and invites me to do the same, but I excuse myself, saying that I never sleep out. She then shows me the coverall which sets the mind at rest, and, finding it too thick, I refuse it. She says that thin ones cost three livres and that everyone considers them too expensive.

"Give me a thin one."

"I have a dozen; but the dealer will not sell them singly."

"I will buy the dozen."

"Very well."

She rings, and a girl comes in whom she orders to bring her the package on her toilet table. The girl's face and her modest bearing strike me, and I tell her so.

"She is fifteen," she says; "but she's a silly goose and won't do anything because she claims to be a virgin."

"May I inspect her?"

"She won't let you. Ask her and you'll see."

The girl comes back with the package. I put myself in condition to order her to choose me one which fits well, and she sulkily begins looking and measuring.

"This one doesn't fit properly," I say, "try another"; and another and another, until I suddenly splash her and no mistake, her mistress laughs, and she, indignant at my scurvy trick, throws the whole packet in my face and angrily leaves. Having no further desire to do anything, I pay her for the coveralls and I leave. However, the girl whom I had treated so badly comes to light my way, and I make it up to her generously, giving her a louis. Very much surprised, she begs me not to tell her mistress.

"Is it true, my dear, that you still have your maidenhead?"

"Perfectly true, Monsieur."

"And why won't you let yourself be inspected?"

"Because it revolts me."

"You'll have to make up your mind to it, for otherwise, pretty as you are, one is at a loss what to do with you. Will you let me?"

"Yes, but not in this house."

"Then where?"

"Have someone bring you to my mother's house tomorrow morning, and I'll be there. Your hire valet knows the way."

Returning to my inn, I ask the valet if he knows the girl who lighted me down, and he replies that he does and that he had been astonished to see her there because he thought she was a decent girl.

"You shall take me to her mother's house tomorrow morning."

"Gladly."

The next morning he takes me at ten o'clock to a wretched one-story house on the outskirts of the city, where I see a woman spinning flax and children eating bread. She asks me what I want.

"Your daughter is not here?"

"No. And if she were, do you take me for her bawd?"

Just then the girl arrives, and the infuriated mother throws a bottle at her head which would have killed her if she had not missed her aim. I step between them, raising my cane, the children scream, my valet comes in and shuts the door; but the woman's rage does not abate, she calls her daughter a whore at the top of her voice, she orders her to leave the house, she says she is no longer her mother, and I can hardly hold her. My valet tells her not to shout so loud because of the neighbors, and she answers:

"Hold your tongue, you pimp."

I give her an écu, she throws it in my face, whereupon I open the door and go out with the poor girl, my valet snatching her from the hands of her mother, who had taken her by the hair. I am booed and jostled by the mob which followed me and which would have torn me to pieces if I had not taken refuge in a church, which I left by a different door a quarter of an hour later. I have never in all my life escaped from a greater danger. What saved me was my fear of angering the town mob, for I knew its ferocity.

Two hundred paces before I reach my inn I am joined by the girl, who is clinging to my valet's arm.

"Knowing how savage your mother is," I ask her, "how could you make me run such a risk?"

"I thought she would respect you."

"Try to stop crying. I don't know how I can be of use to you."

"I shall certainly not go back where I was yesterday. There is nothing for me but the streets."

I ask my valet if he knows some decent woman who would give her lodging, for which I would pay; he replies that he knows a place where furnished rooms are let; I tell him to go there and I will follow. He enters a house, where an old man shows me rooms on every floor. The girl says she needs only a lodging for six francs a month, and the man goes up to the attic, opens a garret with his key, and says:

"This one is six francs; but I must have the month's rent in advance and I warn you that my door is locked at ten o'clock and that no one must ever spend the night with you."

I saw a bed with coarse sheets, but clean; two chairs, a table, and a chest of drawers. The window was glazed and had blinds. I ask the man how much he will take per day to board her, and he says twenty sous, with two sous for the maid who will bring up her meals and do her room. The girl answers that she is satisfied, and she pays the month's rent and twenty sous for meals that day. I leave her there, saying that I will see her again.

Going downstairs with the old man, I ask him for a room for myself; and he gives me one at a louis, which I pay him on the spot. He gives me a skeleton key which

fits the street door so that I can enter at any hour I
please. He says that he cooks in his own part of the
house and that he will prepare meals for me at whatever
price I stipulate.

After doing this good deed, the source of which appeared to be a virtue, I dined alone, then went to a large
coffeehouse, where I saw the agreeable Knight of Malta
playing.[2] He left off when he saw me, putting in his
purse the ten or twelve louis he had won. After asking
me if I had been satisfied with the girl with whom I had
supped, and hearing that I had done nothing, he asked
me if I should like to have him introduce me to his
dancer, and we went there. We found her at her toilet
table having her hair arranged by a hairdresser. She received me with the jocularity which is appropriate to
old acquaintance. She did not interest me; but for the
Knight's sake I showed no sign of it.

After the hairdresser left, she had to dress for the
theater, and she did not stand on ceremony. The Knight
helped her change her shift, which she did with the
greatest freedom, though asking my pardon. I said with
a laugh that she had indeed made me uncomfortable;
she refuses to believe it, she comes to me to learn the
truth and, finding that I have lied, she calls me a milk-
sop.

There is not a city in France in which light women are
as profligate as they are in Marseilles. Not only do they
pride themselves on refusing nothing; they are the first
to offer the man what he perhaps does not dare ask for.
She showed me a repeating watch on which she had got
up a lottery at twelve francs a ticket, and offered me
one, saying that she still had ten. I took them all, I paid
her five louis, then I made her a present of the tickets.
She ran to kiss me, telling her Knight that I could cuckold him whenever I wished. He replied that nothing
would please him better. He invited me to sup with her,
and politeness prompted me to accept; but after supper

the only pleasure I enjoyed was watching the Knight pay her his respects in bed. I found him much less well endowed than Dolci.

After wishing them good night I left them on the pretext of my poor health, and I went to the furnished room in which I had placed the unfortunate girl. Having the key, I entered the house; the maidservant got up to show me to my room. It was midnight. I asked her if I might go to the garret, and she took me there at once. She knocked, and when the girl heard my voice she opened the door, and I sent the maid to wait for me in my room. I sit down on her bed; I ask her if she is satisfied, and she replies that she is happy.

"Then I hope I shall find you kind, and I shall come to bed with you."

"You may do whatever you please; but I warn you that I have given myself to a lover, though it was only once; but that's enough to keep you from finding me quite intact. Forgive me if I lied to you yesterday. I could not guess that you would love me."

Gentle as a lamb, she lets me lay bare all her beauties, feast on them with my eyes, explore them with my hands, and devour them with my mouth, and the mere thought that I was to become possessed of this treasure sets my soul on fire; but her obedient manner distresses me.

"My dear Rosalie" (such was her name), "your submissiveness shows me that you do not love me. Why do you not kindle to my desires?"

"I do not dare; I am afraid you will suspect me of pretending."

Both artifice and deceit are capable of such an answer; but at that moment it could be given only by candor. Impatient to clasp her in my arms, I quickly strip off everything which could lessen my pleasure, I lie down beside her, and a moment later I am surprised to find that she had lied when she said she had had a lover. I tell her so.

"Never," I say, "did a girl tell that sort of lie."

"I am glad that you think it is not true; but it is only too sure that I had a lover, and this is how.

"Two months ago my mother, though hot-tempered, loved me. I worked as a seamstress, I earned twenty and sometimes even thirty sous a day, and I gave it all to her; I'd never had a lover, and I didn't care; I laughed at people praising me for being virtuous when I had no idea that I was being anything of the kind. I had been brought up from childhood never to look young men I met in the street in the face and never to answer when they said silly things to me.

"Well, two months ago a rather good-looking young man, a native of Genoa and a merchant in a small way, made my mother's acquaintance by bringing her some fine cotton stockings to wash. When he saw me he didn't say much in my praise; but all that he said was perfectly honorable, I liked him, and he began coming to our house every evening; my mother was always present, sitting near me, but he never even took my hand to kiss it. My mother, very pleased to see that the young man loved me, often scolded me for not putting myself out to be polite to him. He was to leave for Genoa in a small ship which he owned, carrying merchandise, and he had assured us he would come back in the spring of the following year and would then declare his intentions, which would depend on his still finding me well behaved and, above all, without a lover. No more was needed. Considering him my future husband, my mother often let me talk with him at the door of our house until midnight. When he left I shut the door and got into bed beside her. I always found her asleep.

"Four or five days before he was to leave he persuaded me to walk fifty paces from our house with him to drink a glass of good muscatel at the shop of a Greek merchant who served customers all night. We spent only half an hour alone there together, and it was on that day that I first let him give me a few kisses. If when I got back to the house I had found my mother awake I would have told her all about it, for the pleasure I had felt seemed to me perfectly innocent.

"On the next day but one, urged to grant him the same favor, I consented, and love began to gain ground. The caresses we exchanged no longer seemed innocent, for we knew that we had gone beyond the bounds of decency; even so, we forgave ourselves because we had managed to abstain from the final act.

"Again on the next day but one, my lover having to weigh anchor that night, he took leave of my mother, and after she had gone to bed I did not hesitate to grant him a pleasure which I desired as much as he did. We went to the usual place, we ate to make us thirsty, we drank to quench our thirst, and our heated senses so emboldened our love that, forgetting our duty, we believed we were achieving a triumph. After our defeat we went to sleep, and, on waking to the light of day, we recognized the sin we had committed. We rose more melancholy than happy, and I went home, where my mother, who was already up, received me in more or less the same way as you saw her do yesterday. I assured her that marriage would wipe out the shame of my crime, and at this confession she took up a stick, with which she would perhaps have killed me if I had not taken to my heels.

"I spent the whole morning in a church, and at dinnertime, not knowing where to go, I was wandering through the streets when I met a woman I knew whose trade was finding situations for maidservants. I asked her if she might have a situation for me, and she replied that she had been asked for a girl that morning; but that the mistress of the house was a courtesan and hence I would run the risk of becoming the same. I replied that I was sure I could defend myself, and the woman placed me in the house of ill fame where you found me. The young lady was pleased to see me and even more pleased when,

in answer to her questions, I said that I had never been
with a man. But I heartily repented of having told her
that lie.

"During the week I spent in the abandoned woman's
house I was treated every day to the most outrageous and
humiliating affronts that ever a girl endured. All the
men who came there had no sooner seen me and been told
that I was a virgin than they wanted to have me; they
immediately offered me five or six louis, but I had to
begin by letting them inspect me. I refused, and they
made fun of me. Five or six times a day I had to witness
the brutal excesses of the men who came to amuse themselves with my mistress, and when they were ready to
leave at night and I lighted them down the stairs, they
assailed me with the coarsest insults because I refused to
do what they wanted for a twelve-sou piece; then they
gave me half a copper,[3] saying that I must be rotten with
the pox. When I went up to my garret to bed I barred
my door; I thought I would kill myself when you came
last evening and treated me in a way more shameful
than I thought it possible to imagine; but when you left
you were so reasonable and so generous that I not only
forgave you, I loved you, believing that you were the
man whom Providence had sent me and, above all, the
man to calm my mother and persuade her to let me come
home, being sure that my lover, returning in the spring
and finding me there, would marry me. But since this
morning I have lost all faith in my mother, who apparently believes I am a prostitute. Now I am yours, if you
want me, and I forever renounce my lover, well knowing
that I have become unworthy of him. Take me for your
servant, and I will love you and you alone as faithfully
as if I were your wife, and you will never find any ambition in me."

Whether they sprang from virtue or from weakness, I
know that Rosalie saw my tears before I saw hers. But

Amorous Trifling at Supper

Listening Girl

she shed them in torrents when she saw that I was touched.

"I think," I said, "you have only one shift."

"And another, which I happened to have in my pocket. Everything I owned was left at my mother's."

"Set your heart at rest, my dear Rosalie, tomorrow you shall have everything you may need, and tomorrow evening you shall sup with me in the room I have rented on the third floor. I will take care of you, sleep in peace."

"Then you pity me?"

"I believe, my dear child, that I love you."

"God grant it!"

This heartfelt "God grant it" sent me away laughing, and the maidservant, who had been waiting two hours for me, stopped scowling[4] when she saw a six-franc piece. I ordered her to tell her master I would eat a fast-day supper in my room with Rosalie and that I liked to eat well.

I went to the "Thirteen Cantons," truly in love with the poor girl, whose real story I had finally heard from her own beautiful lips. I felt she had shown so much virtue that she seemed not yet to have committed any sin. I decided never to abandon her. It is the decision to which one always comes when one is in love.

The next morning I went out on foot with my hire valet, instructing him to take me to some ready-made establishment where I could buy my unfortunate Rosalie everything she needed in the way of attire which, though not luxurious, would not suggest poverty.

At fifteen she had the figure of a girl of twenty, with a fully developed bosom and everything in excellent proportion. I did not go wrong in a single measurement. I spent my whole morning making the purchases, and my valet took her a small trunk containing two dresses, shifts, petticoats, stockings, handkerchiefs, bonnets, gloves, slippers, a fan, a work bag, and a mantle. De-

lighted with having thus prepared a delicious spectacle
for my soul, I could scarcely wait to enjoy it at supper.

The Knight of Malta dropped in and invited himself
to dine with me, and I was glad of it. Afterward he
persuaded me to go to the theater, for, he told me, it
being a day on which the subscriptions were suspended,
I should see the best people in Marseilles in the boxes and
no light women in the amphitheater, for on these days
they could get in only by paying. He introduced me to
a woman who received people of standing at her house,
and she invited me there; but I declined, saying that I
had to leave. However, it was an acquaintance which
proved useful in connection with what was to befall me
not long after I arrived in Marseilles for the second time.
Her name was Audibert.[5]

I did not wait for the end of the play before going to
see Rosalie, whom I really believed I did not recognize
when she appeared before me. She was a tall brunette
with black eyes, narrow eyebrows, delicate features in a
face without much color and white as a lily. Her cheeks
had two dimples which appeared only when she smiled,
and there was one on her chin. Her lower lip, of the
most brilliant carmine and protruding a little beyond
the upper, seemed made to receive a kiss and keep it
from falling. All this made up a rare countenance, one
of those which impress because they speak and make one
long to know what they are saying. To see Rosalie's
beauty rightly one had to see her smiling, and until then
I had always seen her sad; sadness had vanished and
given place to the sweetness of gratitude and satisfaction.
Examining her attentively, I was proud of my handiwork; but I had to get over my surprise quickly, for I
could not but apprehend that she might be afraid I was
passing an unfavorable judgment on her. So I hastened
to impart my thoughts to her, ending by assuring her
that, she being such as God had made her, I should ex-

pose myself to eternal ridicule if I kept her with me as a
servant.

"You shall, my dear Rosalie, be my indubitable mistress, and my servants shall show you the same respect
they would show my wife."

At that Rosalie, as if restored from death to life, said
what my various kindnesses had made her feel, her confused expressions flooding my soul with joy, for I was
certain I was hearing no tricks of art.

Having had no mirror in her garret, she had dressed
without using one. I saw that she did not dare go to a
large mirror which was there, I urged her to look at herself, and I saw her laugh; she said she was inclined to
think she was in disguise. She praised the tastefulness
and simplicity of her dress, and she vented her anger at
the thought that her mother would consider it all sinful.

"You must forget your cruel mother. You look like a
lady of quality, and I shall feel proud in Genoa when I
am asked if you are my daughter."

"In Genoa?"

"Yes, Genoa. You turn pale?"

"It is from surprise, for I may well see a man there
whom I have not yet forgotten."

"Do you want to stay here?"

"No, no! Love me. Be sure that I prefer you, and not
from mercenary motives."

"Now you want to cry. Let us embrace each other, my
angel."

She came to my arms and showered me with the sweet
tears she could not hold back. In this state we sat down
at table, waited on by the only maidservant in the house.
We had dishes even tastier than those I was given to eat
at the "Thirteen Cantons." I ate cuttlefish, which are
known as *sipions*[6] and which I found delicious, eel livers,
a crab more delicate than those from the Atlantic; I ate
like an Apicius[7] and was put out to find that Rosalie
could not eat.

"Have you the failing, dear heart, of not liking to eat well?"

"No one has a better appetite than mine, and I have an excellent digestion, as you will see when my heart and my soul have become a little more accustomed to the joy which overwhelms me."

"But you are not drinking either, and this wine is excellent. If you like the Greek's muscat I will send for some. It will remind you of your lover."

"If you want to be completely kind to me, pray in future spare me the greatest mortification to which you can subject me."

"I will subject you to none, my dear Rosalie—please forgive me. It will not happen again."

"When I see you I am in despair because I did not know you before I knew him."

"That feeling is enough, my dear one; it is sublime just because you have drawn it only from your beautiful soul. You are beautiful and virtuous, for you yielded only to love, and when I think that you are mine I am in despair because I am not sure that you love me, for my Evil Genius wants me to believe that if I had not rescued you I should not see you loving."

"Evil Genius indeed! Certainly, if I had met you in the street without knowing you I should not have fallen madly in love with you; but I am equally certain that I should have found you pleasing. I feel that I love you, and that it is not because of your generosity, for I feel, too, that if I were rich and you poor I would do anything for you; but I do not want that. I prefer being in your debt to seeing you in mine. That is all I know, and all that my intelligence can compass. You must guess the rest."

It was midnight; we were still at table; and I see the old master of the house asking me if I am satisfied.

"Not merely satisfied, but grateful. Who prepared this supper?"

"My daughter; but it is expensive."

"Hang the expense, my friend; you will be satisfied with me as I am with you, and tomorrow night you shall serve me the same sort of supper; and the charming young woman you see there will feel better and will eat."

"She will have a good appetite in bed. The same thing happened to me sixty years ago. You laugh, Mademoiselle?"

"I am laughing at the pleasure you must take in remembering it."

"You are right. And that is why I forgive young people all the sins they commit for love."

"You are a wise man," I said.

"If he is wise," said Rosalie when he had gone, "my mother is a great fool."

"Would you like me to take you to the theater tomorrow?"

"No, no—please not! I would obey you, but it would distress me. No theater and no walks. How people would talk! Nothing in Marseilles; but everything anywhere else, and gladly."

"Just as you please. But you shall have this room. No more garret. We shall leave in three days."

"So soon?"

"Yes. You shall tell me tomorrow anything you need for traveling which I might overlook."

"Another lined mantle, half-length boots, a nightcap, combs, a powder bag, a powder puff, a pot of pomade, and a prayer book so that I can go to mass."

"Then you can read?"

"Read and write."

"Giving me such an order is real proof of your love; one cannot love without reliance. Don't fear that I may forget anything; but you shall see to the boots yourself; there is a bootmaker ten paces from here; you can have your measurements taken at once."

With all this talk I prepared Rosalie for the delicious night we spent together. We slept for seven hours, which were preceded and followed by two of caresses. We got up at noon knowing each other intimately. Rosalie addressed me as *"tu,"* she no longer talked of gratitude, she had become used to happiness, and she laughed scornfully at her past afflictions. She came running to me in season and out of season, and in her enthusiasm she called me her child, who had brought her happiness, she devoured me with kisses, and, in short, she made me happy; and since in this life nothing is real except the present, I enjoyed it, dismissing the images of the past and loathing the darkness of the always dreadful future, for it offers nothing certain except death, *ultima linea rerum* ("the final boundary line of all things").[8]

My second night with Rosalie was more delightful than the first, for, having eaten a good supper and drunk sufficiently though moderately, in bed she was able to refine upon the pleasures of Venus and to surrender with less reserve to the furies she inspires.

I gave her a gold needle, with which to amuse herself tatting, and a watch. She said that she wanted one and would never have dared to ask me for it; but seeing that such a fear of displeasing me by asking me for something was a sign of little confidence in me, she promised, kissing me again and again, that in future she would not hide the slightest of her fancies from me. Thus did it please me to instruct her, and I was proud to think that the education I should give her would make her perfect.

On the fourth day I instructed her to be ready to get into my carriage as soon as I came to her room to give her my arm down the stairs. I told neither Leduc nor Costa anything; but I had told Rosalie that I had two servants with whom I often talked in order to laugh at the stupid things they said, but that she must be very reserved with them and beware of indulging in the slightest familiarity; she must give them absolute orders, never doubting that they would be obeyed immediately, but without pride, and must not let any soft-heartedness keep her from telling me if my servants failed in any way to show her respect.

So I set out from the "Thirteen Cantons" with four post horses, having relegated Leduc and Costa to the coachman's seat. My hire valet, whom I had paid liberally, had seen to tying Rosalie's trunk behind the carriage. I had the coachman stop at the door of the house in which she was waiting for me; I went to her room for her, and, after thanking the kind old man, who was sorry to see so likable a girl leave, I seated her in my carriage, ordering the postilions to take the road to Toulon, which I wanted to see before going to Italy. We reached it in five hours.

My dear Rosalie supped with me, maintaining a dignified manner, chiefly to impress Leduc, who claimed it was Costa's place to stand behind her chair. Without looking at him I told Rosalie that it was he who would have the honor to wait on her and to dress her hair whenever she wished; at that he gave in, making her a bow.

The next day we went to see the port,[9] and it was the Commandant himself who, happening to be there, did us the honor of showing us everything; I generously accorded him that of giving Rosalie his arm; and I had little difficulty in persuading him to stay to dinner with us.

Though with absolutely no experience of society, the girl spoke little but always well and responded with great charm to all the attentions and compliments which the amiable Commandant paid her.

In the afternoon he took us to see the arsenal, and politeness demanded that I accept his invitation to supper. There was no question of introducing Rosalie. It was the Commandant who introduced his wife, his daughter, and his son to me. I saw with pleasure that my young sweetheart held her own with women of fashion even

better than with men. The ladies paid her every warm
attention she could wish, and she received them as if to
the manner born, with modesty and deference and that
sweetness of manner which is the infallible sign of a
good upbringing.

I was urgently invited to dinner the next day, but I
took my leave. She jumped on my neck for joy when,
back at the inn, I told her I had been thoroughly pleased
with her.

"But," she said, "I'm always afraid of being asked
who I am."

"In good company in France, my dear child, no one
will ever ask you such a stupid question."

"But if I had been asked, how should I have answered?"

"By a subterfuge."

"What's that?"

" 'Please, Madam,—or Sir,—ask my traveling companion.' "

"I understand. It's called a subterfuge because it
evades the question; but shouldn't I be rude if I answered that way?"

"Yes, but not as rude as the person who questioned
you."

"And what would you answer if you were asked the
same question?"

"That would depend on who asked it. If I didn't want
to tell the truth, I should not be at a loss for things to
say. In the meanwhile, I thank you for being interested
in my lessons. Keep asking. You are my jewel, and it
is my part to set you and make you shine. Let us go to
bed, for we must leave early tomorrow so that we shall
be at Antibes[10] the day after."

In that city I engaged a felucca[11] for Genoa, and, intending to return to France by the same route, I put my
carriage in a stable, under a written agreement to pay
six francs a month.

We left Antibes early; but two hours later, a strong wind having come up, and I seeing that my angel was dying with fear, I would not allow the sail to be hoisted. I had the felucca rowed into the harbor of Villefranche,[12] and, to find a good lodging, I hired a carriage and went to Nice,[13] where the bad weather obliged me to remain for three days.

I thought it my duty to make my bow to the Commandant, who was an old officer named Paterson.[14] The first thing he asked me was if I knew a Russian who went by the name of Charles Ivanov. I replied that I had seen him in a house in Grenoble.

"He is said to have escaped from Siberia and to be the youngest son of the Duke of Kurland."

"I have been told so too, but I know nothing about it."

"He has gone to Genoa, where a banker is said to have instructions to give him twenty thousand scudi; nevertheless, he found no one here who would give him a sou. I sent him to Genoa at my own expense to rid the city of him."

I was very glad that he had left before I arrived. An old officer named Ramini,[15] who was staying at my inn, asked me if I would take charge of a packet which Monsieur de Saint-Pierre,[16] the Spanish Consul, had to send to the Marchese Grimaldi in Genoa. I took charge of it with pleasure as soon as I learned that he was the same Marchese Grimaldi I had just seen in Avignon. Ramini also asked me if in Avignon I had met a Madame Stuard, who had spent two weeks in Nice with her so-called husband, penniless, never saying a word, enchanting everyone by her beauty, and not vouchsafing anyone so much as a smile. I told him she was no longer in Avignon and that it was I who had given her the means to leave there.

"But," I added, "how did she manage to get away from here without money?"

"Nobody knows. She left in a carriage, and the innkeeper was paid. I am very curious about her. The
Marchese Grimaldi told me she refused a hundred louis
he offered her and that she had treated a Venetian in
the same fashion. Perhaps you are the man."

"I am he; but I gave her the money nevertheless."

Commandant Paterson came to see me toward nightfall, and I saw that he was enchanted by my beautiful
Rosalie. What amused me in this city, where one ought
to be bored and in which the midges devour foreigners
in preference to the inhabitants, was a small faro bank
at the coffeehouse,[17] at which I made Rosalie play too.
Lucky on each of the three days, she won twenty Piedmontese pistole.[18] She put them in a little purse; and
she told me afterward that her one wish was to have a
purse with money in it. I was cross with her because, by
not having confided this wish to me, she had broken her
promise; but we made up without too much difficulty.

Thus did I bind her to me, hoping that I would keep
her all the rest of my life and that, living happily with
her, I should not need to run from one beauty to another.

The weather having turned fair, we set sail at nightfall and the next morning landed in Genoa, which I had
never seen. I put up at the "Santa Marta" inn,[19] where,
for decency's sake, I took two adjoining rooms, having
my servants sleep in a closet next door.

The next morning I sent the package to Signor Grimaldi by Costa and later left my visiting card at the door
of his palazzo.

I had a valet whom I engaged take me to a linen
draper's, where I bought enough linen to keep Rosalie
busy making up her deficiencies in that department. My
gift gave her the greatest pleasure.

We were still at table when the Marchese Grimaldi
was no sooner announced than he embraced me in person and thanked me for having taken charge of his
packet. The first thing he asked me was for news of

Madame Stuard, and after hearing the whole story he laughed and said he did not know what he would have done in my place.

As he was looking at Rosalie with great attention, I said that she was a young lady whose goodness interested me as much as her beauty. I told him I wanted to find her a decent girl who could serve her as chambermaid, sew with her, go out with her dressed in the costume of the country, and above all speak good Italian to her so that she could learn it, for I wanted to be able to introduce her in Florence, Rome, and Naples.

"Why will you not accord the city of Genoa such a great pleasure? I offer to introduce the young lady everywhere, beginning with my own house, by any name and style you may designate."

"She has very good reasons for seeing no one here."

"That is enough. Do you expect to spend some time here?"

"A month at most. Our pleasures will consist in seeing the city and its surroundings and going to the theater.[20] We shall spend agreeable hours at table, where we shall daily eat such excellent mushrooms[21] as we have eaten today."

"A delightful program, I could not offer you a happier life than the one you propose to lead here. I will try, Mademoiselle, to find you a girl who will serve you well in all capacities."

"You, Monsieur? You are very kind to take such an interest in me."

"My interest is infinite, and even greater now that I have the illusion that I am in Marseilles."

Rosalie blushed, for she did not know that she rolled her r's and hence a man who had traveled could instantly tell her native country; but I immediately enlightened her and so set her mind at rest.

I having asked Signor Grimaldi how I could obtain the *Journal des Savants*[22] and the *Mercure de France*[23] and all such publications, he promised to send me a vendor who would see to it. He said as he left that he would come to breakfast with me the next day if I would allow him to make me a present of his chocolate, which he promised himself I would find excellent. I replied that he could not give me a more welcome present.

After he left she asked me to take her to a milliner's, where she wanted to buy ribbons and other things she needed, paying for them with her own money and striking her own bargain without my interfering.

"With all my heart. And afterwards we will go to the play."

At the milliner's, who was French, I found my little mistress charming; she assumed a lofty air, pretended to know everything, ordered bonnets of the latest fashion, bargained, and spent five or six louis with great aplomb. I said when we left that I had been taken for her lackey and that I would have my revenge. So saying, I take her to a jeweler's shop, and I buy handsome paste buckles, earrings, and a necklace without letting her say a word, I pay the price asked, and we go out.

"My dear friend, what you bought is charming, but you don't know how to spend your money. If you had bargained you would have saved at least four louis."

We went to the play; but since she did not understand a word of it she was so bored that at the end of the first act she asked me to take her back to the inn. I found a small chest which Signor Grimaldi had sent me, containing twenty-four pounds of chocolate. I told Costa, who had boasted of his skill in preparing it, that when Signor Grimaldi arrived the next morning he was to serve us three cups of it.

He came at nine o'clock with a merchant who sold me two large pieces of the finest cotton, with a pattern of flowers in various colors on a white ground, made in Peking, from which Rosalie was to have two *mezzaro*[24] made so that she could go about Genoa with her head covered according to the custom of the city, as the *zendale*[25] is used in Venice and the mantilla[26] in Madrid.

I thanked him heartily for the generous present of chocolate he had sent me, which we found exquisite. Costa strutted when he heard Signor Grimaldi praise him for the foam he had ordered him to whip up; and a moment later Leduc announced a woman by a name unknown to me. Signor Grimaldi said she was the mother of the chambermaid I had asked him to procure for me.

I see a very well-dressed woman followed by a girl of twenty-three or twenty-four, whom, merely glancing at her, I find very pretty. The mother, after thanking the Marchese Grimaldi, introduces her daughter to Rosalie, describes all her accomplishments, says that she is a good girl, assures her that she will serve her faithfully and that she can go out with her honorably. She could speak French, she would find her cheerful and willing. That done, she told her how much a lady she had served had given her per month besides her board, and she ended by asking her not to make her eat with the servants, for her daughter's only weakness was insisting on being respected. Her name was Veronica.[27] Rosalie, after agreeing to everything, said that insisting on being respected was not a weakness, for one could only demand respect by being respectable.

"So I will keep her, and I hope she will love me."

Veronica takes her hand, and Rosalie, with modest and affable dignity, lets her kiss it. The mother leaves, telling her daughter that she will at once send her all her clothes, and Rosalie takes her to her room to begin giving her her orders.

I felt it incumbent on me to thank the nobleman most particularly, for I thought it obvious that his choice of such a chambermaid had been made more for my sake than for Rosalie's. I said that I would not fail to wait upon him and that I would ascertain at what hours he received. He said that I could easily find him at his casino in Sampierdarena,[28] where he often spent the night.

A F T E R H E left, seeing that Rosalie was very busy with Veronica, I went and amused myself translating *L'Écossaise*,[1] to have it played by the troupe then at Genoa, whom I thought quite good actors.

At dinner, finding Rosalie sad, I asked her the reason.

"That Veronica," she said, "is prettier than I am."

"She is nothing compared with you; and you are my only beauty; but to reassure you I will ask Signor Grimaldi tomorrow to tell her mother she must take her home and to find you another chambermaid who is very ugly instead."

"No, because he would think I am jealous, and that would distress me."

"Then cheer up, for it pains me to see you sad."

"Well then, my dear, you will see me gay again as soon as I am sure you do not love her."

"I can assure you that I did not even see her eyes."

"What an idea of the Signore's to give me such a pretty maid! Did he want to play a trick on me?"

"On the contrary, he wanted to convince you that you need fear comparison with nobody. Are you satisfied with her?"

"She works very well, and she is most respectful. She doesn't speak four words to me without calling me *Signora,* and whatever she says to me in Italian she immediately explains in French. In a month I shall be speaking it so well that we won't need to take her to Florence with us. I've ordered Leduc to move out of the closet and sleep somewhere else; and I will send her dinner from our table. I will treat her well; but remember to reassure me."

"That will be easy enough, for I cannot see that there will be anything in common between her and me."

"Then you forgive me for having felt afraid?"

"You would not have felt so if you loved me less."

"I thank you, but keep my secret."

I made up my mind never to look at Veronica, for I loved my Rosalie too much to cause her the slightest distress.

I spent the day without going out, translating *L'Écossaise,* and the next morning I stayed at Signor Grimaldi's[2] until noon.

I got a man to show me the way to the banker Belloni's[3] office, where I changed all the gold coins I had into Florentine zecchini;[4] and when I made myself known the head of the house did me every honor. I had some twelve or fourteen thousand Roman scudi on Belloni and twenty thousand on Lepri.[5]

I bought a piece of calencar[6] to keep Rosalie occupied, for she did not want to go to the theater again. I went by myself, and, returning to the inn, I found Signor Grimaldi with her and Veronica, giving them advice about the dress they were working on. I embraced the

Senator,[7] then thanked Rosalie for having received him, saying gently that she ought to have left off sewing.

"Ask him, my dear, if he didn't force me to go on. He offered to leave."

With that, leaving Veronica to work on alone, she rose and, playing the role of mistress admirably, she managed to persuade the Marchese to sup with us, thus divining my wish. He ate almost nothing, for he did not usually sup; but I saw with pleasure that my jewel enchanted him. I thought I had nothing to fear from a man of sixty, besides which I was very glad to seize the opportunity to give Rosalie the education proper to a woman of standing, who cannot hope for the approval and applause of the best society unless she flirts.

Rosalie, though a novice in the art, and indeed unaware that such an art existed, nevertheless made me admire nature; she spoke to Signor Grimaldi in a manner from which a thinker could read that she wanted to foster his inclination by giving him hope. When he left she told him that she would be grateful if on another occasion he would dine less well, for she was curious to see him eat.

I took her in my arms a moment later to devour her with kisses, asking her where she had learned to converse with people of the great world.

"It is you, my dear, who speak to my soul; you tell me with your eyes whatever I should say and do."

After having Costa copy out my translation of *L'Écossaise,* I put it in my pocket and went with it to Rossi,[8] the head of the troupe of actors, who, as soon as he learned that I would make him a present of it, offered to have it performed at once. I gave him the names of the actors I had chosen, and invited him to come to dine at the "Santa Marta" with them to hear it read and to give out the parts, which I wished to assign myself.

Rosalie was delighted to dine with the three actresses and the actors who were to perform the play and to hear herself constantly being called Signora Casanova,[9] and

even more so to see that it pleased me; Veronica interpreted all the words she did not understand.

As soon as they were seated in a circle they asked me
to tell them the names of the characters I had decided
they were to play; but they could not shake me: I told
them that they must listen to the play, each not knowing
what part I intended for him, but that he would be told
immediately afterward. They all submitted to my decree,
and just when I was ready to begin reading the Marchese
Grimaldi arrived and, at the same time, the banker
Belloni, come to return my visit. I was very glad to have
them present at the reading, which lasted only an hour
and a quarter.

After receiving the approval of the players, who by
their praise of the situations convinced me that they had
all listened to the whole play, I told Costa to give out
the parts to the names I had indicated. I then saw both
the leading lady and the leading man dissatisfied—she
because I had given her the part of Lady Alton, he
because I had not given him the part of Murray;[10] but
they had to put up with it. I invited them to dinner on
the next day but one, for a reading rehearsal of the play.

The banker Belloni invited me to dinner the next day
with my lady, who very politely declined, and Signor
Grimaldi willingly let her persuade him to keep her
company in my stead.

At dinner at the banker's I was surprised to see the
impostor Charles Ivanov, who, instead of pretending not
to know me, came forward to embrace me; I drew back
and made him a bow. Some of the people present may
have attributed it to respect. He was richly accoutered;
he talked constantly, affecting a certain haughty melancholy, and on the subject of politics he spoke rather in-
telligently. The conversation having turned to the Court
of Russia, where Elisabeth Petrovna[11] was then reigning,
he said nothing but sighed and turned away, pretending
to dry his tears. At dessert he asked me if I had news

of Madame Morin,[12] saying, as if to recall her to my mind, that it was at her house we had supped together; I replied that I knew she was in good health. His servant who waited on him at table wore a yellow livery with red braid. After dinner he found an opportunity to say that he urgently needed to talk with me.

"And I never to let it appear that we are in private communication anywhere."

"You can, by saying no more than a word, put me in a position to obtain a hundred thousand scudi, and I will give you fifty thousand."

I turned my back on him, and in Genoa I did not see him again.

Back at the inn, I found Signor Grimaldi teaching Rosalie Italian. He said that she had given him an exquisite repast, and that she must make me happy. Though observing all the proprieties, Signor Grimaldi was in love with her; but I remained unafraid. As he left she prevailed on him to attend the reading rehearsal of *L'Écossaise* the next day.

When the actors arrived, seeing a young man with them whom I had never seen before, I asked Rossi who he was.

"He is the prompter."

"No prompter. Send him away."

"We cannot do without a prompter."

"I will do the prompting. Send him away."

He sent him away, but the women especially refused to listen to reason. They said that even supposing they knew their parts as well as they knew their Paternoster they were sure to forget them if they did not see him in his box.

"He won't need to prompt us, but we have to see him."

"Very well," I said to the actress who was playing Lindane,[13] "I will get into the box myself, and I will see your underdrawers."

"She doesn't wear any," said the first lover.

"You don't know anything about it," she rejoined.

This exchange put us in a gay mood, and the votaries of Thalia[14] promised me that they would not need a prompter. I was well pleased with them at the reading rehearsal. They asked only three days to be ready to speak their parts from memory, and I was satisfied.

They came, but without the actress who played Lindane and the actor who played Murray. They were both ill, but Rossi vouched for them. I took the part of Murray, inviting Rosalie to read Lindane. She whispered to me that she could not read Italian well enough and did not want to set the actors laughing. She said that Veronica might read the part.

"Very well."

She asks Veronica if she will read it, and she says she does not need to read it since she knows it by heart.

"So much the better."

I laughed to myself, remembering Soleure. Chance was forcing me to talk love to Veronica, to whom, during the two weeks she had been with us, I had never addressed a word. I had not even really looked at her face, such was my dread of Rosalie's love taking alarm.

What I feared happened. At the scene in which I had to take Veronica's hand and say to her: *Sì, bella Lindane, debbo adorarvi* ("Yes, beautiful Lindane, I cannot but adore you"),[15] all present applauded, for I spoke the words as they should be spoken. I glance at Rosalie, and I am in despair to see her uneasy, though she was trying to hide it. But Veronica's acting amazed me; she blushed furiously when, taking her hand and pressing it, I said I adored her; it was impossible to act a girl in love better. We set the date for the final dress rehearsal at the theater, and the players, to excite curiosity, began announcing the date of the first performance a week beforehand, putting up bills in these terms: "We shall give *L'Écossaise* by Monsieur de Voltaire, translated by an unknown hand, and we shall perform it without a prompter.''

But how hard I found it after that rehearsal to soothe Rosalie! She would not be consoled, she wept and, thinking she was reproaching me, said the most touching things. She said that I was in love with Veronica and that I had translated the play on purpose to tell her so.

After I convinced her that she was wrong by good arguments and by tokens of the most loyal affection, she at last became calm, and the next day she asked my forgiveness, saying that she wanted me to cure her of her jealousy by talking to Veronica in her presence at every opportunity. She did more. Having got up first, she sent me a cup of chocolate by Veronica herself, who I saw was as astonished as I.

From that day on she showed no more signs of jealousy, and she was more courteous than ever to the girl, who was decidedly intelligent and with whom I saw that I could easily have fallen in love if my heart had been free.

On the day of the first performance she sat with her in a box I had taken, where Signor Grimaldi never left her side. The play was an unqualified success. The very large theater in Genoa was filled not with the populace but with the noblest and wealthiest in that great city. The actors, playing without a prompter, were pronounced excellent, and what they thought extraordinary was that the public demanded five more performances. Rossi, perhaps hoping that I would give him another play, asked my permission to present my supposed wife with a lynx-fur pelisse, which she greatly cherished.

But now for an unfortunate remark which, by my own fault, troubled the fair soul of that angel incarnate, whose happiness God nevertheless allowed me to assure.

''I have reason,'' she said to me one day, ''to suspect that I am pregnant. How my soul will rejoice if I can give you a pretty little boy!''

"If he is born at such and such a time, he will surely be mine, and he will be dear to me."

"And if he should be born two or three weeks earlier you would not be sure of it?"

"No, but I shall love him: he will be yours. I will provide for him even so."

"He could only be yours, I am sure of it. This time I really am unhappy. It is impossible, my dear, that I conceived by P-i,[16] for he was with me only once, and very imperfectly, whereas you know how lovingly we have been together so many times."

"Ah, my dear, do not weep, I implore you. You are right. What I told you is possible, but it is not likely. The child shall be mine, I will never doubt it, calm yourself."

"How can I calm myself now that I know you believed there might be any doubt about it?"

We said no more on the subject, but I often saw her sad and thoughtful. Tenderly amorous, I held her in my arms for hours on end, and she gave herself to love, but her pleasures seemed often to be interrupted by sighs which were not in harmony with the security an amorous soul should feel. I sorely repented of having troubled her with my stupid calculations.

A week or ten days later she came to me and gave me a sealed letter, saying that the hire valet had given it to her, taking advantage of a moment when I would not see him. She said that she felt insulted. I send for him and I ask him from whom he had received the letter.

"A young man whom I do not know gave me a scudo to do him the favor of delivering the letter to the Signora without your seeing it, and promised me two if I would bring him the answer tomorrow at the Banchi.[17] I did not think I was doing anything wrong, for the Signora was at liberty to tell you."

"That is true, but I shall dismiss you because the Signora, who, as you see, has not unsealed the letter, considers that by acting as you did you showed her disrespect.''

I told Leduc to pay him off, and so he was dismissed. I open the letter and I see that it is signed ''P-i.'' Rosalie leaves me and goes to her room to sew with Veronica. Here is the letter:

''I saw you, my dear Rosalie, enter a sedan chair when you came out of the theater escorted by His Excellency the Marchese Grimaldi, my godfather. I did not deceive you. I still intended to go to Marseilles in the spring and marry you, as I promised. I love you faithfully, and if you are willing to become my wife I am ready to give you my hand at once in my parents' presence. If you have done anything wrong, I will never reproach you with it, for I recognize that I am the cause of it. Tell me if you are willing for me to go to Signor Grimaldi and explain my intentions to him; I hope that he will have the goodness to vouch to you for me. I am also ready to receive you, without making any difficulties, from the hands of the gentleman with whom you are living, if you have not become his wife. Consider, if you are free, that your honor becomes spotless as soon as he who seduced you marries you.—P-i.''

''There,'' I said to myself, ''is an honorable man who deserves Rosalie, and here, in my own person, is a very dishonorable one if I do not let him have her, unless I instantly marry her. Rosalie shall decide.'' I call her, I give her the letter to read, she hands it back to me, and she asks me if I advise her to accept P-i's proposal. I reply that if she accepts it I shall die of grief, but that my honor demands that, if I will not give her up, I must marry her, and that I am ready. She flings herself on my neck, she says she loves no one but me, and that it is not true that my honor demands that I marry her.

''My dear Rosalie, I adore you, but I beg you to believe that you cannot know better than I do what my honor demands. If this P-i is a man of means who can make

you happy, I must, even if it kills me, either advise you
to accept his hand or offer you mine.''

''Neither. We need be in no hurry. If you love me I
am happy. I love you alone. I will not answer his letter.
I want to hear no more of P-i.''

''I will never mention him to you again, you may be
sure; but you will see that the Marchese Grimaldi will
do something about it.''

''So he will; but you can be no less sure that he will
speak of it to me only once.''

''And to me too.''

After this treaty of alliance, I decided to leave upon
receiving the letters for Florence and Rome for which
I had asked Signor Bragadin.[18] I lived with my dear
Rosalie in the sweet peace of love; she was no longer
jealous; the Marchese Grimaldi alone was the honorable
witness of our happiness.

It was five or six days after P-i's letter was written
that Signor Grimaldi, at his casino in Sampierdarena,
said that he was very glad to see me for he wished to
speak to me about a matter which should be of interest.
Instantly guessing what it must be, and knowing what
my answer must be, I asked him to speak. Here is what
he said:

''A worthy merchant of our city came to me the other
day to present his nephew, whose name is P-i. He told
me that he was my godson, and I was convinced of it;
he asked for my protection, and I replied that I would
consider it my duty to be of use to him whenever the
occasion arose; as his godfather, I owed him that.

''Thereupon my godson, left alone with me, told me
that he had known your mistress in Marseilles before
you did, that he had promised to return there and marry
her in the spring of next year, that he had seen her come
out of the theater here with me, that he had followed her,
that he had learned she was living with you, that he had
been told she was your wife, that he had not believed it,

that he had written her a letter, which had come into your hands, in which he told her that he was ready to marry her, and that he had not received an answer. He had decided to appeal to me to learn if Rosalie accepted his proposal, and in that case he made bold to hope for my countenance, acquainting me with his entire financial condition so that I could vouch for him and be convinced that he was in a position to make her happy. I replied that I would speak about the matter to you and would let him know the outcome.

"Before speaking to you I inquired into the young man's financial situation and I learned that he already disposes of a considerable capital, that he has good morals and an excellent reputation on the Exchange. In addition, he is heir to all the property of the uncle who brought him to me. Tell me what answer I shall give him."

"You shall answer him that Rosalie thanks him and begs him to forget her. You know that we shall leave in three or four days. Rosalie loves me as much as I love her, and she will find me ready to marry her whenever she wishes it."

"That is clearly spoken. But I believe that to a man of your nature freedom must be far more precious than marriage. Will you permit me to discuss the matter with Rosalie myself?"

"You do not need my permission. Speak to her; but, of course, not as if you were speaking on my behalf, for, adoring her as I do, I cannot give her any reason to suppose that I could want her to leave me."

"If you object to my acting in the matter, speak out."

"On the contrary, I shall be delighted that you can swear I am not my dear Rosalie's tyrant."

"I will speak to her this evening."

To give the Marchese leisure to talk with her I did not come home until suppertime; he supped with us, and, after he left, she told me all that he had said. He had

told her what he had told me; she had answered him as
I had answered him, with only the addition that she had
begged him not to mention P-i to her again; and he had
promised not to say another word about him.

It was over and done with; we prepared to leave
Genoa.

Three or four days after Signor Grimaldi had last
talked to Rosalie on the subject of P-i, when we believed
he had put the matter out of his mind, he asked me to
bring her to dine with him at Sampierdarena. She had
never been there, and he wanted her to see his garden
before we left. We accepted.

So at noon the next day we are at his charming casino.
We find him with an elderly couple whom he introduces
to us, and he introduces me by my name and the young
lady as my companion.

We all go to walk in the garden, and the couple take
Rosalie between them, treating her with the most courteous amiability; she replies in kind, she is gay, she speaks
Italian with them; the compliments she receives flatter
her; after half an hour's stroll dinner is announced, we
go to the dining room, I see six places. I guessed what
was to come, but it was too late. We sit down at table,
and just then in comes a young man. The Marchese tells
him he is late and very quickly introduces him to me as
Signor P-i, his godson and the nephew of the lady and
gentleman who were present. He makes him sit down at
his left, Rosalie was at his right, and I was seated beside
her. I see her turn deathly pale; I was shaking from
head to foot with rage. I find the Genoese aristocrat's
procedure hard to swallow; it was a surprise, an unfor-
givable affront put upon Rosalie and me, which demanded that I avenge it in blood; and in the tumult of
my soul I yet understand that I must champ the bit.
What could I do? Take Rosalie's arm and leave with
her? I thought of it; and, foreseeing the consequences,
I did not have the courage to do it. I never spent a more

torturing hour at table. Neither she nor I ate anything, and the Marchese, who served the guests, was wise enough to pretend not to notice that we sent back our plates untouched. During the whole dinner he talked to no one but P-i or his uncle on the subject of his business. When dinner was over he told the former that he could go about his occupations, and, after kissing his hand, he left.

He was a young man about twenty-four years of age, of middling stature, of undistinguished but good-natured and honest countenance, extremely respectful in manner, who spoke without brilliance but with good sense. I decided that he was not unworthy of Rosalie, but I trembled to think that I could not see her become his wife except by losing her. After he left, the Marchese chided his uncle for never having introduced the young man to him, as he could certainly have been useful to him in his business.

"But I am sure," he added, "that I shall be of use to him in future, and that I will help him to fortune."

Thereupon the uncle and aunt, who must have known everything, bestowed all kinds of praise on him, saying, as if in passing, that, having no children, they were delighted to see that he who would inherit all they possessed enjoyed His Excellency's countenance. They could not wait to see the young lady from Marseilles to whom he was engaged and to welcome her to their arms as their own daughter.

It was then that Rosalie, unable to bear more, said to me that she felt she would be ill if I did not escort her back to the inn at once, and I took leave of the Marchese, forcing myself to remain controlled. I saw that he was taken aback. Not knowing what to say, he beat about the bush; he told her that he hoped her indisposition would come to nothing, that he should not have the honor to see her that evening, but that he would not fail to do so the next day; and he gave her his arm to her sedan chair.

As soon as we were back at the "Santa Marta" and

alone together we began to breathe again and to relieve our troubled souls with talk. She rightly felt that the Marchese had played a detestable trick on us; she decided that I must write him a note asking him not to trouble to visit us again. I assured her that I would find a way to avenge her; I said that I did not think it advisable to write him a note, but that we should hasten our departure and receive him the next day in a manner which would make him realize all our indignation. Serious bearing, purely formal greetings, politeness, complete concealment, and above all no reply to anything he might say concerning what he had done. Speaking of P-i, she said that if he loved her he was to be pitied, that she thought him honest, and that she could not hold his being at the dinner against him, since he might not have known that his presence at it was an affront to her.

"I thought I should die," she said, "when our eyes met; afterward he was not in a position to see me, and I do not know if he looked at me when he left."

"No, he looked at me, and I pity him too. He is a decent fellow."

"The worst is over, and I hope I shall have a good appetite at supper. Did you hear his aunt? She was apparently in the plot; she said she was ready to treat me like her own daughter. I think she is a very good woman."

After a good supper Love and Morpheus helped us to forget the affront the Marchese had put upon us, and to such effect that when we woke we were able to laugh at it. He came toward nightfall and, approaching me with a look of mortification, said that he had been unpardonably at fault in surprising us as he had done, and that he was ready, if the fault could be repaired, to accord me whatever satisfaction I might ask of him. Rosalie, not giving me time to reply, said that if he felt that he had treated us improperly, we considered ourselves adequately avenged and hence satisfied, and also under the necessity of being on our guard against him on every occasion, though it was difficult to foresee another, since we were on the verge of leaving.

After this proud answer she curtsied to him and went to her room. Thus left alone with me, he spoke as follows:

"Being immeasurably interested in your mistress's welfare, and knowing from experience that it is very improbable she can long be happy in any other situation than that which a girl of her character attains by marrying a young man of the character of my godson P-i, I resolved to make you both acquainted with him, for Rosalie herself knew him only very slightly. To accomplish this, I used a stratagem which I admit was dishonorable but which I trust you will forget for the sake of my good intention. I wish you a good journey, I hope that you will long live happily with this charming girl, I ask you to let me have news of you and to count on my friendship, my influence, and my best endeavors under all circumstances. So much for that. It remains for me only to confide one thing to you, in order that you may have a just idea of the young man's excellent character, whom, by his own avowal, Rosalie alone can make happy. He did not confide to me what you are about to hear until he saw that I would not undertake to deliver a letter which he had written to Rosalie, despairing of conveying it to her in any other way.

"After assuring me that Rosalie had loved him, and that hence she could feel no aversion to him, he added that if perhaps she could not resolve to become his wife because she believed she was pregnant he was content to defer the marriage until after she had borne her child, provided she would be willing to remain in Genoa in some place where her presence would be known to him alone. He offers to defray all her expenses, accompanying his proposal by a very wise consideration. Her being brought to bed too soon after her marriage, he said, would reflect on his honor and stand in the way of the affection which his parents should feel for his children.''

He had scarcely finished speaking before Rosalie enters and surprises us with these words:

''If Signor P-i has not told you it is possible that I am pregnant by him, he is a very honorable young man; but it is I who tell you so. It seems to me very unlikely, but it is still a possibility. Tell him that I will remain in Genoa until after my delivery if I am pregnant, or until I am sure that I am not, and in that case I will go to join my friend here wherever he may be. The time at which I am delivered will show me the truth. If I am convinced that my child is Signor P-i's, tell him that he will find me ready to become his wife, and if he is himself convinced that it cannot be his, he must resign himself to forgetting me. As for my expenses, and the place where I shall stay, tell him he is not to take any steps in the matter or to concern himself with it in any way.''

My astonishment left me half dazed. The Marchese asked me if I authorized him to convey her message, and I replied that I could have no will but Rosalie's. He left well satisfied.

''So you want to leave me?'' I asked Rosalie.

''Yes, my dear; but not for long, if I can count on your constancy. My heart, and your honor and mine, command me, if I am pregnant, to make P-i certain that it is not by him, and you at the same time that it can only be by you.''

''I shall have no doubt of it, my dear Rosalie.''

''You have already doubted it, and that is enough. Our separation will cause me tears, but it is necessary for the peace of my soul. I hope that you will write to me; and after my delivery it will be for you to tell me how I am to join you, and if I am not pregnant we shall be able to meet again at the latest toward the end of this winter.''

''I must consent to whatever is your wish. I think you should go to stay in a convent, and I see no one but the

Marchese to find one for you and to look after you like a father. Shall I speak to him about it? I will leave you money enough for your expenses.''

''It will be no great amount; there is no need for you to speak to Signor Grimaldi, for he will offer me his services himself. Honor demands it of him.''

She was right; and I admired her intelligence in her knowledge of the human heart, of the conduct befitting a nobleman, and of the laws of honor. The next morning I saw that the Russian adventurer had fled an hour before the police arrived to take him to prison on the complaint of the banker, who had found a letter of credit he had presented him to be a forgery. He had fled on foot, abandoning everything; so the banker lost very little.

The next morning the Marchese came to tell Rosalie that P-i had found nothing to object to in her plan and that he hoped she would be willing to become his wife after her delivery even if her calculations showed that the child was not his.

''He is free to entertain the hope,'' she said with a smile.

''He hopes, too, that you will occasionally grant him the honor of visiting you. I have spoken to the Superior of the XXX convent, who is distantly related to me; you will have two rooms, a decent woman who will keep you company, wait on you, and even deliver you if that proves to be necessary. I have settled the price of your board by the month, and every morning I will send you a confidential man of mine who will confer with your waiting woman and convey all your orders to me. I will myself visit you from time to time at the grating when you give me permission.''

It was now my duty to thank the Marchese. I said that it was to him that I entrusted my dear Rosalie, and that I intended to leave on the day after she had gone alone to the convent he had found for her, giving the Superior a letter which he would have the goodness to write for her. He wrote it at once, and Rosalie having told him that she wanted to pay all her expenses herself, he put in writing the terms to which he had agreed. When he left she told him that she would retire to the convent the next day and that she would be delighted to see him at the grating the day after that. He promised he would be there.

We spent the sad night which two souls in love could not but spend when reason had commanded them to part. Complaints, consolations, endless alternatives, and promises which we were sure we would keep but which had yet to be confirmed by Destiny, into whose councils no mortal has ever been admitted.

She spent the whole morning packing with Veronica, who wept and at whom I did not look because I was angry with myself for finding her attractive. Rosalie would accept no more than two hundred zecchini from me, saying that, if she needed it, I could easily find a way to send her money. After asking Veronica to take good care of me during the two or three days I had decided to stay on in Genoa, she dropped me a silent curtsy, and she left, escorted to her sedan chair by Costa. Two hours later a servant of Signor Grimaldi's came for all her things, and I remained alone and very sad until the nobleman himself arrived to ask me to give him supper, at the same time advising me to have Veronica sup with us.

"She is an excellent girl," he said, "whom you really do not know and whom you will not be sorry to know better."

Though somewhat surprised, I at once went and asked her to do me the favor. She accepted the invitation, assuring me that she was sensible of all the honor I did her.

Nothing short of being the greatest fool on earth could have prevented me from seeing clearly that the wily Genoese had perfectly accomplished his purpose, tricking me as if I had been the rawest novice. Despite my having good reasons to hope that Rosalie would return to me, I foresaw that he would set about persuading her otherwise so artfully that he would succeed. I could only pretend to be aware of nothing and let things take what course they would.

His Excellency was nearly sixty years of age, a great epicure, a heavy gambler, rich, eloquent, an accomplished politician, highly regarded in his native country, who had long lived in Venice in order the better to enjoy his freedom and the pleasures of life, and who contrived to return there after being Doge despite the law[19] which forbids patricians who have been granted that high office to leave their country again. In spite of the friendliness which he always showed me he was able to maintain a tone of superiority which awed me. If he had not known that he possessed this ascendancy he would not have dared to trick me into dining with P-i. He made a dupe of me, and it became my part to win his esteem by resolving to act as I acted. It was from gratitude that he undertook to smooth my way to the conquest of Veronica after he made me fall in love with her.

At table, where I said almost nothing, he engaged her in arguments, and she shone. I clearly saw that she was delighted to convince me that she was more intelligent than Rosalie. Nothing could have been more calculated to displease me. Grimaldi, who was put out to see me gloomy, forced me to join in the conversation by leading Veronica to say that I was right to remain silent after the declaration of love which I had made to her and which she had received with disdain. Very much astonished, I said that I did not remember having loved her, still less having told her so. But I had to laugh when she replied that on that day her name was Lindane.

"Such a thing," I said, "can happen to me only in a play. The man who declares his love by words is a fool, he should speak only by his attentions."

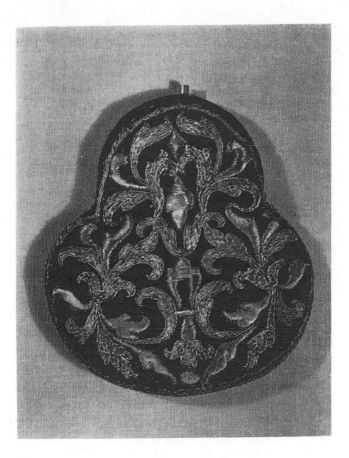

Lady's Coin Purse of Green Damask

An Unpleasant Surprise

"Even so, the Signora took fright."

"Not a bit of it. She was fond of you."

"I know it; nevertheless she was jealous."

"If she was, she had no reason to be."

Our dialogue greatly amused the Senator, who said to me as he left that he would pay his first visit to Rosalie the next day and would bring me news of her at supper. I said that I would expect him. Veronica, after accompanying me to my room, asked me to let my servants wait on me, for, "The Signora being no longer there, people might suspect the worst."

I said she was right, and I rang for Leduc.

The next morning I received a letter from Geneva. It was from my friend the Syndic,[20] who said that he had presented Monsieur de Voltaire, on my behalf, with my translation of *L'Écossaise*, together with the very polite letter in which I asked him to excuse me for having made bold to turn his beautiful French prose into Italian. He said in so many words that he had pronounced my translation bad.

This news, and his impoliteness in not answering my letter, so irritated and offended me that I became that great man's enemy. From then on I criticized him in all the works I published, thinking to avenge myself by wronging him. It is I whom my critics will wrong if my works reach posterity. I will be reckoned among the Zoïluses[21] who dared to attack the great genius. The only wrong he did was seen in his invectives against religion. If he had been a good philosopher he would never have said anything on the subject, for even supposing that all he said of it was true, he should have known that the populace needs to live in ignorance for the sake of the general peace of the nation. *Vetabo qui Cereris[22] sacrum vulgarit arcanae sub iisdem sit trabibus*, etc. ("I will deny my roof to him who has revealed the rites of mystic Ceres").[23]

CHAPTER VI

*I am in love with Veronica. Her sister. Ruse
against ruse. My victory. Mutual disappointment.*

NOT LIKING to eat alone, I ordered two places set.
Veronica, after supping with us, deserved the distinction. Seeing only Costa behind my chair, I asked him
where Leduc was; he said that he was ill; I told him to
stand behind the Signorina's chair; he obeyed me with a
smile. How absurd is the pride of servants! I thought
Veronica prettier than usual. Her bearing, free and reserved as occasion demanded, convinced me that she could
easily have played the role of princess in select company.
Feeling distressed to see that she attracted me, I sadly
consoled myself with the knowledge that her mother was
to come for her that day. Such was the state of my soul.

We were at dessert when her mother came. She immediately made a pretense of thanking me for the honor
I did her daughter. I reply that it was she who did me
honor, for she was beautiful, intelligent, and good.

"Thank the Signore," she said, "for his three presents,
for you are ugly, stupid, and ill-behaved. Oh, the slut!

You are dining with the Signore and I see that your shift is dirty.''

"Excuse me, Mother, I put it on clean this morning."

"Permit me to say, Signora," I said to her mother, "that a shift can hardly look white against her skin."

My compliment made the mother laugh and greatly flattered the girl. When her mother told her she had come to take her home she replied that she was not sure she would be doing me a favor by leaving me twenty-four hours before my departure; and I added that on the contrary she would be doing me an ill turn.

"In that case," said her mother, "decency demands that I send you her younger sister, who will sleep with her."

I told her it was the thing to do, and I left them together.

Veronica was proving to be a difficulty, for I had found her too attractive at table, and, knowing myself, I must fear an attempt at resistance worse than death.

Her mother came in to wish me a good journey and the girl began busying herself with my linen. I sat down to write.

Toward nightfall a maid comes in with her sister Annetta,[1] who, after lowering her *mezzaro*,[2] kissed my hand, then joyfully embraced her sister. The maid, after putting down a package, left. Very curious to see Annetta's face, I at once called for lights. I saw a very young girl of a blondeness whose equal I had never seen. Her hair, her eyebrows were even whiter than her skin, which their excessive fairness darkened a little. She was so short-sighted that she was nearly blind; but her blue eyes were beautiful and very large. If the enamel of her teeth had not been tinged with yellow the girl could have passed for a rare beauty. The poor girl shuddered away from the strong light. She stood there, apparently content that I should examine her, showing the upper halves of two little breasts which seemed to be of marble and which informed my speculative mind that her entire body was of the same whiteness. Veronica was not generous in this respect; one saw that her bosom must be extremely beautiful, but it was always covered by a kerchief even when she was most negligently dressed; she made her sister sit down beside her and at once gave her some sewing to do. Finding it distressing to watch her, for in order to sew she had to hold the cloth an inch from her eyes, I told her that, at least at night, she need not do needlework, and she stopped as if out of obedience.

The Marchese Grimaldi arrived, and Annetta, whom he had never seen, was as much of a surprise to him as she was to me. He passed his beneficent hand over her pretty little bosom, the humble Annetta not daring to protest, and congratulated her on it.

A girl who, by the little she allows a man to see, makes him curious to see the rest has already gone two thirds of the way toward making him fall in love; for what is love if it is not a kind of curosity? I defy anyone to produce a more powerful curiosity in nature. Annetta had already made me curious.

Signor Grimaldi told Veronica that Rosalie asked her to stay with me until I left. I saw that Veronica was as astonished as I was by her insistence. I then told the Marchese to inform Rosalie that she had anticipated her wish and for that reason had sent for her sister Annetta.

"Two," he replied, "are better than one."

We then went to the other room, where he told me that Rosalie was content, and I should congratulate myself on having made her a happy woman, that he was sure she would become one, and that he was only sorry there was every reason why I should not go to see her.

"You are in love with her," I said.

"Certainly, and I regret being an old man."

"That makes no difference. She will love you dearly, and if P-i becomes her husband she can never feel anything toward him but cold friendliness. You shall write me at Florence how she will have received him."

"Remain here three more days and you will know. I believe you have no urgent business, stay here; these two girls will keep you entertained."

"It is precisely because I foresee they may do so that I want to leave tomorrow. Veronica terrifies me."

"I did not think you were a man to be terrified."

"I am afraid she has set out to torment me, for I think she is one to make a parade of virtue. I can love only Rosalie."

"Speaking of Rosalie, here is a letter she wrote you."

I unseal it and I go to a window to read it. Here is what it contained:

"My dear one. You leave me in the hands of a fond father, who will not let me want for anything until the time when I shall be in no further doubt concerning my condition. I will write you at whatever address you give me. If Veronica pleases you I should be wrong to feel jealous at this time. I believe she cannot resist you, and that she will drive away your sorrow, which really distresses me. Write me a line before you leave." [3]

I gave it to the Marchese to read, and I saw that he was touched.

"Yes," he said, "she will find me a fond father; and, if it becomes her duty to marry my godson, if he does not treat her well he shall not have her long. She will be happy even after my death. But did you see what she says to you about Veronica? I don't believe she is a Vestal,[4] though I have heard no gossip about her."

I had ordered four places set; so Annetta joined us at the table without waiting to be asked. Seeing Leduc, I told him that if he was ill he could go to bed.

"I am in good health."

"So much the better. Be off with you. You shall wait on me at table in Leghorn."

I saw that Veronica was delighted with his dismissal.

I determined to make love to her openly, treating her to meaning remarks at table while the Marchese addressed amusing ones to Annetta. Having turned the conversation to my journey, I asked him if I could have a felucca for Lerici[5] the next day.

"At whatever hour you wish, and with as many rowers; but I hope you will stay on for three or four days."

"No, for the delay might cost me dear."

Glancing at Veronica, I saw her smile. When supper was over, I having set myself to question Annetta, the Marchese talked with Veronica for a quarter of an hour, then came to me and said that he had been urged to ask me to stay for another three days or at least for supper the next day.

"Very well. We will talk about the three days at supper tomorrow."

The Marchese was exultant, and Veronica showed that she was pleased by my yielding. After he left I asked her if I might send Costa off to bed. She answered that, since her sister was with her, no one could suspect anything wrong. So she began dressing my hair for the night, while Annetta went to her room to unpack her things. To all my soft speeches she made no answer. When I was ready to go to bed she wished me good night, I make to embrace her, and her refusal surprises me. I tell her that I need to speak to her and to have her answer, and I invite her to sit down beside me.

"Why did you refuse me a pleasure which, after all, is only a token of friendship?"

"Because it is impossible that, being what we are, we should be merely friends; and we cannot be lovers."

"Why cannot we be lovers, since we are free?"

"I am not free from the prejudices for which you care nothing."

"I thought your mind was superior to—"

"A pitiful superiority which is always its own dupe!

What would become of me if I gave in to the feeling you inspire in me?"

"I expected that, my dear Veronica. No. The feeling I inspire in you is not love. It would be like mine. Love tramples on the prejudices which fetter it."

"I admit that you have not yet turned my head, but I know that when you go away I shall be sad for a time."

"If that is so it will not be my fault; but tell me what I can do to make you happy during the short time I shall be here."

"Nothing, because neither of us can be sure of anything about the other."

"And for that reason I am sure I shall never marry until I shall have become my mistress's friend."

"In other words, when you have ceased to be her lover."

"Precisely."

"You want to end where I want to begin."

"I wish you happiness; but it is staking too much. It seems to me, beautiful Veronica, that we could play at love unscathed, spending some happy hours together which prejudice would not have time to trouble."

"It is possible; but the mere thought of it frightens me, for it might undo me. Oh, no! Let me alone. Look, there is my sister taking fright because she sees me defending myself."

"Very well, I see that I am wrong. Rosalie was mistaken."

"What! What can she have thought?"

"She writes me that she thinks you kind."

"She is very fortunate if she has not had reason to repent of having been too kind."

She went off to bed, and so did I, regretting that I had approached her. I promised myself that I would leave her to her morality, whether genuine or feigned. But when I woke I saw her coming to my bedside so

sweetly that I at once changed my plan. I thought she
had repented and I hoped to find her made of better
stuff upon my second attack. I assumed a demeanor
to match hers, and I breakfasted joking with her and
her sister, and I did the same at dinner and until the
evening, when Signor Grimaldi, arriving and finding us
so gay, felt obliged to offer us his congratulations. Seeing that Veronica received them as if she deserved them,
I thought I was sure to have her after supper, and in
my exultation I promised them I would stay on for four
days instead of three.

"Good for you, Veronica!" he said. "Always exer-
cise your rights as you have done on this occasion. Nature created you to have absolute dominion over those
who love you."

It seemed to me that she should say at least a word
or two to lessen the Marchese's certainty; but not a bit
of it, she became more beautiful, she triumphed; I
looked at her with the abashed humility of a captive
proud of his chains. I was magnanimous enough to take
her performance for a sure augury of my imminent victory. I avoided any private conversation with Marchese,
so that I should not be obliged to enlighten him if he
questioned me. When he left, he said that he would not
have the pleasure of supping with us again until the next
evening but one.

"Did you observe," she asked me as soon as we were
alone, "how willing I am to let people believe what they
please? I would rather be taken for kind, since that's
the word for it, than be suspected of being ridiculous,
for that is the charming epithet with which people honor
a girl who has principles. Isn't that so?"

"No, my beautiful Veronica, I will never call you ridiculous; but I will say that you hate me if you make
me spend an infernal night by refusing yourself to my
love as you did yesterday. Let me tell you that at table
you set me on fire."

"Oh, calm yourself, please! Tomorrow evening I won't set you on fire. Please, please, let me alone! Oh, this time—"

What roused her to anger was that, pulling her down with me onto the sofa, I pushed my hand too hard to the point where it could go no farther. She quickly fled, and three or four minutes later I saw her sister come to undress me. I gently told her to go to bed too, since I had to spend several hours writing; and, in order not to see the innocent child leave in humiliation, I opened my strongbox and gave her a watch.

"It's for my sister?"

"No, it is for you."

I allowed her to kiss my hand, and in my troubled state I wrote Rosalie a letter four pages long, which I burned without rereading it. After that I wrote her a reasonable one, in which, not even mentioning Veronica, I said that I would leave the next day.

I went to bed very late, extremely ill pleased with myself, for I considered that, whether she loved me or not, I had failed her both as a lover and as a man of honor. I rang at noon, and I was still more certain of my mistake when I saw only Annetta. As soon as Costa withdrew I asked her how her sister was, and she told me she was sewing. I wrote her a note in which, asking her pardon, I assured her I would not offend her again. I begged her to reappear as if nothing had happened. I was drinking my coffee when I saw her come in with mortification too plainly displayed in her face for me not to feel the whole weight of it. I told her that she need only put up my curls, for I intended to take a walk outside the city and not return to the inn until evening.

"I shall," I said, "have a good appetite for supper, and afterward you will have nothing to fear and no need to send Annetta to me."

I went out of the city and after walking for two hours stopped at a village tavern where I ordered an omelet.

Not having the strength to return to Genoa on foot, I asked for a carriage; but there was none. The tavern-keeper gave me a horse, with a man on foot to guide me and bring back the horse. Night was falling, and we had six miles to go. Rain was my companion all the way to Genoa, where I arrived at eight o'clock soaking wet, dying of cold and fatigue, and with the whole upper part of my thighs chafed raw by the rough saddle, which had torn my satin breeches. After having Costa change all my clothes, I told him to have supper served. I see Annetta and do not see Veronica; she tells me that she is in bed with a bad headache and hands me a letter she had written me. Here it is:

"I went to bed at three o'clock with one of the bad headaches to which I am subject. I already feel better and am sure I can wait on you tomorrow. I tell you this because I do not want you to imagine that I am angry or feigning. I believe you are truly sorry for having humiliated me, and for my part, I ask you to forgive me, or to feel sorry for me, if my way of thinking does not accord with yours."

"Go and ask her," I said, "if she would like us to have supper at her bedside."

She came back at once to say that her sister thanked me and requested that I let her sleep.

So I supped with Annetta, observing with pleasure that she drank only water; but she ate more than I did. My passion for her sister kept me from thinking of her; but I saw that if my heart were not otherwise engaged she would have attracted me. At dessert I decided to get her tipsy and make her talk about her sister. I gave her a glass of muscat from Lunel.[6]

"I drink nothing but water."

"Do you dislike wine?"

"No; but as I'm not used to it, it would go to my head."

"Then you shall go to bed and sleep the better."

She found it excellent, and she laughed when I gave her a second glass, and after that I turned the conversation to her sister, about whom she said every possible good thing with perfect sincerity.

"I love her, and she cannot bear me; she refuses my slightest caresses."

"She can only resist your caresses from fear that you will cease to love her."

"Do you think she is right to make me suffer?"

"No. But if you love her you ought to forgive her."

Annetta's reasoning was only too sound; but at the third glass she said she could no longer see anything and we left the table. The girl already attracted me a little too much; but I promised myself not to make any approach to her, for I feared I should find her too compliant. *Nolo nimis facilem dificilem que nimis* ("I want a woman neither to give in too easily nor to resist too much").[7] She was a good, gentle girl, who, at the age of fourteen and without experience, could not know her own rights. She might have thought that opposing what I might do to her would be rudeness. Only a rich, voluptuous Mussulman can relish that sort of thing.

So I ask her to tuck my hair under my nightcap, intending to send her off to bed at once; but before she leaves I tell her to bring me a jar of unscented pomade.

"What do you want it for?"

"To put on the raw spots from the accursed saddle on which I rode six miles. It will relieve the smarting, and I shall be well tomorrow. I must send for Costa, for I dare not ask this little service of you."

"Do you think I'd know how?"

"It's easy; but I fear to impose on your willingness."

"I understand the reason. But being so short-sighted, how am I to see the raw places?"

"On the bed. Put the candles on the night table."

"There they are; but don't have Costa do you the

same service tomorrow morning, for he'd think it must have been me or my sister who took care of you this evening."

"Will you be as willing again tomorrow?"

"I or my sister, for she will get up very early."

"Not your sister, for she'd be afraid of giving me too much pleasure by touching me there with her beautiful hands."

"And I'm afraid of hurting you! Am I doing it right? What a state your poor skin is in!"

"My dear Annetta, that's not all."

"I'm so short-sighted. Turn around."

"Here I am."

But then I see her laugh at what chance shows her and what the service she was rendering me obliged her to touch. I think I can wager that, short-sighted as she is, she had never seen it so well before and that she must be enjoying it; I become sure of it when I see her straying hand rub where there are no raw spots. At that, unable to bear more, I take her hand to make her stop.

I had to laugh when I saw her motionless and serious, still holding the jar of pomade, and asking me if she had done it right.

"You are, my dear child, an angel incarnate, and I am sure you know what kind of pleasure it was which you have given me. Can you come and spend an hour with me?"

"Wait."

She goes, and she shuts my door, but without turning the key; I feel sure she will come back when she sees that her sister is asleep. She does not come, I get up and go to the door; I see her undress, get into bed, and put out the candle. I go back to bed, still with some hope, and I am not deceived. Five or six minutes later I see her come to my bedside in her shift.

"Come quickly to my arms, my angel, for it is very cold."

"Gladly; my sister is asleep, and I am sure she suspects nothing. Even if she wakes the bed is wide and she won't notice that I am not in it. I give myself to you; do as you will with me; but on condition that you will think no more of my sister."

"I find no difficulty, dear heart, in promising you that and swearing to it."

I found Annetta intact, and it did not occur to me to doubt it in the morning when I saw that the victim had not stained the altar with blood. It has often happened to me. I have learned from experience that no legitimate conclusions can be drawn from either a flow of blood or the lack of it. A girl can be convicted of having had a lover only if he has made her pregnant.

Annetta left me after two hours of encounters, and on waking I saw her at my bedside with Veronica and was delighted to observe not the least sign of a misunderstanding between them. Veronica told me that diet and sleep had, as always, cured her completely. I was in the same situation. Her sister Annetta had completely cured me of the curiosity about her with which she had inspired me. I felt it, and I congratulated myself on it.

At supper Signor Grimaldi, seeing me gay and calm, supposed it was because matters had been brought to a conclusion. I promised to dine with him the next day at Sampierdarena. I went there, and I gave him a long letter for Rosalie, whom I did not expect to see again except as the wife of P-i. But I did not tell her so in my letter.

The same day, supping with the two girls, I devoted equal attention to them both, and Veronica, doing up my hair in curl papers, said, when she was left alone with me, that now that she saw I had become reasonable she loved me far more. I replied that my supposed reasonableness was due to my having given up hope of conquering her.

"My beautiful Veronica, I have made my decision."

"Then your love was a little thing."

"It was a scarce born infant. You had only to foster it till it was mature, and then it could easily have remained alive."

Not knowing what to answer, she wished me a sound sleep and went to her room. Annetta did not come to pay me the visit for which I hoped; I did not know what to conclude.

I saw her in the morning when I rang. She said that her sister was ill in bed and had spent the night writing; and she gave me the letter. At that I saw why Annetta had not come.

The letter, which was very long, and which I returned to her, very nearly made me laugh. After some stuff as boring as it was beside the point, she said that she had refused to yield to my desire because she loved me with all her heart and dared not risk losing me as soon as she had satisfied my momentary fancy. She offered to surrender to my desires if I would grant her the same position which Rosalie had occupied in respect to me. I must leave Genoa with her, giving her a written undertaking, which Signor Grimaldi was to sign, by which I would promise to marry her at the end of a year, settling a dowry of fifty thousand Genoese lire on her, or, if I did not want to marry her, I was to give her the same amount, leaving her perfectly free. If she bore a child during the time we lived together I must agree to leave it with her when we separated, whether it was a girl or a boy which she had brought into the world. On these conditions she consented to become my mistress at once and to grant me all the favors I might ask.

This silly scheme showed me clearly that poor Veronica lacked the intelligence she needed if she was to make me her dupe. I was sure that Signor Grimaldi was not its author and that when I informed him of it he would laugh.

Annetta, bringing me my chocolate, said that her sister made bold to expect an answer to her letter. I said she should have one. I rose and went at once to take it to her in person, carrying her letter, which I immediately returned to her. I found her sitting up in bed, where her scanty attire might have seduced me if her idiotic scheme had not destroyed whatever good opinion of her I still entertained.

I sat down on her bed, and Annetta left the room, even shutting the door; but she told me afterward that she listened.

"Why write to each other," I asked her, "when we can talk?"

"One is oftener more at ease," she replied, "in writing than in speaking."

"That is true in politics and in business matters, where the parties try to trick each other; but in matters of the heart I am not of your opinion. Love, my dear, clears the board: no written undertakings, no guarantees; give yourself to me as Rosalie did, and begin by coming to my arms this very night, without my making you any promises. Trust in love. That is a plan which does honor to us both and which, if you wish, I will submit to Signor Grimaldi's approval. Your scheme, if it is not dishonorable to you, at least bears very poor witness to your intelligence, for it could be accepted only by a fool completely devoid of common sense. It is not possible that you love the man to whom you make such a proposal, and I am sure that Signor Grimaldi would be indignant at it and refuse to have anything to do with it."

My proud reply did not abash her. She said that she did not love me enough to give herself to me without knowing under what conditions. I replied that, on my side, I no longer loved her enough to obtain possession of her under those she had prescribed. After that I left her, and I ordered Costa to inform the master of the felucca that I wanted to sail at dawn the next day. Determined to do so, I went and took leave of the Marchese,

who told me he had that morning brought P-i to see
Rosalie, who had received him tolerably well. I was delighted to hear it. I commended her to his care again,
but there was no need of it.

In that one year two women whom I loved to distraction, both of them abounding in good qualities, and with
whom I would never have parted if it had depended
on me alone, were both taken from me by the clever
scheming of two old men whom I unintentionally helped
to fall in love with them. They made both women's fortunes; but by indirection it was to me that they did the
greatest good, for they rid me of them. They must both
have known that my own fortune, though apparently
ample, had no solid foundation. In the course of my
history my reader will become convinced of it.

I spent the day watching Veronica's and Annetta's
conscientious efforts to pack my things properly. I
would not let Leduc and Costa join in. Veronica, neither
gay nor sad, appeared to have resigned herself and
talked to me as if there had never been the least difference between us. It made me very glad. After supper
they went to bed, and Annetta pressed my hand in a way
which told me that she would pay me a visit. I was very
glad of it; I felt it my duty to make her a present of
fifty zecchini without Veronica's knowledge, for I had
no wish to do as much for her. I put the roll on my night
table, and I gave it to her as soon as she arrived.

After telling me that Veronica was asleep, she asked
me what I would have done if Veronica had accepted the
offer I had made her to receive her in my bed.

"I heard everything," she said, "and I knew that you
love her."

"I was certain, my dear, that she would never bring
herself to do it. I love no one but you."

But a half hour later we are surprised by the presence
of Veronica, who, candlestick in hand, encourages her
generous sister by a great burst of laughter. I laugh too,

not letting her leave my arms. Veronica had on nothing but her shift, she was beautiful, and I had no reason to be angry with her.

"You have come," I said, "to interrupt our pleasures and to cause pain to a sister whom you will henceforth scorn."

"I shall always love her."

"A slave to love, she has given herself to me without conditions."

"She had better sense than I did."

"You mean that?"

"I mean it."

"Very good. Then kiss her."

At this invitation she puts the light down on the night table, takes Annetta from me, and covers her with kisses. The scene goes to my soul. I invited her to lie down beside her, making room for her, and she comes in between the sheets. I feel that she is deathly cold, and the beauty of the spectacle, which I could never have anticipated, allures and transports me. I cannot resist making a pause. A full commentary alone can raise my enjoyment to its pinnacle. So talk there shall be.

"Is this charming trick you are playing on me premeditated?" I asked the two sisters. "And you, Veronica, were you playing a part this morning, or are you doing so now?"

"There was no premeditation. I was sincere this morning, and I am being sincere as you see me now. I hatched an absurd plot, which I beg you to forget, and I am being rightly punished for it; but it is in your power to end my punishment this instant."

"How?"

"By saying you forgive me, and proving it to me."

"I forgive you; but how can I prove it?"

"By continuing to make love to my dear sister without being troubled by my presence."

It was the acme of comedy, and my enthusiasm went

to my head. I must not let myself descend to a passive
role.

"What do you say, my soul?" I ask my little blonde.
"Your sister, heroic beyond praise, wants only to be the
spectator of our amorous exploits. Do you not feel generous enough to let her play a part?"

"No, my dear; but you shall be the generous one tomorrow night, putting on the same play with only the
difference that Veronica shall act my role, while I, following the example she will set us tonight, shall be the
spectator with the greatest pleasure."

"That would be perfect," said Veronica in a tone
which belied her words, "if the Signore had not decided
to leave at dawn."

"I shall stay, charming Veronica, if only to convince
myself that you are adorable."

"And that I love you."

I could not ask her to make herself clearer, and I
would gladly have given her proof of my gratitude then
and there; but that would have been at Annetta's expense, and I should most unforgivably have spoiled the
pure and charming play of which she was the author;
but every time I recall this agreeable incident in my
life I see that the play was composed by beauteous Nature and that Annetta was only the leading actress in
it. Veronica, determined that, as spectator, she would
not enter in, settled herself on her side, plumping up a
pillow to lean her elbow on and resting her face on her
hand. I began the farce as my part demanded, sure that
I should play it to perfection as long as the spectator
continued to watch the action. My eyes were fixed on
her; she must have attributed it to politeness; but in the
end she realized that I had put all my confidence in the
interest she would show in the proceedings. Annetta saw
nothing, her short-sighted eyes could not make out the
direction of mine. Each time our pantomime displaced
the coverlet, Veronica would put it back, each time offer-

ing me, as if by chance, a new picture and enjoying the
instantaneous effect it made on my soul, which eagerly
strove to demonstrate how lively an impression her
charms made on it. Warmed to generosity, in the end
she displayed all her treasures to me, smiling to show
me she was glad I should read her thought. She must
have surmised that the play I was putting on was really
only the rehearsal for the one I was to act with her on
the following night, and her imagination could not but
add to its charms. I had the same thought.

.What obliged me to break off the pretty game was
Costa, who came knocking at my door to tell me the
felucca was ready. Furious at the interruption, I went
to the door and told him to pay the captain for the day
and order him to be ready the next morning. Going
back to bed, I saw that my two companions were delighted with my probity.

We must certainly have been in need of sleep, but,
equally certainly, the play must not be allowed to end
by the always untimely accident of an interruption; it
must be only an intermission, and I must take advantage
of a respite which nature made necessary. I proposed an
ablution, which made Annetta laugh and which Veronica
declared was courteous, appropriate, and justified. The
refreshment not being part of the main action, I easily
persuaded her to imitate us; the two sisters rendered
each other mutual services in different postures, all of
them such that I found the role of spectator preferable
to any other.

After the drying, whose gentle tickling is properly
accompanied by soft laughter, we returned to the stage
where I was to perform the last act. I could scarcely wait
to acquit myself, and I was sure I should bring it off with
honor, counting, of course, on Annetta. Without her the
dialogue could not be sustained. But the girl was too
young; as I had foreseen, she forgot her part. The cruel
god who played the trick on her was Morpheus. Veronica

laughed when she saw her asleep, and I had to laugh too
when I found that she was as if dead. It was a case of
bringing her back to life, and Love has only the power
to awaken. This dénouement had all the appearance of
a catastrophe. ''What a pity,'' Veronica's eyes said;
but she said it only with her eyes. She was wrong, as I
was—she for not taking Annetta's part without asking
my permission, I for waiting for her to invite me. I
thought I ought to refrain from infringing on the play
which was not to be acted until the next night. Veronica
went to her own bed to sleep, and I slept with Annetta
until noon.

We spent the day most interestingly in discussions of
what had befallen us, and, having decided to eat only one
meal, we did not sit down at table until nightfall. We
spent two hours there, satisfying our appetites with exquisite dishes and defying Bacchus to make us fear his
power. We rose when we saw Annetta overcome by irresistible sleep. However, we did not consider this slight
mishap enough to spoil our little play. Annetta as spectator had no possibility of enjoyment, and Veronica's
dazzling charms would occupy me in a way which made
it quite unnecessary to look at any others. We went to
bed, and, she in my arms and I in hers, we spent more
than an hour without moving but without accomplishing
anything. Though she became aware of the reason, politeness prevented Veronica from telling me what it was, as
modesty kept her from complaining of it. She concealed
whatever she may have felt and continued to caress me,
but I was furious. I could not understand it at all. Such
a disaster had never befallen me except immediately
after a long labor whose consummation had been sealed
with my blood, or as the result of a surprise violent
enough to obliterate all my natural faculties, as had
been the case with Genoveffa when, coming out of the
Great Circle, I had expected to be struck by lightning.[8]
But in the situation in which I found myself, in the

prime of life, with a girl who had everything to delight, who charmed me, whom I had wanted to find willing and tender, and whom I saw ready to refuse me nothing of all that I might, or could, ask of her—this was something I could not conceive and which made me positively desperate.

Reduced at last to dropping our masks and talking sense, I was the first to lament my misfortune.

"You did too much yesterday," she replied, "you drank too many liqueurs at supper. Do not be upset, my dear, for I am sure you love me. Stop trying to force nature, for your efforts will only weaken it. It seems to me that a calm sleep is the only remedy you need employ in order to become a man again. I have no need of it, but do not be concerned for me. Go to sleep. We will make love afterward."

After this brief discourse, which I found equally wise and tactful, Veronica turned her back to me and I did likewise. I saw that I could hope everything from sleep, and I determined to sleep, but in vain. The same nature which refused me the ability to work denied me the power to enjoy rest. My eager senses would not relax; they had no need of the relaxation I wanted, and they had no idea that their furtherance could have anything to do with what I needed to put me in a condition to satisfy my amorous desires. On the contrary, my burning senses wanted to remain awake in order to witness my enjoyment; and, far from doing me the kindness to relax, they could not but be angry with me, and they had every right to complain that, by my lack of judgment, I had dulled the vigor I needed to satisfy Love, whose activity and divine joy is that which most interests them and that in which they take part, amid charms which never fail to be present.

It is thus that, in my frenzy and my inability to sleep, I tried to console myself, indulging in physico-metaphysical analyses and arguing on the side of my senses to give me abundant reason for blaming only myself. When I ended I felt satisfied. Satisfied to find myself guilty! Strange satisfaction; but the only one capable of making happy a philosopher overwhelmed by a misfortune. The man who is in the wrong gains a great victory, if, after pleading his cause to himself, he succeeds in convincing himself of it. This is the only happiness I enjoy today when I converse with myself. In all my life no misfortune has befallen me except by my own fault, and I attribute almost all the good fortune I have enjoyed to the chances of life—which, to tell the truth, is a little unjust and humiliating; but such is man. I should go mad, I believe, if in my soliloquies I found that I was unhappy without its being my own fault, for I should not know where the fault lay unless I would admit that I was stupid. I know I am not stupid. Stupidity resides in an idiotic neighbor of mine[9] who is pleased to maintain that the brutes reason better than we do. "I will grant you," I answered him, "that they reason better than you do, but not better than I do." This answer made him my enemy, even though it admitted half of his thesis.

Veronica spent three hours in the arms of sleep and was surprised when I told her I had been unable to enjoy a moment's rest. She found me the nullity she had left me, and she finally lost patience when I tried a little too hard to convince her that the misfortune did not come from any ill will on my part. Tempted to attribute it to herself, and at the same time mortified by the thought that such a thing was possible, she undertook to break the spell which made me unfit. To achieve her end she used remedies which I thought were infallible; and I should have been in the wrong not to leave her to her own devices; but it was all effort thrown away. My despair became as great as hers when I saw her give up, discouraged, humiliated, and angry to the point of tears. She departed without a word, leaving me under the painful necessity of spending two or three hours before

Aurora's return in solitude. My baggage was all ready. My insomnia did not leave me.

At daybreak Costa came to tell me that the wind was strong and contrary and that the felucca could not confront it.

"We will leave," I replied, "when the weather permits."

At that I got up, lit a fire, and fell to writing. Two or three hours later, feeling sleepy, I got into bed, and I enjoyed a sleep of eight hours. On waking I felt calm, but with no desire for amusement. The two sisters were delighted, and I thought I detected a certain scorn in Veronica; but she might be justified, and I should have made a mistake to remark on it. Before we sat down at table I presented her with a hundred zecchini, and I did the same to the kind Annetta, who did not expect it, for she thought she had already received enough.

Toward midnight the captain of the felucca came to tell me that the weather was fair, and I took leave of them. I saw Veronica weep, but I knew why. I set sail for Derici with my two valets, and I went ashore there the next morning, immediately taking post horses for Leghorn. But here is a small yet instructive event worthy of the gravity of this history and not unworthy of being imparted to a reader who reads it with pleasure.

CHAPTER VII

A clever swindle. Passano at Leghorn. Pisa and Corilla. My opinion of squint eyes. Florence. I meet Teresa again. My son. La Corticelli.

AS I am watching the four horses being harnessed for me, a man whose face I do not trouble to notice comes up and asks if I wish to pay for the stage in advance or at the post station.

"I will pay now. Here is a portoghese,[1] bring me the change."

"At once."

Ten minutes later, just when I was going to ask for the change from my portoghese, up comes the post master and asks me for the money for my stage.

"I have already paid it, and I am waiting for the change from a portoghese. Wasn't it to you that I gave it?"

"To me? I beg your pardon."

"Then to whom did I give it?"

"You should know that."

"Damnation, it can only have been to one of your men."

I raise my voice. I am surrounded; the post master asks who had had a portoghese from me; no one knows anything about it. I swear, I curse, then I see I am in the wrong, I pay over again, and I laugh at the clever scoundrel who had tricked me so cleverly. So it is that one learns to live. From that day on I have never paid post except on good grounds. There is no country in which the rascals are more cunning than they are in Italy, if we except ancient and modern Greece.

At Leghorn I had scarcely put up at the best inn[2] before I am told that the theater[3] is open. Unfortunately I take a notion to go to it; one of the actors recognizes me, he comes up, he is delighted to see me, I invite him to supper, he introduces me to a man who calls himself an excellent poet and a great enemy of the Abate Chiari,[4] whom I disliked because he had composed a virulent satire[5] on me and I had not had my revenge. I tell him to come to supper too. The self-styled poet was Genoese, his name was Giacomo Passano,[6] and he had written three hundred sonnets against the Abate Chiari. He said that if he could get them printed the Abate would die of rage. I laughed. Having his manuscript in his pocket, he read me a dozen of them; I found them mediocre. When a sonnet is mediocre it is bad, for it should be sublime.

If I had taken time to study the man's face further than to suppose him some fifty years of age I should have known him for a scoundrel; but his sonnets against Chiari preoccupied me. On the title page of his manuscript I read: *La Chiareide di Ascanio Pogomas.*[7]

"It is," he said, "a perfect[8] anagram of my family and baptismal names; I beg you to admire its felicity."

This stupid remark still makes me laugh. Every one of his sonnets was a piece of flat rigmarole ending by saying that the Abate Chiari was a *coglione.*[9] He did not prove it, but he said it, and that might be enough to pain the Brescian priest, who was no *coglione* but a wit

and a poet, and who, if he had known the theater, would
have surpassed Goldoni,[10] for he had a better command
of the language. This word *coglione,* which properly
means "testicle," is used in Italy to mean "fool," as
couillon in French means "dolt" and in German "cad."
One cannot say a more insulting word to a German than
Kujon or to a Frenchman than *faquin.*

For civility's sake I told Passano that he should get
his *Chiareide* printed.

"I should like to sell it to a printer, for I am not rich
enough to have it printed at my own expense, and the
printers here are all ignorant starvelings; then, too, the
press is restricted; the word *coglione* would be declared
obscene. If I could go to Switzerland I am sure I could
manage it there; but I haven't six zecchini. I would
really go on foot."

"And how," I said, "would you live in Switzerland,
where there are no actors?"

"I can paint miniatures. Look."

He then puts in my hands some oval ivory tablets
measuring three or four inches, on which I see lubricious
nudes, poorly drawn and even more poorly painted. I
promise to give him a recommendation for Bern, and
after supper I write the letter for him and I give him
six zecchini to take him there. He insisted on giving me
six of his pictures; but I refused them. I was stupid
enough to recommend him to Monsieur M. F.,[11] father
of the charming Sara. I told him to write to me at Rome
in care of the banker Belloni.

The next day I went to dine in Pisa at the "Hussar"
inn,[12] where I stayed for two days. From an Englishman
I bought a very pretty carriage which seated two and
had a folding seat for two more. It was this Englishman
who took me to call on the celebrated poetess Corilla,[13]
whom I wanted to meet. She did me the favor to im-
provise, and she enchanted me, not by her singing or
her beauty but by the delightful things she said in good

verse and in perfect Italian. She was squint-eyed, as the ancients depicted Venus[14]—the reason for which I have never been able to guess, for the Goddess of Beauty squinting always seemed to me a great incongruity. It was said that when Corilla, as she sang, fixed her squint eyes on any man in the company she was sure to make him fall in love with her. Thank God, she did not fix them on me very much; apparently she did not like me.

In Florence I found lodgings near the Ponte alla Carraia[15] at Doctor Vannini's,[16] who told me at once that he was "unworthily" a member of the Accademia della Crusca.[17] I took an apartment the windows of which looked out on the embankment of the Arno, next to a beautiful terrace. I also took a town carriage and a hire lackey, immediately dressing the coachman and the lackey in the blue and red livery of Signor Bragadin. I did not want to impose on anyone, but I wanted to make an impression. The next day I went out alone on foot, wearing a redingote, to see Florence and be seen by no one, and in the afternoon I went to the theater[18] to hear the Arlecchino Roffi,[19] whose reputation was greater than his talent, and to judge the Florentine style of delivery, which was highly praised and which I did not like. Only Pertici[20] pleased me. Unable to sing any longer because he had grown old, he had turned actor.

The next day I presented myself to the banker Sasso Sassi, on whom I had a large letter of credit, and after dining alone I dressed for the occasion and went to the opera in the Via della Pergola,[21] taking a seat in a box near the orchestra more to see the actresses than to hear the music, which has never transported me.

But what a surprise when I see the prima donna! I instantly recognized Teresa,[22] whom, after she dropped the mask of Bellino, I had left in Rimini at the beginning of the year 1744—the very Teresa whom I would certainly have married if Signor de Gages had not had me put under arrest. Seventeen years later I see her on the stage, beautiful, fresh, and she seems to me just as young as when I had left her. I thought her a miracle; I was decided that it must be someone else, when, singing an aria, she happens to turn her eyes on me, and from then on they never leave my face. That convinced me that I was not mistaken. At the end of her aria she goes off, and she is scarcely in the wings before she turns and signals me with her fan to come and speak to her.

I leave the box with my heart beating in a way for which I did not understand the reason; for, preserving the happiest memory of Teresa, I felt no guilt toward her except for not having answered her last letter, which she had written me from Naples thirteen years before. I made my way to the pit, more curious to see what the consequences of the interview would be than to learn all that must have happened to her in the course of seventeen years, which, in those days, seemed to me a century.

I come to a door through which one went up to the stage, and I see her at the top of a short stairway giving orders to the doorkeeper to let me enter. I approach her and we both remain mute. I take her hand and I put it against my chest so that she can feel my heart, which seemed to be trying to leap out.

"I cannot do as much here," she said, "but I thought my surprise would send me falling into the orchestra, and I do not know, my dear friend, how I managed to finish my aria. Alas! I have to sup out, I shall not sleep tonight; I expect you tomorrow at eight o'clock. Where are you staying?"

"At Vannini's."

"What name are you using?"

"The same." [23]

"When did you arrive here?"

"Yesterday."

"Shall you remain long in Florence?"

"As long as you wish."

"Are you married?"

"No."

"Accursed supper! What a day! Leave me, I have to go on. Good-by until tomorrow at seven."

A moment earlier she had said "at eight." I go to the parterre, and I remember that I have asked her neither her name nor her address; but I could easily find out all that. She was playing the part of Mandane.[24] At this distance I seem to see her even better, and I find her without an equal in the action with which she animated her recitative. I ask a very well-dressed young man who is sitting beside me the name of so great an actress.

"Then you have arrived in Florence only today?"

"Yes, Signore."

"Well then, her name is the same as mine because she is my wife; and my name is Cirillo Palesi,[25] at your service."

I bow to him, and I remain mute and as if I had fallen from a great height. He might have considered it impertinent if I had asked him where he lived. Teresa married to this handsome young man! And it is precisely her husband I bump into when I want to inquire about her!

I have not the strength to stay through the opera. I cannot wait to be alone so that I can reflect on this fantastic adventure, on the visit I was to make to the married Teresa the next morning at seven, for I must go by what she had said last, and on what her husband will say to me when he sees me. I feel my old fire rekindled, and I think I am not sorry to have found her married.

I go out, and I tell my lackey to call my carriage; he replies that I cannot have it until nine o'clock. The weather was so cold that the coachman had gone to the stable.

"Then we will walk. Tell me," I said, "what is the name of the *prima virtuosa*?"

"Her name was Lanti; but for the last two months it has been Palesi. I can tell you there is nothing to be done there. She is rich, and she married a young man who has nothing and no profession.''

''Where does she live?''

''At the end of this street. We shall pass her door. She lives on the second floor.''

After that I said no more to him, so that I could devote my attention to the route I was to take alone the next morning.

I ate scarcely a bite and went to bed at once, ordering Leduc to call me at six o'clock.

''It is not light until seven.''

''I know that.''

''Very well.''

So at seven o'clock I am at the door of my first great passion. I go up to the second floor, I ring, and a woman who opens the door for me asks me if my name is Casanova.

''Yes.''

''The Signora told me that you would come at eight o'clock; but it does not matter, go into this room, I will wake her.''

Five or six minutes later I see her husband approach me politely in his nightcap, saying that his wife was getting up and would come; but I nearly laughed when, after staring at me for a time, he said:

''Was it not you, Signore, who asked me my wife's name yesterday evening?''

''I am the man, I thought I knew her, and my good luck saw to it that I should ask her husband. The friendship, Signore, which I shall always feel for you will be the same as that which I have always felt for her.''

But there she is, beautiful as a star. She enters with open arms, I open mine, and we embrace like two fond friends, or like lovers enjoying the happiness of a moment for which they have longed. After a brief pause for thought, we embrace again, then she tells her husband to sit down. She draws me to a sofa, letting her tears flow freely, I cannot hold back mine; but a moment later, wiping our eyes, we happen to turn them on Signor Palesi's face, and we cannot help bursting out laughing. His amazement was too comic.

"You see my father," she said to him, "and more than my father, for I owe him everything. Happy moment, which I have awaited for ten years!"

Hearing me called "father," her husband stared at me again; but the emotion of the situation did not permit me to laugh. I was not quite two years older than Teresa; but fondness takes the name of father to mean whatever it chooses.

"Yes, Signore," I said, "she is my daughter, she is my sister, an angel without sex, she is a living treasure, and she is your wife.

"I did not," I said to her, "answer your last letter—"

"I know everything. You were in love with a nun, you were imprisoned under the Leads, and when I was in Vienna I heard of your prodigious escape. A false presentiment made me certain that I should see you there. Afterward I learned of your vicissitudes in Paris and Holland; but after you left Paris I could get news of you from no one. But here we are, and I shall die content. When I tell you all that has happened to me during these ten years you will hear some fine tales. Now I am happy. There is Signor Palesi, of Rome, who married me two months ago; we love each other, and I hope you will be his friend as you are mine."

I then rose to embrace him, and he came to meet me, though with extreme embarrassment, for he could not imagine what attitude he should assume toward me, who was now father, now brother, now friend. He did not know if he must be prepared to put up with me as the lover of his dear wife. It was she who, to reassure him, went and embraced him most heartily, making me the spectator of a second scene which I pretended to find very agreeable, but which annoyed me, for in that half hour Teresa had rekindled in me all the fire with which I had begun to burn for her at Ancona when Don Sancho Pico[26] introduced me to her.

Signor Palesi asked me if I would be pleased to breakfast, joining them for a cup of excellent chocolate which he whipped himself, and I replied that I was passionately fond of chocolate. He went off at once to make it.

Thereupon Teresa fell into my arms, saying:

"Let us embrace a hundred times this first day, my dear friend, and afterward leave it at that, since such is the decree of destiny. Tomorrow we shall meet again only as two fond friends; our transports at this happy moment are too well justified for us to restrain them."

After satisfying some of our fire, finding that we were as we had been when we parted in Rimini, we breathed again, and we resumed our places.

After reflecting a little:

"You must know," she said, "that I am still in love with my husband and determined never to deceive him. What I did just now did not depend upon me, and we must both forget it. It is over. Let it suffice us to know that we still love each other, and to have no possible doubt of it. In future, my dear friend, let us avoid any opportunity to be alone together. Does that make you sad?"

"I find you bound, and I am free. We would not have parted again; you have just rekindled all my old fire; I am the same, and happy that I have been able to prove it to myself and unhappy that I can no longer hope to possess you; I find you not only married but in love. Alas! I have delayed too long; but if I had not stopped in Genoa I should be equally unhappy. You shall know all when occasion serves. Meanwhile, I will obey no other laws than those you will prescribe for me. Your husband, I believe, does not know our story; so I must let nothing out, must I not?"

Girl in Her Bedroom

"Nothing; for he has no knowledge of my affairs, and I am very glad he shows no curiosity about them. He knows, like everyone else, that I made my fortune in Naples, where I say I went at the age of ten. Such things are falsehoods which harm no one, and which in my profession I must prefer to a number of truths which would injure me. I claim I am twenty-four—what do you say to that?"

"I would say you are telling the truth, though I know you are thirty-two."

"You mean thirty-one. When I met you I could not have been more than fourteen."

"I thought it was fifteen."

"Possibly; but tell me, please, do I look more than twenty-four?"

"I swear that you do not even look that. But in Naples—"

"In Naples a gazetteer might know everything; but nobody listens to such people. But I am waiting to see you at what will be one of the most interesting moments in your life."

"One of the most interesting moments in my life? When?"

"Permit me to say no more. I want to enjoy your surprise. But let us speak of something essential. How are you off? If you need money I am in a position to return yours to you with all the interest you can demand. My husband controls nothing; all that I have is my own. I have fifty thousand ducati del regno[27] at Naples, and the same amount in diamonds. Tell me how much you need. Quick, for the chocolate is coming."

Such was Teresa. Deeply moved, I was about to throw myself on her neck before answering her, when the chocolate arrived. Her husband entered, followed by a chambermaid who was a beauty and who carried three cups of chocolate on a silver-gilt tray. Palesi kept us entertained while we were drinking it, wittily describing

the nature of his surprise when he saw that the man who
had got him out of bed at seven o'clock was the same
one who had asked him his wife's name the previous evening at the theater. Teresa's laughter, accompanied by
mine, was not displeasing to the Roman, who I thought
appeared jealous only for propriety's sake.

Teresa said that at ten o'clock a rehearsal of all the
arias from the new opera was to be held at her house,
that I was welcome to remain for it and dine with her
afterward, and to spend the whole day there if I had
nothing better to do. I replied that I would not leave
her until after supper to let her go to bed with her
fortunate husband. At these words Signor Palesi cordially embraced me, as if to say that he was grateful to
me for not having raised obstacles to his exercising his
rights.

He was no more than twenty or twenty-two years old,
he was blond, and too good-looking for a man, for, such
as he was, all mankind of either sex owed him approba-
tion. I could not but forgive Teresa for having fallen in
love with his pretty face, for I knew the power of a
beautiful countenance only too well; but I disapproved
of her having made him her husband, for a husband ac-
quires sovereign rights.

Teresa's young chambermaid came in and said that my
carriage was at the door.

"Will you permit my hire lackey to come in?" I
asked Teresa. "Who," I said to the scoundrel, "ordered
you to come here with my carriage?"

"No one; but I know my duty."

"Who told you I was here?"

"I guessed it."

"Go call Leduc and come here with him."

I told Leduc to pay him for three days, to take away
his livery, and ask Doctor Vannini for another valet of
the same stature who did not "guess." When the impertinent fellow begged Teresa to intervene for him, she
told me I had done well.

At ten o'clock I saw all the actors and actresses arrive, together with a number of devotees of music, who all kissed her hand and whom she received most graciously. The rehearsal, which went on for three hours, bored me to extinction. I spent my time talking with Palesi, whom I liked for his never asking me where or when or how I had known his wife.

At the end of the rehearsal one of the actresses, a girl from Parma named Redegonda,[28] who had a male role and sang well, stayed for dinner with Teresa, and a moment later a young ballerina from Bologna named Corticelli,[29] whom she had also invited, arrived and at once kissed her hand. The girl's budding charms struck me; but, being full of Teresa at the moment, I paid her no special attention. After another moment I see a very stout old abate, of a bland and smiling countenance, who enters with stately steps and, looking at no one but Teresa, approaches and kisses her hand, going down on one knee in the Portuguese fashion. Gracious and smiling, Teresa makes him sit at her right; I was at her left. I at once recognize the Abate Gama,[30] whom I had left in the household of Cardinal Acquaviva[31] in Rome seventeen years earlier; but I give no sign of it. He had aged greatly, but it was he. The philandering old man, who had eyes only for Teresa, treated her to stale compliments and had not yet looked at anyone. Hoping that he will not recognize me, I avoid looking at him and I flirt with La Corticelli. Teresa calls me to order, saying that the Signor Abate wishes to know if I recognize him. At that I look at him, I pretend surprise, I rise, and I ask if I have the pleasure of seeing the Abate Gama.

"Himself," he replies, rising and taking me by the head to give me a number of kisses, in perfect accord with the combination of subtle policy and great curiosity which I knew to make up his character and which I have portrayed for my reader in the first volume of these memoirs.

After this beginning it can be imagined that we talked

endlessly. He gave me news of Barbaruccia, of the Marchesa G., of Cardinal S. C.,[32] and he told me how he had passed from the service of Spain to that of Portugal, in which he still continued; but suddenly a figure appears which absorbs and bewilders all the faculties of my soul. A youth of perhaps fifteen or sixteen, but with the sort of maturity which an Italian can attain at that age, enters and bows to the whole company. I being the only person present who did not know him, Teresa presents him to me unabashed, saying:

"He is my brother."

I receive him as I should, but flabbergasted, not having had time to recover myself. This supposed brother of Teresa's was the image of me, except that he was not as dark; I instantly see that he is my son; nature had never been more indiscreet; it was the surprise which Teresa had promised me, and which she had cunningly arranged so that she should have the pleasure of seeing it in my face. In her first letters from Naples she had never written me that she was pregnant, and it had never occurred to me that she might be.

It seemed to me that Teresa should have avoided this meeting, for everyone present had eyes, and no more was needed to discern that the youth must be either my son or my brother. I give her a glance, but she turns away; the youth was looking at me in such confusion that he paid no attention to what his sister was saying to him. The others simply looked back and forth from his face to mine, and, convinced that he was my son, could only conclude that I had been the intimate friend of Teresa's mother, if it was true that she was his sister, for at the age she appeared to be it was impossible to suppose that she was his mother. Nor was it possible to conclude that I was Teresa's father, for I looked almost as young as she did.

What began to please me greatly was the youth's fine bearing and the intelligence he showed as he discoursed in the Neapolitan dialect, which he spoke very markedly. Teresa had me dine between herself and him. I found him well informed and with manners such as a Neapolitan upbringing rarely bestows. Teresa told him he should begin speaking Tuscan.

"It is only six months," she said to me, "since he left the custody of the man who brought him up and who taught him everything he knows, and especially music, which is his passion. You shall hear him at the harpsichord. I am eight years his elder."

Whether it was nature, prepossession, self-esteem, or whatever the reader may please, I rose from the table so enchanted with this son of Teresa's that I embraced him with such affection that the whole company applauded. I invited Teresa to dine with me the next day, together with everyone present.

"I too?" La Corticelli asked.

"You too."

After dinner the Abate Gama told me to choose between having him to breakfast or coming to breakfast with him the next morning, because he was dying to spend two hours alone with me. I invited him to my inn.

As soon as everyone had left, Don Cesarino (for such was the handsome youth's name) asked me if I would take him to the promenade with me. I embraced him and replied that he could go in my carriage with his brother-in-law, for I must not leave his sister alone. Palesi agreed.

As soon as we were alone I congratulated her on Cesarino.

"He is," she replied, "the happy fruit of our love. Happy, because he has everything to make him so. It is the same Duke[33] with whom I left Rimini who provided for his upbringing; I confided my secret to him as soon as I found that I was pregnant. I was delivered without anyone's knowing it, and it was he who sent him to nurse at Sorrento and had him baptized by the name of Cesare Filippo Lanti. He left him there until he was nine, then put him to board with a competent man, who saw that he received an excellent education and taught him music. From his earliest childhood he has always known me as his sister, and you cannot imagine my joy when I found that the older he grew the more he looked like you. I always considered him a sure pledge of our union, certain that it would take place as soon as we met again, for every time I looked at him I thought it impossible that he would not produce the same effect on your soul as he did on mine. I was sure that you could not refuse to make such a charming creature your legitimate son by marrying his fond mother.

"When the Duke died,[34] I left Naples, leaving him to board in the same place under the protection of Prince della Riccia,[35] who never thought him anything but my brother. Your son commands a capital of twenty thousand ducati del regno, the interest on which is paid to me and of which he does not know; but I let him want for nothing. My heart bleeds because I cannot tell him I am his mother; for I think he would love me all the more. You cannot imagine the pleasure I felt today when I saw your surprise and afterward observed how quickly you fell in love with him."

"And the resemblance?"

"It pleases me. Can it lead people to believe anything except that you were my mother's lover? Let it be so. My husband believes that is the source of the friendship between us, at which he might well have taken offense this morning when he saw our transports. He told me last night that Cesarino might be my brother on his mother's side but not on his father's, for he had seen his father at the theater and he could certainly not be mine. If I have children by Palesi all my property will go to them on my death; and if not it will go to Cesarino. My property is in trustworthy hands, even if Prince della Riccia should die."

She then took me to her bedroom, where she opened a strongbox which contained all her jewels and over fifty thousand ducati in good securities. In addition she had a large quantity of plate, and her talent, which assured her of leading roles in any theater in Italy.

I asked her if our son had yet had a love affair.

"I do not think so," she answered; "but I think my chambermaid is in love with him. I will keep my eyes open."

"Give him to me. I will teach him the way of the world."

"Ask anything of me, but leave me your son. Know that I never kiss him for fear of going mad. If you knew how good he is and how much he loves me, for I satisfy all his wishes. What will people say in Venice four months from now when they see the Casanova who escaped from the Leads become twenty years younger?"

"So you are going to Venice for La Sensa?"[36]

"Yes; and you are going to Rome?"

"And to Naples, to see my friend the Duke of Matalona."[37]

"I know him. He already has a son[38] by the daughter of the Duke of Bovino,[39] whom he married, a charming woman who was able to make a man of him. Everyone in Naples knows he was impotent."

In such talk we passed the day until Cesarino arrived with his brother-in-law. At supper my son won all that he had not earlier conquered of my paternal affection. He was sprightly and had all the Neapolitan vivacity. He wanted me to hear him at the harpsichord, at which he accompanied himself in some Neapolitan songs which made us laugh heartily. Teresa did nothing but look from him to me and from me to him, then she embraced her husband and exclaimed that to be happy in this world one must be in love.

So I spent that day, which was one of the happiest of my whole life.

CHAPTER VIII

La Corticelli. The Jewish impresario cudgeled.
The pretended Charles Ivanov and the trick
he plays on me. Arbitrary order to leave Tus-
cany. I arrive in Rome. My brother Giovanni.

AT NINE o'clock the next morning the Abate Gama
was announced; he began by weeping for joy to see me,
after so many years, in such good health and in the
prime of life. The reader sees that he must have praised
me to my face. However intelligent one may be, however
well one may know those who practice it, having one's
ears tickled is gratifying. The mild-mannered Abate,
extremely amiable and without an iota of malice, but
curious both by nature and by his occupation—such, in
short, as I have portrayed him in my first volume—did
not wait for any urging on my part to tell me his whole
story for the past seventeen years, making it a lengthy
business by recounting its various episodes in all possible
detail. He had passed from the service of Spain to that
of Portugal, and as Secretary of Embassy to Commander
Almada,[1] he had been obliged to leave Rome because
Pope Rezzonico[2] would not allow His Most Faithful
Majesty[3] to punish the Jesuits who, though they had

only broken his arm, had intended to kill him.[4] Gama
traveled about Italy, corresponding with Almada and
the famous Carvalho[5] and waiting for the end of the
quarrel so that he could return to Rome; that was his
whole story. But the eloquent Abate made it last for an
hour, expecting that I would pay him in the same coin
with a detailed account of my adventures; we both displayed our talent—the Abate by lengthening out his
story, I by shortening mine, not without the minor pleasure of balking his curiosity. He asked me perfunctorily
what I was going to do in Rome, and I replied that I
was going to see the Pope to ask him to persuade the
State Inquisitors[6] to pardon me. It was not true; but
if I had told him truthfully that I was going there
simply to amuse myself he would not have believed me.
He who tells the truth to unbelieving ears prostitutes
truth; it is murder. The Abate asked me to do him the
favor of corresponding with him, and I promised to do
so; then he told me that he was in position to show me
his friendship by introducing me to the Marchese Botta-
Adorno,[7] then Governor of Tuscany,[8] who was said to
be a friend of the Emperor Francis I,[9] then reigning,
and I replied that he would be doing me a great honor.
He brought up the subject of Teresa, whereupon he
found me constipated; I told him that she was a child
when I had known her family in Bologna, and that her
brother's resemblance to me could only be chance. On
my table he saw something very well written, and he
asked me if it was my secretary who had such a good
hand. Costa, who was present, answered him in Spanish
that it was he. The Abate then exhausted himself in
compliments, ending by asking me to send Costa to him
to copy some letters. I did not hesitate to answer that I
urgently needed the young man all day. He wanted him
only in order to make him talk. Such are the curious.

Curiosity, which moralists refuse to number among
the passions, is a noble quality of mind whose laudable

object is to know all of nature: *nihil dulcius quam omnia scire* ("nothing is sweeter than to know all things"); however, it is a thing of the senses, for it can arise only from perception and sensation. But curiosity is a vice when it seeks only to pry into the affairs of others, whether the man possessed by it tries to obtain knowledge of them directly or indirectly, whether he tries to discover them in order to be of service to the person he sounds or to use what he discovers for his own advantage; it is always a vice, or a disease, for the mind of a man curious by nature is never at rest. Discovering a secret is perpetrating a theft. I am not speaking of the kind of curiosity which, relying on the abstruse sciences, tries to know the future or things which are not in nature; it is the daughter of ignorance and superstition, and they who dally with it are fools; but the Abate Gama was no fool; he was curious by nature, and he was paid to be curious. Having some visits to make, he left me, promising that he would return at dinnertime.

Doctor Vannini brought me a new hire valet, vouching for him. He was from Parma and of the same height as the first; I told Leduc to give him the livery. I warned the innkeeper-academician that I wanted a creditable dinner, and I was served accordingly.

The first to arrive was La Corticelli, together with her mother, who went by the name of "Signora Laura," [10] and her brother, a violinist who looked like a girl. Her mother told me that she never let her daughter dine alone with strangers. I replied that in that case she had only to go home or to leave her there and accept two scudi to dine with her son wherever she pleased. She took the two scudi and departed, saying she felt sure she was leaving her in good hands.

Her daughter made such amusing comments on this little dialogue between her mother and myself, laughing so heartily, that it was on that very day I began to love her. She was thirteen years of age, and looked only ten; she was well built, extremely fair, gay, with a sense of humor; but I do not know how or with what in her I could have fallen in love. She begged me to protect her against the Jewish opera impresario.[11] In the contract he had given her he had undertaken to have her dance a *pas de deux* in the second opera, and he had not done so. She asked me to force the Jew to abide by his undertaking. I promised to send the Jew word to come and talk with me.

The next to arrive was the Parmesan actress Redegonda, tall and beautiful. Costa, who was Parmesan too, told me she was the sister of my hire valet. In two or three minutes of questioning I found Redegonda worthy of attention. The Abate Gama arrives, and he congratulates me on finding me between the two pretty girls. I make him take my place, and he begins flirting with them; they laugh at him, but he persists. I saw that he thought he was pleasing them; and I well understood that vanity could prevent him from knowing he was making himself ridiculous; but I did not foresee that when I reached his age I might be like him. Indeed, I did not give it a thought. Unhappiness is the lot of the old man who does not know what he is or understand that the same sex which he attracted in his youth cannot but scorn him as soon as he shows that he still has pretensions though age has deprived him of all the qualities required to please.

My beautiful Teresa arrived last, with her husband and Cesarino, who had on a very fine coat; I embraced him after fulfilling the same obligation to his mother; and I sat down at table between them. The Abate Gama took the place between Redegonda and La Corticelli, and it was he who enlivened the meal with his witty remarks. I laughed to myself, seeing how attentively my hire valet changed his sister Redegonda's plate, while she plumed herself on being entitled to honors to which he could not aspire; she seized an opportunity to say to me:

"He's a good lad who, unfortunately, has no talent."

I had purposely put in my pocket an enameled gold box on the cover of which was my portrait, painted on the enamel in the form of a medallion and a very good likeness. I had had it made in Paris as a present for Madame d'Urfé; and I had not given it to her because the painter had made me too young. I had filled the box with the excellent Havana snuff which Monsieur de Chavigny[12] had given me and which Teresa liked very much, and I was waiting for her to ask me for some so that I could take it from my pocket.

It was the Abate Gama, who had some very good snuff in a box from Orihuela,[13] who passed it to Teresa, and she passed him some of hers in a snuffbox of light-colored tortoise shell, encrusted all over with gold, than which nothing could be handsomer. Gama finds fault with Teresa's snuff; I pronounce it good, but I venture to say that mine is better. With that I take out my snuffbox and offer her a pinch, holding it open. She could not see the portrait. She agrees that the snuff is excellent.

"In that case, Signora, shall we exchange?"

"Gladly. Give me a piece of paper."

"There's no need for that. Snuff is exchanged in whatever boxes it happens to be in."

So saying, I put Teresa's box in my pocket, and I hand her mine closed. When she sees the portrait she gives a cry which startles the company, and she cannot refrain from printing a kiss on the medallion.

"Look," she immediately says to Cesarino. "It is your portrait."

Cesarino looks at it in astonishment, and the box makes the round of the table. Everyone says it is my own portrait made ten years earlier but that it could pass for Cesarino's. Teresa is mad about it and swears the box shall never leave her hands, she gets up from the table and embraces her dear brother several times. I saw that the Abate Gama's politic mind was busily drawing conclusions from the little incident. He left toward nightfall, saying that he expected me for breakfast the next morning.

I spent the day flirting with Redegonda and Teresa, who, seeing that the girl attracted me, advised me to speak out and promised to invite her to visit her whenever I liked. But Teresa did not know her well.

The next morning the Abate Gama gave me a cup of exquisite chocolate; he said that he had sent word to Marshal Botta and that he would come for me at four o'clock to present me to him. Then, as ever the slave of his curiosity, he politely reproached me for having said nothing about my great wealth in my brief account of my adventures.

"My wealth, Signor Abate, is not great; but I have friends whose purses are open to me."

"If you have true friends you are rich. But they are very scarce."

Leaving him, I went to visit Redegonda, to whom I would gladly have given the preference over La Corticelli. She received me in a room in which I saw her mother, her uncle, and three or four children, her brothers and sisters.

"Have you not another room in which to receive your friends?"

"I do not need another room, for I have no friends to receive."

"Have the room and you will have friends. This one is all very well for receiving relatives, but not people who, like myself, come to pay homage to your charms and your talent."

"My daughter, Signore," said her mother, "has very little talent and no charms."

"Yet I find her most pleasing."

"That is an honor for her, and she will receive you whenever you come to see her, but in no other room than this."

"Here I am afraid I inconvenience you. Good-by, Signora."

I went to Teresa's and told her about my visit, and we laughed over it. She said she would be glad to see me at the opera in her *camerino*,[14] which I could enter by giving a testone[15] to the man who stood guard at the little stairway leading to the stage.

The Abate Gama came to fetch me to introduce me to Marshal Botta. I saw a man in every way worthy of respect. He was famous because of the Genoese affair.[16] He was commanding the Austrian army in person when the people of Genoa, angry at the presence of foreigners who were there only to subjugate their country, revolted and drove them out of the city. But for that the ancient Republic would have perished. He was with some Florentine ladies and gentlemen, whom he left in my honor. He talked to me of Venice like a man who knew my country well, and, after making me talk at length about France, he seemed satisfied. In his turn he talked of the Russian Court, where he had been when Elisabeth Petrovna, who still reigned, so easily ascended the throne of her father,[17] Peter the Great. He said that only in Russia did politics know the art of using poisons.

At the hour when the opera began, the Marshal withdrew, and everyone left. After taking home the Abate, who naturally assured me that I had made a very good impression on the Marshal, I went to the opera too, where, at the price of a testone, I went up to Teresa's *camerino*, to find her pretty chambermaid dressing her. She advised me to go to Redegonda's *camerino*, where, as she had to dress as a man, she might let me see charming things.

I had myself shown to it, and her mother did not want me to stay, for her daughter was just then dressing in male attire; but when I assured her I would turn my back she gave me permission, saying that I could sit at her toilet table. Now there was a large mirror on the toilet table, which admirably enabled me to see for nothing all of Redegonda's most private treasures, especially when she awkwardly put her legs into her breeches. She lost nothing by it, for I would have signed any conditions in order to obtain her favors. I thought it impossible she did not know that, seated where I was, I must see everything, and the idea increased my flame. I turned when her mother gave me permission, and, in her disguise as a man, admired this girl of twenty-one who was perfectly proportioned and five feet tall.

As soon as Redegonda was dressed she went out; whereupon I was able to talk with her privately in the wings.

"I am on fire," I said, "charming Redegonda, and I feel that I shall die if you do not make me happy. Do not pretend: as you know that in your mirror I saw the whole of you, and I cannot imagine you capable of having set me aflame only to drive me to despair."

"What can you have seen? I don't know what you're talking about."

"Come now. It's possible; but answer me. That's what matters. What am I to do to have you?"

"To have me? I do not understand such language. I am a decent girl."

"I believe it; and you must believe that after you have loved me you will not be anything else. Speak out, for I must know my fate this instant."

"I cannot say anything but that you are at liberty to come to see me."

"At what hour will you be alone?"

"Alone? Never."

"Very well, then, let your mother be present; it will not matter. If she is wise she will pretend not to see, and I will give you a hundred ducati each time."

"Really, either you are mad or you do not know me."

When, a quarter of an hour later, I recounted the whole incident to Teresa she advised me, after laughing heartily, to go at once and offer the mother the hundred ducati, and, if she refused them, to consider it good riddance and try my luck elsewhere.

I go back to the *camerino,* where she is alone.

"Signora, I am a foreigner, and I shall leave in a week or ten days; I am rich and in love with your daughter. Will you bring her to sup with me this evening, and be obliging? I will give you a hundred zecchini, and after that you shall ruin me."

"To whom do you think you are speaking? Your effrontery amazes me. Inquire who I am, and inquire into my daughter's behavior. You are the first person in the world who has dared to address me in such a manner."

"Then good-by, Signora."

"Good-by, Signore."

I find Redegonda in the wings, and I repeat the dialogue to her word for word. She bursts out laughing.

"Did I do right, or wrong?"

"More right than wrong; but if you love me come to see us."

"Come to see you now!"

"Why not? Who knows?"

"Who knows? You do not know me. Hope poisons me, my beautiful Redegonda; that is why I spoke to you clearly."

Determined to put the girl out of my mind, I went to sup with Teresa, where I spent three delicious hours which made my soul rejoice. The next day, having a great deal of writing to do, I did not go out, and toward evening I saw La Corticelli before me with her mother and her brother. She had come to hold me to my promise that I would protect her against the Jewish impresario who would not let her dance the *pas de deux* as he had undertaken to do in the contract. I said she should come to breakfast with me the next morning and I would talk to the Jew in her presence, provided he would come; I promised to send for him. Needing to finish my letters and to refrain from eating, I told Costa to serve them supper.

After finishing my correspondence, feeling in the mood for amusement, I have the little madcap sit beside me and I flirt with her in a fashion to which Signora Laura could make no objection; but I am a little surprised when the youth comes to join in.

"You are not a girl," I say.

Thus apostrophized, the rascal shows me that he is a boy, but in such a scandalous way that his sister, who was sitting on my lap, gives a great burst of laughter and throws herself into her mother's arms at the other end of the room, where, after eating a good supper, she had respectfully retired. When he sees his sister gone, the little scoundrel treats me to a gesture which annoys me, and I give him a light box on the ear. I rise and I ask Signora Laura for what purpose she has brought me this catamite. The only answer she gives me is:

"Isn't he a very pretty boy?"

I told her to leave, giving the Giton[18] a scudo to make up to him for the box on the ear. He took it, kissing my hand.

I went to bed laughing over the incident, for, such as nature made me, the wristband game[19] could never have been anything but the consequence of an intoxication produced by a great friendship.

The next morning I sent Costa to the Jew with a message asking him to come and hear something I had to tell him. A little later La Corticelli arrived with her mother, and the Jew came as we were breakfasting.

After setting forth La Corticelli's grievance to him, I read him his contract and I told him quietly that I could easily find means to make him abide by his undertaking.

After offering various excuses, whose insubstantiality La Corticelli herself proved to him, he ended by promising me he would see the ballet master that day and instruct him to have her dance with a partner whom he named to me and who, by her account, would be very glad to compose a *pas de deux* for her. After thus settling the matter, I let them leave.

I went to the Abate Gama's, to go on to dinner at Marshal Botta's, who had sent us an invitation. It was at this dinner that I made the acquaintance of the Chevalier Mann,[20] the English Resident, who was the idol of Florence, a man of wealth, amiable, a great lover of the arts, and with excellent taste. The next day I paid him a visit, and in his small garden, the furnishings of his house, his pictures, and his choice books, I saw the man of genius. After returning my visit he invited me to dinner, and he was kind enough also to invite Signora Palesi, her brother, and her husband. After dinner Cesarino delighted the company at the harpsichord. The conversation turning to resemblances, the Chevalier Mann showed us some miniature portraits of amazing beauty. Shortly before she left, Teresa told me gravely that she had kept me in mind.

"I told Redegonda," she said, "that I would come for her and keep her for supper with me and send her home afterward. Come to supper too, have your carriage wait at my door, and you shall be the one to take her home. You will have her alone with you only a few minutes, but that is something. I would wager that you will find her submissive."

"You shall hear the whole story tomorrow. I will not fail to be at your supper."

I got there at nine o'clock. Teresa receives me as one receives an unexpected friend, I tell Redegonda that I congratulate myself on finding her there, and she replies gaily that she had not expected to have the pleasure of seeing me. At supper no one had any appetite; only

Redegonda ate very heartily and laughed a great deal at all the stories I told her. After supper Teresa asks Redegonda if she wishes to have a sedan chair sent for or if she will let me take her home; she replies that, if I will be so kind, there is no need for a sedan chair. This answer makes me sure of everything. Good nights are said, embraces exchanged, I give her my arm, which she presses, we go down, her brother opens the carriage door; Redegonda gets in, I get in after her, and when I go to sit down, I find the place taken, I hear a great shriek of laughter and Redegonda saying to me:

"It's my mother."

I should have made a joke of it, but I did not have the strength. Redegonda sat down on her mother's lap. I coldly asked her why she had not come upstairs to supper with us. When we reached her door the *virtuosa's* mother said I might come up, but I excused myself, and for good reason. If she had done the slightest thing to annoy me I would have boxed her ears, and the man they had in the house looked too much like a cutthroat.

In my fury, I think of going to La Corticelli's; the hour was unwonted, and I had never been there; but no matter. I needed to calm myself, and I was almost certain I should find the Bolognese girl accommodating and Signora Laura unable to resist money.

My lackey shows me the way to her room.

"That will do. Go and wait for me in the carriage."

I knock, I knock again, the family wakes:

"Who is there?"

I give my name, the door is opened, I enter in darkness, and I hear Signora Laura say she is going to light a candle, and that if I had let her know she would have waited up for me despite its being so cold; and in fact I felt as if I were in an icehouse. I hear La Corticelli laughing, I grope for her bed, I find it, I put in my hand, and I touch the too obvious tokens of the male sex. I guess it is her brother, and I see him by the light of the

candle her mother has lighted. I see his sister lying in
the same bed laughing, with the covers drawn up to her
chin because, like her brother, she was stark naked.
Despite my freedom from prejudice on the subject, such
infamous behavior disgusts me.

"Why," I ask Signora Laura, "do you not keep your
son in bed with you?"

"What harm can I fear? They are brother and sister."

"It is not good."

The catamite makes off and gets into his mother's bed,
and La Corticelli says in her Bolognese dialect, which
immediately sets me laughing, that it was neither good
nor bad, since she loved her brother only as a brother
and he loved her only as a sister. She ended by saying
that if I wanted her to sleep alone I had only to buy
her a bed, which she would take with her when she went
back to Bologna.

Talking and gesticulating, she unwittingly let me see
a third of her nudity, and I saw nothing worth seeing,
nevertheless it was ordained that I should fall in love
with her skin, for it was all she had. If she had been
alone I would have gone further with her; but, her
mother and her brother being there, I feared scenes
which might anger me. I gave her ten zecchini to buy
herself a bed, and I left her.

I took refuge in my inn, cursing all the execrable
mothers of *virtuose*.

I spent the whole of the next morning with Monsieur
Mann in the gallery,[21] where in the course of five or six
visits I saw marvels in the way of paintings, statues,
and engraved gems. Before going to dine with the Abate
Gama, whom I had invited, I went to tell Teresa the
story of my two adventures of the night before, and we
laughed over them. She said that if I absolutely needed
a girl I had only to take La Corticelli, who certainly
would not keep me languishing.

At table the Abate Gama, talking politics in good

earnest, asks me if I would be willing to represent the Court of Portugal in a certain matter at the congress which, all Europe believed, was to be held in the city of Augsburg.[22] He assured me that if I did well in the post, which he would be glad to solicit for me, I could be sure that if I went to Lisbon afterward I could get whatever I might want from the Court. I replied that he would find me ready to undertake anything of which he thought me capable, that he had only to write to me, and that I would see to it that he always had my address. It was at that moment that I first felt the strongest possible desire to become a diplomat.

That evening at the opera I talked to the ballet master, to the dancer who was to be my protégée's partner, and to the Jew, who confirmed his promise that she should dance the *pas de deux* three or four days later and every day for the rest of the Carnival. La Corticelli told me she already had a bed and invited me to supper with her. I promised I would go.

Being sure that I would pay for everything, her mother had sent out to a cookshop for a supper for four, which was good enough, and several flagons of the best Florentine wine; in addition there was a clarified wine called "ogliatico" or "aleatico," [23] which I found excellent, but the mother, the son, and the daughter, who were not accustomed to drinking so well, became tipsy. The mother and son went off to bed without ceremony, and the little madcap did likewise, urging me to follow her example. I did not dare, the cold was intense, there was no fire in the room, and her bed had only one cover; if I had undressed I should have caught a cold. She gave herself to me and tried to assure me that I was her first lover, and I pretended to believe her. I left after spending two hours with her, promising to spend the following night with her on condition that she would heat the room with a brazier and would buy another cover, and I left her fifty zecchini.

The next day a letter which I received from Grenoble interested me greatly. Valenglart wrote me that La Roman had left for Paris with her aunt, having become convinced that if they did not go what the horoscope declared could never come true.

So they would never have gone there if I had not taken it into my head to cast them a fantastic horoscope, for even if astrology had been a science I knew nothing about it. We find countless events in real history which would never have occurred if they had not been predicted. This is because we are the authors of our so-called destiny, and all the "antecedent necessities" of the Stoics are chimerical; the argument which proves the power of destiny seems strong only because it is sophistical. Cicero laughed at it. Someone whom he had invited to dinner, who had promised to go, and who had not appeared, wrote him that since he had not gone it was evident that he had not been *iturus* ("going to go"). Cicero answers him: *Veni ergo cras, et veni etiamsi venturus non sis* ("Then come tomorrow, and come even if you are not going to come").[24] At this date, when I am conscious that I rely entirely on my common sense, I owe this explanation to my reader, despite the axiom, *Fata viam inveniunt* ("Destiny finds the way").[25] If the fatalists are obliged by their own philosophy to consider the concatenation of all events necessary, *a parte ante* ("a priori"), what remains of man's moral freedom is nothing; and in that case he can neither earn merit nor incur guilt.[26] I cannot in conscience admit that I am a machine.

Having gone to the theater to see La Corticelli rehearse her *pas de deux*, I saw her in possession of a fine pelisse. When the other ballerinas caught sight of me they treated me to scornful looks; but my favorite, proud of being preferred, came to speak to me and give me playful pinches.[27]

At supper I found that Signora Laura had provided a large brazier and another cover on the bed. She showed me all the things her daughter had bought for herself and complained that she had not provided clothes for her brother. I pacified her by giving her six zecchini.

In bed I found the girl neither in love nor passionate but amusing. She made me laugh, and I found her accommodating. She needed no more to keep me constant. I gave her a watch and promised to sup with her on the next day but one. By then she should have danced her *pas de deux.*

But I was surprised when I saw her appear only in ensembles.

I go to sup with her as I had promised, and I find her wretched; she tells me, with tears, that I must avenge her for the insult, that the Jew put the blame on the tailor but he was lying. I try to calm her by promising her everything, I spend several hours with her, and I go back to my inn resolved to avenge her after making inquiries.

The next morning early I send Costa to tell the Jew to call on me. He answers that he knows what I want, and that if La Corticelli was not dancing in this opera she would dance in the next.

I then saw what had to be done, but I also saw that I must pretend to take the thing lightly. I summoned Leduc, I told him the whole story, saying that I would be dishonored if I did not avenge myself. I told him that he alone could give me the satisfaction of arranging a good cudgeling for the scoundrel, who by breaking his word to me had given me such an obvious proof of his disregard. I promised him twenty zecchini. I impressed the importance of secrecy on him. He asked me for twenty-four hours before he gave me a positive answer.

The next morning he came to my bedside to tell me that during the preceding day he had devoted himself entirely to acquiring a knowledge of the Jew's person and of the house in which he lived, asking information from no one.

"Today," he said, "I will not let him out of my sight; I shall know at what hour he goes to bed, and tomorrow you shall hear the rest."

"Be prudent, and before you entrust the business to anyone consider carefully."

The next day he tells me that if he goes home at the same hour and takes the same road, he will have the cudgeling before he gets to bed.

"What men have you chosen?"

"No one but myself, on whom I can rely, and you shall not give me the twenty zecchini until the whole town is telling the story. After cudgeling him I will go back for my redingote where I will have left it and I will re-enter the inn by the back door, going off to bed without anyone seeing me. Even Costa will be able to swear that I cannot possibly be the man who cudgeled him if anyone should say so. However, I will have pistols in my pocket in case I have to defend myself."

The next morning he comes to dress my hair and I see he is calm. But as soon as he sees that I am alone he gives me the news that the thing is done.

"The Jew," he said, "instead of running threw himself on the ground, his shouts brought a few people, and I slipped away. I don't know if I killed him, for two blows landed on his head."

"I should be sorry if you did."

I was invited to dinner at Teresa's, where the guests were Signor Sassi, the first castrato, and the Abate Gama. I hear the pretty story told. I say I am sorry, though he is a scoundrel. The castrato says he is not sorry, and that he is sure people will say it was he who made him the present.

"They are saying," the Abate said to me, "that it is you who had it done, and for good reason."

"It will not be easy to discover who is behind it," I replied, "for the rascal has gone too far with many decent people."

The subject was dropped at last, and we dined in high spirits.

The Jew got up from bed a few days later with a plaster on his nose, and the thing was generally attributed to me; but when nothing was discovered the affair was finally forgotten. Only La Corticelli, as wild with joy as she was scatterbrained, talked as if she were sure it was I who had avenged her and was furious with me for refusing to admit it.

With all this to entertain me, I was not thinking of leaving Florence in any hurry, when Doctor Vannini handed me a letter which someone had left with him. I open it in his presence and I find a bill of exchange for two hundred Florentine scudi drawn on Sasso Sassi,[28] at which Vannini looks and says it is good. I retire to my room to read the letter and I see that it is signed "Charles Ivanov."

He wrote me from the posthouse inn at Pistoia[29] that, still without luck or money, he had told his story to an Englishman who was leaving Florence for Lucca and who had generously made him a present of two hundred scudi, giving him the enclosed bill of exchange, which he had written in his presence. It was payable to bearer.

"I do not," he wrote, "dare to come to Florence myself for fear I shall be recognized and arrested because of the unfortunate business at Genoa. So I beg you to take pity on me, to send someone to collect the amount, and forward it to me here at once so that I can leave after paying my host."

The favor the poor wretch asked of me was very small; but I might compromise myself, for not only might the bill be false but even if it were good it would proclaim me a friend of his and in correspondence with him, a man whose name and description had been published in the gazettes. I decide to return his note to him in person. I go to the post station alone, I have two horses harnessed, and I go to the posthouse inn at Pistoia; the innkeeper himself takes me to the scoundrel's room and leaves me. I remained there only three or four minutes to tell him, handing him back his bill, that Signor Sassi knew me and that I did not want to give anyone grounds for supposing that I had any sort of connection with him. I advise him to give the bill of exchange to the inn-keeper, who will simply go with it to Signor Sassi and bring him the money. He says he will take my advice, I leave him and return to Florence.

No later than the next day but one, I see Signor Sassi and the innkeeper from Pistoia in my room. Signor Sassi shows me the note for two hundred scudi, saying that the person who had given it to me had swindled me because, firstly, it was not in the lord's handwriting, and, secondly, the said lord, having no money in his bank, could not draw on him.

"This man here," he said, "discounted the bill, the Russian left, he comes to me for his money, I tell him the bill is forged, and he replies that it was you who brought it to the Russian in person and that, knowing you, he did not hesitate to discount it; he claims that you should reimburse him."

"I? He is mad."

I then tell Signor Sassi the whole story, I show him the letter in which the Russian had sent me the bill, I summon Vannini, who had brought me the letter and who was ready to swear that he had seen the bill of ex-change. Signor Sassi tells the innkeeper from Pistoia that he is mistaken in claiming that I should reimburse him, but the innkeeper sticks to his guns; he insists on my reimbursing him, going so far as to say that I must be in league with the Russian to swindle him.

At that I run for my cane, the banker holds me, and the innkeeper decamps. Signor Sassi tells me that I am in the right, that I should pay no attention to what the innkeeper had said to me in his anger, and he leaves.

The next day I received a note from the head of the

police, who is called the Auditor,[30] in which he asked me
to call on him. I had no choice but to do so. As a foreigner, I must go and learn what he had to say to me.
After receiving me politely enough, he tells me in so
many words that I must reimburse the Pistoian innkeeper for the two hundred scudi he had given the
Russian, since he would never have given them to him
if he had not seen me bring him the note; I reply that,
as a judge, he cannot sentence me to pay unless he believes I am an accomplice in the swindle. Instead of
answering me *ad unguem* ("precisely") he repeats that
I must pay.

"Signor Auditore, I will not pay."

He then rings, bowing to me, and I leave. I go to the
banker Sassi and give him an account of the conversation I had just had with the Auditor, he is amazed, I
beg him to go to him and make him listen to reason, he
is willing, and he goes. I told him that I was to dine at
the Abate Gama's.

When I told Gama the whole story he was indignant.
He said he foresaw that the Auditor would stick to his
guns, and that if Signor Sassi did not succeed I should
inform Marshal Botta of the entire affair.

"That is unnecessary, for, after all, the Auditor cannot force me to pay."

"He can do worse."

"What?"

"Send you an order to leave."

"If he has that power I shall be surprised if he dares
to abuse it to such an extent; but rather than pay I will
leave. Let us go to the Marshal."

We go there at four o'clock, and we find that the
banker Sassi is with him and has already informed him
of the situation. Sassi, obviously mortified, tells me that
the Auditor refused to listen to reason and that if I want
to remain in Florence I must pay; I reply that I will
leave when I receive the order, and that I will publish

an account of this crying injustice. The Marshal tells me that the Auditor's decision is beyond belief and that he regrets he cannot interfere in the matter, but that I will do well to leave rather than pay.

Early the next morning a man brought me a letter from the Auditor, which I have mislaid, in which he told me that, my case being such that the usual legal steps could not be taken to make me pay, he had no choice but to order me to leave Florence within three days and Tuscany within five. His responsibility for the security of the city empowered him to give me this order. He said that I would be free to return as soon as His Imperial Highness the Grand Duke, to whom I was free to appeal, had disapproved of his decision.

I answered this *Cassian*[31] judge by only two lines, saying that his order would be executed to the letter.

After thus accepting my sentence, I put everything in order for my departure, and I spent the three days, during which I kept the Auditor's letter in my pocket, amusing myself at Teresa's, at the Chevalier Mann's, and at La Corticelli's, promising her that I would come to fetch her in person during Lent and spend a few days in Bologna with her. During the three days the Abate Gama was with me constantly. My great pleasure was the general distress which I saw in my friends and the execration bestowed on the Auditor. The day before I left, the Marchese Botta invited me to a dinner for thirty, and I spent that last day with my dear Teresa, both of us promising to maintain a regular correspondence in future. I left the next morning, and reached Rome in thirty-six hours.

It was an hour after midnight. The great city can be entered at any time; a foreigner is at once sent to the Customs Office,[32] which is always open, where his baggage is examined. The customs officials are strict only in regard to books. I had thirty or more, all hostile to religion or to the virtues it prescribes. I knew this, and I had resigned myself to giving them up without an argument, for I needed to get to bed at once. The clerk who examined my baggage politely told me to count them and leave them with him, assuring me that he would bring them all to me the next day at the inn to which I was going. I assented, and he kept his word. I gave him two zecchini.

No sooner is the examination over than I am in the Piazza di Spagna and in front of the "City of Paris";[33] such was the name of the inn which had been recommended to me. The whole household was asleep, my arrival rouses someone, I am asked to wait in a small room on the ground floor while a fire is made in the apartment I am to occupy. All the chairs were littered with dresses, petticoats, or shifts, I hear a girl in bed, covered up so that I see only her head, telling me to sit on her bed, in which another girl was asleep. I see a smiling mouth and two eyes which look like carbuncles. I praise them and ask her to let me kiss them. She answers only by putting her head under the coverlet; but I slip my hand beneath it and halfway down her figure and, finding her stark naked, I withdraw it, asking her to forgive me if I have been too inquisitive. I think I see that she is grateful for my kindness in restraining my curiosity.

"Who are you, my beautiful angel?"

"I am Teresa Roland,[34] daughter of the innkeeper, and this is my sister."

"You are seventeen?"

"Not quite."

"I can hardly wait to see you up and in my room tomorrow."

"Are there ladies in your party?"

"No."

"Too bad. We never go up to gentlemen's rooms."

"Won't you hold the coverlet a little lower? It keeps you from talking."

"It's too cold."

"Charming Teresa, your eyes scorch my soul."

She puts her head under the coverlet again, I seize the opportunity once more to advance my hand, she curls up, I take her by surprise, and I am sure that the angel is female.

It is enough. I withdraw my hand, again asking her pardon, and I see her little face reassured, smiling, red as fire, showing just a trace of anger but at the same time of consent. I was about to treat her to a discourse full of love, sentiment, and passion when a pretty maid entered and told me to go up.

"Good-by until tomorrow," I said to the charming Teresa, who answered only by turning over to resume her sleep.

After ordering dinner for one o'clock I go to bed and I sleep until noon, all my dreams being of this new Teresa. Costa tells me he has found the house in which my brother is living[35] and has left a note there. This was my brother Giovanni, who must then have been thirty years of age and who was in Rome studying under the famous Mengs,[36] who was at that time deprived of his pension because of the war, which obliged the King of Poland to live in Warsaw, the Prussians having occupied his Electorate of Saxony. It had been ten years since I had seen this brother.

I was still at table when I saw him appear before me. After embracing each other and spending an hour talking, he giving me a brief account of the little happenings of his life and I of the great ones of mine, he ended by saying that I should at once leave this inn, where it was expensive to live, and lodge where it would cost me nothing, in the house of the painter Mengs, who had an apartment which was unoccupied. As for meals, he said there was a cookshop in the same street. I reply that I have not the strength of mind to change lodgings because I have fallen in love with one of the innkeeper's daughters; and I tell him the story of the previous night. He laughs and replies that it is not love but a passing fancy, which I can still pursue, and he persuades me. I promised I would go to lodge with him the next day, and we went out together to walk about Rome a little.

I at once go to La Minerva[37] to call on Donna Cecilia,[38] and I am told that she had died two years earlier. I inquire where her daughter Donna Angelica[39] lives, I go there, I find her in, she gives me a poor reception, even to the point of saying that she scarcely remembers having met me. I leave her, and I feel no regret; she seems to me to have become ugly. I obtain the address of the doctor, the printer's son, who was to have married Barbaruccia,[40] and I put off visiting him until some other day, according the same treatment to my kind Father Giorgi,[41] who enjoyed the highest reputation in Rome. I also inquire for Don Gaspare Vivaldi[42] and am told that he is living in the country. My brother then took me to call on Signora Cherufini,[43] and this time I enter a house of the highest fashion. He introduces me, the lady receives me in the Roman manner, I find her charming and her daughters[44] even more so; but their swains of every description are too numerous, there is a glitter which annoys me, and the young ladies, one of whom was as pretty as a Cupid, seem too polite to everyone. I am asked an interesting question, I reply in a manner which should inspire a second, and I am not asked it. I do not care. I see that in this house I should lose something of my intrinsic value, and that the reason for it was the rank of the person who had brought me there. I hear an abate saying to another who is looking at me:

"He is Casanova's brother."

I tell him he should have said it was Casanova who was my brother, and he replies that it makes no difference. An abate says that it does make a difference, we talk, and we become good friends. It was the celebrated Abate Winckelmann,[45] who twelve years later[46] was murdered in Trieste.

Cardinal Alessandro Albani[47] arrives, Winckelmann introduces me; and His Eminence, who was nearly blind, says a great many things to me; none of them worth hearing. As soon as he learns that I am the man who had escaped from the Leads he rudely says that he is amazed that I have the effrontery to come to Rome, where at the least request from the Venetian State Inquisitors an *ordine santissimo*[48] would oblige me to leave. Nettled by such a warning, I bitterly reply that he had chosen the wrong ground on which to condemn me for effrontery, since I ran no risk in Rome.

"It would be the State Inquisitors," I said, "who could be taxed with effrontery if they dared to ask for me, since they would be unable to state for what crime they had deprived me of my freedom."

My short and tart reply silenced the Cardinal, who, ashamed to have taken me for a fool, said not another word. I never again set foot in the Casa Cherufini. We returned to the "City of Paris" with the Abate Winckelmann, whom my brother persuaded to stay to supper with us. The Abate bore a strong resemblance to the Abbé de Voisenon.[49] The next day the three of us went to the Villa Albani[50] to see the Cavaliere Mengs,[51] who was living there, being engaged in painting a ceiling.[52]

My host Roland, knowing my brother, came to pay me a visit while we were supping. I told the man, who was from Avignon and fond of good living, that I was sorry to leave his establishment to lodge with my brother because I had fallen in love with his daughter Teresa, though I had talked with her only a quarter of an hour and seen nothing of her but her head.

"You saw her in bed, I wager."

"Exactly. I want to see her out of it. With all due respect, may I ask you to have her come up?"

"Gladly."

She came up, delighted to have her father summon her. She had an elegant figure, her manner was cheerful and frank, and she could pass for pretty, though her

The Singer

Piazza of the Church of the Fathers of the Oratory, Florence

only striking feature was her eyes. My enthusiasm diminished; but my brother, without saying a word to me, took such a fancy to her that, a year later,[53] he let himself be trapped. The young Teresa had the art to make him marry her, and two years later he took her with him to Dresden, where I saw her five years afterward with an infant. She died of consumption ten years later.

The next morning at the Villa Albani I saw for the first time the indefatigable painter Mengs, who was truly great in his art, but no less great an eccentric in society. However, I found him pleasant and glad that he could lodge me in Rome, to which he expected to return in a few days with his whole family. But what astonished me was the Villa Albani. Cardinal Alessandro had had it built, and, to satisfy his taste for antiquities, he had allowed nothing to be used in its construction except antique materials. Not only the statues and vases but all the columns and even the pedestals were Greek, and, being a great connoisseur and a shrewd Greek himself,[54] he had done it all at very little expense. Then, too, he often bought on credit, like Damasippus;[55] so no one could say that he was ruining himself. If a sovereign had wanted to erect the same building *Attalicis conditionibus* ("regardless of expense"),[56] it might have cost him fifty millions.

Not being able to have antique ceilings, he had them painted by Mengs, who was admittedly the greatest and most painstaking painter of this century and who most unfortunately died in the middle of his career,[57] without ever having trained a single good successor, for my brother never did anything to deserve the name of his pupil.

1761.

I shall have much more to say about Mengs when I am in Spain, that is, in the year 1767.

I had scarcely settled in with my brother, rented a

fine carriage, and dressed my coachman and hire valet in livery before I waited on Monsignor Cornaro,[58] an Auditor of the Rota,[59] with the intention of making my way into the best society after arranging to be presented to His Holiness; but Monsignor Cornaro, fearing that, as a Venetian, he might compromise himself, introduced me to Cardinal Passionei,[60] who mentioned me to the sovereign pontiff; but before being granted this honor, here is what happened to me on my second visit to this most unusual Cardinal, an enemy of the Jesuits, a man of intelligence, and graced with a rare knowledge of literature.

CHAPTER IX

Cardinal Passionei. The Pope. Mariuccia.
I arrive in Naples.

HE RECEIVED me in a great room in which he was busily writing; a minute later he put down his pen. He could not give me permission to sit, for there were no chairs. After saying that he would inform the Holy Father that he had seen me, he added that Monsignor Cornaro might have thought of someone better, since the Pope did not like him.[1]

"He chose to set esteem above liking."

"I do not know if he esteems me; but I know that he knows I do not esteem him. I liked and esteemed him as a cardinal, but since he has become Pope he has shown himself too much the *coglione*."[2]

"The Sacred College should have elected Your Eminence."

"Certainly not, for, intolerant as I am toward all that I consider wrong, I should perhaps have made too clean a sweep, and God knows what would have happened. The only member of the conclave with the qualities to be

elected Pope was Cardinal Tamburini.[3] But come tomorrow, for I hear people arriving.''

How my soul rejoiced when I heard none other than
His Eminence call the Pope a *coglione* (fool) and commend Tamburini! I immediately noted it down in my
records. But who may this Tamburini be? After dinner
I put the question to Winckelmann, for when one would
learn one should seek out a philosopher.

''Tamburini,'' he said, ''is deserving of respect for his
virtues, his character, his far-seeing intelligence, and his
firmness. He has never concealed what he thinks of the
Jesuits. He despises them, and that is why Passionei
commends him. I, too, believe that he would be a great
Pope.''

But here is what I heard in Rome nine years later at
the Prince of Santa Croce's[4] from a tool of the Jesuits,
who were then at their last gasp:[5] The Benedictine Cardinal Tamburini was impious; on his deathbed he demanded the viaticum without first making his confession.
I hear that, and I say nothing. The next day I asked
someone who should know the truth of the matter and
who could have no reason to hide it. He said that the
Cardinal had himself celebrated mass three days earlier,
and so it must be concluded that if he did not ask for a
confessor it was because he would have had nothing to
tell him.

Woe unto those who love truth and who do not know
enough to seek it at its source. I hope, my dear reader,
that you will not find it hard to forgive me my digressions.

So the next day I go to see the Cardinal, and he at
once puts down his pen, saying that I had done well by
coming early to tell him the story of my escape, of which
he had heard wonders.

''Willingly, Your Most Excellent Eminence, but it is
a long story.''

"So be it. I have heard that you tell it well."

"Shall I sit on the floor?"

"Oh no, your coat is too handsome."

He rings. He tells the gentleman who enters to have a seat brought, and a lackey brings me a stool. A seat without arms or a back makes me angry, I tell my story badly, and in a quarter of an hour it is all over.

"I write better than you speak," he said, "and if you do not believe me read this at your leisure, it is a funeral eulogy on Prince Eugene;[6] I make you a present of it. You may go to kiss the Holy Father's foot tomorrow at ten o'clock."

Back at the house and thinking of the odd character of this Cardinal, a man of intelligence yet haughty, vain, and talkative, I decide to make him a handsome present. It was the *Pandectarum Liber unicus,*[7] which my Swiss acquaintance M. F.[8] had given me at Bern and for which I had no use; it was a folio, well bound and in a good state of preservation. It was a gift which, as the chief Librarian of the Vatican, he should prize, the more so since he had a fine library of his own[9] under the care of my friend Winckelmann. So I write His Eminence a short letter in Latin, and another to Winckelmann, who was to present the code to him as an offering from me. I thought this rare book was more than a fair exchange for his funeral oration, and I hoped that on another occasion he would not leave me to ask for a stool. I sent it to the Abate at once by Costa.

The next morning at the appointed hour I go to Monte Cavallo.[10] I needed to be neither introduced nor announced to the Holy Father, for any Christian is at liberty to appear before him once he sees the door open; besides, he had known me in Padua when he occupied the episcopal throne there;[11] nevertheless, I had preferred to have my visit arranged beforehand.

I had scarcely entered and kissed the holy cross depicted on his holy slipper before, laying one hand on my left shoulder, he said that he remembered the time I left his reception at Padua as soon as he began chanting the Rosary.

"I have, Most Holy Father, much greater sins to reproach myself with; so I have come to prostrate myself at your feet to receive absolution for them."

He then gave me his blessing with an ample gesture and asked me what favor I wished to ask of him.

"Your Holiness's intercession, so that I can freely return to Venice."

"We will speak to the Ambassador and give you our answer afterward. Do you often go to see Cardinal Passionei?"

"I have been there three times; he gave me his funeral oration on Prince Eugene, and to show him my gratitude I have sent him the *Pandects* as a present."

"Has he received it?"

"I believe so."

"If he has, he will send Winckelmann to pay you for it."

"That would be to treat me like a bookseller. I will not accept any payment."

"In that case he will send you back the code, we are certain. That is his habit."

"If His Eminence sends me back the code I will send him back the funeral oration."

At that the Pope laughed so hard that he was seized by a fit of coughing, and, after spitting, he laughed again.

"We shall be pleased to know the end of this incident, without the world's being informed of our harmless curiosity."

After these words a benediction given with an even more ample gesture informed me that my audience was ended.

As I left, an elderly Abate approached me, asking me

in surprised tones if I was the Casanova who had escaped from the Leads.

"I am he."

"And you do not remember me? I am Momolo,[12] gondolier in those days for the Ca' Rezzonico." [13]

"Then you have become a priest?"

"Certainly not, but here we all dress as priests. I am first *scopatore*[14] (sweeper) to the Most Holy Father."

"I heartily congratulate you, and I beg you to excuse me if it makes me laugh."

"Laugh away, for my wife and my daughters laugh too every time they see me dressed as a priest. Come to see us."

"Where do you live?"

"Behind Trinità dei Monti.[15] Here is my address."

"You shall see me this evening."

I returned to the house, delighting in the thought that I was to spend the evening with the family of a Venetian gondolier. Dining with my brother, I told him nothing of my conversation with the Pope, but I invited him to accompany me on my visit to the gondolier turned *scopatore santissimo*.

But after dinner in comes the Abate Winckelmann, on purpose to tell me that I was high in the good graces of his Cardinal; that the code I had sent him was rare and valuable and in better condition than the one in the Vatican.[16]

"I have come," he said, "to pay you for it."

"I wrote His Eminence that I was making him a present of it."

"He does not accept presents of books, for he wants it for his own library and being Librarian of the Vatican he fears slander."

"That is understandable, but the code cost me nothing, so I do not wish to sell it. Tell the Cardinal that I will be honored if he will accept it as a present."

"He will send it back to you."

"And I will send him back his funeral oration. I will not take presents from someone who refuses to accept them."

And so it was: On the next day the Cardinal sent me back my book, and within the hour I sent him back his funeral oration, writing him that I had found it a masterpiece. My brother emphatically pronounced me wrong, but I paid no attention. Toward nightfall we went to the house of the Abate Momolo, who was expecting me and who had announced me to his family as a prodigy.

After introducing my brother to him, I examine all the members of the family one by one: his wife, four daughters, the eldest of whom was twenty-four, and two little boys; they were all ugly. I was there; it was for me to stay there and try to enjoy myself. In addition, the place smelled of poverty, for the *scopatore* had to live on two hundred scudi a year. For all that, the worthy man no sooner saw me seated than he told me he wanted to give me supper, though it would be only a polenta[17] and pork chops.

"Will you permit me to send to my house for six bottles of Orvieto[18] wine?"

"It is for you to say."

I immediately wrote Costa a note ordering him to come with the six bottles and a ham. A half hour later he arrived with my hire valet, who was carrying the basket, and all the girls exclaimed:

"What a handsome young man!"

I see Costa delighted, I ask the Abate Momolo if he wants to invite him for supper, all the girls say yes, and I tell him to stay. Delighted to be so honored, Costa immediately goes to the kitchen to help Momolo's wife make the polenta.

A cloth is spread on a large table, and a half hour later a polenta big enough to feed twelve hungry people is brought in and placed on it, followed by a large casserole filled with pork chops.

There is a knock at the street door; the boy says it is Signora Maria and her mother. I see all the girls make wry faces at the news.

"Who sent for them?" asks one.

"What do they want here?" asks another.

"They are hungry," says the father; "they shall share the food which Providence sends us."

I see the two starvelings come in: a very pretty girl of modest bearing and a sad-looking mother who seemed ashamed of her poverty. The girl at once apologizes, she says she would not have come if she had known that strangers were present. Momolo alone answers her greeting, saying that she has done well to come, and he places a chair for her between my brother and myself. I then look at her closely, and I find the poor girl a perfect beauty.

The family fall to eating, no more is said. The polenta is excellent, the pork delicious, the ham perfect; in less than an hour not a sign remains that anything to eat had ever been on the table; but the Orvieto wine continues to keep the company in high spirits. The conversation turns to the lottery,[19] which was to be drawn on the next day but one, and all the girls report the numbers on which they had risked three soldi. I tell them that if I could be sure of only one number I should be satisfied; young Mariuccia, who was on my right, said that if one number was enough for me she could give it to me. I laugh at her offer; but she does not laugh, she tells me in all seriousness that she is sure of twenty-seven. I ask the Abate Momolo if one can still stake, and he replies that the lottery does not close until midnight and that he would himself go and stake; I thereupon give him forty scudi in notes of hand and I tell him to put twenty scudi unconditionally on twenty-seven, of which I made a present to the five girls at the table, and twenty scudi on twenty-seven coming out fifth[20] for myself. He goes, and comes back a quarter of an hour later with the two

tickets. Mariuccia thanks me and says she is sure she will
win; but that she has doubts about my ticket, for it was
not certain that her number would come out fifth.

"But I am certain of it because you are the fifth girl
I have seen in the house."

My explanation made everybody laugh. Momolo's wife
said I would have done better to give the forty scudi to
the poor, and her husband told her to be still, for she
had no idea how clever I was. My brother laughs, but he,
too, tells me I have done a foolish thing. I reply that I
have taken a chance. I adroitly press the modest Mariuccia's hand, she presses mine with all her strength, and
I understood all that she meant. I left them about midnight, asking Momolo to repeat the supper on the next
evening but one, so that we could rejoice over our winnings in the lottery.

On the way home my brother said that if I had not
become rich as Croesus I must be a fool; but he agreed
with me that Mariuccia was as beautiful as an angel.

The next day Mengs came to Rome, and I supped
with him and his family. He had an ugly though good-
hearted sister[21] who was talented; she had been in love
with my brother, who, when she spoke to him, did not
look her in the face. She painted portraits in miniature
which were excellent likenesses, and I believe she is still
living in Rome with her husband Maroni.[22] She said to
me one day that my brother would not treat her so
scornfully if he were not the most ungrateful of men.

Mengs's wife[23] was pretty, virtuous, very scrupulous in
performing all the duties of a wife and mother, and very
submissive to her husband, whom she could not have
loved because he was not lovable. He was stubborn and
cruel, and always got up from the table drunk; but
when he dined out he had the good sense to drink only
water. His wife had the patience to serve as his model
for all the nudes he had occasion to paint. She told me
one day that her confessor had ordered her to obey her

husband in this respect without protest, for otherwise he would have taken another model, whom he would have enjoyed before painting her and so would have sinned.

After supper everyone was tipsy. Winckelmann turned somersaults on the floor with Mengs's children, male and female, who adored him. The learned man liked to frolic with the young in the manner of Anacreon and Horace: *Mille puellarum, puerorum mille furores* ("Passions for a thousand girls, a thousand boys").[24] What happened to me one day at his house is worth recording.

Early that morning I go without knocking into a small room in which he was usually alone copying out some antique inscription, and I see him hastily leave a boy, at the same time quickly setting his breeches to rights. I pretend to have seen nothing, immersed in admiring an Egyptian idol which was behind the door of the room. The Bathyllus,[25] who was indeed very pretty, leaves; Winckelmann comes to me laughing and says that, after the little I had seen he did not think he could keep me from deducing the rest, but that he owed himself a kind of justification, which he begged me to hear.

"Know," he said, "that not only am I not a pederast, but that all my life long I have declared it inconceivable that the inclination could have exercised such an attraction on the human race. If I said this after what you have just seen, you would pronounce me a hypocrite. But here is the truth of the matter. In the long course of my studies I first came to admire, then to idolize the ancients, who, as you know, were almost all of them b[uggers] [26] without concealing the fact, while a number of them even immortalized the charming objects of their love by their poems and even by magnificent monuments. Indeed, they went so far as to cite their inclination as testimony to their morality—for example, Horace, who, to prove to Augustus and Maecenas that he was beyond the reach of calumny, defied his enemies to prove to him that he had ever incurred the guilt of adultery.[27]

"In the light of this obvious truth, I scrutinized myself, and I felt a kind of disdain and even of shame because in this respect I did not in the least resemble my heroes. At considerable cost to my self-esteem, I felt that I was in a way contemptible, and, unable to convict myself of stupidity merely by cold theory, I decided to seek the light of practice, hoping that by analyzing the thing my mind would gain the illumination it needed in order to distinguish the true from the false. Having so resolved, I have been applying myself to the matter for the past three or four years, choosing the prettiest Smerdiases[28] in Rome; but all to no avail: when I set to work, *non arrivo* ('I get nowhere'). To my dismay I always find that a woman is preferable in every respect. But, quite aside from my seeing nothing wrong in that, I am afraid of acquiring a bad reputation, for what would people say in Rome, or anywhere else where I am known, if it could be said of me that I have a mistress?"

The next day I went to pay my respects to the Pope.

Seeing the Abate Momolo in the first antechamber, I begged him to bestow his best attention on the evening's polenta, then I was shown into the presence of the Holy Father, who at once said to me:

"*The Venetian Ambassador*[29] *has told us that, if you desire to return to your country, you must present yourself before the Secretary of the Tribunal.*" [30]

"I am ready to do so, if Your Holiness will give me a letter of recommendation in your own hand. Without such a letter, I will never expose myself to the risk of being shut up in a place from which the invisible hand of God released me by a series of miracles."

"You are wearing a very handsome coat, which you certainly did not put on to offer prayers to God."

"True, most Holy Father, but I did not put it on to go to a ball either."

"We know the whole story of the returned presents. Admit that you gratified your pride."

"But at the same time humbling an even greater pride."

Seeing the Pope smile, I went down on one knee and begged him to grant me his kind permission to present my code of the *Pandects* to the Vatican Library; by way of answer I received only a benediction, which in Papal language signifies: "Rise, your prayer is granted."

"We will send you," he said, "a token of our *singular affection,* without your having to pay the customary registration fee."

A second benediction told me to leave. I was curious to see the token of his "singular affection" which the Pope had promised me.

I at once sent my code to the library by Costa, then I dined with Mengs. Someone brings the five numbers drawn in the lottery, and my brother looks at me. I did not remember that I had played.

"Twenty-seven," he said, "came out fifth."

"So much the better, we will be gay."

My brother tells the whole story to Mengs, who replies: *"Follies sometimes turn out luckily; but they are follies none the less."*

I told him that I would go at once to Naples to enjoy the fifteen hundred Roman scudi[31] which Fortune had sent me; and the Abate Alfani[32] says that he will come with me as my secretary. I make him promise to do so.

I invited Winckelmann to come and eat polenta at the Abate Momolo's, leaving it to my brother to show him the way there, then I went to see my banker, the Marchese Belloni,[33] to settle my accounts and obtain from him a letter of credit on a banker in Naples. I commanded nearly two hundred thousand francs, I had at least ten thousand scudi in jewels, and thirty thousand florins at Amsterdam.

Toward nightfall I go to Momolo's, where I find Winckelmann and my brother; but instead of finding the family joyous, they seem to me sad. Momolo said his daughters were angry because I had not staked on the number coming out fifth for them as I had for myself. They had twenty-seven scudi each[34] and they were gloomy, whereas two days earlier they had not had a copper and they were gay. More and more clearly I perceive that the true source of gaiety is in the mind which is free from cares.

Costa puts on the table a basket in which there are ten cornucopias of sweetmeats. I say that I will distribute them when everyone is at the table. Momolo's second daughter tells me that Mariuccia is not coming, but that they will send her two cornucopias.

"Why isn't she coming?"

"They had a quarrel yesterday," Momolo answered, "and Mariuccia, who is really in the right, left saying that she would not come again."

"You ungrateful creatures!" I said to them, though not harshly. "Consider that day before yesterday she brought you good luck. It was she who gave me the twenty-seven. In short, find a way to bring her here, or I will leave and take the cornucopias with me."

Momolo said that it would serve them right.

The mortified girls beg their father to go and persuade her to come, but he replies that they must go themselves, and in the end they decide to go with Costa; two would be enough. Mariuccia lived next door.

A half hour later I see them come back triumphant and Costa proud that his mediation had succeeded in reconciling the girls. At that I distributed my cornucopias.

The polenta came with the pork chops; but after them the Abate Momolo, whose acquaintance with me had brought two hundred scudi[35] into his house in one day, gave us choice dishes and excellent wines. Mariuccia's manner set me on fire. Since I could only press her hand, she could reply only by pressing mine in return; but I needed no clearer language to be certain that she loved me. Going down the stairs with her, I asked if I could not talk with her in some church; she replied that I should go the next morning at eight o'clock to Trinità dei Monti.

At seventeen or eighteen years of age, Mariuccia was tall, had a very good carriage, and seemed carved by the chisel of Praxiteles.[36] She was fair, but her fairness was not that of a blonde, which with its unrelieved brilliance almost suggests that she has no blood in her veins. Mariuccia's fairness was so alive that it offered the eyes a rosy bloom which no painter could ever have caught. Her black eyes, very large and prominent, and always in motion, had a dew on their surface which seemed a coating of the finest enamel. This imperceptible dew, which the air very easily dissipated, was continually restored by the rapid blinking of her lids. Her hair was gathered into four heavy braids, which joined at her neck to form a beautiful boss, yet not so tightly as to restrain a quantity of little curls which everywhere escaped from it, more especially to ornament her high and broad forehead with a random pattern as artless as it was unstudied. Living roses animated her cheeks, and sweet laughter dwelt on her beautiful mouth and her fiery lips, which, neither quite meeting nor quite parted, showed only the extremities of two perfectly even rows of teeth. Her hands, on which neither muscles nor veins were visible, appeared long in proportion to their breadth. This Roman beauty had not yet been seen by a connoisseur; it was to me that chance presented her in a blind alley where she lived in the darkness of poverty.

I did not fail to be at the church she had named at eight o'clock the next morning. As soon as she was sure I had seen her she went out, and I followed her. She stopped at a great ruined building and sat down on the highest steps of a long stairway, saying that no one would think of climbing it and so I could talk to her freely.

"Charming Mariuccia," I said, sitting down beside her, "you have made me fall madly in love with you; tell me what I can do for you; for, hoping to be granted your favors, my chief thought must be to deserve them."

"Make me happy, and I shall not find it hard to surrender to your love in return for your bounty, for I love you too."

"Then what can I do to make you happy?"

"Free me from the poverty which overwhelms me and from the constraint to which I am subjected by living with my mother, who means well but who, being devout to the point of superstition, damns my soul by dint of trying to assure my salvation. She even criticizes my cleanliness because it might make me pleasing to men. If you had given me as charity the money you enabled me to win in the lottery, she would have made me refuse it because you might have given it to me with evil intentions. She lets me go to mass alone only because our confessor assured her that she might let me do so; but I should never dare to stay out a minute longer, except on feast days, when I may stay at church two or three hours performing my devotions. So we can see each other nowhere but here. But this is what is needed if you want to make me happy and have the means to do it: a young, handsome, well-behaved young man, an excellent wigmaker, saw me at the *scopatore*'s two weeks ago; the next day he waited for me at the church door and gave me a letter. In it he declares his love, and he says that if I can bring him a dowry of four hundred scudi he will marry me, setting up shop as a wigmaker and buying the necessary household furnishings. I replied that I was poor and that I had only a hundred scudi, in the form of charity vouchers, which were in the hands of my confessor. By now I have a hundred more, for if I married my mother would give me the fifty of her winnings.[37] Hence you can ensure my happiness by obtaining another two hundred scudi in charity vouchers and taking them to my confessor, who is a saintly old man who loves me and would never tell anyone that he had them from you.''

''I do not need to go looking for charity vouchers; I will take your confessor two hundred scudi today, and you shall see to the rest. Give me his name. I will tell you the outcome tomorrow morning, but not here, for the cold and the wind are killing me. Leave it to me to find a room where we shall be safe and at our ease and where no one can ever guess that we have spent an hour. You shall see me at the church, and you shall follow me.''

Mariuccia gave me the old Minimite's name and promised to follow me the next morning. With gratitude depicted on her features, she received all the tokens of affection which she could receive and I give in the tormenting place where we were, but they amounted to so little that I left her on the stroke of nine o'clock much more in love with her than before and very impatient to have her in my arms the next day in a room which I must set about procuring. It was the first thing I did.

I leave the ruined palazzo, and, instead of going down toward the Piazza di Spagna, I retrace my steps and enter a narrow, dirty street in which there are a few humble houses. I see a woman coming out of one of them to ask me if I am looking for somebody.

''I am looking,'' I reply, ''for a room to rent.''

''There is none here, but you will find any number on the Piazza.''

''That I know; but I want it here, not to save expense but to be sure I can spend an hour in the morning in it with someone in whom I am interested. I will pay whatever price is asked.''

''I understand, and I would oblige you myself if I had two rooms; but my neighbor has one on the ground floor, and I can go and speak to her if you will wait a moment. You may go in.''

I enter a hovel, where I see poverty and two little boys writing out their lessons. Five or six minutes later the woman comes back and tells me to accompany her; I go, leaving ten or twelve paoli[38] on the table, from which she takes them, kissing my hand. She shows me into the next house, where I find an empty room on the ground floor, and another woman who says she will let me have the room cheap if I will pay her three months in advance, that is, three Roman scudi, and will agree to supply all the furniture I may need.

"I will pay you the three scudi on the spot; but I cannot undertake to supply the furniture. See to it yourself, and let me have the room all furnished at three o'clock today. I will pay you twelve scudi."

"Twelve scudi? What furniture do you want?"

"A bed, a small table, four chairs, and a burning brazier of charcoal, for it is deathly cold here. I will come only occasionally, early in the morning, and I will always leave before noon."

"In that case, come at three o'clock and you will find my bed and everything else you have asked for."

I give her the three scudi, I promise to come back at three o'clock and I leave. So that is done.

I go at once to Trinità dei Monti, I ask for the father confessor, and I am shown to his room. I see a French monk who appears to be sixty years of age and whose fine, handsome countenance inspires confidence.

"Reverend Father, at the house of the Abate Momolo, *scopatore santissimo,* I saw a girl named Maria, whose father, XX, lives at Tivoli, and her mother with the girl herself. I fell in love with her, and I found an opportunity to tell her so and to offer her money to seduce her; she replied that instead of making her criminal offers I ought to use my influence to obtain her some charity vouchers which would enable her to marry a suitor who had presented himself and who would make her happy. Her reprimand touched me, but it did not cure me of my criminal passion. I talked to her a second time, and I told her that I wanted to give her two hundred scudi for nothing and that I would take them to her mother. She replied that I would cause her ruin, for she would believe that the money was payment for a crime and would refuse to accept it. She said it was to you, her confessor, that I should take it, and at the same time speak to you on her behalf so that the marriage she has in view can take place. So here is the money, which I bring you, wishing to have nothing further to do with the matter. I shall leave day after tomorrow for Naples, and I hope that on my return I shall find her married.''

He took the hundred zecchini[39] and gave me a receipt; then he said that, by showing an interest in Mariuccia, I became the protector of an innocent dove, that she had been confessing to him for five years, and that he often ordered her to go to communion without hearing her confession because he knew her well enough to be certain that she was incapable of committing a mortal sin. He added that her mother was a saint, he promised me that he would see the marriage concluded after he had inquired into the character of the young man to whom she wished to give herself, and he assured me that no one should ever know from whom she had received this assistance.

After having thus arranged the whole matter to my satisfaction, I went to dine with Mengs and was easily persuaded to go to the opera at the Teatro Aliberti[40] with his whole family. But I did not fail to go first to the little room I had rented, to see if it was furnished. I found everything in it which I had ordered, I paid twelve scudi, and received the key to the room from the mistress of the house. She assured me that I would find it heated every day at seven o'clock in the morning.

My impatience to see the next day arrive made me find the whole opera bad and kept me awake the whole night.

The next morning even before the appointed hour I go to Trinità dei Monti; Mariuccia arrives a quarter of an hour later, I see her, I leave, she follows me at a distance, and I enter the house and open the door of my room, which I find heated. A moment later I see Mariuccia, apprehensive and uncertain, I lock the door, and, clasping her in my arms, I restore all her courage. I tell her about my visit to her confessor, and I end by showing her the receipt he had made out for the two hundred scudi and by assuring her that he would himself take steps to arrange her marriage. I urge her to make me happy, telling her that the time is passing quickly, she replies that we have almost three hours before us, for she has told her mother that she would perform her devotions to thank God for the hundred scudi they had won[41] in the lottery.

Full of my happiness and reveling beforehand in the pleasures in which I was to immerse my senses, I clasp Mariuccia in my arms, I cover her face with fiery kisses, and, undressing her little by little, I lay all her charms bare before me, and my soul rejoices to meet not the slightest resistance. Mariuccia does not anticipate my desires, but, pliable by nature, she abandons herself to my appetite, never daring to take her eyes from mine for fear that they will stray to some place which will give them too easy a triumph over the expiring remnants of her modesty.

But now she is in the bed, motionless and ready to succumb. It is the moment when, whether more or less fortunate than she in having no shame to conquer, I must make haste. The sacrifice was perfect, and I had no cause to doubt the purity of my victim. Other symptoms, far dearer to a soul in love, made mine certain that Mariuccia had never loved until that moment. But she did more. Pleasure makes pain precious. She assured

me she had felt none, and at the second assault I saw
her completely possessed by Venus.

The clock of Trinità dei Monti pealed the imperious
strokes of ten o'clock into our ears. We quickly dressed.
Having arranged to leave for Naples the next morning,
I assured Mariuccia that only the hope of clasping her
in my arms again before her wedding day would make
me hasten my return to Rome. I promised to take her
confessor another hundred scudi that day, which would
make it possible for her to use the hundred she had won[42]
in the lottery on clothes. I told her that I would spend
the evening at the Abate Momolo's and should be delighted to see her there; but that we must behave in a
manner calculated to dissipate whatever suspicions of
an understanding between us might have arisen.

As she departed, she assured me that she knew she
had surrendered to love far more than to interest. Leaving last, I informed the mistress of the house that I
would not reappear there for ten or twelve days; and
I went at once to the Minimite monastery to give my
angel's kindly confessor the hundred scudi I had promised her.

When I told the old monk that I was giving them to
him so that Mariuccia could use the hundred she had
won in the lottery for buying dresses and making shifts,
he assured me that he would himself go to her house
immediately after dinner both to persuade her mother
to consent to it and to speak privately with her daughter
in order to obtain the address of the youth who wanted
to marry her. When I returned from Naples I learned
that he had punctually fulfilled his undertaking.

At two o'clock in the afternoon a *cameriere* of His
Holiness sent in word that he had come to see the Cavaliere Mengs. We were all at table. He at once asked him
if I was staying in his house, and Mengs introduced me.
He immediately delivered to me, on his Most Holy Master's behalf, the cross of the Order of the Golden Spur,[43]

together with a diploma sealed with the Papal seal and
declaring me, as a Doctor of Civil and Canon Law, an
Apostolic Prothonotary *extra urbem*.[44] Expressing my
gratitude for this high honor, I assured the personage
that I would go the next day to thank my new sovereign
and ask his blessing. Mengs, as my confrère, immediately
embraced me; but I had been granted the privilege of
expending nothing. The Cavaliere Mengs had had to
pay twenty-five scudi to have his diploma drawn up.
They say at Rome that *sine effusione sanguinis non fit
remissio* ("without shedding of blood is no remis-
sion").[45] Everything costs money, and with money one
can obtain everything, in the Holy City.

I immediately hung the cross around my neck on a
broad poppy-red ribbon.[46] This is the color of the order
of the gilded soldiers of San Giovanni Laterano,[47] "companions of the palace," in Latin *comites palatini*, which,
translated once again, gives "counts palatine." Poor
Cahusac,[48] author of the opera *Zoroastre*, went mad in
Paris about this time when the Papal Nuncio made him
a count palatine in the same way. As for me, I did not
go mad, but I was so delighted with the decoration that
I at once asked Winckelmann if I could have my cross
set with diamonds and rubies; he said I was at liberty
to do so, and that he knew where I could buy one already
set, which I could have for a thousand scudi and which
had cost more. I bought it the next morning as soon as
I saw it, to make a show with it in Naples. I never dared
to wear it in Rome. When I appeared before the Holy
Father to thank him I put the cross in my buttonhole
in due observance of modesty. I gave up wearing the
cross five years later in Warsaw when the Palatine of
Russia, Prince Czartoryski,[49] asked me what I was doing
with it.

"*It's a drug on the market,*" he said, "*only charlatans
wear it any more.*"

But it is the present which the Popes give to Ambassadors, even though they know that these give it to their valets; it is very easy to pretend not to know something and to go quietly on in the same old way.

That evening Momolo gave a supper for me to celebrate my installation; but I made it up to him by opening a bank at faro. I was dexterous enough to lose forty scudi, sharing them out equally among the whole family and showing no partiality to Mariuccia. She found an opportunity to tell me that her confessor had come to her house, that she had given him all the necessary information concerning the young wigmaker, and that he had persuaded her mother to spend the hundred scudi on clothes for her.

Having observed that the Abate Momolo's second daughter was in love with Costa, I told her that I would be off to Naples the next morning but that I was leaving him for her, hoping on my return to find a marriage contract between them, that it would meet with my approval, and that I would even be glad to defray the expense of the wedding. The fact is that Costa did not marry the girl at that time, for fear I was marrying her off to him in order to have the use of her. He was a consummate fool. He proceeded to marry her the next year, after robbing me. We will speak of him again when the time comes.

The next morning, after breakfasting well and fondly embracing my brother, I set off in my fine carriage with the Abate Alfani, preceded by Leduc on horseback. I reached Naples at a time when the whole city was in a state of alarm because the fatal volcano was threatening to erupt.[50] At the last post station the post master showed me the will left by his father, who had died after the eruption of 1754: he said that the eruption by which God intended utterly to destroy the sinful city of Naples would take place in the winter of 1761; hence he advised me to go back to Rome. Alfani declared there was no doubt about it, we must obey the voice of God. The event was foretold, hence it would infallibly happen. Thus it is that certain people reason.

CHAPTER X

*My short but enjoyable stay in Naples. The
Duke of Matalona, my daughter, Donna Lucrezia. My departure.*

IT IS impossible either to express or to conceive how
greatly my soul rejoiced when I found myself once more
in Naples, where eighteen years earlier I had made my
fortune on my return from Martorano.[1] I had gone there
only to pay the Duke of Matalona the visit which I had
promised him when he was in Paris; but before waiting
on that nobleman I wanted to inquire after all my old
friends.

So I went out early on foot, first to make myself known
to the banker who was Belloni's correspondent. After
accepting my letter of credit he gave me the number of
bank notes I asked for, assuring me that no one should
know anything of our dealings.

Leaving his place of business, I went to the house in
which Don Antonio Casanova[2] had lived. I was told that
he was living on an estate he had bought near Salerno,
and of which he bore the name with the title of Marchese.
I go and inquire after Palo;[3] he had died and his son

was living at Santa Lucia with a wife and children. I intended to go to see him, but I never found the time for it. I next ask where the advocate Castelli[4] is living; he was the husband of my dear Donna Lucrezia, with whom I had been so much in love at Rome; I could scarcely wait to see her, and I was in ecstasy at the thought of the pleasure we should feel when we met again. I am told that he has long been dead and that his widow lives twenty miles from Naples. I promise myself that I will visit her. I knew that Don Lelio Caraffa[5] was still alive and resided in the Palazzo Matalona.[6]

So I go to dine, then I dress and take a hackney carriage to the Palazzo Matalona. The Duke was still at table; but no matter, I am announced; he comes out to see who it is, he recognizes me, he gives a cry, he embraces me, he at once does me the honor to address me in the second person singular, he introduces me to his wife, who was a daughter of the Duke of Bovino,[7] and to all the very numerous company. I tell him that I have come to Naples only to pay him the visit I had promised him in Paris.

"Then it is only right that I should put you up; let someone go at once to the inn at which Casanova *s'est débarqué* ['disembarked'] and bring all his luggage here and, if he has a carriage, put it in my stable."

I accept.

A fine-looking man who was at the table no sooner heard the name Casanova than he said to me gaily:

"If you bear my name, you must be a bastard of my father's."

"Not of your father's," I replied, "but of your mother's."

My riposte is applauded, the man comes and embraces me, and the misunderstanding is explained. Instead of hearing "Casanova," he had heard "Casalnuovo,"[8] and the gentleman was none other than the Duke of that fief.

"You know," the Duke of Matalona said to me, "that I have a son."[9]

"I was told so, and I found it hard to believe; but now I am no longer surprised. I see a princess who could not fail to perform the miracle."

The Duchess blushes, without vouchsafing me a look, but the company clap their hands, for it was well known that before his marriage the Duke of Matalona was supposed to be impotent. His son is summoned, I say that he looks like him; a cheerful monk who was seated beside the Duchess says he does not, and she coldly gives him a slap in the face, which he receives with a laugh.

In less than half an hour my banter endeared me to the entire company with the marked exception of the Duchess, who maintained a deliberate haughtiness which took the ground from under my feet. She was beautiful, but lofty as the clouds, deaf and mute in season and out of season, and always in control of her eyes. I labored for two days to persuade her to converse with me, and finally, despairing of success, I left her to her pride.

The Duke showed me to my apartment and, seeing my Spaniard, asked me where my secretary was, and when I said he was the Abate Alfani, who had assumed the office so that he could stay in Naples incognito, he replied that he had been well advised to do so, for he had cheated a great many people with his pretended antiquities.[10]

He took me to see his fine stable, where there were superb horses, then his picture gallery, then his library, and finally his private apartment and his choice books, which were all forbidden. After that he made me swear not to breathe a word of what he was going to read me. It was a scathing satire[11] on the whole court, of which I understood nothing. I never kept a secret more faithfully.

"You shall come with me," he said, "to the Teatro San Carlo,[12] where I will introduce you to the most beautiful ladies in Naples, and to which you may go whenever you wish; when you want to be completely free you shall go to my box on the third tier, which is always open to my friends. In that way the opera will cost you nothing. I will also introduce you at my mistress's box, to which you may go when you please.''

''What, my dear Duke! You have a mistress?''

''Yes, for form's sake, for I love only my wife; nevertheless people believe I am in love with her and am even jealous because I never introduce anyone to her and do not allow her to receive visitors.''

''And the Duchess, young and charming as she is— does not object to your having a mistress?''

''My wife cannot be jealous of her, because she knows that I am impotent with all the women on earth except with her.''

''I take it you are not joking, but I find it hard to believe. Can a man have a mistress he does not love?''

''But I do love her, for she is divinely intelligent and she amuses me; but she does not interest me physically.''

''That is possible; I suppose she is ugly.''

''Ugly? You will see her this evening. She is pretty and only seventeen years old, she speaks French, her mind is unprejudiced, and she is well-bred.''

At the hour for the opera he takes me to the great theater, he introduces me to several ladies, all of them ugly. In the great middle box I saw the very young King,[13] surrounded by many members of the nobility dressed richly but without taste. The whole parterre and all the boxes were full, the latter all covered with mirrors and illuminated inside and out because of an anniversary.[14] The effect was most striking.

He takes me to his private box on the third tier and introduces me to his friends; they were the most brilliant minds in Naples. I laughed to myself at those who do not believe that the intelligence of a nation is far more dependent on its climate than on education.[15] Such critics should be sent to Naples. What intelligence! Boerhaave,[16] the great Boerhaave, if he had been in Naples, would have known the nature of sulphur far better from its effects on plants, and even more clearly from its effects on animals. Nowhere but in that country is water the only remedy needed to cure any number of diseases which, in our country, would be deadly without the art of pharmacy.

The Duke, who had vanished, returns and takes me to the box in which his mistress was seated in company with a respectable-looking woman. As he enters he says:

"Leonilda mia, ti presento il cavalier Don Giacomo Casanova veneziano amico mio" ("My Leonilda, I beg to introduce my friend the Chevalier Don Giacomo Casanova, of Venice").

She receives me affably and modestly, and she renounces the pleasure of listening to the music for that of talking with me. When a girl is pretty it takes but a moment to find her so; if her charms must be examined to elicit a favorable judgment they become dubious. Donna Leonilda was striking. I smiled, glancing at the Duke, who had told me that he loved her as a father loves his daughter and that he kept her only for fashion's sake; he understands me, and he says I must believe what he had told me. I reply that it is incredible, and with a sly smile she says that *anything that is possible is credible.*

"I admit that," I said, "but one is free to believe or not believe when a thing seems unlikely."

"Exactly; but I think believing is quicker and easier. You arrived in Naples yesterday, it is incredible, yet it is true."

"What is incredible about it?"

"Can anyone believe that a stranger would come to Naples at a time when everyone there is in terror?"

"And indeed I felt afraid until this moment, but now I have no fear at all. If you are in Naples St. Januarius[17] cannot but protect it. You laugh?"

"I am laughing at an amusing idea. If I had a suitor with a face like St. Januarius's he would reap no favors."

"Is the saint so very ugly?"

"You can decide that for yourself when you see his statue."

The bantering tone which she had taken was one which was but a step from friendship and frankness. The charms of the mind are superior to the spell of beauty. I bring up the subject of love, and she discourses on it in masterly fashion.

"If love," she says, "is not followed by possession of the loved object it can only be a torment, and if possession is forbidden one must not allow oneself to love."

"I agree, and the more so because even the enjoyment of a beautiful object is not a true pleasure if it has not been preceded by love."

"And if love has preceded it, it accompanies it—of that there is no doubt. But one may doubt if love follows it."

"That is true, for possession is often the death of love."

"And if it is not dead in both the persons who love each other, that is murder, for the one of them in whom love survives is left unhappy."

"That is indubitable, Madame,[18] and from this argument, based on the most irrefutable dialectic, I must infer that you condemn the senses to perpetual starvation. That is cruel."

"God preserve me from such Platonism. I condemn love without enjoyment as severely as I do enjoyment without love. I leave you to draw the inference."

"Love and enjoy, enjoy and love, turn and turn about."

"Exactly."

My conclusion set her laughing, and the Duke kissed

her hand. The duenna, who did not understand a word of French, listened to the opera; but I!

I was beside myself. These things were being said by a seventeen-year-old girl as pretty as a Cupid. The Duke now recited a ribald epigram by La Fontaine on enjoyment and desires, which is found only in the first edition[19] and of which the first four lines are as follows:

> *La jouissance et les désirs*
> *Sont ce que l'homme a de plus rare,*
> *Mais ce ne sont pas vrais plaisirs*
> *Dès le moment qu'on les sépare.*

("Enjoyment and desires are man's rarest possessions, but they cease to be true pleasures as soon as they are separated.")

I said that I had translated the epigram, with the six following lines, into Italian and Latin, and that in Italian it had taken me twenty lines to say what La Fontaine said in ten, whereas I said it all in six in my Latin translation. Donna Leonilda said she was sorry she did not know Latin.

In polite Neapolitan society the first token of friendship which a gentleman or a lady bestows on a new acquaintance is to use the second person singular in addressing him. Both parties are then more at their ease; but this mode of address entails no diminution in the respect which they owe each other.

Donna Leonilda filled me with admiration; if one does not recover from it, it becomes adoration, then irresistible love. The opera, which lasted five hours, came to its end without my realizing how long it was.

After the young prodigy left with her duenna the Duke told me that we must part unless I liked gambling.

"I am not averse to it with the right sort of players."

"Excellent. Then come with me. You will be with ten or twelve men of my stamp at a faro bank, then a cold supper; but it is a secret, for gambling is forbidden. I will vouch for you."

He takes me to the Duke of Monteleone's[20] and up to the fourth floor, where, after passing through ten or twelve rooms, I find myself in one in which a mild-looking banker was dealing; before him were silver and gold coins to the value of three or four hundred zecchini. The Duke makes me sit down beside him, introducing me as his friend. I go to take out my purse, but I am told that play there is on one's word and that one pays at the end of twenty-four hours. The banker gives me a *livret*[21] and a basket in which, between singles and doubles, there are a thousand counters. I say that each counter will be worth a Neapolitan ducat; that completes the ceremonies. In less than two hours I lose my whole basket, and I stop. Then I sup very gaily. The supper consisted of an enormous dish of macaroni and ten or twelve dishes of various sorts of shellfish. On the way home I never gave the Duke time to indulge in those condolences on one's losses which are always irksome. I kept him delightfully occupied with talk of Donna Leonilda.

Early the next morning the Duke sent me word that if I wanted to go to kiss the King's hand with him I must dress for the occasion. I put on a coat of rose-colored short-napped velvet embroidered with gold spangles, and I kissed the King's hand, which was swollen with chilblains.[22] He was nine years old. The Prince of San Nicandro[23] brought him up as far as in him lay, but he became an accomplished monarch, affable, tolerant, just, and generous, although too unceremonious, which, in a king, is a serious fault.

I had the honor of dining at the right of the Duchess, who, after looking at my coat, felt obliged to say that she had seldom seen a finer.

Johann Joachim Winckelmann

Pope Clement XIII, Carlo Rezzonico

"By such means, Signora, do I attempt to preserve my person from too thorough a scrutiny."

She smiled. When we rose table the Duke took me downstairs with him to the apartment of his uncle Don Lelio, who remembered me well. I kissed the venerable old man's hand, asking him to forgive my youthful escapades. He told his nephew that eighteen years earlier he had chosen me to be the companion of his studies,[24] and he was very glad to hear me give a brief account of all my vicissitudes in Rome when I was in the service of Cardinal Acquaviva.[25]

After an hour of conversation he asked me to come to see him often.

Toward evening the Duke told me that if I wanted to go to the opera buffa at the Fiorentini[26] it would please his mistress if I went to see her in her box, and he gave me the number of it; he said that he would come for me toward the end of the performance and that we would sup together as we had done on the previous evening.

I did not need to order horses harnessed. There was always a coupé in the courtyard awaiting my orders.

At the Teatro dei Fiorentini I found the opera already begun. I enter the box in which Donna Leonilda was sitting, and she receives me with these honeyed words:

"*Caro Don Giacomo*, it is a great pleasure to see you again."

She saw fit not to address me in the second person singular. The girl's alluring features struck me as being not unfamiliar, but I could not remember what young woman it was of whom she reminded me. Leonilda was a beauty; her hair was light chestnut, a color which is above suspicion, and her beautiful black eyes at once listened and questioned. But what enchanted me, and what I found entirely new, was that when she told a story she spoke with her hands, her elbows, her shoulders, and often with her chin. Her tongue did not suffice her to express all that she wanted to convey.

The conversation turning to La Fontaine's epigram, which I had not wanted to recite to her entire because it was licentious, she said that it could only provoke a smile.

"I have a room," she said, "which the Duke has had hung for me with Chinese designs representing a quantity of the postures in which the people of that country make love. We go there sometimes, and I assure you[27] they do not arouse the slightest sensation in me."

"That may be due to a defect in temperament, for when I see things of that sort well drawn they set me on fire; and I am amazed that when you look at them with the Duke you do not feel tempted to put some of them into practice."

"We feel only friendship for each other."

"That is not easy to believe."

"I could swear that he is a man; but I could not swear that he is capable of giving a woman any substantial proof of love."

"He has a son."

"True. And, according to him, he can love only his wife."

"That is nonsense, for you are a woman to inspire desires, and a man who could be familiarly in your company without his senses responding to it ought to kill himself."

"I am delighted, *caro Don Giacomo,* to learn that you love me, but since you are staying in Naples only a few days you will easily forget me."

"A curse on gaming, for we could spend charming evenings together."

"The Duke told me that you lost a thousand ducati without flinching last night. I take it that you are unlucky."

"Not always, but when I play on the same day on which I have fallen in love I am sure to lose."

"You will win this evening."

"Today I made my declaration; I shall lose again."

"Then don't play."

"They would say I'm afraid of losing or that I have no money."

"Then I hope you will win, and that you will come and tell me so at my house tomorrow morning. You can come with the Duke."

He arrives, and he asks me if I have enjoyed the opera. It is she who answers that we can tell him nothing about the opera because we had spent the whole time talking of love. She asks him to bring me to her house the next morning so that I can tell her I have won. The Duke replies that it is his turn, that he will be the dealer, but that he will bring me to breakfast with her whether I win or lose.

We left, and we went to the same place, where all the players were waiting for my Duke. It was a company of twelve, each of whom provided the bank in turn. They insisted that this made their chances equal. The idea made me laugh. Nothing is more difficult than to establish equality among players.

The Duke of Matalona takes his place, draws out his purse, and puts two thousand ducati in gold, silver, and bank notes on the table, asking the company to excuse him if he is doubling the amount of the bank in compliment to the stranger.

"Then I, too," I said, "will risk two thousand ducati, and no more, for at Venice people say that the prudent player must never lose more than he can win. So each of my counters will be worth two ducati."

So saying, I take from my pocket ten bank notes of a hundred ducati each and give them to the banker who had won them from me the evening before. War is declared, and in less than three hours, staking only on one card and with the utmost prudence, I lose my entire basket. That ended it. I had some twenty-five thousand ducati; but I had declared that I would not lose more,

I was ashamed to go back on my word. I have all my life been dismayed by losing, but I have always had the strength of mind to conceal it; my natural gaiety was doubled precisely because it was forced by art. This has always gained me the good will of the company and opened resources to me. My appetite for supper was none the worse, and my ebullience made me think of so many laughable things to say that I succeeded in entirely dissipating the low spirits of the Duke of Matalona, who was in despair at having won so large a sum from a stranger who was his guest and whom people might think he had entertained only in order to win his money. He was the perfection of courtesy, lavish, rich, generous, and a man of honor.

On the way back to his palazzo he could not bring himself to say that he was not in need of money, that he would give me all the time I wanted to pay him; he rightly feared to wound my feelings; but before he went to bed he could not refrain from writing me a short note in which he said that if I needed credit at his banker's he would stand surety for me for whatever amount I might require. I replied that I was duly sensible of his courtesy and that if I should be in need of money I would accept his generous offer.

The next morning I went to his room early to embrace him and remind him that we were to breakfast with his beautiful mistress. He put on morning dress, as I had done, and we walked to the Fontana Medina[28] and the pretty house near it in which the angel lived.

She was still in bed, not naked but sitting up, modestly charming, beautiful as the day, wearing a dimity corset laced with wide rose-colored ribbons. She was reading *Le Sopha,* by the elegant Crébillon the Younger.[29] The Duke sat down on the foot of her bed, while I could only stand in a sort of daze, looking at her enchanting face, which I seemed once to have known and even to have loved. It was the first time that I saw her well. Laughing to see me so distracted, she told me to sit down in a small armchair at her bedside.

The Duke said that I was very glad to have lost two thousand ducati to him, for my loss made me sure that she loved me.

"*Caro il mio* Don Giacomo, I am sorry I told you that you would win, you would have done better not to play: I should love you just as much, and you would be richer by two thousand ducati."

"And I two thousand ducati the poorer," said the Duke with a smile.

"But I shall win this evening, charming Leonilda," I said, "if you will grant me some favor today. Otherwise I shall lose my soul and die in a very few days here at Naples."

"In that case, dear Leonilda," said the Duke, "you must grant him some small token."

"That I cannot."

The Duke told her she might dress and come to breakfast in the Chinese room, and she began to obey him at once, being neither too generous in what she let us see nor too miserly in what she managed to hide from us —a procedure which is sure to set any man on fire who has already been captivated by a woman's pretty face and intelligence and manners. Nevertheless I saw her beautiful bosom; it was a theft, but one which I could never have committed if she had not permitted it. On my side, I pretended I had seen nothing.

During the moments of distraction which a woman permits herself when she is dressing, she maintained with much ingenuity that a sensible girl should be more chary of her favors with a man whom she loves than with one whom she does not love, for the simple reason that she must always be afraid of losing the former while she has no interest in keeping the latter.

I said that in time she would find the contrary to be true in my case; and she replied that I was wrong.

The Chinese designs which covered the room in which we breakfasted were admirable rather for their coloring and their drawing than for the amorous acts they represented.

"On me," says the Duke, "they have no effect whatever"; and, so saying, he shows us his nullity. Leonilda does not look, but I was shocked; however, I concealed it.

"I am," I said, "in the same case, but I do not care to convince you of it."

The Duke says he does not believe it, he puts out a hand, and he finds that I am not lying; he shows his astonishment, and, withdrawing his hand, says that I must be as impotent as he is. I deny his conclusion and I say that to convince him of the contrary I had only to look into Leonilda's eyes, he asks her to look at me, she turns and fixes her eyes on mine, the Duke puts out his hand to the place of proof once more, and he finds he is wrong. He makes to uncover me, but I oppose him; he persists, he laughs, and I let him go on; in a sweet access of ardor I seize Leonilda's hand and, never taking my eyes from hers, I press it to my lips, and the Duke withdraws his wet hand, exclaiming, laughing, and getting up to fetch a towel. Leonilda has seen nothing, but she succumbs to uncontrollable laughter, as do I and the Duke. It was one of those delicious little games which so effectually stimulate Love, who, ever a child, revels in the play and laughter whose nectar makes him immortal. In playing it all three of us transgressed certain limits, though we managed to remain within certain others. We ended it with embraces, and Leonilda's lips pressed to mine sent me away with the Duke, plunged in the intoxication of the love which fetters the mind.

On the way I told the Duke that I would not see his mistress again unless he would relinquish her to me, declaring that I was prepared to marry her and give her a dowry of five thousand ducati.

"Speak to her, I will raise no objection. You shall learn from herself what property she has."

I went to dress, and when the bell rang went down to dinner. The Duchess was surrounded by a large company. She had the goodness to say she was sorry I had had bad luck.

"Fortune, Signora, is changeable; but your kind concern is bound to bring me luck. I shall win this evening."

"I doubt it, your opponent this evening will be Monteleone, who is very lucky."

Reflecting on the state of my gambling ventures after dinner, I decided to play for cash, first so that, in case I was overwhelmed, I should not endanger my honor by losing more on my word than I could pay, secondly in order to relieve the banker of any fear that I would be short when I was cleaned out for the third time, and thirdly in the hope that the change of system would also change my luck.

I spent four hours at the San Carlo in Leonilda's box, finding her more elaborately dressed and more brilliant than she had been on the previous days. I told her that the love she had inspired in me was of a kind which could tolerate neither rivals nor delay nor the slightest possibility of future inconstancy.

"I have told the Duke that I am prepared to marry you, giving you a dowry of five thousand ducati."

"What was his answer?"

"That I should make the proposal to yourself, and that he will raise no objection."

"And we will leave together."

"At once. After that only death can separate us."

"We will talk tomorrow morning. You will make me happy."

The Duke arrives, she tells him that there is no more question of anything between us but marriage.

"Marriage," he replied, "is the one thing in the world

which must be considered the most before it is undertaken.''

"But not too much, for as long as one is considering
it one does not marry; in any case we have no time for
that, since Don Giacomo has to leave.''

"If it is to be a marriage,'' he said to me, "you can
put off your departure, or return after becoming for-
mally engaged to my dear Leonilda.''

"No putting it off, my dear Duke, and no returning.
We have made up our minds, and if we are mistaken we
shall have all the time we need to repent.''

The Duke laughs, he says we will discuss it the next
day, and we go to our circle, where we find the Duke of
Monteleone dealing with a well-stocked bank before him.

"I have bad luck,'' I said to him, "when I play on my
word, so I hope you will permit me to play for cash.''

"As you please—it makes no difference. I have made
you a bank of four thousand ducati, so that you can
recoup your losses.''

"And I promise to break it or to lose four thousand.''

So saying, I draw from my pocket six thousand ducati,
in paper as always, I give two thousand to the Duke of
Matalona, and I begin playing for a hundred ducati.
After a very long session I broke the bank; and, the
Duke of Matalona having left, I returned to his palazzo
alone. When I told him the good news the next morning
he embraced me and advised me always to play for cash.
A great supper which the Princess della Valle[30] was
giving would keep our circle of players from meeting
that day. So we went to say good morning to Donna
Leonilda, putting off discussing our marriage until the
morrow, and we spent the rest of the day looking at the
wonders of nature in the environs of Naples. At the great
supper I saw the highest nobility of Naples, and great
lavishness.

The next morning the Duke told me that I could go
alone to his mistress's, where, having business, he would

come later, and I went; but he did not come. For this reason we could settle nothing in the matter of our marriage. I spent two hours alone with her; but, as I felt I must be ruled by her inclinations, she found me amorous only in words. When I left her I again swore that it rested entirely with her to leave Naples with me, bound by marriage to my destiny until death.

The Duke asked me, with a smile, if, after spending the whole morning alone with his mistress, I still wanted to marry her.

"More than ever. What have you in mind?"

"Nothing. And since that is how things stand we will talk tomorrow."

That evening at Monteleone's I found a personable-looking banker with much gold before him; the Duke told me he was Don Marco Ottoboni.[31] He was holding the cards in his left hand, and he drew the card very well with his right, but he held the pack so tightly in his hand that I could not see it.

I decide to play for a ducato. With persistent bad luck, I lost only eighteen or twenty ducati after five or six deals. The banker politely asks me why I am staking such small sums against him.

"Because," I reply, "when I do not see at least half the pack I am afraid I shall lose."

The next night I broke the bank of the very amiable and very rich Prince del Cassaro,[32] who asked me to give him his revenge, inviting me to supper at a pretty house he had at Posilipo,[33] where he lived with a *virtuosa*[34] with whom he had fallen in love at Palermo. He also invited the Duke of Matalona and three or four others. This was the only occasion on which I dealt at Naples. I made him a bank of six thousand ducati, after telling him that, as I was on the eve of my departure, I would play only for cash. He lost ten thousand ducati and stopped only because he had no more money. Everyone made off, and I would have stopped too if the

Prince's mistress, who was playing on her word after losing thirty or forty once,[35] had not been in arrears another hundred. I continued to deal, hoping that she would recoup; but I finally put down the cards at two o'clock in the morning, saying that she should pay me in Rome.

Since I was determined not to leave Naples without having seen Caserta,[36] and since Donna Leonilda was of the same mind, the Duke sent us there in a very comfortable carriage drawn by six mules, whose trot was faster than a horse's gallop. During the journey I first heard the voice of her duenna.

It was on the day after our journey to Caserta that we settled the particulars of our marriage in a conversation which lasted two hours.

"Leonilda there," said the Duke, "has her mother living on an estate not far from the city with an income of six hundred ducati a year which I settled on her for life when I bought a piece of property which her husband left her; but Leonilda is not dependent on her. She relinquished her to me seven years ago, and I at once gave her a life annuity of five hundred ducati, which she will bring you as her dowry together with all her diamonds and a fine wardrobe. Her mother has confided her entirely to my love and to my word of honor that I would arrange an advantageous marriage for her. I had her educated, and when I became aware of her cast of mind I cultivated it, freeing her from all prejudices except the one which makes it a girl's duty to keep herself for him whom Heaven has destined to be her husband; and you can be certain that you will be the first man whom my dear Leonilda will clasp to her bosom."

I told him to have the deed for her dowry drawn up and to add to it five thousand ducati del regno, which I would pay over to him when the marriage contract was signed; he said that he would guarantee them himself by a mortgage on a country house which was worth twice as much, and, turning to Leonilda, who was weeping for joy, he said that he would send for her mother, who would be delighted to sign her marriage agreement.

Her mother was living at Sant'Agata in the household of the Marchese Galiani.[37] It was a day's journey from Naples. He said that he would send his carriage for her the next day, that the day after that we would sup together, and on the following day we would settle everything with the notary and would go at once to the little church in Portici, where a priest would marry us, he undertaking to secure a dispensation from publishing the banns. On the day after the wedding her mother would return to Sant'Agata with us, we would dine with her there, and we would continue our journey with her blessing.

At this conclusion to his discourse, I shuddered, then I laughed; but Leonilda, for all her intelligence, fell fainting into the arms of the Duke, who revived her, calling her his "dear daughter" and kissing her again and again. At the conclusion of the scene we all three dried our tears.

From that day on I did not play again. I had won fifteen thousand ducati, I considered myself a married man; it was my part to conduct myself with prudence.

The next day, at supper with Leonilda and the Duke after the opera at the San Carlo,

"What will my mother say," she asked me, "when she sees you tomorrow evening?"

"She will say that you have done a foolish thing to marry a stranger whom you have known for only a week. Have you written her my name, my country, my situation, my age?"

"I wrote her these three lines: *'Come tomorrow, my dear Mama, to sign my marriage contract with a man whom I receive from the hands of His Grace the Duke and with whom I shall leave for Rome on Monday.'*"

"And here are my three lines," said the Duke:
" '*Come at once, my dear friend, to sign your daughter's
marriage contract and give her your blessing, for she has
wisely chosen a husband who could be her father.*' "

"That's not true," said Leonilda, coming to my arms;
"she'll think you're an old man, and I don't like it."

"Is your mother old?"

"Her mother," said the Duke to me, "is a charming
and very witty woman no more than thirty-seven or
thirty-eight years old."

"What is she doing in Galiani's house?"

"Being an intimate friend of the Marchesa, she lives
with her family, but she pays board."

The next morning, having various small matters of
business to dispose of and needing to go to my banker
to give him all my bank notes and obtain his draft on
Rome, only excepting the five thousand ducati I was to
pay over at the signing of the contract, I told the Duke
to expect me at Leonilda's about suppertime.

At eight o'clock I enter the room, in which they were
standing with their backs to the fireplace, the Duke between the mother and the daughter.

"Ah! There he is!"

I look first at the mother, who, the instant I appear,
gives a piercing cry and sinks onto the sofa. I stare at
her, and I see Donna Lucrezia Castelli.

"Donna Lucrezia!" I say, "how happy I am!"

"Let us recover our breath, my dear friend. Sit down
here. You are going to marry my daughter."

I sit down; I understand it all; my hair stands on
end, and I sink into the gloomiest silence. The astonishment was Leonilda's and the Duke's; they saw that we
knew each other; but beyond that they could not go. I
think of that past time and of Leonilda's age, and I see
that she could be my daughter; but I considered that
Donna Lucrezia could not be sure of it, for she was living

with her husband, who was not yet fifty and who loved her. I rise, I take a light, and asking the Duke and Leonilda to excuse me, I request the mother to go into the next room with me.

The woman I had so greatly loved in Rome has scarcely sat down beside me before she says:

"Leonilda is your daughter,[38] I am sure of it; I have never considered her anything else, my husband himself knew it, and he made no protest; he adored her. I will show you her baptismal certificate, and after seeing the date of her birth you can calculate for yourself. My husband never touched me in Rome, and my daughter was not born prematurely. Do you remember that my late mother must have read you a letter in which I wrote her that I was pregnant? That was in the January of 1744. In six months she will be seventeen. It was my dear husband himself who gave her the name Leonilda Giacomina at the baptismal font, and when he played with her he always called her Giacomina. This marriage, my dear friend, horrifies me, yet you can understand that I will not oppose it, for I should not dare tell the reason. What do you think? Have you really the courage to marry her? You hesitate. Can it be that you have consummated the marriage before contracting it?"

"No, my dear friend."

"I breathe again."

"She has none of my features."

"That is true. She looks like me. You weep, dear friend."

"Who would not weep? I am going into the other room, and I will send you the Duke. You understand that he must be told all."

I enter, and I tell him to go and speak with Donna Lucrezia. Leonilda, aghast, comes and sits on my lap and asks me what is the matter. My distress keeps me from answering, she kisses me, trembling, and she sheds tears with me. We remained there mute for half an hour, until the Duke returned with Donna Lucrezia, who, alone of the four of us, had assumed a reasonable attitude.

"But my dear daughter," she said to Leonilda, "this unpleasant mystery must be revealed to you; and it is from your mother herself that you shall learn it. Do you remember what name my late husband often called you, when, holding you in his arms, he caressed you?"

"He called me 'charming Giacomina.' "

"That is the name of this gentleman here. He is your father. Go and kiss him as a daughter, and if he has been your lover forget your crime."

It was then that the pathos of the tragedy undid us. Leonilda ran to embrace her mother's knees, and, despite the tears which choked her, said:

"I have never loved him except as a daughter."

The scene then became dumb show, except that the sound of the tears and kisses of the two admirable creatures gave it life, while the Duke and I, the supremely interested witnesses of the spectacle, were like two marble statues.

We remained at table for three hours, always sad, always talking, and passing from reflection to reflection on this more unhappy than happy recognition, and we separated at midnight unaware that we had eaten nothing.

We knew that the next day at dinner we should discuss the incident more coolly and sensibly; we were sure that nothing would stop us from taking the wisest course, and without any difficulty, for there was no other.

On the way the Duke talked aloud to himself, making countless reflections on what moral philosophy may denominate "prejudice." That the union of a father with his daughter is horrible by nature no philosopher will make bold to say; but the prejudice in this regard is so strong that one must have a thoroughly depraved mind to trample it underfoot. It is the fruit of a respect for the laws which a good education has inculcated in a noble soul; and, so defined, it is no longer prejudice, it is duty.

This duty can also be considered natural in that nature inspires us to grant to those we love the same goods which we desire for ourselves. It would seem that what is most conducive to reciprocity in love is equality in everything, in age, in situation, in character; and at first sight one does not find this equality between father and daughter. The respect which she owes to him who had given her being raises an obstacle to the kind of affection she must feel for a lover. If the father takes possession of his daughter by virtue of his paternal authority, he exercises a tyranny which nature must abhor. Our natural love of good order likewise causes reason to regard such a union as monstrous. The offspring of it are bound to be marked by confusion and insubordination; in short, such a union is abhorrent from every point of view; but it is no longer so when the two individuals love each other and have no knowledge that reasons which have nothing to do with their mutual affection ought to prevent them from loving each other; and incestuous relations, the eternal subjects of Greek tragedies, instead of making me weep make me laugh, and if I weep at *Phèdre,*[39] it is Racine's art which makes me do so.

I went to bed, but I could not sleep. The sudden transition I had to make from carnal to fatherly love caused all my moral and physical faculties the deepest distress. I slept for two hours, after deciding that I would leave the next day.

On waking and finding my decision very wise, I go to communicate it to the Duke, who was still in bed. He replied that everyone knew I was soon to leave and that such haste would be interpreted unfavorably. He advised me to take a broth with him and to consider my projected marriage a joke.

"We will," he said, "spend these three or four days

gaily, and we will apply our minds to dismissing the gloomy aspects of this untoward incident and even giving it a comic cast. I advise you to renew your affair with Donna Lucrezia. You must have found her as she was eighteen years ago; she cannot possibly have been better.''

This little discourse reduces me to reason. To forget the projected marriage was certainly the best course I could take; but I was in love, and the object of love is not like some piece of merchandise for which, when one cannot have it, one can easily substitute another.

So we went to Leonilda's together, the Duke in his usual spirits, but I pale, undone, the perfect picture of gloom. What immediately surprises me is to find gaiety. Leonilda flings herself on my neck, calling me ''dear Papa,'' her mother addresses me as ''dear friend,'' and my eyes and my soul are held captive by her face, in which eighteen years had been unable to harm a single feature.

We enact a mute scene, embracing each other again and again at intervals; Leonilda gives me, and receives, any quantity of kisses, regardless of what desires they may arouse in us; it was enough for her to be certain that, knowing who we were, we should be able to resist them. She was right. One grows used to everything. It was shame which dissipated my gloom.

I tell Donna Lucrezia about the strange welcome her sister had accorded me in Rome, and we begin laughing; we recollect the night at Tivoli,[40] and the remembered images soften us. After a short silence I tell her that if she would like to come to Rome with me simply to visit Donna Angelica I would undertake to bring her back to Naples at the beginning of Lent. She promises to give me an answer the next day.

Dining between her and Leonilda, and having to forget the latter, it is not surprising that all my old flame was rekindled. Whether it was due to her gay banter, or to my need to love, or to the excellence of the dishes and the wines, at dessert I offered her my hand.

"I will marry you," I said, "and the three of us will set off together on Monday, for now that Leonilda is my daughter I cannot leave her in Naples."

At this proposal my three table companions looked at one another, and no one answered me.

After dinner, overtaken by sleepiness, I had to lie down on the bed, and I did not wake until eight o'clock, when I was surprised to see only Donna Lucrezia, who was writing. She comes to me, she says I have slept for five hours, and that she had not gone to the opera with her daughter and the Duke so that I should not be left alone.

Recollecting an old love in the presence of an adorable woman reawakens it, desires are rekindled, and the strength with which they return is boundless. If the two persons are still in love, neither yields to the other in eagerness; they feel as if they were regaining possession of a treasure which belongs to them and which a series of harsh circumstances has long forbidden them to enjoy. Such we became in an instant, with no preamble, no idle talk, no preliminaries, and even with no feigned attacks, in which one or the other cannot but be playing a role. Immersed in the sweetness of a happy silence, we surrendered ourselves to the one true author of nature, to love.

I was the first to break the silence during the first intermission. If a man has a mind which sees the amusing side of things, will it not continue to be of the same cast during the delightful repose which follows an amorous victory?

"Here I am again," I said, "in the charming country which undid me to the sound of gunfire and drums the first time I dared to explore it in the dark." [41]

She could not but laugh, and, memory joining in, we recollected in turn all that had happened to us at Testac-

cio and Frascati and Tivoli.[42] We passed them in review
only to laugh, but what are the subjects for laughter
which two lovers who are alone together bring up except
an excuse to celebrate the festival of love once more?

At the end of the second act, in the enthusiasm which
love crowned and content leaves in the soul,

"Let us," I said, "be each other's until death; let us
thus assure ourselves that we will die happy; we are of
the same age, and we can even hope to die at the same
time."

"It is my dearest wish, but stay in Naples and leave
Leonilda to the Duke. We will frequent society, we will
find her a husband worthy of her, and our happiness will
be complete."

"I cannot settle in Naples, my dear. Your daughter
was ready to leave with me."

"Say 'our daughter.' I see that you wish you were
not her father. You love her."

"Alas! I am very sure that my passion for her would
be stilled as long as I could live with you; but I answer
for nothing if you should not be there. She is charming,
and her mind captivates me even more than her beauty.
Being sure that she loved me, I renounced attempting
to seduce her only for fear of making her distrust me.
Such an apprehension on her part might have lessened
her fondness. I aspired to her esteem, I did not want to
trouble her innocence. I wanted to possess her only
legitimately and with a right equal to hers. My dear,
we have created an angel. I cannot understand how the
Duke—"

"The Duke is impotent. Now you understand all."

"How can he be impotent? He has a son."

"He is impotent, I tell you."

"Nevertheless—"

"Nevertheless. He is impotent, and he knows it."

"Let me see you as I did at Tivoli."

"No, for a carriage is stopping."

How Leonilda burst out laughing when she saw her mother in my arms! She gave us countless kisses. The Duke arrived a moment later, and we supped very gaily. He declared me the happiest of mortals when I told him I should spend the night honorably with my wife and my daughter; and he was right: I was the happiest of mortals in those days.

> *Quand'ero in parte altr'uom da quel ch'io sono.*
>
> ("When I was in part a different man from the man I am.")[43]

After he left, it was Leonilda who undressed her mother, while, after wrapping my hair in a kerchief, I threw my clothes into the middle of the room. She tells her daughter to get into bed beside her.

"Your father," she says, "will confine his attention to your mother."

"And I," she replies, "will give mine to you both"; and, on the other side of the bed she undresses completely and gets in next to her, saying that as her father I was at liberty to see all my handiwork. Her mother is proud of her, she praises her, and she rejoices to see that I find her beautiful. It sufficed her that she was in the middle and that it was only upon her that I extinguished the fire with which she saw that I was burning. Leonilda's curiosity delighted me to the soul.

"So is that what you did," she asked me, "when you engendered me eighteen years ago?"

But the moment which leads Lucrezia to the death of love has come, just when, to spare her, I feel it my duty to withdraw. Moved to pity, Leonilda sends her mother's little soul on its flight with one hand and with the other puts a white handkerchief under her gushing father.

Lucrezia, grateful for her daughter's fond ministrations, turns her back to me, clasps her in her arms, gives her countless kisses, then, turning to me again, says in moving tones:

"There, look at her, she is unstained, touch if you want to, nothing has suffered harm, she is as I made her."

"Yes," said Leonilda, laughing, "look at me and kiss Mama."

Alas! I loved her mother, otherwise nothing would have saved her from my fury. The combat began again and did not end until we fell asleep.

What waked us was the rays of the sun.

"Go and draw the curtain, dear daughter," says her mother.

At that Leonilda, naked as my hand, obediently goes to draw the curtain, showing me beauties of which, when one is in love, one has never seen enough. Alas! Coming back to bed, she lets me bestow my kisses on all that I saw; but as soon as she sees me on the edge of the precipice she slips away and gives me to her mother, who receives me with open arms and imperiously orders me to not spare her but to make her another Leonilda. At the end of the encounter, which was a very long one, I believed I had obeyed her, but my blood, which she saw when I yielded to exhaustion, left her doubtful.

"You have accustomed me," she said, "to this frightening phenomenon."

After assuring the innocent Leonilda that it was of no consequence, we dressed, and the Duke of Matalona arrived. It was Leonilda who gave him an account of all our nocturnal labors. In the wretchedness of his impotence he could not but congratulate himself on not having witnessed them.

Determined to leave the next day so that I should be in Rome in time to enjoy the last week of the Carnival, I used all my powers of persuasion on the Duke to assure myself that a present I had determined to bestow on Leonilda would not be refused. It was the dowry of five thousand ducati which I would have given her if she could have become my wife. The Duke decided that her being my daughter was all the more reason why she should accept the amount as a dowry. She accepted it, smothering me with caresses and making me promise that I would come back to Naples to see her when I learned that she was married. I promised, and I kept my word.

Since I had decided to leave the next day, the Duke wanted me to see all the Neapolitan nobility in his palazzo at a great supper of the kind I had seen at the Princess della Valle Piccolomini's. So he left me with my daughter, saying that we would meet again at the supper. We dined together, and we spent the rest of the day within the bounds prescribed to a father and daughter. The large amount of blood I had lost the night before may have contributed to my share in our abstention. We did not embrace until the very last moment of our parting, which the mother felt as keenly as did the daughter.

I went off to dress for the supper. When I took leave of the Duchess, she addressed me in these words:

"I am sure that you will always recollect Naples with pleasure."

No one could doubt it. After showing my generosity to the Duke's household, I left as I had arrived. That nobleman, who died three or four years later, escorted me to the door of my carriage.

CHAPTER XI

Accident to my carriage. Mariuccia's wedding.
Flight of Lord Lismore. My return to Flor-
ence and my departure with La Corticelli.

WITH MY Spaniard riding ahead and Don Ciccio
seated beside me, I am sound asleep in an excellent four-
horse carriage when I am startled awake by a violent
jolt. It was midnight when my carriage was overturned
in the middle of the highway, beyond Francolisi[1] and
four miles from Sant'Agata. Alfani, who was under-
neath me, was screaming from the pain in his right arm,
which he thought was broken and which afterward
proved to be only dislocated. My Leduc, coming back,
told me that the two postilions had fled and that they
might have gone to take the news to highway robbers.

I easily got out of the carriage through the door which
was above me; but Alfani, unable, between his age and
his disabled arm, to make his own way, had to be pulled
out. We managed it in a quarter of an hour. His piercing
shrieks made me laugh because of the strange oaths with
which he interlarded his silly prayers to St. Francis of
Assisi, his patron.

For my part, accustomed to being overturned, I suffered no damage. It depends on the position one assumes. Don Ciccio may have hurt his arm because he put it outside.

From the carriage I take my dueling pistols, having short ones in my pocket, my carbine, and my sword. I tell Leduc to mount and go looking for armed peasants in the vicinity, money in hand. Meanwhile, Don Ciccio having lain down on the hard ground groaning and in no condition to resist robbers,[2] I make my own preparations to sell them my fortune and my life at the highest price. My carriage being close to the ditch, I unhitch the four horses, I tie them to the wheels and the pole in a circle, and I station myself behind them with my five firearms.

In this predicament I could not help laughing at poor old Alfani, who was writhing exactly like a dying dolphin on the seashore and who uttered the most horrible execrations when a mare whose back was turned to him took it into her head to empty her bladder on him. There was nothing to be done; he had to put up with the whole stinking rain and to forgive my laughter, which I had not the strength to hold in.

The darkness of the night and a strong north wind made my situation still more trying. At the least sound I heard, I cried, "Who goes there?" threatening death to anyone who should dare to advance. I had to spend two whole hours in this tragicomic situation.

Leduc finally arrived at full gallop, shouting at the top of his voice and followed by a band of peasants, each with his lantern, come to my rescue. There were ten or twelve of them, all armed with muskets, and all ready to obey my orders.

In less than an hour the carriage was put back on its four wheels, the horses were harnessed, and Don Ciccio was restored to the seat he had occupied. I sent all the peasants away well satisfied, keeping only two who, serving as my postilions, brought me to the posthouse at Sant'Agata[3] at daybreak. The row I raised there was terrifying:

"Where is the post master? Someone go fetch me a notary, for the first thing is to make a statement. I insist on an indemnity; and the postilions who overturned me on an excellent road, where a spill is impossible unless it is done on purpose, shall be at least sentenced to the galleys."

A wheelwright arrives; he looks over my carriage and finds the axle broken, a new one must be made at once, and the verdict is that I will have to stay there at least one day.

In need of a surgeon, Don Ciccio goes without telling me to the Marchese Galiani,[4] whom he knew[5] and who comes in person to ask me to stay in his house until my carriage is repaired. I accept his invitation. He orders my carriage put in his stable at once.

The Marchese Galiani was as learned as he was courteous—courteous in the Neapolitan fashion, without ceremony. He was not as brilliant as his brother,[6] whose wit was effervescent, and whom I had known in Paris as Embassy Secretary to the Count of Cantillana.[7] The Marchese who offered me his hospitality was a mathematician; at that time he was writing a commentary on Vitruvius,[8] which he afterward published; but *ploravere suis non respondere favorem speratum meritis* ("they lamented that their merits did not meet with the gratitude for which they had hoped").[9] He introduced me to his spouse,[10] whom I knew to be the intimate friend of Donna Lucrezia; she was an excellent wife and mother, with several young children. Don Ciccio was immediately put to bed, and a surgeon was summoned, who, after examining him thoroughly, eased his mind by assuring him that it was only a dislocation, or, in his language, a "luxation."

At noon we hear a carriage arriving at a fast trot; we go to the window, and I see Donna Lucrezia getting out of it.

She comes up the stairs, she embraces the Marchesa, and, not in the least surprised to see me, asks me what chance has brought me here. She tells the Marchesa that I am an old friend of her late husband's and that she had just seen me again in Naples at the Duke of Matalona's.

After dinner I asked this creature made for love if we could spend the night together, and she showed me that it was absolutely impossible. I repeated my offer to marry her at Sant'Agata and take her with me, and she replied that if I really loved her I had only to buy an estate in the Kingdom, where she would come to live with me and would not demand that I marry her except in case she gave me children.

I should have lived happily with that charming woman, but I loathed the idea of settling down anywhere. In Naples I could have bought an estate which would have made me rich; but I should have had to adopt a prudent course of conduct which was absolutely foreign to my nature. After supper I took leave of the entire company, and I left at dawn so that I should be in Rome the next day. I had only fifteen stages[11] to cover on a very good road.

Arriving at Carillano,[12] I see an Italian two-wheeled carriage known as a *mantice*. Two horses were being harnessed to it. I needed four; I get out, and I hear my name spoken. I turn, and there, sitting under the hood beside a young and pretty girl, is Signora Diana, the Prince del Cassaro's[13] *virtuosa*, who owed me three hundred once. She said that she was going to Rome and that she was very glad we should make the journey together.

"We shall spend the night," she said, "at Piperno." [14]

"Signora, I shall not stop until I reach Rome."

"We shall get there tomorrow just the same."

"I know that, but I sleep better in my carriage than I do in the poor beds one finds in these inns."

"I dare not travel at night."

"Then we shall meet again in Rome."

"That's not right. You see that I have only a fool of a valet and my chambermaid, who is no braver than I am, and besides the wind is cold and this is an open carriage. I will come in yours."

"I have my old secretary with me, who broke his arm day before yesterday."

"Shall we dine together at Terracina?[15] We will talk."

"Very well. We will dine there."

We ate well. We were to arrive at Piperno after dark; Signora Diana again urged me to spend the night there. She was blonde and too fat, I found her unappetizing, but her chambermaid attracted me. I finally promise that I will sup with her, put her under the innkeeper's protection, and then leave, for I could not waste ten hours at the post station.

At Piperno I find an opportunity to tell the chambermaid that if she promises to be kind to me that night I will stay there.

"I will come to your bed," I say, "and you may be sure I will make no noise; your mistress will not wake."

She promises, and she even lets one of my hands assure me that she will be kind.

After supper they go off to bed; I go to wish them good night, and I see them. I cannot be mistaken, the door is open; I knew what I needed to know. After putting out the candle I go off to bed too. A half hour later I make my way to their bed, and my hands encounter the Signora Diana. It was obvious. The chambermaid had told her the story, and they had changed places. I could not possibly be mistaken, I did not need to use my eyes, my hand had sufficiently convinced me. I paused, hesitating between two ideas, both of which would adequately avenge me for the trick. The first was to get into bed with her, the other to dress and leave at once. The latter prevailed. I woke Leduc, and he the innkeeper, I paid, I had horses harnessed, and I went to Rome. I saw Signora Diana three or four times at the Barbary horse race,[16] and we saluted each other from a distance; if I had thought she would pay me I would have gone to see her.

I found my brother, Mengs, and Winckelmann cheerful and in good health, and Costa very glad to see me back. I at once ordered him to tell the Abate Momolo that I would go to his house for polenta that evening and that he need make no preparations. I ordered Costa to see to providing a supper for twelve. I was sure that Mariuccia would be present, for Momolo knew that I enjoyed seeing her.

As the Carnival[17] was to begin the next day, I hired a landau for the entire week. This is a carriage seating four, the hood of which can be lowered either in front or behind and in which people drive on the Corso[18] every day of that week from twenty-one to twenty-four o'clock. They go masked, or unmasked if they choose; they wear all sorts of masking costumes on foot and on horseback; they throw sweetmeats to the populace, they hand out satires, pasquinades, pamphlets. The lordliest people in Rome mingle with the humblest, there is general confusion, and the Barbary horses race down the middle of the Corso between the landaus, filled with spectators, which are drawn up to left and right. Toward nightfall the whole crowd makes off to fill the theaters for operas, plays, pantomimes, and rope-dancing exhibitions, in all which entertainments the performers have to be whole men or castrati. People also go to inns and pothouses, where all the rooms are full of patrons eating with might and main, as if they never ate except on those days.

I at once went on foot to the banker Belloni's[19] to

deposit my money and obtain a letter of credit on Turin, where I was to see the Abate Gama and be entrusted with the mission from the Court of Portugal to the Congress of Augsburg, on which all Europe was counting. After that I went to look at my room behind Trinità dei Monti, where I hoped to see Mariuccia the next morning. I found everything in good order.

In the evening the Abate Momolo greeted me with cries of joy, and his whole family did likewise. His eldest daughter said with a smile that she was sure I would be glad if she sent for Signora Maria; I replied that she was quite right; and a few minutes later I saw her arrive with her pious mother, who at once told me that I should not be surprised to see her daughter better dressed, for she was to be married in three or four days. I congratulated her, and all the girls together asked her: "To whom, to whom?" Whereupon Mariuccia blushed and said very modestly to one of Momolo's daughters:

"You know him; he is So-and-So, who has seen me here and who is going to open a wigmaker's shop."

Her mother adds that it was Father XXX, her confessor, who had arranged the marriage and who had in his keeping the four hundred scudi which her daughter would bring him as her dowry. Momolo adds that he is an upright young man, who would have married his daughter if she had had such a sum.

I see that the girl is mortified, I comfort her, I tell her that her turn will come, and she takes me at my word. She believed I could not fail to know that she was in love with Costa and that I was planning to have him marry her. Nothing was further from my thoughts. Her idea was confirmed when I told Costa to use my landau to take all Momolo's daughters to the Corso the next day, well masked, for they must not be recognized; I told him to hire clothes from the Jews. They were delighted.

"And Signora Maria?" the jealous sister asked me.

"Signora Maria," I replied, "is about to be married;

so she must not attend any entertainment except with
her fiancé.''

Her mother applauds me; whereupon the clever girl
at once pretends to be mortified. I then turn to the Abate
Momolo and ask him to do me the favor of inviting
Mariuccia's fiancé to supper, and he promises he will do
so.

Being very tired, and having let Mariuccia see me, I
had nothing further of consequence to do. So I asked
the company to excuse me, and, after wishing them all
good appetites, I went home.

The next morning at seven o'clock I did not need to
enter the church. Mariuccia saw me, followed me, and
we were alone in our little room. She needed to talk to
me, I was eager to hear all her news, but such talk would
have infringed on love. We had only an hour before us,
and when one is making love one does not spend time
chatting. We did not even bother to undress. As she put
on her hood after we exchanged a last kiss, she finally
told me that she was sure she would be married on the
last day but one of the Carnival, that her confessor had
arranged everything, that I had done well to ask Momolo
to invite her future husband to supper, and that we could
spend four hours together on the coming Sunday, the
eve of her wedding day. She left after that, and I slept
for a good hour.

On my way back to the house[20] I meet a carriage
driven at high speed and preceded by a courier. A young
nobleman dressed in black and wearing a blue ribbon[21]
puts out his head, calls my name, and orders the carriage
stopped. I am greatly surprised to see Lord Tallow,[22]
whom I had met in Paris at his mother's, the Countess
of Lismore,[23] who was separated from her husband and
the kept mistress of Monsieur de Saint-Albin,[24] the
Archbishop of Cambrai. He was a natural son of the
Duke of Orléans, Regent of France.

Lord Tallow was a handsome young man, full of wit

and talent, but unbridled in his pursuit of all the vices.
Knowing that he was not rich, I was surprised by the
style in which I saw he was traveling and even more by
the blue ribbon. He hastily says that he is going to dine
at the Pretender's,[25] but that he will sup at home; he
invites me, I accept. He was lodging in the house of the
English tailor in the Piazza di Spagna.

I went there, after laughing my fill at the comedy at
the Tor di nona,[26] where I saw Costa with all the *scopatore*'s daughters.

But I was very pleasantly surprised when, entering
Lord Tallow's apartment, I saw the poet Poinsinet.[27]
He was a short young man, ugly, amusing, full of inspiration and talent for the theater. He would have shone
in the French Parnassus if five or six years later he had
not most unfortunately fallen into the Guadalquivir and
been drowned.[28] He was on his way to Madrid to make
his fortune.

"What are you doing in Rome, my dear friend? And
where, pray, is Lord Tallow?"

"He is in the next room; but he is no longer Tallow,
he is Earl of Lismore, his father having died recently.
You know that he was an adherent of the Pretender. I
left Paris with him, gladly seizing such an opportunity
to see Rome without spending a copper."

"Then His Lordship has become rich?"

"Not yet; but he will be, for his father's death makes
him the master of an immense fortune. It is true that
everything is confiscated; but that makes no difference,
his claims are incontestable."

"Then he is rich in claims; but how did he become a
Knight of one of the French King's orders?"

"You are joking. That's the blue ribbon of the Order
of St. Michael,[29] the Grand Master of which is the Elector
of Cologne, who has just died. His Lordship, who, as you
know, plays the violin extremely well, happening to be
at his court in Bonn, played him a concerto of Tartini's.

The gracious prince, not knowing how to give him any substantial token of his esteem, presented him with the ribbon you saw. You cannot imagine how pleased His Lordship was by the present, for when we return to Paris everyone who sees him go by will think it is the Order of the Holy Ghost.''

We enter the drawing room, where we find His Lordship with the guests he had invited to supper. He comes to embrace me, calls me his dear friend, and, one by one, names to me all the persons who made up his select company: seven or eight girls, each prettier than the one before; three or four castrati, all fit to play women's parts to perfection in the Roman theaters; and five or six abati, husbands to all wives and wives to all husbands, who boasted of it and defied the girls to be more shameless than they. Yet the girls were not what would be called public prostitutes;[30] they were music lovers, devotees of painting, and dabblers in libertine philosophy. In this company I was a greenhorn. I see a respectable-looking man who is leaving; His Lordship asks him:

''Where are you going, Prince?''

He replies that he does not feel well. His Lordship tells me that he is the Prince of Chimay,[31] a subdeacon, and that he is seeking permission to marry in order to keep his illustrious family from becoming extinct. I praised his foresight.

At supper, where we were twenty-four, we may have emptied a hundred bottles. Everyone rose from the table intoxicated, except for myself and the poet Poinsinet, who had drunk only water. It was then that the great orgy began. It is impossible to describe all the excesses I saw; but a great libertine can imagine them. A castrato and a girl offered to undress in the next room, stipulating that they would keep their heads covered and lie in bed on their backs. They defied anyone to go in to see them and be able to decide which was male and which female. Bets were laid, and they went. We all entered, and no

one ventured to decide. We were allowed only to look. I
offered to wager His Lordship a hundred scudi against
fifty that I would say which was the female. The probabilities were equal, and His Lordship accepted. I won,
but there was no question of his paying me. This first
act of the orgy ended with the prostitution of the two
naked bodies. They defied all the men in the company to
sodomize them, everyone set to work with the exception
of myself and Poinsinet, and no one succeeded; but afterward we were treated to the spectacle of five or six copu-
lations, in which the abati shone by alternating between
the active and passive roles. I alone was respected. His
Lordship, who had not shown a sign of life throughout
the debauch, attacked poor Poinsinet; he defended himself in vain, he had to let himself be undressed and put
in the same condition as His Lordship, who was stark
naked too. We gathered around them. His Lordship took
up his watch and offered it to the first person who could
give either Poinsinet or himself an erection.[32] The hope
of winning the watch put the girls, the abati, and the
castrati on their mettle. Everyone wanted to be first; it
was decided to write each name on a slip of paper and
draw them. This was the most interesting part of the
drama for me, who, during the whole incredible performance, never felt the slightest sensation, except that
I laughed, chiefly at the distress exhibited by Poinsinet,
who was reduced to being afraid of having an erection,
since the drunken Earl swore that if he made him lose
his watch he would have him pitilessly sodomized in the
presence of all the actors. The scene, and the drama,
ended when there was no one left with any hope of winning the watch. However, the secret of the Lesbians was
employed only by the abati and the castrati; the girls
would not use it; they wanted to preserve their right to
look down on those who had employed it. It was pride
rather than shame which stood them in good stead. They
were afraid of employing it to no purpose.

Promises before Signing the Marriage Contract

Orgiastic Scene

What I gained from this hellish debauch is a better knowledge of myself. I risked my life. I had only my sword, and I would certainly have used it if His Lordship, in his Bacchic frenzy, had taken it into his head to force me to behave like the others, as he had done to poor Poinsinet. I have never understood what reason or what power made him respect me, for he was drunk. When I left, I promised him that I would come again whenever he sent me word, but I was firmly determined never to return there. Once outside of the stinking rooms, I thought I was restored to life. All sorts of foul things littered the floor of the abominable stage. Nevertheless I went to bed well satisfied to have witnessed a spectacle whose like I had never seen before and which I never saw equaled later.

Toward evening he came to see me on the pretext of returning my visit; he was on foot, he said that he did not care to see the Barbary horse race, and he invited me to take a walk with him at the Villa Medici.[33] I accept. I congratulate him on the immense fortune he must have inherited in order to live as he was doing, and he replies, laughing, that his entire capital is some fifty scudi, that he has no letter of credit, that his father had left nothing but debts, and that he already owed three or four thousand scudi.

"I am amazed that you are given credit."

"I am given credit because everyone knows that I have drawn a bill of exchange for two hundred thousand francs on Pâris de Montmartel.[34] But in five or six days it will come back protested, and I shall not wait until that awkward moment to make my escape."

"If you are certain it will be protested I advise you to leave today, for since the sum is so large the advice might be sent sooner."

"No, for I still have a slim hope. I have written my mother that I am ruined if she does not find a way to pay the amount to the banker on whom I drew, and in that case my bill will be accepted. You know my mother loves me.''

''I also know that she is not rich.''

''That is true; but Monsieur de Saint-Albin is so; and, between ourselves, I believe he is my father. Meanwhile, my creditors are almost as calm as I am. All those girls you saw would, if I asked them, give me all they possess, for each of them expects a substantial present this week, but I don't want to cheat them. The one I shall cheat, if I have to, is the Jew who wants to sell me this ring for three thousand zecchini, whereas I know it is worth only a thousand.''

''He will track you down.''

''I defy him to find me.''

It was a straw-colored solitaire of nine or ten carats. He left, asking me to say nothing. This harebrained wastrel did not arouse the slightest feeling of pity in me. I saw in him a wretch who would end his days in some fortress or who would kill himself if the idea occurred to him.

I went to sup at Momolo's, where I found the wig-maker, Mariuccia's fiancé. She had sent Momolo word that, her father having come from Palestrina on account of her marriage, she could not be present at the supper. I admired my dear Mariuccia's tactfulness; and through-out the supper I devoted my entire attention to the young man, in whom I found all that Mariuccia could wish. He was good-looking, sensible, and modest, and everything he said revealed an admirable frankness and probity. These characteristics, which would do honor to a great king, were nevertheless those of a wigmaker, whose dis-tant prospect of succeeding in life was bounded by his wigs. He told me in the presence of Tecla (she was Momolo's daughter) that it was she who would have made him happy if she had had means to help him open a shop, and that he must thank God for having made the

acquaintance of Mariuccia, who, after hearing him, had
found a true father in God in her confessor. I asked him
where he would hold the wedding party, and he said it
would be at the house of his father, a gardener, who lived
on the farther side of the Tiber, and that he had already
decided to give him ten scudi for the expenses because he
was poor.

How I wanted to give him ten scudi then and there!
But how was I to do it? I should have betrayed myself.

"Is your father's garden pretty?" I asked him.

"Not pretty; but very well kept. Since he owns the
land he has made one which he hopes to sell and which
yields twenty scudi a year; I should think myself fortunate if I could buy it."

"What is the price of it?"

"Two hundred scudi."

"That is a bargain. Listen to me. I met your intended
here, and I found her in all ways worthy of happiness.
She deserves a decent young man like yourself. Tell me
what you would do if I gave you two hundred scudi here
and now to buy your father's garden?"

"I would add the garden to my wife's dowry."

"Excellent. Here are two hundred scudi, which I entrust to the Abate Momolo because I do not yet know you
well enough. The garden is yours as part of the dowry
of your future wife."

With that, I give him the money, which he hands to
Momolo, who undertakes to make the purchase the next
day; whereupon the young man kneels to kiss my hand,
shedding tears of gratitude. All the girls cry, and so do
I; but all these different tears had different sources: it
was an alliance between vice and virtue. I made the
young man rise and embraced him. He ventured to invite
me to the wedding; I declined. I merely said that I would
be glad if he would come to supper at Momolo's on Sunday; it was the eve of his marriage. I asked Momolo to

arrange for Mariuccia and her father to be present too. I was sure I should see her Sunday morning. It would be for the last time.

It was seven o'clock when we met, and, having four hours before us, we went to bed. She began by telling me that everything had been arranged at her own house the day before, in the presence of her father, her fiancé, her confessor, the notary, and Momolo, who, having tendered the receipt from her fiancé's father, had included the garden in the contract for her dowry. She said further that her father confessor had found means to give her twenty scudi for the notary's fee and the expenses of the wedding.

"This evening," she said, "we shall sup together at Momolo's, and you did very well to arrange it. Nobody can say a word. My fiancé adores you. You did very well, too, to decline to come to my wedding at Trastevere.[35] The house would have been too poor for you, and the talk afterward would have made my future less happy."

"How will you manage if your husband takes it into his head to find fault with your physical condition, which he may expect to find intact?"

"My caresses, my sweetness, and my clear conscience, which do not even let me give it a thought, are my assurance that my husband will not think of it either."

"But if he brings it up?"

"It would hardly be tactful; but what is to keep me from answering, with all the sincerity of seeming innocence, that I don't know what he is talking about, that I have no knowledge of these things?"

Four hours passed very quickly. We parted, taking leave of love and shedding sweet tears.

After the Barbary horse race, which I attended with Mengs's family, who amused themselves throwing sweetmeats from a bag I had filled for them into the landaus we overtook, we went to the Teatro Aliberti, to which the castrato[36] who was playing the leading woman's part was drawing the entire city. He was the favorite of Cardinal Borghese, with whom he was invited to sup alone every evening.

The *virtuoso* sang very well, but his principal attraction was his beauty. I had seen him strolling at the Villa Medici, dressed in men's clothes, and though his face was handsome enough he had not made an impression on me, for one saw at once that he was not a whole man; but on the stage, dressed as a woman, he was a firebrand.

It would seem that a man dressed as a woman could not but be known for what he was if he let too much of his chest be seen; but it was precisely by so doing that the little monster bewitched everyone in the audience. Tightly laced in a very well-fitting corset, he had the figure of a nymph, and few women could show a firmer and more enticing bosom than his. The illusion he created was such that it was impossible to resist it. One looked, the spell acted, and one had either to fall in love or be the most stolid of all Germans. When he walked across the stage waiting for the *ritornello*[37] of the aria he was singing his gait was imposing, and when he swept his gaze over the boxes his black eyes revolved so tenderly and modestly that they ravished the soul. It was obvious that, as a man, he meant to foster the love of those who loved him as such and who would not have loved him if he had not been a man; but that he also meant to inspire love in those who, to love him, had to think of him as really a woman. Yet Rome, the Holy City, which thus drives the whole human race to become pederasts, refuses to admit it as she refuses to admit the existence of an illusion which she does everything possible to foster in the minds of audiences.

"You are right," replied a celebrated Monsignore of the wristband game[38] to put me off; "yes, you reason very soundly. Why do they allow this castrato to exhibit his beautiful breasts and at the same time insist that he be known to be a man and not a woman? And if women

are forbidden to appear on the stage[39] so that the senses
shall not be excited into becoming the victims of their
charms, why seek out men endowed with the same attrac-
tions who deceive and seduce the senses and give rise to
desires far more sinful than the natural desire aroused
by real women? It is stubbornly maintained that to suppose pederasty so easy and so common is to malign the
human race, and even that falling in love with these
artificial creatures is matter for laughter, because those
who do so are all bound to find they have been hoodwinked when it comes to conclusions; but would to God
that it were so! Far from feeling hoodwinked, they throw
themselves into the thing with gusto and even come to
take such pleasure in the subterfuge that a great many
people who are lacking neither in intellect nor in common
sense prefer these gentlemen to all the prettiest girls in
Rome.''

''The Pope would do well to put a stop to this practice.''

''I say no. One could not have a beautiful actress to
supper alone without causing a scandal; and one can
have a castrato to supper. It is true that afterward one
goes to bed with him; but no one is supposed to know
that; and if it becomes known no one can swear that
there has been any wrongdoing, for after all he is a man,
whereas one cannot go to bed with a woman except to
enjoy her.''

''True, Monsignore. The chief thing is to make certainty impossible, for well-bred people never pass judgment on uncertain grounds.''

Having seen the Marchesa Passarini,[40] whom I had met
in Dresden, in a box with His Highness Don Marcantonio
Borghese,[41] I went to make my bow to them. The Prince,
who had known me in Paris ten years earlier, invited me
to dine with him the next day. I went, and he was not
at home; I was told that I could dine even so, I left. On
the first day in Lent he sent me his valet with an invita-

tion to sup at the Marchesa's, whom he was keeping. I promised to go, and he waited for me in vain. Pride, the child of stupidity, never loses its mother's nature.

After the opera at the Aliberti I went to sup at Momolo's, where I saw Mariuccia with her father, her mother, and her fiancé. I was impatiently awaited. It is not difficult to make people happy if one confines one's efforts in that direction to those who deserve happiness. I supped delightfully in the company of these poor and honest people. It is possible that my satisfaction arose from my vanity, I knew that I was the author of the happiness and the joy I saw portrayed on the handsome faces of the bride and groom; but vanity itself must be held dear by him who, examining himself, finds that it has often been the cause of his doing good. After supper I made a small bank at faro, obliging everyone to play for counters, for none of them had a copper, and I saw to it that the bank was broken. After that we danced, despite the prohibition issued by the Pope, who believed that dancing was damnation and permitted gambling. His successor Ganganelli[42] did just the opposite. My present to the young couple was purposely small in order to avoid suspicion; I let them have my landau so that they could drive on the Corso and enjoy the Carnival, and I ordered Costa to take a box for them at the Teatro Capranica.[43]

Intending to leave Rome on the second day in Lent, I went to receive the Holy Father's blessing at twenty-two o'clock, just when the whole city was on the Corso. He received me most graciously. He said he was surprised I was not watching the great show with everyone else. He kept me for a good hour, talking of Venice and Padua, and when I again commended myself to his good offices in the matter of a pardon which would permit me to return to Venice, he told me to commend myself to God.

On the next day, which was the last day of the Carnival, I went to the Corso on horseback, dressed as Pulcinella,[44] throwing sweetmeats into all the landaus in which I saw children and finally emptying my basket on Momolo's daughters, whom I saw in my landau with Costa. Toward nightfall I went and took off my costume, then went to Momolo's, where I was to see Mariuccia for the last time. Our supper party was much the same as the one on the previous Sunday; but what was new to me, and very interesting, was that I saw Mariuccia married and that I thought her husband had a different attitude toward me from the one I had observed in him the first time I had seen him.

Wanting to know all, I found an opportunity to sit down beside Mariuccia at a time when we could talk freely. She gave me a detailed account of the whole of the first night, and she praised all her husband's excellent qualities. He was gentle, in love, even-tempered, and had become her fond friend after she had confided to him that I was her only benefactor.

"And he did not suspect," I asked, "a secret understanding between us and a few meetings?"

"Not in the least. I told him that what you had done to make me happy had been entirely through my confessor, after you had spoken with me only once in the church, where I had informed you of the good chance I had of being married to him."

"And you think he believed you?"

"I am sure of it; but even if he didn't, isn't it enough if he pretends to?"

"Certainly; I should even think more highly of him, for I would rather you were married to an intelligent man than to a fool."

This faithful narrative from Mariuccia's lips was the reason why, when I said good-by to the whole company, having to leave on the next day but one, I embraced the wigmaker, presenting him with my watch, and gave his wife a handsome ring of the same value. After that I went home to bed, telling Costa and Leduc that we would begin packing the next day.

But the next morning at nine o'clock I received a note from Lord Lismore, in which he asked me to go alone to the Villa Borghese[45] about noon to talk with him. Though I clearly foresaw what he would have to say to me, I went. I was in a position to give him some good advice, and my friendship for his mother made it my duty to go.

Since he was waiting for me where I could not fail to pass, he comes to meet me and hands me a letter from his mother, which he had received the day before and in which she told him that Pâris de Marmontel had just sent her a note saying that he had received a draft on her for two hundred thousand francs issued at Rome by him, which he would honor if she would be so good as to supply the funds. She had replied that she would let him know within three or four days if she could transfer the amount to him. She told her son that she had only asked for the delay to gain him time, which he should use to reach some place of safety, for he could be sure that his draft would be protested.

I hand him back her letter and tell him he must vanish.

"Give me the means, by buying this ring. You would not know that it does not belong to me if I had not told you so in confidence."

I arranged to meet him again at four o'clock, and I went to have the stone, which had been removed from the setting, appraised by one of the leading jewelers in Rome. After telling me that he knew the stone he declared it worth as much as two thousand Roman scudi. I took them to him, five hundred in gold and fifteen hundred in paper which he was to take to a banker who would give him a bill of exchange on Amsterdam for the amount in bank notes. He said that he would leave alone at nightfall and ride at full gallop to Leghorn, taking only a small courier's satchel with his absolute necessities and especially his precious blue ribbon. I wished him a good

journey and kept the stone, which I had set in Bologna
ten days later.

On the same day I obtained a letter of introduction
from Cardinal Francesco Albani[46] to Monsignor Onorati,
the Nuncio,[47] in Florence, and another from the painter
Mengs to the Chevalier Mann,[48] whom he asked to put
me up. I was going to Florence for La Corticelli and for
my dear Teresa, and I counted on the Auditor's pretending not to know that I had returned to Tuscany in spite
of the unjust order he had given me, and the more so
if the Chevalier Mann should be putting me up.

On the second day of Lent the news of Lord Lismore's
disappearance was the talk of the city. The English tailor
was ruined, the Jew who owned the ring in despair, and
all the scapegrace's wretched servants turned out into
the street almost naked, for the tailor had despotically
confiscated whatever he could lay his hands on, saying
that it must all be the property of the swindling Lord
who had ruined him.

The comic side of the tragedy was enacted for me by
Poinsinet, who appeared before me clad in a redingote
under which he had on nothing but his shirt. The host,
having seized everything he possessed, had threatened to
send him to prison when he had told him he was not in
His Lordship's service.

"I haven't a copper," he said, "or another shirt, I
know nobody, and I see nothing for it but to throw myself into the Tiber."

He was not destined to drown in the Tiber, but in the
Guadalquivir, in Spain. I lightened his despair by telling him that he was at liberty to come to Florence with
me, but no farther, for I had someone waiting for me in
Florence. So he stayed with me, sedulously composing
verses until the moment of my departure.

My dear brother Giovanni gave me a most beautiful
onyx. It was a cameo representing a bathing Venus in
bas-relief. It was a genuine antique, twenty-three cen-

turies old, for with a very strong lens one could read the name of the sculptor Sostratus.[49] I sold it two years later in London to Dr. Maty[50] for three hundred pounds sterling, and it may still be in the British Museum.

So I set off with Poinsinet, whose gloom kept me entertained with the most amusing ideas. On the next day but one I arrive in Florence, going directly to Vannini's, who makes an effort to conceal his surprise at seeing me. I at once wait on the Chevalier Mann, whom I find at table alone; he receives me cordially, reads Mengs's letter, and asks me if the matter between the Auditor and myself has been settled, I say it has not, and I see him look chagrined, he tells me frankly that he would compromise himself if he put me up, that I had been ill advised to return to Florence.

"I am only here in passing."

"That is all very well; but you must realize that you cannot avoid going to see the Auditor."

I promise him I will do so, and I go back to my inn. No sooner have I entered my room than a police officer comes to tell me that the Auditor wishes to speak with me and will expect me early the next morning. The order annoys me, and in my ill-humor I decide to leave rather than to obey a command which was an insult to me. With this idea in mind, I set out; I go to Teresa's, I am told that she has left for Pisa; I go to La Corticelli's, she falls on my neck and makes all the Bolognese grimaces appropriate to the occasion. It is a fact that, though she was pretty enough, the only real attraction the girl had for me was that she made me laugh.

I give her mother money, ordering her to make us a good supper, and I go out with the girl, telling her that we will take a walk. I escort her to my inn, I leave her with Poinsinet, then I call Costa and the innkeeper into the other room. In his presence I order Costa to leave the next morning with Leduc and all my effects and to come to Bologna, where he will find me lodged at the

"Pilgrim." [51] The innkeeper departs. I then order Costa
to leave Florence with Signora Laura and her son, telling
her, as was true, that I had gone ahead with her daughter; I tell Leduc the same. After that I take Poinsinet
aside and give him ten zecchini, asking him to find lodgings elsewhere. He weeps with gratitude and tells me
that he will leave on foot the next morning for Parma,
where he is sure that Monsieur Dutillot[52] will not leave
him without succor.

I go back to the room in which La Corticelli was, I tell
her to come with me; she thinks we are going back to her
mother's; but, without enlightening her, I go to the post
station, I have two horses harnessed to a chaise, and I
order the postilion to drive to L'Uccellatoio,[53] the first
post station on the road to Bologna.

"But where are we going?" she asks me.

"To Bologna."

"And Mama?"

"She will come tomorrow."

"Does she know it?"

"No; but she'll know it tomorrow when Costa tells her
and takes her and all my luggage with him."

La Corticelli declares it an excellent joke, she laughs,
and we set off.

*I arrive in Bologna. I am expelled from Mo-
dena. I go to Parma and to Turin. The beautiful Jewess Leah. The milliner R.*

LA CORTICELLI had a mantle well lined with
fur, but the fool who was carrying her off did not have
even a cloak. The wind was very cold; nevertheless I
would not stop. I was afraid of being followed and forced
to return, which would have caused me the keenest mortification. A scudo which I gave the postilion to drink
my health induced him to go at full gallop. I thought the
wind would blow me away on the crest of the Apennines;
but nothing could stop me for more than the three or
four minutes required to change horses. The postilions
thought I was a prince abducting the girl who was with
me. The idea of being taken for the heroine of an ab-
duction made the little madcap laugh at the top of her
lungs for all the five hours it took us to make forty miles.
We left Florence at eight, and I did not stop until an
hour after midnight at a post station in Papal territory,
where I had nothing more to fear. The name of the station was "The Ass Unloads";[2] the name set my feather-

brained companion laughing, and we went upstairs. The whole household was asleep, but the racket I made and three or four paoli which I at once distributed among the servants got me a fire lighted and set everyone scurrying to prepare a repast of some sort. We were dying of hunger and cold. The innkeeper told us there was nothing to eat, but I laughed at him; he had butter, eggs, macaroni, rice, Parmesan cheese, bread, and good wine; and the idiot did not see that we had the ingredients for an excellent meal. I got my way; and I had a bed made up which astonished the innkeeper, for I had insisted that all the bed furniture from four others should be used in making it up. La Corticelli, who was eating like a madwoman, suddenly said, "What will Mama say?" and burst into such hysterical laughter that she seemed on the verge of expiring.

We went to bed at four o'clock in the morning after ordering that we be waked when a four-horse English carriage[3] arrived. Stuffed with macaroni as we were, and tipsy from Chianti and Montepulciano,[4] we did not feel like making love, and when we woke what sports we indulged in amounted to very little. It was an hour after noon; we were ready to eat; and the innkeeper, following my instructions, gave us a very good meal. But when I saw darkness fall without having seen my carriage arrive I began to wonder what could have happened; however, La Corticelli refused to hear of anything untoward. I went to bed after supper, having decided to send the post master's son to Florence if my party did not arrive during the night. They did not arrive, and I dispatched an express messenger to Costa to learn what had happened; for if there had been violence of any kind I would have gone back to Florence myself, despite La Corticelli, who would have been very averse to returning.

The messenger I sent left at noon and came back at two o'clock to tell me that my party would arrive in less than an hour. My carriage was being drawn by horses supplied by a *vetturino,* and was followed by a two-horse calèche in which there were an old woman and a boy.

"It's Mama!" said La Corticelli, "Oh, how we'll laugh! We must have a good meal got ready for her and let her tell her whole amazing story, which she will remember to her dying day."

Costa told me that he had been delayed for twenty-four hours because the Auditor, to avenge himself for my having disregarded his order, had sent word to the post station to refuse my servants horses, but that a certain Agresti, who was not subject to the order, had given him horses, undertaking to get him to Bologna in two days and a half. But here is the discourse delivered by Signora Laura, which rejoiced her daughter's soul:

"I got supper ready, as you ordered me, and I spent more than ten paoli, as you will see, and which you will repay me, for I'm a poor woman; but just think how anxious I was when I saw hour after hour pass and never saw you come back. At midnight I sent my son to Vannini's to find out what had become of you, and imagine my grief—for I'm a mother—when my son came back and said no one at your inn knew anything about you. I spent the night without ever going to bed, and in the morning I went to the authorities and complained that you'd carried off my daughter and demanded that they send someone after you to make you bring her back; but think of it! they laughed at me and told me I shouldn't let her leave my house with you unless I went with her too. What slander!"

"Slander," said La Corticelli.

"Certainly, for it was as much as to tell me that I had consented to my daughter's being carried off, which those vermin had no reason to suppose, because if I'd consented to it I wouldn't have gone to them for justice. After that I went to Doctor Vannini's, where I found your valet, who assured me you'd gone to Bologna, where I'd find you if I'd follow your carriage, and you'll pay for it,

I hope, for that's what I arranged with the *vetturino*. But let me tell you: what you've done is too much for a joke.''

I consoled her by assuring her that I would pay for everything. We left the next morning, and we arrived in good time at Bologna, where I went to stay at La Corticelli's, sending my valets to an inn from which I had meals brought in for the whole family. I spent a week there, in the course of which my madcap mistress, who knew a quantity of girls as giddy as herself, procured me pleasures so delicious that I sigh every time I recall them to my aging memory. There are cities in Italy where one can procure all the pleasures which a sensual man finds in Bologna; but they are nowhere to be had so cheaply or so easily or so freely. In addition, one eats and drinks very well there, one strolls under the arcades, and one finds not only wits but men of learning in the sciences. It is a pity that—whether because of the air or the water or the wine—one contracts a slight case of the itch, which gives the Bolognese the pleasure of scratching, and that is not so trifling a pleasure as one might think when the itching is not too intense. Especially during the month of March the ladies use their fingers with enchanting grace to scratch their hands.

I left La Corticelli about the middle of Lent, wishing her a good journey too, for she was about to go to Prague, where she had been engaged for a year as second ballerina. I promised I would go to fetch her in person and take her to Paris with her mother. The reader will see how I kept my word.

It was sheer whim which led me to stay in Modena, which I reached the same day. The next morning I go out to see paintings, I return for dinner, and I find a boor awaiting me with an order from the government to continue my journey at latest the next day. I call the innkeeper, and I make him repeat the order in his presence. I told him I had understood. He goes.

"Who is that man?" I ask the innkeeper.

"A constable."

"And the government sends me a constable?"

"The person who sent him can be no one but the Bargello."[5]

"Then is the Bargello the Governor of Modena? The low scoundrel!"

"Low scoundrel! Don't let anyone hear you. All the aristocrats speak to him. He manages the opera;[6] the greatest noblemen eat at his table and so gain his good will."

"But why does this noble Bargello expel me from Modena?"

"I have no idea. Go and talk with him. You will find a man of parts."

Instead of going to see the blackguard,[7] I go to see the Abate Testagrossa;[8] still alive and then resting on his laurels, he was a man who, despite his humble birth, had distinguished himself by his intelligence and whom his master the Duke of Modena[9] had judged worthy to conduct political negotiations for him at several courts. This Abate, who had made my acquaintance in Vienna in 1753, after greeting me most graciously, was greatly annoyed to hear what had just befallen me.

"What can I do?" I ask him.

"Leave, for the man is capable of treating you even more insultingly."

"I will leave. But could you do me the favor of acquainting me with the reason for this strange proceeding?"

"Come back this evening."

That evening the Abate told me that the Bargello, as soon as he had seen my name in the register, had guessed that I was the same Casanova who had escaped from the Leads, and, one of his duties being to guard the city against suspicious persons, he hastened to order me to leave.

"I am surprised," I said, "that, telling me this, you do not feel ashamed for the Duke of Modena. What an outrage! What deliberate subversion of morality and even of the good of the State!"

The next morning, just before I get into my carriage, a tall, robust man between twenty-five and thirty years of age, with the look of a cutthroat, asks me for a word in private.

"If you will stop in Parma for only three days," he says, "and will now promise on your honor that you will give me fifty zecchini when I come to ask you for them and you have learned for a certainty that the Bargello has been killed, I promise to kill him myself by blowing out his brains with my carbine tonight."

"I thank you," I said, "and I beg you to let him die his natural death. Here is a scudo; go and drink my health."

It is certain that if I had been sure the villain was not setting a trap for me I should have given him the promise he asked for; but I feared a plot. I reached Parma the next day and put up at the post station inn, giving the name of Chevalier de Seingalt, which I still bear; for once a man of honor takes a name to which no one else can lay claim it is his duty to keep it. I had then borne it for two years,[10] though I often added it to my family name.

I had scarcely reached Parma before I dismissed Costa; but a week later, the day before my departure, I took him back. His father, a violinist and very poor, had a large family to provide for.

I inquired for Monsieur d'Antoine,[11] and he was no longer there; and the Director of the Mint, Dubois-Chatellerault,[12] was in Venice. He was there by permission of the Infant-Duke, to set up a coining press,[13] and he did it very well; but it was not used. Venetian coins are not milled. Republics are superstitiously attached to their old ways; they fear that the slightest change of any kind is likely, or indeed is bound, to have an effect on the constitution which will be detrimental to the State. *Ne tangas Camerinam* ("Touch not Camerina").[14] The Venetian government is still as rigidly Greek[15] in spirit as it was at the birth of the Republic.

My Spaniard, who was delighted when I dismissed Costa on arriving in Parma, was annoyed when I took him back.

"He is no profligate," he said, "he is sober, he does not frequent bad company; but I believe he is a thief precisely because he makes a point of not cheating you in small matters. You will be his victim. He's waiting to gain your entire confidence before he makes his move. That's not my way; I'm a bit of a cheat, but you know me."

The rascal saw better than I did. Five or six months later Costa stole fifty thousand scudi from me. Twenty-three years later—that is, in 1784—I found him in Vienna as valet to Count Hardegg,[16] and, finding him poor, I was tempted to get him hanged. I proved to him, documents in hand, that I could do it. At that he took refuge in tears and in the pity of an honest man named Bertrand who was in the household of the Sardinian Ambassador. This Bertrand, whom I esteemed, so worked on me that I heroically pardoned him. When I asked the wretch what he had done with all he had stolen from me in money and jewels he said he had lost it all by furnishing the funds for a *biribissi*,[17] that it had been his own associates who had cleaned him out. In that same year he had married Momolo's daughter, who had left him very soon afterward.

But to continue.

At Turin I went to lodge in a private house in which the Abate Gama, who was expecting me, was staying. I took the whole apartment on the second floor, laughing at the sermon on economy which he immediately preached me. Having assured him again that I would be ready to go to Augsburg whenever the representatives of the belligerent powers had assembled there, he assured me, on his side, that I would receive credentials in May and that he himself would give me all the necessary instructions. I was supremely gratified by this mission.

After making adequate arrangements with the mistress of the house for my meals I went to the coffeehouse, where the first person I saw was the self-styled Marquis Desarmoises, whose acquaintance I had made at Aix-en-Savoie. The first thing he told me was that games of chance were forbidden and that the ladies I had met at Aix would undoubtedly be delighted to see me again. As for himself, he said that he lived by playing backgammon, despite his not being lucky with dice, for in backgammon knowledge of the game outweighed bad luck. I could well understand that, with luck favoring neither player, the one who knew the game better would win, but I did not understand how the opposite case was possible.

We went to walk on the beautiful promenade leading to the citadel,[18] where I saw a quantity of pretty girls. Turin is the city of Italy in which the sex has all the charms for which love can hope, but in which the police are the most troublesome; and, the city being small and very populous, the spies know everything; it follows that the only freedom one can enjoy there is that which one obtains by taking the greatest precautions and employing the services of clever bawds, whom one must pay very well, for, if they are caught, they risk being punished with a severity nothing short of barbarous. Neither public prostitutes nor kept women are allowed there, which is most gratifying to the married women, as the ignorant police should have foreseen. For the same reason the devotees of the wristband game[19] make holiday there.

Among the beauties I see, only one impresses me so much that I ask about her. Desarmoises knew them all. He said that she was the famous Leah,[20] a Jewess and unconquerable, having resisted the attacks of the most celebrated amateurs of the sex in Turin; that, her father being a horse dealer, there was no difficulty in going to her house, but that there was nothing to be done there. I determine to take my chances, and he promises he will guide me to her house. I invite him to dine with me; on our way we encounter Monsieur Z.[21] and two or three more of the people who had been at Aix, I bestow and receive compliments, but I am not of a mind to call on any of them or even to leave a visiting card at the Marquis de Prié's[22] door.

Immediately after dinner he shows me the way to the Jewish horse dealer's outside the Porta del Po.[23] I ask him if he has a good saddle horse for sale; he sends a boy to the stable to bring one out; meanwhile, into the courtyard comes his charming daughter to receive compliments on her charms. I find her beyond praise. Slender, at most twenty-two years of age, dressed tastefully but without affectation, wearing no cap over hair whose blackness was just softened by a touch of powder, complexion of lilies and roses, lively and eloquent eyes which, under proud brows, declared war on all who came to conquer them. Her whole appearance betokened intelligence and social grace. Lost in ecstatic contemplation, I did not see the horse in front of me. Though my thoughts are elsewhere, I manage to examine it, looking at all its points as if I am an expert, I open its mouth, I inspect its feet and knees, I give it a sudden blow on the back, I feel its ears, I make it walk, trot, and gallop, and I tell the Jew that I will come the next day in top boots to ride it. It was a dapple gray, and priced at forty Piedmontese pistole, which comes to about a hundred zecchini. The beautiful Leah tells me that the horse is gentleness itself and that its amble is as fast as any other horse's trot.

"I have tried it several times," she says, "and if I were rich it would be mine."

"Then you would both be happy, for I am sure that it has loved you ever since you rode it. I will not buy it until I see you on its back."

She blushes, her father says she must do me the favor; she consents; I promise I will be there at nine o'clock in the morning.

I keep my word, and I find her dressed in riding clothes. What a body! What a likeness to the Callipygian Venus[24] in her hips, her thighs, her knees! I had already fallen under the spell. She mounts like the most nimble Spaniard, and I mount another horse which is standing ready for me. I accompany her everywhere, the horse went very well, but my thoughts were all of her. Returning to the house at a walk I tell her that I will buy the horse, but as a present for her, and that if she will not accept it she shall not see me again. The only condition I make is that she will ride it in the morning whenever I ask her to do me the favor. I say that I will stay in Turin five or six weeks, that I had fallen in love with her on the promenade, and that buying the horse had been only a pretext for gaining the sweet satisfaction of seeing her and declaring my passion. She replies, very sensibly, that the friendship she had inspired in me was infinitely flattering and that the generous present I was making her was not necessary to assure me of her own. That the condition I imposed on her was one which she cherished and that she would take pleasure in accepting the present I offered her even if she were not sure that her father would be displeased if she refused it; she ended by asking me to give her the horse in her father's presence, repeating my stipulation that I would not buy it if she refused it.

This I proceeded to do. Her father, whose name was Moses, thought it an excellent bargain, he congratulated his daughter, accepted, tendered me a receipt for the forty pistole I gave him, and invited me to breakfast with him on the following day.

The next morning Moses received me with the utmost respect. The charming Leah, in female attire, said that if I wanted to ride she would quickly dress as she had done the day before, and I replied that we would ride another day; but her father, who was always thinking of money, said that if I liked driving he could sell me a very pretty phaeton with two excellent horses. His daughter said he should show them to me, and he went off to order the horses harnessed.

"I will look at the carriage," I said to Leah, "but I will not buy it, for I have no use for it."

"You could go driving with the lady whom you love."

"With you. But perhaps you would not dare."

"Why not, in the country, outside of Turin?"

"Very well, I will look at it."

Her father drives up in the phaeton, I go downstairs with Leah, and I look at the carriage and the horses; I find them very attractive.

"You can have the whole rig for only four hundred zecchini; after Easter anyone who wants it will have to give me five hundred for it."

We get in with Leah, we drive a mile and return to the house. I tell Moses I will give him my answer the next day; he leaves, and I go upstairs again with Leah.

"The rig," I say, "is certainly worth four hundred zecchini, and tomorrow I will pay them with pleasure; but on the same conditions on which I bought the horse, and with one more—that you will grant me all the favors which are granted to love."

"You speak very clearly. I reply no less clearly. I am a decent girl and I am not for sale."

"Permit me to tell you, my beautiful Leah, that all women, decent or not, are for sale. When a man has the time, he buys them with his attentions, and when he is in a hurry, as I am, he has recourse to presents and money."

"Then he takes the wrong course; he would do better to inspire love by the assiduity of his attentions."

"Nothing would make me happier; but, I repeat, I am in a hurry."

Her father comes back, and a moment later I leave, saying that if I could not return on the morrow I would come some other day and we would talk about the phaeton.

It was clear that Leah had taken me for a spendthrift ready to become her dupe. She would have liked to get the phaeton on the same terms on which she had got the horse. For my part, I had been prepared to lose a hundred zecchini; but that must suffice. My course must be to suspend my visits and see what would result between Leah and her father, who, with his love of money, must be very much displeased that she had not found some way to make me buy the phaeton, whether by giving or not giving herself to me, for that could not matter to him. I was sure that in the end I should see them come to me.

It was on Saturday that I saw the beautiful Jewess on the promenade at the citadel.

"We see nothing more of you," she said; "either come to breakfast with me tomorrow morning or I will send you the horse."

I promised I would come, and I kept my word. She had me breakfast with her aunt, who was there only for propriety's sake, and after breakfast she put on riding clothes in my presence, but with her aunt still there. She stepped out of her skirt, under which she already had breeches, then took off her corset and put on a jacket, letting me see what I pretended not to see; but she knew what she was about. She asked me to arrange her jabot, and in doing so I touched what had previously engaged only my sight. I knew that she had a plan, and that my success depended entirely on foiling it. I had hopes of victory.

Her father arrived just as we were mounting; he said that if I would buy the phaeton and the horses he would let me have them for twenty zecchini less. I replied that it lay with his daughter to make me do whatever she pleased when we came back from our ride.

We set off at a walk, and she says that, having told her father that she could make me buy the carriage and horses, I ought to buy them so that he would not be angry with her.

"Buy them," she says, "on the understanding that you will not give them to me until you are sure that I love you. I promise we will go driving alone together whenever you please, so long as we do not get out anywhere; but I think you no longer care about that, your affection was only a passing fancy."

"To convince you that mine was not a passing fancy, I will buy the phaeton and have it put in a coach house in Turin and I will keep the horses in a stable and not use them; but if you do not make me happy within a week I will sell them."

"Come tomorrow." [25]

"I will come, but I want a pledge of your affection this morning."

"This morning? I couldn't."

"I will go upstairs with you; and when you change your clothes you can grant me some favors."

Back at the house, we get out, and she astonishes me by telling her father that the phaeton is mine and he has only to have the horses harnessed. The Jew laughs, he goes up with us, and Leah confidently tells me to count out the money.

"I haven't it on me, but I can give you a note."

"Here are pen and paper."

I immediately write the banker Zappata to pay 380 zecchini at sight. The Jew leaves to collect them, and Leah remains alone with me.

"By your trust in me," she says, "you have rendered yourself worthy of my heart."

"Then quick—get undressed."

"No. My aunt is in the house, she might come in, and I daren't lock the door. You shall be content with me tomorrow. But now I'm going to undress; so you go into that closet. You shall come out as soon as I am in women's clothes again."

I consent, and she locks me in. Looking at the door from bottom to top, I see a crack high up between the two leaves, I get on a stool, and I see the whole room, and Leah sitting before me on a sofa and immediately beginning to undress. She changed her shift, took off her shoes and stockings, wiped her feet, examined a toenail, took down her breeches, a button dropped off, and she bent to get it from under the sofa; there was no end to the postures in which she exhibited herself, and I felt certain she knew I was at the crack. I could not refrain from masturbating.

When she was dressed she opened the door; I fall on her neck, I tell her I have seen everything, she will not admit it, I try to enforce my rights, she resists, and in comes her father, thanking me and saying that his house and everything in it are at my service, after which he gives me a receipt for 380 zecchini. I leave thoroughly vexed, and I return to my lodging in the Via Po[26] in the phaeton. I put it in my coach house, and I send the horses to a stable, keeping the coachman. I was of a mind not to see Leah again. She had pleased me in her postures, but the pleasure she had given me had arisen entirely from an irritation which Love could not but abhor. She had forced him to be a thief, and the starving child had given in; but when afterward he thought he had the right to demand the same fare freely given and was refused it, scorn took the place of esteem. Leah would not admit that she was a whore, and my love would not consent to be a cheat.

I made the acquaintance of an amiable Chevalier, a man of letters, a soldier, and a great lover of horses, whose only fault was horse-faking. He introduced me to several families of consequence; but I did not cultivate them; for I had no wish to be drawn into the sentimental relationships which were all that they offered; what I wanted was substantial pleasures, for which I was willing to pay cash. The Chevalier de Brézé[27] was not the man I needed. He bought my phaeton and the horses for thirty zecchini less than I had paid for them, and he left for the country. A Signor Baretti,[28] who had known me at Aix-en-Savoie and who acted as croupier for the Marquis de Prié, took me to call on La Mazzoli,[29] a former dancer, then being kept by the Cavaliere Raiberti,[30] a cold, very gentlemanly personage who directed the Department of Foreign Affairs. La Mazzoli, who was not pretty, had several girls come to her house for me, but I did not find any of them worthy to take the place of Leah, whom I thought I no longer loved. I was mistaken.

The Cavaliere Coconà,[31] who had the pox at the time, offered me his mistress; she was a seamstress, whom, despite all she said to me, I never dared to touch. After a week I stopped seeing her. His brother Count Trana, whom I had also known at Aix, introduced me to Signora Sc.,[32] who tried to inveigle me into committing a crime. My Good Genius kept me from it. Count Trana cleared himself. Not long afterward his uncle died and he became rich. He married and was unhappy.

I was bored; and Desarmoises, who regularly ate at my table, became uneasy. I was thinking of going to Milan. He advised me to make the acquaintance of a French milliner, of some celebrity in Turin, known as ''La R.'' [33] She employed seven or eight girls, who sewed for her in a room next to her shop. He thought that, if I went about it in the right way, I could get one of them. Since I had money I did not think it would be difficult. I went to La R.'s shop to buy some black blond-lace which

I wanted to send to Venice. On entering I was surprised to see Leah, who was bargaining for a number of things she had chosen and which she protested were too dear. She said, reproachfully but kindly, that she had thought I must be ill; I replied that I had been busy. She attracted me. I told her she would see me the next day. She invited me to a Jewish wedding party, at which, she said, I would find a large crowd. I knew that it would be entertaining, and I promised to go. After bargaining for a long time without coming to terms, Leah left, and La R. was going to put away all the gewgaws at which she had been looking, when I said that I would buy them myself. She smiled, I paid her, and she asked me where I was staying and at what time she should send me my purchases.

"You might do me the honor, Signora, of coming to breakfast with me tomorrow morning and bringing them yourself."

"I cannot leave my shop, Signore."

"Then by whom will you send them?"

Despite her thirty-five years, La R. attracted me. I told her that I wanted some black blond-lace. She opened a door and asked me to follow her. I was surprised to see seven or eight girls, all of them pretty, so busy working that they scarcely looked at me. La R. opens several cupboards and takes out magnificent lengths of blond-lace. With my eyes and my attention on the girls, I said that I wanted enough to make two Venetian *bautte*.[34] She knew what they were. In Venice they were the height of luxury. The lace cost me more than a hundred zecchini. She told two of her girls to take it to me the next day together with all the things which Leah had refused and I had bought.

"Yes, Mama."

They rise, and I find them charming. I go back to her shop with La R. and, sitting down at her counter, I praise the beauty of her apprentices, but I say—which was not true—that I would have preferred her to any of them. She declines my proffered homage, saying frankly that she has a lover, and an instant later she tells me he is at the door.

In comes the Comte de Saint-Gilles.[35] He was an old man who could no longer make any possible pretensions to gallantry. I thought that La R. had been trying to hoodwink me; but the next day I learned that she had told me the unvarnished truth. I had met him at the "Change"[36] coffeehouse; I left him with his fair one after making him a bow.

The next morning the pretty girls came, and I ordered chocolate, but they refused it. After giving me my purchases they were about to leave; but I suddenly thought of telling them to take Leah all the things she had chosen and to come back afterward and tell me how she had received the gift. They agreed to do so and waited while I wrote her a note. I could not give the two girls the slightest indication of my affection, for I had not dared to shut my door and the mistress of the house and her ugly daughters found a hundred excuses for constantly coming and going. But when they returned I waited for them at the foot of the stairs, and after giving them a gold pistole[37] I told them they had only to say the word and it was in their power to make my heart theirs. They said that Leah had graciously accepted my handsome present and that she was expecting me.

In the afternoon I pass La R.'s shop, she is alone, she calls to me, and I am glad to go and sit at her counter. She thanked me for my generosity to her girls, and she asks me if I am very much in love with the beautiful Jewess. I tell her frankly that I love her but that, having had no success, I had acted accordingly; she congratulates me, saying that she is nothing but a cheat whose only thought was to fleece the men who were taken with her charms.

"Perhaps that is also the principle of your charming girls."

"My girls are accommodating only when I tell them that they may be so."

"Then I commend myself to your kind offices, for they would not accept even a cup of chocolate from me."

"Their behavior is forced on them; you do not know Turin. Are your lodgings satisfactory?"

"They are excellent."

"Are you perfectly free there? Can you have anyone you choose to supper and do anything you like in your rooms? I am sure you cannot."

"So far I have had no occasion to try it; but I believe—"

"Do not deceive yourself. Everyone in the house is a spy for the police."

"Then you think I could not ask you to supper with one or two of your apprentices?"

"I should take good care not to go. The whole of Turin would know of it, and people would say what was not true."

"And if I went to lodge elsewhere?"

"It is the same everywhere; but I know a house in which you could live as you choose and to which my girls, if proper precautions were taken, could even come to bring you anything you might buy at my shop."

"Where is the house? I will do whatever you tell me to do."

After saying that I must not confide in any Piedmontese, she gave me the address of a small furnished house in which no one lived except the old caretaker and his wife. She said that I could rent it by the month, and that if I paid in advance no one would even ask my name. The house was some two hundred paces from the citadel, the last in an unfrequented street, with a back gate which gave onto the countryside and which I could even enter by carriage.

I went there at once; I found it answered her description in every detail, I rented it for a month, and the very next night I slept there. La R. admired my dispatch.

The next day I went to the wedding to which Leah had invited me, and which I found entertaining; but I resisted all the arts with which she tried to lure me back into her toils. However, I rented a closed carriage from her father, having it sent to my house and putting the horses in my stable; I was thus able to go wherever I pleased and enter and leave at any hour. It was just as if I were outside the city. I had to give the address of my new lodging to the ever too curious Abate Gama, and I thought I had good reason to hide nothing from Desarmoises, whom his poverty made completely dependent on me; nevertheless my door was closed to everyone except when I ordered it opened to people whom I expected. I could not doubt the fidelity of Costa and my Spaniard.

In that auspicious house I had, one by one, but always accompanied by another, all of La R.'s girls, the last of whom, whose name was Vittorina, was obstructed and did not know it. La R., who did not know it either, had given her to me as a virgin, and I was forced to believe her such for the two hours during which I hoped for victory; but finally, exhausted by my efforts, I decided to see what was the matter, candle in hand. I saw the fleshy membrane pierced by a hole so small that the head of a pin would scarcely pass through it. Vittorina herself urged me to put my little finger in by force, but to no purpose. The attempt caused her not the slightest pain, but what was in the way was only flesh. It was the outer extremity of her vagina, which nature by the purest chance had made impenetrable in her case. It condemned Vittorina to die a virgin unless some skillful surgeon performed the celebrated operation on her—the same one which was performed on Signorina Cherufini[38] soon after Signor Lepri[39] married her.

"Your little god Hymen," I said "defies the most vigorous Love to seat himself on his altar."

The poor girl wept.

When I told La R. the story she laughed and said that it could make Vittorina's fortune. It was Count de La Pérouse[40] who had Vittorina's obstruction removed some years later. When I came back from Spain I saw her pregnant.

Early in the morning on Maundy Thursday Moses and his daughter Leah came to see me. I was not expecting them. I greeted them cordially. They did not dare appear in Turin during our holy days. I advised them to spend them with me, and I realized that I should have no great difficulty in persuading them when I saw the scoundrel show me a ring he wanted to sell me. I said that I might buy it from his daughter, and he hoped that I would make her a present of it, but I disappointed him. I kept them for dinner and supper, and I gave them a room with two beds, in which they slept very comfortably.

The next morning, seeing that I had not yet bought the ring and having business, he asked me to let him use my carriage all day, saying that he would come back toward nightfall, at the beginning of his Sabbath, to go home with his daughter. After he left I bought the ring for six hundred zecchini, but on the conditions I laid down, and, being in my house, Leah could not cheat me. She refused me nothing; and in the evening her father was as pleased as I was—but not Leah, who expected that when she left I would give her a present. I told her that I would take it to her in person.

On Easter Monday a man brought me a note summoning me to the police office.

Entrance Hall of the
Palazzo dei Conservatori, Rome

At the Grating in a Nunnery

*My victory over the Vicario, the Superintend-
ent of Police. My departure. Chambéry. Desarmoises's daughter. Monsieur Morin. M. M.
of Aix. The boarder. Lyons. Paris.*

SURPRISED BY such a summons, which promised
me nothing pleasant, I dress and go by sedan chair to the
office of the Vicario.[2] He was seated at a large table,
with eighteen or twenty people standing about him. He
was a man sixty years of age, with half of his nose concealed by a black patch because of a malignant ulcer.

"I have had you summoned here," he said, "to order
you to leave[3] in three days at the latest."

"You have no right, Signore, to give me such an order;
so I will not leave until it suits me."

"I will have you expelled by force."

"Indeed! I cannot resist force; but I hope you will
think it over, for in a well-governed city it is unheard
of to expel a man who is doing nothing illegal and who
has a hundred thousand francs in the hands of a banker."

"So much the better. In three days you can pack and
make arrangements with your banker. I advise you to
obey: the order comes from the King."[4]

"If I left I should become an accomplice in your injustice; but since you speak in the King's name I will instantly wait on His Majesty. I am sure that he will revoke the unjust order which you have so publicly given me."

"Has not the King power to make you leave?"

"Yes, but only by using force if I resist. He also has the power to sentence me to death, but he has to supply the executioner to carry out the sentence on me."

I had met the Cavaliere Raiberti at the house of a dancer he was keeping; he was the First Secretary in the Department of Foreign Affairs. I have myself carried to his office,[5] and I tell him the whole story, ending by saying that I must have an audience with the King, for I had made up my mind I would not leave of my own free will. The worthy man advises me to go instead to speak with the Cavalier Ossorio,[6] who was then in charge of Foreign Affairs and who had the King's ear. I like his advice, and I at once wait on the Marchese Ossorio; he was a highly intelligent Sicilian. After telling him all the circumstances, I ask him to bring the matter to His Majesty's attention, since, considering the Vicario's order unjust, I was determined not to leave. He promised he would speak to the King and told me to come back the next day.

I went to dine with the Abate Gama, thinking that I would be the first to bring him the news. But not a bit of it: he knew that I had been ordered to leave and how I had answered the Vicario, and when I told him that I was still determined not to obey he did not dare to condemn my firmness. He assured me that, if I left, he would send me all the necessary instructions at whatever address I should give him.

The Cavalier Ossorio received me the next morning in the most affable manner. The Cavaliere Raiberti had spoken to him on my behalf. He said that he had spoken to the King and to Count d'Aglié[7] as well, and that I could stay; but that I must go at once to speak further with the latter, who would give me what time I might need to finish my business in Turin.

"I am waiting," I said, "for instructions from the Court of Portugal for the Congress to be held in Augsburg, which I shall attend."

"Then you believe that the Congress will be held?"

"No one doubts it."

"There are those who believe it will come to nothing. I am delighted to have been of service to you, and I shall be glad to hear how the Vicario receives you."

So I go to the Vicario, who no sooner sees me than he says that the Cavalier Ossorio had told him I had business which obliged me to remain in Turin a few more days, and so I might stay.

"But no doubt you can tell me approximately how many days you will need."

"I have no way of knowing precisely, for I am awaiting instructions from the Court of Portugal in regard to the Congress which is to be held at Augsburg. I think I might leave for Paris in a month; and if I am delayed longer than that I will do myself the honor of informing you."

"I shall be glad if you will."

I at once went back to the Cavalier Ossorio, who said with a smile that I had caught the Vicario, for I had set an indefinite time. But what a titbit it was for the politic Gama when I told him that the Cavalier Ossorio doubted if the Congress would be held! Nevertheless, I again assured him that I would go to Augsburg and that I would leave in three or four weeks.

La R. lavished congratulations on me, for she could not but be delighted that I had humiliated the Vicario; but we thought it best to give up the little suppers with her girls at my house. Having already had them all, I did not find this small sacrifice too painful. I continued in this course until the middle of May, when I left Turin after receiving from the Abate Gama a letter for Lord Stormont,[8] who was to be the Plenipotentiary for England at Augsburg. It was with him that I was to work in the matter of my mission.

Having decided to see Madame d'Urfé before going to Germany, I wrote to her asking her to send me a letter to Monsieur de Rochebaron,[9] at Lyons, which I might have occasion to use. Intending also to stop at Chambéry for three or four days to pay a visit at the convent grating to M. M., for whom I sighed every time I remembered her, I asked Signor Raiberti for a letter for that city; and I wrote to my friend Valenglart at Grenoble to remind Madame Morin that she had promised to show me a resemblance at Chambéry.[10]

But now for another inauspicious event, considering the very harmful consequences it had for me.

Five or six days before I left Turin, I see Desarmoises appear before me at ten o'clock in the morning, looking very downcast.

"I have just received an order," he said, "to leave Turin within twenty-four hours."

"Do you know the reason for it?"

"It is because yesterday at the Caffè del Commercio[11] I contradicted Count Scarnafigi[12] when he said that the writer of the *Gazette de Berne* was in the pay of France; he left the place in a rage, I followed him to make him listen to reason, but in vain; he apparently lodged a complaint, and tomorrow early I shall have to decamp."

"You are French, and since you can claim the protection of the Ambassador,[13] you would make a mistake in leaving so precipitately."

"In the first place the Ambassador is away, and in the second place my barbarous father disowns me. I would rather leave. I will wait for you in Lyons. I only ask you to lend me another hundred scudi, which I will repay you."

I gave him the small amount, and he left the next day

at dawn. I told him that I would stop for some days in Chambéry.

After obtaining a letter of credit on Augsburg I left, and the next day I crossed the Mont Cenis on mules—I, Costa, Leduc, and my carriage. Three days later I reached Chambéry, putting up at the only inn,[14] where all travelers are obliged to lodge.

Seeing a very pretty young lady come out of the room next to mine, I ask the maid who she is, and she says she is the wife of a young man who was staying in bed recovering from a sword thrust he had received four days before on his way from France.

Leaving my room to go to the post station for the letter Valenglart was to have written me, I stop before my neighbor's, the door of which was open, and offer her my services as her fellow lodger; she asks me to come in; I see a handsome young man sitting up in bed, and I ask him how he feels. His wife tells me that the surgeon had forbidden him to talk because of a sword thrust in the chest which he had received half a league away on the road from France, that he hoped to be cured in a few days and continue his journey to Geneva. Just as I am about to leave, the maid comes in and asks me if I will sup alone in my room or with Madame. I reply, laughing at her blunder, that I will sup in my room, that I have not the pleasure of the lady's acquaintance; the latter replies that it would be an honor and a pleasure if I would sup with her, and her husband says the same in a whisper; so I say that I will gladly avail myself of his kindness. Whether she was married or unmarried, she was charming. When I found her escorting me to the stairs I took the liberty of kissing her hand, which in France is a tender yet at the same time respectful declaration of love.

I hurry to the post station, and I find two letters, one from Valenglart telling me that Madame Morin would come to Chambéry if I would send a carriage for her. I open the other letter, and I see that it is signed Desarmoises. He wrote me from Lyons. He said that on his way from Chambéry he had met his daughter in a carriage with "a scoundrel" who had carried her off and that he had pinked him in the body with his sword but had been unable to stop the carriage which was taking them to Chambéry. He asked me to make inquiries and to persuade his daughter to return to Lyons, and, if she refused, to go to the police for assistance, acting in the name and at the behest of her unhappy father, who demanded her return; he assured me they were not married, and he implored me to use whatever means were in my power to do him this service of friendship. He asked me to answer him at once by express messenger, sending me his address.

I had no need to make inquiries. His daughter could only be my neighbor; but I was very far from taking any steps to send the charming creature back to Lyons.

Returning to the inn, I sent Leduc to Monsieur Valenglart in Grenoble with a four-seated carriage and a letter containing another addressed to Madame Morin, in which I told her that, since I had stopped at Chambéry only for her, I would await her convenience. After that I joyfully abandoned myself to the promising adventure which Fortune was offering me. Mademoiselle Desarmoises and her abductor had inspired me with feelings of the fondest friendship; I did not stop to discover if what was leading me on was vice or virtue.

I enter their room, and I see the surgeon dressing the young man's wound. It was not dangerous; it was suppurating. After the surgeon left, I congratulate him, I recommend diet and silence, and I return to my room for the rest of the day until suppertime, after handing Mademoiselle Desarmoises, in his presence, the letter I had just received from her father. I was sure that she would come and speak to me.

A quarter of an hour later I see her appear before

me, looking downcast. She hands me the letter, asking me what I intend to do.

"Nothing. I shall consider myself fortunate if you will enable me to be of service to you."

"I breathe again."

"Could you believe anything else of me? The moment I saw you, you interested me. Are you and he married?"

"No, but we shall be as soon as we reach Geneva."

"Sit down and tell me the whole story. I know that your father has the misfortune to be in love with you and that you shun him."

"So he has told you that; I am glad of it. A year ago he arrived in Lyons, and a quarter of an hour later I took refuge with a friend of my mother's, for I cannot spend so much as an hour with him except at the risk of suffering the most monstrous violence. The young man whom you saw in bed is the only son of a merchant in Geneva; my father himself brought him to our house two years ago, and we immediately fell in love. After my father left, he asked my hand of my mother, who, my father being in Marseilles, did not feel that she had the right to decide my future. She wrote to him in Marseilles, and he replied that he would make up his mind when he returned to Lyons. Meanwhile my lover went to Geneva, where he obtained his father's consent to our marriage, and he came back to Lyons with all the necessary information and an excellent letter of recommendation to Monsieur Tolosan.[15] When my father arrived last year I fled, as I told you, and my lover had Monsieur Tolosan himself ask for my hand on his behalf. My father said he would answer him when I had come home. Monsieur Tolosan told me I should return to my father's house, and I replied that I would do so if my mother would come to fetch me and take me under her protection; but when Monsieur Tolosan told her this she said she knew her husband too well to bring me back home. He again asked my father for his consent, but to no purpose. A

week or ten days later he left, then we learned that he
was at Aix-en-Savoie, then at Turin, and finally, seeing
that my father would not make up his mind, my lover
proposed that I go away with him, having Monsieur Tolosan himself assure me that he would marry me in
Geneva; my mother consented. So we set off a week ago.
By ill luck we took the road through Savoy and met my
father not far from this city. He recognized us, he made
the carriage stop, he comes to me, he tries to force me to
get out, I scream, my lover takes me in his arms, my
father seizes his sword and plunges it into his body.
Seeing people coming in response to my cries and the
coachman's, and believing that he had killed my lover,
he got on his horse again and fled at full gallop. I will
show you the sword stained halfway up with blood,
though the wound is only three inches deep.''

"I have to answer his letter. I am trying to think
how best to obtain his consent for you.''

"There is no need of that. We shall be none the less
married and none the less happy without it.''

"That is true; but you cannot so lightly disregard
your dowry.''

"What dowry? He has nothing.''

"But when your grandfather the Marquis Desarmoises
dies, he will be rich.''

"That's a fairy tale. My father has nothing but a
small annuity for having served for thirty years as a
courier. His father has been dead for twenty years. My
mother and my sister live by the work of their hands.''

Very much surprised by the shameless effrontery of a
man who, after imposing on me in such a fashion, now
put me in a position to discover the whole extent of his
imposture, I said nothing more. We went to supper and
spent three hours at the table. We talked of nothing but
the situation, and the wounded man had only to listen to
me to know what I thought on the subject. At nineteen,
Mademoiselle Desarmoises had every quality to attract.

She wittily ridiculed the foolish passion with which, she told me, her father had loved her madly from the time she was eleven years old.

"And you always resisted him?"

"I resisted him only when he tried to carry his playing with me too far."

"And did that go on long?"

"Two years. I was thirteen when, seeing that I was ripe, he tried to make off with the fruit; but I screamed and jumped out of his bed stark naked and took refuge in my mother's, who from that day on would not let me sleep with him again."

"So you slept with him? How could your mother allow it?"

"She did not think he could love me like a lover, and I had no idea there was anything wrong in it. I believed that all he did to me and wanted me to do to him was only play."

"But you saved the jewel."

"I kept it for my lover."

At that the poor wounded man, weak though he was from hunger, laughed, and she rose from the table and gave him a quantity of kisses. I was in a state of excitement, for her faithful narrative had set the girl before my mind's eye more than stark naked. I thought that if I had been in her father's place she would not have escaped me so easily, and I forgave him for having forgotten in his love that she was his daughter. When she escorted me to my room I made her feel the effect her narrative had produced on me, and she laughed; but since my servants were there, I had to let her go.

The next morning very early I wrote to her father that his daughter was determined not to leave her lover, who was only slightly wounded, and that at Chambéry she was completely safe under the protection of the laws. I went to her room to show her my letter, and, finding her at a loss to express her gratitude, I asked her lover to permit her to embrace me; he opened his arms and said:

"And me too."

My hypocritical love then donned the mask of fatherly affection. I called them my children, and I offered them my purse full of gold if they needed it. The surgeon comes, and I go back to my room. Madame Morin arrived at eleven o'clock with her daughter, preceded by Leduc cracking his whip. I ran to embrace her, thanking her again and again for the favor she was doing me. The first piece of news she gave me was that her niece Mademoiselle Roman[16] was the King's mistress, lived in a fine house in Passy,[17] was five months gone with child [18] and on the way to becoming the Queen of France, as my divine horoscope had predicted.

"At Grenoble," she said, "no one talks of anything but you, and I advise you not to go back there, for you would never be allowed to leave. You will have the whole nobility at your feet and every woman who is eager to know her daughter's destiny. The whole town now believes in judicial astrology, and Valenglart is exultant. He has wagered a hundred louis against fifty that she will give birth to a prince; he is sure he will win; if he loses he will be laughed at."

"He will win. I am going to Paris, and I hope you will give me a letter to Madame Varnier, who will arrange for me to have the pleasure of seeing your niece."

"It is only right that you should, and I will give you a letter to her tomorrow."

I introduced Mademoiselle Desarmoises to her by her lover's family name, after asking her if she would stay for dinner. So she joined the three of us, and after dinner we went to the convent, where M. M., as soon as her aunt was announced, came down to the grating very much surprised at her visit and even more so when she saw me. When Madame Morin introduced me she told me that she had seen me five or six times at the spring at Aix, but that I could not recognize her for she had always gone there veiled. I admired her tact and her presence of mind. I thought she looked even more beautiful. After we spent an hour talking of Grenoble and M. M.'s old friends she left us to ask the Abbess to come down, and to fetch a young girl boarder of whom she was fond and whom she wanted to introduce to Madame Morin.

I availed myself of the opportunity to tell that lady that she was quite right about the resemblance and to ask her to do me the favor of arranging for me to breakfast with her[19] the next morning and of giving her a dozen pounds of chocolate which I had at my lodging. She urged me to give them to her myself.

She came back to the grating with the Abbess, two other young nuns, and the boarder, who was from Lyons and pretty enough to eat. While I, as in duty bound, took on all the nuns, Madame Morin told her niece that I wanted to try some chocolate which I had brought from Turin, if her lay sister would prepare it. M. M. told me to send her the chocolate, saying that she would be delighted to breakfast with us the next morning and with the nuns who were there.

I sent it to her as soon as we were back at the inn, and we supped in Madame Morin's room, still in the company of Mademoiselle Desarmoises, whose charms dazzled me more and more; but I talked to her only of M. M., with whom she felt sure I had had an intrigue at Aix.

The next morning, after the breakfast, I told her she would not find it so easy to give me a dinner for twelve at which we would all be seated side by side at the same table; she replied that we would all be at the same table, the only difference being that half of it would be in the convent and the other half, cut off by a grating, would be in the visiting room. I then said it was something I should like to see, if she would permit me to pay for it; and she consented. So the dinner was fixed for the next day. M. M. undertook to arrange everything and to invite six nuns; I said I would send her the wines. It was Madame Morin who, knowing my tastes, told her to spare no expense.

After escorting Madame Morin, her daughter, and Mademoiselle Desarmoises back to the inn I called on Monsieur Magnan,[20] to whom I had a letter of introduction from the Cavaliere Raiberti, and asked him to find me some good wines, and he gave me all sorts of them in more than sufficient quantities. I sent them to M. M.

Monsieur Magnan was a pleasant-looking, intelligent man, very well off, who lived in a very comfortable house outside the city and had a pleasant wife who had not yet lost her bloom and nine or ten children, among them four very pretty girls, the eldest of whom was nineteen. He was passionately fond of good living, and to convince me of it he invited me to dinner on the next day but one.

After having spent all day in the convent visiting room we would have supped in the wounded man's room in order not to leave him alone, if the surgeon had not told us he must be allowed to sleep.

The next day we went to the visiting room at eleven o'clock, and at noon dinner was announced. The table was a charming sight. The guests numbering twelve, two thirds of them were beyond the grating, for the nuns, counting the boarder, numbered eight and we only four; the grating was between us; but the table appeared to be continuous. I was seated beside M. M.; but to no purpose, for the wall was between us up to the sill, and above that was the grating. At my left I had Mademoiselle Desarmoises, who needed no help in keeping the nuns entertained with amusing stories. We who were outside had Costa and Leduc to wait on us, while the nuns within were waited on by their lay sisters. The abundance of dishes, the bottles, and the conversation made the dinner last three hours; we were all tipsy; and but for the grating I could easily have possessed all the eleven females present, who were in no state to reason. Mademoiselle Desarmoises had become so gay that, if I had not kept her in check, she would have scandalized all the nuns. I could not wait to have her alone with me in some place where nothing would interfere with my forcing her to quench the flame which, at no cost to herself, she had set raging in my soul from the beginning to the end of this unique dinner.

After coffee we removed to another visiting room where we remained until nightfall. Madame Morin took leave of her niece, and the exchange of thanks between the nuns and myself, in which each side tried to outdo the other, went on for a quarter of an hour. After I had told M. M. in everyone's hearing that I would do myself the honor of seeing her again before my departure, we went home, very well pleased with the occasion, which still delights me every time I remember it.

Madame Morin left me a letter to her cousin Madame Varnier, and I promised to write her from Paris whatever I managed to learn about her niece. She drove away at eight o'clock in the morning, preceded by my Spaniard, whom I ordered to convey my compliments to the caretaker's whole family. I went to dine with the pleasure-loving Magnan, finding everything delicious. I promised him I would stay with him whenever I was in Chambéry, and I kept my word.

Leaving Magnan's house, I went to call on M. M., who at once came to the grating alone. After thanking me for visiting her, and for having contrived to make such a brilliant occasion of it under the cloak of her aunt, she said my coming had disturbed her peace of mind.

"I am ready, my dear, to climb the garden wall more nimbly than your ill-omened lover."

"Alas! Believe me, you are already spied on. Everyone

here is sure that we knew each other in Aix. Let us forget
all, my dear friend, and so spare ourselves the torture
of vain desires."

"Give me your hand."

"No, it is over. I still love you, but I cannot wait to
know that you are gone. Your leaving will give me a
true proof of your affection."

"You amaze me. You appear to be in perfect health;
you look more beautiful than ever; I know that you are
made for love. I do not understand how you can be
content to live in continual abstinence."

"Alas, when one cannot have the reality, one plays at
it. I will not hide it from you that I love my young
boarder. It is a love which fosters my peace of mind; it
is an innocent passion; her caresses suffice to quench a
flame which would kill me if I did not diminish its inten-
sity by make-believe."

"And your conscience does not suffer?"

"What I do does not trouble me."

"But you know it is a sin."

"And I confess it."

"And what does your confessor say?"

"Nothing. He absolves me, and I am happy."

"And does your little boarder confess too?"

"Of course; but she sees no reason to tell her confessor
what she does not consider a sin."

"I am astonished that her confessor has not enlightened her, for enlightening the young mind is a great
pleasure."

"Our confessor is a wise old man."

"Then I must leave without receiving so much as a
kiss from you?"

"Nothing at all."

"May I come tomorrow? I shall leave the next day."

"Yes; but I will not come down alone, for the nuns
might imagine something. I will bring my little boarder.

Then nothing can be said. Come after dinner, but to the other visiting room.''

If I had not known M. M. at Aix her religion would have surprised me; but such was her character. She loved God, and she did not believe that he would fail in mercy because she had not had the strength to overcome nature. I returned to the inn annoyed that she would have nothing more to do with me, but sure that Mademoiselle Desarmoises would make up to me for it.

I found her sitting on the bed beside her lover, whom diet and fever had made extremely weak; she said she would come to supper in my room in order to let the patient rest, and the patient pressed my hand to show me his gratitude.

Having dined all too well at Magnan's, I ate very little; but Mademoiselle Desarmoises, who had not dined, ate and drank with ravenous appetite. She enjoyed my amazement. After my servants left I challenged her to drink glass for glass of punch with me, and it put her in the state of gaiety which wants nothing but to laugh and which laughs to find itself entirely deprived of will power and reason. However, I cannot say that I took advantage of her state of intoxication, for, all her natural voluptuousness being aroused, she could not wait to join in all the pleasures which I urged upon her until two o'clock in the morning, when, both incapable of more, we parted.

After sleeping until eleven o'clock I went to see her in her room, where I found her as fresh as a rose. When I asked her at what hour she wished to dine she replied in the most enchanting manner that she would rather save her appetite for supper. Her lover remarked to me, calmly and politely, that it was impossible to keep up with her.

''At drinking,'' I said.

''At drinking,'' he replied, ''and at something else too.''

She laughed, and hurried to kiss him.

This brief dialogue convinced me that Mademoiselle Desarmoises must adore the young man, for in addition to his being very handsome he was of just the temperament she needed. I went and dined alone. Leduc arrived from Grenoble just as I was leaving to see M. M. He told me that the caretaker's daughters had made him put off his departure while they wrote to me; and he gave me three letters and three dozen pairs of gloves which they had sent me as a present. Their letters were entirely devoted to urging to come and spend a month with them. I had not the courage to return to a town where, with the reputation I had made, I should have had to cast every girl's horoscope or become the most boorish of men by refusing her the favor.

After sending my name in to M. M. I entered the visiting room which she had indicated, and a moment later I saw her before me with the boarder who was the object of her affection. She was not yet twelve years of age, and her face denoted an alliance between sweetness and subtlety; dark, tall, well built, and tightly laced in a corset, she showed her entire bosom, delighted that those who saw it could not think she took pride in it, since all that she displayed was the place for what love might hope to find there. It was easy to guess what the unseen part of her figure was like, and her interesting face impelled one to judge most favorably of all the rest. I told her at once that she was very pretty and that she could not fail to make the man happy whom Heaven had destined to be her husband. I knew that the compliment would make her blush. It is cruel, but it is precisely there that seduction begins. A girl of her age who did not blush would be either an idiot or thoroughly indoctrinated and experienced in all the practices of libertinism. Nevertheless, the source of the blush which rises to a youthful face when its owner is confronted with an alarming idea is a puzzling problem. It may be modesty, it may be shame, and it may be a mixture of the two. It is a conflict between vice and virtue, in which virtue usually succumbs, being overthrown by those henchmen of vice, the desires. Knowing the boarder from what M. M. had told me, I could not but know what caused her to blush.

Pretending not to have noticed her blushing, I talked with M. M. for a moment, then returned to the attack. She had already recovered her composure.

"How old are you, my charming child?"

"Thirteen."

"You're mistaken, darling," said M. M. "You're not quite twelve yet."

"The time will come," I said, "when, instead of adding to your age, you will subtract from it."

"I will never lie, I'm very sure of that."

"Then you want to become a nun?"

"I have not yet received my vocation; but nothing will oblige me to lie even if I live in the world."

"You will begin to lie as soon as you have a lover."

"Then my love will lie too?"

"Of course he will."

"If that were the way of it, love would be a very base thing, but I don't believe it, for I love my dear friend here and I never hide the truth from her."

"But you will not love a man as you love a woman."

"Exactly the same."

"No, for you don't sleep with her, and you would sleep with your lover."

"That makes no difference. My love would be the same."

"What! You wouldn't rather sleep with me than with M. M.?"

"No indeed, for you are a man and you would see me."

"Then you must know you are ugly."

At that she turned to M. M. with her pretty face red as fire, asking her if she was really ugly. She replied, bursting with laughter, that on the contrary she was very pretty, and she took her between her knees. I said that her corset was too tightly laced, for her waist could not possibly be so small. She replied that her corset was so loose that I could put my hand under it. I said that I did not believe it, whereupon she turned her little boarder so that her side was toward me and against the grating and told me to put out my hand; at the same time she pulled up her dress. I put my hand under it, and I found that M. M. was right, but I cursed the shift and the grating which prevented my arm from going farther.

"I believe," I said to M. M., not withdrawing my hand, "that this is a little man; may I convince myself of it?"

But at the same time that I asked her permission, my hand went to work without waiting for it to be granted, and to such good purpose that I convinced and more than convinced myself not only that the boarder was a charming little girl but that M. M. took no less pleasure than she did in my curiosity. The little girl drew away, bestowing a kiss on her dear friend, whose smiling countenance assured her that she had not committed any great sin in letting herself be thus explored; but, on my side, surprise had almost stupefied me. The little girl asked permission to absent herself for a moment. I must have been the cause of it.

"Are you aware," I said to M. M., "that the revelation you have procured me makes me unhappy?"

"Why?"

"Because, having found your boarder charming, I am dying to devour her."

"I'm sorry, for you cannot do any more than you have done; but even if it were possible I would not let you have her, for you would spoil her for me."

"Give me your hand."

"Certainly not. I don't want to see."

"But you are not angry with my hand or with my eyes."

"On the contrary, if you have had pleasure I am very glad, and if you have awakened desires in her she will love me the more."

"Oh that the three of us could be together in perfect freedom!"

"Impossible."

"Are you sure no one saw us?"

"Perfectly sure."

"The sill of this grating kept many charms from me."

"Why didn't you go to the other one? It is lower."

"Let us go there."

"No, for I couldn't think up a reason."

"I will come tomorrow, and I will leave for Lyons at nightfall."

The little girl returned, and I rose and stood facing her. I had a quantity of charms on my watch chains, and I had not had time to rearrange my clothing properly. She noticed it at once; and my charms gave her curiosity a very plausible pretext.

"You have a lot of pretty things there," she said. "May I look?"

"As much as you like, and touch them too."

At that, M. M., foreseeing what would happen, said that she would return. In no time at all I made the too curious boarder lose all her interest in the charms. She did not try to hide her amazement or the pleasure she took in satisfying her curiosity about an object entirely new to her and all of whose parts she found herself at perfect liberty to examine. She desisted from her investigation when she was startled by an eruption the agreeable sight of which I took the greatest pleasure in providing for her.

Seeing M. M. slowly returning, I quickly rang down the curtain and seated my self. My watches being still on the sill, she asked the little girl if she had found the charms pretty; she answered yes, but soberly. In less than two hours she had made so long a journey that she had good reason to be thoughtful. I spent the rest of the day telling M. M. the whole story of my journey to Grenoble, Marseilles, Genoa, Rome, and Naples, promising that I would come to finish it the next day at the same hour. The little girl said that she was curious to know how I had ended matters with the Duke of Matalona's mistress.

Back at the inn, I supped with Mademoiselle Desarmoises, and after paying her the due tribute of a lover I went off to bed, assuring her that it was entirely on her account that I was still delaying my departure. The next day, after dining with her, I went to the convent visiting room. After sending in my name to M. M. I went to the grating with the low sill.

She came alone, but at once told me that the little girl would soon follow her.

"Yesterday," she said, "you set her on fire; she told me everything and she indulged in every kind of wantonness, each time calling me her husband. You have seduced her, and I am very glad you are leaving, for I believe she would go mad. Wait till you see how she is dressed."

"Are you sure she won't tell?"

"Perfectly sure. All I ask is that you do nothing to her in my presence. When I see that the time has come, I will leave."

In she comes, as gay as possible, with a dress which is open in front and a skirt which reaches only halfway down her legs.

She has scarcely sat down before she reminds me that I had left off my story with Donna Leonilda in bed, and I go on to the end when her mother showed her to me stark naked. At that M. M. left, and the little girl quickly asked what I had done to assure myself that my daughter was a virgin. Stretching out my arm and putting my hand into the opening of her skirt, I made her feel what

I had done, enjoying her emotion, which she did not trouble to hide. She then gave me her hand, so that I could use it for the same purpose; but M. M. came back.

"It doesn't matter," the little girl said, "I've told her everything; she's kind, she won't tell."

I went on with my story, and when I finally came to the place where I described the charming obstructed girl and recounted all the efforts I had vainly made to satisfy her, the little boarder became so curious that, to enable me to teach her, she exposed herself in the most charming of all postures. M. M., seeing that I had risen, fled just as I was about to break my promise to her; but the boarder told me to kneel on the sill and leave it to her. I obeyed, guessing her intention. She was moved to eat me, and she may have hoped to swallow me; but the too great pleasure she aroused in my soul liquefied my heart. She did not leave me until she was convinced of my exhaustion. I sat down, and in gratitude pressed my lips to the sweet mouth which had sucked the quintessence of my soul and my heart.

I left the two angels toward the end of the day, saying good-by and promising that I would see them again the following year.

Back at the inn, I took leave of the wounded man, whom I vainly urged to make free of my purse; he assured me that he was not in need of money. I promised him I would oblige Desarmoises to refrain from proceeding against him if he ever went back to Lyons, and I kept my word. His fiancée came to sup with me and to sport until midnight, when she left me so that I could go to sleep until daybreak, when I had ordered horses.

I arrived in Lyons the next day, going to lodge at the "Parc" [21] and at once sending word to Desarmoises. I told him, concealing nothing, that his daughter's charms had seduced me, that her future husband was a most amiable young man, and that he had every reason to consent to their marriage, though he had no need of his consent. He did all that I demanded of him when I said that I could continue to be his friend only on that condition. He drew up a document, signed by two witnesses, which I sent to the wounded man in Chambéry by express messenger the same day.

Desarmoises insisted on my dining with his wife and his younger daughter in his mean house. The girl had not the slightest charm, and his wife filled me with pity.

Since I had to go to Paris, I gave him the money he needed to wait for me in Strassburg with my Spanish valet. Monsieur de Rochebaron was in the country. I thought I was wise to take only Costa with me, but I was wrong. I took the road through the Bourbonnais, and I reached Paris on the third day, going to lodge at the Hôtel du Saint-Esprit[22] in the Rue Saint-Esprit.

Since I needed to go to bed I at once wrote a note to Madame d'Urfé, sending it to her by Costa. I promised that I would go to dine with her the next day. Costa was quite handsome but spoke French very badly and was rather stupid, so I was sure that Madame d'Urfé would take him for some extraordinary being. She replied that she awaited me with the utmost impatience.

"Tell me," I said to Costa, "how the lady received you and how she read my note."

"She looked at me in a mirror, speaking words which I could not understand; after that she burned incense, walking around the room three times. Then she looked at me closely, smiled, and told me to wait outside for her answer."

VOLUME 7 • NOTES

CHAPTER I

1. *St. Aloysius Gonzaga:* The Jesuit Luigi Gonzaga (1568-1591) was canonized in 1726 for the purity of his life.
2. *St. Anthony of Padua:* Born at Lisbon in 1195, died at Padua in 1231; he was first an Augustinian, and became a Franciscan in 1220; a great preacher, he was canonized in 1232.
3. *Correggio:* Antonio Allegri da Correggio (1494-1534), famous painter of the Italian Renaissance. To which of his works C. refers appears to be indeterminable.
4. *Madame Z:* Cf. Vol. 6, Chap. XI, n. 2.
5. *Marquis:* Giovanni Antonio II Turinetti, Marquis de Prié (Priero) et Pancalieri, well-known gambler and adventurer (cf. Vol. 6, Chap. XI).
6. *Desarmoises:* Not certainly identified (cf. Vol. 6, Chap. X, n. 88). For C.'s previous and subsequent relations with him, see Vol. 6, Chap. XI, and Vol. 7, Chaps. XII and XIII. He was acting as C.'s croupier.
7. *Made in England:* Condoms were said to have been invented in England and were manufactured there from the end of the 17th or the beginning of the 18th century.
8. *Schmit:* Nothing is known of this person; perhaps he was an Englishman named Smith. For Roxburghe, see Vol. 6, Chap. VI, n. 8.
9. *How . . . Sir:* C. writes, by ear: *oudioudou ser.*

CHAPTER II

1. *Valenglart:* C. writes now "Valenglar," now "Valenglard," now "Valenglart." The person so designated is probably either François Léonard Le Roy, Marquis de Valenglart, or Jean Antoine Le Roy, Vicomte de Valenglart.

2. *Princess of Estouteville:* Agnès Marie, Duchess (not Princess) of Estouteville (1732-1756), née d'Urfé.

3. *Outside of the city:* Probably in the village of La Tronche, noted in the 18th century for its fine country houses, most of which belonged to prosperous citizens of Grenoble.

4. *The Isère:* The River Isère, which flows through Grenoble and enters the Rhone near Valence.

5. *Concert:* From 1747 concerts were given at Grenoble in a room in the town hall which long bore the name "Salle des Concerts."

6. *Lebel:* Probably a fictitious name, used by C. to designate the major-domo of the French Ambassador in Soleure, Anne Théodore Chavignard de Chavigny (cf. Vol. 6, Chaps. VI-IX).

7. *Ratafia:* A liqueur distilled from cherries, for which Grenoble was famous.

8. *Visnat:* Also vichnak, a kind of honey water with cherries.

9. *Yusuf Ali:* Turkish merchant in Constantinople (cf. Vol. 2, Chaps. IV ff.). C.'s "seventeen years" would put him in Constantinople in 1743; actually, he cannot have gone there until 1745.

10. *Tallow candles . . . Venetian:* As a Venetian, C. was accustomed to wax candles.

11. *Zappata:* Banker in Turin (cf. Vol. 6, Chap. XI).

12. *Saute, Marquis:* "Jump, Marquis": self-congratulatory exclamation often used in soliloquy by a pretended Marquis in Regnard's comedy *La Joueur* ("The Gambler"; 1696). By C.'s time it had become proverbial.

13. *Morin:* Advocate in Grenoble; nothing more is known of him.

14. *Judicial astrology:* Astrology as concerned with foretelling the futures of individuals and nations (in contradistinction from "natural astrology," which foretells the motions of the heavenly bodies).

15. *Roman-Coupier:* Anne Roman-Coupier, also Coppier (1737-1808), daughter of the court clerk Jean Joseph Roman Coppier, of Grenoble; from 1761 to 1765 she was the mistress of Louis XV, who ennobled her as Baroness of Meilly-Coulonge; in 1772 she married Gabriel Siran, Marquis de Cavanac.

16. *Seventeen years of age:* She was born in 1737, so she was 23 at the time of which C. is writing.

17. *Quadrille:* Old card game played with 2 packs of cards from which the 8's, 9's, and 10's have been removed.

18. *Gloves:* Grenoble was celebrated from the 17th century for its leather industry and the manufacture of gloves.

19. *Louis:* A louis was worth 24 francs (livres).

20. *Bourchenu de Valbonnais:* Jean Pierre Moret de Bourchenu, Marquis de Valbonnais (1651-1730), member of the Grenoble Parlement and author of 2 historical works on Dauphiné. Presumably C. had previously seen one of his books, so that he was able to bring out the well-known name at the right moment in Grenoble.

21. *My daughter:* The lady who here addresses C. is Madame Bailly de Montcarra; her husband was President of the Grenoble Parlement and a nephew of the Marquis de Valbonnais. Their daughter was later an acquaintance of the young Stendhal.

22. *Discredited astrology:* The period of the Enlightenment attacked belief in prodigies and astrology, beginning with Fontenelle's *Histoire des oracles* (1687) and Bayle's *Pensées diverses sur la comète* (1682).

23. *Madame de Maintenon:* Françoise d'Aubigné, Marquise de Maintenon (1635-1719), married the writer Pierre Scarron (died 1660) in 1652; in 1669 she became the mistress of Louis XIV and, after the death of the Queen in 1683, his second wife.

24. *America:* The Marquise de Maintenon lived from 1645 to 1647 with her parents on the island of Martinique in the West Indies; after her father's death in the latter year she returned to France with her mother.

25. *Had lovers:* The references to Madame de Maintenon's alleged lovers in Saint-Simon's *Memoirs* are probably fiction.

26. Already quoted by C. in Vol. 5, Chap. VIII, as by Pico della Mirandola.

27. *Eighteenth year:* Cf. note 16 to this chapter.

28. *Madame Varnier:* Marie Madeleine Varnier, née Roman-Coupier, elder sister (not aunt) of Mademoiselle Roman; from 1749 she had lived in Paris as a procuress; she was

well acquainted with Louis XV's First Gentleman of the Bedchamber, Dominique Guillaume Lebel (1696-1768).

29. *The Café de Foy:* Still famous in the 19th century as a rendezvous of chess players; it was near the Palais-Royal.

30. *Is your aunt:* Cf. note 28 to this chapter.

31. *Doblones de a ocho:* Spanish gold coins (cf. Vol. 1, Chap. X, n. 29).

32. *Sister order of "Mops":* The "Mopsorden," a para-Masonic order which also admitted women, was founded in 1740, probably by the Elector Clemens August of Cologne, in reaction to Pope Clement XII's bull against Freemasonry. It rapidly spread through Germany as well as through Holland and France (Ordre du Carlin) but in 1775 was replaced by new Masonic lodges which also admitted women.

33. *Charles Ivanov:* Adventurer whose name (variously spelled) appears in contemporary documents.

34. *Kurland:* Ernst Johann (Ivan) Biron, Duke of Kurland (1690-1772), favorite of Czarina Anna Ivanovna, banished to Siberia from 1740 to 1762. By his wife Bengina Gottliebe von Trotha he had 2 sons, Peter (1724-1800) and Karl (1728-1801), Baron von Treyden.

35. *Before leaving to see Mademoiselle Roman:* Text: "avant d'aller à Roman." If this reading of the Brockhaus-Plon edition is correct, "Roman" can here be only a place name. But since it is not documented as such in France, Mrs. Helen Wolff has conjectured: "d'aller à La Roman," and the translation has been made accordingly.

36. *Monteynard:* Louis François, Marquis de Monteynard (died after 1774), French General, Minister of War from 1771 to 1774; in 1772 he signed the marriage contract between Anne Roman and Gabriel Siran, Marquis de Cavanac.

CHAPTER III

1. *By water:* C.'s memory must have been at fault here. In all probability he made only a part of the more than 120-mile journey from Grenoble to Avignon by boat; traffic on the Isère is undocumented.

2. *"Saint-Omer" inn:* The Hôtel de Saint-Omer still exists in the Rue du Lim as in Avignon.

3. *Mademoiselle Astrodi:* Marguerite Astrodi, also Astraudi (after 1733 - after 1778), youngest daughter of an Italian actor and an actress of the Comédie Italienne in Paris; she was a dancer there.

4. *Sous:* The sou was a copper coin worth one-twentieth of a franc.

5. *Stuard:* Adventurer, also known as Tuard, Baron Stuart de Frisot, or Baron Neisen; his alleged wife was Marie Anne Constance Louise Des Grafs, daughter of an advocate of Aix-la-Chapelle, who ran away from home and became an adventuress.

6. *"Cascade":* The celebrated source of the River Sorgue is just outside the village of Vaucluse; in rainy seasons it overflows in a waterfall nearly 100 feet in height.

7. *Laura de Sade:* According to tradition the Laura whom Petrarch celebrated in some 300 poems was Laura de Noves, who married Hughes de Sade in 1325 and died in 1348. Petrarch says that he saw his Laura for the first time in the church of St. Clare in Avignon in 1327. He moved to Vaucluse 10 years later and lived there for some time.

8. *The theater:* The theater in Avignon was built in 1732 on the Place d'Oulle, now the Place Crillon; it was demolished in 1824.

9. *Vice-Legate:* In 1309, under political pressure from King Philip IV of France, Avignon became the seat of the Papacy; it was not until 1417, after the end of the Great Schism, that Rome again became the center of the Catholic Church. From 1348 until the French Revolution Avignon formed part of the Papal States and was governed by a Vice-Legate.

10. *Salviati:* Gregorio Salviati (1722-1794), Papal Vice-Legate in Avignon from 1760, Cardinal from 1777.

11. *The beautiful Astrodi whom all Paris knew:* Rosalie Astrodi (1733 - after 1756), singer, dancer, and actress with the Comédie Italienne, elder sister of Marguerite Astrodi (see note 3 to this chapter); after first being the mistress of the Count of Egmont, in 1756 she married the Sieur Pajot de Villiers.

12. *Egmont:* Gui Félix Pignatelli, Titular Count of Egmont, Prince of Gavre (1720-1753), Grandee of Spain, officer in the French service.

13. *Petits écus:* The petit écu was worth 3 francs, the gros écu 6.
14. *The ancient bridge:* The famous "Pont d'Avignon" of the nursery rhyme, properly the Pont Saint-Bénézet; built in Roman times and rebuilt at the end of the 12th century. Of its original 18 arches only 3 remain.
15. *Hermitage:* A celebrated wine from Tain-l'Hermitage, on the Rhone. White Hermitage is not bottled until it is 4 years old.
16. *Dolci:* A Dolci, or Doulcy (first name not recorded), was captain of the Swiss Guard at the Papal Palace in Avignon in 1760.
17. *L'Isle:* C. writes "Lille"; but the reference can only be to L'Isle-sur-la-Sorgue, a village on the road from Avignon to Vaucluse.
18. *Apt:* C. doubtless left his carriage in Vaucluse, not in Apt, which is nearly 20 miles east of Vaucluse.
19. Francesco Petrarca, *Le Rime* (ed. Carducci-Ferrari-Contini), beginning of Canzone CXXVI.
20. *Allatius:* Leo Allatius (Latinized form of Allacci) (1586-1669): Greek scholar and theologian, librarian in Rome; he wrote a book on the birthplace of Homer (*De patria Homeri,* 1640), which various authorities supposed to be the island of Chios in the Aegean Sea.
21. *Arquà:* Petrarch retired to the village of Arquà in the Eugaenean Hills, south of Padua, in 1368 and died there in 1374; his tombstone stands in front of the village church.
22. Petrarca, "Il Trionfo della Morte," I, last verse.
23. *"Messer Francesco d'Arezzo":* Petrarch came from Arezzo, in Tuscany; "Messer(e)" is the old Italian equivalent for the present title of respect, "Signor(e)."
24. *Where:* C. writes *p* . . . (for *putain*).
25. *Grimaldi:* Gian Giacomo Grimaldi, Marchese di Campo Tejar (1705-1777), Genoese patrician, Doge of Genoa from 1756 to 1758.
26. *Bussy:* Presumably a member of the noble family of Bussy or Bussy-Rabutin.
27. *I'm off:* C. writes (and underlines), *Je m'en y vas,* thus convicting the innkeeper of speaking poor French.
28. *Non-Conformity:* C. writes *non-conformisme,* a word rarely

used in the 18th century; Bossuet imported it into French (from English) in 1688 in his *Histoire des variations des églises protestantes.* It was originally applied to those who opposed the royal edict prescribing a uniform liturgy in all churches.

29. *Lepi:* Two brothers named Lepi were dancers with the Comédie Italienne in Paris in 1756; the hunchbacked actress to whom C. refers was probably their sister.

30. *Florentine kiss:* A kiss in which the giver pinches the receiver's cheeks between thumb and middle finger.

31. *Auditor:* Title of an official of an ecclesiastical court.

32. *The Golden Age:* Perhaps a reference to the famous chorus in Tasso's *Aminta* (I, 2) in praise of the Golden Age, when *S'ei piace, ei lice* ("Whatever gives delight is lawful").

33. *Lend . . . a hand:* Original, *donne la diligence,* which may have a technical erotic meaning, especially since C. subsequently makes the noun a verb *(diligencier).* However, the translator has not been able to find any such usage. The difficulty is only compounded by C.'s later *que je lui fisse la même chose* ("[let] me do the same thing to her").

34. *Ganymede:* In Greek mythology a beautiful youth with whom Zeus (Jupiter) fell in love and whom he translated to Olympus as cupbearer of the gods.

35. *Costa:* Gaetano Costa (ca. 1734-1801), of Parma; he was C.'s secretary from 1760 to 1761 and later became valet to Count Hardegg in Vienna.

36. *Pistoria:* Physician to King Fernando VI of Spain (C. writes "Pistorin").

37. *Council of Trent:* Church Council which sat from 1545 to 1563 and was instrumental in launching the Counter-Reformation.

38. *A three and a zero:* In French the city of Trent is "Trente" and the number 30 is *"trente."*

39. *Parlement:* Before the French Revolution Aix-en-Provence was the seat of one of the 12 provincial Parlements (high judicial courts).

40. *"Thirteen Cantons":* The Auberge des XIII Cantons was a Swiss hostelry on the Cours Belzunce; it ceased to exist during the 19th century.

41. *The play:* Plays were performed in the Théâtre Vacon,

which was located in the street of the same name from 1738
to 1789.

42. *Amphitheater:* See Vol. 3, Chap. VIII, n. 46.

CHAPTER IV

1. *Knight of Malta:* In his *Confutazione della storia del go-
verno veneto di Amelot de Houssale* (Amsterdam, 1769), C.
names him. He was a Chevalier de Forbin.

2. *Playing:* C. writes *qui jouait à la Marseillaise.* It is impossible to determine if the meaning is "playing in the manner of Marseilles" or "playing Marseillaise." The former is
more probable, since no record has been found of a game so
named.

3. *Half a copper:* Text: *six blancs.* The term *blanc* was applied to 2 coins, either of which was worth less than a sou.

4. *Stopped scowling:* C. writes: *se défroigna.* There is no such
verb in French; but, *pace* the commentators who go as far
afield as *defronçer,* it is an easy neologism on the basis of
renfrogner. C. had an ear even if he was a poor speller.

5. *Audibert:* A certain Madame Audibert (died after 1772)
maintained a gaming room in Marseilles.

6. *Sipions:* Marseillaise dialect for French *sèches.*

7. *Apicius:* There were 4 Romans of this name who were famous for their gastronomy. Of these the best known, and
hence the one to whom C. most probably refers, was M.
Gavius Apicius, who lived in the reigns of Augustus and
Tiberius and who, legend relates, took poison for fear of
starving to death when his fortune was reduced to an amount
equivalent to several million dollars.

8. Horace, *Epistles,* I, 16, 79.

9. *The port:* In the 18th century Toulon was one of the chief
ports in Europe. During the War of the Austrian Succession
there was a great naval battle off Toulon, in which ships of
the French, Spanish, and English fleets were engaged.

10. *Antibes:* Ancient seaport, founded by the Greeks as An-
tipolis, a few miles east of Cannes on the French Riviera. The
distance between Toulon and Antibes is some 85 miles.

11. *Felucca:* Small Mediterranean vessel, used in the coastwise

trade, usually with 2 masts and lateen rigged. The word is derived from the Arabic.

12. *Villefranche:* A small port a few miles east of Nice. Hence C. had to travel back to Nice.

13. *Nice:* Italian Nizza; until 1860 the capital of a Savoyan duchy which belonged to the Kingdom of Sardinia; in that year Savoy was ceded to France by Italy.

14. *Paterson:* James Paterson (1692-1765), of Scottish descent, from 1716 in the service of the Kingdom of Sardinia, from 1752 to 1763 Governor of Nice.

15. *Ramini:* Jean Antoine Ramini (died 1770), ennobled in 1727 by the purchase of a part of Villevieille; he was probably not an officer but an advocate.

16. *Saint-Pierre:* Gallicized form of the name of Antonio de San Pedro (1706-1790), born in Seville, ennobled by King Carlos III in 1783, from 1749 Spanish Consul in Nice.

17. *The coffeehouse:* Nice would appear to have had but one such establishment at the time; its proprietor was a certain Jean Ramos.

18. *Piedmontese pistole:* Gold coin (also known as doppia di Piemonte), worth 24 Piedmontese lire.

19. *"Santa Marta" inn:* The most celebrated hostelry in Genoa, near the church of the Annunziata; it was opened early in the 17th century.

20. *The theater:* There were 3 theaters in Genoa at the time: the Teatro del Falcone, opened in the middle of the 17th century; the Teatro S. Agostino, opened early in the 18th century and probably the one to which C. went; and the smaller and more recent Teatro delle Vigne (also known as Il Teatrino).

21. *Excellent mushrooms:* The mushrooms from the chestnut woods of Liguria were then famous throughout Europe and were exported dried. In the neighborhood of Genoa they were cultivated more especially about Val de Vara, some 20 miles west of the city.

22. *Journal des Savants:* The oldest French, and indeed European, literary and scientific periodical; it was founded in 1665, principally to publish articles and reviews by members of the various royal academies.

23. *Mercure de France:* Weekly journal, founded in 1672 as

Mercure galant, and published from 1717 under the title *Mercure de France.* (The present periodical by the same name began publication in 1890.)

24. *Mezzaro:* Or *mezzaru,* a head covering made from an Oriental material and worn by Genoese women.

25. *Zendale:* Or *zendado,* a fichu worn by Venetian women; cf. Vol. 1, Chap. VII, n. 21.

26. *Mantilla:* The Spanish mantilla is a scarf of silk, or more commonly of lace, worn over the head by women.

27. *Veronica:* Probably Veronica Alizeri (born 1734), daughter of Nicolò and Caterina Alizeri, née Frassineto, impoverished aristocrats.

28. *Sampierdarena:* Suburb of Genoa; it still contains many fine villas belonging to Genoese families.

CHAPTER V

1. *L'Écossaise: Le Café, ou l'Écossaise,* comedy by Voltaire, first performed in 1760 (cf. Vol. 6, Chap. V).

2. *At Signor Grimaldi's:* At Grimaldi's palazzo in Fossatello, near Genoa.

3. *Belloni:* Genoese banker; there was a well-known banker of the same name in Rome (see Chap. IX of this volume).

4. *Florentine zecchini:* The zecchino of Florence was a gold coin bearing the arms of Florence, the lily (*giglio*), and hence known as *zecchino gigliato*; its value was 24 Tuscan lire. C. writes "sequins *gigliati.*"

5. *Lepri:* Genoese banker.

6. *Calencar:* A fine colored fabric from India.

7. *Senator:* The constitution of the Republic of Genoa was very similar to that of Venice. However, from 1533, the Doge was elected for only 2 years (instead of for life, as in Venice). He was the head of the Senate, also called the "Signoria," which was composed of 12 members likewise elected for 2 years. In addition there were the so-called "senatori di camera," a body made up of 8 Procurators and the former Doges and which had charge of the public finances; Grimaldi belonged to this latter body, having been Doge from 1756 to 1758.

8. *Rossi:* Pietro Rossi (1720 - after 1778), Venetian actor and theater director. His company was then playing at Genoa in the Teatro S. Agostino. Voltaire's *L'Écossaise* is known to have been in Rossi's repertory, but in the translation by Goldoni. Nothing has been discovered concerning performances of the play in C.'s translation.

9. *Signora Casanova:* It follows that in Genoa C. did not call himself de Seingalt.

10. *Lady Alton . . . Murray:* The former is the scheming villainess, the latter the lover, in *L'Écossaise*.

11. *Elisabeth Petrovna:* 1709-1762, daughter of Peter the Great and Catherine I; Czarina from 1741 to 1762.

12. *Madame Morin:* Cf. Chap. II of this volume (C.'s stay in Grenoble).

13. *Lindane:* Heroine of *L'Écossaise*.

14. *Thalia:* The Muse of comedy and of the theater in general.

15. *L'Écossaise,* Act V, scene 3; Voltaire's French runs: *Je vous adore, je le dois.*

16. *P-i:* Laforgue expanded this to Preti; in Vol. 9, Chap. III, C. calls him Paretti, probably a fictitious name; in any case, no information about him except what C. gives has come to light.

17. *The Banchi:* The Piazza Banchi, which still exists near the port in the old part of the city; it took its name from the many banks of which it was the site in the Middle Ages.

18. *Bragadin:* Matteo Giovanni Bragadin (1689-1767), Venetian patrician, Senator, and faithful friend to C. (cf. Vols. 2 ff.).

19. *After being Doge . . . law:* Grimaldi was Doge of Genoa from 1756 to 1758. There was no written law in Genoa that former Doges might not leave the Republic; possibly a customary law to that effect had become established with the passage of time. There is no indication that Grimaldi's travels were frowned on by the Republic.

20. *My friend the Syndic:* See Vol. 6, Chap. X, n. 27.

21. *Zoïlus:* Of Amphipolis in Macedonia, Greek rhetorician (probably 3rd century B.C.), known for his carping and malicious criticism of Homer. (For a different explanation by C. of his hostility to Voltaire, see Vol. 6, Chap. X, p. 246.)

22. *Cereris:* The text has *Cesaris* but the Brockhaus-Plon edi-

tion so abounds in obvious typographical errors—e.g., to cite only the nearest to hand, Vol. 7, p. 104, line 15: *comme le premier; acteur elle* (*sic:* for *comme le premier acteur; elle*)—that it cannot bear any witness in such a case. If the very conditionally announced facsimile of the ms. ever appears, it will be interesting to see if C., for all his indifferent spelling, ever went so far astray.

23. Horace, *Odes,* III, 2, 26-28 (where the reading is *Cereris;* see the previous note).

CHAPTER VI

1. *Annetta:* Probably Maria Anna Alizeri (born after 1734), younger sister of Veronica (cf. this volume, Chap. IV, n. 27).
2. *Mezzaro:* See note 24 to Chap. IV of this volume.
3. *"My dear one . . . before you leave":* In the manuscript this letter shows many erasures, perhaps because C. was trying to reconstruct it in the absence of the original. The issue is confused by the fact that a manuscript found at Dux provides a variant version of this part of the memoirs, in which the episode with Veronica and Annetta is related differently.
4. *Vestal:* Name applied to the 6 priestesses of the Roman goddess Vesta; they were required to be virgins.
5. *Lerici:* Small port on the Gulf of La Spezia.
6. *Lunel:* Town and wine district in western Provence, some 15 miles from Montpellier.
7. Martial, *Epigrams,* I, 57, 2.
8. *Genoveffa . . . lightning:* See Vol. 2, Chap. XI, and Vol. 3, Chap. I.
9. *A neighbor of mine:* Allusion to C.'s quarrels with the physician O'Reilly, who lived in Oberleutensdorf, near Dux. In 1792 C. composed a satire on him, entitled: *Passe-temps de Jacques Casanova de Seingalt pour le carnaval de l'an 1792 dans le bourg de Oberleutensdorf.*

CHAPTER VII

1. *Portoghese:* Gold coin, originally minted at the end of the 15th century and the beginning of the 16th under King

Emanuel of Portugal and soon imitated in other European countries; value, 10 ducati.

2. *The best inn:* Presumably the "Croce di Malta," also known as the "Croce d'Oro."

3. *The theater:* Until 1782 there was only one theater in Leghorn, the Teatro delle Commedie, also called Teatro di San Sebastiano after the nearby church; the street is still named Via della Commedia.

4. *Chiari:* Pietro Chiari (1711-1785), Jesuit, Professor of Oratory at Modena (1736-1737), Court Poet to the Duke of Parma; he later settled in Venice, where he wrote plays and novels.

5. *Satire:* Chiari attacked C. in a satirical novel, *La Commediante in Fortuna* (Venice, 1755); cf. Vol. 4, Chap. IX.

6. *Passano:* Giacomo Passano (died ca. 1772) used the anagrams Ascanio Pogomas and Cosimo Aspagona; actor, writer, and adventurer.

7. *La Chiareide . . . :* The manuscript of this work is in the Biblioteca Estense in Modena; its 1200 verses against Chiari have never been printed. C. is wrong in stating that the sonnets all end alike.

8. *Perfect:* The text has *purissimo*.

9. *Coglione:* The word, as C. explains a few lines further on, means "testicle"; it is commonly used as a term of abuse in Italy. The French *couillon*, a derivative from *couille*, is used in the same sense.

10. *Goldoni:* Carlo Goldoni (1707-1793), the greatest Italian comic dramatist of the 18th century.

11. *M. F.:* Louis de Muralt-Favre (1716-1789), Swiss government official (cf. Vol. 6, Chap. VIII).

12. *"Hussar" inn:* Until 1943 there was a Caffé dell'Ussero on the Lungarno Regio (now Lungarno Pacinotti); it may well have been an inn during the 18th century.

13. *Corilla:* Maria Maddalena Fernandez, née Morelli (1727-1800), whose name as a member of the Arcadian Academy was "Corilla Olimpica"; poetess famous for her improvisations, for which she was crowned at Rome in 1776.

14. *As the ancients depicted Venus:* Some ancient authorities held that Venus squinted; cf. Varro, *Saturae Menippeae*, 344, and Petronius, *Satyricon*, LXVIII.

15. *Ponte alla Carraia:* Built in 1218 and then called Ponte Nuovo (in distinction from the earlier Ponte Vecchio), it was several times destroyed and finally rebuilt in 1559 from plans by the architect Bartolomeo Ammanati. Blown up in 1944 during the Second World war, it was rebuilt in its old form.

16. *Vannini's:* The hostelry of Attilio Vannini in the Borgo Ognissanti, Florence, enjoyed an excellent reputation in the 18th century. He was a doctor of letters, not of medicine.

17. *Accademia della Crusca:* The Accademia Nazionale della Crusca, or Accademia Furfuratorum, took its name from its purpose, which was to guard the purity of the Italian language by separating the chaff (*crusca*) from the wheat. It was founded by Cosimo I de' Medici in 1540. In 1591 it began to compile a dictionary. This work, though it was never completed, acquired great authority. It is unlikely that Vannini was ever a member of the Academy.

18. *The theater:* The Teatro del Cocomero, in the street of the same name; it survived until 1930, when it became a cinema (Teatro Nicolini).

19. *Roffi:* Giovanni Roffi (died after 1780), Tuscan actor and theater director, famous for his interpretation of the role of Arlecchino.

20. *Pertici:* Pietro Pertici, who appeared first as a singer from 1731 to 1744, and, from 1748, as an actor; from 1751 to 1756 he played in Florence with a company of his own.

21. *The opera in the Via della Pergola:* At the Teatro della Pergola, built about the middle of the 17th century in the street of the same name, and still standing.

22. *Teresa:* For C.'s account of his meeting with Teresa, then masquerading as the castrato Bellino, his discovery of her true sex, and his subsequent affair with her, see Vol. 2, Chaps. I and II. There C. calls her only by her first name; in the present chapter he gives her the surname Lanti; in Vol. VIII he gives her husband's name as Palesi; it is not until Vol. X that he reveals her real name: Angela Calori (born 1732, died ca. 1790).

23. *"The same":* This would seem to indicate that C. did not use the name Chevalier de Seingalt during this visit to

Florence. But a contemporary document shows that he registered at Vannini's hostelry as "Cavaliere Sangalli."

24. *Mandane:* None of the operas produced at the Teatro della Pergola in 1760 and 1761 contained such a role. C. is obviously trying to conceal the identity of Teresa, who was a famous singer.

25. *Cirillo Palesi:* Presumably a fictitious name for Angela Calori's husband.

26. *Sancho Pico:* See Vol. 2, Chap. I.

27. *Ducati del regno:* The ducato del regno was a gold coin of the Kingdom of Naples, minted from the 16th century.

28. *Redegonda:* C. met her again at Turin in 1762 and at Brunswick in 1764; she may have been a certain Signora Blizzi.

29. *Corticelli:* Maria Anna Corticelli (1747-1767 or '73), Italian dancer.

30. *Gama:* Giovanni Patrizio da Gama de Silveira (ca. 1704-1774), born in Lisbon, made a Roman citizen in 1735 (cf. Vol. 1, Chaps. IX and X).

31. *Acquaviva:* Troyano Francisco Acquaviva d'Aragona (1696-1747); Cardinal from 1732; Spanish Ambassador in Rome from 1737 (cf. Vol. 1, Chaps. IX and X).

32. *Barbaruccia . . . the Marchesa G. . . . Cardinal S. C.:* Barbara Dallacqua, the Marchesa Caterina Gabrieli, Cardinal Prospero Colonna di Sciarra; acquaintances of C. during his first stay in Rome (cf. Vol. 1, Chap. X).

33. *The same Duke:* Francisco Eboli, Duke of Castropiñano (1688-1758), of Spanish descent, Neapolitan General and diplomat.

34. *When the Duke died:* In 1758.

35. *Della Riccia:* Bartolomeo de Capua, became Prince della Riccia in 1732, and died, the last of his line, in 1792.

36. *La Sensa:* The Fiera della Sensa, the great fair held yearly in Venice at Ascensiontide, at which time the theaters were open.

37. *Matalona:* Carlo Caraffa, Duke of Matalona (Maddaloni) (1734-1765), married Vittoria Guevara in 1755 (cf. Vol. 1, Chap. IX).

38. *A son:* Marzio Domenico V (1758-1829); his marriage

(1774) to Donna Maria Josefa de Cardenas, Countess of
Acerra, was annulled by Pope Pius VI on the ground of
impotence, the same infirmity which had been attributed to
his father.

39. *Daughter of the Duke of Bovino:* Vittoria Guevara was the
daughter of Innico Guevara, Duke of Bovino, and his wife
Eleonora.

CHAPTER VIII

1. *Almada:* Francisco, Marquês de Almada (Almeida, Almeda)
y Mendoça, Portuguese Ambassador in Rome from 1757 to
1760 and from 1769 to after 1799.
2. *Rezzonico:* Carlo Rezzonico (1693-1769), Cardinal at Padua
from 1743, Pope, as Clement XIII, from 1758.
3. *His Most Faithful Majesty:* Title of the King of Portugal.
4. *Intended to kill him:* Allusion to the attempted assassina-
tion of King Joseph Emanuel I (1715-1777) on Sept. 3,
1758, which was generally ascribed to the Jesuits. The
petition to the Pope to empower the King to punish the
suspected Jesuits was dismissed by Clement XIII. Thereupon the all-powerful Minister, the Marquês de Pombal,
banished the Papal Nuncio from Lisbon and the Jesuits
from Portugal (1759) The Portuguese Ambassador in Rome
left the city on July 7, 1760, and did not return to it until
1769; the Abate Gama followed him back in 1770.
5. *Carvalho:* Sebastião José de Carvalho e Mello, Marquês de
Pombal (1699-1782), Prime Minister of Portugal from 1757
to 1777.
6. *State Inquisitors:* The 3 State Inquisitors (Inquisitori di
Stato) constituted the highest court in the Republic of
Venice. In 1755 they sentenced C. to indefinite imprisonment
under the Leads.
7. *Botta-Adorno:* Antonio Ottone, Marchese Botta-Adorno
(1688-1774), Austrian diplomat, field marshal, and supreme
commander of the Austrian troops in Italy; Governor of
Tuscany from 1757 to 1766.
8. *Governor of Tuscany:* In accordance with a treaty concluded among Austria, France, and Spain in 1735, Duke

Franz Stephan of Lorraine was declared the heir to Tuscany. The Duke having married the Empress Maria Theresa in 1736, on the death of the last Grand Duke of the Medici family the Grand Duchy of Tuscany became a possession of the Hapsburgs and was administered by a Governor.

9. *Francis I:* Franz Stephan of Lorraine (1708-1765), Emperor of Austria from 1745 (cf. the previous note).

10. *Signora Laura:* Laura Corticelli, née Citti (also Cilli or Cigli), married to Antonio Corticelli.

11. *Impresario:* According to information furnished by the Biblioteca Comunale of Florence, the Teatro della Pergola was under the direction of the impresario Compostov from 1760 to 1761.

12. *Chavigny:* Anne Théodore Chavignard, Chevalier de Chavigny (1689-1771), French Ambassador in Soleure (Solothurn) from 1753 to 1762 (cf. Vol. 6, Chaps. V ff.).

13. *Orihuela:* Village in southern Spain, between Alicante and Murcia.

14. *Camerino:* Dressing room.

15. *Testone:* Originally a French silver coin called "têton" because it displayed the King's head; it was minted in France from the reign of Louis XI (1461-1483), and until the introduction of the franc in 1567 was the most important French coin. It was imitated in Rome and Tuscany from the 16th century. Value: 40 soldi.

16. *The Genoese affair:* In the War of the Austrian Succession Genoa sided with Spain, France, and the Kingdom of Naples in 1745. In Sept. 1746 the city was taken by the Austrian forces under the command of the Marchese Botta-Adorno; but they were driven out as early as Dec. of the same year by a popular uprising and were unable to retake the town.

17. *So easily ascended the throne of her father:* Elisabeth Petrovna, daughter of Peter the Great, caused the Regent Anna Leopoldovna and her son Ivan VI to be poisoned in Dec. 1741, banished the Regent's supporters to Siberia, and had herself proclaimed Czarina.

18. *Giton:* Name of a boy catamite in the *Satyricon* of Petronius (died A.D. 66).

19. *The wristband game:* Text, *le manège de la manchette* = pederasty.

20. *Mann:* Sir Horatio (Horace) Mann (1701-1786); he came to Florence in 1738 as the English Chargé d'affaires, was appointed Resident in 1740, Envoy Extraordinary in 1765, and Plenipotentiary in 1782. He does not mention C. in his letters to Horace Walpole, but he was one of the subscribers to C.'s translation of the *Iliad* (1775-76).

21. *The gallery:* The celebrated gallery in the Palazzo degli Uffizi (built by Vasari from 1560 to 1574) and containing, among other treasures, the rich collection of paintings and other works of art assembled by the Medicis.

22. *Augsburg:* In March 1761 France and her allies proposed a congress at Augsburg to end the Seven Years' War; the proposal came to nothing because of the conditions laid down by Frederick the Great. The war was not ended until 1763, by the Peace of Hubertusburg.

23. *Aleatico:* The name of a sweet red muscat wine of Tuscany, as well as the name of a grape which is also cultivated in other parts of Italy.

24. Since neither the anecdote nor the passage cited occurs in Cicero's letters, C.'s source remains unknown.

25. Vergil, *Aeneid*, X, 113; C. quotes it frequently (e.g., in a somewhat similar context, in Vol. 1, Chap. VI, p. 158).

26. *Merit . . . guilt:* C. uses exactly the same language in his "Preface" (see Vol. 1, p. 25).

27. *Playful pinches:* The word in the manuscript, which is said to be "almost illegible" at this point, is printed as "ciguenaudes," presumably for *chiquenaudes*.

28. *Sasso Sassi:* Florentine banker.

29. *Pistoia:* The town of Pistoia is some 20 miles northwest of Florence, at the foot of the Apennines. The inn referred to is the "Albergo della Serena."

30. *Auditor:* The Florentine Chief of Police was still called the "Bargello" in the 18th century; however, the official in charge of the entire police of the Grand Duchy of Tuscany was called the "Auditore Fiscale"; in 1760 he was Count Roberto Pandolfini.

31. *Cassian:* From G. Cassius Longinus, Roman jurist of the first century A.D., head of the Cassian (also Sabinian) school of jurisprudence, which was anti-liberal.

32. *Customs Office:* From the end of the 17th century the

Dogana di Terra was on the Piazza di Pietra (near the Piazza Colonna); all foreigners arriving by land were obliged to go there immediately, accompanied by a customs officer. All books and manuscripts were confiscated and were not returned to the owner until they had been examined by a representative of the Church.

33. *"City of Paris":* Text: *Ville de Paris.* The name of the hostelry conducted on the Piazza di Spagna by Carlo Roland of Avignon (died 1785), was the "Albergo di Londra" ("London Inn"). However, in 1770 he opened a second hostelry, named the "Ville de Paris," on the Piazza Caetani (now Piazzetta dei Trinitari), near the present Corso. Since C. later stayed at the "Ville de Paris" (in 1771), his error is understandable. (For C.'s previous meeting with Roland and his earlier history, see Vol. 1, Chap. IX, and *ibid.*, n. 46.)

34. *Teresa Roland:* 1744-1779, daughter of the innkeeper Carlo Roland; she married C.'s brother Giovanni in 1764.

35. *The house . . . is living:* From 1752 Giovanni Casanova had been living in the house in which Raphael Mengs resided, Via Vittoria 54, near the Piazza di Spagna.

36. *Mengs:* Anton Raphael Mengs (1728-1779) was appointed first Court Painter to King Augustus III of Poland in 1749 and granted a pension of 1600 thalers. During the Seven Years' War the King had to leave Dresden and fled first to Königstein, then to Poland. Though Mengs had received permission to work in Rome, his pension ceased to be paid him at this time. He remained in Rome, and in 1754 became a director of the Capitoline Academy, founded by Pope Benedict XIV.

37. *La Minerva:* District of Rome, named from the Church of Santa Maria sopra Minerva, near the Pantheon.

38. *Donna Cecilia:* C. called her "Donna Cecilia Monti" in Vol. 1, Chap. IX; according to J. Rives Childs, she was in all probability Cecilia d'Antoni; mother of "Donna Lucrezia" (probably Anna Maria d'Antoni, who married the painter Alessio Vallati in 1734), and of "Donna Angelica" (probably Lucrezia d'Antoni, who married a certain Filippo Tomassi in 1745). For C.'s relations with them, cf. Vol. 1, Chaps. IX and X.

39. *Donna Angelica:* See the foregoing note and Vol. 1, Chap. X.

40. *The doctor . . . Barbaruccia:* The references are to Barbara Dalacqua and her lover (cf. Vol. 1, Chaps. IX and X).

41. *Giorgi:* Antonio Agostino Giorgi (1711-1797), Procurator General of the Augustinian Order and Librarian of the Biblioteca Angelica in Rome (cf. Vol. 1, Chaps. IX and X).

42. *Vivaldi:* Marco Tomaso Niccolò Gaspare, Marchese di Vivaldi (1699-1767); he lived in Marino, south of Rome (cf. Vol. 1, Chap. IX).

43. *Signora Cherufini:* Countess Francesca Cherufini, née Gherardi (1709-1778), mistress of Cardinal Alessandro Albani; her receptions, conducted in the style of a French *salon* in the present Palazzo Frascara (Piazza Pilotta 3), were among the most brilliant literary and social functions in Rome.

44. *Her daughters:* Vittoria, known as "Tolla," born ca. 1742, and Maddalena, known as "Nena," born 1746; the former married Giuseppe Lepri (died 1774) in 1764, the latter married Count Gianfrancesco Maffei, of Cesena, in 1776.

45. *Winckelmann:* Johann Joachim Winckelmann (1717-1768), celebrated German antiquarian, studied Protestant theology at Halle, was converted to Catholicism in 1754, went to Rome in 1755 with a stipend, became librarian to Cardinal Archinto in 1757, and, after the latter's death in 1758, librarian to Cardinal Albani, was appointed Keeper of Antiquities at the Vatican Library in 1763. Though he never received minor orders Winckelmann dressed as an abate from 1757.

46. *Twelve years later:* Winckelmann was robbed of his money and murdered at an inn in Trieste in 1768, hence 8 years after the time of which C. is writing.

47. *Albani:* Alessandro Albani (1692-1779), Cardinal from 1721, Imperial Ambassador in Rome from 1746, Librarian of the Vatican.

48. *Ordine santissimo:* A Papal ordinance.

49. *Voisenon:* Claude Henri de Fusée de Voisenon (1708-1775), celebrated French writer of the period and member of the Académie Française (cf. especially Vol. 3, Chap. X).

50. *Villa Albani:* Now the "Villa Torlonia"; it is outside the

old city wall, just north of the Porta Salaria; it was built
by Carlo Marchionni from 1743 to 1763 for Cardinal Alessandro Albani, who with the help of his friend the antiquarian Winckelmann made it the repository of a precious collection of antique sculpture. Napoleon I had nearly 300
works of art from the collection conveyed to Paris; only a
small proportion of them was returned in 1815.

51. *Cavaliere Mengs:* Mengs was made a Knight of the Order
of the Golden Spur (see note 43 to the following chapter)
in 1758, probably in recompense for 2 portraits of Clement
XIII which he painted.

52. *Painting a ceiling:* Mengs worked on his celebrated ceiling painting "Parnassus" in the Villa Albani from 1760 to
1761.

53. *A year later:* Giovanni Casanova did not marry Teresa
Roland until May 1764, and took her to Dresden with him
in the autumn of the same year. Her first son was baptized
there as Carolus Xaverius Vincentius Franciscus on Dec. 24,
1765.

54. *Greek:* C. puns on the slang meaning of "Grec": "sharper."

55. *Damasippus:* Brutus Damasippus, Roman artist and art
dealer of the first century B.C., known in his time as un-
trustworthy in business (cf. Horace, *Satires,* II, 3, 16 ff., and
Juvenal, VIII, 185-186).

56. Horace, *Odes,* I, 1, 12. Attalus III Philometor, King of
Pergamum 138-133 B.C., left his fabulous wealth to the
Roman people.

57. *Died in the middle of his career:* Mengs died in 1779 at the
age of 51.

58. *Cornaro:* Giovanni (Zuane) Cornaro, also Corner (1720-
1789), Venetian patrician, Auditor of the Rota from 1758,
Governor of Rome 1776, Cardinal 1778.

59. *Rota:* The Sacra Romana Rota is the Papal court of appeal
for ecclesiastical suits. The 16 judges have the title "Auditor."

60. *Passionei:* Domenico Passionei (1682-1761), from 1731 to
1738 Papal Nuncio in Vienna, made a cardinal and secretary
of the Papal "brevia" in 1738, Librarian of the Vatican from
1755; he was an outspoken enemy of the Jesuits and corresponded with Voltaire.

CHAPTER IX

1. *The Pope did not like him:* As a Benedictine, Cardinal Passionei was a strong opponent of the Jesuits, whom Pope Clement XIII favored.

2. *Coglione:* Cf. note 9 to Chap. VII of this volume. The gloss further on in the text is C.'s.

3. *Tamburini:* Fortunato Tamburini (1683-1761), of Modena; Benedictine; made a cardinal in 1743.

4. *Santa Croce:* Antonio Publicola, Prince of Santa Croce (1736 - after 1800).

5. *At their last gasp:* Allusion to the abolishment of the Jesuit Order by Pope Clement XIV in 1773.

6. *Funeral eulogy on Prince Eugene:* Cardinal Passionei's *Oratio funebris in Principem Eugenium* was published at Vienna in 1737; the Italian version of it, *Orazione in morte di Francesco Eugenio principe di Savoia,* at Padua in the same year. The Cardinal had composed it in 1736, when he was Nuncio in Vienna.

7. *Pandectarum liber unicus:* The *Pandects* or *Digests* is a collection of excerpts from the writings of Roman jurists, made by direction of the Emperor Justinian and published in the 6th century as *Corpus juris.* C. later refers to it as "the code."

8. *M. F.:* Louis de Muralt-Favre (1716-1789) (cf. note 11 to Chap. VII of this volume).

9. *A fine library of his own:* Cardinal Passionei's library was housed in the Palazzo della Consulta, on the Quirinal; after his death it was combined with the Biblioteca Angelica. Winckelmann was not its librarian, but had free access to it.

10. *Monte Cavallo:* The Palazzo di Monte Cavallo, on the Quirinal, was the summer residence of the Popes.

11. *Occupied the episcopal throne there:* Clement XIII was Bishop of Padua from 1743 to 1758 (the year in which he was elected Pope).

12. *Momolo:* Giovanni Righetti, of Venice; C.'s "Momolo" is apparently meant to conceal Mariuccia's family name; Righetti's daughter Tecla married Gaetano Costa, C.'s secretary, in 1763.

13. *Ca' Rezzonico:* Many Venetian palazzi are called Ca', from "casa" (house). The Ca' Rezzonico belonged to the patrician family of the same name, of which Pope Clement XIII (Carlo Rezzonico) was a member.

14. *Scopatore:* Designation of the servant whose duty it was to sweep and clean the Pope's rooms. The gloss immediately following in the text is C.'s.

15. *Trinità dei Monti:* Church and monastery of the Minimite Order, on Monte Pincio, built in 1493 by Charles VIII of France and dedicated to St. Francis of Paola; the church was restored in 1774 and dominates the Piazza di Spagna from the top of the Scala di Spagna.

16. *Vatican:* The celebrated Biblioteca Apostolica Vaticana (often abbreviated to "Vaticana") was founded by Pope Martin V in 1417.

17. *Polenta:* Italian dish, prepared from corn meal.

18. *Orvieto:* A kind of muscatel wine produced in the vicinity of Orvieto, in north-central Italy.

19. *Lottery:* As appears from the sequel, the lottery was of the *lotto genovese* type (cf. Vol. 5, Chaps. II ff., especially note 23 to Chap. II, and note 19, below).

20. *Coming out fifth:* Out of 90 numbers, 5 were drawn. Players could stake on 1, 2, 3, 4, or 5 numbers. It was also possible to stake on the order in which numbers would be drawn, as C. does in this instance; winners under these conditions received a proportionately higher return.

21. *Sister:* Theresia Concordia Mengs (1725-1806).

22. *Maroni:* Anton Maron, also Antonio Maroni (1733-1808), painter; though of Viennese origin, from 1756 he lived in Rome almost exclusively.

23. *Mengs's wife:* Margherita Teresia Geltrude, née Guazzi (1729-1778).

24. Horace, *Satires,* II, 3, 325.

25. *Bathyllus:* Name of a handsome youth loved by the Greek poet Anacreon.

26. *B[uggers]:* C. writes *b* . . . (for *bougres*).

27. *Augustus . . . adultery:* Both the Emperor Augustus and Gaius Cilnius Maecenas (1st century B.C.) were patrons of Horace. C. may refer to Horace's defense of himself in *Satires,* I, 6, 68-70, which is addressed to Maecenas. No

passage in Horace's works corresponds exactly to C.'s description; however, admissions of homosexual love occur here and there in the *Odes* and *Epodes*.

28. *Smerdias:* Another youth loved by Anacreon (cf. note 25 to this chapter); the name was often applied in a general sense to a catamite, as Winckelmann uses it here.

29. *The Venetian Ambassador:* Alvise V Sebastiano Mocenigo (1725-1780), Venetian patrician, Ambassador of the Republic of Venice in Rome from 1760 to 1761.

30. *Secretary of the Tribunal:* The Secretary of the Council of Ten was one of the most powerful members of the Venetian government (cf. Vol. 1, Chap. IV, n. 37).

31. *Roman scudi:* The Roman scudo was a silver coin worth 10 paoli or 100 baiocchi.

32. *Alfani:* Francesco Maria Alfani (died 1798), related to the Galiani family, art collector. This is the first time C. mentions him.

33. *Belloni:* The Marchese Girolamo Belloni (died 1761), director of the Roman banking house of the same name; author of a then celebrated treatise on commerce (1750), which gained him the title of Marchese.

34. *Twenty-seven scudi each:* C. Later implies (p. 196) that the four girls' winnings totaled 200 scudi. Still later he makes Mariuccia say (p. 198) that her mother had won 50 scudi, then (p. 202) that her own and her mother's winnings totaled 100 scudi. C. (p. 192) having shown her mother to disapprove of his having bought lottery tickets for the 4 girls, it seems unlikely that she bought one for herself; and his account leaves no room for him to have bought one for her. In a final discrepancy, C. promises Mariuccia (p. 203) that he will take another 100 scudi to her confessor so that she can spend her 100 from the lottery on clothes.

35. *Two hundred scudi:* See the previous note.

36. *Praxiteles:* Celebrated Greek sculptor (4th century B.C.).

37. *The fifty of her winnings:* See note 34.

38. *Paoli:* The paolo was a silver coin of the Ecclesiastical State worth 10 baiocchi; 10 paoli were equivalent to 1 scudo.

39. *The hundred zecchini:* Here the Roman zecchino, a gold coin worth approximately 2 scudi; first minted under Pope Benedict XIII (1724-1730).

40. *The Teatro Aliberti:* Also known as Teatro delle Dame and built by Antonio Aliberti in 1717, it was on the Via Margutta near the Via Babuino; it was demolished about the middle of the 19th century.

41. *The hundred scudi they had won:* See note 34.

42. *The hundred she had won:* See note 34.

43. *Order of the Golden Spur:* It was founded by Pope Pius IV in 1559 to reward Catholics who had distinguished themselves in science and art. Highly prized in the 16th century, the cross was later so generously distributed that it came to be little regarded.

44. *Apostolic Prothonotary extra urbem:* The title of Apostolic (Papal) Prothonotary originated in the 14th century and was applied to all notaries in the service of the Holy See. *Extra urbem* signifies "outside the city [of Rome]."

45. Hebrews, IX, 22.

46. *Hung . . . neck . . . ribbon:* This was contrary to the regulations, according to which the cross was only to be worn attached to the buttonhole by a narrow red ribbon. C. obeys the regulation later when he calls on the Pope wearing the cross.

47. *Gilded soldiers . . . Laterano:* Knights of the Order of the Golden Spur bore the title "Aureatae Militiae Equites" or "Comites Palatini Lateranenses," from the former seat of the Pope, the Lateran, or from the Church of San Giovanni in Laterano there.

48. *Cahusac:* Louis de Cahusac (1700-1759), advocate in Toulouse and man of letters; he wrote the libretto of the opera *Zoroastre* (1749), with music by Rameau. C. had translated the libretto into Italian in Dresden (cf. Vol. 3, Chap. X). Cahusac did become insane toward the end of his life, but hardly for the reason C. alleges.

49. *Czartoryski:* August Aleksander, Prince Czartoryski (1697-1782), of Polish extraction, was Palatine of what was then called "Red Russia" (Eastern Galicia, Volhynia, and Podolia).

50. *Threatening to erupt:* The eruption of Vesuvius began on Dec. 23, 1760, and continued for 7 days.

CHAPTER X

1. *Martorano:* In central Calabria, near Cosenza (cf. Vol. 1, Chap. VIII).
2. *Antonio Casanova:* A relative of C.'s in Naples (cf. Vol. 1, Chap. IX).
3. *Palo:* Gennaro Palo, of Naples, to whom the Bishop of Martorano had given C. a letter of introduction (cf. Vol. 1, Chaps. VIII and IX).
4. *Castelli:* Husband of Donna Lucrezia; the name is probably fictitious (cf. note 38 to Chap. VIII of this volume).
5. *Caraffa:* The Marchese Lelio Caraffa, Duke of Arienzo, of the ducal family of Matalona (Maddaloni), died 1761.
6. *Palazzo Matalona:* Or Maddaloni; it was on the Via Toledo (cf. Vol. 1, Chap. IX).
7. *Daughter of the Duke of Bovino:* Carlo Caraffa, Duke of Matalona (Maddaloni) (1734-1765), was married in 1755 to Vittoria Guevara, of the ducal house of Bovino (cf. Vol. 3, Chap. IX).
8. *Casalnuovo:* Antonio Como, Duke of Casalnuovo.
9. *A son:* Marzo Domenico V, the last Duke of Matalona (Maddaloni) (1758-1829), son of Duke Carlo Caraffa and Vittoria Guevara.
10. *Pretended antiquities:* Francesco Maria Alfani (died 1798) was often accused at the time of selling spurious antiquities.
11. *Scathing satire:* The Duke of Matalona was imprisoned in the fortress of Gaeta in 1756 for composing a satirical comedy; this may be the work to which C. refers.
12. *Teatro San Carlo:* One of the most celebrated theaters in Italy. It was built under King Charles Bourbon and dedicated in 1737; the present building was not constructed until 1817.
13. *The very young King:* King Ferdinand IV of Naples (1751-1825) had ascended the throne in 1759.
14. *An anniversary:* The reference is presumably to the gala performance of the opera *Attilio Regolo* (libretto by Metastasio, music by Jomelli) given Jan. 12, 1761, on the occasion of the King's birthday.

15. *Intelligence . . . education:* C. may here be unconsciously echoing Montesquieu's *Esprit des lois*.

16. *Boerhaave:* Hermann Boerhaave (1668-1738), celebrated physician and professor at the University of Leiden.

17. *Januarius:* Italian, San Gennaro; the patron saint of Naples; his relics are preserved in the cathedral (cf. Vol. 3, Chap. VII, n. 29).

18. *Madame:* As appears from the sequel, they are speaking French.

19. *In the first edition:* Contrary to C.'s statement, this epigram is not by La Fontaine and is not included in any edition of his works. It is doubtless by one of his many 18th-century imitators.

20. *Monteleone:* Fabrizio Mattia Pignatelli, Duke of Monteleone (1718-1763).

21. *Livret:* The 13 cards dealt to each player in faro.

22. *Chilblains:* From his letters it appears that King Ferdinand IV was still complaining of his chilblains in 1821.

23. *San Nicandro:* Domenico Cattaneo, Prince of San Nicandro, Duke of Termoli and Count of Aversa, appointed Grand Master of the Crown Prince Ferdinand's household in 1755 and President of the Council of Regency in 1759.

24. *Companion of his studies:* See Vol. 1, Chap. IX.

25. *Vicissitudes . . . Acquaviva:* See Vol. 1, Chaps. IX and X.

26. *The Fiorentini:* The Teatro dei Fiorentini or, more properly, Teatro di San Giovanni dei Fiorentini, named from the adjoining church and also known as the Commedia Nuova, was built in 1618 and still exists.

27. *You:* At this point Leonilda begins to address C. in the second person singular.

28. *Fontana Medina:* One of the most beautiful fountains in Naples, built in the second half of the 16th century by M. A. Naccherino and Pietro Bernini (father of the celebrated Giovanni Lorenzo), and several times relocated. In C.'s day it was in the Strada delle Corregge (now Via Medina, near the Piazza del Municipio).

29. *Crébillon the Younger:* Claude Prosper Jolyot de Crébillon (1707-1777), usually known as Crébillon fils to distinguish him from his father, the celebrated tragic dramatist Prosper

Jolyot de Crébillon; well known as a writer of sometimes licentious stories, among them *Le Sopha* (1745).

30. *Princess della Valle:* Margherita Piccolomini d'Aragona, Princess della Valle di Scafati, née Caracciolo.

31. *Don Marco Ottoboni:* Perhaps a younger brother of Alessandro Ottoboni-Buoncompagni-Ludovisi, Duke of Fiano (1710 - before 1766).

32. *Cassaro:* Cesare Gaetani e Lanza, Prince del Cassaro.

33. *Posilipo:* Hilly district on the Gulf of Naples, a favorite site for residences even in Greek and Roman times because of its magnificent view; now practically a part of the city of Naples.

34. *Virtuosa:* Her name, it appears from the following chapter, was Signora Diana. Three singers or actresses (*virtuose*) by the same name are recorded in the annals of the Italian stage at this period; but little more is known of them than their names, and it is impossible to determine which, if any, of them was the Prince's mistress.

35. *Once:* The oncia (plural, once) was a silver coin of the Kingdom of Naples worth 3 ducati or 30 carlini; there were also gold once, which were worth twice as much.

36. *Caserta:* The city of Caserta, some 20 miles north of Naples, was and still is famous for its great royal palace in a park with impressive fountains. The Palazzo Reale, containing some 1200 rooms, is one of the largest buildings in Italy; it was begun in 1752 and completed in 1774 by L. Vanvitelli.

37. *Galiani:* The Marchese Bernardo Galiani (1724-1772 or '74), elder brother of the celebrated Abbé Galiani, owned an estate at Sant'Agata di Sessa.

38. *Your daughter*: Leonilda's authenticity has been questioned because, in a notation in C.'s hand found at Dux in which he acknowledged having been the father of a child by Donna Lucrezia, he first wrote *un fils de* ("a son by"), then crossed it out and substituted *une fille de* ("a daughter by"). It is, however, possible that he wrote *fils* as the equivalent of Italian *figlio*, which can be used in the sense of "child," without specification of sex.

39. *Phèdre:* The theme of Racine's famous tragedy (1677) is

the incestuous love of Phaedra, wife of King Theseus of Athens, for Hippolytus, his son by a previous marriage.

40. *Tivoli:* C. had first spent a night with Donna Lucrezia in Tivoli (see note 42, below).

41. *Gunfire . . . dark:* Allusion to the circumstances which defeated C.'s first attempt to make love to Donna Lucrezia (cf. Vol. 1, Chap. IX).

42. *Testaccio . . . Tivoli:* The scenes of C.'s successful pursuit of Donna Lucrezia in Rome (cf. Vol. 1, Chaps. IX and X).

43. Petrarch, *Canzoniere,* Sonnet X, line 4.

CHAPTER XI

1. *Francolisi:* On the road from Naples to Rome, between Capua and Sant'Agata.

2. *Robbers:* Attacks by highway robbers on this mountainous stretch of road were dreaded into the 19th century.

3. *Sant'Agata:* The first post station on the road from Naples to Rome.

4. *Galiani:* The Marchese Bernardo Galiani (cf. note 37 to the preceding chapter).

5. *Whom he knew:* The Abate Francesco Maria Alfani (died 1798) was related to Bernardo and Ferdinando Galiani, since their sister Settimia was married to an Andrea Alfani.

6. *His brother:* Ferdinando Galiani was Secretary to the Neapolitan Ambassador in Paris from 1759 to 1769; his brilliant wit soon made him famous in Parisian society, where he was known as the Abbé Galiani. For C.'s acquaintance with him, see Vol. 5, Chap. IV.

7. *Cantillana:* José María Carmelín Enrique Baeza y Vicentello, Count of Cantillana, Marqués de Castromonte, Montemayor y el Aguila (1714-1770), Spanish grandee; he was the Spanish Ambassador in Paris from 1753 to 1770. C. writes *le comte de Cantillana Montdragon,* the latter presumably a slip for "Castromonte" or "Montemayor."

8. *Vitruvius:* Vitruvius Pollio (88-26 B.C.), Roman architect, author of *De Architectura.* Bernardo Galiani's edition of it, *L'architettura di M. Vitruvio Pollione, colla traduzione italiana,* had already been published at Naples in 1758.

9. Horace, *Epistles*, II, 1, 9-10.

10. *His spouse:* The Marchesa Agnese Galiani, née Mercadante, married to Bernardo Galiani in 1745.

11. *Stages:* A stage corresponded to two hours' travel by carriage.

12. *Carillano:* So C.; but he appears to have made the name of a nonexistent town out of that of a river—the Garigliano —which travelers had to cross by boat.

13. *Cassaro:* Cesare Gaetani e Lanza, Prince del Cassaro. On what follows, cf. Chap. X of this volume. For once, see *ibid.*, n. 35.

14. *Piperno:* Post station between Terracina and Rome.

15. *Terracina:* Town on the Gulf of Gaeta, at the point where the Appian Way, after traversing the Agro Pontino from the north, reaches the sea.

16. *Barbary horse race:* The "Corsa [Palio] dei Barberi" was run at Rome every year during the last 3 days of January.

17. *The Carnival:* The Carnival proper began at Rome 8 days before Ash Wednesday; in 1761 it lasted from Jan. 17th to Feb. 3rd.

18. *Corso:* Still one of the busiest streets in Rome, the Corso extends from the Piazza Venezia to the Piazza del Popolo.

19. *Belloni:* Either Girolamo Belloni (see note 33 to Chap. IX of this volume) or his son Francesco, who took over the bank on the death of his father in 1761.

20. *The house:* Presumably Mengs's house, where C. had lodged on his previous visit to Rome (see Chap. VIII).

21. *Blue ribbon:* In France the blue ribbon designated a Knight of the Order of the Holy Ghost (Ordre du Saint-Esprit); cf. Vol. 3, Chap. IX, n. 32.

22. *Tallow:* James Daniel O'Bryan, Viscount Tallow (1736-after 1794), became Earl of Lismore in 1759.

23. *The Countess of Lismore:* Elizabeth O'Bryan (ca. 1711-1787), wife of Daniel O'Bryan, Viscount Tallow, Earl of Lismore (died 1759), from whom she was separated for many years, and mother of James Daniel O'Bryan (see the preceding note).

24. *Saint-Albin:* Charles de Saint-Albin (1698-1764), illegitimate son of the French Regent by a dancer; from 1723 Archbishop of Cambrai.

25. *The Pretender:* James Edward Francis, called "The Old Pretender," was the son of James II, who was dethroned in 1688; his adherents called him James III. There was an ardent group of Jacobites in Rome, who formed the Pretender's court.

26. *Tor di nona:* This theater occupied the site of an old jail of the same name on the left bank of the Tiber opposite the Castel Sant'Angelo. First built in 1660 by Jacques d'Alibert, it was rebuilt in 1733 and 1798 and finally demolished in 1866.

27. *Poinsinet:* Antoine Alexandre Henri Poinsinet de Noirville (1735-1769), French poet and dramatist.

28. *Drowned:* Poinsinet, who was traveling through Spain with a troupe of actors, was drowned while bathing in the Guadalquivir near Cordova.

29. *Order of St. Michael:* The Order (Ordre de chevalerie des protecteurs de l'honneur divin, sous la protection du saint Archange Michel) was founded in 1693 by Joseph Clemens, Duke of Bavaria and Elector of Cologne. It was dissolved in 1918.

30. *Prostitutes:* C. writes *p* . . . (for *putains*).

31. *Chimay:* Not the Prince, who did not take ecclesiastical orders, but probably his younger brother Philippe Gabriel Maurice de Hennin-Liétard (born 1736).

32. *Erection:* C. writes *ferait ban.* . . .

33. *Villa Medici:* Villa with celebrated gardens, on Monte Pincio near the church of Trinità dei Monti, built in 1560 by Annibale Lippi for Cardinal Ferdinando de' Medici; seat of the French Academy in Rome from 1802.

34. *Pâris de Montmartel:* Jean Pâris de Montmartel (1690-1760), French Comptroller-General and Court Banker.

35. *Trastevere:* Literally, "across the Tiber"; old quarter of Rome on the right bank of the Tiber.

36. *The castrato:* Probably Giovanni Osti, nicknamed Giovannino di Borghese. However, in the year of which C. is writing (1761), Cardinal Francesco Borghese (1697-1759) was no longer alive.

37. *Ritornello:* An instrumental passage occurring as a prelude or refrain in a vocal composition.

38. *Of the wristband game:* See note 19 to Chap. VIII of this volume.

39. *Women are forbidden to appear on the stage:* The prohibition was issued by Pope Sixtus V in 1587. In 1686 it was modified to apply only to theaters in Rome and the Ecclesiastical State.

40. *The Marchesa Passarini:* Since C. had met her in Dresden, she may have belonged to the German branch of the Passarini (or Passerini) family, which also had branches in Rome and Florence.

41. *Borghese:* Marcantonio Nicolò Borghese (1730-1800), from 1763 Prince of Sulmona and Rossano.

42. *Ganganelli:* Giovanni Vincenzo Antonio Ganganelli (1705-1774); Cardinal 1759; Pope, as Clement IV, 1769.

43. *Teatro Capranica:* A small theater, opened in 1678 by the Marchese Pompeo Capranica in his palazzo near the Church of Santa Maria in Aquiro, next to the Pantheon. Performances of *opera buffa* were given there from 1754 to the middle of the 19th century. It is no longer used.

44. *Pulcinella:* One of the masks of the *commedia dell'arte* (cf. Vol. 2, Chap. V, n. 7).

45. *Villa Borghese:* Also known as Villa Pinciana, built in 1615 for Cardinal Scipione Borghese on Monte Pincio. In C.'s day it was outside the city proper. In 1902 it was given to the City of Rome.

46. *Albani:* C. probably here refers to Cardinal Alessandro Albani (1692-1779), whom he has mentioned in Chap. VIII of this volume. However, his nephew Gianfrancesco Gaetano Albani (1720-1803), who was likewise a cardinal, was also present in Rome at the time.

47. *Onorati:* Bernardino Onorati (1724-1807), Archbishop of Sidonia *in partibus,* Nuncio in Venice (not Florence) 1767-1775, Bishop of Senigallia from 1777.

48. *Mann:* See note 20 to Chap. VIII of this volume.

49. *Sostratus:* Greek architect who designed and built the Pharos of Alexandria.

50. *Maty:* Matthew Maty (1718-1776), first a practicing physician, later Librarian of the British Museum and Secretary of the Royal Society.

51. *The "Pilgrim":* Al Pellegrino, Bolognese inn opened in the

15th century and well known in the 18th (cf. Vol. 2, Chap. III).

52. *Dutillot:* Guillaume Léon Dutillot (or Du Tillot) (1711-1774), major-domo to the ducal house of Parma from 1749, minister from 1756 to 1771. He had played a part in C.'s separation from Henriette (cf. Vol. 3, Chap. IV).

53. *L'Uccellatoio:* The post station, the first on the road from Florence to Bologna.

CHAPTER XII

1. *Chapter XII:* A marginal note in C.'s hand at the beginning of this chapter reads: *"64 pages supprimés"* ("64 pages deleted"). Since the narrative continues without a break, the reference would seem to be to an earlier version.

2. *"The Ass Unloads":* Text: "l'âne décharge"; C. literally translates "Scaricalasino," which was the name of a post station on the road from Florence to Bologna. The place, which is near the Passo della Raticosa, some 40 miles north of Florence, is now called Monghidoro.

3. *English carriage:* English coachmaking was then as recognizable abroad as English tailoring is today.

4. *Montepulciano:* Old hill town in Tuscany, south of Arezzo, long famous for its excellent wine.

5. *Bargello:* Title of the chief of police, first used in Florence then adopted by other Italian cities. The Bargello of Modena was appointed directly by the Duke of Ferrara and also bore the title Governatore ("Governor"); his position was one of great power.

6. *Manages the opera:* There were several theaters in Modena in the 18th century; the most important among them was the Teatro Ducale. It is possible that the Bargello, as Governor of the City, exercised considerable influence on the direction of the theaters.

7. *Blackguard:* C. writes "J . . . F . . ." for "Jean Foutre," more or less equivalent to modern American "son of a bitch."

8. *Testagrossa:* The Abate Antonio Testagrossa (died 1761), diplomat in the service of the Duke of Modena (cf. Vol. 3, Chap. XII).

9. *The Duke of Modena:* Francesco III Maria d'Este (1698-1780), Duke of Modena, Reggio, and Mirandola from 1737.

10. *Two years:* C. first mentions the name Chevalier de Seingalt in his memoirs in the course of his account of his stay in Switzerland (April-July 1760; cf. Vol. 6, Chap. V, n. 7). The time is now early March of 1761. It is not known when he actually assumed the name.

11. *D'Antoine:* Count François d'Antoine-Placas, Gentleman of the Bedchamber to the Duke of Parma (cf. Vol. 3, Chaps. IV and V).

12. *Dubois-Chatellerault:* Baron Michel Dubois-Chatellerault, also Chateleraux (1711 - ca. 1776), Director of the Parmesan Mint, but only until 1756 (cf. Vol. 3, Chaps. IV and V).

13. *A coining press:* Until 1755 Venetian coins were struck by means of a hammer; Dubois-Chatellerault took a coining press to Venice and published a small book on the work he did there: *Gravures représentant les différentes machines servant à la fabrication des Monnayes au Balancier contruites à Venise pour le service de la Sérenissime Républiqᵗe* (Parma, 1757).

14. *"Touch not Camerina":* Allusion to a Greek legend concerning the town of Camerina (now Torre di Camerina) in southern Sicily. According to Herodotus, the town was visited by plague. Despite the command of the Delphic oracle not to touch the swamp which surrounded the town, the inhabitants drained it. The plague ceased. But the next time the town was attacked it was easily taken, for the enemy soldiers were able to cross the drained swamp. Vergil alludes to the story in *Aeneid,* III, 700 ff.

15. *Greek:* Until the 9th century Venice was a dependency of the Eastern Roman Empire; its economic and political relations with Byzantium-Constantinople remained close in later centuries.

16. *Hardegg:* Johann Joseph Franz de Paula, Count Hardegg (born 1741), Court Cupbearer of Austria and Enns.

17. *Biribissi:* A popular gambling game in Italy in the 18th century, somewhat resembling roulette.

18. *The citadel:* Built in 1565 by order of Emanuele Filiberto, Duke of Savoy, and considered a masterpiece of military architecture in its day. In 1857 it was demolished except for

the central tower, which now houses the Artillery Museum.

19. *Wristband game:* See note 19 to Chap. VIII of this volume.

20. *Leah:* C. writes "Lia." Neither she nor her father Moses ("Moyse") has been identified.

21. *Monsieur Z.:* Unidentified member of the group whom C. met at Aix-les-Bains (cf. Vol. 6, Chaps. X and XI).

22. *Prié:* See note 5 to Chap. I of this volume.

23. *Porta del Po:* The 4 ancient gates of the city were destroyed by the French after the Battle of Marengo (1800).

24. *Callipygian Venus:* Celebrated Greek statue of Aphrodite, then in the Palazzo Farnese in Rome, now in the National Museum, Naples. The epithet means "having beautiful buttocks."

25. *"Come tomorrow":* The following 7 lines in the ms. are so heavily crossed out that they are indecipherable.

26. *Via Po:* Opened in 1675, and one of the principal streets of what was then the new city; it runs from the Piazza Castello to the Po.

27. *Brézé:* Giovacchino Argentero, Marchese di Bersezio and Conte di Bagnasco, known as the "Marquis de Brézé" (1727-1796); man of letters and bibliophile.

28. *Baretti:* Paolo Antonio Francesco Alessio Baretti (ca. 1740 - after 1794).

29. *La Mazzoli:* Anna Maria Teresa Mazzoli, also Mazzola (died after 1771), Italian singer and dancer; she is known to have appeared in Turin in 1761. She was secretly married to Raiberti (see the next note), but he acknowledged the marriage only on his deathbed.

30. *Raiberti:* Cavaliere Carlo Adalberto Flaminio Raiberti-Nizzardi (1708-1771), from 1761 Turinese Secretary of State for Foreign Affairs.

31. *Coconà:* Nothing is known of this person or of his brother Count Trana. Three letters from a Count Coconà di Trana to C., written in 1762 and 1763, are among the mss. preserved at Dux.

32. *Signora Sc.:* In all probability a member of the noble family of Sclopis, which had resided in Turin from the 17th century.

33. *La R.:* Unidentified.

34. *Bautte:* Singular, *bautta;* short cloak with a hood, worn

either as part of the Venetian masking costume or separately when masking was forbidden.

35. *Saint-Gilles:* Count Vittorio Francesco Vignati di San Gillio (ca. 1705-1769), known as the "Comte de Saint-Gilles," illegitimate son of King Victor Amadeus II of Sardinia.

36. *"Change":* The Caffè del Cambio, now Ristorante del Cambio, opened in 1711 and named from the fact that post horses were changed there.

37. *Gold pistole:* Piedmontese pistole (cf. Chap. IV, n. 18).

38. *Cherufini:* The Countess Vittoria Cherufini (born ca. 1742); the operation referred to was performed on June 21, 1769. She bore a daughter in 1775.

39. *Lepri:* Giuseppe Lepri (died 1774) married Vittoria Cherufini in 1764.

40. *La Pérouse:* Gian Giacomo Marcello Gamba della Perosa (1738-1817), known as the "Comte de la Pérouse," married Angelica Tizzoni in 1759.

CHAPTER XIII

1. *Chapter XIII:* A marginal note at the beginning of this chapter reads: "Desunt 22 paginae" ("22 pages missing"). Here again, however, there is no break in the narrative (cf. note 1 to the preceding chapter).

2. *Vicario:* In Turin the administration consisted of the Vicario (or Superintendent of Police), who was appointed directly by the King, of 2 syndics, and of 60 decurions over whom the Vicario presided. His functions were both administrative and judicial.

3. *Order you to leave:* Letters found at Dux show that C.'s expulsion from Turin did not take place until the fall of 1762, during his second stay in that city. Such chronological errors are not infrequent in the memoirs.

4. *The King:* Charles Emmanuel III of Sardinia (1701-1773).

5. *His office:* The offices of the Secretary of State for Foreign Affairs were in a palazzo built by King Carlo Emanule I near the royal palace.

6. *Ossorio:* Giuseppe d'Ossorio-Alarcon (1697-1763), of Sicilian

extraction, from 1725 diplomat in the service of the King of Sardinia, from 1750 Minister of Foreign Affairs.

7. *D'Aglié:* Count Francesco di San Martino d'Aglie (died 1791), Vicario (Police Prefect) of Turin from 1759.

8. *Stormont:* David Murray, Viscount Stormont, Earl of Mansfield (1727-1796), English diplomat and statesman.

9. *Rochebaron:* François La Rochefoucauld, Marquis de Rochebaron (1677-1766), French Lieutenant-General and Commandant of Lyons. It was in his house that C. met the person who was instrumental in his becoming a Freemason (cf. Vol. 3, Chap. VII).

10. *Valenglart . . . Madame Morin . . . a resemblance at Chambéry:* See this volume, Chap. II. When Madame Morin saw the portrait of the Venetian M. M. she had promised to take C. to see the second M. M. in her convent the next time he came to Chambéry.

11. *Del Commercio:* C. presumably means the Caffè del Cambio mentioned earlier.

12. *Scarnafigi:* C. writes "au comte Scarnafis"; probably Giuseppe, Count of Ponte de Scarnafigi (cf. Vol. 6, Chap. XI, n. 3).

13. *The Ambassador:* François Claude, Marquis de Chauvelin (1716-1773), French commander and diplomat, French Ambassador in Turin from 1754 to 1765 (cf. Vol. 6, especially Chap. V).

14. *The only inn:* There were several hostelries in Chambéry in the 18th century; C. probably refers to the inn at the post station, outside the old city walls.

15. *Tolosan:* This person has not been identified.

16. *Mademoiselle Roman:* See Chap. II of this volume.

17. *House in Passy:* The house was in the Grand-Rue, at the corner of the Rue de Passy and the present Rue Gavarni, in the 16th Arrondissement; it was demolished in 1880.

18. *Five months gone with child:* Her son, Louis Aimé de Bourbon, known as "l'Abbé de Bourbon," was born in 1762, but died in Naples of smallpox in 1787.

19. *Her:* I.e., M. M.

20. *Magnan:* Possibly a certain "Monsieur de Magnan" mentioned in Horace Walpole's letters as an adventurer who spoke 14 languages.

21. *"Parc"*: Well-known hostelry, opened in 1755, on the Place des Carmes in Lyons.
22. *Hôtel du Saint-Esprit:* There were no less than 26 inns bearing this name ("the Holy Ghost") in Paris toward the end of the 18th century, but there was no street officially so named. However, contemporary documents sometimes refer to the Rue des Vieilles Garnisons in the 9th Arrondissement as "Rue Saint-Esprit."

HISTORY OF MY LIFE

Volume 8

CONTENTS
Volume 8

LIST OF PLATES

Volume 8

VOLUME 8

CHAPTER I[1]

*My stay in Paris and my departure for Strass-
burg, where I find La Renaud. My misfortunes
in Munich and my unhappy stay in Augsburg.*

---

*AT TEN o'clock in the morning, refreshed by the
pleasant feeling that I was once more in Paris, which, for
all its imperfections, is so attractive that no city in the
world can dispute its right to be considered the city of
cities. I went to see my dear Madame d'Urfé, who received me with open arms. She told me that young
D'Aranda was well and that, if I wished, she would have
him to dine with us the next day. I said I should be glad
to see him, then I assured her that the operation by which
she was to be reborn a man would take place as soon as
Querilinte,[2] one of the three heads of the Rosy Cross, had
been freed from the dungeons of the Inquisition in Lisbon.*

*"That is why," I added, "I must go to Augsburg in
the course of the next month, where, on the pretext of
a mission I have obtained from the government, I shall
confer with Lord Stormont[3] with a view to securing the
adept's release. To that end, Madame, I shall need a good*

*letter of credit and some watches and snuffboxes to
bestow as occasion demands, for we shall have to win
over some of the profane.''*

*"I will gladly see to all that, my dear friend, but you
need be in no hurry, for the Congress is not to assemble
until September.''*

*"It will never be held, Madame, believe me; but the
ambassadors of the belligerent powers will confer even so.
If, contrary to my expectations, a congress should be
held I should have to go to Lisbon.[4] In any case I promise you we shall meet again this winter; I shall have to
devote the two weeks I shall spend here to defeating a
plot of Saint-Germain's.''*

*"Saint-Germain! He would not dare come back to
Paris.''*

*"On the contrary, I am certain he is here now, but he
is in hiding. The government messenger who ordered
him to leave for London convinced him that the English
Ambassador was not taken in by the demand for his
surrender which Count d'Affry made to the States General in the King's name.'' [5]*

*This whole tale was built on nothing but probabilities,
and it will be seen that I guessed right.*

*Madame d'Urfé then congratulated me on the charm-
ing girl who had left Grenoble at my instigation.[6] Valenglart had written her the whole story.*

*"The King adores her,'' she said, ''and she will soon
make him a father. I went to see her in Passy with the
Duchess of Lauraguais.'' [7]*

*"She will give birth to a son who will make France
happy, and thirty years from now you will see wonderful things,[8] which I am unfortunately forbidden to tell
you before your transformation. Did you speak to her
of me?''*

*"No, but I am sure you will find means to see her, if
only at Madame Varnier's.''*

She was right. But now for what chance brought to

pass, as if to urge the excellent woman on to ever more insane delusions.

About four o'clock we were talking of my travels and our plans, when she took a fancy to go to the Bois de Boulogne. She asked me to accompany her, and I acceded to her request. When we were near Madrid [9] we got out of the carriage and, making our way deep into the wood, sat down under a tree.

"It was eighteen years ago today," she said, "that I fell asleep alone in the very place where we are. While I slept the divine Horosmadis[10] descended from the sun and stayed with me until I woke. As I opened my eyes I saw him leave and ascend to Heaven. He left me pregnant with a daughter, whom he took from me ten years ago, doubtless to punish me for having so far forgotten myself for a moment as to love a mortal after him. My divine Iriasis[11] looked like him."

"Are you perfectly certain that Monsieur d'Urfé was not her father?"

"Monsieur d'Urfé never had intercourse with me again after he saw me lying beside the divine Anael." [12]

"He is the Genius of Venus. Was he squint-eyed?"

"Extremely so. Then you know that he squints?"

"I also know that in the amorous crisis he ceases to squint."

"I did not notice that. He, too, left me because of a sin I committed with an Arab."

"He had been sent to you by the Genius of Mercury,[13] who is Anael's enemy."

"It must be so, and it was a grievous misfortune."

"No, your meeting with him made you fit for transformation."

We were walking toward the carriage when suddenly Saint-Germain came in sight; but as soon as he noticed us he turned back and disappeared into another walk.

"Did you see him?" I said. "He is working against us, but our Geniuses made him tremble."

"I am thunderstruck. I shall go to Versailles tomorrow morning to tell the Duke of Choiseul he is here. I wonder what he will say."

When we were back in Paris I took leave of the lady and went on foot to call on my brother, who lived near the Porte Saint-Denis.[14] He received me with cries of joy, as did his wife, whom I found very pretty but very unhappy, for Heaven had refused her husband the power to prove that he was a man, and she had the misfortune to be in love with him. I say the misfortune, for her love made her faithful; otherwise, since her husband treated her very well and left her perfectly free, she could easily have remedied her misfortune. She was consumed with grief because, having no idea that my brother was impotent,[15] she imagined that he deprived her of the object of her desires only because he did not reciprocate the love she felt for him; and her mistake was excusable, for her husband looked a Hercules, and indeed he was one in every respect except that in which she wished to find him so. Her grief brought on a consumption, of which she died five or six years later.[16] She did not die to punish her husband, but we shall see later that her death did in fact prove to be a punishment to him.

The next day I called on Madame Varnier to give her Madame Morin's letter. I was cordially received, and she was so good as to tell me that there was no one whose acquaintance she would rather make than mine, for her niece had told her so many things about me that she was extremely curious to learn more. Curiosity is well known to be woman's greatest infirmity.

"You shall see my beautiful niece, Monsieur," she added, *"and she herself will tell you all her circumstances and the state of her heart."*

She immediately wrote her a note and enclosed Madame Morin's letter in the same envelope.

"If you want to know what answer my niece sends me," said Madame Varnier, *"stay for dinner."*

I accepted, and she immediately gave orders that she was at home to no one.

The little Savoyard who had taken the letter to Passy returned at four o'clock with a note in these words: "The moment when I see the Chevalier de Seingalt again will be one of the happiest of my life. Arrange to have him at your house day after tomorrow at ten o'clock, and if he cannot be there then, please let me know."

After hearing the note read and undertaking to be there on time, I left Madame Varnier and called on Madame du Rumain,[17] who made me promise to devote a whole day to answering a quantity of questions she wanted to ask me, in which I should need the help of my oracle.

The next day I heard from Madame d'Urfé the amusing reply the Duke of Choiseul had made to her when she told him she had met the Count of Saint-Germain in the Bois de Boulogne.

"It does not surprise me," the Minister had said, "since he spent the night in my study."

The Duke, a man of wit and, above all, a man of the world, was of an expansive nature and could keep secrets only in highly important matters; very different in this respect from the would-be diplomats who think they lend themselves importance by making a mystery of trifles whose concealment is of no more consequence than their revelation. It is true that Monsieur de Choiseul rarely thought anything important; and in fact if diplomacy were not the science of intrigue and craftiness, if morality and truth were the foundation of affairs of state, as they should be, secrecy would be more ridiculous than necessary.

The Duke of Choiseul had pretended to disgrace Saint-Germain in France so that he could have him in London as a spy; but Lord Halifax[18] was not taken in; he even declared it a clumsy stratagem; but such are the civilities

which all governments exchange, lest they be found
wanting in their own estimation.

Young D'Aranda, after lavishing caresses on me, asked
me to come to breakfast with him at his boarding school,
assuring me that Mademoiselle Viard would be delighted
to see me.

The next morning I took good care not to miss my
appointment with the beautiful Mademoiselle Roman. I
was at Madame Varnier's a quarter of an hour before the
dazzling brunette arrived, and I awaited her with pal-
pitations of the heart which showed me that the small
favors I had managed to obtain had not sufficed to
quench the fire she had kindled in me. When she appeared, her full figure rather overawed me. A sort of
respect which I felt that I owed to a child-bearing sultana
kept me from approaching her with demonstrations of
affection, but she was far from thinking she deserved
more respect than when I had known her in Grenoble,
poor but untouched. She said as much without mincing
her words, after cordially embracing me.

"People think I am happy," she said, "everyone en-
vies my lot; but can one be happy when one has lost one's
self-respect? It is six months since I have really laughed,
whereas in Grenoble, poor and almost without the necessities of life, I laughed naturally, out of a gaiety on which
there was no constraint. I have diamonds, laces, a splendid house, carriages, a beautiful garden, maids, a lady
in waiting who perhaps despises me; I am treated like
a princess by the highest ladies of the Court, who come
to see me familiarly; yet not a day goes by in which I
do not suffer some mortification."

"Mortification?"

"Yes, petitions thrust upon me, in which I am asked to
beg some favor and which I am obliged to refuse, making
the excuse that I am powerless since I dare not ask anything of the King."

"But why not?"

"*Because I cannot speak to my lover without having the monarch before my eyes. Ah! happiness is in simplicity, not in pomp.*"

"*It is in conforming to one's condition, and you must make every effort to rise to the height of that which destiny has decreed for you.*"

"*I cannot; I love the King and I am always afraid of displeasing him. I always think he gives me more than I deserve; that is why I do not dare to ask any favors of him for others.*"

"*But the King would be happy, I am sure, to prove his love to you by granting you what you ask for the people in whom you show an interest.*"

"*I believe so, and it would make me happy, but I cannot prevail on myself; I have a hundred louis a month for pin money; I distribute them in charity and presents, but sparingly, so that I can reach the end of the month. I have got it into my head, mistakenly no doubt, but ineradicably, that the King loves me only because I do not importune him.*"

"*And do you love him?*"

"*How could I help it? Perfectly polished, kind, gentle, handsome, amorous, and tender, he has everything needed to conquer a woman's heart.*"

"*He is always asking me if I am satisfied with my furniture, my clothes, my servants, my garden, if I want anything changed. I kiss him, I thank him, I tell him that everything is as it should be, and I am happy to see him pleased.*"

"*Does he ever speak to you of the scion you are going to bestow on him?*"

"*He often says that in my condition I must take every care of my health. I have reason to hope that he will recognize my son as a prince of the blood; the Queen being dead,[19] he ought in conscience to do so.*"

"*You may be sure he will.*"

"*Oh, how I shall love my son! What happiness to be*

sure it will not be a girl! But I do not say a word about
that to anyone. If I dared tell the King about your horoscope I am sure he would want to know you; but I am
afraid of slander."

"And so am I, my dear. Continue to keep silent on the
subject; and may nothing come to trouble a happiness
which can only increase and which I am glad to have
procured for you."

We did not part without shedding tears. She left first,
after embracing me and calling me her best friend. I
remained alone with Madame Varnier to regain my composure, and I said that instead of casting her horoscope
I ought to have married her.

"She would have been happier. You may not have
foreseen either her shyness or her lack of ambition."

"I can assure you, Madame, that I did not reckon on
either courage or ambition in her. I lost sight of my own
happiness, thinking only of hers. But what is done is
done. Yet I should be consoled if I saw her perfectly
happy. I hope it will come, especially if she bears a son."

After I dined with Madame d'Urfé we decided to send
D'Aranda back to his boarding school so that we should
be freer for our cabalistic activities; then I went to the
opera,[20] where my brother had arranged to meet me to
take me to supper at Madame Vanloo's,[21] who received
me most cordially.

"You will have the pleasure," she said, "of supping
with Madame Blondel and her husband."

The reader will remember that she was Manon Balletti,
whom I was to have married.

"Does she know I am here?" I asked.

"No, I wanted to have the pleasure of seeing her
surprise."

"I am grateful to you for not having wanted to enjoy
mine. We shall meet again, Madame, but for today I bid
you good-by; as a man of honor I feel that I cannot

permit myself ever to be in any place where Madame Blondel is."

I departed, leaving the company aghast, and, not knowing where to go, I took a hackney carriage and went to sup with my sister-in-law, who was most grateful to me for coming. But through the whole supper the charming woman did nothing but complain of her husband, who should not have married her since he knew he was incapable of fulfilling the functions of a man toward a woman.

"Why did you not make the experiment before you married him?"

"But was it proper for me to make the advances? And then who could suppose that such a fine man would be good for nothing? Here is the story. I was dancing, as you know, at the Comédie Italienne[22] and was being kept by Monsieur de Saincy,[23] treasurer of the ecclesiastical bursary. It was he who brought your brother to my house. I liked him and it was not long before I saw that he was in love with me. My lover advised me that it was a perfect opportunity to give me a settled position by arranging a marriage. With that idea in mind I conceived the plan of granting him nothing. He would come to see me in the morning, often finding me alone in bed; we talked, he appeared to become ardent, but it all ended in kisses. I was waiting for a formal declaration, which would bring about what I then wanted. It was at that juncture that Monsieur de Saincy settled an annuity of a thousand écus on me, making it possible for me to retire from the stage.

"Spring having come, Monsieur de Saincy invited your brother to spend a month in the country, taking me with him, and, in order to maintain an appearance of perfect decency, it was agreed that I should be introduced as his wife. The proposal was acceptable to Casanova, who thought it only a joke and probably did not suppose it

*could lead to anything. So he introduced me as his wife
to my lover's entire family as well as to his relatives—
Councillors in the Parlement, officers, men about town—
and their wives, who were all women of high fashion. It
amused him that the plot of the comedy gave him the
right to insist that we sleep together. I could not refuse
without putting myself in a most deplorable light; in
any case, I was far from averse to making the concession,
I saw in it only a quick road to what I most wanted.*

*"But how can I tell you? Your brother, devoted and
showing me countless proofs of his love, having me in
his possession for thirty nights in succession, never
reached the conclusion which cannot but seem so natural
under such circumstances."*

*"But you should have drawn the inference that he was
impotent, for unless he was made of marble, or had taken
a vow to remain chaste under the strongest of tempta-
tions, his behavior was impossible."*

*"So it seems to you; but the fact is that he showed him-
self neither capable nor incapable of giving me proofs of
his ardor."*

"Why did you not make sure yourself?"

*"Vanity, even mistaken pride, kept me from discover-
ing the truth. I did not even suspect it, I indulged in a
thousand ideas which flattered my self-esteem. I thought
that, truly loving me, he might well fear to put me to the
test before I was his wife. This kept me from descending
to the humiliating course of trying to find out for myself."*

*"All that, my dear sister-in-law, might have been
natural, though decidedly unusual, if you had been an
innocent girl; but my brother knew perfectly well that
you had more than passed through your novitiate."*

*"That is very true; but what fantasies will not arise in
the mind of a woman who is in love and whom love and
self-esteem spur on in equal measure."*

"Your reasoning is very sound, but a trifle belated."

"*I know it only too well. Finally we came back to Paris, he to his lodging, I to my little house, he continuing to court me, I receiving him and at a loss to understand such strange behavior. Monsieur de Saincy, who knew that nothing of consequence had taken place between us, made conjecture after conjecture and could not solve the puzzle. 'No doubt he is afraid of getting you with child,' he said, 'and so being obliged to marry you.' I began to believe it myself; yet I thought it a strange line of reasoning for a man in love.*

"*Monsieur de Nesle,*[24] *an officer in the French Guards and married to a pretty woman who had made my acquaintance in the country, went to your brother's to call on me. Not finding me there, he asked him why I was not living with him. He replied quite frankly that I was not his wife and that it had only been a joke. Monsieur de Nesle came to me to ask if it were true, and, when he learned that it was, he asked me if I would be averse to his forcing Casanova to marry me. I replied that, on the contrary, I should be delighted. That sufficed him. He went to your brother and told him that his wife would never have consented to associate with me on equal terms if he had not himself introduced me to her as his wife, a situation which had entitled me to enjoy all the privileges of good society; that his imposture was an insult to the whole company; and that he must atone for it by marrying me within the week or fighting a duel to the death with him. He added that if he fell in the duel he would be avenged by all the men whom his action had also offended. Casanova laughed and replied that, far from fighting a duel in order not to marry me, he was ready to break more than one lance to get me. 'I love her, and if I am to her liking I am perfectly ready to give her my hand. Be so good,' he added, 'as to take it upon yourself to prepare the way, and I will be at your orders whenever you please.'*

"*Monsieur de Nesle embraced him, promised he would*

*see to everything, then came to me with the news, which
made me completely happy, and within the week the
thing was done. Monsieur de Nesle gave us a splendid
supper on our wedding day, and from then on I have
been his wife in name. But it is an empty title, for, despite the ceremony and the fatal 'yes,' I am not married,
for your brother is completely impotent. I am unhappy,
and it is entirely his fault, for he must have known himself. He deceived me most horribly."*

*"But he was forced into it; he is less to be censured
than pitied. I pity you, too; yet I blame you, for after
having gone to bed with him for a month without his
giving you a single proof of his virility, you could not
but suspect the truth. Even if you had been a complete
novice Monsieur de Saincy should have set you right;
for he must know very well that no man can lie beside a
pretty woman, hold her naked in his arms for such a long
time, and not find himself, despite his will, in a physical
condition which will force him to reveal himself, unless
he is completely without the faculty which constitutes his
essence."*

*"It seems perfectly true when I hear you say it, yet
neither of us ever thought of it, he looks such a Hercules."*

*"I see only one remedy for your situation, my dear
sister-in-law: you must either have your marriage annulled or take a lover; and I think my brother is too
reasonable to object to that."*

*"I am perfectly free, but I cannot think of either a
lover or a divorce; for the wretch treats me so well that
my love for him only grows, which doubtless increases
my unhappiness."*

*I saw that the poor woman was so wretched that I
would gladly have consented to console her; but it was
out of the question. Yet her confiding in me had soothed
her grief for the moment, I congratulated her on it, and*

after kissing her in a way which showed her that I was not my brother, I wished her good night.

The next day I went to see Madame Vanloo, who told me that Madame Blondel had charged her to thank me for not having stayed, but that her husband had asked her to tell me that he was very sorry not to have seen me in order to let me know how greatly he was indebted to me.

"He would seem to have found his wife a virgin, but it is not my fault, and he is indebted for it to no one but Manon Balletti. I am told he has a pretty baby,[25] that he lives in the Louvre, and that she lives in another house in the Rue Neuve-des-Petits-Champs.[26]

"It is true, but he sups with her every evening."

"An odd arrangement for a married couple!"

"A very good one, I assure you. Blondel wants to have his wife only as a conquest. He says it keeps love alive, and that, never having had a mistress worthy to be his wife, he is very happy to have found a wife worthy to be his mistress."

I devoted the whole of the next day to Madame du Rumain, considering knotty questions with her until the evening. I left her well satisfied with the answers. The marriage of her daughter, Mademoiselle Coëtanfao, to Monsieur de Polignac, which took place five or six years later,[27] was the result of our cabalistic calculations.

The beautiful stocking-seller[28] of the Rue des Prouvaires, whom I had loved so ardently, was no longer in Paris. A certain Monsieur de Langlade[29] had carried her off, and her husband was living in poverty. Camilla[30] was ill, and Corallina[31] had become a Marquise and titular mistress of the Count of La Marche,[32] son of the Prince of Conti, to whom she had given a son whom I knew twenty years later, when he wore the Cross of Malta and bore the name of Chevalier de Montréal.[33] Several other young women whom I had known had

become widows and gone to live in the provinces, or were
otherwise inaccessible.

Such was Paris in my day. Women, intrigues, and
principles changed there as quickly as the fashions.

I devoted a whole day to my old friend Balletti,[34] who
had retired from the stage after the death of his father
and had married a pretty ballet girl; he was experiment-
ing with the herb melissa, hoping to succeed in discovering the philosopher's stone.

I had a pleasant surprise in the lobby of the Comédie
Française[35] when I saw the poet Poinsinet, who, after
embracing me several times, told me that at Parma Monsieur Dutillot had overwhelmed him with favors.

"He did not get me a position," he said, "for in Italy
no one knows what to do with a French poet."

"Have you any news of Lord Lismore?"[36] I asked
him.

"Yes, he wrote to his mother from Leghorn, saying
that he was going to India and that if you had not been
so good as to give him a thousand louis he would now be
in prison in Rome."

"I am very much interested in his welfare, and I
should be glad to call on Milady[37] with you."

"I will tell her you are in Paris, and I am sure she
will invite you to supper, for she is most eager to talk
with you."

"How are you getting on here?" I asked him. "Are
you satisfied with Apollo?"[38]

"He is not the god of the Pactolus;[39] I haven't a sou;
I have no room, and I shall be glad to be indebted to you
for a supper if you will invite me. I will read you Le
Cercle,[40] which the actors have accepted, and which I
have in my pocket. I am sure it will be a success."

Le Cercle was a short play in prose, in which the poet
ridiculed the jargon of the physician Herrenschwandt,[41]
brother to the Herrenschwandt I had met in Soleure.
And in fact it proved to be a great success.

I took him to supper, and the poor votary of the Muses ate like four. The next day he came to tell me that the Countess of Lismore expected me for supper.

I found the lady, who was still beautiful, with Monsieur de Saint-Albin,[42] *Archbishop of Cambrai, her aged lover, who spent the entire revenue of his archbishopric on her. This worthy Prince of the Church was one of the natural sons of the Duke of Orléans, the celebrated Regent of France, by an actress. He supped with us, but he never opened his mouth except to eat, and his mistress talked to me of nothing but her son, whose intelligence and talents she praised to the skies, whereas Lord Lismore was really nothing but a wastrel; but I felt I must play up to her. It would have been cruel to contradict her. I left, promising that I would write to her if I ever met her son.*

Poinsinet, who was hearthless and homeless, as the saying goes, came to spend the night in my room, and the next day, after making him take two cups of chocolate, I gave him money enough to rent a room. I did not see him again, for some years later he was drowned, not in Hippocrene[43] *but in the Guadalquivir. He told me that he had spent a week at Monsieur de Voltaire's and that he had hurried back to Paris to obtain the Abbé Morellet's*[44] *release from the Bastille.*

I had nothing more to do before leaving Paris, and I was only waiting for some clothes I was having made and a cross, in rubies and diamonds, of the order which the Holy Father had conferred on me.[45]

I expected everything in five or six days, when an unfortunate incident forced me to leave hurriedly. Here is the incident, which I record reluctantly, for it was a piece of imprudence on my part which very nearly cost me my life and my honor, to say nothing of more than a hundred thousand francs. I am sorry for the fools who, falling into misfortune, complain of Fate, whereas they have nothing to complain of but themselves.

I was walking in the Tuileries about ten o'clock in the morning when I had the bad luck to encounter La Dazenoncourt[46] with another girl. La Dazenoncourt was a ballet girl at the Opéra whose acquaintance I had vainly tried to make before my last departure from Paris. Congratulating myself on the fortunate chance which had thrown me in her way at just the right moment, I approached her, and I did not have much trouble in persuading her to accept a dinner at Choisy.[47]

We walked toward the Pont Royal,[48] and, taking a hackney coach there, set off. After ordering dinner, when we were going out to stroll in the garden, I saw a hackney coach stop and two adventurers whom I knew get out of it with two girls who were friends of the two I was escorting. The accursed hostess, who happened to be at the door, came and told us that if we were willing to be served together she would give us an excellent dinner; I said nothing, or rather, I gave in to the "yeses" of my two light-o'-loves. As it turned out, the dinner was excellent, and after paying, just as we were about to return to Paris, I noticed that I was without a ring which I had taken off during dinner to show it to one of the two adventurers, whose name was Santis,[49] and who had said he wanted to examine it. It was a very pretty miniature, the diamond setting of which had cost me twenty-five louis. I politely asked Santis to return my ring; he replied with the greatest coolness that he had already returned it.

"If you had returned it," I replied, "I should have it, and I do not."

He sticks to his assertion; the girls said nothing, but Santis's friend, a Portuguese named Xavier, had the effrontery to tell me that he had seen him return it to me.

"You are a liar," I say, and, seizing Santis by the neckerchief, I tell him that he shall not leave until I have my ring. But, the Portuguese having at the same time risen to help his friend, I fall back a step and, sword in

*hand, repeat my accusation. The hostess arriving and
setting up an outcry, Santis tells me that if I will allow
him a few words aside he will convince me. Guilelessly
believing that, ashamed to give me back my ring in the
presence of so many people, he would restore it to me
in private, I sheathed my sword, crying:*

"Let us go."

*Xavier got into the hackney coach with the four girls
and they returned to Paris. Santis followed me behind
the Château, and there, assuming a smile, he said that,
wanting to play a joke, he had put my ring in his friend's
pocket but that he would give it back to me in Paris.*

*"That is a lie," I said; "your friend claims that he
saw you return it to me, and you let him go. Do you
think I am ninny enough to be taken in by such a trick?
You are a pair of robbers."*

*So saying, I put out my hand to seize his watch chain,
but he falls back and draws his sword. I draw mine, and
I am scarcely on guard before he makes a lunge at me, I
parry it, close in on him, and run him through. He falls,
calling for help. I sheathe my sword and, leaving him
to his own devices, find my coach and set off for Paris.*

*I got out at the Place Maubert[50] and made my way to
my hotel by a roundabout route. I was sure that no one
would have come to my lodging in search of me, for even
my landlord did not know my name.*

*I spent the rest of the day packing my trunks, and
after ordering Costa to put them on my carriage I went
to see Madame d'Urfé and informed her of what had
happened, asking her, as soon as what she was to give
me should be ready, to deliver it to Costa, who would
rejoin me at Augsburg. I should have told her to send
it all to me by one of her servants, but my good Genius
had abandoned me that day. Then, too, I did not think
that Costa was a thief.*

*Back at the Hôtel du Saint-Esprit,[51] I gave the scoun-
drel my instructions, telling him to waste no time and*

to keep his mouth shut, and giving him the money he would need for the journey.

I left Paris in my own carriage, with four hired horses which took me as far as the second post station, and I did not stop until I reached Strassburg, where I found Desarmoises[52] *and my Spaniard.*

Having nothing to do in that city, I wanted to cross the Rhine immediately, but Desarmoises persuaded me to go to the "Ghost" with him to meet a pretty woman who had put off leaving for Augsburg only in the hope that we might make the journey together.

"She is a young lady whom you know," said the pretended Marquis, "but I had to give her my word of honor not to tell you her name. She has only her chambermaid with her, and I am certain that you will be glad to see her."

My curiosity conquered. I follow Desarmoises and I enter my room, in which I see a pretty woman but one whom I do not at first recognize. My memory returning, I see that she is a dancer whom I had thought charming when I saw her on the stage in Dresden eight years earlier. At that time she belonged to Count Brühl,[53] *Master of the Horse to the King of Poland, the Elector of Saxony; but I had not even tried to pay my court to her. Finding her now with the most luxurious appointments and ready to leave for Augsburg, I instantly began imagining what pleasure such a meeting had in store for me.*

After expressing a delighted recognition on either side, we arranged to leave together for Augsburg the next morning. The beauty was going to Munich, but as I had nothing to do in that small capital we agreed that she should go there alone.

"I am certain," she said, "that you will decide to come there yourself, for the envoys of the powers which are to take part in the Congress will not go to Augsburg until some time in September."

We supped together, and the next day we set out, she in her carriage with her chambermaid and I in mine with Desarmoises, preceded by Leduc on horseback; but at Rastadt we changed our arrangements, for La Renaud [54] thought she would awaken less curiosity if she rode in my carriage instead of staying in her own, and Desarmoises willingly occupied her place beside her maid. It did not take us long to become intimate. She informed me of her situation, or at least seemed to do so, and I confided to her everything which it was not in my interest to conceal. I told her that I had a mission from the Court of Lisbon; she believed me, and I believed that she was going to Munich and Augsburg only to sell her diamonds.

The conversation having turned to Desarmoises, she said that I could perfectly well continue my association with him but that I should not allow him to style himself "Marquis."

"But," I replied, "he is the son of the Marquis Desarmoises, of Nancy."

"He is nothing but an old courier to whom the Department of Foreign Affairs pays a small pension. I know the Marquis Desarmoises who lives in Nancy, and who is not as old as he."

"In that case he can hardly be his father."

"The innkeeper at the 'Ghost' knew him when he was a courier."

"How did you happen to meet him?"

"We dined together at the public table. After dinner he came to me in my room and told me he was waiting for someone in order to leave for Augsburg, and that we might make the journey together. He mentioned your name, and after asking him a few questions I concluded that it could be none other than you, and here we are, to my great pleasure. But one word more: I advise you to give up false names and false titles. Why do you call yourself Seingalt?"

"It is my name, my dear; but that is no reason why people who have long known me may not call me Casanova as well, for I am both. You should be able to understand that."

"Yes, I understand it. Your mother is in Prague, and since she receives none of her pension[55] because of the war, I think she may be in rather straitened circumstances."

"I know that, but I do not forget my duty as a good son, I have sent her money."

"I congratulate you. Where shall you lodge in Augsburg?"

"I shall rent a house, and if it would please you I will make you its mistress and you shall do the honors of it."

"A charming idea, my friend! We will give good suppers there and spend the night gaming."

"That's a delightful plan."

"I undertake to find you an excellent cook; Bavarian cooks are justly famous. We shall cut a fine figure at the Congress, and everyone will say we are madly in love with each other."

"It goes without saying, my dear, that I tolerate no trifling in the matter of fidelity."

"For that, my friend, you may trust me. You know very well how I lived in Dresden."

"I trust you, but not blindly, I warn you. In the meanwhile, let us drop ceremony between us: call me tu. *It is love's way."*

"Very good! Kiss me."

My beautiful Renaud did not like traveling at night because she liked not to stint herself at supper and to go to bed when her head began to turn. The heat of the wine then made her a Bacchante difficult to satisfy; but when I was exhausted I asked her to let me alone, and she had no choice but to obey.

Arrived at Augsburg, we were going to stop at the "Three Moors," [56] but the innkeeper, though saying that *he would give us a good dinner, told me that he could not put me up, because the French Envoy[57] had taken the entire inn. I decided to call on Signor Carli,[58] to whom I had a letter of introduction, and he immediately found me a pretty house with a garden, which I rented for six months and which La Renaud liked very much.*

No one was yet in Augsburg. Having to go to Munich, La Renaud put it to me that I would be bored during her absence and so persuaded me to accompany her. We put up at the "Stag,"[59] where we found excellent lodgings; Desarmoises went to stay elsewhere. My business having nothing to do with my new companion, I gave her a carriage and a lackey for her own use and did the like for myself.

The Abate Gama had given me a letter from the Commendatore Almada[60] for Lord Stormont, the English Ambassador to the Court of Bavaria.[61] That nobleman being in Munich, I hastened to acquit myself of my commission. He received me very well, and assured me that when the time came he would do everything in his power, Lord Halifax having informed him of the entire business. On leaving his British Lordship I went to wait on Monsieur de Folard,[62] the French Ambassador, to whom I presented a letter which Monsieur de Choiseul had sent me through Madame d'Urfé. Monsieur de Folard received me most cordially and invited me to dinner for the next day, and on the day after that he presented me to the Elector.[63]

During the four ill-fated weeks which I spent in Munich the French Ambassador's house was the only one I frequented. I call the four weeks "ill-fated" and with good reason, for during that period I lost all my money, I pawned more than forty thousand francs' worth of jewels, which I never redeemed, and finally, and worst of all, I lost my health. My assassins were none other than La Renaud and Desarmoises, he who owed me so much and repaid me so ill.

The third day after my arrival in Munich I was obliged
to pay a private call on the Dowager Electress of Saxony.[64] It was my brother-in-law,[65] who was in that princess's service, who insisted on my doing so, saying that I
could not avoid it, for she knew me and, in any case, had
already made inquiries about me. I had no reason to repent of my politeness, for the Electress received me well
and made me talk a great deal; she was curious, like all
idle people who are not self-sufficient because they cannot
find resources enough either in their native intelligence
or in their education.

I have done many foolish things in my lifetime; I confess it as frankly as Rousseau,[66] and with less egotism
than that unfortunate great man; but among them there
have been few as absurd as my going to Munich when I
had nothing to do there. But I was passing through a
crisis; it was a period during which my fatal Genius
had proceeded in crescendo from folly to folly ever since
the time I left Turin and even since the time I left
Naples. My fall at night, my evening at Lismore's, my
association with Desarmoises, my excursion to Choisy, my
trust in Costa, my affair with La Renaud, and, above all,
my incredible ineptitude in letting myself be fleeced at
faro at a court where the gamesters who held the bank
were reputed to be the most skillful in Europe at im-
proving upon luck. There, among others, was the famous,
the infamous Afflisio,[67] the associate of Duke Frederick
of Zweibrücken,[68] whom that prince gilded with the
title of his aide-de-camp and whom everyone knew to be
the cleverest scoundrel imaginable.

I played every day, and, frequently losing on my word,
the straits to which my obligation to pay the next day
reduced me caused me intolerable anxiety. When I had
exhausted my credit with the bankers I had to turn to
the Jews, who lend only against pledges, and it was
Desarmoises who acted as my go-between, together with
La Renaud, who ended by laying hands on everything I

*owned. Nor was that the worst service she did me; she
infected me with a disease which was devouring her, but
which, confining its ravages to her inner organs, left her
exterior intact and all the more perilous because her
fresh complexion seemed to indicate the most perfect
health. In short, that serpent dispatched from hell for
my destruction had brought me so completely under her
spell that I neglected the disease for a month because
she had the art to persuade me that her reputation would
be ruined if I put myself in a surgeon's care during our
stay in Munich, since every hanger-on at Court knew that
we were living together as man and wife.*

*When I reflect on it I cannot comprehend such an in-
credible submission to her wishes on my part, especially
when, with every passing day, I added fresh virulence to
the poison she had instilled into my veins!*

*My stay in Munich was a kind of damnation, or rather,
in the course of that fatal month I experienced every
possible form of it, as if all the pains suffered by the
souls of the lost had joined to give me a foretaste of
hell. Renaud loved gambling, and Desarmoises dealt for
her on equal shares. I would never play at their table,
for the false Marquis cheated remorselessly and often
with more impudence than skill. He invited disreputable
people to my lodging, entertaining them at my expense;
afterwards when they began to play there were scandalous scenes every evening.*

*The Dowager Electress of Saxony caused me the most
intense mortification the last two times I had the honor
of conversing with her.*

*"Everyone here is aware, Monsieur, that you are liv-
ing with La Renaud and of the kind of life she leads in
your house, possibly without your knowledge," that
princess said to me; "it is very much to your discredit,
and I advise you to have done with it."*

*She did not know that everything forced me into it.
I had been gone from Paris a month, and I had still*

*heard nothing either from Madame d'Urfé or from Costa.
I could not guess the reason, but I began to suspect my
Italian's fidelity. I also feared that my kind Madame
d'Urfé had died, or had recovered her sanity, which
would have had the same result for me; and the condition
I was in made it impossible for me to return to Paris
to find out what it was so essential I should know, both
for my peace of mind and for the replenishment of my
purse.*

*So I was utterly without resources; and what made
me suffer the most was my being forced to admit to myself that I was experiencing the first symptoms of failing
powers, the usual result of age; I no longer had the
careless confidence which is bestowed by youth and the
consciousness of strength, yet I had not been sufficiently
matured by experience to mend my ways. Nevertheless,
the habit of resolute action which I owed to my character
was not quite dead in me: I took a sudden leave of La
Renaud, telling her that I would expect her in Augsburg.
She made no attempt to detain me but promised that
she would join me as soon as possible, since she was on
the verge of selling her jewels advantageously. I set out,
preceded by Leduc and very well content that Desarmoises chose to remain with the unworthy creature whose
ill-omened acquaintance I owed to him. Arriving at my
charming house in Augsburg, I went to bed, resolved not
to leave it until I was rid of the poison which was devouring me. Signor Carli, my banker, recommended a
certain Kephalides,[69] a pupil of the celebrated Faget,[70]
who some years previously had rid me of a similar af-
fliction in Paris. Kephalides was considered the best
surgeon in Augsburg. After examining me he assured
me that he would cure me by sudorifics without recourse
to the ever ominous lancet. So he began by putting me
on the strictest diet, prescribed baths, subjected me to
mercury massages. I endured this treatment for six*

weeks, and, far from being cured, I felt worse than I had done when he took me in hand. I was terrifyingly thin, and I had two monstrously big inguinal tumors. I had to submit to their being opened, but the painful operation, in addition to nearly costing me my life, accomplished nothing. He clumsily cut the artery, bringing on a hemorrhage which was stopped only with difficulty and which would have killed me except for the care of Signor Algardi,[71] a Bolognese physician who was in the service of the Prince-Bishop of Augsburg.

On my declaring that I had had enough of Kephalides, Algardi proceeded to prepare, in my presence, ninety pills containing eighteen grains of manna.[72] I took one of these pills in the morning, washing it down with a large glass of diluted milk, and another in the evening, after which I took some barley water, and that was all I had in the way of nourishment. This heroic remedy restored me to health in two and a half months, during which I suffered intensely; but I did not begin to put on flesh again and recover my strength until toward the end of the year.

It was during this period of suffering that I learned the details of Costa's flight with all the diamonds and watches and snuffboxes and linen and embroidered coats, packed in an excellent trunk, which Madame d'Urfé had entrusted to him for me, together with the hundred louis she had given him for traveling expenses. The kind lady sent me a bill of exchange for fifty thousand francs, which she had fortunately not had time to give to the man who had robbed me, and the sum arrived most opportunely to rescue me from the state of indigence to which my bad conduct had reduced me.

At this same time I suffered another disappointment which I felt very keenly: I discovered that Leduc was robbing me. I would have forgiven him if he had not driven me to take public measures which I could not

avoid except at the cost of my honor. Nevertheless I kept
him until I returned to Paris at the beginning of the
following year.

Toward the end of September, when it became certain
that the Congress would not be held, La Renaud passed
through Augsburg with Desarmoises on their way back
to Paris; but she did not dare come to see me for fear I
would make her return my various goods and chattels,
of which she had taken possession without notifying me,
and she doubtless supposed that I was informed of her
rascality. Four or five years later in Paris she married
a certain Böhmer,[73] the same man who gave the Cardinal
de Rohan the famous diamond necklace,[74] believing it
was intended for the unfortunate Marie Antoinette,
Queen of France. She was in Paris when I returned
there, but I made no effort to see her, wanting to forget
everything if that were possible. I considered it a necessity, for of all the things I did during that ill-fated year
what I saw as the most detestable was my own course of
behavior, or rather, my own self. However, I would not
have so far slighted the infamous Desarmoises as to de-
prive myself of the pleasure of cutting off his ears if he
had given me time to do it; but the old scoundrel, who
no doubt foresaw what treatment I had in store for him,
took to his heels. He died, penniless and consumptive, in
Normandy not long afterward.

No sooner was my health restored than, forgetting all
my past sufferings, I went back to amusing myself.
Annemirl,[75] my excellent cook, who had been idle for so
long, had to work hard to satisfy my gluttonous appetite;
for three weeks I was prey to a ravenous hunger, which,
however, my nature required in order to restore my person to its original corpulence. My landlord the engraver
and his pretty daughter Gertrude, whom I had eat with
me, watched me in a kind of stupor and feared fatal re-
sults from my intemperance. My dear Dr. Algardi, who
had saved my life, predicted a dyspepsia which would

*bring me to the grave; but my need to eat was stronger
than his arguments; I paid no attention, and I was right;
for by dint of eating well I recovered my original constitution, and I soon felt perfectly capable of renewing
my offerings on the altar of the god for whom I had just
suffered so greatly.*

*My cook and Gertrude, both young and pretty, made
me amorous, and, gratitude entering in, I tendered my
love to them both at once; for I had foreseen that, attack-
ing them one at a time, I should have conquered neither.
In addition, I knew that I had not much time to lose, for
I had promised Madame d'Urfé that I would sup with
her on the first day of the year 1762 in an apartment
which she had furnished in the Rue du Bac.*[76] *She had
decorated it with the magnificent tapestries which had
been woven for René of Savoy*[77] *and on which all the
operations of the Great Work*[78] *were depicted. She had
written me that she had been in Choisy and had there
learned that the Italian Santis, whom I had stretched on
the ground with a thrust which had run him through, had
been imprisoned in Bicêtre*[79] *for fraud after recovering
from his wound.*

*Gertrude and Annemirl kept me pleasantly entertained
during the remainder of my stay in Augsburg, but they
did not captivate me to the point of making me neglect
good society. I spent my evenings very pleasantly in
visits to Count Max Lamberg,*[80] *who was residing at the
Prince-Bishop's Court with the title of Grand Marshal.
His wife,*[81] *a charming woman, had everything to attract
good company in large numbers. At the Count's I made
the acquaintance of Baron Sellentin,*[82] *a captain in the
Prussian service, who was stationed in Augsburg to re-
cruit for his master. What especially drew me to Count
Lamberg was his literary genius.*[83] *Possessing a scholarly
mind of the highest order and, above all, a vast erudition,
he published several works which are highly esteemed.
I maintained a correspondence with him which ceased*

only at his death, which occurred by his own fault four years ago, in 1792. I say "by his own fault," but I should have said "by the fault of his physicians," who treated him with mercury for a malady with which Venus had nothing to do and which only served to defame him after his death.

His widow, as charming as ever, still lives in Bavaria, beloved by her friends and her daughters, for all of whom she arranged excellent marriages.[84]

During this time a small down-at-heels troupe of actors, my fellow countrymen, arrived in Augsburg, and I got them permission to perform in a wretched little theater. Since they occasioned a little incident which amuses me because I am the hero of it, I will give it to my readers in the hope of pleasing them.

Comte de Saint-Germain

Walking in a Formal Garden

CHAPTER II

*The actors and the play. Bassi. The girl from
Strassburg. The female count. I return to
Paris. I arrive in Metz. The beautiful Raton
and the false Countess of Lascaris.*

---

*AN UGLY woman, but lively and talkative in the
Italian manner, having gained admission to my house,
begged me to intercede with the magistrate to grant the
troupe[1] to which she belonged permission to perform.
She was ugly, but she was Italian and poor, and, not
even asking her name or trying to find out if the troupe
was worth the effort, I promised to do what I could for
her, and I had no difficulty in obtaining the favor she
sought.*

*Having gone to the first performance, I saw with sur-
prise that the leading actor was a Venetian with whom,
twenty years earlier, I had studied at the Seminary of
San Cipriano.[2] His name was Bassi,[3] and, like myself, he
had renounced the priesthood. His destiny had made him
take up the trade of actor, and from all appearances
he was miserably poor, whereas I, whom chance had
launched on a course which was all vicissitudes, appeared
to be wealthy.*

31

*Curious to learn of his adventures, and impelled both
by the kindly feeling which draws us toward the friends
of our youth and especially our schoolmates, and by a
wish to enjoy his surprise when he recognized me, I
went to him on the stage as soon as the curtain fell. He
recognized me instantly and, after embracing me, introduced me to his wife,⁴ the woman who had come to
speak with me, and his daughter,⁵ who was thirteen or
fourteen years of age and very pretty and whose dancing
I had watched with pleasure. Nor did he stop there; seeing that I was cordial to him and to his family, he turned
toward his fellow actors, whose director he was, and
bluntly introduced me to them as his best friend. Hearing
that appellation and seeing me dressed like a nobleman,
with a cross on my breast, the good people insisted that
I was a famous cosmopolitan charlatan⁶ who was expected at Augsburg, and Bassi made no attempt to un-
deceive them, which surprised me.*

*When the troupe had taken off their theatrical rags
and put on their everyday ones, Bassi's ugly wife took
my arm and marched me away, saying that I should sup
with her. I let her lead me, and before long we arrived
at a lodging such as I had imagined. It was an immense
room on the ground floor, which served at once as kitchen,
dining room, and bedroom. A long table, half of which
was covered by a ragged cloth which showed signs of
having done service for a month; on the other end of it
was a filthy pot in which someone was washing a few
earthenware dishes which had been left there since dinner
and were to be used at supper. A single candle, stuck in
the neck of a broken bottle, lighted the den, and since
there were no snuffers Bassi's ugly wife supplied the
deficiency very skillfully with thumb and index finger,
then unceremoniously wiped her hand on the tablecloth
after throwing the bit of wick on the floor.*

*An actor, the odd-job man for the troupe, who wore
long mustaches because he played only murderers and*

highway robbers, served an enormous dish of reheated meat swimming in a muddy liquid honored with the name of sauce; and the ravenous family fell to dipping it up with pieces of bread which, in the absence of knives and forks, they tore from the loaf with their fingers or simply with their teeth; but since they were all doing it, no one had the right to turn up his nose. A large pot of beer passed from mouth to mouth, and amid this abject poverty gaiety animated every face, making me ask myself, "What is happiness?" To conclude the meal the actor-cook set down a second dish filled with pieces of fried pork, which was finished off with great relish. Bassi did me the favor of excusing me from sharing in this appetizing banquet, and I was grateful to him.

After this barrack-room fare he gave me a brief account of his adventures, all of them as unremarkable as the poor devil to whom they had happened; meanwhile his pretty daughter, sitting on my lap, did her best to make me believe she was innocent. He ended his story by saying that he was going to Venice,[7] where he was sure he would make his fortune during the Carnival. I wished him all possible luck, and when he asked me what my profession was I took it into my head to tell him I was a doctor.

"It's a much better trade than mine," he said, "and I am happy that I can give you a valuable present."

"And what may that be?" I asked.

"It is," replied Bassi, "the Venetian theriaca,[8] which you can sell for two florins the pound and which will cost you only four groschen."[9]

"I shall be glad to accept it. But tell me—are you satisfied with what you took in?"

"I can't complain for a first performance; I paid all my expenses and had enough left over to give each of the actors a florin. But I don't know how I am to play tomorrow, for my company is in revolt, and they say they won't play unless I give them a florin each in advance."

"They really don't ask very much."

"I know that, but I haven't a copper and have nothing to pawn; otherwise I'd satisfy their demands, and they would be sorry afterward, for I'm sure to make at least fifty florins tomorrow."

"How many of you are there?"

"Fourteen, counting my family. Can you lend me ten florins? I'll return them to you tomorrow after the performance."

"Gladly; but I should also like to have you all to supper at the inn nearest the theater. Here are ten florins."

The poor devil could scarcely find words to express all his gratitude and undertook to order the supper at a florin a head, as I had instructed him to do. I needed to be amused and to laugh at the sight of fourteen famished actors eating with ravenous appetites.

The troupe played the next day, but since twenty or thirty people at most attended the performance poor Bassi took in barely enough to pay for the musicians and the lights. He was in despair and, far from being able to repay me, came to beg me to lend him another ten florins, always in the hope of a good house the next day. I comforted him by saying that we would talk about it after supper and that I would expect him at the inn with his whole troupe.

By dint of liberal applications of wine from the Margravate[10] I made the supper last three hours, the reason being that a girl from Strassburg,[11] the soubrette of the troupe, at once so captured my interest that I began to think of possessing her. Endowed with a most attractive figure and a delicious voice, the girl kept me roaring with laughter by pronouncing Italian in the incongruous accent of Alsace, accompanying it with gestures which were at once pleasing and comic and which gave her a charm not easy to describe.

Determined to gain possession of the young actress no

*later than the next day, before leaving the inn I ad-
dressed the assembled troupe as follows: "Ladies and
gentlemen, I engage you for a week at fifty florins a day,
but on condition you will perform for my benefit and that
you will pay the expenses of the theater. It is understood
that you will set the price of tickets at whatever figure
I name, and that five members of the company, whom I
shall be free to designate, shall sup with me every evening. If the receipts come to more than fifty florins you
will divide the surplus among you."*

*My proposal was greeted with cries of joy, and, ink,
pen, and paper being brought, the two parties bound
themselves by a formal agreement.*

*"For tomorrow," I said to Bassi, "I will leave the
tickets at the same price as yesterday and today; for day
after tomorrow, we shall see. You and your family will
sup with me tomorrow, together with the young lady
from Strassburg, whom I would not dream of separating
from her dear Arlecchino."*

*The next day he announced a carefully chosen bill of
a nature to draw a large audience; nevertheless the
parterre was occupied by only a score of common people
and the boxes remained almost empty.*

*At supper Bassi, the promise of whose bill had been
well kept in the performance, came to me in great embarrassment and handed me ten or twelve florins. I took
them, saying, "Courage," and I divided them among my
guests. We had a good supper, which I had seen to ordering without their knowledge, and I kept them at table
until midnight, giving them good wine and playing
countless pranks with Bassi's daughter and the girl from
Strassburg, who were on either side of me, and paying
no attention to the jealous Arlecchino, who sulked because of the liberties I took with his mistress. The latter
accepted my caresses rather ungraciously, for she hoped
that Arlecchino would marry her and she did not want
to make him angry. At the end of supper we rose, and*

I took her in my arms, laughing and giving her caresses which doubtless seemed too suggestive to her lover, who snatched her from me. For my part, finding his lack of tolerance a trifle ill-bred, I took him by the shoulders and kicked him out of the room, which treatment he received with great humility. However, the scene became dismal, for the beauty began crying bitterly. Bassi and his ugly wife, long since hardened to their trade, laughed at the poor weeping creature, and Bassi's daughter told her that it was her lover who had first failed in respect to me; but she went on whimpering and ended by saying that she would not come to supper with me again unless I made her lover return to her.

"I promise to mend the matter so that everyone will be content," I said; and four zecchini which I put into her hand so far restored her good humor that before long there was not a cloud in the sky. She even tried to convince me that she was not cruel and would be still less so if I would avoid arousing Arlecchino's jealousy. I promised to do whatever she wished, and she made every effort to convince me that she would be perfectly compliant at the first opportunity.

I ordered Bassi to announce on the bills for the next day that tickets for the parterre were two florins and for the boxes a ducat[12] but that the gallery would be open free to the first comers.

"We shall have nobody," he said in alarm.

"That may be so, but we shall see. You must ask the police for twelve soldiers to maintain order, I will pay for them."

"We'll need them for the rag, tag, and bobtail that will come to storm the free places; but the rest of the house—"

"I repeat; we shall see. Do as I wish, and whether it succeeds or fails, we will laugh at supper as we always do."

The next day I went to see Arlecchino in his little

garret, and by giving him two louis and promising to respect his mistress I made him as pliant as a glove.

Bassi's handbills set the whole city laughing. Everyone said he was mad; but when it came out that the speculation was the manager's and that the manager was I, it was my turn to be called mad—but what did I care? That evening the gallery was packed an hour before the performance, but the parterre was empty and so were the boxes, except for Count Lamberg, the Abate Bolo,[13] of Genoa, and a young man whom I suspected to be a woman in disguise.[14]

The actors outdid themselves, and the applause from the gallery made it a most animated performance.

When we got to the inn Bassi gave me the three ducats which were the evening's receipts, but I of course made him a present of them; for him, they meant the beginning of affluence. At table I sat between his wife and his daughter, leaving my beauty from Strassburg beside her lover. I told the manager to continue the same course, to let people laugh if they chose, and I made him promise to give his best plays.

When the supper and the wine had put me in high spirits, seeing that I could accomplish nothing with the girl from Strassburg because of her lover, I let myself go with Bassi's little daughter, who let me do whatever I pleased, while her father and mother only laughed and the fool of an Arlecchino fumed because he could not do the same with his Dulcinea.[15] But when, at the end of supper, I showed him the little Bassi in a state of nature and myself in the costume of Adam before he ate the fatal apple, the fool made to leave, taking the girl from Strassburg by the arm and urging her to leave with him. At that, in the most serious and commanding tone, I ordered him to mind his manners and stay where he was, and he, dumbfounded, merely turned his back; but his beauty did not follow his example; instead, on the pretext of defending the little Bassi, who had already lodged me without difficulty, she cleverly assumed such a position that it both increased my pleasure and rewarded her with as much of the same as my straying hand could give her.

This bacchanalian scene having fired Bassi's wife, she began urging her husband to give her a proof of his conjugal affection, to such effect that he yielded to her solicitations, while the modest Arlecchino, who had gone to the fireplace, remained there motionless with his head in his hands. Profiting by his posture, the girl from Strassburg, surrendering to nature, let me do whatever I pleased; so giving her the place on the edge of the table from which I had just released Bassi's daughter, I accomplished the Great Work in all its perfection, and the violence of her embraces proved to me that she had taken at least as active a part in it as I.

At the conclusion of the orgy I emptied my purse on the table, and I enjoyed the eagerness with which the company shared a score of zecchini.

Fatigue and intemperance, at a time when I had not yet fully recovered my strength, had made me sleep long and late. I had only just risen when I received a summons to appear at the Town Hall before the burgomaster on duty.[16] I hastened to dress and set out, being extremely curious to know for what I was wanted. I knew that I had nothing to fear. When I appeared, the magistrate addressed me in German, but I turned a deaf ear, and with good reason, for I knew scarcely words enough in that language to ask for the most necessary things. Informed of my ignorance, he at once began speaking to me in the un-Ciceronian and pedantic Latin which is commonly found in German universities.[17]

"Why," he asked, "do you use a false name?"

"My name is not false. Inquire of the banker Carli, who paid me fifty thousand florins."

"I know that, but your name is Casanova; so why do you use the name Seingalt?"

"*I assume it, or rather I assumed it, because it is mine. It belongs to me so legitimately that if someone dared to use it I should challenge his right to it by every means, public and private.*"

"*And how does the name belong to you?*"

"*Because I created it; but that does not keep me from also being Casanova.*"

"*Sir, either the one or the other. You cannot have two names at the same time.*"

"*Spaniards often have half a dozen names,*[18] *and so do the Portuguese.*"

"*But you are neither Portuguese nor Spanish, you are Italian; and after all how can anyone create a name?*"

"*It is the simplest and easiest thing in the world.*"

"*Explain yourself.*"

"*The alphabet belongs to everyone; there's no denying that. I took eight letters, and I combined them in such a way as to produce the word Seingalt. The word thus formed pleased me, and I adopted it as my surname, in the firm conviction that, since no one ever bore it before me, no one has the right to deny it to me, still less to bear it without my permission.*"

"*That is a very far-fetched idea; but you support it with an argument which is more specious than well grounded; for your name can only be your father's name.*"

"*I think you are mistaken, for the name you bear yourself by right of inheritance did not exist from all eternity; it must have been invented by one of your ancestors who had not received it from his father, even if your name were Adam. Do you admit that, Your Worship?*"

"*I am obliged to; but it is something new.*"

"*There you are mistaken. Far from being new, it is very old, and I undertake to bring you tomorrow any number of names all invented by perfectly respectable people who are still alive and who enjoy them in peace without anyone's taking it into his head to summon them*

to the Town Hall to account for them, unless they dis-
avow them when and as they please, to the detriment of
society."

"But you will admit that there are laws against false
names?"

"Yes, against false names; but I repeat that nothing
is more true than my name. Yours, which I respect without knowing it, cannot be truer than mine; for it is possible that you are not the son of the man whom you believe to be your father."

He smiled, rose, and escorted me to the door, saying
that he would ask Signor Carli about me.

As it happened I had to go there myself, and I did so
at once. The story set him laughing. He told me that the
Burgomaster was a Catholic, a worthy man, rich and
rather stupid—in short, a good soul who could be han-
dled without any difficulty.

The next morning Signor Carli came to me for breakfast and invited me to go to the Burgomaster's with him.

"I saw him yesterday," he said, "and in a long discussion I had with him I turned his arguments against
him to such purpose that he is now entirely of your
opinion."

I accepted the invitation with pleasure, for I foresaw
that I should find good company there. I was not mistaken: there were charming women and several agreeable
men. Among others I noticed the disguised woman whom
I had seen at the theater. I set myself to observe her
during dinner, and I was soon convinced that I had
guessed right. Yet everyone spoke to her as if she were
a man, and she played her part very well. For my part,
wanting a little amusement and unwilling to have it supposed that I was taken in, I accosted her on the level of
polite pleasantry, but confining my remarks to the sort
of amorous persiflage which one addresses to a woman,
and in my allusions, my ambiguous phrases, I expressed
if not certainty as to her sex at least something more than

doubt. She pretended to notice nothing, and the company was not far from laughing aloud at what it thought my mistake.

After dinner, when we were taking coffee, the pretended gentleman showed a certain canon the portrait set in a ring which he wore. It was the portrait of a young lady who was present, and a very good likeness, which was not difficult since the original was ugly. This did not shake my conviction, but I began to wonder when I saw him kiss her hand with mingled fondness and respect, and I stopped my jesting. Signor Carli seized an opportunity to tell me that the gentleman, for all his feminine appearance, was a man, and indeed on the eve of marrying the young lady whose hand he had kissed.

"That may be so," I replied, "but I find it very hard to believe."

However, the fact is that he married her during the Carnival and received a very considerable dowry; but at the end of a year the poor deceived girl died of grief, and it was only on her deathbed that she told the reason. Her stupid parents, ashamed of having been so grossly taken in, did not dare to say anything and got the swindling female out of sight, but not before she had made sure of the dowry. The story, which soon came out, still sets the good citizens of Augsburg laughing, and gave me, though a little too late, a great reputation for perspicacity among them.

I continued to enjoy the favors of my two female table companions and the girl from Strassburg, who cost me some hundred louis. At the end of a week I released Bassi from our agreement with some money in his pocket. He continued to give performances, returning to the usual prices for tickets and putting an end to the free places in the gallery. He did rather well.

I left Augsburg about the middle of December.

I was very melancholy because of the charming Gertrude, who believed she was pregnant and who could not make up her mind to go to France with me. I would gladly have taken her with her father's consent, for he, not intending to find a husband for her, would have been delighted to get rid of her by giving her to me as my mistress.

We shall speak of this good-hearted girl five or six years hence, as we shall of Annemirl, that excellent cook, to whom I made a present of four hundred florins. She married some time later, and on my second visit to Augsburg[19] I was grieved to find her unhappy.

I set out, with Leduc on the coachman's seat, never having been able to forgive him, and when we reached Paris and were in the middle of the Rue Saint-Antoine, I made him get down with his trunk and left him there, giving him no letter of recommendation, despite his entreaties. I never heard of him again, and I still regret him, for he was an excellent servant, though with many grave failings. I should perhaps have remembered the important services he had rendered me in Stuttgart, Soleure, Naples, Florence, and Turin; but I was indignant at his impudence in compromising me before the magistrate in Augsburg,[20] where I should have been dishonored if my presence of mind had not put me in possession of the means to convict him of a theft for which, but for that, I should have been adjudged guilty.

I had done a great deal by saving him from the hands of the law, nor had I failed to reward him liberally each time I had had occasion to congratulate myself on his loyalty or his obedience.

From Augsburg I traveled to Basel by way of Constance, where I put up at the most expensive inn[21] in Switzerland. The proprietor, whose name was Imhof, was the king of fleecers; but I found his daughters agreeable, and after amusing myself there for three days I continued my journey. I reached Paris on the last day of the year 1761, going directly to the apartment in the Rue du

Bac which my good angel Madame d'Urfé had furnished for me with equal forethought and elegance.

I spent three whole weeks in those charming rooms without going anywhere, in order to convince the kind lady that I had returned to Paris for no other reason than to keep my promise to accomplish her rebirth as a man.

We spent the three weeks making the necessary preparations for that divine operation, preparations consisting in paying the appropriate devotions to each of the Geniuses of the seven planets on the days sacred to them. After these preparations I was to go to a place which would be made known to me only through the inspiration of the Geniuses and there obtain possession of a virgin, the daughter of an initiate, and impregnate her with a male child by a method known to no one except the Brothers of the Rosy Cross. The child was to be born alive, but with only a sensitive soul.[22] Madame d'Urfé was to receive him into her arms the instant he came into the world and keep him with her, in her own bed, for seven days. At the end of the seven days she was to die, pressing her mouth against that of the child, who would thus receive her intelligent soul.

After this exchange it would be for me to bring up the child by the virtue of the magistery[23] which was known to me, and as soon as he had reached his third year Madame d'Urfé was to become conscious of herself, and I was then to begin initiating her into perfect knowledge of the Great Doctrine.

The operation had to be performed on the day of the full moon in April, May, or June. Above all, Madame d'Urfé was to make a will in due form leaving all her property to the child, whose guardian I was to be until its thirteenth year.

In her insane exaltation, she considered the possibility of the operation a self-evident truth, and she was on fire with impatience to see the virgin who was to be its chosen vessel. She begged me to hasten my departure.

By making the oracle deliver itself in these terms, I had hoped to arouse some repugnance in her, since, after all, she would have to die, and I counted on the natural love of life drawing the thing out. But finding just the opposite, I saw that I must keep my promise to her, at least in appearance, and go to fetch the mysterious virgin.

I saw that I needed an unscrupulous hussy whom I should have to instruct in her role and I thought of La Corticelli. She must, I knew, have been in Prague for nine months, and I remembered that in Bologna I had promised I would go to see her before the end of the year. But I had just come back from Germany, bringing no very pleasant memories with me, and I thought the journey too long for the season and especially for so trifling a matter. I decided to spare myself the discomfort of such an expedition and I settled on summoning her to France, at the same time sending her the necessary money and telling her where I would meet her.

Monsieur de Fouquet,[24] a friend of Madame d'Urfé's, was the Intendant[25] of Metz; I was sure that if I waited on that nobleman with a letter from his dear friend he would give me a distinguished reception. In addition, the Count of Lastic,[26] her nephew, whom I knew very well, was there with his regiment. These considerations determined me to choose that city as the place where I would meet the virgin Corticelli, who could hardly guess that I intended her to play such a role. Madame d'Urfé having given me as many letters as I wanted, I left Paris on January 25, 1762, loaded with presents and with a generous letter of credit, which I did not use because my purse was well stocked.

I did not take a servant, for after Costa's theft and Leduc's treachery I thought I no longer dared to trust one. I reached Metz in two days and went to lodge at the

"King Dagobert," an excellent inn, where I found the Swedish Count Lewenhaupt,[27] whom I had met at the house of the Princess of Anhalt-Zerbst,[28] mother of the Empress of Russia, who lived in Paris. He invited me to supper with the Duke of Zweibrücken, who was traveling to Paris, alone and incognito, to visit Louis XV, whose faithful friend he remained until his death.

The day after I arrived I took my letters to the Intendant, who invited me to dine at his table every day. Monsieur de Lastic was not in Metz, which I regretted, for he would have added greatly to the pleasure of my stay in that beautiful city. On the same day I sent La Corticelli fifty louis, writing her to come to meet me with her mother as soon as she was at liberty, and to get someone who knew the road to accompany her. She could not leave Prague until the beginning of Lent, and to make sure that she would not fail me I promised her in my letter that I would make her fortune.

In four or five days I knew the city perfectly, but I avoided assemblies in order to go to the theater,[29] where an actress in the comic opera company had captivated me. Her name was Raton,[30] and she was only fifteen years old, reckoning in the manner of actresses, who always steal two or three years from the account if they can manage no more—a weakness which almost all women share and which we must forgive them, for youth is their greatest advantage. Raton was less beautiful than attractive, and what made her an object of envy was that she had set a price of twenty-five louis on her first fruits. One could spend a trial night with her for a louis; the twenty-five were due only if the investigator proved able to bring the undertaking to its due conclusion.

It was well known that several officers and young councillors at the Parlement had attempted the operation without succeeding, and each of them had paid his louis.

The thing was too unusual not to excite my curiosity, and I could not resist making the trial. So I lost no time

*in calling on her, but, not wanting to be duped, I took
my precautions. I told the beauty that she must come to
sup with me, that I would give her twenty-five louis if
I was completely happy, and, if I was not, she should
have six instead of one, provided she was not obstructed.
Her aunt assured me that I would not find that deformity
in her. I remembered Vittorina.*[31]

*Raton came to supper with her aunt, who, when dessert
was served, retired to spend the night in an adjoining
room. The girl was a masterpiece in the perfection of
her forms, and I felt not a little uneasy at the thought
that I was to have her entirely at my disposition, amenable, laughing, and defying me to conquer a fleece, not of
gold* [32] *but of ebony, which the flower of the youth of
Metz had sought to conquer in vain. The reader will
perhaps think that, since I no longer enjoyed the vigor
of my youth, the vain efforts which so many others had
expended should have discouraged me; but not at all, I
knew myself, and I laughed at them. Those who had
made the attempt were Frenchmen who were better
versed in the art of taking fortresses by storm than in
that of outwitting the art of a conscienceless girl determined to elude them. An Italian, I knew all about that,
and I had made such preparations that I had no doubt
of victory.*

*But they proved unnecessary, for as soon as Raton was
in my arms, aware from the way in which I attacked her
that trickery would accomplish nothing, she frankly
yielded to my desires, wasting no time in attempting the
elusive tactics which, to unseasoned combatants, made
her appear to be what she no longer was. She gave herself freely, and, when I promised to keep her secret, she
paid me ardor for ardor. It was no new thing to her;
hence I should not have needed to give her the twenty-
five louis; but I was satisfied, and, having very little regard for this kind of priority, I recompensed her as if I
had been the first to bite the apple.*

I kept Raton at a louis a day until La Corticelli arrived, and she could not help being faithful to me for I never let her out of my sight. I felt so much the better for a diet of this girl, who was thoroughly likable, that I very much repented having bound myself to wait for my Italian accomplice, whose arrival was announced to me just as I was leaving my box to go home. My temporary valet said in a loud voice that "Her Ladyship my wife," my daughter, and a gentleman had just arrived from Frankfort and were waiting for me at the inn.

"Idiot!" I said, "I have no wife and no daughter."

Which did not prevent everyone in Metz from learning that my family had arrived.

La Corticelli threw herself on my neck, laughing as always, and the old woman introduced the worthy man who had escorted them from Prague to Metz. He was an Italian named Monti, long settled in Prague, where he gave Italian lessons. I saw to it that Signor Monti and the old woman were comfortably lodged; then I took the little madcap to my room, finding her changed for the better: she had grown taller, her forms had gained in definition, and her charming manners added all that was needed to make her a very attractive girl.

CHAPTER III

I return to Paris with La Corticelli, transformed for the occasion into the Countess Lascaris. The abortive hypostasis. Aix-la-Chapelle. Duel. Mimi d'Aché. La Corticelli betrays me, but only to her own undoing. Journey to Sulzbach.

"WHY DID you let your mother call herself my wife, you scatterbrain? Do you think I can take it as a compliment? If she wanted to pass you off as my daughter she should have given it out that she was your governess."

"My mother has her own ideas; she'd rather be whipped than be taken for my governess, because in her mind there's no difference between a governess and a bawd."

"She's an ignorant fool; but we'll make her listen to reason of her own free will or by force. But I see you are well set up; have you made your fortune?"

"At Prague I captivated Count N . . . ,[1] and he was generous. But before anything else, my dear friend, I beg you to send Signor Monti back. The worthy man's family is in Prague, and he cannot stay here long."

"You are right; I will see that he is sent back at once."

The coach was to leave that evening for Frankfort;

I summoned Monti and, after thanking him for his kindness, I paid him liberally, and he left well pleased.

Having nothing further to do in Metz, I took leave of my new acquaintances, and on the next day but one I slept at Nancy, whence I wrote to Madame d'Urfé that I was returning with a virgin, the last descendant of the Lascaris[2] *family which had reigned in Constantinople. I asked her to receive her from my hands at a country house which belonged to her family, where we should have to remain for some days to perform certain cabalistic ceremonies.*

She replied that she would expect me at Pont-Carré,[3] *an ancient castle four leagues from Paris, and that she would there receive the young princess with all the cordiality she could wish for: "I have all the more reason to do so," she added in the exaltation of her insanity, "because the Lascaris family is connected with the D'Urfés, and because I am to be reborn from the offspring of this favored virgin." I saw that my course should be not to cool her enthusiasm but to hold it in check and moderate its manifestations. So I immediately wrote to her on the subject, explaining why she must treat her as no more than a countess, and I ended by announcing that we should arrive, with the young Lascaris's governess, on Monday in Holy Week.*

I spent ten or twelve days in Nancy, instructing my young scatterbrain and convincing her mother that she must content herself with being the most humble servant of the Countess Lascaris. I found it a very difficult task; I had not only to make it plain that her hope of affluence depended on her complete submission, I even had to threaten that I would send her back to Bologna alone. I was sorely to repent of my persistence. The woman's obstinacy was an inspiration of my Good Genius, who wanted to guard me against the greatest mistake I have made in all my life!

We arrived at Pont-Carré on the appointed day.

Madame d'Urfé, whom I had informed in advance of the hour of our arrival, had the drawbridges of the castle lowered and stood in the gateway surrounded by her entire household, like a general ready to surrender the place to us with all the honors of war. The dear lady, who was insane only because she had an excess of intelligence, gave the pretended princess a reception so flattering that she would have been astounded by it if I had not taken care to forewarn her. She embraced her three times with truly maternal tenderness, addressed her as her "very dear niece," and recited her own genealogy and that of the house of Lascaris to show her how she came to be her aunt. What most pleasantly surprised me was that my Italian madcap heard her out with polite dignity and did not once laugh, though the whole comedy must have struck her as extremely funny.

As soon as we had retired to the apartment the fairy performed some mysterious fumigations, and censed the newcomer, who received the homage with all the modesty of an opera goddess and then threw herself into the arms of the priestess, who received her with the greatest enthusiasm.

At table the Countess was animated, gracious, talkative, which won her the heart of Madame d'Urfé, who was not at all surprised to hear her chatter away in French. Madonna Laura, who knew only her native Italian, was not present. She had been given an excellent room, where her meals were brought to her and which she never left except to go to mass.

The castle of Pont-Carré was a sort of fortress, which, in the days of the civil wars,[4] had withstood more than one siege. It was square, as its name indicated, flanked by four crenelated towers, and surrounded by a wide moat. The rooms were huge and richly furnished, but in the old fashion. The air was infested with venomous gnats, which ate us up and produced extremely painful swellings on our faces, but I had undertaken to spend a

*week there, and I should have found it hard to invent
a pretext for shortening the time. Madame d'Urfé had a
bed for her niece set up beside her own, and I was not
afraid she would attempt to assure herself of her virginity, for the oracle had forbidden it, upon pain of
destroying the effect of the operation, which we fixed for
the fourteenth day of the April moon.*

*On that day we supped temperately, then I went to
bed. A quarter of an hour later Madame d'Urfé brought
me the virgin Lascaris. She undressed her, perfumed her,
draped her in a magnificent veil, and, when she had put
her beside me, remained, wishing to be present at the
operation which was to result in her being reborn nine
months later.*

*The act was consummated in due form, and when that
was done Madame d'Urfé left us alone for that night,
which was very well employed. After that night the
Countess slept with her aunt until the last day of the
moon, at which time I was to ask the oracle if the young
Lascaris had conceived by my efforts. It might well be
the case, for nothing had been spared to achieve that end;
but I thought it wiser to make the oracle reply that the
operation had failed because the youthful D'Aranda had
seen the whole performance from behind a screen. Madame d'Urfé was in despair; but I comforted her by a
second answer in which the oracle told her that what it
had been impossible to accomplish during the April moon
in France could be accomplished outside of the kingdom
during the May moon, but that she must send the prying
youth, whose influence had been so adverse, a hundred
leagues from Paris for at least a year. The oracle also
stipulated how D'Aranda was to travel: he must have a
tutor, a manservant, and all his appurtenances in perfect
order.*

*The oracle had spoken; no more was needed. Madame
d'Urfé at once thought of an Abbé whom she liked, and
D'Aranda was sent to Lyons,[5] with a warm letter of rec-*

*ommendation to her relative, Monsieur de Rochebaron.[6]
The lad was delighted to travel and never learned anything of the little slander I had permitted myself in
order to get him out of the way. What made me take this
action was not empty whim. I had seen beyond peradven-
ture that La Corticelli was in love with him and that
her mother was fostering the intrigue. I had twice surprised her in her room with the youth, who was interested
in her only as a young adolescent is interested in all
girls; and my disapproval of my Italian accomplice's
designs became, in Signora Laura's mind, an unwar-
ranted opposition to her daughter's inclination.*

*Our business now was to think of some place abroad
where we could go to repeat the mysterious operation.
We decided on Aix-la-Chapelle, and in five or six days
everything was in readiness for the journey.*

*La Corticelli, angry with me for having spirited away
the object of her love, reproached me vehemently and
from then on began to behave badly toward me; she
even went so far as to indulge in threats if I would not
summon back the "pretty boy," as she called him.*

*"You have no right to be jealous," she said, "and I
am my own mistress."*

*"Quite so, my beauty," I replied, "but I have a right
to prevent you from behaving like a prostitute in the
situation in which I have placed you."*

*Her mother flew into a rage and told me that she
wanted to go back to Bologna with her daughter; and
to soothe her I promised I would take them both there
after our journey to Aix-la-Chapelle.*

*However, I did not feel easy, and, fearing difficulties,
I hastened my departure. We left one May day in a
berlin in which I accompanied Madame d'Urfé, the pretended Countess Lascaris, and a maid, her favorite,
named Brougnole.[7] A two-seated cabriolet followed us;
it was occupied by Signora Laura and another maid.
Two menservants in full livery sat on the outside seat*

of the berlin. We rested one day in Brussels and another in Liège. At Aix⁸ we found a great number of distinguished foreigners, and at the first ball Madame d'Urfé presented my Lascaris to two Princesses of Mecklenburg⁹ as her niece. The pretended Countess received their embraces calmly and modestly, and she attracted the particular attention of the Margrave of Bayreuth¹⁰ and of the Duchess of Württemberg,¹¹ who together took possession of her and did not leave her until the end of the ball. I was on tenterhooks for fear that my heroine would betray herself by some piece of theatrical repartee. She danced with a grace which won her the attention and applause of the whole company; and it was I who was complimented on her performance. I suffered martyrdom, for I thought the compliments were malicious; it was as if everyone had divined the ballerina disguised as a countess, and I believed I was dishonored. Having found an opportunity to speak privately to the young madcap, I begged her to dance like a young lady of station and not like a ballet girl, but she was proud of her success and had the impudence to answer that a young lady might well be able to dance like a dancer and that she would never dance badly to please me. This behavior so disgusted me with her that, had I known how, I would have got rid of her then and there; but I silently swore that she would escape nothing by waiting; and, be it a vice or a virtue, vengeance never ceases to burn in my heart until it has been satisfied.

On the morning after the ball Madame d'Urfé made her a present of a casket containing a very fine watch set with brilliants, a pair of diamond earrings, and a ring adorned with a rose diamond weighing fifteen carats. All together they were worth sixty thousand francs. I took charge of them, lest it should occur to her to leave without my consent.

Meanwhile, to ward off boredom, I gambled, I lost my money, and I made bad acquaintances. The worst

of them all was a French officer named *D'Aché*,[12] who
had a pretty wife and an even prettier daughter. The
girl very soon captured the place in my heart on which
La Corticelli by now had only a slight hold; but as soon
as Madame *d'Aché* saw that I preferred her daughter
she refused to receive my visits.

I had lent *D'Aché* ten louis; so I thought I could complain to him of his wife's behavior toward me; but he
curtly replied that if I went to the house only for his
daughter, his wife was in the right; that his daughter
was a girl who could well find a husband, and if my
intentions were honorable I had only to declare them
to her mother. Nothing in all this was offensive except
his tone, and I took offense at it; however, knowing that
he was a coarse brute, a drunkard, and always ready
to fight over a "yea" or a "nay," I decided to say nothing and forget his daughter, not wanting to become involved with a man of his kind.

I was in this frame of mind and almost cured of my
fancy for his daughter, when, four days after our conversation, I entered a billiard room where *D'Aché* was
playing with a Swiss named *Schmit*,[13] an officer in the
Swedish service. As soon as *D'Aché* saw me he asked me
if I would bet him the ten louis he owed me. The game
was just beginning; I replied:

"Yes, that will make it twenty or nothing. I accept."

Toward the end of the game *D'Aché*, seeing that he
was losing, made an unfair stroke so obvious that the
marker told him so to his face; but *D'Aché*, for whom
the stroke won the game, takes the money which was in
the stake bag and puts it in his pocket, paying no attention to the marker's adjurations or to those of his opponent, who, seeing that he has been cheated, makes to hit
the blackguard across the face with his cue. *D'Aché*,
who had warded off the blow with his arm, instantly
draws his sword and runs at *Schmit*, who was unarmed.
The marker, a sturdy young man, caught *D'Aché* around

the waist and prevented murder. The Swiss leaves, saying:

"*We shall meet again.*"

The scoundrel, who had cooled down, looks at me and says:

"*Now we are quits.*"

"*Very much so.*"

"*I'm glad of that; but, the devil take it, you could have spared me an insult which dishonors me.*"

"*So I could, but I was under no obligation to do it. Besides, you must know what your rights are. Schmit was without his sword, but I believe he is a man of mettle, and he will give you satisfaction if you have courage enough to return his money to him, for, after all, you lost.*"

An officer whose name was De Pienne[14] took me aside and said that he would himself pay me the twenty louis which D'Aché had pocketed, but that Schmit must give him satisfaction, sword in hand. I did not hesitate to promise him that the Swiss would fulfill the obligation, and I undertook to bring him an affirmative reply the next day in the place where we then were.

I had no doubt that I should do as I had said. A gentleman who carries a weapon must always be ready to use it, whether in avenging an insult to his honor or in giving satisfaction for an insult he may have offered. I know that this is a prejudice which, rightly or wrongly, is called "barbaric," but there are social prejudices to which no man of honor can deny allegiance, and Schmit impressed me as being a thorough gentleman.

I went to him at daybreak the next morning; he was still in bed. As soon as he saw me,

"*I am sure,*" *he said,* "*that you have come to ask me to fight D'Aché. I am more than ready to burn powder with him, but on condition that he shall first pay me the twenty louis he stole from me.*"

"*You shall have them tomorrow morning, and I will*

be with you. D'Aché's second will be Monsieur de Pienne."

"Well and good. I shall expect you here at daybreak."

I saw De Pienne two hours later, and we arranged the meeting for six o'clock in the morning on the following day, with two pistols. We chose a garden half a league from the city.

At daybreak I found my Swiss waiting for me at the door of his lodging, humming the "Ranz-des-Vaches," of which his fellow countrymen are so fond. I thought it a good omen.

"You have come," he said. "Let us be off."

On the way he said:

"I have never fought except with a gentleman, and I find it hard to kill a scoundrel; that should be work for a hangman."

"I understand," I said, "that it is very distasteful to risk one's life against such people."

"I risk nothing," said Schmit with a laugh, "for I am certain to kill him."

"Certain?"

"Perfectly certain, because I shall make him tremble."

He was right. The secret is infallible when one knows how to employ it and when one is in the right against a coward. We found D'Aché and De Pienne at the appointed place, and we saw five or six people who could have been there only out of curiosity.

D'Aché took twenty louis from his pocket and handed them to his opponent, saying:

"I may have been mistaken, but I mean to make you pay dearly for your brutality."

Then, turning to me:

"I owe you twenty louis," he said.

I did not answer him.

Schmit, having put his money in his purse with the utmost calm, and making no reply to the other's boasting, took his station between two trees about four paces apart, *drew a pair of dueling pistols from his pocket, and said to D'Aché:*

"You have only to place yourself at ten paces' distance and fire first. The space between these two trees is the place where I choose to walk back and forth. You may walk too, if you wish, when it is my turn to fire."

No one could have explained his intentions more clearly or have spoken more calmly.

"But," said I, "we must decide who is to have the first shot."

"There is no need of that," said Schmit, "I never fire first; in any case the gentleman has that right."

De Pienne placed his friend at the specified distance, then he retired with me, and D'Aché fired at his opponent, who was slowly walking back and forth without looking at him. Schmit turned around with the greatest composure and said:

"You missed me, sir; I was sure you would; try again."

I thought he was mad, and I expected some kind of discussion between the parties. But not a bit of it. D'Aché, thus given leave to take the second shot, fired and again missed his opponent, who, without a word, but in a firm and confident manner, fired his first shot into the air, then, aiming at D'Aché with his second pistol, hit him in the center of the forehead and stretched him dead on the ground. Putting his pistols back in his pocket, Schmit instantly set off, unaccompanied, as if he were continuing his walk. I left two minutes later, when I was certain that the unfortunate D'Aché was lifeless.

I was in a daze, for such a duel seemed to me a dream, something out of a romance, rather than a reality. I could not get over it, for I had not detected the slightest change on the impassive countenance of the Swiss.

I went to breakfast with Madame d'Urfé, whom I found inconsolable, for it was the day of the full moon, and at exactly three minutes past four o'clock I was to accomplish the mysterious creation of the child from whom she was to be reborn. But the divine Lascaris, who was to be the chosen vessel, was writhing on her bed, feigning convulsions which would make it impossible for me to accomplish the work of fecundation.

On hearing an account of this disaster from the heart-broken Madame d'Urfé, I affected a hypocritical grief, for the dancer's spitefulness served my turn to perfection, first because she no longer aroused the slightest desire in me, second because I foresaw that I could make use of the incident to avenge myself and punish her.

I lavished consolations on Madame d'Urfé, and, after consulting the oracle, I found that the young Countess Lescaris had been defiled by a black Genius, and that I must go in search of the predestined girl whose purity was under the protection of the higher Geniuses. Seeing the mad Madame d'Urfé perfectly content with the oracle's promises, I left her and went to see La Corticelli, whom I found on her bed, with her mother beside her.

"So you are suffering from convulsions, my dear," I said.

"No, I am perfectly well; but I shall go on having them until you give me back my jewel casket."

"You have become naughty, my poor child, and it has come from taking your mother's advice. As for the casket, if you continue to behave in this way you may never get it back."

"I will tell all."

"No one will believe you, and I will send you back to Bologna without a single one of the presents Madame d'Urfé has given you."

"You will have to give me back the casket when I announce that I am pregnant—as in fact I am. If you do not satisfy me I shall go and tell the old fool everything, no matter what may happen."

Greatly surprised, I stared at her without saying a word, but I was considering how best to get rid of the im-

*pudent wench. Signora Laura said, with perfect calm,
that it was only true that her daughter was with child,
but that it was not by me.*

"Then who made her pregnant?" I asked her.

"Count N . . . , whose mistress she was in Prague."

*I did not think it possible, for she showed no signs of
being with child, but, even so, it might be the case. Forced
to think of some course which would foil the scoundrelly
pair, I left the room without a word and shut myself
up with Madame d'Urfé to consult the oracle concerning
the operation which was to make her happy.*

*After a quantity of questions more obscure than the
oracles which the Pythia delivered from her tripod at
Delphi,[15] the interpretation of which I consequently left
to my poor infatuated Madame d'Urfé, she herself discovered—and I took great care not to contradict her—
that the young Lascaris had gone mad. Fostering all her
fears, I succeeded in making her read in the reply of a
cabalistic figure that the princess had failed to answer
our expectations because she had been defiled by a black
Genius hostile to the Rosicrucian Order; and, being now
well launched, she added of her own motion that the girl
must be pregnant with a gnome.*

*She then drew up another figure to learn how we were
to go about attaining our end without fail, and I so directed her that she found she must write to the moon.[16]*

*This extravagance, which should have brought her back
to reason, filled her with joy. Her enthusiasm was that
of a mystic in ecstasy, and I became certain that even if
I had tried to prove the groundlessness of her hopes I
should have wasted my breath. At most she would have
concluded that a hostile Genius had corrupted me and
that I was no longer a perfect Rosicrucian. But I was
far from undertaking a cure which would have been so
disadvantageous to me and of no use to her. If nothing
else, her infatuation made her happy, and no doubt a
return to the truth would have made her the reverse.*

In short, she received the command to write to the moon all the more joyously because she knew the devotions in which that planet delights and the form of ceremony with which it must be approached; but she could not perform it without the help of an adept, and I knew that she counted on me. I said that I would be hers to command, but that we must wait until the first phase of the coming moon, which fact she knew as well as I did. I was very glad to gain some time, for, having lost a great deal at cards, I could not leave Aix-la-Chapelle before I received the sum represented by a bill of exchange which I had drawn on Monsieur D. O.[17] in Amsterdam. In the meanwhile we agreed that, since the young Lascaris had gone mad, we would pay no attention to anything she might say in her insane fits, for, her mind being in the power of the evil Genius who had taken possession of her, it was he who put the words into her mouth.

However, her condition deserving our pity, we agreed that, to lighten her lot as much as possible, she should continue to eat with us, but that in the evening, when we rose from supper, she should go to bed in her governess's room.

After having thus disposed Madame d'Urfé not to believe anything La Corticelli might say to her, and to give her whole thought to the letter she must write to the Genius Selenis,[18] who inhabits the moon, I set seriously about finding means to replace the money I had lost, which the cabala could not do for me. I pawned La Corticelli's casket for a thousand louis, and went to deal at an English club,[19] where I could win much more than I could with Frenchmen or Spaniards.

Three or four days after D'Aché's death his widow wrote me a note asking me to call on her. I found her with De Pienne. She told me in sorrowful tones that, her husband having contracted many debts, his creditors had seized everything, so that she could not pay the expenses *of a journey to throw herself and her daughter on the mercy of her family in Colmar.*

"*You are,*" *she went on,* "*the cause of my husband's death; I ask you for a thousand écus; if you refuse me I will sue you in court, for, the Swiss officer having left, there is no one else I can sue.*"

"*What you have permitted yourself to say surprises me, Madame,*" *I rejoined coldly,* "*and but for my respect for your misfortune, I should reply with the acerbity which your behavior cannot but inspire in me. In the first place I have not a thousand écus to throw away, and even if I had them, your threatening tone would be little calculated to induce me to make such a sacrifice. In addition, I am curious to see how you could possibly go about suing me. As for Monsieur Schmit, he fought like a brave man and a gentleman, and I have yet to understand what you could gain by suing him if he had remained here. Good-by, Madame.*"

I had scarcely got fifty paces from the house, when I was joined by De Pienne, who said that before Madame d'Aché sued me it was for us to go to some private place and cut each other's throats. Neither of us was wearing a sword.

"*Your intention is scarcely flattering,*" *I said calmly;* "*indeed, it has a certain brutality which does not encourage me to involve myself with a man whom I do not know and to whom I owe nothing.*"

"*You are a coward.*"

"*I might be one if I imitated you. What you may think of me leaves me completely indifferent.*"

"*You will be sorry.*"

"*Perhaps, but meanwhile I give you due warning that I never go about without a pair of pistols in good condition and that I know how to use them. Here they are,*" *I added, drawing them from my pocket and cocking the one in my right hand.*

At sight of them the bully gave a curse and fled in one direction while I made off in the other.

Not far from where this scene had taken place I ran into a Neapolitan named Militerni,[20] then a Lieutenant-Colonel and Aide-de-Camp to the Prince of Condé, who was in command of the French army. Militerni was a man who enjoyed life, always ready to oblige and always short of money. We were friends, and I told him what had just happened.

"I should be sorry," I said, "to become involved with De Pienne, and if you can dispose of him for me I promise you a hundred écus."

"It can doubtless be done," he replied; "I will tell you more tomorrow."

And in fact he came to me the next morning and announced that my cutthroat had left Aix at daybreak in obedience to a formal order from his military superior, and at the same time he gave me an unrestricted passport from the Prince of Condé.

I admit that I was gratified by the news. I have never feared to cross swords with the first comer, though I have never sought the barbarous pleasure of shedding a man's blood; but this time I felt an intense aversion to involving myself with a man whom I had reason to believe was no more scrupulous than his friend D'Aché. So I heartily thanked Militerni, at the same time giving him the hundred écus I had promised him, which I considered too well spent to regret them.

Militerni, a past master at jesting and a tool of Marshal d'Estrées,[21] was not without either intelligence or education; but he lacked discipline and, to some extent, refinement. Withal, he was a most agreeable companion, for he was imperturbably good-humored and he had a considerable knowledge of the world. Made a Field Marshal in 1768, he went to Naples and married [22] a rich heiress, whom he left a widow a year later.

The day after De Pienne left, I received a note from

Performance by a Small Company of Actors

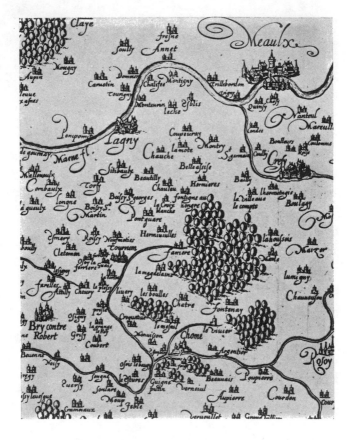

Surroundings of the Château de Pont-Carré

Mademoiselle d'Aché asking me, on behalf of her mother, who was ill, to call on her. I replied that she would find me at such-and-such a place at an hour which I specified, where she could tell me whatever she wished.

I found her at the appointed place with her mother, who came despite her pretended illness. Complaints, tears, reproaches—nothing was spared. She called me her "persecutor," and said that the departure of De Pienne, her only friend, had reduced her to despair, that she had pawned all her possessions, that she had no further resources, and that I, being rich, ought to help her if I was not the basest of men.

"I am far from being insensible to your misfortunes, Madame, and though I am not so to your insults I cannot refrain from telling you that you proved yourself the basest of women by inciting De Pienne, who may be an honorable man, to murder me. In short, rich or not, though I owe you nothing, I will give you what you need to take your things out of pawn, and I may even escort you to Colmar myself; but you must consent to my giving your charming daughter some first proofs of my love here and now."

"And you dare to make this horrible proposal to me?"

"Be it horrible or not, it is the proposal I make you."

"Never."

"Good-by, Madame."

I called the waiter to pay for the refreshments I had ordered, and I put six double louis in the girl's hand, but the proud mother, seeing it, forbade her to accept them. I was not surprised, despite her indigence, for the mother was charming and indeed a better prize than her daughter, and she knew it. I should have given her the preference, and so have ended all protest—but whim! In love, there is no accounting for it. I felt that she must hate me, and the more so because, since she did not love her daughter, she was humiliated to find her a preferred rival.

My departure leaving me still holding the six double louis which pride or pique had refused, I went to the faro bank and decided to sacrifice them to Fortune; but that capricious goddess, as haughty as the proud widow, refused them as she had done, and, having left them five times on one card, I very nearly broke the bank then and there. An Englishman named Martin offered to go halves with me; knowing him to be a good player, I accepted his proposal, and in eight or ten deals we managed so well that, after taking the casket out of pawn, I found not only that my other losses were made good but that I was also ahead by a considerable sum.

In the meanwhile La Corticelli, thoroughly angry with me, had revealed everything to Madame d'Urfé, telling her the true story of her life, of our acquaintance, and of her pregnancy. But the more truth she put into her account, the more the good lady was confirmed in her idea that the girl was mad, and she only laughed with me over the supposed insanity of my Italian traitress. She put all her trust in the instructions which Selenis was to give her in his answer.

For my part, however, being unable to overlook the girl's behavior, I decided to send her to eat in her mother's room, seeing to it that I alone kept Madame d'Urfé company and assuring her that we should easily find another chosen vessel, since the young Lascaris's madness made her wholly unfit to participate in our mysteries.

It was not long before the widow D'Aché, under the stress of need, found herself obliged to give me her Mimi; but I conquered her by kindness and, in the beginning, by so far respecting appearances that she could pretend to know nothing. I redeemed all the things she had pawned; and, satisfied with her behavior, though her daughter had not yet yielded entirely to my ardor, I formed the plan of taking them both to Colmar with Madame d'Urfé. To persuade the lady to perform this good action without suspecting its real motives, it oc-

curred to me to make her receive the order from the moon in the letter she was awaiting from that planet; I was certain that, under such circumstances, she would obey blindly.

The way in which I contrived the exchange of letters between Selenis and Madame d'Urfé was as follows.

On the day determined by the phase of the moon we went to sup together in a garden outside the city,[23] where, in a room on the ground floor, I had prepared everything necessary for the ceremony; I had in my pocket the letter which was to come down from the moon in reply to the one which Madame d'Urfé had carefully prepared and which we were to send to its address. A few paces from the ceremonial chamber I had arranged to have a large bath filled with the perfumes pleasing to the luminary of the night, which we were to enter together at the hour of the moon, which on that day was an hour after midnight.

When we had burned the aromatics and sprinkled the perfumes appropriate to the worship of Selenis and recited the mystic prayers, we undressed completely, and, holding my letter concealed in my left hand, with my right I escorted her to the edge of the bath, in which was an alabaster cup filled with spirits of juniper, which I ignited, meanwhile uttering cabalistic words which I did not understand and which she repeated after me, handing me the letter addressed to Selenis. I burned the letter in the juniper flame on which the full moon was shining, and the credulous Madame d'Urfé assured me that she had seen the characters she had written ascending along the luminary's rays.

After that we got into the bath, and the letter which I held concealed in my hand, written in silver on glazed green paper, appeared on the surface of the water ten minutes later. As soon as Madame d'Urfé saw it she took it up reverently and left the bath with me.

After drying and perfuming ourselves, we dressed again. When we were in a state of decency I told Madame

*d'Urfé that she might read the letter, which she had laid
on a perfumed white satin cushion. She obeyed, and a
visible gloom descended on her when she read that her
hypostasis was put off until the arrival of Querilinte,
whom she would see with me at Marseilles in the spring
of the following year. The Genius further told her that
the young Countess Lascaris could only do her harm,
and that she must leave it to me to get rid of her. He
ended by ordering her to instruct me not to leave in Aix
a woman who had lost her husband and who had a
daughter whom the Geniuses had destined to be of great
service to our Order. She was to arrange for her to travel
to Alsace with her daughter and not let them out of her
sight until they had arrived there, so that our influence
would protect them from the dangers by which they
were threatened if they were left to themselves.*

*Madame d'Urfé, who, her madness aside, was extremely
kindhearted, recommended the widow to me with all the
warmth of fanaticism and humanity and was extremely
impatient to learn their whole story. I coldly told her
whatever I thought proper to strengthen her in her
resolve and promised to introduce the ladies to her as
soon as possible.*

*We returned to Aix, and we spent the rest of the
night together, discussing all the matters which filled her
imagination. Everything being favorable to my plans, I
devoted myself entirely to arranging for the journey to
Alsace and to obtaining complete possession of Mimi
after having so well deserved her favors by the service
I was doing her.*

*The next day I was lucky at cards, and, to crown my
day, I went to enjoy the grateful surprise of Madame
d'Aché when I informed her that I had decided to take
her to Colmar myself with her Mimi. I said that I must
begin by introducing them to the lady whom I had the
honor of accompanying, and I asked her to be ready the
next day, for the Marquise was impatient to make her
acquaintance. I clearly saw that she found it hard to*

convince herself that what I was telling her was true, for she assumed that the Marquise was in love with me, and she could not reconcile that idea with Madame d'Urfé's eagerness to put me in the company of two women who might well be dangerous rivals.

I went for them the next day at an hour we had agreed upon, and Madame d'Urfé received them with a cordiality which must greatly have surprised them, for they could not know that they owed it to a recommendation direct from the moon. The four of us dined together, and the two ladies conversed like women of the world. Mimi was charming, and I paid her particular attention, of which her mother well knew the reason and which the Marquise attributed to the esteem in which the Rosicrucians held her.

In the evening we all went to the ball, where La Corticelli, always bent on causing me every possible annoyance, danced in a manner forbidden to well-born young ladies. She performed entrechats à huit, *pirouettes, caprioles, mid-leg* battements—*in short, all the acrobatics of an opera ballet girl. I was in torment! An officer who perhaps did not know that I gave myself out to be her uncle, or perhaps only pretended not to know it, asked me if she was a professional dancer. I heard another officer behind me saying that he thought he had seen her dance at the theater in Prague during the last Carnival. I realized that I must hasten my departure, for I foresaw that the wretched girl would end by costing me my life if we remained in Aix.*

Madame d'Aché having, as I said, the manners of good society, completely won the approval of Madame d'Urfé, who thought that she saw a new favor from Selenis in her amiability. Feeling that, after the services I was doing her in so marked a manner, she owed me some gratitude, Madame d'Aché pretended not to feel well and left the ball first, so that when I took her daughter home I found myself alone with her and under no constraint. Taking advantage of this favorable circumstance,

I spent two hours with Mimi, who proved to be so amenable, so willing, and so passionate that when I left her I had nothing more to desire.

On the third day I furnished the mother and daughter with traveling clothes, and, in an elegant and roomy berlin which I had secured, we all set out happily from Aix. A half hour before leaving I made an acquaintance the consequences of which were disastrous later on. A Flemish officer, whom I did not know, accosted me and described his destitute situation so feelingly that I could not help giving him twelve louis. Ten minutes later he brought me a note in which he acknowledged his indebtedness and stated the time at which he would repay me. The note showed me that his name was Malingan.[24] My reader shall learn the sequel ten months hence.

Just as we were leaving I directed La Corticelli to a four-seated carriage in which she was to travel with her mother and two maids. She shook from head to foot; her pride was wounded, and for a moment I thought she would go out of her mind; tears, insults, curses—nothing was spared. I remained unmoved, and Madame d'Urfé, laughing over the insane vagaries of her supposed niece, showed that she was very glad to be seated opposite me and beside the protégée of the powerful Selenis; while Mimi seized every opportunity to show how happy she was to be in my company.

We arrived at Liège the next day at nightfall, and I suggested to Madame d'Urfé that we spend the following day there, for I wanted to hire horses to travel to Luxembourg by way of the Ardennes; it was a detour in which I indulged myself in order to possess my charming Mimi the longer.

Having risen early, I went out to see the city. On my way toward the great bridge, a woman so closely wrapped in a black mantilla that only the tip of her nose was visible comes up to me and asks me to follow her to a house of which she points to the open door.

"As I have not the honor of your acquaintance," I said, *"prudence does not permit me to accept your invitation."*

"You know me," she replied, and, taking me to the corner of the next street, she uncovered her face. The reader may imagine my surprise: it was the beautiful Stuard, whom I had encountered in Avignon, the insensible statue of the Fountain of Vaucluse.[25] I was very glad to see her again.

Curious, I follow her and go up with her to a room on the second floor, where she greets me most lovingly. It was no use, for, despite her beauty, I bore her a grudge and I rejected her advances; doubtless because I was in love with Mimi, who made me happy and whom I wished to please by keeping myself entirely for her. However, I took three louis from my purse and gave them to her, asking her to tell me her story.

"Stuard," she said, *"was only my traveling companion; my name is Ranson, and I am kept by a rich landowner. I have come back to Liège after suffering much."*

"I am very glad," I said, *"that you are well situated now, but you must acknowledge that your behavior in Avignon was as preposterous as it was silly. But let us say no more about it. Good-by, Madame."*

I went back to my hotel to write the Marchese Grimaldi[26] an account of my meeting with La Stuard.

We set off again the next day and spent two days crossing the Ardennes.[27] It is one of the strangest landscapes in Europe, a vast forest whose tales of ancient chivalry furnished Ariosto with such beautiful pages on the subject of Bayard.[28]

Amid this immense forest, which contains not a single city, and which one must nevertheless cross to get from one country to another, one finds almost none of the comforts or even the necessities of life.

One would search it in vain for vices and for virtues and for what we call *"manners."* The inhabitants are

*without ambition, and, unable to have correct ideas of
the truth, they hatch monstrous notions concerning nature, the sciences, and the powers of men who, in their
opinion, deserve the epithet "wise." It is enough to be
a physician to gain the reputation of being an astrologer,
and still more a magician, among them. Yet the Ardennes
are well populated, for I have been assured that they
contain twelve hundred churches. The inhabitants are
kindly, even obliging, especially the girls; but in general
the fair sex does not deserve that epithet there. In this
vast district, the entire length of which is watered by
the Meuse, lies the city of Bouillon,[29] a hole if ever there
was one, but in my time it was the freest city in Europe.
The Duke of Bouillon[30] was so jealous of his jurisdic-
tional rights that he preferred his prerogative to all the
honors which could have been paid him at the Court of
France.*

*We stopped one day at Metz, where we paid no visits,
and in three days we arrived at Colmar, where we left
Madame d'Aché, whose good graces I had won. Her family, who were very well off, received both mother and
daughter with the greatest affection. Mimi shed many
tears when we parted, but I comforted her by promising
to see her again before long. Madame d'Urfé, whom I
had prepared for the separation, felt it very little, and
for my part I did not find it hard to console myself. At
the same time that I congratulated myself on having
contributed to the happiness of the mother and daughter,
I bowed to the secret counsels of Providence.*

*The next day we went to Sulzbach,[31] where Baron
Schaumbourg,[32] an acquaintance of Madame d'Urfé's,
gave us a cordial reception. I should have been bored in
the dreary place had it not been for cards. Madame
d'Urfé, feeling in need of company, encouraged La Corticelli to hope for the return of my good graces and,
with them, of hers. The wretched creature, who had
used every means to cross me, seeing how easily I had*

*foiled her plots and how deeply I had humiliated her,
had changed her role: she had become docile, obliging,
and submissive. She hoped to regain some part of the
esteem which she had so completely lost, and she thought
that victory was at hand when she saw that Madame
d'Aché and her daughter had remained behind in Colmar.
But what she had most at heart was neither my friendship nor the Marquise's, but the casket, for which she
no longer dared to ask me and which she was not to see
again. By her pleasantries at table, which made Madame
d'Urfé laugh heartily, the madcap managed to inspire
some twinges of desire in me; but the compliments of
that kind which I paid her did not lead me to lessen my
severity in the least; she always slept with her mother.*

*A week after we arrived at Sulzbach I put Madame
d'Urfé in the care of Baron Schaumbourg and went to
Colmar, where I expected to be happy in love. I was
disappointed, for I found the mother and the daughter
both preparing to be married.*

*A rich merchant who had loved the mother eighteen
years earlier, seeing her a widow and still beautiful, felt
his old fire rekindled, offered his hand, and was accepted.
A young advocate found Mimi to his taste and asked her
in marriage. The mother and the daughter, who, besides
considering it a good match, feared the consequences of
my love, hastened to give their consent. I was made
much of by the family, and supped with a numerous and
choice company; but seeing that I could only be in the
ladies' way and be bored myself while hoping for some
momentary favor, I bade them good-by and the next
day returned to Sulzbach. There I found a charming
woman from Strassburg by the name of Salzmann[33] and
three or four gamesters who said that they had come to
take the waters and who gave me advance notice of
several female table companions, whose acquaintance
the reader will make in the next chapter.*

CHAPTER IV

I send La Corticelli to Turin. Helena initiated into the mysteries of Love. I pay a visit to Lyons. I arrive in Turin.

MADAME SAXE possessed every quality to command the homage of a man given to love; and if she had not had a jealous officer who never let her out of his sight and who looked threateningly at anyone who dared to show his admiration by aspiring to please her, she would probably not have been without ardent admirers. The officer was fond of piquet,[1] but he insisted that Madame should always sit at his side, and she seemed happy to be there.

In the afternoon I played with him, and we went on in this way for five or six days. I got tired of it then, for as soon as he had won ten or twelve louis from me he would get up and leave. The officer's name was D'Entragues;[2] he was handsome, though thin, and lacked neither intelligence nor the tone of good society.

Two days had passed since we had played together, when he came to me after dinner and asked if I would like him to give me my revenge.

"*I am not interested,*" *I said,* "*for you and I do not play in the same way. I play for my pleasure, because play amuses me, whereas you play to win.*"

"*What do you mean? You insult me.*"

"*That is not my intention; but each time we have played together you have left me in the lurch after an hour.*"

"*You ought to be grateful to me, for, not being my equal at play, you would perforce have lost a great deal.*"

"*That may be so, but I do not believe it.*"

"*I can prove it to you.*"

"*I accept; but the first to stop playing shall lose fifty louis.*"

"*I accept, but money on the table.*"

"*I never play otherwise.*"

I order the waiter to bring cards and I go to my room for four or five rolls of fifty louis. We begin playing at five louis a hundred, each of us first setting fifty louis aside for the wager.

It was three o'clock when we sat down to play, and at nine D'Entragues said we might go to supper.

"*I am not hungry,*" *I replied,* "*but you are free to get up if you want me to put the hundred louis in my pocket.*"

He laughed and went on playing, but the beautiful lady scowled at me, which I gave no sign of noticing. All the people who were looking on went to supper, then came back to keep us company until midnight; but at that hour we were left alone. D'Entragues, who now saw what he had let himself in for, said not a word, and I opened my mouth only to reckon my points; we played on steadily and quietly.

At six o'clock in the morning the water-drinkers began to pass by, and they all congratulated us on our tenacity, clapping their hands, at which we only scowled. Louis were heaped up on the table; I lost a hundred, yet the game was going my way.

At nine o'clock the beautiful Saxe arrived, and a few moments later Madame d'Urfé with Baron Schaumbourg. The two ladies joined in advising us to take a cup of chocolate. D'Entragues consented first, and, thinking that I was on my last legs, he made bold to say:

"Let us agree that the first who asks for food or who leaves the table for more than a quarter of an hour or who falls asleep on his chair will lose the wager."

"I take you at your word," I cried, "and I accept any other more stringent condition you may be pleased to propose."

The chocolate arrives, we take it, and then go on playing. At noon we are summoned to dinner, but we reply together that we are not hungry. About four o'clock we were persuaded to take some broth. When supper-time came everyone began to think the thing was being carried too far, and Madame Saxe proposed that we divide the stake. D'Entragues, who had won a hundred louis from me, would have been glad to accept her proposal, but I refused it, and Baron Schaumbourg declared that I was within my rights. My opponent could have let the wages go and stopped playing; he would still have been ahead; but avarice kept him from doing so even more than pride. For my part, the amount by which I was behind meant something to me, but very little in comparison with the point of honor. I looked fresh, while he looked like a disinterred corpse, his thinness lending itself to the macabre effect. As Madame Saxe continued to insist, I said that I profoundly regretted my inability to yield to the solicitations of a charming woman who in every respect deserved far greater sacrifices, but that in the present case there was a certain element of nice honor, and so I was resolved either to win or not to yield the victory to my antagonist until I dropped dead.

By speaking in these terms I hoped to accomplish two things: to frighten D'Entragues by my firmness and to anger him by making him jealous; certain that a jealous man sees double, I hoped that his skill would suffer accordingly and that in winning the fifty louis of the wager, I should not have the heartbreak of losing a hundred to his superior skill at play.

The beautiful Madame Saxe gave me a scornful look and left, but Madame d'Urfé, who believed that I was infallible, avenged me by saying to Monsieur d'Entragues, in a tone of the deepest conviction:

"My God, Monsieur, how I pity you!"

The people who had been with us before supper did not come back; we were left to continue our combat alone. We played all night, and I paid as much attention to my opponent's face as I did to my cards. The more I saw that it was becoming troubled, the more blunders he made; he mixed up his cards, he scored incorrectly, and often made wrong discards. I was scarcely less exhausted than he; I felt my strength failing, and I hoped every minute to see him drop dead, for fear that I should be beaten despite my strong constitution. I had won back my money at daybreak, when, D'Entragues having gone out, I took him to task for having stayed away longer than a quarter of an hour. This trumped-up quarrel left him the worse and roused me—at once the natural result of our different temperaments, a gamester's stratagem, and a subject of study for the moralist and the psychologist; and my trick succeeded because it was not planned beforehand and could not be foreseen. The same thing holds true for army commanders: a military stratagem must come to a captain's mind from the existing circumstances, from the concatenation of events, and from a habit of instantly grasping the connections and the distinctions between men and between things.

At nine o'clock Madame Saxe arrived; her lover was losing.

"Now, Monsieur," she said to me, "it is for you to yield."

"Madame, in the hope of being agreeable to you, I am ready to withdraw my stake and end the matter."

These words, uttered in a tone of marked gallantry, aroused the anger of D'Entragues, who added sharply that it was now his turn to say he would not stop until one of us dropped dead.

"You see, most amiable lady," I said, with a look which, in my state, must have been more bleary than lovelorn, "that I am not the more obstinate of the two."

We were served a dish of broth, but D'Entragues, who was in the last stage of exhaustion, had no sooner swallowed it than he became so ill that he reeled in his chair, broke into a sweat, and fainted. He was quickly carried off, and I, after giving six louis to the marker, who had stayed up for forty-two hours, and putting my money in my pocket, instead of going to bed made my way to an apothecary's shop, where I took a mild emetic. Having then gone to bed, I slept lightly for some hours, and about three o'clock I dined with the best of appetites.

D'Entragues did not reappear until the next day. I expected a quarrel of some sort, but night brings counsel, and I was mistaken. As soon as he saw me he came and embraced me, saying:

"I accepted an insane wager, but you have given me a lesson I shall remember all the rest of my life, and I am grateful to you for it."

"I am very glad of it, if only the effort has not injured your health."

"No, I feel perfectly well, but we shall not play together again."

"I hope at least that we shall not play against each other."

Eight or ten days later I gave Madame d'Urfé the pleasure of taking her to Basel with the pretended Lascaris. We put up at the inn of the notorious Imhoff, who fleeced us; but his "Three Kings" was the best hostelry in the town. I said earlier, I believe, that one of the peculiarities of Basel is that noon there is at eleven o'clock,[3] *an absurdity due to a historical circumstance which the Prince of Porrentruy*[4] *explained to me but which I have forgotten. The citizens of Basel are said to be subject to a kind of madness of which they are cured by the waters of Sulzbach but which recurs soon after they are at home again.*[5]

We should have spent some time in Basel but for an incident which tried my patience and caused me to hasten our departure. It was as follows:

Need had forced me to forgive La Corticelli to some extent, and when I came home early, after supping with the rattlebrained creature and Madame d'Urfé, I would spend the night with her; but when I came home late, which happened rather often, I slept alone in my own room. The hussy likewise slept alone in a small room adjoining her mother's, through which one had to pass to enter hers.

Having come home an hour after midnight and not feeling sleepy, after putting on my dressing gown I take a candle and go to visit my beauty. I was somewhat surprised to find the door of Signora Laura's room ajar, and just as I was about to go in, the old woman reached out and caught me by my dressing gown, begging me not to enter her daughter's room.

"Why?" I said.

"She was very ill all evening, and she needs sleep."

"Very well, I will sleep too."

So saying, I give the old woman a push, I enter the girl's room, and I find her in bed with someone who hides under the coverlet.

After contemplating the tableau for a moment I began laughing, and, sitting down on the bed, I asked her who the fortunate mortal was whom it was my duty to throw out the window. Beside me on a chair I saw the person's coat, breeches, hat, and cane; but, having good pistols in my pockets, I knew I had nothing to fear; however, I did not want to make a noise.

Trembling all over, she took my hand and implored me with tears in her eyes to forgive her.

"He is a young nobleman," she said, "whose name I do not know."

"A young nobleman whose name you do not know, you cheat? Very well! He shall tell it to me himself."

As I utter the words I take a pistol and, with one vigorous hand, uncover the bird who should not have laid in my nest if he expected to escape punishment. I saw a young man whom I did not know, with his head wrapped in a madras kerchief but otherwise naked as a little Adam, as was my vixen. He turned his back to reach for his undershirt, which he had thrown down beside the bed, but, seizing his arm, I kept him from moving, for the mouth of my pistol spoke an irresistible language.

"Who are you, my fine young gentleman, if I may ask?"

"I am Count B.,[6] *Canon of Basel."*

"Do you think you are performing an ecclesiastical function here?"

"Oh no, Monsieur, I beg you to forgive me and Madame too, for the guilt is entirely mine."

"That is not what I asked you."

"Monsieur, Her Ladyship the Countess is perfectly innocent."

I was in a fortunate frame of mind, far from being angry, I could scarcely keep from laughing. The tableau had a certain charm for me, because it was at once comic and voluptuous. The combination of the two cowering nudities was genuinely lascivious, and I remained in contemplation of it for a good quarter of an hour, uttering not a word and trying to resist the strong temptation I felt to get into bed with them. I overcame it only be-

cause I feared that I should find in the Canon a fool incapable of worthily playing a role which, in his place, I should have sustained to perfection. As for La Corticelli, since it never cost her anything to change on the instant from tears to gaiety, she would have played hers ravishingly; but if, as I feared, I had found myself dealing with a fool, it would have degraded me.

Convinced that neither of them had divined what was taking place in my mind, I rose, ordering the Canon to dress.

"This incident," I said to him, "must never be divulged; but you and I will at once repair two hundred paces away and engage each other at point-blank range with these pistols."

"Ah, Monsieur," my gentleman cried, "take me wherever you like and kill me if you please, for I was not born to fight."

"Really?"

"Yes, Monsieur; and I took orders only to escape that fatal obligation."

"Then you are a coward who will take a cudgeling?"

"Anything you please; but you would be a barbarian, for love blinded me. I entered this room only a quarter of an hour ago; Her Ladyship was asleep and so was her waiting woman."

"Tell that to someone else, liar!"

"I had only just taken off my undershirt when you came in, and before that I had never been face to face with this angel."

"That," said the wench, "is as true as the Gospels."

"Do you know that you are two shameless scoundrels? And you, my fine Canon, seducer of girls, you deserve that I should have you grilled like a little St. Lawrence." [7]

Meanwhile the wretched Canon had put on his clothes.

"Follow me, Monsieur," I said in a tone calculated to freeze him, and I led him into my room.

"What will you do," I asked him, *"if I forgive you and let you leave this house without a stain on your honor?"*

"Ah, Monsieur, I will leave in an hour at the most and you will never see me here again; and wherever you meet me in future you will be sure to find me a man ready to do anything to serve you."

"Very well. Go, and in future remember to take better precautions in your amorous adventures."

After thus sending him off, I went to bed thoroughly satisfied with what I had seen and what I had done; for it left me with a perfectly free hand in respect to the little cheat.

As soon as I got up the next morning I went into La Corticelli's room and ordered her, calmly but peremptorily, to pack her things, forbidding her to leave her room until she got into the carriage.

"I will say I am ill."

"Do as you please, but no one will pay any attention, no matter what you say."

Without waiting for her to protest further, I went to Madame d'Urfé and, telling her the story of the night and enlarging on the comic side of it, I made her laugh heartily. It was just what I needed to put it into her mind to ask the oracle what we should do after this flagrant proof of the young Lascaris's having been polluted by the black Genius in the guise of a priest. The oracle replied that we must leave the next day for Besançon, that from there she must go to Lyons with all her servants and wait for me, while I took the young Countess and her governess to Geneva, where I would arrange to have them sent back to their native country once and for all.

The amiable visionary was delighted with the decree and saw in it only a proof of the kindness of her good Selenis, who thus afforded her the pleasure of seeing young D'Aranda[8] again. As for me, we agreed that I

*should meet her in the spring of the next year to perform
the great operation which would cause her to be reborn
from herself as a man. She considered the operation infallible and perfectly consonant with common sense.*

*Everything was ready for the next morning, and we
left, Madame d'Urfé and I in the berlin, La Corticelli,
her mother, and the two maids in the other carriage.
When we reached Besançon Madame d'Urfé left me,
taking her servants with her, and the next day I set out
for Geneva with the mother and daughter. I put up, as
always, at the "Scales."*

*During the whole journey not only did I not address
a word to my companions, I did not even honor them
with a look. I had them eat with a valet from Franche-
Comté* [9] *whom I had decided to engage on Baron Schaumbourg's recommendation.*

*I called on my banker to ask him to find me a reliable
vetturino* [10] *to take two unaccompanied women in whom
I was interested to Turin. At the same time I gave him
fifty louis for a bill of exchange on that city.*

Back at the inn, I wrote to the Cavaliere Raiberti, [11]
*sending him the bill of exchange. I told him that three
or four days after receiving my letter he should expect
the arrival of a Bolognese dancer and her mother with
a letter of introduction. I asked him to put them to board
in a decent house and to pay the charges on my account.
At the same time I said he would do me a great favor if
he could arrange for her to dance, even gratis, during
the Carnival, and told him to warn her that if I heard
anything to her discredit when I arrived in Turin I
would abandon her.*

*The next day one of Monsieur Tronchin's clerks came,
bringing me the* vetturino, *who said that he would be
ready to leave as soon as he had dined. After confirming
the agreement he had made with the banker, I sent for
the two Corticellis, and I said to the* vetturino:

"Here are the two persons whom you are to convey,

*and they will pay you immediately after they arrive in
Turin, safe and sound with their baggage, in four and
a half days, as specified in the contract, one copy of
which they will take with them and you the other.*"

An hour later he came to load the carriage.

La Corticelli dissolved into tears. I was not cruel
enough to let her go without some consolation. She had
been sufficiently punished for her bad behavior. I had
her dine with me, and, handing her the letter of introduction to Signor Raiberti and twenty-five louis, eight
of which were for the usual expenses, I told her what I
had written to that gentleman, who, in accordance with
my instructions, would see that she wanted for nothing.
She asked me for a trunk in which there were three
dresses and a magnificent mantle, which Madame d'Urfé
had intended to give her before she went mad; but I
told her we would talk about it in Turin. She did not
dare to mention the jewel casket, and only wept; but she
aroused no pity in me. I left her far better off than I
had taken her; for she had beautiful dresses, linens,
jewels, and a very fine watch I had given her. It was
more than she had managed to deserve.

At the moment of leaving I escorted her to the carriage, less for politeness' sake than to commend her to
the vetturino again. When she had gone, feeling relieved
of a great burden, I went to call on my Syndic,[12] whom
my readers will not have forgotten. I had not written to
him since my stay in Florence; he must have put me
out of his mind, and I looked forward to enjoying his
surprise. And in truth it was extreme; but after the
first moment he threw himself on my neck, embraced
me a dozen times, shedding tears of joy, and finally said
that he had lost all hope of seeing me again.

"What are our dear little friends doing?"

"They are as well as can be. You are still the subject
of their conversations and of their fond regrets; they
will be mad with joy when they learn that you are here."

"You must not let them wait to hear the news."

"Certainly not; I shall go and tell them that we will all sup together this evening. By the way, Monsieur de Voltaire has let the Duke of Villars have his house and has gone to live at Ferney." [13]

"That's all the same to me, for I do not intend to visit him [14] *this time. I shall stay here two or three weeks, and I devote them entirely to you."*

"You will make several people happy."

"Before you go out, be so kind as to let me have writing materials for three or four letters; I will make good use of my time until you come back."

He gave me the freedom of his desk, and I wrote at once to my late housekeeper, Madame Lebel, [15] that I should spend some three weeks in Geneva and that if I were sure I should see her again I would gladly go to Lausanne. Unfortunately for me, I also wrote to Bern, to Ascanio Pogomas, otherwise Giacomo Passano, [16] the bad poet and enemy of the Abate Chiari, whom I had met in Leghorn. I told him to go to Turin and wait for me. At the same time I wrote to my friend M. F., [17] to whom I had given him a letter of recommendation, to give him twelve louis for the journey.

My evil Genius made me think of the man, who was of imposing stature and had all the look of an astrologer, with the idea of presenting him to Madame d'Urfé as a great adept. A year from now you shall see, my dear reader, whether I had reason to repent of trusting in that ill-omened inspiration.

That evening, as the Syndic and I were on our way to visit our pretty cousins, I saw a fine English carriage for sale, and I exchanged it for mine, giving a hundred louis to boot. While I was bargaining for it, the uncle of the beautiful theologian [18] who maintained theses so learnedly, and to whom I had given such sweet lessons in physiology, recognized me, came to embrace me, and invited me to dine at his house the next day.

Before we reached the dwelling of our lovable young friends the Syndic informed me that we should find with them a very pretty girl who had not yet been initiated into the sweet mysteries.

"So much the better," I said. "I will act accordingly, and perhaps I shall be the one to initiate her."

I had put in my pocket a jewel box in which I had a dozen very pretty rings. I had long known that such trifles take one very far.

The moment when I met those charming girls again was, I confess, one of the most agreeable in my life. In their welcome I saw joy, satisfaction, candor, gratitude, and love of pleasure. They loved one another without jealousy, without envy, and without any of those ideas which could have made them think less well of themselves. They considered themselves worthy of my esteem precisely because they had lavished their favors on me without any thought of degradation and under the impulsion of the same feeling which had drawn me to them.

The presence of their new friend obliged us to limit our first embraces to the conventional demonstrations which are called "decent," and the young novice granted me the same favor, blushing and not raising her eyes.

After the usual remarks, the commonplaces of which one delivers oneself after a long absence, and a few double meanings which made us laugh and gave the young Agnes[19] matter for thought, I told her that she looked as beautiful as a Cupid, and that I would wager that her mind, no less beautiful than her ravishing figure, was free from certain prejudices.

"I have," she answered modestly, "all the prejudices which are inculcated by honor and religion."

I saw that I must be careful not to shock her, use tact, and play for time. It was not a fortress to be taken by assault in a sudden attack. But, as usual, I fell in love with her.

The Syndic having spoken my name,

"Ah," cried the girl, "then are not you, Monsieur, the gentleman who two years ago discussed some very strange questions with my cousin, the pastor's niece? [20] *I am very glad to have the opportunity to make your acquaintance."*

"I am happy to make yours, Mademoiselle, and I hope that when she spoke of me your charming cousin said nothing to prejudice you against me."

"Quite the contrary, for she esteems you highly."

"I shall have the honor of dining with her tomorrow, and I shall not fail to thank her."

"Tomorrow? I shall arrange to be there, for I am very fond of philosophical discussions, though I dare not put my word in."

The Syndic praised her prudence and her discretion so warmly that I clearly saw he was in love with her and that, if he had not yet seduced her, he must be looking far and wide for a way to accomplish it. The beautiful girl was named Helena. [21] *I asked the young ladies if the beautiful Helena was our sister. The eldest replied with a sly smile that she was a sister but that she had no brother, and, having thus enlightened me, ran to embrace her. After that the Syndic and I outdid ourselves paying her honeyed compliments, saying that we hoped to become her brothers. Helena blushed, but answered not a word to all our gallantries. Having then displayed my jewel box and seen all the young ladies enchanted by the beauty of my rings, I managed to persuade them to choose the ones they liked best, and the charming Helena followed her companions' example and paid me with a chaste kiss. Soon afterward she left us, and we were once again able to enjoy our old freedom.*

The Syndic had good reason to be in love with Helena, for the girl possessed not only all that is required to please but all that is needed to inspire a violent passion; but the three friends had no hope that they could prevail upon her to join in their pleasures, for they insisted that her feeling of modesty in the presence of men could not be conquered.

We supped very gaily, and after supper we returned to our sports, the Syndic, as usual, being merely the spectator of our exploits and very well satisfied to be no more than that. I passed the three nymphs in review twice in succession, cheating them for their own good and sparing them when I was forced to yield to nature. At midnight we parted, and the good Syndic saw me to the door of my lodging.

The next day I went to dinner at the pastor's, where I found a number of guests, among them Monsieur d'Harcourt[22] and Monsieur de Ximénès,[23] who told me that Monsieur de Voltaire knew I was in Geneva and hoped to see me. I answered him only by a low bow. Mademoiselle Hedwig, the pastor's niece, paid me a very flattering compliment which pleased me less than the sight of her cousin Helena, who was with her and whom she presented to me, saying that, having become acquainted, we should not lack opportunities to meet. It was what I most wanted. The twenty-year-old theologian was beautiful and appetizing, but she did not have that je ne sais quoi which is so piquant, the something of bitter-sweet which heightens even voluptuousness. However, her friendship with her cousin was all that I needed to enable me to inspire a favorable feeling in that young lady.

We had an excellent dinner, during which the conversation turned only on indifferent matters; but at dessert the pastor invited Monsieur de Ximénès to put some questions to his niece. Knowing this scholar by reputation, I expected some problem in geometry, but I was mistaken, for he asked her if a mental reservation suffices to justify the person who makes it.

Hedwig modestly replied that, despite the case in which a lie might become necessary, a mental reservation was always a fraud.

"Then tell me how Jesus Christ could say that the

time at which the world would end was unknown to him." [24]

"He could say it because he did not know."

"Then he was not God?"

"The conclusion is false because, God having all power, he has the power to be ignorant of futurity."

The word "futurity," [25] *so aptly coined, seemed to me sublime. Hedwig was enthusiastically applauded, and her uncle went around the table to embrace her. I had a very natural objection on the tip of my tongue, and one which, arising out of the subject, might have embarrassed her; but I wanted to ingratiate myself with her and I said nothing.*

Monsieur d'Harcourt was next urged to question her, but he replied with Horace, nulla mihi religio est.[26] *Thereupon Hedwig, turning to me, said that she could not help thinking of the amphidromia,* [27] *a pagan festival:*

"But I wish," she added, "that you would ask me a question concerning something difficult which you could not resolve yourself."

"You make it easy for me, Mademoiselle."

"So much the better, you won't have to think so hard."

"I am trying to think of something new. I have it. Will you grant me that Jesus Christ possessed all the qualities of mankind in the highest degree?"

"Yes, all, except its weaknesses."

"Do you reckon the procreative power among its weaknesses?"

"No."

"Then be so kind as to tell me what would be the nature of the creature which would have been born if Jesus Christ had seen fit to give the woman of Samaria a child."

Hedwig turned fiery red. The pastor and the entire company looked at one another, and I fixed my eyes on the beautiful theologian, who was thinking. Monsieur d'Harcourt said that we must send for Monsieur de

*Voltaire to resolve so thorny a question; but, Hedwig
raising her eyes with a meditative look which seemed to
declare her ready to answer, everyone fell silent.*

*"Jesus Christ," she said, "had two perfect natures in
perfect equilibrium; they were inseparable. So if the
woman of Samaria had had carnal knowledge of our
Redeemer she would certainly have conceived; for it
would be absurd to suppose so important an act in a
God without admitting its natural consequence. At the
end of nine months the woman of Samaria would have
given birth to a male, not a female, child; and this
creature, born of a human woman and a man-God, would
have been one fourth God and three fourths man."*

*At these words all the company clapped their hands,
and Monsieur de Ximénès admired the logic of the cal-
culation; then he said:*

*"As a natural consequence, if the Samaritan's son had
married, the children issuing from his marriage would
have possessed seven eighths of humanity and one eighth
of divinity."*

*"Unless he had married a goddess," I added, "which
would have markedly changed the proportions."*

*"Tell me," Hedwig went on, "exactly what proportion
of divinity the child would have had in the sixteenth
generation."*

*"Wait a moment and give me a pencil," said Monsieur
de Ximénès.*

*"There is no need to calculate," I said; "he would
have had a particle of the spirit which animates you."*

*Everyone echoed this gallantry, which was not dis-
pleasing to her to whom I addressed it.*

*The beautiful blonde set me on fire by the charms of
her mind. We rose from the table and gathered around
her, and she demolished all our compliments with the
most perfect courtesy. Having taken Helena aside, I
asked her to induce her cousin to choose one of the rings
from my box, which I had taken care to refill the evening*

before; the charming girl willingly undertook the com-
mission. A quarter of an hour later Hedwig came to
show me her hand, and I was pleased to see the ring she
had chosen; I kissed her hand with delight, and she must
have guessed, from the ardor of my kisses, all that she
had inspired in me.

That evening Helena gave the Syndic and the three
friends an account of all the questions which had been
asked at dinner, not forgetting the slightest detail. She
spoke easily and with grace; I did not once need to
prompt her. We begged her to stay for supper, but,
taking the three friends aside, she convinced them that
she could not; but she told them she would be able to
spend two days at a country house they had on the lake,
if they would themselves ask her mother to permit it.

At the Syndic's request the three friends called on
her mother the next day, and on the day after they set
out with Helena. That evening we went to supper with
them, but we could not spend the night there. The Syndic
was to take me to a house not far away where we would
be very well lodged. That being so, we were in no hurry;
and the eldest, eager to please her friend the Syndic,
told him that he might leave with me whenever he
pleased and that they were going to bed. So saying, she
took Helena's arm and led her to her room, and the
two others went to theirs. A few minutes after they left,
the Syndic entered the apartment to which Helena had
gone, and I repaired to the two other girls.

I had spent scarcely an hour between my two little
friends when the Syndic appeared and interrupted my
erotic diversions by asking me to leave.

"What have you done with Helena?" I asked him.

"Nothing, she is an intractable fool. She hid under
the covers and refused to look at the amusements in
which I indulged with her friend."

"You should have addressed your attentions to her."

"I did so, but she repulsed me time after time. I am

exhausted. I have given up, and I am sure I shall get nowhere with the wildcat unless you undertake to tame her."

"How am I to do that?"

"Go to dine with them tomorrow; I shall not be there, for I have to spend the day in Geneva. I will come for supper, and if we could get her tipsy!"

"That would be a pity. Leave it to me."

So the next day I went by myself and asked them if I might dine with them, and they entertained me in the full sense of the word. When we went for a walk after dinner the three friends, anticipating my wish, left me alone with the beautiful recalcitrant, who resisted my caresses and my pleadings and almost made me lose all hope of taming her.

"The Syndic," I said, "is in love with you; and last night—"

"Last night," she interrupted me, "last night he amused himself with his old sweetheart. I have no objection to everyone's acting as he pleases and sees fit; but I wish to be left free in my own acts and tastes."

"If I could succeed in possessing your heart, I should consider myself happy."

"Why do you not invite the pastor to dinner somewhere with my cousin? She would take me with her, for my uncle is fond of all those who love his niece."

"I am very glad to know that. Has she some man who is in love with her?"

"Not one."

"How is that possible? She is young, pretty, gay, and, what is more, highly intelligent."

"You do not know Geneva. Her intelligence is precisely the reason why no young man dares declare himself her lover. Those who might be attracted by her person avoid her because of her mind, for they would be left with nothing to say in the middle of a conversation."

"But are the young men of Geneva so ignorant?"

"*Generally speaking. However, it is only right to say that many of them have received good educations and done well in their studies; but taken as a whole, they have a great many prejudices. No one likes to pass for a fool or an ignoramus; and then the young men here simply do not run after intelligence or a good education in a woman. Far from it. If a young lady is intelligent or well educated, she has to hide it carefully, at least if she hopes to marry.*"

"*I see now, charming Helena, why you did not open your mouth during your uncle's dinner.*"

"*I know that I have no talents to hide. So that was not the reason which made me silent that day, and I can tell you, without vanity as without shame, that it was pleasure which kept my mouth closed. I admired my cousin, who talked of Jesus Christ as I might talk of my father and who did not fear to show her knowledge of a subject which any other girl would have pretended not to understand.*"

"*Pretended, even though she knew more about it than her grandmother.*"

"*It is part of our ways, or rather of our prejudices.*"

"*You reason admirably, my dear Helena, and I already sigh for the dinner party which your kindness has suggested to me.*"

"*You will have the pleasure of being with my cousin.*"

"*I know her merits, beautiful Helena; Hedwig is amiable and interesting; but, believe me, it is especially because you will be present that the thought of the dinner delights me.*"

"*What if I did not believe you?*"

"*You would be wrong, and you would cause me great sorrow, for I love you dearly.*"

"*Despite that, you tried to deceive me. I am sure that you have given tokens of your affection to the three young ladies, whom I greatly pity.*"

"*Why?*"

"*Because none of them can suppose that you love only her.*"

"*And do you think such delicacy of feeling makes you happier than they?*"

"*Yes, I do; though in this matter I am completely inexperienced. Tell me frankly if you think I am right.*"

"*Yes, I think you are.*"

"*You charm me; but if I am right, admit that by trying to associate me with them you do not give me such a proof of love as would convince me that you love me as I should wish to be convinced of it.*"

"*Oh, I admit that too, and I sincerely ask your pardon. But now, divine Helena, tell me how I am to go about inviting the pastor to dinner.*"

"*It is not difficult. Simply go to his house and invite him; and if you want to be sure that I shall be present, ask him to invite me with my mother.*"

"*Why with your mother?*"

"*Because he was very much in love with her twenty years ago and still loves her.*"

"*And where can I give the dinner?*"

"*Is not Monsieur Tronchin your banker?*"

"*Yes.*"

"*He has a fine pleasure house on the lake; ask him for it for a day; he will lend it to you gladly. Do that, but say not a word about it to the Syndic or his three friends; we will tell them afterward.*"

"*But do you think your learned cousin tolerates my company?*"

"*More than tolerates it, you may be sure.*"

"*Very well, it will all be arranged tomorrow. You are to return to the city day after tomorrow, and I will set the dinner for two or three days later.*"

The Syndic joined us toward nightfall, and we spent the evening gaily. After supper, the young ladies having gone to bed as on the previous evening, I went into the room of the eldest while my friend went to see the two younger sisters. I knew that whatever I might undertake in order to bring Helena to terms would be unavailing; so I confined myself to a few kisses, after which I wished them good night, then I went to pay the younger sisters a visit. I found them sleeping soundly, and the Syndic in solitary boredom. I did not cheer him when I told him I had not been able to obtain a single favor.

"I see beyond doubt," he said, "that I shall be wasting my time with that little idiot, and in the end I shall have to make the best of it."

"I think," I replied, "that it is your most advisable course, and the sooner the better, for dangling after an insensible or capricious beauty is being her dupe. Good fortune should be neither too easy nor too difficult."

The next morning we went to Geneva together; and Monsieur Tronchin seemed delighted to be able to do me the favor I asked of him. The pastor accepted my invitation and said he was sure I would be glad to make the acquaintance of Helena's mother. It was easy to see that the worthy man cherished a tender feeling for the lady, and, if she reciprocated it a little, that could only be favorable to my plans.

I expected to go to supper that evening with the three friends and the charming Helena in the house on the lake, but a letter brought by an express messenger obliged me to leave for Lausanne at once; my former house-keeper, Madame Lebel, whom I still love, invited me to sup with her and her husband. She wrote me that she had no sooner received my letter than she had persuaded her husband to take her to Lausanne; she added that she was sure I would leave everything to give her the pleasure of seeing me again. She told me the hour at which she would arrive at her mother's.

Madame Lebel is one of the ten or twelve women whom I loved the most fondly in my happy youth. She had everything one could ask to make a happy marriage if it had been my destiny to enjoy that felicity. But with my character I may have done well not to bind myself irrevocably, though at my present age my independence is a sort of slavery. If I had married a woman intelligent enough to guide me, to rule me without my feeling that I was ruled, I should have taken good care of my money, I should have had children, and I should not be, as now I am, alone in the world and possessing nothing.

But let us renounce digressions on a past which cannot be recalled; since I am happy in my memories, I should be mad to create useless regrets.

Having calculated that, by leaving at once, I could reach Lausanne an hour before my dear Dubois, I did not hesitate to give her that proof of my esteem. I must tell my readers here that, though I loved the woman, occupied as I then was with another passion, no hope of amorous pleasure entered into my haste. My esteem for her would have sufficed to hold my love in check, but I also esteemed Lebel, and I should never have allowed myself to risk clouding the happiness of two such friends.

I hastily wrote the Syndic a note, saying that important and unexpected business obliged me to leave for Lausanne, but that on the next day but one I should have the pleasure of supping with him and the trio of friends in Geneva.

At five o'clock I reach the house of Madame Dubois, dying of hunger. The good woman's surprise at seeing me was extreme, for she did not know that her daughter was coming to visit her. Without spending much time on compliments, I gave her two louis to procure us a supper such as I needed.

At seven o'clock Madame Lebel arrived with her husband and an eighteen-months-old child, whom I had no difficulty in recognizing as mine without his mother's telling me so. Our interview was entirely happy. During the ten hours we spent at table we bathed in joy. At daybreak she set out for Soleure, where Lebel had business. Monsieur de Chavigny[28] sent me countless compliments.

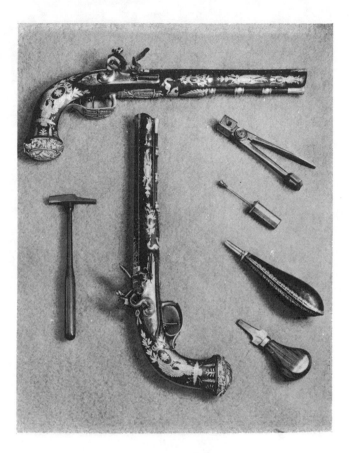

Pair of Dueling Pistols with
Accessory Implements

Playing Cards

Lebel assured me that the Ambassador showed his wife innumerable kindnesses, and he thanked me for the present I had made him in relinquishing her to him. I could see for myself that he was happy and that he made his wife happy.

My dear housekeeper talked to me of my son. She said that no one suspected the truth, but that she knew the state of the case, as did Lebel, who had religiously observed the agreement not to consummate their marriage until the two stipulated months had passed.

"The secret," said Lebel, "will never be known, and your son will be my heir, either alone or with my children if I have any, which I doubt."

"My friend," his wife said to him, "there is someone who suspects the truth, and will suspect it the more as the child grows; but we have nothing to fear on that score; the person is paid to keep the secret."

"And who, my dear Lebel," I asked her, "is this person?"

"It is Madame de . . . ,[29] who has not forgotten you, for she speaks of you often."

"Will you be so good, my dear, as to convey my compliments to her?"

"Gladly, my friend, and I am sure she will be delighted."

Lebel showed me my ring, and I showed him her wedding ring,[30] giving him a splendid watch with my portrait for my son.

"You shall give it to him, my friends," I said, "when you consider that the time has come."

We shall meet this child again at Fontainebleau twenty-one years hence.[31]

I spent more than three hours giving them a detailed account of all that had happened to me during the twenty-seven months since we had seen one another. As for their story, it was not long; their life had the uniformity which befits untroubled happiness.

Madame Lebel was still beautiful; I did not find her changed at all; but I had changed. She declared that I was less fresh and less gay than I had been when we parted; she was right, the ill-omened Renaud had played havoc with me and the false Lascaris had caused me great concern.

After the tenderest embraces the couple set off for Soleure and I went back to dine in Geneva; but, badly needing rest, far from going to supper with the Syndic and his three friends, I wrote him that, being indisposed, I should not have the pleasure of seeing him until the morrow, and I went to bed.

The next day, which was the eve of the day I had set for my dinner at Tronchin's country house, I ordered the innkeeper to furnish me with a repast in which he was to spare no expense. I did not forget to stipulate the best wines, the finest liqueurs, ices, and everything needed for a punch. I told him that we should be six, for I foresaw that Monsieur Tronchin would be of the company. I was not mistaken, for he was there at his charming house to do us the honors of it, and I had no difficulty in persuading him to stay. In the evening I thought it best to let the Syndic and his three friends into the secret of the dinner in the presence of Helena, who pretended to know nothing about it, saying that her mother had told her that she would take her to dinner somewhere.

"I am delighted," she added, "to learn that it is to be nowhere but in Monsieur Tronchin's pretty house." [32]

My dinner was such that the greatest epicure could have asked nothing better, and Hedwig really furnished all its charm. The astonishing girl discoursed on theology so pleasantly, and made reason so attractive, that it was impossible not to feel the strongest persuasion even when one was not convinced. I have never seen a theologian able to attack and discuss the most abstruse points of that science with such facility, copiousness, and true dignity as that young and beautiful girl, who set me completely on fire during the dinner. Monsieur Tronchin, who had never heard Hedwig, thanked me again and again for procuring him such a pleasure, and, obliged to leave just when we rose from table, he invited us to repeat the occasion on the next day but one.

A thing which greatly interested me during dessert was the encomium which the pastor delivered in commemoration of his old fondness for Helena's mother. His amorous eloquence waxed in proportion as he moistened his throat with champagne and Cyprus wine or with liqueurs from the Indies. Her mother listened to him with satisfaction and matched him glass for glass; the young ladies, however, had drunk only sparingly, as had I. Nevertheless the variety of beverages and especially the punch had produced their effect, and my beauties were a little tipsy. Their gaiety was charming but extreme. I took advantage of this general well-being to ask the two superannuated lovers' permission to take the young ladies for a stroll in the garden at the edge of the lake, and it was granted with all cordiality. We went out arm in arm and a few minutes later were out of everyone's sight.

"Are you aware," I asked Hedwig, "that you have won Monsieur Tronchin's heart?"

"I should not know what to do with it. Besides, the honest banker asked me rather stupid questions."

"You must not suppose that everyone is able to ask them within your compass."

"I must tell you that no one ever asked me one which pleased me as much as yours did. A stupid and bigoted theologian who was at the end of the table appeared to be scandalized by your question and still more by my answer."

"Why, may I ask?"

"He insists that I should have answered you that Jesus Christ could not have impregnated the woman of

Samaria. He said he would explain the reason to me if I were a man, but that since I was a woman, and especially an unmarried girl, he could not permit himself to say things which might suggest ideas to me when I reflected on the composite God-man. I wish you would tell me what the fool would not."

"I am willing, but you must allow me to speak to you clearly and to suppose that you are acquainted with the construction of a man."

"Yes, speak clearly, for there's no one here to hear us; but I must confess that I know nothing about the construction of a man except from theory and reading. No practical knowledge, of course. I have seen statues, but I have never seen, still less examined, a real man. And you, Helena?"

"I have never wanted to."

"Why not? It is good to know everything."

"Very well, charming Hedwig, your theologian was trying to tell you that Jesus was not capable of an erection."

"What is that?"

"Give me your hand."

"I feel it, and it is as I had imagined it would be; for without this phenomenon of nature man could not impregnate his spouse. And that fool of a theologian maintains that it is an imperfection!"

"Yes, for the phenomenon arises from desire; witness the fact that it would not have taken place in me, beautiful Hedwig, if I had not found you charming, and if what I see of you did not give me the most seductive idea of the beauties I do not see. Tell me frankly if, on your side, feeling this stiffness does not cause you a pleasant excitation?"

"I admit it, and precisely in the place you are pressing. Do not you, my dear Helena, feel as I do a certain itching here while you listen to the very sound discourse to which Monsieur is treating us?"

"Yes, I feel it, but I feel it very often where there is no discourse to excite it."

"And then," I said, "does not Nature oblige you to relieve it in this fashion?"

"Certainly not."

"But it does!" said Hedwig. "Even in sleep our hand goes there instinctively; and without that relief, I have read, we should be subject to terrible maladies."

Continuing this philosophical discussion, which the young theologian sustained in a masterly manner and which gave her cousin's beautiful complexion all the animation of voluptuous feeling, we arrived at the edge of a superb basin of water with a flight of marble stairs down which one went to bathe. Though it was chilly our heads were heated, and it occurred to me to ask them to dip their feet in the water, assuring them that it would do them good and that, if they would permit me, I would have the honor of taking off their shoes and stockings.

"Why not?" said the niece. "I'd like it."

"So should I," said Helena.

"Then sit down, ladies, on the top step." And they sit, and I, placing myself on the fourth step below, fall to taking off their shoes and stockings, praising the beauty of their legs, and for the moment showing no interest in seeing anything above the knee. I took them down to the water, and then there was nothing for it but that they should pull up their dresses, and I encouraged them to do so.

"Well," said Hedwig, "men have thighs too."

Helena, who would have been ashamed to show less courage than her cousin, was not slow to follow her example.

"Come, my charming Naiads," [33] *I said, "that is enough; you might catch cold if you stay in the water longer."*

They came up the stairs backward, still holding up their skirts for fear of wetting them; and it was my part to dry them with all the handkerchiefs I had. This agreeable office allowed me to see and to touch in perfect freedom, and the reader will not need to have me swear that I made the most of the opportunity. The beautiful niece told me that I was too curious, but Helena accepted my ministrations in a manner so tender and languishing that I had to use all my will to keep from going further. Finally, when I had put on their shoes and stockings, I said that I was in raptures at having seen the secret beauties of the two most beautiful girls in Geneva.

"What effect did it have on you?" Hedwig asked me.

"I do not dare tell you to look; but feel, both of you."

"You must bathe too."

"That is impossible, getting ready takes a man too long."

"But we still have two full hours to stay here with no fear of anyone coming to join us."

Her answer made me see all the good fortune which awaited me; but I did not choose to expose myself to an illness by entering the water in the state I was in. Seeing a garden house a short distance away and certain that Monsieur Tronchin would have left it unlocked, I took them there, not letting them guess my intention.

The garden house was full of pot-pourri jars, charming engravings, and so on; but what was best of all was a fine, large couch ready for repose and pleasure. Sitting on it between the two beauties and lavishing caresses on them, I told them I wanted to show them what they had never seen, and, so saying, I exposed to their gaze the principal effective cause of humanity. They stood up to admire me; whereupon, taking them each by one hand, I gave them a factitious consummation; but in the course of my labors an abundant emission of liquid threw them into the greatest astonishment.

"It is the word," [34] I said, "the great creator of mankind."

"How delicious!" cried Helena, laughing at the desig-
nation "word."

"But I too," said Hedwig, "have the word, and I will
show it to you if you will wait a moment."

"Sit on my lap, beautiful Hedwig, and I will save you
the trouble of making it come yourself, and I will do it
better than you can."

"I believe you, but I have never done it with a man."

"Nor have I," said Helena.

Having made them stand in front of me with their
arms around me, I made them faint again. Then we all
sat down, and, while I explored their charms with my
hands, I let them amuse themselves by touching me as
they pleased, until I finally wet their hands with a
second emission of the humid radical, which they curi-
ously examined on their fingers.

After restoring ourselves to a state of decency, we
spent another half hour exchanging kisses, then I told
them they had made me half happy, but that to bring
their work to completion I hoped they would think of a
way to grant me their first favors. I then showed them
the little protective bags which the English invented to
free the fair sex from all fear. These little purses, whose
use I explained to them, aroused their admiration, and
the beautiful theologian told her cousin that she would
think about it. Become intimate friends and well on the
way to becoming something more, we made our way
toward the house, where we found the pastor and
Helena's mother strolling beside the lake.

Back in Geneva, I went to spend the night with the
three friends, and I took care to keep my victory over
Helena concealed from the Syndic; for the news would
only have renewed his hopes, and he would have wasted
his efforts and his time. Without the beautiful theologian,
even I would have obtained nothing from her, but since
she greatly admired her cousin she would have feared to

fall too far below her if she refused to imitate her in the freedoms which, in her, were the measure of her freedom of mind.

Helena did not come that evening, but I saw her the next day at her mother's, for politeness demanded that I go to thank the widow for the honor she had done me. She received me in the friendliest fashion and introduced two very pretty young ladies who were boarding in her house and who would have interested me if I had intended to make a long stay in Geneva; but since I had only a few days to spend there, Helena deserved all my efforts.

"Tomorrow," the charming girl said, "I shall be able to tell you something at Monsieur Tronchin's dinner, and I think that Hedwig will have hit upon a scheme for satisfying your desires in perfect freedom."

The banker's dinner was admirable. He took great pride in showing me that the repast provided by an innkeeper can never rival one offered by a rich householder who has a good cook, a choice cellar, beautiful silver, and porcelain of the finest quality. We were twenty at table, and the occasion was in honor both of the learned theologian and of myself in my role of wealthy stranger who spent his money freely. Among the guests I found Monsieur de Ximénès, who had come from Ferney expressly to be present, and he told me that I was expected at Monsieur de Voltaire's; but I had stupidly made up my mind not to go there.

Hedwig shone. The guests gained consideration only by their questions. Monsieur de Ximénès asked her to do her best to justify our first mother for having deceived her husband into eating the fatal apple.

"Eve," she said, "did not deceive her husband; she only cajoled him, in the hope of giving him an added perfection. Besides, Eve did not receive the prohibition from God himself, she had received it from Adam; in *what she did there was only cajolery, not deceit; then, too, it is probable that her womanly good sense refused to let her think the prohibition serious."*

At this answer, in my opinion full of sense, intelligence, and tact, two learned Genevans, and even the young prodigy's uncle, began muttering. Madame Tronchin gravely told Hedwig that Eve had received the prohibition from God himself, as had her husband; but the young lady replied only by a humble:

"I beg your pardon, Madame."

Madame Tronchin, turning to the pastor in alarm:

"What do you say, Monsieur?"

"Madame, my niece is not infallible."

"I beg your pardon, dear Uncle, but I am as infallible as Holy Scripture when I speak in accordance with it."

"Quick, a Bible! let us see!"

"Hedwig, my dear Hedwig . . . you are right after all. Here is the passage.[35] The prohibition preceded the creation of the woman."

Everyone applauded, but Hedwig, calm and modest, did not change her expression; only the two learned men and Madame Tronchin could not recover their calm. Another lady having asked her if, in good conscience, one could believe that the story of the apple was allegorical, she said:

"I do not think so, Madame, for the allegory could be applied only to copulation, and it is established that it did not take place between Adam and Eve in the Garden of Eden."

"But the learned hold different opinions on that point."

"So much the worse for those who deny it, Madame; for Scripture speaks clearly on the point; it says in the first verse of the fourth chapter that Adam did not know Eve until after his expulsion from the terrestrial paradise, and that then she conceived Cain."

"Yes, but the verse does not say that Adam did not know Eve until then, hence he could have known her before."

"That I cannot admit, for if he had known her earlier she would have conceived, since I should find it absurd to suppose that the act of generation could take place between two creatures proceeding immediately from the hands of God, and hence as perfect as it is possible for a man and a woman to be, without its natural effect following."

This answer made the whole company clap, and everyone whispered words of commendation for Hedwig into his neighbor's ear.

Monsieur Tronchin asked her if one could establish the immortality of the soul by reading only the Old Testament.

"The Old Testament," she replied, "does not teach that doctrine; but without its being mentioned there, reason establishes it; for what exists must necessarily be immortal, since the destruction of a real substance is contrary to nature and reason."

"Then I will ask you," the banker resumed, "if the existence of the soul is established in the Bible."

"The idea of it is inescapable. Where there is smoke there is always fire."

"Tell me if matter can think."

"That I shall not tell you, for it is not within my competence; but I will tell you that, believing God to be all-powerful, I cannot find any adequate reason for inferring his inability to give matter the faculty of thinking."

"But what do you believe yourself?"

"I believe that I have a soul by means of which I think; but I do not know if after my death I shall remember through my soul that I had the honor of dining at your table today."

"Then you believe that your memory may not be a

*part of your soul? But in that case you would no longer
be a theologian."*

*"One can be a theologian and a philosopher, for phi-
losophy harms nothing, and to say 'I do not know' does
not mean 'I know.' "*

*Three quarters of the guests exclaimed in admiration,
and the beautiful philosopher enjoyed seeing me smile
with pleasure as I listened to the applause. The pastor
wept for joy and whispered to Helena's mother. Suddenly, turning to me,*

*"I should like," he said, "to hear you ask my niece a
question."*

*"Yes," said Hedwig; "but let it be new or none at
all."*

*"You put me in a quandary," I replied, "for how am
I to be sure that what I ask you is new? Nevertheless,
tell me, Mademoiselle, if, to comprehend a thing, one
must consider its principle."*

*"There is no comprehending it otherwise; and that is
why God, having no principle, is incomprehensible."*

*"God be praised, Mademoiselle! your answer is what
I hoped it would be. That being admitted, be so good as
to tell me if God can know his own existence."*

*"Now I'm at the end of my rope; I don't know how
to answer. What a cruel question, Monsieur!"*

"Then why did you ask me for something really new?"

"But that's only natural."

*"I thought, Mademoiselle, that the newest thing would
be to put you in a quandary."*

*"What a compliment! Gentlemen, be so good as to
answer for me and teach me."*

*Everyone beat about the bush, but no one said anything
conclusive. Then Hedwig, entering into the discussion
again, said:*

*"Nevertheless, I think that, since God knows all things,
he must know his own existence; but please do not ask
me how that is possible."*

"Good," I said, "very good! and no one can say any more on the subject."

All the guests thought me a flattering atheist, so superficially are people of fashion accustomed to judge; but I did not care whether I was an atheist or a believer in their eyes.

Monsieur de Ximénès asked Hedwig if matter had been created.

"I do not recognize the word 'created,'" she said. "Ask me if matter was formed, and I will answer in the affirmative. The word 'created' cannot have existed, for the existence of the thing itself must precede the formation of the word which designates it."

"Then what meaning do you give to the verb 'to create'?"

"'To make out of nothing.' You see the absurdity, for you must suppose the precedent nothing. . . . I am delighted to see you laugh. Do you think that nothing *is susceptible of creation?"*

"You are right, Mademoiselle."

"Now, now," said a guest, frowning, "not entirely, not entirely."

Everyone burst into laughter, for the contradicter seemed not to know what to say.

"Tell me, please, Mademoiselle, who your teacher was in Geneva," said Monsieur de Ximénès.

"My uncle there."

"No, no, my dear niece, for may I die if I ever told you all that you have brought out today. But, gentlemen, my niece has nothing to do; she reads, thinks, and reasons, perhaps too boldly; but I love her because she always ends by saying she knows nothing."

A certain lady, who until then had not spoken, politely asked her to define "spirit."

"Madame, your question is purely philosophical; so I will tell you that I know neither spirit nor matter well enough to be able to define them satisfactorily."

"But in accordance with the abstract idea you must have of the real existence of spirit—since, admitting a God, you cannot but have an idea of what spirit is—tell me how you suppose that it can act on matter."

"One cannot build solidly on an abstract idea. Hobbes[36] calls them 'empty ideas'; one can entertain them, but one should let them alone, for when one tries to explore them one ends in confusion. I know that God sees me, but I should make myself wretched if I tried to convince myself of it by reasoning, for, arguing from our perceptions, we must admit that one can do nothing without organs; now since God cannot have organs, for we conceive him as a pure spirit, philosophically speaking, God cannot see us any more than we can see him. But Moses and several others saw him, and I believe it without examining it."

"You are well advised to do so," I said, "for if you examined it you would find it impossible. But if you read Hobbes you risk becoming an atheist."

"I have no fear of that, for I cannot even conceive the possibility of atheism."

After dinner everyone wanted to compliment the truly astonishing girl, so that I could not speak with her alone even for a moment to tell her of my love; but I went aside with Helena, who said that her cousin was to go to supper at her mother's with the pastor the next day.

"Hedwig," she added, "will stay, and we will sleep together, as we do every time she comes to sup with her Uncle. The question, then, is whether, for the sake of spending the night with us, you will be willing to hide in a place which I will show you tomorrow morning at eleven o'clock. Come at that hour to call on my mother, and I will find an opportunity to show you your hiding place. You will not be comfortable there, but you will be safe, and if you become bored, you can entertain yourself by remembering that we shall be thinking a great deal about you."

"Shall I stay hidden long?"

"Four hours at most, because at seven o'clock the street door is closed and is not opened again except to people who ring."

"And if I had to cough in the place where I shall be, would it be heard?"

"It is possible."

"That is a great difficulty. All the rest is nothing; but no matter, I will risk everything for the sake of the greatest happiness, which I accept with my whole heart."

The next day I called on the widow, and Helena, as she showed me out, pointed to a closed door between the two flights of stairs.

"At seven o'clock," she said, *"you will find it unlocked, and when you are inside you must bolt it shut. When you come, take care to choose a moment to enter it when no one will see you."*

At a quarter to seven I was already shut in the closet, where I found a chair—a piece of good luck, for otherwise I should have been able neither to lie down nor to stand erect. It was a miserable hole, and I knew from the smell that it was used to store hams and cheeses; but there were none in it at the time, for I took pains to grope to left and right to find my bearings a little in the thick darkness. Shuffling cautiously along in all directions, I felt something soft, I put my hand on it, and recognized linen. It was a napkin in which there was another and then two plates between which was a fine roast chicken and a piece of bread. Directly beside it I found a bottle and a glass. I was grateful to my beautiful friends for having thought of my stomach; but I had dined well, and rather late by way of precaution, so I put off paying my respects to the cold repast until the hour of fulfillment should be more nearly come.

At nine o'clock I set to work, and since I had neither a corkscrew nor a knife I had to break the neck of the bottle with a brick which I was luckily able to pull out *of the rotting floor which supported me. It was an old Neuchâtel* [37] *wine, and delicious. In addition, my chicken was truffled to perfection, and the two stimulants showed me that my nymphs had some notion of physiology or that chance had seen fit to serve my turn. I should have spent my time patiently enough in this retreat had it not been for the rather frequent visits of one or another rat, which announced its presence by its loathsome smell and caused me nausea. I remembered that I had suffered the same annoyance at Cologne on a like occasion.* [38]

At last ten o'clock struck, and a half hour later I heard the voice of the pastor as he went downstairs talking; he charged Helena not to play any tricks with his niece during the night and to sleep soundly. I then remembered Signor Rosa, who, twenty-two years earlier, left Signora Orio's [39] *house in Venice at the same hour; and, reflecting upon myself, I found that I had changed greatly without becoming more reasonable; but if I was less sensible to pleasure I thought that the two beauties who awaited me were far superior to Signora Orio's nieces.* [40]

In my long career as a libertine, during which my invincible inclination for the fair sex led me to employ every method of seduction, I turned the heads of several hundred women whose charms had overwhelmed my reason; but what was always my best safeguard is that I was always careful not to attack novices, girls whose moral principles or whose prejudices were an obstacle to success, except in the company of another woman. I early learned that what arouses resistance in a young girl, what makes it difficult to seduce her, is lack of courage; whereas when she is with a female friend she gives in quite easily; the weakness of the one brings about the fall of the other. Fathers and mothers believe the contrary, but they are mistaken. They commonly refuse to entrust their daughter to a young man, whether for a ball or a walk; but they yield if the girl has one of her friends as a chaperone. I repeat for their benefit:

they are mistaken; for if the young man knows how to go about it their daughter is lost. A false shame prevents both girls alike from offering an absolute resistance to seduction, and as soon as the first step has been taken the fall comes inevitably and quickly. If the friend permits the theft of the slightest favor in order to save herself from blushing, she will be the first to urge her friend to grant a greater one, and if the seducer is skillful the innocent novice will, without realizing it, have gone too far to turn back. Then, too, the more innocent a girl is, the more unacquainted she will be with the methods and the end of seduction. Without her being aware of it, the lure of pleasure draws her on, curiosity enters in, and opportunity does the rest.

It is possible, for example, that without Helena I should have succeeded in seducing the learned Hedwig; but I am sure that I should never have conquered Helena if she had not seen her cousin grant me freedoms and take liberties with me which they must have regarded as the very reverse of what modesty and decorum demanded of a well-brought-up girl.

Since, though I do not repent of my amorous exploits, I am far from wanting my example to contribute to the corruption of the fair sex, which deserves our homage for so many reasons, I hope that my observations will foster prudence in fathers and mothers and thus at least deserve their esteem.

Soon after the pastor left, I heard three soft knocks on the door of my hiding place. I opened it, and a hand as soft as satin took mine. All my senses reeled. It was Helena's hand, she had electrified me, and that moment of happiness had already repaid me for my long wait.

"Follow me quietly," she whispered as soon as she had closed the door again, but in my happy impatience I clasped her fondly in my arms, and, making her feel the effect which her mere presence produced on me, I also assured myself of her complete docility.

"*Restrain yourself, my friend,*" *she said,* "*and let us go up quietly.*"

I groped my way after her, and, at the end of a long, dark corridor, she led me into an unlighted room, closing the door behind us; then she opened the door to another room, where there was a light and in which I saw Hedwig almost undressed. She came to me with open arms as soon as she saw me, and, kissing me ardently, expressed the most lively gratitude for my having been so patient in so dreary a prison.

"*My divine Hedwig,*" *I said,* "*if I did not love you to distraction I would not have stayed a quarter of an hour in that dreadful hole; but you have only to say the word and I will spend four hours there every day as long as I remain here. But let us not waste time, my friends; let us go to bed.*"

"*You two go to bed,*" *said Helena;* "*I will spend the night on the couch.*"

"*No, no, my cousin!*" *cried Hedwig,* "*you must not think of it. Our destinies must be one and the same.*"

"*Yes, divine Helena, yes,*" *I said, going to embrace her,* "*I love you both equally; and all this ceremoniousness only makes us lose precious time during which I could prove my fond ardor to you. Do as I do. I shall undress and get into the middle of the bed. Come quickly to my sides, and you will see if I love you as you deserve to be loved. If we are safe here I will keep you company until you tell me to leave; but I implore you not to put out the light.*"

Quick as a wink, philosophizing the while on shame with the beautiful theologian, I offered myself to their gaze in the nudity of a second Adam. Blushing, perhaps fearing to lose my esteem by too much holding back, Hedwig let the last veil of modesty fall, citing St. Clement of Alexandria,[41] *who says that shame resides only in the shift. I eulogized her beauties, the perfection of her forms, hoping thus to encourage Helena, who was un-*

*dressing slowly; but an accusation of false modesty from
her cousin had more effect than all my prodigal praises.
And at last the Venus appears in the state of nature, at
a loss how best to employ her hands, covering part of
her most secret charms with one and a breast with the
other, and seeming to be aghast at all that she cannot
hide. Her bashful confusion, the struggle between expiring modesty and voluptuousness, held me spellbound.*

*Hedwig was taller than Helena, her skin was whiter,
and her bosom twice as full; but Helena had more animation, smoother forms, and a bosom modeled after that of
the Medicean Venus.*[42]

*When Helena, emboldened little by little, arrived at a
parity with her cousin, we spent a few moments admiring one another, then we went to bed. Nature spoke imperiously, and we asked nothing better than to obey.
Having donned a protective covering which I did not fear
would break, I made Hedwig a woman, and, when the
sacrifice was completed, she said, covering me with kisses,
that the moment of pain was nothing in comparison with
the pleasure.*

*Helena, six years younger than Hedwig, soon had her
turn; but the finest fleece I have ever seen offered some
resistance; she parted it with her two hands and, jealous
of her cousin's success, though she could not be initiated
into the mystery of love without a painful rupturing,
she uttered only sighs of happiness, responding to my
efforts and seeming to rival me in tenderness and ardor.
Her charms and her motions made me shorten the sweet
sacrifice, and when I left the sanctuary my two beauties
saw that I needed rest.*

*The altar was cleansed of the victims' blood and we
performed a salutary ablution together, delighting in
serving one another.*

*My existence was renewed under their agile and curi-
ous hands, and the sight filled them with joy. I then told
them how much I needed to renew my happiness during*

all the time I was to remain in Geneva, but they sighed and said it was impossible.

"In five or six days we may be able to arrange another such joyful meeting; but that will be all. Invite us," said Hedwig, "to supper at your inn tomorrow, and chance may give us the opportunity for a sweet theft."

I agreed to do so.

The mood taking us again, since I knew my nature and cheated them when I saw fit, I filled their cup of happiness for several hours, changing from one to the other five or six times before I exhausted my powers and reached the paroxysm of consummation. Between times, seeing them docile and eager, I made them assume all the most difficult of the Aretine's postures,[43] which inexpressibly amused them. We lavished our kisses on whatever aroused our admiration, and once when Hedwig had her lips fastened to the mouth of the pistol the charge exploded and poured over her face and her bosom. She was completely delighted, and, in the role of eager student of physiology, entertained herself by watching out the end of the eruption, which they declared a wonder. The night seemed short to us, though we had not wasted a minute of it, and at daybreak the next morning we had to part. I left them in bed, and I had the good luck to leave the house without being seen.

After sleeping until noon I got up and, having made my toilet, I went to call on the pastor, whom I treated to a fervent eulogy of his charming niece. It was the best way of getting him to come to supper the next day at the "Scales."

"We are in the city," I said, "so we can remain together as long as we wish; but try to bring the amiable widow and her charming daughter."

He promised to do no less.

That evening I went to see the Syndic and the three friends, who inevitably found me a trifle cold. I pretended I had a bad headache. I told them I was giving a supper for the learned theologian, and I invited them to attend it with the Syndic; but I had foreseen that the latter would decline because it might give rise to talk.

I saw to it that the most exquisite wines were the chief ingredient of my supper. The pastor and his lady drank heartily, and I encouraged their inclination to the best of my ability. When I saw that they had reached the point to which I wished to bring them, with their heads slightly muddled and entirely occupied with their old memories, I made a sign to the two beauties, who left the room as if in search of a place to which to retire. Pretending to show them the way to it by going out with them, I took them into another room, telling them to wait for me.

Going back and finding my two veterans completely occupied with each other and scarcely aware that I was there, I made punch, and, after serving them, I said I would take some to the young ladies, who were amusing themselves looking at engravings. I did not lose a minute, and I made several appearances which they found most interesting. Such stolen pleasures have an inexpressible charm. When we were more or less satisfied, we all went back together and I proceeded to mix another bowl of punch. Helena praised the engravings to her mother, urging her to go and look at them with us.

"I don't care to," she said.

"In that case," Helena resumed, "let us go and look at them again."

Finding her ruse delightful, I left with my two heroines, and we accomplished prodigies. Hedwig philosophized on pleasure, saying that she would never have known it if I had not chanced to make her uncle's acquaintance. Helena said nothing; but, more voluptuous than her cousin, she swooned like one of Venus's doves, and returned to life only to die an instant later. I admired this amazing capacity, though it is common enough; she passed from life to death fourteen times while I was accomplishing a single operation. It is true that I was running my sixth race, and that, to enjoy her happiness, I sometimes slowed my own pace.

Before we parted I promised I would call on Helena's mother every day for the sake of learning which night would be the one I could spend with them before I left Geneva. We parted at two o'clock in the morning.

Three or four days later Helena hurriedly told me that Hedwig would sleep with her that night and that she would leave her door open at the same hour.

"I will be there."

"And I will be there to lock you in, but you will be in the dark because the maid might notice a light."

I was prompt, and as ten o'clock struck I saw them come in full of joy.

"I forgot to tell you," said Helena, "that you would find a chicken here."

I was hungry, I devoured it in an instant, and then we gave ourselves to happiness.

I was to leave on the next day but one. I had received two letters from Signor Raiberti. In one of them he told me that he had followed my instructions in regard to La Corticelli; and in the other that she would probably be engaged to dance during the Carnival as first figurante. I had nothing more to do in Geneva, and, in accordance with our arrangement, Madame d'Urfé was waiting for me in Lyons. I had to go there. In this posture of affairs, the night that I was to spend with the two charming girls was my last business in Geneva.

My lessons had borne fruit, and my two pupils had become past mistresses in the art of receiving and giving pleasure. But during the intervals joy gave place to sadness.

"We shall be wretched, my friend," said Hedwig, "and we would be ready to follow you if you would provide for us."

"I promise you, my dears, that I will return before the

end of two years," I said; and they did not have to wait
so long.[44] We went to sleep at midnight and, waking at
four o'clock, resumed our sports until six. A half hour
later I left them, completely exhausted, and I spent the
whole day in bed. In the evening I went to see the Syndic
and his young friends. There I found Helena, who had
the wit to pretend to be no more saddened by my departure than the others, and, the better to hide her
stratagem, she let the Syndic kiss her as he did the three
friends. For my part, imitating her trick, I begged her
to convey my farewells to her learned cousin and ask her
to excuse me for not going to take leave of her in person.

I left very early the next morning and arrived at
Lyons the following evening. I did not find Madame
d'Urfé there; she had gone to Bresse,[45] where she had
an estate. I found a letter from her telling me that she
would be very glad to see me there, and I went there
without losing a moment.

She received me in her usual fashion, and I at once
informed her that I must go to Turin to wait for
Federico Gualdo,[46] then head of the Rosicrucian Order,
and I made the oracle reveal to her that he would come
to Marseilles with me and there would make her happy.
It followed from this oracle that she must not think of
returning to Paris before we had seen each other. The
oracle further told her that, until she heard from me,
she was to wait in Lyons with the little D'Aranda, who
lavished caresses on me, begging me to take him to Turin.
The reader can well imagine that I managed to put him
off.

Back in Lyons, it took Madame d'Urfé two weeks to
get me fifty thousand francs which I might need for my
auspicious journey. During the two weeks I became well
acquainted with Madame Pernon,[47] and I spent a considerable sum of money at the establishment of her husband, a rich manufacturer, for materials for an elegant
wardrobe which I had made. Madame Pernon was beauti-

ful and intelligent. She had a Milanese lover named Bono,[48] *who acted as agent for a Swiss banker by the name of Sacco.*[49] *It was through Madame Pernon that Bono arranged to have his banker give Madame d'Urfé the fifty thousand francs which she then gave me. She also gave me the three dresses which she had promised to La Lascaris, but which La Corticelli never saw. One of the dresses was of rarely beautiful sable. I left Lyons accoutered like a prince and set out for Turin, where I was to find the famous Gualdo, who was none other than the perfidious Ascanio Pogomas whom I had sent there from Bern. I thought it would be easy for me to make the clown play the role I had in mind for him. I was cruelly deceived, as my reader will see.*

I could not resist spending a day in Chambéry to see my beautiful nun. I found her beautiful, calm, and contented, but still grieving for the loss of her young boarder,[50] *who had been married.*

Arriving in Turin at the beginning of December,[51] *I found La Corticelli at Rivoli,*[52] *where Signor Raiberti had told her to expect me. She gave me a letter from that amiable man, in which he told me the address of the house which he had rented for me, since I did not want to stay at an inn, and in which I immediately installed myself and my possessions.*

My old acquaintance. Signora Pacienza. Agata.
Count Borromeo. A ball. Lord Percy.

WHEN WE arrived in Turin La Corticelli went to her lodging; I promised I would go to see her.

I found my apartment very comfortable and the rent reasonable, but I increased it by taking the kitchen too. Having a great deal of money, I wanted to invite my friends to suppers. Signor Raiberti at once found me a good cook. After accounting to me for the money he had spent for La Corticelli, he gave me the remainder and advised me to call on Count d'Aglié,[2] who already knew that La Corticelli belonged to me. He told me that Signora Pacienza,[3] who was boarding her, had orders never to leave me alone with her when I chose to pay her a visit. This struck me as odd, but since I did not care I refrained from complaining. He said that her behavior until then had been irreproachable, and I was very glad to hear it. He advised me to speak to the ballet master Dupré[4] and persuade him to give her lessons, for which I would pay, so that he would have her dance some *pas de deux* during the Carnival. I promised the worthy man, who supposed I was in love with her, that I would do as he said, and, leaving his house, I went to the Vicario.[5]

After smilingly welcoming me back to Turin, he said that he knew I was keeping a dancer.

"But I warn you that the respectable woman with whom she is boarding has been ordered not to let her receive visitors except in her presence, even though she is with her mother."

"This strictness pleases me, Signore, and the more so since I do not believe her mother is very scrupulous. The Cavaliere Raiberti, to whom I recommended her, knew my intentions, and I am delighted that he has fulfilled them so well. It is my wish that she shall make herself worthy of your protection."

"Do you expect to spend the Carnival here?"

"Possibly, if Your Excellency approves."

"It will depend entirely on your good behavior. Have you seen the Cavalier Ossorio?"[6]

"I shall pay him my respects today or tomorrow."

"Kindly convey my compliments to him."

He rang, and I left. The Cavalier Ossorio received me in his office at the Ministry of Foreign Affairs and greeted me most graciously. After I gave him an account of the visit I had just made to the Vicario he asked me, with a smile, if I willingly submitted to the decree which forbade me to see my mistress. I replied that I did not care, and, giving me a sly look, he replied that my indifference might not be to the taste of the respectable woman who had orders to watch over her.

He had said enough; but it was true that the constraint which prevented me from visiting the little vixen freely rather pleased me. I knew that it would start talk, and I was curious to see the consequences.

Back at my apartment I found the Genoese Passano,[7] the bad poet and bad painter, who had been in Turin a

month waiting for me and whom I had destined to appear
before Madame d'Urfé in the role of a Rosicrucian.

After having him sup with me, I gave him a room on
the fourth floor, telling him to send out for his meals and
not to come down to my apartment unless I sent for him.
I found him an insipid storyteller, ignorant, ill-disposed,
and given to drink. I was already sorry that I had taken
him into my service; but it was done.

Curious to see how La Corticelli was lodged, I went
there, taking with me a piece of material I had bought
in Lyons to make her a winter dress. I found her with
her mother in the room occupied by her hostess, who said
she was very glad to see me and that she would be pleased
to have me come to family dinner there as often as I
liked. La Corticelli and her mother took me to her room,
and the hostess followed us.

"Here," I said to the girl, "is something to make you
a dress."

"Is it a present from the Marquise?"

"It is from me, if you will accept it."

"But I am supposed to have three dresses which she
gave me."

"But you know on what conditions. We will discuss
it another time."

She unfolds the material and finds it to her liking:

"But it must be trimmed," she says.

La Pacienza says she will send someone to tell the
milliner to bring trimmings. She lived in the same street.
No sooner is she gone than Signora Laura says that she
is sorry she cannot receive me except in the hostess's
rooms.

"You are certainly very glad not to have that privilege."

"I thank God for it morning and night."

I give her the look she deserves, and a few minutes
later I see Vittorina[8] and another girl bringing trimmings. I ask her if she is still with La *R.*,[9] she blushes

and says yes. La Corticelli chooses the trimming, I tell
the girls that I will go to pay their mistress, and they
leave. La Pacienza sends for a dressmaker, who comes to
measure La Corticelli, and the latter says that she needs
a corset, showing me her figure. After joking with her
about her former big belly, the fruit of her affair with
Count Nostitz,[10] I give her all the money she may need
and take my leave. Escorting me to the stairway, she
asks me when she will see me again, and I reply that I
have no idea.

It is obvious that if I had been in love with the girl
I would not have left her in the woman's house a single
day; but what amazed me was that she should think me
tolerant to such a degree, though my manner was just
the reverse.

After having called on the bankers on whom I had bills
of exchange, among them Monsieur Martin,[11] whose wife
was well known for her beauty, I ran into Moses,[12] who
took me to see Leah, who had married. As soon as she
told her husband my name he put himself out to welcome
me, but, finding Leah big with child, I felt no desire for
her. I did not go back there again.

I could not wait to visit La R., and I found her no
less impatient to see me, Vittorina having brought her
news of me. Sitting at her counter facing her, I had the
pleasure of listening to her account of all the amorous
intrigues in Turin. She told me that, of all the girls she
had when I left Turin, only Vittorina and Caton[13] were
still with her, but that she heard from them. Vittorina
was in the same state as that in which I had left her;
but a nobleman who was in love with her was going to
send her to Milan. The nobleman was Count de la Pérouse,[14] with whom I became well acquainted in Vienna
three years later. I shall speak of him at the proper time
and place. La R. told me mournfully that in consequence
of some unfortunate incidents in which the police had
been obliged to intervene she had been forced to promise

Count d'Aglié that in future she would send her girls
only to ladies, and so, if I found that any of them pleased
me, I could get to know them only by taking them somewhere on feast days and Sundays, after obtaining intro-
ductions to their parents. She showed them to me in her
workroom, but I found none of them especially interesting. She talked to me about Signora Pacienza, and when
I told her I was keeping La Corticelli and described the
hard conditions to which I had submitted, her indignation was so vehement that it set me laughing.

"The woman," she said, "is not only a spy for Count
d'Aglié but a bawd well known to the whole city; but I
am surprised that the Cavaliere Raiberti did not send
her to lodge with La Mazzoli." [15]

She stopped protesting when I told her that the Cavaliere had good reasons for doing as he had done, and
that I had mine for being very glad that La Corticelli
was where she was rather than anywhere else.

Our conversation was interrupted by a customer who
came to ask for silk stockings. Hearing him speak of
dancing, I asked him where the ballet master Dupré
lived.

"I am he, at your service."

"I am very glad to have the opportunity to speak
with you. Signor Raiberti told me that you would be kind
enough to give some lessons to a dancer of my acquaintance."

"He mentioned it to me this morning. You must be
the Chevalier de Seingalt."

"I am."

"The young lady can come to me every morning at
nine o'clock."

"Certainly not; you will go to her at whatever hour
you find convenient; and I will pay you, hoping that
you will train her to the point of dancing in other than
ensembles."

"I will go to see her today, and I will tell you to-

morrow what I can make of her; but I shall have to speak
frankly. I charge three Piedmontese lire per lesson.''

''That is not much. I will call on you tomorrow.''

''It will be an honor, here is my address. If you come
in the afternoon you will find me rehearsing a ballet.''

''Are rehearsals not held at the theater?''

''Yes, but at the theater no one may come in during
a rehearsal. It is the Vicario's order.''

''But you may receive whomever you please.''

''Certainly; still, I could not receive the ballerinas if
it were not for my wife, whom the Signor Vicario knows
and trusts.''

''You shall see me at the rehearsal.''

Thus it was that the accursed old Vicario, with his
rotten nose, exercised his tyranny wherever those who
love pleasure go to seek it.

At the good Mazzoli's I found two notables, whom she
introduced to me after telling me their names. The one,
very old, very ugly, and wearing the Order of the White
Eagle,[16] was Count Borromeo;[17] the other, youngish and
lively, was a Count A. B.,[18] of Milan. I learned from her
afterward that the two noblemen paid her assiduous
court to please the Cavaliere Raiberti, whose good offices
they needed in order to obtain certain rights or privileges
with respect to their estates, which were under the juris-
diction of the King of Sardinia. The Milanese A. B. was
penniless, and the lord of the Borromean Islands[19] was
also very short of money. He had ruined himself over
women, and, unable to live any longer in Milan, he had
retired to the most beautiful of his islands in Lake
Maggiore, where he enjoyed a perpetual spring. I paid
him a visit when I returned from Spain, but I will give
an account of it when I come to that time.

The conversation turning to my lodging, La Mazzoli,
always the busybody, asked me if I was satisfied with my
cook.

''I have not yet tried him; but I will do so tomorrow,

if you will honor me by coming to supper with these gentlemen.''

The invitation was accepted, and she promised to bring her dear Cavaliere, who, if he were informed in advance, would not dine. His health obliged him to eat only once a day.

At the ballet master Dupré's I saw all the male dancers and all the ballerinas, with their mothers, who stood apart admiring them and watching over their mantles and muffs. Strangely enough, one of the mothers was beautiful and fresh. Dupré, after introducing me to his wife, who was young and pretty but, being consumptive, had given up dancing, told me that if Signorina Corticelli would apply herself he would do miracles with her. She came running up and, assuming an air of privilege, told me she needed ribbons and to have some bonnets made. All the ballerinas were looking her up and down,[20] whispering to one another. Not answering her by so much as a word, I took two Piedmontese pistoles from my pocket and gave them to Dupré, saying that they were for three months of lessons he was to give the young lady, for which I was glad to pay him in advance. I saw the general astonishment, and I enjoyed it, but without letting my enjoyment appear.

I sat down at a distance. Considering all the girls I saw there, I see one who is striking. Fine figure, delicate features, noble bearing, and a patience, which I find supremely interesting, toward a dancer who, when he was not satisfied with her, treated her to coarse language; she bore it all, but with unmistakable scorn depicted on her charming countenance. I approach the young and beautiful woman whom I had noticed taking care of a mantle when I entered, and I ask her where I can find the mother of the pretty ballerina who interested me.

''I am she,'' she replied.

''You? Your looks belie it.''

"I was very young when I had her."

"I have no doubt of that. Where are you from?"

"I am from Lucca, a widow and poor."

"How can you be poor when you have a daughter as pretty as yourself?"

She looks at me and makes no answer. A moment later Agata[21] (such was the girl's name) comes up and asks for a handkerchief to wipe her face. I give her mine, white and fresh and scented with attar of roses; she wipes off her sweat with it, praising the perfume, then offers to give it back to me, and I refuse it, saying that she should have it washed. She smiles and tells her mother to keep it. I ask her if I may take the liberty of calling on her, and she replies that her hostess does not allow her to receive visitors unless she is present. This cursed restriction was in force everywhere in Turin.

At my supper, which was the first, I was surprised by the excellence of my cook. I have always thought that nowhere in the world does one eat as well as in Turin; but it is also true that the countryside itself produces the exquisite viands which the skillful cooks there prepare with an art which makes them delectable. The wines, too, may be preferred by many epicures to those from elsewhere. Game, fish, fowl, veal, herbs, truffles—everything is exquisite. It is a crying shame that strangers in that fortunate country are restricted, and that its people are not the most honest in Italy. Obviously, the brilliant beauty of the fair sex there is due to the air of the place and even more to the good food. I easily prevailed upon Signorina Mazzoli and the two Milanese Counts to do me the same honor every day. The Cavaliere Raiberti could not make a definite engagement, but he promised he would take pot luck from time to time.

At the *opera buffa* at the Teatro Carignano,[22] I saw on the stage the Parmesan Redegonda[23] whose favors I had failed to obtain in Florence. She noticed me in the parterre and gave me a smile. I wrote her a note the

next morning, offering her my services if her mother had
changed her way of thinking. She replied that her mother
was still of the same mind, but that if I could get La
Corticelli to come to supper at my lodging she could
come with her. Since their mothers would have been
present, I did not answer her.

About this time I received a letter from Madame du
Rumain, who sent me one from the Duke of Choiseul
addressed to Monsieur de Chauvelin,[24] the French Ambassador in Turin, for which I had asked her. I had
known that amiable man at Soleure, as my reader may
remember, but I wanted to have better warrant for calling on him. So I delivered the letter, and, after reproaching me for having supposed that I needed it, he
took me to see his charming wife,[25] who received me
most graciously. Three or four days later he invited me
to dinner, where I found the Venetian Resident, Imberti,[26] who said he was very sorry he could not present
me at Court. Informed of the reason, Monsieur de Chauvelin offered to present me himself; but I thought it
proper to decline. It would have been a great honor, but
I should have been more noticed and hence less free.

Count Borromeo, who honored my table every day,
maintained a certain dignity, and, since he always came
with La Mazzoli, seemed neither to lower himself nor to
need my hospitality; but Count A. B. availed himself of
it more frankly. After a week or ten days he told me that
my tolerance of his presence made him truly grateful to
Eternal Providence, for, as his wife could not send him
any money, he would not have had the means to pay for
his dinner at the inn. He showed me her letters and,
praising her merits, often said that he hoped to put me
up in his house in Milan and that I would value her as
she deserved. He had been in the Spanish service and,
being garrisoned in Barcelona, had fallen in love with
her and married her. She was twenty-six years of age,
and he had no children.[27] Having written her that I had

The Sweet Sacrifice

Dancing Lesson

several times opened my purse to him and that I expected
to spend half of the Carnival in Milan,[28] he had prevailed upon her to invite me to stay in their house. She
wrote to me wittily, and I soon found the correspondence
so interesting that I promised her I would go there, which
I should never have done, for, knowing that he was poor,
I ought to have seen that it was not right for me to
become a burden to him and that, determined not to do
so, I should have to pay a very high price for his hospitality; but in such a case a feeling of curiosity has
much the nature of love. I imagined the Countess A. B.
was born to make me happy, as I alone was destined to
make her so and to arouse the jealousy of all the ladies
in Milan. Having a great deal of money, I could not wait
to seize the opportunity to shine by spending lavishly.

Meanwhile, going every morning to Dupré's, where I
always found Agata, come to take her lesson, in less than
two weeks I was desperately in love with her. Madame
Dupré, won over by several presents I had given her,
graciously received my avowal of my passion, and, by
keeping Agata and her mother to dinner with her, had
made it possible for me to be alone with the girl several
times in her own room, where I had declared myself,
and I had obtained a few favors; but they were so
trifling, and our meetings were so brief, that my desires,
far from being extinguished, had increased. Agata told
me again and again that everyone knew I was keeping
La Corticelli, and that not for anything in the world
would she give people occasion to say that, prevented as
I was from going to my mistress, she was only my second
choice. In vain did I swear that I did not love her and
that I was keeping her only because, if I abandoned her,
I would compromise Signor Raiberti. She would not
listen to reason; she insisted on a resounding break which
would show all Turin that I loved only her and despised
the other. On that condition she promised me her heart.

Determined to do what I could to satisfy her and to

assure my own happiness, I asked Dupré to give a ball at my expense in some house outside the city and to arrange that all the dancers and singers of the fair sex who were engaged for the Carnival in Turin should be there. No one else was to dance. The male dancers were to be only escorts, among whom he would distribute tickets priced at one ducato, and each escort would have the right to bring a lady with him. But these ladies were not to dance. To prevail upon Dupré to carry out my scheme, and to assure him that his profits would be large and that the tickets would not be thought too dear, I told him I would pay whatever the supper and all the usual refreshments would cost him, together with the hire of the carriages or sedan chairs with which he was to furnish all the *virtuose* who would dance at the ball. No one was to know that it was I who was paying these expenses. He promised, and, certain of making a handsome profit, he set to work. He found a very suitable house for the ball, he invited the *virtuose,* he prepared fifty tickets, which he distributed in three or four days, and he chose a day when there were no performances in Turin. Only Agata and her mother knew that the project was of my invention and that I was paying the greater part of the expenses; but the day after the ball the whole city knew it.

Agata, declaring that she did not have a dress pretty enough to set her off, had one made under the direction of Dupré's wife, whom I gladly paid. She promised to dance all the contradances with me and to return to Turin with no one but Madame Dupré.

On the day of the ball I dined at the Duprés' in order to be present when she put on her dress. It was of stuff from Lyons manufactured that year, so the pattern was entirely new; but the trimming, of which Agata did not know the value, was of Alençon point.[29] La R., who had put it on the dress, had been ordered to say nothing, as had Madame Dupré, who was well versed in laces.

Just as she was about to leave I told her that the earrings she had on were not in keeping with the rest of her costume. Madame Dupré said that they really were not as pretty as they should be and that it was a pity. Agata's mother said she had no others.

"I have some paste girandoles[30] with me," I said to them, "which I could lend you. They are very brilliant."

I had purposely put in my pocket the earrings which were in the jewel case Madame d'Urfé had intended to give her niece, the young Countess Lascaris. I take them out, and the mother and daughter pronounce them very pretty. Madame Dupré adds that one would say they were genuine stones. I put them in Agata's ears, she looks at herself in the mirror, and, admiring their sparkle, she swears that real ones could not be any more brilliant. I say nothing.

They all go to the ball, and I go home, where I have my hair given a hasty combing, and, after putting on a handsome coat, which Pernon[31] had had embroidered for me, I go to the ball, which I find well begun. I see Agata dancing a minuet with Lord Percy.[32] He was a son of the Duchess of Northumberland who spent money lavishly but foolishly.

I see the most beautiful ladies in Turin, who, being spectators, could imagine that the ball was being given for them. I see all the foreign envoys, among them Monsieur de Chauvelin, who tells me that so charming an occasion lacked only the charming housekeeper I had had at Soleure. I see the Marquise de Prié[33] and the Marquis, who, not caring to dance, was playing quinze, with his mistress sitting opposite him and beside her an impolite player who would not let her see his card. She sees me and pretends not to know me. The trick I had played on her at Aix was not of a kind to be forgotten.

The minuets end, Dupré arranges the contradance, and I am glad to see the Cavaliere di Villa Faletta[34] take his place at the head of it with La Corticelli. I take Agata, who was warding off Lord Percy, telling him that she was engaged for the whole evening. She told me with a smile that everyone thought her girandoles were genuine, and that she let it pass.

After the contradance everyone took ices, then there was another contradance, then some minuets, and those who wanted to eat went to the well-stocked buffet, where I observed that Dupré had not been sparing. The Piedmontese, who are always calculating, said that Dupré would lose a great deal on it, for bottles of champagne were being emptied one after another.

Needing to rest, as did I, Agata had sat down beside me, and I was telling her of my love when Madame de Chauvelin came up with a foreign lady. I rise to give her my place, and Agata does likewise, but she makes her sit down beside her and praises her dress, especially the lace. The foreign lady praises the fire of the girandoles and says it is a pity that after a certain time such stones lose all their luster. Madame de Chauvelin says these will never lose it because they are genuine beyond the possibility of doubt; she questions Agata, who, not daring to say they are genuine, says they are paste and that it was I who had lent them to her. At that Madame de Chauvelin laughs and says I have deceived her, for no one lends earrings set with paste stones. Agata blushes, I say nothing either way, and, at Madame de Chauvelin's behest, I dance a minuet with Agata, who danced it to perfection. Madame de Chauvelin tells me that she still remembers our having danced together at Soleure, and that we shall dance again at her house on Twelfth Night.[35] I thanked her with a deep bow.

We danced contradances until four o'clock in the morning, and I went home after seeing Agata leave with La Dupré and her mother.

I was still in bed the next day when her mother was announced, with the addition that she demanded most urgently the "honor" of speaking with me. I had her shown in, and, making her sit down, prevailed on her to drink chocolate. Having thus broken her fast, and finding herself alone with me, she took from her pocket the earrings I had lent her daughter and said, with a laugh, that she had come to return them to me; but that she had just shown them to a jeweler, who had offered her a thousand zecchini for them. After laughing and telling her, as I took the earrings, that the jeweler was mad and that she ought to hold him to his word, for the earrings were worth only four louis, I began flirting with the pretty mother to such good purpose that I kept her with me for an hour, giving her, and myself receiving from her, all the tokens of a lively affection. After the act, which left us both looking somewhat surprised, she said with a laugh that she ought to tell her daughter what way I had taken to convince her that I loved her.

"I love you no less," I replied, "and, if you don't avoid being alone with me, I think it hardly possible that what has just happened between us will not always happen. The only favor I ask of you is not to stand in the way of my aspiring to the same favor from Agata, whom I adore."

"And I will ask you to do me a favor too. Tell me if these girandoles are really genuine, and what your intention was when you put them in Agata's ears."

"They are genuine, and my intention would be to leave them with her as a reminder of my love."

The good mother sighed and, rising to leave, told me to invite her to supper with Monsieur Dupré and his wife as often as I pleased. She departed, of course leaving me my earrings.

Such was this unexampled paragon of honesty among mothers of ballerinas. She could not tell me more than she had told me in a few words, or announce my good fortune with greater magnanimity.

The following day I invited Dupré and his wife, with Agata and her mother, to sup with me on the next day but one, in addition to my usual company. But now for an odd adventure which befell me that same day just as I was leaving Dupré's.

I run into my temporary lackey, a great scoundrel but a worthy fellow on this occasion, who, almost out of breath, triumphantly announces that he has come looking for me to tell me he had that very moment seen the Cavaliere di Villa Faletta enter the alley in which La Pacienza lived and that he could have gone there only to pay La Corticelli an amorous visit.

Curious to see if the restrictions laid upon me were in force for him, I go there, and I find the bawd with Signora Laura. They tried to stop me, but I push them away, I open the door, and I see the gallant rise, doing his best to restore himself to decency. She did not stir.

"Excuse me, Signora," I said, "if I came in without knocking."

"Wait a moment, wait a moment."

But I was already in the street. Full of the adventure, which made me the most contented of mortals, I go to tell it to the Cavaliere Raiberti, who, seeing me laugh, laughs at it too; but he agrees that I am right when I ask him to inform La Pacienza that La Corticelli is no longer at my charge and hence will receive not another soldo from my pocket.

"I imagine you will not complain to Count d'Aglié?"

"Only fools complain."

This little incident would have passed unnoticed if want of caution had not made it public. The first indiscretion was committed by Villa Faletta, who, remembering that he had met my valet in the street when he was on his way to La Pacienza's, supposed he had gone running to warn me. He found him toward noon and accused him of being a spy. The brazen fellow answered that his duty was to serve his master well, and the Cavaliere gave him a caning. Without saying anything to me, the valet went and complained to the Vicario, who at once sent for Villa Faletta and asked him what reason he had thought he had for caning the valet. Villa Faletta told him the whole story. Signor Raiberti lost no time in going to tell La Pacienza that La Corticelli was no longer at his charge or at mine, and, not stopping to hear what she began saying in her own defense, he left her. Reporting the incident to me the same evening, he said that, as he went down the stairs, he had met a police officer, who was apparently on his way to summon her at the Count's order.

The next day, just as I was leaving my apartment to go to the Marquis de Chauvelin's ball, I was surprised to receive a note from Count d'Aglié in which he asked me most politely to call on him in order to hear something he had to say to me. I immediately have my chairmen take me to the Count's house.

He received me privately, and, after making me sit down near him, he delivered a long discourse, of which the general purport was that I should forget the little incident, all the details of which were known to him.

"That is my intention, Signore. I shall never again in my life go to see La Corticelli, nor shall I give her another thought either for good or for evil, and I shall always be the Cavaliere di Villa Faletta's most humble servant."

"Oh, that is no reason for abandoning her. I will see that you receive what satisfaction you may require from La Pacienza, and I will send the girl to board with an honest woman of my acquaintance, where you will be very well received and perfectly free."

"I despise La Pacienza, La Corticelli, and her mother; they are swindlers whom I do not want to see again."

"You had no right to force your way into a room, the door of which was shut, in a house which was not yours."

"If I did not have it, I am in the wrong; but you will permit me to inform His Majesty of the whole affair and to abide by his judgment."

"La Corticelli claims that, far from her being in your debt, you owe her a great deal, and she says that the girandoles which you gave your new mistress belong to her. She maintains that they are a present she was given by the Marquise d'Urfé, whom I know."

"She is lying; but since you know the lady, write to her, she is in Lyons. If she answers you that I owe the wretched girl anything, I will do my duty. I have a hundred thousand francs in the hands of the bankers of this city to pay for the girandoles if it should appear that I had no right to dispose of them."

The Vicario then rose, and I made him a bow. At the French Ambassador's ball I found the thing so generally known that, in sheer boredom, I ceased to answer people who spoke to me about it. Everyone told me that it was a matter of no moment, to pay any attention to which was beneath my honor. The Cavaliere di Villa Faletta went so far as to say that, if I abandoned La Corticelli for such a trifle, he would consider it his duty to *give* me satisfaction.

"It will be enough," I replied, "if you do not *demand* it of me."

So saying, I shook his hand. He said no more.

But it was the Marquise de Prié, his sister, who, after we had danced together, really launched an attack on me. She had charms, and it would have lain entirely with her to conquer me, but fortunately, either she did not think of it or she did not realize what justice I did to her merits.

Three days later a lady who wielded great power in Turin and exercised a sort of supervision over all theatrical intrigues, and to whose patronage all the *virtuose* aspired, took it into her head to send for me, dispatching her command by a valet in livery. Guessing what she wanted to talk to me about, I went on foot and wearing a redingote. She began by mentioning the matter to me in the most affable manner, but since her face did not interest me, I told her in so many words that La Corticelli was a girl for whom I no longer felt the slightest inclination and that I abandoned her without regret to the gallant Cavaliere with whom I had found her *in flagrante delicto*. She left me, saying that I would be sorry, for she would publish a little story which she had already read and which would not be to my credit. The lady's name was De Saint-Gilles.[36]

A week later I read in manuscript[37] an account of all that had happened between La Corticelli, Madame d'Urfé, and myself, which everyone in Turin could have read but which was so badly written and so full of nonsense that no one could read it through. It had no effect on me, and I left Turin two weeks later without having troubled to see her again. But I saw her six months later in Paris, and we will speak of it when we come to that time.

The day after Monsieur de Chauvelin's ball I had my dear Agata and her mother, Dupré and his wife, La Mazzoli, and my two Milanese noblemen to supper, as I had arranged. It was for the mother to act in such a way that the girandoles would rightfully enter Agata's possession; hence, all ready for the sacrifice, I left it to the dear priestess to arrange the order of ceremonies.

So it was she who, as soon as she had sat down at the table, told the company that all Turin was saying I had made her daughter a present of two earrings which were worth five hundred louis and which, according to La Corticelli, were hers and hers alone.

"I do not know," she went on, "either if the earrings are genuine or if they belong to La Corticelli; but I know it is not true that Agata has been made a present of them by this gentleman here."

"No one will doubt it from now on, my dear friend,"

I said to her, taking the earrings from my pocket and putting them in Agata's ears, "for I now make her a present of them and I confirm the valuation placed on them, and the proof that they belong to me is that I give them to her."

The whole company applauded, and Agata, overcome with gratitude, promised me with her eyes all that I could desire. We then talked of La Corticelli's affair with Villa Faletta and of all that was being done to make me continue to support her. The Cavaliere Raiberti said that, in my place, he would have answered Madame de Saint-Gilles, and even the Vicario, by offering to continue paying for her board, but purely as an act of charity and giving the money to one or the other of them. I replied that I would be glad to do so, and that he could count on my promise. No later than the next morning the worthy man called on Madame de Saint-Gilles to settle the matter, and I put the necessary money in his hands; but the wretched manuscript containing the whole story was published nevertheless. The Vicario sent La Corticelli to the same house in which Redegonda was living, but he left La Pacienza in peace.

After supper we all put on black dominoes, except the Cavaliere, and went to the ball at the Teatro Carignano, from which I ran away with Agata, who gave herself to me that night, and to such good purpose that from then on we no longer subjected ourselves to any restraints. At the suppers I gave in my house I was perfectly free, and the Vicario could do nothing to trouble my love affair with that charming girl, whose fortune it was God's will that I should make, in a most extraordinary way, when she showed me that she was worthy of it six or seven years later, as the reader will see if I do not tire of writing my memoirs.

We were so much in love, and so perfectly at peace in our enjoyment of each other, that we could not possibly have parted of our own free will, had it not been for an event which compelled us to submit our mutual passion to the wholesome light of our reason. But for that event, I should have spent at least the whole Carnival in Turin, and I should have put off until Lent going to Milan to visit the Spanish Countess A. B., whom I imagined to be a wonder of nature. Just at this time her husband the Count, having finished his business at the Court of Turin, returned to Milan, embracing me and shedding tears of gratitude, for he could not have left Turin if I had not given him what he needed for the expenses of the journey after paying his debts, which, however, amounted to very little. So it is that vice often allies itself with virtue, or dons the mask of it; but in this instance the dupe was myself and I did not care to open my eyes. All my life long I have been absorbed in vice and at the same time a worshiper of virtue.

Lord Percy, whom I have mentioned, was in love with Agata, he followed her everywhere, he waited for her in the wings, he never missed a rehearsal, and he called on her every day, despite the fact that her hostess, a woman of the type of La Pacienza, never left her to him unchaperoned. Agata always refused his presents, but she could not prevent her hostess from accepting everything that the young Englishman sent her from the inn and all kinds of wines and liqueurs; by all which means he hoped to bribe her into finally getting him Agata, who, completely indifferent to him, told me everything. Sure of her heart, I laughed, and I was not displeased that the young man's fruitless assiduity should set off my success. The whole city knew that Agata was faithful to me, and the Englishman became so convinced of it that he believed the only way left him to attain his purpose was to become acquainted with me.

He came one morning to ask me for breakfast, and, reasoning like an Englishman, he thought he could declare his passion to me and propose an exchange which made me laugh.

"I know," he said, "that you have long loved the singer Redegonda and have never succeeded in having her; I offer her to you in exchange for Agata, and tell me what you want to boot."

After laughing heartily I say that I might consider the thing possible, but first of all we must see if the two pieces of merchandise would consent to the change of ownership:

> *Sì come amor si regga a questa guisa*
> *Che vender la sua donna o permutarla*
> *Possa l'amante, nè a ragion si attristi*
> *Se quando una ne perde una n'acquisti.*

> ("As if love's laws were such that the
> lover may sell his lady or exchange her
> and has no reason to be pained when,
> losing one, he gains another.")[38]

"For my part," His Lordship replies, "I am sure of Redegonda's consent."

"So far so good; but on mine, I am doubtful of Agata's."

"You need not doubt it."

"What grounds have you?"

"She will be reasonable."

"She loves me."

"And Redegonda loves me as much."

"And do you think she loves me?"

"I have no idea; but love you she will."

"Have you discussed it with her?"

"No, but that does not matter. I will see to it. What I must know now is if my scheme is agreeable to you, and what boot you will ask, for your Agata is worth more than my Redegonda."

"We will talk about that later. Allow me to begin by discussing it with her, and I will bring you my answer at your lodging tomorrow morning."

His scheme amused me, and I decided I would see

what would come of it. I was surprised that the young
Lord had gained possession of Redegonda, for her mother
had always overawed me.

Agata laughed heartily that evening when I informed
her of Lord Percy's proposal, and when I asked her if
she would consent to the exchange she said she would do
whatever I wished and that she advised me to accept it
if he offered me boot enough to make it worth my while.
I saw that she was joking, but we both became curious
to see how he would go about settling the thing.

So I went to breakfast with him the next morning,
and I told him that Agata accepted his proposal, but
that, for my part, I wanted to be convinced that Redegonda accepted it too and to learn how she expected to
arrange for us to live together. He said that the four
of us should meet, well masked, at the first ball at the
Teatro Carignano, which we would leave to sup together
in a place which belonged to him, and that we would
strike our bargain there.

Accordingly we masked, we went to the ball, and, as
soon as we recognized one another, we left, and the four
of us got into a carriage which belonged to Lord Percy
and were driven to the door of a house which I knew;
but my surprise was not small when I saw La Corticelli
in the room we entered. I called the young coxcomb
aside and told him that such behavior was unworthy of
a gentleman. He replied, with a laugh, that he had
thought he would be gratifying me, and that, La Corticelli being the boot, I could not but be satisfied.

I refused his carriage. Not wanting to go back to the
ball, we took sedan chairs to return to my apartment.

CHAPTER VI

I relinquish Agata to Lord Percy. I leave for Milan. "The Pilgrim" at Pavia. The Countess A. B. Disappointment. The Marchese Triulzi. Zenobia. The two beautiful Marchese Q.[1] Barbaro the Venetian.

THUS IT was that Count d'Aglié had punished La Corticelli by sending her to board elsewhere. Soon become Redegonda's intimate friend, she did exactly as she pleased. The good part of it was that no one in Turin ever learned the story, and I took care not to tell it; but Lord Percy did not give up the idea of obtaining possession of Agata, and here is how he accomplished it. He was a prodigal who had a great deal of money and who, setting no value on it, used it to satisfy all his whims. In a country where it was scarce, it opened all doors to him.

Two or three days after this event Agata told me that the impresario of the opera at Alessandria[2] had come to her to engage her as second ballerina, offering her sixty zecchini[3] for the whole period of the Fair, and that she had promised to answer him the next day. She asked me if I advised her to accept the engagement.

"If you love me, my dear Agata, you will spend a

whole year without engaging yourself to any theater. I will not let you want for anything, and I will pay for a teacher who will perfect you, and then you will not dance anywhere except as first ballerina, and you will demand at least five hundred zecchini.''

''Mother says that accepting an engagement will not prevent me from studying, but that, on the contrary, the practice will make me better and better.''

''You don't need sixty zecchini. If you accept the proposal you will dishonor me. If you love me you will tell the impresario that you want to spend a year without dancing.''

''It seems to me I would do better to ask him for an exorbitant sum.''

''You are right. Tell him that you insist on being first ballerina and that you demand five hundred zecchini.''

''I will do it tomorrow morning.''

She kept her word, and she told me, bursting out laughing, that the impresario had not seemed surprised at what she had demanded. After thinking it over for a few minutes, he left, telling her that he needed time to make up his mind and that she should see him again.

''It would be amusing if he took me at my word.''

''If he does, we shall have to find out if he is either mad or a beggar thinking of declaring bankruptcy.''

''And if he is solvent?''

''You must accept.''

''And then? Have I talent enough to be first ballerina? There won't be a dancer who will want to dance with me.''

''I will find you a dancer at once, and you will have talent enough; but you will see that nothing will come of this.''

I was mistaken. The impresario came back, offered her a written engagement,[4] and at that she sent for me. I at once asked the man what security he could give to vouch for his own solvency. He answered that the banker

Martin would sign his undertaking, after which I could make no objection. He wrote out his agreement, she wrote out hers, which I signed, and I went to inform the Cavaliere Raiberti, who, knowing the impresario, was surprised that Monsieur Martin would answer for him; but we learned all the next day, though the thing was supposed to be kept secret.

The real impresario was Lord Percy, who wanted to obtain possession of Agata at any cost, and I could no longer oppose his scheme. I could have continued to live with her, and even have so arranged matters that the young man would never become her lover; but I had to meet Madame d'Urfé in France after Easter, and, peace having been made,[5] I was absolutely determined to visit England. I adopted the course of becoming the young Lord's friend, making him free of my society, and seeing how he would go about ingratiating himself with Agata, who simply could not bear him.

In less than a week we became intimate friends, supping together every evening either at his lodging or at mine, Agata always being present with her mother. I easily came to the conclusion that she could soon become his fond mistress, despite his not being handsome, and that, loving her as I did, I ought not to stand in the way of her good fortune. I decided to leave for Milan. Madly in love with her, the young Englishman did not let a day pass without making her some costly present, and I had to swallow this sort of insult; but I was tired of doing so. However, Agata never gave me any reason to complain or any ground for believing that her new lover's assiduity had diminished the feelings which made her so dear to me. She listened to all my advice, she promised to follow it, and she followed it. The Englishman made her rich; but she did not leave the theater until she was in Naples, where we shall find her again a few years hence.

Though I am of a character which forbids me to take

presents from my equals, the Englishman made me one
so unusual as to force me to accept it. On my telling him
that I was about to go to England for the first time and
that he would greatly honor me if he would give me a
letter to his mother the Duchess,[6] he took a portrait of
that lady from his pocket, saying:

"Here is the letter of introduction I give you, and
tomorrow I will write her that you will deliver her portrait to her in person unless she will let you keep it."

"Her Ladyship will see that I aspire to that favor."

There are a number of ideas which can enter no heads
but English ones. But Count A. B.[7] was summoning me
to Milan, and his Countess had asked me to bring her
two large pieces of taffeta.

After taking leave of all my acquaintances I set out
for Milan with a letter of credit from the banker Zappata
on Greppi.[8] At parting from Agata I shed tears, but
less copiously than did she and her mother, who was
always telling me that she could never have forgiven
a rival if it had not been her own daughter. I sent Passano to Genoa, where his family was, giving him enough
to live on until I arrived. Having dismissed my valet
from Franche-Comté[9] for good reasons, I took another,
and I set out in company with the Cavaliere di Rosignano,[10] traveling by way of Casale,[11] where there was
opera buffa.

The Cavaliere di Rosignano, a handsome man and a
good officer, fond of wine and women and even fonder
of boys, amused me because, though not lettered, he
knew Dante's *Divine Comedy* by heart. It was the only
book he had read, and he quoted from it in season and
out of season, interpreting the passages just as he pleased.
It was an absurdity which often made him intolerable in
society, but which afforded much amusement to those
who knew the great poet well and admired his beauty.
However, the proverb which warns us to beware of the
man who has read only one book[12] remains true. The

Count of Grissella,[13] his brother, was not like him. He
was a truly lettered man, and one whose erudition was
allied with all the qualities of the wit, the statesman, and
the affable companion. Berlin knew and admired him
when he resided there as Ambassador for the King of
Sardinia.

Having found nothing interesting at the opera, I went
to Pavia, where, though I knew no one, I was immediately
presented to the Marchesa Corti[14] in her great box at
the theater, where she received all strangers who appeared to be of consequence. Here in the year 1786 [15] I
made the acquaintance of her noble son, who honored me
with his friendship and who died young in Flanders, a
Major-General. My tears paid him unavailing homage.
His virtues made him regretted by all who knew him.
Had he lived, he would have attained the highest ranks,
but *Vitae summa brevis spes nos vetat inchoare longas*
("The shortness of life forbids us to entertain distant
hopes").[16]

I stopped in Pavia for only two days; but it was decreed that something should befall me there which
would make me talked about.

During the second ballet of the opera a ballerina costumed as a pilgrim held out her hat toward the stage
boxes in the course of her *pas de deux*, as if asking for
alms. I was in the Marchesa Corti's box. When I saw
the ballerina below me I dropped my purse into her hat.
It contained eighteen or twenty ducati. She put it in her
pocket, smiling, and the parterre applauded. I asked the
Marchese Belcredi,[17] who was beside me, if she had anyone keeping her, and he replied that she had only a
French officer, whom he pointed out to me in the parterre,
who was penniless. He said that he constantly went to
visit her.

Back at my inn, I was supping with Signor Basili,[18]
a colonel in the service of Modena, when I saw the ballerina come in with an elderly woman and a young girl;

they were her mother and her sister. She came to thank me for having been the instrument of Divine Providence, for their poverty was extreme. As I had nearly finished supper, I invited them to supper on the next day, and they promised to come.

Delighted so easily to have conferred happiness on a girl upon whom I had no designs, the next day, just as I was dressing to dine at Basili's, I was told by Clairmont (such was my new valet's name) that a French officer was asking to speak to me. I have him shown in, and I ask him what I can do for him.

"I offer you three courses, Monsieur Venetian, and I leave the choice to you. Either countermand the supper tonight, or invite me too, or come out with me now to a place where we can measure swords."

Clairmont, who by then was making up my fire, does not give me time to answer; he seizes a half-burned and still blazing stick of wood and runs at the madman, who does not see fit to wait for him. At the noise he made getting down the stairs at full speed, the valet of the inn came running and stopped him, thinking he had stolen something; but Clairmont made the fellow release him and, still carrying his burning brand, returned to tell me the outcome of the farce, which at once became the talk of the city. My valet, proud of his exploit and sure of my approval, said that I could go about without apprehension, for the loud-mouthed coward had not drawn his sword against the waiter, who, dressed as he was and with only a knife in his hand, had sturdily taken him by the collar.

"*But in any case,*" said Clairmont, "*I will go about with you.*"

I told him that, this time, he had done well, but that henceforth he was not to interfere in my concern; he replied that my concerns were his, and to prove it he inspected my pocket pistols and, finding no powder in the pans, he looked at me with a smile and filled them.

The majority of French servants, who have a good reputation, are like Clairmont; but they always think they are more intelligent than their masters, and when they find they are right they become the master, they steal from him, tyrannize over him, and even show their disdain of him, which the fool thinks he must pretend not to notice. But when the master is the more intelligent, the Clairmonts are excellent.

As the Frenchman wore a uniform, the innkeeper of the "St. Mark" immediately sent a full report to the police, who expelled the desperate wretch from the city the same day. Colonel Basili said at dinner that only a Frenchman would think of going to attack a man in his own room for such a reason; but I proved to him that he was wrong. Poverty and love, combined with a mistaken notion of courage, breed inordinate conduct in every country in the universe.

At supper the "Pilgrim" thanked me for having delivered her from the penniless wretch, who bored and frightened her by constantly saying he would kill himself. The next day I dined at the celebrated Carthusian monastery,[19] and toward nightfall I arrived in Milan, going to stay at Count A. B.'s, where I was not expected until the following day. The Count presented me to his wife before I went to my room, in which I had to wait for a fire to be made. Signora A. B., pretty, though too short, would have pleased me had it not been for a gravity which was inappropriate for a first arrival at her house. After the customary compliments, I said that my valet would bring her the taffeta which her husband had asked me to get for her. She replied that her priest would at once reimburse me for what it had cost me. The Count showed me to my room, then left me until suppertime. The room was good enough, but I was determined to leave the next day if the Spanish Countess did not change her attitude. I could grant her only twenty-four hours to do so.

At supper, at which we were four, the Count, lively and eager to bring me out and to conceal his wife's distant manner from me, talked constantly. I answered him in kind, always addressing the Countess in order not to leave her in a silence which could not but injure her in my estimation; but she contributed only some smiles and dry monosyllables to the conversation, never raising her rather fine black eyes from the dishes, which she declared unappetizing. This observation she made to the priest, who was the fourth at table, and with whom she talked affably.

As I was very fond of the Count, I was distressed to find his wife morose. I examined her carefully to find at least some reason in her charms to forgive her for her ill-humor; but I felt offended when I noticed that whenever she was sure I was looking at her profile she deliberately avoided my scrutiny by turning her head toward the Abate and addressing him for no good reason. I laughed to myself both at her scorn and at her intention, for, since she had not impressed me, I felt safe from any pain which her calculated tyranny could have caused me. After supper my valet brought in the two pieces of taffeta, which were to be used to make her a domino on hoops, such as the fashion at the time demanded.

The Count, who saw me to my room, begged me when he left to excuse his wife's Spanish ways, assuring me that I would find her a good creature as soon as we had come to know each other. The Count was poor, his house was small, his furniture shabby, the livery of his only lackey was threadbare, his table linen was old, his dishes were of stoneware, and one of his Countess's two chambermaids did the cooking. He had no carriage. Clairmont informed me of all this in the course of telling me that he was lodged in a small room next to the kitchen together with the lackey who had served at table.

For my part, having only one room and having three trunks, I was very uncomfortable. It was on waking

that I decided to find a good apartment. As soon as the
Count came to bid me good morning and ask me what
I took for breakfast, I said that I had enough Turinese
chocolate for his whole family; he said that his wife liked
it but that she took it only when it was prepared by her
maid. I immediately gave him six pounds of it, asking
him to persuade her to accept it and to swear to her
that if she wanted to pay me for it I would keep it for
myself. He said she would accept it and thank me for
it. He undertook to have my carriage put in a carriage
house, to rent me a good coach, and to answer for the
fidelity of a temporary lackey he would find for me.

A moment after the Count left, I see the Abate who
had supped with us. He was a man forty years of age,
who, in return for seeing to the running of the house,
lived in it and ate with his masters. He said mass every
day at San Giovanni in Conca.[20] As soon as he was
alone with me the priest asked me point-blank to say
that he had paid me the three hundred Milanese lire,[21]
which were the price of the two pieces of taffeta, when
the Countess asked me if I had received them.

"Signor Abate," I replied, laughing heartily, "if Her
Ladyship asks me that impertinent question I shall tell
her the truth, and it will amuse me."

"She will ask you, I am sure, and you will be the
cause of her ill-treating me."

"Will she have any reason?"

"None."

"Then go and tell her that I make her a present of
them, and that if she wants to pay me I am in no hurry."

"I see that you know neither her nor the circumstances of this house. I will speak to the Count."

A quarter of an hour later the Count comes to tell me
sadly that he owes me a great deal of money, which he
hopes to repay during Lent, and that I will be doing him
a favor if I add the value of the pieces of taffeta to his
account. I answered, embracing him, that he had only

to add them to it himself, for it was my habit never to write down the sums of money with which I was only too happy to be able to oblige my friends. I assured him that if his lady asked me if I had received the money for the taffeta I would tell her that he had paid me himself.

While waiting for dinnertime, having been told that the Countess was not receiving, I sat down at a small table to write my letters. On a large table Clairmont laid out several of my coats to air, together with some women's cloaks and a magnificent dress of red *gros de Tours*[22] trimmed with sable which Madame d'Urfé had intended for the wretched Corticelli. I should have given it to Agata[23] if I had continued to live with her, and I should have made a great mistake, for such a dress was suitable only for a woman of rank.

At one o'clock in comes the Count to announce his wife, who was coming to present the best friend of the house; he was a Marchese Triulzi,[24] of about my age, tall, well built, with a slight squint, easy in his manner, and in short with the bearing of a nobleman. He said that he had come both to have the pleasure of making my acquaintance and to warm himself at the fire, for in the whole house there was a fireplace only in my room.

All the chairs being littered, the Marchese takes the Countess and sets her on his knees like a marionette; but she resists, she blushes, she wrests herself away from him, and, seeing him burst out laughing, she says that, old as he is, he has not yet learned to respect women of her kind. While waiting for Clairmont to clear the chairs, the Marchese, noticing women's clothes and the beautiful dress, asked me if I was expecting a woman. I replied that I hoped to find ladies in Milan whom I should think worthy to receive these presents.

"In Venice," I said, "I knew Prince Triulzi.[25] I suppose he belongs to your family."

"He says so, and it is possible; but I do not believe that I belong to his."

Enlightened by this witticism, I did not mention the Prince again.

"You ought," the Count said to him, "to stay to dinner with us, and, since you do not like anything which is not prepared by your own cook, to send out for your dinner."

The Marchese assented, and we ate well. I saw fine china, fine linen, bottles, and adroit servants. I understood everything, and I almost never spoke. The Marchese bore almost the whole burden of the conversation with wit and liveliness, infuriating the Countess, who constantly complained of the familiarity of his address. Yet the Marchese did not intend to humiliate her, for he loved her; he only wanted to make her less haughty. He soothed her by saying that there was not a man in Milan who was more devoted to her than he and who more greatly respected her charms and her birth.

After dinner a tailor came to measure the Countess for the domino, which was to be ready for the ball to be given on the next day but one. To the Marchese's praise of the colors and the fine quality of the two pieces of taffeta, the Countess replied that it was I who had brought them from Turin, and she asked me if I had received my money. I answered that her husband had reimbursed me, and that she had taught me a good lesson.

"What lesson?" the Marchese asked me.

"I flattered myself," I replied, "that Her Ladyship would have considered me worthy to make her so small a present."

"And she would not accept it? Ha, ha, ha!"

"That shouldn't make you laugh," the Countess said to him angrily; "but you laugh at everything."

Still undressed down to her corset, she showed her beautiful bosom and, when she said that she was cold, the Marchese passed his hand over it; but at that she treated him to outrageous insults, which he received with fits of laughter. Toward nightfall she went to the opera[26] with him, but followed by her own lackey in her livery, who got up behind the Marchese's carriage with his two footmen. A quarter of an hour later I got into mine with the Count, and I was pleasantly surprised to see that the leading actress was my dear Teresa Palesi.[27] I was tactful enough not to mention either his wife's charms or the state of his household to the Count. During the second act I went with him to the gaming room, where there were ten or twelve banks at faro. I played, and after losing about a hundred gold ducati, I stopped.

At supper I thought the Countess less unapproachable. She condoled with me on my losses. I replied that they were not worth her condolences.

The next morning Clairmont enters my room with a tall girl who reminds me of the Jewess Leah, as beautiful as she, but with fewer pretensions, for she had come only to offer me her services in the way of looking after my linen and laces. She charms me on the instant. I was in bed, taking my chocolate, I ask her to sit down, and she replies that she will come back when I am up. I ask her if she lives far away, and she answers that she lodges in the same house, on the ground floor, with her father and mother, and that her name is Zenobia.[28] After telling her that I think her beautiful, I ask for her hand to kiss, and, all smiles, she refuses it, saying that her hand is pledged.

"Then you are engaged?"

"To a tailor who will marry me before the Carnival ends."

"Is he handsome and rich?"

"Neither."

"Then why are you marrying him?"

"To be mistress in my own house."

"You are very sensible, and I declare myself your friend. Bring your intended here, I will give him work."

I rise, I order Clairmont to get my soiled linen together, I have him dress my hair hastily in order to go to see La Palesi, and in comes Zenobia with the tailor. I see a dwarf of a fellow whose face makes me want to laugh.

"So you," I said, "are going to marry this charming girl, are you?"

"*Illustrissimo si* ['Yes, my lord']. The banns are already published."

"You are fortunate. When are you to marry her?"

"In ten or twelve days."

"Why don't you marry her tomorrow?"

"You are in a great hurry."

At this answer I burst out laughing. I gave him an embroidered waistcoat, and I told him to measure me for a black domino for the ball the next evening. He said I must give him the taffeta, for he had neither money nor credit, and I give him ten zecchini, saying that he will have both when he is married, and he leaves.

After giving Zenobia some soiled ruffles, which she undertook to wash as good as new, I asked her if she hoped that her husband would not be jealous.

"He is neither jealous nor in love, and he is marrying me only because I earn more than he does."

"With the charms I see that you possess, you could have aspired to wealth."

"I am twenty-two years old and I have waited long enough. I am tired of single life. Besides, the man you saw is intelligent."

"So I observed. But why does he put off marrying you?"

"Because he has no money; and, having relatives, he wants a fine wedding. And to tell you the truth, I like the idea."

"You are right; but I disapprove of the prejudice which prevents you from giving a gentleman who asks for it your hand to kiss."

"It was only to let you know I am to be married. I am not so scrupulous."

"Well and good. I think all the better of you now. Tell your intended that if he will have me as his sponsor your wedding party will be at my expense."

"Really and truly?"

"Really and truly. I will give him twenty-four zecchini, but on condition that he will spend them."

"It will make people talk; but we won't let that trouble us. I will give you his answer tomorrow."

"And a loving kiss now."

"That too."

Zenobia skipped down the stairs, and I went out to present myself to my banker, who at once accepted my letter of credit. After this necessary visit I went to see Teresa, my old passion. As soon as her chambermaid, the same one she had had in Florence, saw me she took me by the hand and led me to her mistress's bed, from which she was about to rise. She received me with tokens of that sincere friendship which strikes those who feel it dumb for the first moments. After we had embraced each other several times she said that six months earlier she had stopped living with her husband Palesi. He having become insupportable, she had settled an income on him which enabled him to live in Rome. She told me that Don Cesarino, our son, was still with her, that she had sent him to board and would show him to me whenever I wished. She said that she was happy, that gossip gave her a lover, but it was not true, and that I could come to see her in perfect freedom and at any time. We recounted our brief stories to each other, but we spent no less than two hours over it. Finding her as beautiful and fresh as she had been when she had made me fall in love with her at Ancona, I asked her if she considered it her duty to remain true to her husband, and she replied that in Florence she had still been in love with him and that if she still pleased me we could renew our ties and live together until death. Upon hearing this I convinced her that I could prove my love to her on the instant. Surrendering to all my caresses, she replied that we would talk of it at our second interview; but she had to put up with seeing herself become the accomplice of my incontinence. After the act I reproached her with being cold. She swore that I was mistaken and that she was delighted to have found me full of fire. I went home in love with her; but my ardor found too many diversions to last long.

The Countess A. B. began to take a milder tone. She told me complacently that she knew where I had spent two hours; but that if I loved the person I ought to give up my visits, for her lover would leave her.

"If he leaves her I will take his place."

"You do well to amuse yourself looking for women who know how to earn your presents. I have been told that you do not give any until you have received obvious proofs of their love."

"That is my principle."

"It is the best way for you to avoid being duped. The lover of the person whom you went to see had one of our ladies, whom he put in very comfortable circumstances. We despise her."

"Why, may I ask?"

"Do you not consider that she made a misalliance? Greppi[29] is a man of no birth."

Showing no surprise at the name Greppi, I replied that ladies who despise another for such a reason can only be absurdly steeped in pride and devoured by envy.

"I am convinced that if they found Greppis, they would all contract misalliances."

The Marchese's arrival prevented her from answering me; she went out with him and I with her husband, who introduced me to a house where I saw a man dealing at faro with a hundred zecchini before him. I played at small stakes, to do as the others were doing, and after

losing twenty ducati I stopped. On the way to the
opera my poor Count told me that I was the cause of
his having lost ten ducati on his word and that he did
not know how to pay them the next day. I gave them
to him. At the opera I lost two hundred at the same
bank at which I had lost a hundred the evening before.
I laughed at the distress of my dear Count, who did not
know that I had a hundred thousand lire in Greppi's
hands besides a hundred thousand in jewels. The Countess, who had seen me lose, thought it the moment to ask
me if I would sell my sable dress.

"I have been told," she said, "that it is worth a
thousand zecchini."

"That is true, Signora; but I will sell everything before I will touch the ornaments which I have reserved
for your fair sex."

"It is the Marchese Triulzi who wants to buy it to
give to someone."

"I am sorry, Signora, that I cannot sell it to him."

She did not answer. Near the door of the theater after
the opera I saw Teresa about to enter a sedan chair. I
leave the Count long enough to tell her that I am sure
she is going to sup with her lover. She whispered in
reply that she would sup by herself, or alone with me
if I had the courage to go there. I saw that she was
astonished when I agreed. She said she would wait for
me. After telling the Count to use my carriage, I took a
sedan chair and went to Teresa's, who arrived just as I
did.

Oh, how we laughed when, sitting side by side, we exchanged our thoughts.

"Knowing," she said, "that you are in love with the
Countess A. B., I was certain you would not come to
sup with me."

"And I, knowing that Greppi is your lover, thought
I would confound you by accepting your invitation."

"Greppi is my friend; if he loves me, I am sorry for

him. He has not yet found the secret of seducing me."

"Do you think he can find it?"

"That is most unlikely, for I am rich."

"And Greppi is still richer."

"Yes, but I do not believe he loves me more than he does his money."

"I understand you, my charmer; you will make him happy if he is brave enough to ruin himself."

"You have guessed it; but it will not happen. Meanwhile, here we are together after twenty years of divorce. You will find me the same, I am sure."

"That is a privilege which nature has granted to your sex alone. You will find me different; and my heart, which is the same, will weep for it; but you will perform miracles."

Teresa did not perform one. After an appetizing but very brief supper we went to bed and surrendered to love; but after two hours filled with amorous furies Morpheus seized on our senses. When we woke our furies were renewed, and I did not leave her until I had wished her good morning with an ardor equal to that with which I had won a sleep of four hours. I went home, and I was pleased to see the beautiful Zenobia in my room; she told me that the tailor was ready to marry her on the following Sunday if I had not been joking in the offer I had made her. To convince her that I had not been joking I immediately gave her twenty-four zecchini. Filled with gratitude, she came to my arms and let me devour her with kisses. She must have attributed it to my open door that she did not see me as she would have seen me if I had not been exhausted by Teresa. However, a long toilet restored me to freshness. After a pleasant drive in my carriage I returned to the Count's, where I found the Marchese Triulzi, who, as usual, was putting the Countess in a fury. He had his own dinner brought in for six, and we dined in high spirits.

The conversation having turned to my dress, the

Countess, like a fool, told him that I was saving it to
give to the lady who would captivate me and make me
happy. The Marchese politely told me that I deserved
favors at a cheaper rate.

"It seems," the Countess said to me, "that you will
give your dress to the person with whom you spent the
night."

I reply that I had spent the night at cards; and just
then Clairmont comes in to tell me that there is an officer outside who wishes to speak with me. I go out, and
I see a handsome young man who comes to embrace me.
I recognize him as Barbaro,[30] son of a Venetian nobleman and brother of the beautiful and famous Signora
Gritti,[31] wife of the Gritti Sgombro[32] who was sentenced
to imprisonment in the citadel of Cattaro,[33] where he
died at the end of a year. I spoke of her ten years ago, as
my reader may remember.[34] Signor Barbaro, her brother,
who had come to see me, had also incurred the disfavor
of the State Inquisitors. We had been good friends in
Venice the year before my imprisonment. After telling
me that he was in the service of the Duke of Modena,[35]
Governor of Milan, he said that, having seen me lose at
Carcano's[36] bank, he had come because of our old friendship to tell me of a sure way for me to make a great
deal of money if I would let him introduce me at a
house where the usual company consisted of young men
who liked play and who could not but lose. He said that
he would deal himself, and that he knew so well what
good luck he had when he held the cards that he was
sure of winning. He ended by saying that he needed me
only to furnish the money for the bank and would ask
me for no more than twenty-five per cent interest. I see
that he does not dare tell me he is an accomplished
sharper. In addition he says that in the house I will
find objects worthy to please me and such that their
seduction would be a delight. I replied that I would
make up my mind after I had seen the company and the

young ladies to whom he wished to introduce me. I engage to meet him at a coffeehouse the next day at three o'clock. He leaves, saying that he hopes he will see me at the ball.

Zenobia's fiancé brought me my domino, and the Countess's tailor had brought her hers. As the ball was to begin after the opera, I went to it to hear Teresa sing; and after losing another two hundred zecchini at Carcano's bank, I go back to the house to undress and put on my domino. The Countess, who was already dressed, tells me that if I will be so kind as to take her to the ball and home again in my carriage she will not send to the Marchese Triulzi's for one, and I reply that I will escort her with the greatest pleasure.

It was on the way to the ball with her that I told her my dress would be hers if she would grant me the honor of sleeping with her.

"You insult me barbarously, and it astonishes me, for it cannot be from ignorance."

"I know everything; but with a little of the proper spirit you can disregard the insult and even pretend to forgive me for it, thus conquering prejudice."

"One can do that when one loves; but admit that your very coarse style of address is more apt to make you hated."

"I employ it because I dislike dragging things out; admit, on your side, that you would be delighted to see me in love and timid."

"I should not care at all, for, such as I know you to be, I feel that I could never love you."

"In that we are perfectly at one, for I do not love you either."

"Bravo! But you would spend a thousand zecchini to go to bed with me. Ha, ha, ha! Is not that ridiculous?"

"Not so very. I want to go to bed with you only to humiliate you, to mortify your pride."

God knows what she would have replied if we had not

In a Box at the Opera

"L'Amour Menaçant"

just then arrived at the theater. We parted, and after boring myself walking about in the crowd I went to the gaming room, hoping to make up my losses. I had in my pocket two hundred Piedmontese gold pistoles, which came to more than five hundred zecchini. I was well supplied with money; but at the rate I was going I was headed for ruin. I sat down at Carcano's bank, and I thought it a good augury when I saw that no one knew me except my poor Count, who followed me everywhere. Punting on only one card, and playing prudently, I spent four hours without being able either to lose all the money I had in front of me or to win a thousand zecchini, which was the sum I had decided on. It was at the last deal that, determined either to win or to lose, I lost all my gold. In the ballroom I found the Countess, who followed me as soon as she saw me, and we went home. On the way she said she had seen me lose a great sum, and that she was very glad of it.

"The Marchese Triulzi," she said, "will give you a thousand zecchini for your dress, and the money will bring you luck."

"And you will have my dress."

"Possibly."

"Signora, you shall never have it in that way, and you know the other. I scorn a thousand zecchini."

"And I your presents and your person."

In my room I found my poor Count, looking mournful and wanting but not daring to condole with me. My good humor gave him the courage to tell me that I could get a thousand zecchini at once for my sable dress from the Marchese Triulzi.

"I would rather give it to your Countess; but she has told me that she would despise it if she had to accept it from me."

"She is mad about it; but, I don't know quite how, you have wounded her pride. Sell it, my friend, and take the thousand zecchini."

"I will answer you tomorrow."

After sleeping for four or five hours I put on morning dress to go to Greppi's, for I had no more cash. I got a thousand zecchini, asking him to talk to no one about my affairs; he replied that my affairs were his and that I could be sure of his discretion. He complimented me on the esteem in which Signora Palesi held me, saying that he hoped we should sup together at her house. I replied that such an occasion would give me the greatest pleasure. Leaving Greppi's, I paid her a visit, which was very short because she had company. I was pleased to find that she knew nothing of my losses at cards or of the money I had in her friend's hands. She said she wanted us to sup together and that she would send me word. I went back to the house, where I found the Count in my room before the fire.

"My wife," he said, "is furious with you, and she will not tell me the reason."

"The reason is that I insist that she shall have my dress only from my hands and purely as a gift. She told me in so many words that if she had to receive it from me she would despise it. Do you think she has reason to be furious?"

"Either it is madness or I fail to understand it; but be so good as to listen to what I have to say. You despise a thousand zecchini, and I congratulate you if you are in a position to despise a sum which would make me happy. Sacrifice a vanity, which seems to me mistaken, to friendship, get a thousand zecchini from the Marchese to lend to me, and let my wife have the dress, which he will certainly give her."

I could not help laughing again and again, grasping all the beauty of the arrangement; but I stopped laughing when I saw the Count red with shame. I embraced him affectionately; then I was cruel enough to say that, all vanity aside, I should be glad to do as he had suggested.

"I will sell my dress to the Marchese whenever you wish," I said, "and I will take his five thousand lire; but on condition that I shall not lend them to you but will give them to your beautiful Countess at a private meeting; but not by force, and I beg you to make that clear to her, but freely, for in receiving the sum she must prepare herself to be not only polite to me but gentle as a lamb. That is my last word."

"I will see."

He left me. An hour later we dined badly—he, the Abate, and I; then I drove in my carriage to the place where Barbaro was to meet me. Tired from the ball, the Countess had not left her bed. I had never seen her room.

Barbaro was punctually waiting for me. He at once got into my carriage and had us driven to a house at the far end of Milan. We go up to the second floor, and he introduces me to a handsome elderly man, a respectable-looking woman, and two young ladies, cousins, of whom it was hard to decide which one deserved to be preferred. He announces me as a Venetian who, like himself, has the misfortune to be out of favor with the State Inquisitors. But he adds that, being rich and a bachelor, I can take the misfortune lightly.

He announced me as wealthy, and I looked the part. The richness of my attire was dazzling. My rings, my snuffboxes, my watch-chains studded with diamonds, together with my diamond and ruby cross which I wore hanging from my neck on a bright red ribbon, made me an imposing personage. It was the Order of the Golden Spur, which I had received from the Pope himself, but at the foot of my cross there was no spur to be seen. No one knew what it was, which pleased me. Those who were curious and who did not dare to ask me were well advised. I stopped wearing the cross in Warsaw in the year 1765, when the Prince Palatine of Russia[37] told me, the first time we were alone together, that I would do well to get rid of such a piece of trash.

"You do not need it," he said, "except to dazzle fools, and here you can enjoy the privilege of not dealing with them."

I followed the advice of a nobleman whose intelligence was profound and who, nevertheless, was the man who removed the first stone from the pedestal which supported the Kingdom of Poland. He ruined it by the very means by which he tried to make it greater.[38]

The old Marchese to whom Barbaro introduced me said that he knew Venice and that, since I was not a patrician, I could not live more happily than by living abroad; he offered me his house and to serve me in whatever way he could. But the two Marchesine seemed to me something above nature. I could not wait to inquire about them from someone who could tell me all, for I could not trust Barbaro.

A half hour later the guests began arriving, on foot and by carriage. I saw well-dressed young ladies and gentlemen, the latter all rivaling one another in paying court to the lady to whom love or politeness bade them give the preference. When the company numbered eighteen or twenty they all sat down at a large table and fell to playing a game called "bankruptcy."[39] After spending two hours over it and losing a few zecchini I went to the opera with Barbaro. I told my fellow countryman that the two Marchesine seemed to me angels incarnate, and that, after offering them my homage, I should see in a few days if they were within my reach; as for the game, I said that I would lend him two hundred zecchini which I did not want to lose and that hence he must guarantee them to me in the most legal form. I said that instead of the twenty-five per cent which he asked of me on the profits from the bank I would give him fifty, that is to say half, which no one was to know, for when I was there I should also punt in all honesty. I told him to come to see me early the next morning, bringing me good written security, if he wanted the money. He embraced me joyously.

With my mind running on the two young ladies who had struck me, I was thinking of going to ask Greppi about them, when I saw the Marchese Triulzi, who was talking with someone. It was in the parterre at the opera. It was he who, seeing me alone, came to me, saying cheerfully that he was sure I had dined badly and that he would be pleased if I would dine at his house every day. Feeling really ashamed, I asked him a thousand pardons if I had not yet gone to pay my respects to him. He said, with a laugh, that he had heard I had made up my mind to sell him my dress, that he was very glad of it, and that he would give me the fifteen thousand lire it was worth whenever I wished. I said he had only to send someone for it the next day. He briefly told me several interesting stories about ladies who were in the first-tier boxes and whose beauty had led me to ask him who they were.

"In such-and-such a church," I said, "I saw two beauties according to all the canons. A person who was beside me said that they were cousins and that their names were the Marchesa Q . . . and the Marchesa F. . . . Do you know them? I am very curious about them."

"They are both charming. It is not difficult to gain admittance to their house, and I believe they are virtuous, for until now there has not been a single story told about them in Milan. However, I know that Signorina F. has a lover, but in the utmost secrecy, for he is the only son of one of our first families. The young ladies unfortunately are not rich, but being, I am assured, highly intelligent, they can hope to make wealthy matches. If you are curious about them I will find someone to take you there."

"Please do not trouble yourself."

After the ballet I went to the gaming room. I heard three or four voices say: ''There he is.'' Carcano bowed to me, made me sit beside him, gave me a pack of cards instead of a *livret,* and I began punting with such constant bad luck that in less than an hour I lost seven hundred zecchini. I should have lost the rest if Carcano, having to go somewhere, had not risen and given the cards to a man whose face I did not like. I went home, and, in order not to be forced to hide my bad humor, I retired to bed.

The next morning Barbaro came for the two hundred zecchini I had promised him. He guaranteed to repay my money, giving me the right to sequestrate his income until his indebtedness was cleared. I went to Greppi's, where I drew two thousand zecchini, in gold and in notes payable to the bearer.

CHAPTER VII[1]

*The Countess humiliated. Zenobia's wedding
at the Cascina dei Pomi. Faro. Conquest of
the beautiful Irene. Plans for a masquerade.*

BACK AT the house, I found the Count with one of
the Marchese Triulzi's menservants, who handed me a
letter in which he said that he was ready to receive the
dress. I sent it to him at once. The Count said that the
Marchese would dine with us and that he would certainly
pay me for it. I replied that I had no doubt of it, and
that I could not wait to receive the sum in order to give
it to the Countess. He said that he had spoken to her,
and that my proposal had set her laughing, but that he
was sure she would make up her mind as soon as the
dress was in her possession. It was a Friday, there was
no opera, and fast-day food was in order. The Marquese
sent his excellent fish dinner, then he came himself, and
after dinner the dress arrived in a pretty basket, and
we saw the Signora very well pleased; she outdid herself
in thanks, which the Marchese turned away with a jest,
adding that if she were wise she would sell it because,
since everyone knew she was not rich, such a fine dress

was not suitable for her. He told her in so many words
that she would be laughed at. To this advice the Countess
replied with insults, saying, among other things, that if
such was his opinion he must be mad, for if the dress
was unsuitable he ought not to give it to her.

At the height of the quarrel a visitor is announced.
It was the Marchesa Menafoglio.[2] She sees the dress,
which was laid out on a table, she declares it magnificent,
she assumes it is for sale, and she says she would be glad
to buy it. The Countess replies tartly that she had not
bought it to sell it again, and the other begs her pardon
for her mistake. The Marchese cannot refrain from
laughing, the Countess becomes furious but conceals it,
and the conversation continues. But after Signora Menafoglio leaves, the Countess gives vent to her anger, heap-
ing insults on the Marchese for having laughed. She
ends at last by saying she has a headache and is going
to bed. The Marchese then gives me fifteen thousand lire,
saying that he is sure they will bring me luck at Carcano's bank, who, he adds, adores me and has asked him
to bring me to dinner at his house, for, having to spend
his nights in the gaming room, he cannot invite me to
supper. I ask him to tell him that I will dine with him
whenever he pleases except on the next day but one, since
I had promised to attend a wedding party at the Cascina
dei Pomi.[3] The two gentlemen congratulate me, they
make it clear that they would like to be of the party,
and I promise to have the beautiful bride invite them,
together with the Countess, provided she is willing to do
so much honor to the company, which will consist only
of townspeople. The Marchese undertakes to persuade
her to go, and he is sure that he can when he learns that
the bride is Zenobia. The Count goes out to see if she
is in the house, he finds her and comes back with her.
The Marchese congratulates her, and, encouraging her to
invite the Countess, takes her by the hand and leads her

to her room; and a half hour later he comes out again, telling us that the Countess has promised to go.

The Marchese having left a quarter of an hour later, the Count says to me that if I have nothing better to do I can keep his wife company, for, having business, he unfortunately has to leave her alone. I reply that I have the thousand zecchini in my pocket and that I am prepared to give them to her if I find her kind. He tells me to wait while he goes to speak with her. I went to my room, where, waiting while the Count was with the Countess, I took fifteen thousand lire in notes to the bearer, which I had received from Greppi, putting away all the gold the Marchese Triulzi had given me.

Just then I see Zenobia bringing me my ruffles. She asks me if I want to buy a piece of fine linen which is not dear, and I say yes. She goes downstairs and comes up again with candles and the linen. I find it fine enough, she says there is enough of it to make a dozen shirts and that it costs only eighteen zecchini. I say I will give it to her if she will grant me her final favors then and there. She says that she loves me but that she will be obliged to me if I will wait until after the wedding.

"No, my dear, I am in a great hurry. Now or never, for I am dying. There, look at the state I am in."

"I see, but it is impossible."

"Why impossible? Do you suppose your dwarf of a fiancé will notice anything?"

"Oh, no! And even if he did, I should think it very funny if he dared open his mouth to reproach me with it."

"He would certainly be in the wrong. So come to my arms."

"I think we should at least lock the door from inside."

"I think not, for we might be heard, and God knows what people would suspect. You can be certain that no one will come."

The charming Zenobia fell into my arms with an amorousness in which there was no play-acting. In the extremity of my pleasure I said again and again that she was made for me and not for her fiancé, who could not possibly appreciate her charms. I told her frankly to send him to the devil and take me in his place, but I had the good luck that she did not believe me. A half hour later I called a halt, surprised and delighted that the Count had not come to interrupt my enjoyment. I suppose that, not knowing I am in my room, he has gone out, and I see Zenobia very well pleased when she sees me ready to begin again. She knew that the festival would last longer. I make myself more comfortable, I display her charms before me in a more seductive light, and I care not that my hair is disarranged by it. A whole hour of encounters at last calmed my fury. During the sweet ecstasy I hear the Count's voice, I tell Zenobia so, I put myself to rights, I give her eighteen zecchini, she leaves, and the Count comes in, laughing and saying that he had seen everything through a crack, which he shows me, and that he had not been bored. He says that his wife is willing to let me keep her company, and, after laughing loud and long, that he is willing too. I smiled and, setting out for her room, begged him to make what use he pleased of my carriage, which was at the door, for I should not go out again.

I enter the Countess's room, where I find her in bed, I go to her, I ask her how she is feeling, she replies "very well," smiling and saying that her husband has restored her to health. I sit down on her bed, and she does not scold me.

"Are you not going out again?" she asks; "you have on your dressing gown and your hair is disarranged."

"I fell asleep and I decided to keep you company, if you will put up with me and be kind and gentle."

"If your behavior toward me is such as it should be,

you may be sure that you will always find me polite."

"And you will love me."

"That will depend upon you; this evening you are sacrificing Count Carcano to me."

"He has won a great deal of money from me, and I foresee that tomorrow he will win fifteen thousand lire I have with me, which the Marchese Triulzi gave me for the dress you would not accept from my unworthy hands."

"You would be very ill advised to go and lose them."

"Of course. And that will not happen if I find you kindly disposed, for I shall give them to you. Will you permit me to lock your door?"

"Why?"

"Because I wish to have the honor of getting under these covers. I am dying of cold, beautiful Countess, and burning with desire."

"Signore, I will never permit that."

"Then good-by. I shall sit in front of a good fire, and tomorrow I will launch an attack on Carcano."

She called me back, saying that I was a horrid man; and at that I locked the door, and I undressed without her seeing me, for she turned her back to me completely. I got into bed beside her, and she, having made up her mind, let me do whatever I wished; but never was an eclipse of nature so favorable to my intentions, I could never get an erection. Keeping her eyes closed, she submitted to my putting her in every possible position and allowed me to use her hand as much as I liked to accomplish the miracle of resurrection. All was in vain.

Pretending to be asleep, she let me do whatever I pleased with her head, and at that she made me feel so sorry for her that I regretted I could not return to life. I left her at last, giving the last thrust of the dagger with these terrible words:

"It is not my fault, Signora, if your charms have no

power over me. I leave you your fifteen thousand lire."

After playing out this scene, I went to my room and to bed.

My reader must despise me, I know, but I advise him to withhold his disapproval for a moment. Very early the next morning the Count entered my room, with his face the picture of satisfaction. He said that his wife felt very well and wished me good morning. I did not expect as much. He said he had been delighted to see that the fifteen thousand lire I had left her were not those which I had received from the Marchese Triulzi, and that he hoped that, as the Marchese had said, his money would bring me luck the following evening. I had not known that there was to be a ball. I told him that I would not go to the opera, but would go instead to the ball and the gaming room, doing my best to make myself unrecognizable. I asked him to buy me a brand-new domino and never to come near me, for I hoped that no one but he would know me. I asked him to let me write, my correspondence being greatly in arrears.

At noon he brought me the domino, which I immediately hid, and we dined with the Countess, whose expression and manner amazed me. Her serenity, her calm, her affability, made me think her a beauty. I was in despair that I had so dreadfully mistreated her. I thought her insensibility inconceivable, it astounded me; I concluded that she must have been asleep during the time I had insulted her so barbarously. Her husband having left us alone together, I told her that I pleaded guilty to being a monster whom she must despise. She replied that she felt she was profoundly indebted to me, and that she did not know in what way I could think I had failed in respect to her and why I called myself a monster. I asked for her hand, but she withdrew it and gave me a very sweet kiss. Repentance gnawed my soul.

After sealing all my letters I masked and I went to the ball, wearing nothing by which I could be recognized.

I took a watch and two snuffboxes which no one had seen, and I even changed the purses in which I carried my money. I sat down at Carcano's bank, and to maintain my incognito I played in an entirely different way. In one purse I had a hundred Spanish quadruples,[4] which amounted to seven hundred zecchini, and in another three hundred Venetian zecchini.[5] It was the gold I had received from Greppi. I began by emptying before me the purse in which I had the hundred quadruples.

In less than an hour I lost all my gold. I rose, and everyone, thinking that I was leaving, was making room for me, when I took out the purse in which I had the three hundred Venetian zecchini. Refusing to sit down again, I stake a hundred of them on a card, which I find second with *paroli* and *sept et la va,* and the banker, with a very satisfied expression, gives me back all my hundred doblones de a ocho. At that, taking a place beside him again, I resume playing, and Carcano seems well pleased. He studied me. I had the snuffbox which the Elector of Cologne had given me with his portrait on it. The banker, in pantomime, asks my permission to take a pinch of snuff, and everyone around the bank examines the portrait. I hear a woman's voice say:

"It is the deceased Elector of Cologne[6] in the robes of Grand Master of the Teutonic Order."

My snuffbox is returned to me. I play by a new system. A single card at fifty zecchini *paroli* and *paix de paroli.* An hour before dawn the bank gave up the ghost. Carcano politely says that if I want to leave all my gold there he will have it weighed, giving me a note to bearer for which his cashier will pay me the entire sum at sight, and I agree, adding my hundred quadruples to the rest. A pair of scales is brought. The gold is weighed, and I am given a receipt for thirty-four pounds of gold, which came to two thousand eight hundred and fifty-six zecchini. Carcano signs the note, and I slowly make my way to the ballroom.

Barbaro, having the practiced eye of any Venetian, recognizes me, comes up, and congratulates me; but seeing that I do not answer, he leaves me. A woman masker, clad in the Greek fashion, with an oriental headdress covered with fine brilliants and a rich girdle below her bosom, which offered a foretaste of its beauties, says to me in falsetto that she wants to dance the contradance with me. I accept. She takes off her gloves, and I see an alabaster hand and feel its softness. I tried in vain to guess who she could be. After the contradance, which had made me sweat profusely, she said that I could go to dry myself in her box; I follow her, and, seeing the banker Greppi, I feel sure that I have danced with Teresa, who, unmasking, congratulates me on my triumph. She says that if she had not seen my snuffbox she would not have known who I was, but that she had revealed my identity only to her friend there. Nevertheless she assures me that I had been recognized by others. I gave Signor Greppi the note to bearer and he immediately gave me a receipt for it. She invited him to supper with me at her house the next day, telling me that we should be four; Greppi wondered who the fourth would be, but not I. I was sure that I should find my dear Cesarino there.

I went down to the ball again, where two female dominoes attacked me from right and left, saying in their falsetto that Messer Grande[7] was waiting for me outside. They ask me for snuff; I give them some from a snuffbox with a secret device which exposed an indecent miniature. I have the impudence to show it, and one of them, after thoroughly examining it, hands me back my box, saying that in punishment for my crime I shall never know who they are; after which they leave me. Very sorry that I have given them reason to take offense, I follow them, and, seeing Barbaro, who knew everyone, I point them out to him, and he tells me they are the Marchesine Q. and F. I am delighted, and I promise him I will go there on the next day but one. He says that everyone at the ball knows me, and that the bank has been doing well, though I must scorn such trifles.

Toward the end of the ball a masker dressed as a Venetian gondolier was accosted by a very charming female masker wearing a *bautta* and a black cloak in the most authentic Venetian style. The female masker challenged the gondolier to convince her he was a Venetian by dancing the furlana⁸ with her. The gondolier accepts the challenge, the orchestra is ordered to play a furlana; but the gondolier, who was obviously Milanese, was hissed. The pretty female masker, on the contrary, danced to perfection. The dance being among my lesser passions, I invite the unknown woman to dance it with me; and, all the onlookers having applauded us, we dance another, and that would have been enough if a girl dressed as a shepherdess but not wearing a mask, and pretty as a Cupid, had not persuaded me to dance yet one more. She danced it superlatively. She executed a double *grand cercle* three times, gliding so perfectly that she seemed not to touch the floor. She left me panting. She whispered my name into my ear, I asked her hers, and she replied that I would learn it if I came to see her at the "Three Kings," ⁹ in such-and-such a room.

"Are you alone?"

"I am with my father and mother, your old friends."

So many adventures! Tired to the point of exhaustion, I go home, but I am allowed to sleep only three hours. I am waked and told to hurry. The Count, the Countess, and the Marchese, all ready for Zenobia's wedding party, tell me that it is not polite to make a bride and groom wait. All three of them congratulate me in the highest terms on the boldness with which I had conquered Fortune. I answer the Marchese that it was his money which had brought me luck; I could no longer keep up a pretense. He said that he knew where his money had gone.

This indiscretion of the Countess's or the Count's surprised me, for I thought it broke the most rudimentary rules of this sort of intrigue. The Marchese said that Carcano had recognized me by the way I opened my snuffbox and that he expected us for dinner.

"He wants," he said, "to lose all his money to you."

"Tell him that I want the same."

We all went to the Cascina dei Pomi, where we found eighteen or twenty townspeople waiting for us, and the bride and groom, who outdid themselves in compliments. We had no difficulty in putting the whole company, whom our arrival had thrown into a state of embarrassment, at their ease. We sat down at table. The bride was seated between the groom and myself. We were twenty-four, and I saw some very pretty "pullets"; but I was too much preoccupied. The dinner, which lasted three hours, was so abundant, and the foreign wines were so exquisite, that I felt certain my twenty-four zecchini had not been enough to pay for it. What made us laugh was the *brindisi* ("toasts"). Everyone proposed rarely ingenious healths in verses improvised on the spur of the moment, and everyone felt called upon to sing. We laughed, but we made them laugh too with our impromptus and our songs, which we succeeded in making no less nonsensical than those which came from the mouths of all these excellent people.

When we rose from the table embraces became the rule; but the Countess could not keep from laughing when she had to embrace the tailor. He took her laughter as a particular favor. A very good orchestra striking up, dancing began. Etiquette demanded that it begin with a minuet by the bride and groom. Zenobia danced it in time, but the tailor made the Countess laugh so hard that we thought she would be ill; however, she had to dance with him while the bride danced with me. In less than an hour there was an end to the minuets, and the contradances began, to last until the end of the ball, when coffee was served to everyone five or six times, together with *confetti*. These are sweets of various kinds, which are made to perfection in Milan.

After I had duly congratulated the groom, he thought it the perfection of good manners when he saw me give my hand to his bride, asking her to grant me the honor of seeing her home. After telling the coachman where he was to go, I took the charming woman in the "extinguisher" position[10] and so kept her till we arrived at her door. Zenobia got out first, but, noticing that testimony of the grossest kind to our crime, which would leave a terrible stain, remained on the most visible part of my gray linen-velvet breeches, I told Zenobia to go up, assuring her that I would come back immediately. I went home, where I quickly put on black breeches. I returned to Zenobia's before her husband had arrived. I saw a large bed in one room, a large tailor's table in another, and a kitchen.

"I am delighted, my dear gossip,[11] to see you well lodged."

"You have changed your breeches."

"Yes. A great stain caused by our exploit made them indecent."

"You did well."

The tailor arrives with his sister. He thanks me, addressing me as "gossip," and he at once asks me how I managed to change my breeches.

"By going home," I replied, "and leaving your wife alone, for which I beg you to forgive me."

"Didn't you see," she asked him, "that the Signore spilled coffee on himself?"

"You should," he said, "have gone home with him."

Then he laughed at his witticism.

"Were you pleased with the wedding party?" he asked me.

"Very much so, but I must reimburse you, dear gossip, for what it cost you in addition."

"Not much, not much, I will send you the account by Zenobia."

I returned home, angry with myself for not having seen that people would notice I had changed my breeches. After saying good-by to the Count, the Countess, and the Marchese, who thanked me for the laughable entertainment which I had provided for them, I went off to bed.

The next morning I set out on foot to see who the girl could possibly be who, after dancing the furlana so well, had told me she was staying at the "Three Kings" with her father and mother, my "old friends."

I arrive at the inn of that name and, speaking to no one, go up to the room for which the girl had given me such exact directions. I enter, and I am very much surprised to see Countess Rinaldi,[12] to whom Zawoiski[13] had introduced me at the Locanda del Castelletto[14] sixteen years earlier. My reader may remember how Signor Bragadin had paid her husband the amount which he had won from me at cards.[15] Signora Rinaldi had aged, but I recognized her instantly. As I had felt only a passing fancy for her, I refrain from dwelling upon memories which do us no honor. I tell her that I am delighted to see her again, and I ask her if she is still living with her husband.

"You shall see him in half an hour."

"Signora, I shall leave, for there are old scores between us which I do not care to recall."

"No, no, be seated."

"Pray excuse me."

"Irene,[16] stop the Signore."

So commanded, the pretty Irene stood at the door, not like a mastiff which, grinding its teeth, threatens death to anyone who thinks of opposing its fury, but like an angel who, with a bewitching look, soothes him whom she stops with a promise of happiness. She struck me motionless.

"Let me go," I say, "we can meet elsewhere, let me go."

"Oh, I beg you, wait for Papa."

So saying, she looks at me so tenderly that her lips draw mine. Irene has conquered; I take a chair, in which, proud of her victory, she comes and sits on my lap, and I give her caresses which she returns with delight. I ask the Signora where she was born, and she replies:

"In Mantua, three months after I left Venice."

"When did you leave Venice?"

"Six months after I made your acquaintance."

"That is odd; if I had had an affair of the heart with you, you could tell me I am her father; and I would believe it, taking the passion she inspires in me to be blood speaking."

"I am amazed that you forget certain things so easily."

"Far from it! I reply that I do not forget those things; but I see all. You want me to renounce the feelings she inspires in me, and I will do so; but she will lose by it."

Irene, whom this brief dialogue has struck dumb, recovers her courage after a moment and says that she looks like me.

"Stay for dinner with us," she says.

"No, for I might well fall in love with you, and a divine law forbids it, according to what your mother claims to be the fact."

"I was joking," her mother replies. "You can love Irene with a clear conscience."

"I believe it."

Irene leaves the room, and, alone with the mother, I tell her that her daughter attracts me, but that I am unwilling either to languish or to be made a dupe.

"Discuss it with my husband. We are in straits, and we are expected at Cremona."

"But your daughter has a lover, and has had others."

"It has never come to anything serious."

"That seems impossible."

"Nevertheless it is true."

But in comes Count Rinaldi[17] with his daughter. He had aged so greatly that I should not have recognized him. He embraces me, and he begs me not to mention the past.

"You alone," he says, "can help me out of my difficulties, by giving me the means to leave for Cremona. I have pawned everything, I am in debt and on the verge of going to prison. No one comes to see me except wretches who are after my daughter, who is the only thing of value that I possess. Here is a pinchbeck[18] watch I went out to sell; it is well worth six zecchini, and I am offered only two."

I take the watch, I give him six zecchini, and I present it to Irene. She says with a laugh that she cannot thank me, for it is her own watch, to which she could lay claim if her father had sold it.

"As it is," she says to him without laughing, "you can sell it again."

After laughing heartily at her repartee, I gave Signor Rinaldi ten zecchini, saying that I was pressed for time and would see him again in three or four days.

Irene, having shown me to the foot of the first staircase, and having convinced me with the sweetest submissiveness that her fair flower had not been picked, received ten more zecchini. I told her that the first time she would come to the ball with me alone I would give her a hundred. She replied that she would tell her papa so.

Returning to the house, and feeling sure that the wretched man would sell me his daughter's first fruits before the next ball, and that I would not know where to take her to possess her in perfect freedom, I see a notice on a door beside a pastry shop. The street was unfrequented; that pleases me, and I decide to rent a room. I speak to the pastry cook, he says the house is his; and

his wife, with an infant at her breast, tells me to go upstairs with her and choose. She takes me to the fourth
floor, where I see only wretched garrets. I refuse them
all. She says that her second floor has four rooms opening
into one another, and that she cannot let one of them
separately. I go to see them, and I at once rent them
all. I go downstairs, I pay the pastry cook the month in
advance which he demanded, and he gives me a receipt,
then he tells me he will prepare meals for myself alone
or with company at whatever price I fix. This is just as
I would have it. I gave him some ordinary name; he did
not learn to whom he had rented his apartment.

I went home, and, having arranged with Barbaro to
spend the afternoon calling on the beautiful Marchesine,
I made a lengthy toilet. After dining poorly enough with
the Countess, who I thought had become affability itself,
but who nevertheless did not attract me, I went to meet
Barbaro. We went on together.

"I have come," I said to them, "to beg your pardon
for having revealed the secret of my snuffbox."

They blushed, and accused Barbaro of indiscretion. I
contemplated the two girls, whom, all prejudice aside, I
thought far superior to Irene, who at the time filled my
mind; but their bearing and the respect which they
seemed to demand terrified me. Irene's situation had
opened the possibility of my asking for everything and
being sure that I would obtain everything; but here I
saw two young ladies of station who displayed all the
haughtiness of noble blood and whom I feared my appearance did not have the power to impress. To judge
from what the Marchese Triulzi had told me, I was sure
that when Barbaro had said they could be had for money
he had been only making a guess.

When a sufficient company had arrived there was talk
of play, and I prepared to punt at small stakes, like
Signorina Q., beside whom I seated myself. Her aunt,
who was the mistress of the house, had introduced me

to a very handsome young man in the Austrian uniform,[19] who sat down at my other side.

My dear Barbaro held the cards like a sharper, and it
began to annoy me. At the end of play, which went on
for four hours, the Signorina beside me was the winner
by a few zecchini; and her brother, my neighbor on the
other side, who, after losing his money, had played on
his word, was in debt by twenty zecchini. The bank won
fifty, including the young Lieutenant's twenty. We all
left, and, since the handsome young man lived at a distance, he did me the honor of getting into my carriage.

On the way Barbaro says that he wants to introduce
us to a Venetian girl who has just arrived; and, the
young officer urging him to do so at once, we go there.
I do not find her pretty, and she does not interest the
young officer either. I pick up a pack of cards and, while
coffee is being made and Barbaro is flirting with the
Venetian girl, I take twenty zecchini from my pocket,
and I invite the young man to lose another twenty to
me on his word. I had no difficulty in persuading him.
While he played, I talked to him of the passion which
his sister the Marchesina had inspired in me, saying
that, since I dared not declare myself, there was no one
else to whom I could turn. My urgency, which in the
beginning he took for a joke, made him laugh. Preoccupied with his play, he answered me vaguely. But
when he observed that, speaking of love, I did not notice
the cards he lost, he began promising me he would speak
in my favor. He won the twenty zecchini from me, immediately paying them to Barbaro, then he embraced me
as affectionately as he would have done if I had made
him a present of the small sum. He promised to use all
his influence on my behalf, and when we parted he assured me he would be able to tell me something the next
time we met.

Since I had promised to sup at Teresa's, I went to the
opera, which had reached the third act. Having entered

the gaming room, I could not resist the temptation to play. I lost two hundred zecchini in a single deal, losing four cards in succession. I stopped, looking very much as if I were trying to save my skin. Carcano said that he hoped every day he would see me arrive with the Marchese Triulzi at his dinner hour.

At La Palesi's I found Greppi waiting for her. A quarter of an hour later she arrived with Don Cesarino, whom I covered with kisses, while Greppi, in the utmost surprise, stared at the boy, whom he could only suppose to be my brother or my son; but when Teresa told him that he was her own brother, he asked me, with a laugh, if I had known her mother well, and I replied that I had. He seemed satisfied.

At the supper, which was very choice, nothing interested me but Cesarino. I found him sensible and well educated, and since the last time I had seen him at Florence he had grown to the point of being very well formed. I rejoiced when I learned that she would keep him with her for the rest of the Carnival. The youth's presence cast a seriousness over our supper, but his mother and Greppi enjoyed it none the less. We left Teresa and Cesarino at one o'clock in the morning, and I went to bed very well pleased with my day, for the loss of two hundred zecchini troubled me not at all.

The next day I received a note from Irene begging me to come to see her. Her father would let her go to the ball with me; she had a domino; but she needed to speak with me. I replied that she would see me in the course of the day. I had promised to dine at Carcano's, and the Marchese had sent word that he expected me at his house, whence we would go together.

I found that admirable gamester in a pretty house tastefully furnished, with two pretty women, one of whom was his mistress, and five or six Marchesi, for in Milan a nobleman cannot be less than a Marchese, just as in Vicenza they are all Counts.[20] In the high spirits which reigned at the dinner he told me that he had first heard of me seventeen years earlier in connection with an encounter I had had at the Cascina dei Pomi with a self-styled Count Celi, a cardsharper from whom I had stolen a dancer whom I had taken to Mantua.[21] I confirmed the story, and I enlivened the company with a detailed account of what had befallen me in Milan with O'Neilan,[22] and at Cesena, where I found Count Celi transformed into Count Alfani. The conversation turned to the ball which was to be given the next day, and when I said I should not go to it everyone laughed. Carcano offered to wager me that he would recognize me if I went to play at his bank. I replied that I would play no more, and he congratulated himself, saying that, though unlucky at punting, I won from him all the same; yet, he added, he would gladly lose everything he possessed to me.

He had a ring with a straw-colored stone almost as beautiful as mine. It had cost him two thousand zecchini; mine had cost me three thousand. He asked me if I would stake it against his, first having them removed from their settings and valued, before going to the opera. I replied that I should be glad to do so, each of us dealing once.

"No, I never punt."

"Make the chances equal for me. Doublets will count nothing, as will the two last cards."

"That would give you the advantage."

"If you can prove that to me I will lose a hundred zecchini. On the contrary, I wager a hundred zecchini that, despite the doublets counting for nothing, and the two last cards likewise, the chances are still in the banker's favor. I will prove it to you beyond doubt, and I will leave it to the decision of the Marchese Triulzi."

I was asked to prove it without wagering.

"The banker's advantages," I said to Carcano, "would be two. The first, which is the lesser, is that, holding the cards in your hand, you need concentrate on nothing except, as is always the case, on never making a misdeal, a concentration which leaves your mind perfectly calm and at ease, whereas the punter loses his head in chimerical speculations in his search for cards whose probability of coming out is more equal than unequal. The second advantage is that of time. The banker necessarily draws the card which is for him a second before he draws the one for the punter. So your luck is determined before your opponent's.''

No one answered me. Only Triulzi said that to establish absolute equality in a game of chance the two players would have to be equal, which is almost an impossibility. Carcano said that to him all this sort of thing was abstraction.

Leaving his house, I went to the ''Three Kings'' to see what Irene wanted to say to me, and to enjoy her presence and desire her before possessing her. When she saw me she fell on my neck, but too eagerly for me to take it for genuine; but when one values pleasure one should not lessen it by philosophizing. If Irene had struck me when she danced the furlana, why could I not have attracted her too, despite my being twenty years older than she was? Her father and mother received me as their savior. The father asked me to go out with him for a moment.

''I beg you,'' he said, ''to forgive an old man whom Fortune has ill-used an impertinent question I shall put to you. Answer me yes or no, and then we will go back. Is it true that you promised Irene a hundred zecchini if she will go to the ball with you tomorrow?''

''It is perfectly true.''

At that the poor old scoundrel took me by the head in a way which almost frightened me; but it was only to kiss me. We went in again, I laughing and he shedding tears of joy. He at once went to relieve his wife's mind, who could not believe him.

But it was Irene who made me laugh, by saying in a feeling tone that I must not suppose they thought her a liar.

"They thought," she said, "that I had misunderstood 'fifty' for a 'hundred'; they don't think I am worth more."

"You are worth a thousand, charming Irene. You stood at the door to keep me from leaving, and your courage pleased me. I want to see you in your domino, for I fear you will be criticized."

"Oh, I'll look well—you'll see!"

"Are those your shoes and your earrings? Have you no other stockings? Have you gloves?"

"I have nothing."

"Send for everything. Have the shopkeepers come here. You shall choose, and I will pay for it all."

It was Signor Rinaldi who left at once to send up a jeweler, a stocking seller, a shoemaker, and a perfumer. I spent some thirty zecchini buying her everything for which she asked and which I thought she needed.

But when I saw her mask without a border of English lace[23] I threw up my hands. Her father at once sent up a milliner, and I gave her an ell of stiffened needlepoint to be sewn around her mask in a frill. It cost me ten or twelve zecchini. Irene was beside herself; and her father and mother looked gloomy, for they thought so much money thrown away.

When I saw her dressed I found her charming. I told her to be ready the next day at the hour of the opera, for before going to the ball we would sup somewhere. When I was about to take leave of them, Rinaldi asked me where I intended to go when I left Milan.

"To Genoa," I replied, "then to Marseilles, then to Paris, then to England for a year."

"Lucky escape from the Leads!"

"I risked my life."

"You certainly deserve your good fortune."

"Do you think so? I use what fortune I have only for my pleasures."

"It shows some restraint that you do not take a mistress with you."

"She would prevent me from enjoying fifty intrigues in every city in which I stay. If I had a mistress with me she would prevent me from taking your charming Irene to the ball tomorrow."

"That is very true."

I went to the opera, where I would have played; but finding Cesarino in the parterre, I spent two delightful hours with him. He opened his heart to me, he begged me to speak to his sister to persuade her to consent to his vocation. He felt invincibly drawn to ships and the sea, and he said that if he could become a merchant his leaning might bring him a great fortune. I promised him I would speak to her.

I ate something with him, and then I went home to bed. The next morning Signorina Q.'s brother came to ask me for breakfast and to tell me that he had spoken to his sister and that she had answered that I must have been making a fool of him, since the life I led made it unthinkable that I should marry.

"I did not tell you I aspired to the honor of becoming her husband."

"You did not tell me so, and I did not tell her so; however, that was her reply."

"Honor demands that I disabuse her this very day."

"You will do well. Go at two o'clock, I am dining there, and, having something to discuss with my cousin, I will leave you alone."

The arrangement pleased me. Seeing him admire a small gold case which was on my night table, I told him that it was a trifle which I made bold to offer him and which he could accept in friendship without the least scruple. He embraced me and put it in his pocket, assuring me he would keep it until the day of his death.

Certain that I should sup with Irene, I went without dinner. The Count having gone the day before to Sant'Angelo,[24] fifteen miles from Milan, leaving the Countess alone, I could not avoid going to her room to ask her to excuse me if I could not have the honor of dining with her. She replied as sweetly as possible that I must feel under no constraint. I clearly saw all the falsity of the role she was playing; but I wanted her to believe that I was taken in by it. It was to my advantage. Prepared to pass for a fool, I told her that I was not ungrateful, and that I could assure her I would make up to her during Lent for the dissipations which prevented me from paying her more assiduous court during the Carnival which was hastening to its end. Replying with a smile that she hoped it would be so, she gave me a pinch of snuff after enjoying one herself; but it was not snuff. She said it was an excellent powder which brought on nosebleed. Sorry that I had taken it, I said with a laugh that since I did not have a headache I should not enjoy it. She replied with a laugh that one did not bleed very much and that it could only do good, and we instantly fell to sneezing together five or six times in succession; I should really have become angry if I had not seen her laugh. However, knowing the properties of sternutatives, I did not think we should bleed, but I was mistaken. She held a large silver bowl close to her head, and I saw her blood. A moment later I had to yield to her insistence that I do the same thing, for she prevented me from catching my blood in my handkerchief. After I had bled twenty or thirty drops the scene was over. Seeing her still laughing, I had to laugh too. We washed with cold water.

"Our mingled blood," she said, still laughing, "will bring an eternal friendship to birth between us."

I asked her for some of the powder, but she refused to give it to me; I asked her what it was called, and she said she did not know. On leaving her, the first thing

I did was to go to an apothecary's to inquire about the
powder, of which I had never heard, and which, but for
what had just happened to me, I should have thought a
fable; but the apothecary knew no more than I did.
However, he told me that euphorbia could sometimes
cause bleeding; but it was not a case of sometimes; the
effect must be certain and infallible, as I was more than
convinced. This little episode gave me cause for serious
thought. The lady was Spanish and must hate me. The
reader will see what was afoot.

I found the handsome officer in the drawing room off
the garden with his cousin, who was writing. Signorina
Q. was in the garden. They had already dined. On the
excuse of leaving them to write, I joined her.

"I am in despair," I said, "over a misunderstanding
which could rightly lead you to think me a tactless fool.
I have come to justify myself, Signorina."

"I guess what you have in mind; but be sure that my
brother means no harm. Indeed, we had better let him
go on believing what he does. Do you think it likely that
I could have supposed you capable of taking such a
step when we do not know each other? I thought it best
to give a matrimonial turn to a courtship on which my
very young brother might otherwise have put an unfavorable interpretation."

"I admire your quickness of mind, and I have nothing
more to say; but I am none the less obliged to your
brother for having had the kindness to let you know
that your charms have captivated me and that there is
nothing in the world I am not prepared to do to convince you of my enduring affection."

"Your declaration does not displease me; but you
would have done better not to acquaint my brother with
your feelings, and even, permit me to say, not to declare
them to me. You could have loved me, I should have
become aware of it and should have pretended not to be
so; under those circumstances, I should have been justi-

fied in putting no constraint upon myself. But as things are now, I must be on my guard. Do you not agree?"

"You transfix me, beautiful Marchesa; never in my life has anyone so thoroughly convinced me of my stupidity. But what I find amusing is that I already knew all that you have told me. You have made me lose my head; but I hope you will not be so cruel as to punish me for it."

"How could I punish you?"

"By not loving me."

"Alas! Does that depend on ourselves? We are forced to love, and then there is no escape."

Interpreting these words to my own advantage, I thought it best to talk of something else. I asked her if she was going to the ball. She answered no.

"You and your cousin will perhaps go incognito."

"We should like to, but it is impossible. There is always someone to recognize us."

"If I might have the honor of serving you, I would wager my life that no one would recognize you."

"I doubt if you would want to trouble yourself over us."

"I like your being a little skeptical. Put me to the test. If you and she can go out alone we will disguise ourselves in a way which will arouse the greatest curiosity, but to no purpose."

"We could go out with my brother and a young lady whom he loves, and we are certain he will say nothing."

"It is a delight to obey you; but it can be only for the ball on Sunday. So I will make arrangements with your brother. Tell him to come to see me, and warn him that even Barbaro must not hear a word of it. You will come to mask in a place to which I will direct you; but we will discuss that later. Now I must be off quietly, to give my instant attention to this most important business."

Sure of succeeding, and having no plan ready for a

masquerade for five persons, I put off racking my brains to a quieter moment, for just then Irene was too much on my mind.

I went home and put on my domino, then I called for her at the "Three Kings." I did not have to go upstairs; she came down immediately, and I took her to my fine apartment, where I ordered the pastry cook to give us a good supper at midnight. We had six hours before us, which the reader can imagine were well employed. We got out of bed thoroughly satisfied, and laughing because we were dying of hunger. Our supper was as choice as it was gay. Irene told me that her father had taught her to deal at faro in a way which made it impossible for her to lose. My curiosity aroused, I give her a new pack of cards, and in five or six minutes she arranges them as she had been taught to do, meanwhile talking and looking at me to keep me from seeing what she is doing. After that I give her the hundred zecchini I owed her, and I tell her to win from me as if she really had to do it. She said very sweetly that, if I always staked on only one card, she was certain always to make me lose it, and she kept her word. I admitted that if she had not told me beforehand I should have noticed nothing. I then saw what great store the old cheat Rinaldi must set by his daughter, who was a real treasure. With her air of gay innocence, timidity, and candor, she was bound to take in even seasoned sharpers.[25] She said in a mortified tone that her talent was of no use to her, because she never found herself in any company but that of beggars; and then, in a feeling tone, at which I could not help laughing, that she loved me so dearly that, if I would take her with me, she would leave her parents to shift for themselves and would win me great sums. She said she was also very skillful at punting when she was not playing against sharpers; whereupon I told her to stake the hundred ducati I had given her at Carcano's bank, to which I would take her.

"You are to stake twenty zecchini on your card," I
said, "and, if you win on it, you will stake *paroli* and
sept et le va, and you will stop playing as soon as you
get it. If three second cards in succession won't come
out for you, you will have lost the hundred ducati; but
I will reimburse you."

At that she threw herself on my neck and asked if she
should give me half if she won, and I thought she would
eat me up with kisses when I said it would be all hers.

We left at once in sedan chairs, and we had no sooner
arrived at the ball, which had not yet begun, than we
went to the gaming room. Carcano, who was doing nothing, at once sent for a pack of cards, pretending not to
recognize me. I saw him smile when he saw that the
pretty masker who was with me was going to play in
my stead. Irene made a deep curtsy when he offered
her the place beside him. She put her hundred zecchini
in front of her, and she began by winning a hundred and
twenty, because, instead of staking *sept et le va,* she
staked *paix de paroli.* Her method pleased me, and I let
her go on playing. At the next deal she lost three cards
in succession, then she won another *paix de paroli.* After
that she lost two more cards, and, after gathering up
her coins, she curtsied to the banker, and we left. But
no sooner were we out of the room than I turned around
to discover the source of heart-rending sobs. I saw the
weeping masker moving away. Irene whispered to me
that she was sure it was her father, who had watched her
play and was weeping for joy. She had two hundred and
forty zecchini in her pocket, and she took them home to
him after amusing herself for three hours. I danced
only one minuet with her. Amorous enjoyment and the
supper had so tired me that I was not capable of more.
Waiting while Irene danced, I sat down in a corner and
fell asleep. I was astonished, on waking, to see that Irene
was looking for me everywhere. I had slept for three
hours. I escorted her to the "Three Kings," where I

Carnival Scene

Matching Knife, Fork, and Spoon,
ca. 1750

restored her to her father and mother. The poor man, beside himself with joy when his daughter gave him the money she had won, told me to wish him a good journey, for he would leave at daybreak. I could not object, and I did not want to, and perhaps he expected the contrary. But at his announcement Irene went into a fury; she told him she wanted to stay with me, and reproached him with always snatching her away as soon as she made a friend. When she saw that I was not taking her side against her father, she wept, then she kissed me, and I left them. The reader will see where I met them again. I went home to bed.

The next morning at eight o'clock I saw in my room the handsome Lieutenant, who, after saying that his sister had told him about the masquerade which I had promised to arrange, said that he had a great secret to confide to me.

"One of the most agreeable noblemen in this city," he said, "my intimate friend, who loves my cousin, and who has more cause to be discreet than all the rest of us, is to be of the party if you have no objection. My sister and my cousin will be delighted if you consent."

"How can you possibly doubt my consent? I have thought about five; now I will think about six. Sunday at nightfall you shall be where I will tell you, we will sup, we will mask, and we will go to the ball. You and I will meet at your sister's tomorrow at five o'clock. Just give me your mistress's measurements and those of your charming cousin's lover."

"My dear mistress is two inches shorter than my sister and my cousin, and she is slender; and my friend is of exactly your build, so that I take you for him every time I see you from behind."

"That will do. Leave everything to me, and now go, for I am curious to know what the Capuchin who is waiting outside wants of me."

I had told Clairmont to give him alms; but he said

he needed to speak to me privately. I could not imagine what a Capuchin could have to say to me privately. I had him shown in, and I shut my door.

"Signore," he said, "pay attention to what I shall tell you, and profit by it. Beware of scorning my words, for you might pay for your scorn with your life. You would repent of it, but your repentance would come too late. After hearing me out, do what I shall have advised you to do, and do not ask me the least question, for I shall not answer you. What will make it impossible for me to answer you is a duty which is laid upon me, and which every Christian must respect. It is the inviolable seal of confession. Consider that my good faith and my words cannot be suspect, since no base interest brings me into your presence. A powerful inspiration alone obliges me to speak to you as I do. It can only be your guardian angel, who, unable to speak to you himself, uses me as the instrument to preserve your life. God in his goodness will not abandon you. Tell me if you feel touched and if I may give you the salutary advice which is in my heart."

"Never doubt it, Reverend Father, speak, give me your advice; your words have not only touched me but filled me with a kind of terror. I promise you I will follow your advice, if acting upon it proves to be contrary neither to my honor nor to the light of my reason."

"Very good. Charity will also prevent you, whatever be the outcome of the matter of which you will acquire knowledge, from compromising me. You will mention me to no one, or say either that you know me or do not know me."

"I promise. Speak, I beg you."

"Before noon today go alone to the Piazza ———— and to such-and-such a house, go up to the third floor, and ring at a door which you will see to your left. Tell the person who will open it to you that you wish to speak to Signora . . . . You will be taken to her room without any difficulty; I am sure that you will not be asked to give your name. When you are in the woman's presence ask her gently to hear you out and to keep what you will confide to her a secret. As you say this, gain her confidence by putting one or two zecchini into her hand. She is poor, and I am sure that your generosity will instantly win you her good will. She will lock her door and will of course tell you to speak. You will then tell her gravely that you will not leave her room until she gives you the little bottle which a maidservant must have delivered to her at nightfall together with a certain note. Remain firm if she resists, make no noise, do not let her leave the room, prevent her from calling anyone, and win her over completely by telling her that you are ready to give her twice the sum of money she will lose by giving you the bottle *and everything that goes with it*. Remember that. *Everything that goes with it*. She will do whatever you want. The amount it will cost you will not be great; but even if it were, your life should be dearer to you than all the gold of Peru. I cannot tell you more. Before I leave, tell me if I may hope that you will go.''

''I will be guided by the inspiration of the same angel who sent you here.''

After he left I was in no mood to laugh. Reason told me to dismiss all this rigmarole and to go nowhere, and a residue of superstition which was always part of my nature prevented me from listening to reason. In addition, the Capuchin had impressed me favorably. He looked honest and worthy of respect. He had convinced me, and I thought I should be a fool if I went against my conviction. At last I suddenly make up my mind, I take the slip of paper on which I had written the names he had given me, I put a pair of infallible pistols in my pocket, and I go to the place, telling Clairmont to wait for me at the Piazza to which I was to go. This was by way of precaution.

Everything happened as the Capuchin had told me it
would. The ugly old woman plucked up courage at the
sight of the two zecchini, and bolted her door. She said
with a laugh that she knew I was in love, and that it
was my own fault if I was not successful; but that she
would give me the means. At these words I at once saw
that I was dealing with a witch. La Bontemps[26] in Paris
had talked to me in the same strain. But upon my telling
her I would not leave her room without the bottle and
everything that went with it, her countenance became
horrible, and she trembled when, holding a pocket knife
in my hand, I prevented her from rising. When I finally
said that I would give her twice the money she would
lose by giving me what I wanted, I saw her become calm
and at ease. She said she would lose six zecchini, but
that I would be glad to give her twelve when I saw
myself, for she had just recognized me. I ask her who
I am, and she astonishes me by telling me my name.
I then feel called upon to take twelve zecchini from my
purse, and when she sees them the old woman is softened
to tears. She assures me that she would not have killed
me, but that she would certainly have made me in love
and unhappy.

"Explain yourself."

"Follow me."

I go with her into a closet in which, in utter astonishment, I see a thousand things whose use it is beyond
common sense to explain. Vials, stones, metals, minerals,
small nails, spikes, tongs, furnaces, coals, misshapen
statues, and I know not what.

"There," she said, "is your bottle."

"What is in it?"

"Your blood mixed with the Countess's, as you can
read in this note."

It was then that I understood what was afoot, and I
am amazed today that I did not burst out laughing.

Instead, my hair stood on end, and I was suddenly bathed in cold sweat.

"What would you have done with this blood?"

"I would have applied it to you."

"What do you mean by 'applied'? How? I do not understand you."

"You shall see."

I was aghast; but instantly the scene changed. The witch opened a box a yard long, and I see a wax statue lying on its back and stark naked; I read my name on it, and, though they are crudely executed, I recognize my features, I see my cross on a ribbon around the idol's neck. The image was like a monstrous Priapus[27] in the parts which are characteristic of that god. The sight is too comical; I succumb to hysterical laughter and sink into a chair until I have recovered my breath.

"You laugh?" said the sorceress. "Woe to you if I had bathed you in those bloods according to my lore! And woe and again woe if afterward I had put the portrait of yourself which you see into the fire."

"Is that all?"

"Yes."

"All this is mine, here are your twelve zecchini. Now light me a fire, for I am going to melt this statue; and as for the blood, permit me to throw it out of the window."

It was accomplished instantly.

The old woman, who was afraid that I would take everything with me, said that I was as good as an angel and, kissing my hand, begged me to forgive her and to tell no one what had taken place between us. I swore to her that the Countess herself should never hear a word of it. What surprised me was that the impenitent witch said that if I would promise her another twelve zecchini[28] she would make the Countess madly in love. I declined, and I left her, advising her to give up her accursed trade, which justly condemned her to be burned alive.

In the Piazza I saw Clairmont and told him to go home. Despite all the money the foul business had cost me, I was not sorry to have learned the whole story and to have followed the advice of the good Capuchin, who honestly believed that I was done for. He must have learned the thing in confession from the person who had taken the blood to the witch. Such are the miracles which auricular confession very often performs in the Roman Catholic religion.

Thoroughly determined never to let the Countess know that I had discovered her horrible crime, I prepared to take the opposite course of treating her in a manner calculated to soothe her and make her forget the barbarous injury I had done her. It was for me to thank Providence that she believed in witchcraft, for otherwise she would have hired assassins, who would have avenged her to the full.

As soon as I got home I took the handsomer of two mantles I had and went to make her a present of it, kissing her hand. It was lined with ermine. Accepting it, she asked me most graciously what the occasion for my making her so fine a present might be. I replied that I had dreamed she was so angry with me that she had bargained with cutthroats to murder me. She blushed and replied that she had not gone mad. I left her when I saw that she was sunk in dark thought. Nevertheless, whether because she decided to forget everything, or because she found no way to avenge herself, I had no cause to complain of her during all the rest of the time I spent in Milan. The Count had come back from his estate. He said that we really must make a visit there at the beginning of Lent. I promised him I would go. The Countess said she would stay in Milan. I went to dress and to think about my masquerade.

CHAPTER VIII

Unique masquerade. My amour with the beautiful Marchesa Q. . . . The deserted girl from Marseilles; I become her rescuer. My departure for Sant'Angelo.

MY PLAN requiring trustworthy accomplices, I thought of two people on whom I could unhesitatingly rely. They were Zenobia's husband, for I needed a tailor, and Zenobia herself, who must be prepared to do whatever might be necessary for the three young ladies whom I wanted to disguise. So, setting out on foot, I went to see the tailor, whom I forced to drop all his work and take me to the most well-stocked secondhand-clothes dealer in Milan. The dealer asked me if the clothes I wanted were to be old or brand-new.

"You have new ones?"

"Yes, Signore, for both men and women."

"First find me a handsome new velvet coat for myself which no one has seen, without silver or gold, and perfectly plain."

He shows me several, and I choose a blue coat lined with white satin. He tells me the price of it, the tailor haggles, and we come to terms; I set it aside, making

him write down the price. It was the coat I intended for
the cousin's lover.

"Find me another handsome coat for a well-built man
three inches shorter than I am."

"Here is a sulphur-yellow one, of short-nap velvet,
lined with satin of the same color."

"I will keep it. Put it there, and write down the
price."

It was the coat which I intended for the officer.

"Find me two women's dresses with petticoats and
brand-new. The ladies are very well built and six inches
shorter than I am."

"Here are two winter ones in different styles, but
both charming."

"I like them. Name the price and set them aside."

One of the dresses was of flame-colored satin, the other
of lilac floss silk. The cousins were of the same height.
I then ask him for a dress for the officer's mistress, two
inches shorter than the other two, and he gives me a
charming striped one. I ask him for fine shirts and shifts,
and he shows me some of batiste. I buy two shirts and
three shifts, trimmed with beautiful lace. I also buy
batiste handkerchiefs and several half-ells of velvet of
different colors, of satin, and of silk, all in small pieces.
I pay about two hundred gold ducati for all his wares;
but on condition that if it becomes known that I bought
them from him, and it can be proven that the information came from him, he shall give me back all my money
and take his merchandise, no matter in what condition
it may be. He agrees to the stipulation, the tailor takes
the lot and accompanies me with it to the furnished
apartment I had rented. After threatening him with
death if he tells anyone a word of what I am about to
have him do, I lock myself into a room with him, I put
the men's clothes on a table, I take a knife from my
pocket, I begin cutting holes in them and then putting
my fingers in and tearing them two or three inches in

one place, two or three inches in another—breeches, waistcoats, coats, linings—meanwhile having all I can do to keep from laughing at the tailor, who thought I had gone mad and expected me to cut his throat.

After giving the two coats sixty wounds of this sort, I placed before the tailor all the half-ells and pieces of velvet and silk of twenty different qualities which I had bought:

"It is your part," I said, "to sharpen your fine wits and mend these clothes, patching the ripped places as badly as possible and using the most ill-matching materials you can wherever you think it best to put them. You see that you have much work to do. I will have food brought to you in another room, and you shall not leave here until your work is finished. I am going to fetch your wife; she will have work too, and she will spend the night with you."

"Are you going to rip the three beautiful dresses to pieces too?"

"Certainly."

"It is murder. My wife will weep."

Before going to fetch Zenobia I bought five pairs of pearl silk stockings, men's and women's gloves, two hats of the finest beaver, caricature masks for men, and three women's masks with beautiful natural faces but serious-looking. I also bought some china plates. I put all this into a sedan chair, into which I handed Zenobia and took her to the pastry cook's.

I found her husband busy choosing the pieces to make patches. Zenobia was aghast, but when she saw me treat the women's dresses as I had treated the men's coats she took fright in good earnest. Her husband restored her courage, and when she saw my intention she understood that I might be in my right mind in terms of the fantastic idea which had come to me. Zenobia even carried my idea further when I told her to put the dresses in such a state that the ladies who would wear them

would inspire love even more than they would do if they
had suffered no injury.

Zenobia tore them at the bosom, at the shoulders, and
she wreaked havoc on the petticoats to the point that
the shift, together with more than half the leg, would
be visible somewhere. I left them to labor, having them
served excellent meals and going to look at their work
three or four times a day, always leaving better satisfied.
The work was not finished until Saturday after dinner.
I dismissed the tailor, giving him six zecchini; but I
keep Zenobia, for the young ladies would need her. I
took care to put in one room powder, pomades and
combs, and whatever well-brought-up young ladies could
wish for. I also left thread and linen ribbons.

The next day at five o'clock I found play well under
way; and, not seeing the young ladies, I went to their
aunt's room, where I found them. They said they were
not playing because Signor Barbaro was too lucky.

"But my brother is winning," said Signorina Q. . . .

The aunt having gone out, they asked me if the Lieutenant had told me that there would be another girl too,
and I assured them that they would be pleased, but not
more than I. I said that I needed to speak to the officer
the next morning.

"Tell us how we shall be disguised."

"In accordance with the orders you gave me."

"I said nothing about it."

"Did you not say that you wanted to be sure that
none of you would be recognized? You will not be recognized."

"But how dressed?"

"In a way to surprise, to arouse the greatest curiosity,
to have followers from the beginning to the end of the
ball. But do not ask me how, for I want to enjoy the
beauty of your surprise. Bolts from the blue are my
passion. You shall learn nothing until after supper."

"You want us to sup?"

"If such is your pleasure. I am a great eater, and I hope you will not be cruel enough to leave me to eat alone."

"No, of course not, since you wish it. We will even eat sparingly at dinner. I am only sorry that you are being put to expense for us."

"It is nothing. When I leave Milan I shall congratulate myself on having enjoyed a pleasure in the company of the two most charming young ladies to be seen in the city." [1]

"How is luck treating you?"

"Carcano wins two hundred zecchini from me every day."

"And you win two thousand from him in one."

"Nevertheless, I am behind."

"You will break his bank on Sunday."

"Would you like me to offer you that spectacle?"

"I should be very glad to see it. My brother told me you do not want to be with us."

"No, for I should be recognized. However, he told me that the person who will be with you resembles me."

"Exactly, except for his complexion, for he is fair."

"He is very lucky. Light wins over dark."

"Not always," said her sister. "You might at least tell us if you are having us dress as men."

"Fie, fie! I never thought of it. I cannot bear a pretty girl dressed as a man."

"That is strange. Tell us why."

"Gladly. If a girl dressed as a man really seems to be a man she disgusts me, for I see that she lacks the charming beauty which is proper to a woman, whose form should be different from a well-built man's."

"And if the girl dressed as a man shows you that she has the beauties which you demand in a beautiful girl?"

"Then I am sorry that she robs me of an illusion, for I like to look only at the face and to imagine the rest."

"But the imagination often deceives."

"I agree. I always fall in love with the face, prepared to forgive all the rest if I am ever granted the favor of seeing it. You laugh."

"I am laughing at the vigor with which you argue."

"Would you like to be dressed as a man?"

"Ah-ha! I expected you would ask us that. After all you have said we can no longer answer you."

After paying my court to them for a good two hours, I left them and went to the pastry cook's, then to the opera, then to lose my money, then to sup with the Countess, who had become gracious, but who, seeing that I did not lie in wait to enter her bedroom, began to relapse into her ill-humor. On Saturday morning I told the officer that I laid only one task on him, but that it must be carried out to the letter and that I must be sure of it beforehand.

"You must, Signore, have a carriage and four horses in the courtyard, which, as soon as all five of you have got into it, will take you at full gallop out one of the gates of Milan, bring you back by another, and take you to the door of the house where you will find me and where you will undress to return home without anyone's seeing you. The carriage and four must leave as soon as you have left it. You will go home by sedan chair. I am sure you will create such an effect at the ball that everyone will want to find out who you are at all costs."

"I give you my word that the instructions you have given me will be faithfully carried out. The person who will see to it is my friend the Marchese F . . . , who is impatient to make your acquaintance."

"Then I will expect you tomorrow at seven o'clock at the house of which you know. You shall all come by sedan chair, and all go to the ball by sedan chair. The carriage and four will be used only for you to make your escape. The thing you must see to is that the coachman is not known; you will not need any servant."

I gave him the key to a box, to which they could go for a rest whenever they saw fit.

For my part, I decided to dress as Pierrot.[2] There is no costume which is a more perfect disguise, for it hides the entire person, not letting even the color of the skin be seen anywhere. The reader may remember what happened to me ten years earlier disguised as Pierrot.[3] The tailor found me a costume, which I had him put with the others, and, provided with a thousand zecchini in two purses, I arrived at the pastry cook's at half past five o'clock, where I found the table laid for supper as soon as the company should arrive. I shut Zenobia up in the room which contained everything necessary for the masquerade.

At exactly seven o'clock I saw the company, and I was delighted to make the acquaintance of the Marchese F . . . , whom I found accomplished. He was handsome, young, and rich, and very much in love with the cousin, whose hand he kissed most respectfully. The Lieutenant's mistress was a jewel; she was mad about him. As they knew that I did not want to show them their disguises until after supper, we immediately sat down at table, and we supped deliciously, for everything was excellent. The Marchese did not know that such a caterer existed. When we were ready to rise I treated them to a little preamble:

"Your masquerade," I said, "for I do not wish to be with you, will represent five beggars in rags, two men and three women. You will each hold a plate as if asking for charity, and, thus clad, you will walk about the ball together. Come with me into this room, and you shall see your beggar's rags."

My pleasure was intense when I saw the disgust with which all five of them received my announcement. They follow me; I open the door of the room, and they see

the beautiful Zenobia, who drops them a curtsy, standing in front of the table on which were the magnificent
dresses reduced to tatters.

"There," I said to the two cousins, "are your dresses;
and there, Signorina, is yours, a little shorter. There are
your shifts, your handkerchiefs, your stockings, and
there is a toilet table at which, with your permission,
your most humble servant there will dress your hair in
true beggar-maid fashion. There are your masks, though
their faces are not as beautiful as yours, and there are
three plates into which the alms for which you beg will
be put; these garters which cost only a soldo will prove
your poverty if anyone chances to see the upper part of
your legs, and these stockings with their holes will show
that you have not a soldo to buy silk to mend them with.
These cords will serve you for buckles, and we will make
holes in your shoes, the backs of which will be trodden
under your heels. These gloves will be in holes too, and
as soon as you have changed shifts the lace around the
neck will be torn here and there."

The three young ladies at once saw the richness of
their disguise. They saw the beauty of the dresses which
had been reduced to rags, and they did not dare to say,
"What a pity!"

"Come and see the clothes of your beggar escorts.
Here they are; I forgot to make holes in the hats. What
do you think of it all? And now, Signorine, close your
door, for you have to change shifts. Let us get dressed
too."

The Marchese F . . . was beside himself at the thought
of the effect the masquerade was bound to produce, for
no one could have devised anything more lavish. It was
impossible not to see that the splendid brand-new garments had been torn on purpose and then patched so
comically that they were a delight. In a half hour we
were dressed. The stockings in holes, the shoes deliberately slashed, the batiste shirts, with their fine lace cuffs,

deliberately torn, the uncombed hair, the masks expressing desperation, and the plates deliberately cracked
around the edges, all together composed the most striking
picture. As for me, it was agreed that my Pierrot costume made me unrecognizable. The young ladies took
longer dressing because of their hair. It hung down their
backs as far as it could go; Signorina Q . . .'s reached
halfway down her legs. They finally opened the door,
and we saw all that a charming girl can display to attract and yet remain within the bounds of decency. I
admired Zenobia's skill in dressing them. The torn petticoats showed their legs, whose whiteness appeared
through the big holes in their stockings; their shifts,
purposely torn under imperfectly patched rents in their
dresses, revealed bits of their beautiful breasts. But the
length to which her hair hung down gave the prize to
Signorina Q. . . .

I showed them how they should walk, how to hold
their heads to arouse pity, and how to hold their fine
handkerchiefs so that the holes in them would prove
their poverty. Beside themselves with delight, they could
not wait to be at the ball; but I wanted to go first in
order to enjoy the pleasure of watching their entrance.
I quickly put on my Pierrot mask, after telling Zenobia
to go to bed, since we should not be back until daybreak.

I enter the ball, and since there are more than a score
of Pierrots, no one looks at me. Five minutes later I see
everyone hurrying to see some arriving maskers, and I
find a place where I am sure I shall see them well. The
Marchese was between the two cousins. Their slow, piti-
able walk awoke interest. Signorina Q . . . , with her
dress of flame-colored satin torn to rags and her hair
which cloaked her, struck the company silent. It was not
until a quarter of an hour later that people began talking again. "What a masquerade! what a masquerade!
Who are they? who are they? I have no idea. I'll find
out." What filled my cup of joy was their bearing.

The orchestra strikes up. Three maskers in dominoes come to ask my beggar maids to dance a minuet; but they decline, showing them their torn shoes. The touch pleased me greatly. After following them about the ball for more than an hour, rejoicing at the success of my masquerade and assured that the general curiosity would only increase, I went to see Carcano, where the play was high. A masker in a *bautta* and cloak in the Venetian fashion punted on a single card, staking fifty zecchini *paroli* and *paix de paroli,* as I had been doing, and lost three hundred; the masker was of my build, and everyone said he was I. Carcano said no. I stake three or four zecchini on a card to have the right to remain, and at the next deal the Venetian masker puts fifty zecchini on one card, gets the *paroli* and the *paix,* and recovers all the gold he had lost, which was there in six piles.

At the deal after that he has the same good luck, he collects his money and goes. The chair being left empty, I take it, and I hear a lady name me and say that I am in the ballroom dressed as a beggar, with four other maskers whom no one knows.

"How as a beggar?" Carcano asks.

"Like beggars, all in rags and tatters, and nevertheless magnificent and at the same time comical. All five of them are asking for alms."

"They ought to be turned out."

I begin putting zecchini on a card chosen at random, and I lose five or six cards in succession; in less than an hour I lose five hundred zecchini. Carcano studied me, everyone said it was not I because I was at the ball dressed as a beggar. In three lucky deals I win all that I had lost, and I go on with the whole pile of gold before me. I stake a good handful of zecchini; I win the card, I go *paroli,* I win, I go *paix,* and there I stop, for the bank is at its last gasp. He pays me, and he sends to the cashier for a thousand zecchini; while he shuffles, I hear voices: "Here come the beggars, here come the beggars." They stand at Carcano's bank, and he looks at the Marchese F . . . and asks him for a pinch of snuff. I then admired a fine bit of characterization which I had not foreseen. The Marchese takes from his pocket a paper in which there are two coppers' worth of snuff, gives him a pinch, and everyone laughs. Signorina Q . . . holds out her plate asking him for alms; he tells her that with such beautiful hair she rouses no pity in him; but that if she wants to stake it on a card he will rate it at a thousand zecchini. Signorina Q . . . holds out her plate to me, I drop as many zecchini as I can gather up with the tips of my fingers into it, and I do the same for the two others.

"Pierrot," said Carcano, "likes beggar maids."

They left. Triulzi said to Carcano that the beggar in the straw-colored coat was certainly I.

"I recognized him immediately," said Carcano, "but who are the women?"

"We'll find out."

"The masquerade is the most expensive anyone could devise, for all the clothes are new."

While waiting for the money, he shuffled. The thousand zecchini arrive. I punt at a hundred, and at the second deal I win everything. He asks me if I want to go on playing, I shake my head, and I show him in pantomime that I will take a note from the cashier. He comes with his scales, and, wanting to go and dance, I give him all the gold I have except some fifty zecchini; he writes a receipt, which Carcano signs, for twenty-nine pounds and some ounces of gold, which came to more than two thousand four hundred zecchini. I get up and, walking lopsidedly after the fashion of Pierrot, I go to the parterre, then to my box in the third tier, where my beggars were, to dry myself, for I was dripping with sweat. I knock, making them understand that it is I, and we fall delightedly to talking of all our adventures. We had all unmasked, but we had nothing to fear, for the boxes on either side of ours were empty. The three beggar maids talk of returning me the alms I had given them; but I replied in such a way that they did not insist. The Marchese F . . . said that he had been taken for me, and that the mistake might lead to something being guessed; I told him that toward the end of the ball I would unmask.

The beggar maids told me that they had their pockets full of sweetmeats, that all the ladies left their boxes to go and look at them, and that they all said that no one could devise a more magnificent masquerade.

"Then you have enjoyed yourselves?"

"Extremely. But we will go down."

"I too, for I want to dance; and as Pierrot I am sure to raise a laugh."

"Do you know how much you gave us in alms?"

"I have no way of knowing exactly; but I am sure that I treated the three of you alike."

"That is true, but it is astonishing."

"I have made the experiment countless times in my life. When someone wins a *paroli* of ten zecchini from me, I put out three fingers; and I am sure to gather up thirty zecchini. I would wager that I gave each of you thirty-eight or forty zecchini."

"Forty, but it's astonishing. We shall remember this masquerade."

"I would wager," said the Marchese, "that no one will imitate us."

"But we ourselves," said the cousin, "wouldn't dare do it a second time."

We resumed our masks, and I preceded them. After making some impertinent exchanges with the Harlequins and Harlequinesses, I saw Teresa[4] in a domino, and, in the most awkward way possible, invited her for the contradance.

"You are," she said, "the Pierrot who broke the bank."

I assented in pantomime. I danced like a demon; I seemed always on the verge of falling, and I always kept my feet.

The contradance over, I escorted her to her box, where Greppi was alone, and she let me go in. They were astonished when I took off my mask, for they thought I was with the beggar maids. I gave Signor Greppi the note to bearer, for which he at once gave me a receipt, and I went down again with my face unmasked, which confounded all the busybodies who thought the Marchese F . . . was I.

Toward the end I left, taking a sedan chair as far as the Piazza Cordusio;[5] then, going through a house, I took another, which carried me to the pastry cook's, where I found Zenobia in bed; she told me she was sure I would come back before the others did. It was the first time I really had her in my arms. I remained there until the trot of four horses told me that my beggars were returning. Zenobia put on her clothes again in a flash. The Marchese and the Lieutenant went to undress, and, when I told the three beggar maids that I might stay because they did not have to change their shifts and stockings, they made no objection. I confined my attention to Signorina Q . . . , admiring all her beauties, of which she saw fit not to be stingy. After dressing her hair Zenobia left to do the same service for the others, whereupon she let me help her put on her dress, allowing my eyes to enjoy the advantage of a great rent in her chemise over her bosom.

"What will you do with your shift, Signorina?"

"It's childish, but we've decided to keep all our things as reminders. With your permission, my brother will see to our receiving whatever we leave here. We are going to bed. Will you come to us this evening?"

"If I were prudent I should shun your presence."

"And if I were really prudent I should not urge you to come."

"What a reply! You shall certainly see me. Dare I ask you for a kiss?"

"Two."

Her brother and the Marchese F . . . left. Two sedan chairs which I had had brought to the door carried the cousins home, and two others for which I sent afterward left with the Lieutenant and his mistress, and the Marchese, left alone with me, said most politely that he wanted to pay me for half of what the masquerade had cost me.

"I foresaw that you would humiliate me."

"I have no such intention, and I will not insist; but you must see that now it is I who am humiliated."

"No, for I count on your intelligence. You see that money costs me nothing. I give you my word of honor that I will let you pay my share in all the diversions at which we may happen to be together during the rest of the Carnival. We will sup here whenever you please; I am at home here. You shall choose the guests, and I will let you pay the bill."

"Excellent. The arrangement is to my taste. Let us be good friends, and I leave you with this charming chambermaid, whose being in Milan unknown to anyone but you I am at an utter loss to understand."

"She is a townswoman, who knows how to keep a secret. Is that not so, Signora?"

"I will die before I will tell anyone that the Signore is the Marchese F. . . ."

"Well spoken. Now see to it that you never break your word. Here is a trifle to remember me by."

He gave her a pretty ring, which she readily accepted, and he left. It was a small rose-cut stone which might be worth fifty zecchini. She put me to bed, and an hour later I sent her off with twenty-four zecchini. I slept until two o'clock, I dined well, I went home to dress, then I went to see La Q . . . , whom, to judge from what she had said to me, I need not expect to find very prudent. Everyone else was playing; she, leaning against a window absorbed in reading, did not notice my arrival. She put the book in her pocket as soon as she saw me and blushed fiery red.

"Oh, I am not indiscreet. I will not tell anyone that I caught you reading a prayer book."

"Pray do not. My reputation would be ruined if people knew that I am devout."

"Have you heard talk of our masquerade? Do people say who the maskers were?"

"No one talks of anything else; and people are sorry for us because we were not at the ball. All hope of finding out who the maskers were is gone, for it is known that a strange carriage, with four horses which went like the wind, conveyed them to the first post, where God knows what road they took. My hair is declared to have been false, which tempts me to prove the contrary; everyone says, too, that you must know them, for otherwise you would not have given them handfuls of zecchini. What is true is that we enjoyed ourselves thoroughly. If you carry out all the tasks that are laid on you so well, you are one in a thousand."

"But it is only from you that I could have accepted such a task."

"Today from me, and tomorrow from some other woman."

"Yes, I see; you must think I am inconstant; but I swear to you that if you found me worthy of your heart your image in mine would never be effaced."

"I am sure you have said that to a thousand girls, and that you scorned them after they had found you worthy of their hearts."

"Oh, I beg of you—do not use the word 'scorn,' or you make me a monster. Beauty captivates me, I aspire to enjoy it. So you see it is impossible that I should scorn a beauty who has given herself to me only for love; I should have to begin by scorning myself. You are beautiful, and I adore you, but you are very much mistaken if you think I could be content to possess you only because of your kindness."

"You want my heart."

"Exactly. It is my only object."

"To make me wretched in two weeks."

"To love you until death. To subscribe to all your commands."

"Would you settle in Milan?"

"Have no doubt of it, if you would make me happy upon that condition."

"The amusing thing is that you deceive me without knowing it, if it is true that you love me."

"Deceiving someone without knowing it is something new for me. If I do not know it, I am innocent."

"But you deceive me none the less if I believe you, for it will not be in your power to love me when you love me no longer."

"It is among possible things, but I reject the poisonous idea. I prefer to believe myself in love with you for ever and ever. Ever since I first met you not a girl in Milan has struck me as pretty."

"Not even the charming one who waited on us, and whom you may have had in your arms until this moment?"

"What are you saying, divine Marchesa! She is the wife of the tailor who worked on your clothes; she went away a half hour after you did, and her husband would not have left her in my house if he had not seen that I needed her to wait on three ladies."

"She is as pretty as a Cupid. Is it possible that you do not love her?"

"How can one love a person whom one knows that a dwarf enjoys whenever he sees fit? The only pleasure the young woman gave me this morning was when she talked to me of you."

"Of me?"

"Will you forgive me if I confess that, being curious, I asked her which of the three girls she must have seen without their shifts was the most beautiful?"

"A libertine's question. Well, what was her answer?"

"That the one with the long chestnut hair was matchlessly beautiful."

"I don't believe a word of it, for I have learned to change my shift modestly, she cannot have seen anything but what even a man might have seen, she was trying to play up to your indiscreet curiosity; if I had such a chambermaid I would turn her out of the house."

"You are angry."

"No."

"Say no as much as you please; I saw your soul in your little outburst. I am in despair that I told you such a thing."

"Oh, it is of no consequence. But I know that men ask chambermaids such questions, and that they answer just as your beauty did, perhaps trying to make you curious about her."

"How could she think she was playing up to me by praising you above the two others, when she did not know you were the one I preferred?"

"If she didn't know it, I am wrong; but she lied none the less."

"She may have made it up; but I do not believe she lied. You laugh, and you enchant me."

"I laugh because I like letting you believe whatever you please. I want to ask you for a favor. Here are two zecchini. Put them on an *ambo*⁶ in the lottery, and give me the ticket when you come to see me, or send it to me. No one is to know about it."

"You shall have it tomorrow. Why do you tell me to send it?"

"Because you may find my company boring."

"Do I seem to? I am very unfortunate. What are your numbers?"

"Three and forty. It was you who gave them to me. Three fingers three times, and each time forty zecchini. I am superstitious. It seems to me you have come to Milan to bring me good fortune."

"Those words from you fill me with joy. You have a little the look of a witch; but at least don't take it into your head, if you don't win the *ambo,* to draw the conclusion that I do not love you, for that would be a monstrous sophism."

"I do not reason as badly as that."

"Do you believe that I love you?"

"Yes."

"May I tell you so a hundred times?"

"Yes."

"And prove it to you in all ways?"

"As for that, I want to know in advance what they are, for those which you might think the most efficacious I might consider perfectly useless."

"I foresee that you will make me languish for a long time."

"As long as I can."

"And when the time comes that you cannot?"

"I will surrender. Does that satisfy you?"

"Yes. But I shall use all my powers to wear you out."

"Do so. Your efforts will please me."

"Will you help me to succeed?"

"Even that."

"Ah, charming Marchesa, you need only speak to make a man happy. I leave your presence all on fire and really happy, not in imagination but really."

I went to the theater, and at Carcano's bank I saw the masker who had won the three hundred zecchini from him the previous evening; he was playing with very bad luck. He was behind by more than two thousand zecchini in counters, and in less than an hour he increased it to four thousand, whereupon Carcano laid down the cards, saying it was enough. He rose, and the masker left. He was a certain Spinola,[7] from Genoa.

"Now tell me," I said, "if I would not have won a wager against you. Admit that you would not have recognized me as Pierrot."

"It is true. But it happened that I had before me the beggar-masker whom I took to be you. You know who he is."

"Absolutely not."

"Everyone says they are all Venetians and that when they left here they went to Bergamo."

I went to sup with the Countess A. B., her husband, and Triulzi, who all believed the same story. Triulzi told me that all the wiseacres had condemned me when I gave the maskers the handfuls of zecchini. I retorted that my action was intended to win the approval of none but fools.

The next day I played the *ambo,* and after dinner I took the superstitious Marchesa the ticket. I was as much in love with her as possible, because I thought she was in love. Her cousin was not playing, so I spent three hours conversing with them on nothing but amorous subjects, holding my own against the pair of cousins, whose beauty and intelligence were of the rarest. I realized, when I left them, that if chance had first put me in the other's company I should have fallen as much in love with her.

We were nearing the end of the Carnival, which in Milan lasts four days longer than in all Christendom.[8] There were three more balls. I played, I lost two or three hundred zecchini each time, and everyone admired my prudence more than my luck. I called on the cousins every day, and every day I hoped for more, though I never obtained anything. She gave me no more than a few kisses, I had never asked her for a meeting. Only three days before the ball I asked her if I might hope to

have her to supper in the same company. She said that
her brother would come to see me the next morning to
tell me what had been arranged. So the Lieutenant arrived, just as I was rejoicing to see the three and the
forty among the five numbers of the drawing. I did not
mention it to him, for his sister had forbidden it.

"The Marchese F . . . ," he said, "invites you to
supper at your place on the night of the ball, with the
same company; but needing to have the masking costumes got ready, and not wanting you to know what
they will be, he asks you to lend him your apartment
and, so that other people will not be let into the secret,
he asks you to engage the same chambermaid you had
before."

"Gladly, gladly."

"Arrange to have her there today about three o'clock,
and let the pastry cook know that you have given him
full powers."

I saw that my dear Marchese F . . . wanted to have
a taste of Zenobia, and I was not displeased. *Fovet et
Favet* ("He forwards and fosters")[9] was my favorite
maxim, and thanks to my kindly nature it still is so
and will be until I die. I went at once to inform the
pastry cook, and I stopped in at the tailor's, who did
not take it at all amiss when I said I had no need of
him and asked him only for my gossip his wife. He said
that at three o'clock he would give her leave for three
days.

In the afternoon I found La Q . . . beside herself
with joy. The winning *ambo* would bring her five hundred zecchini.

"What delights me," she said, "is not the money,
though I am not rich, but the beauty of the idea which
came to me and which I adopted; it is the pleasure I feel
at the thought that this piece of luck comes to me from
you; it is the concatenation of events which imperiously
speaks to me in your favor."

"What does it tell you?"

"That I should love you."

"Docs it tell you, too, that you should prove it to me?"

"Ah, my dear friend, you may well believe it."

She gave me her hand for the first time, and I covered it with kisses.

"Know," she said, "that my first idea was to put all the forty zecchini on the *ambo*."

"And you didn't have the courage?"

"It is not that. I was ashamed. I was afraid of a thought which might have come to you and which you would not have expressed to me. You might have thought that, by giving you all the forty zecchini as my stake, I wanted to let you know that I scorned them, and that would have given you a wrong impression of my character. If you had encouraged me I should have assented at once."

"It never occurred to me! You would now have ten thousand zecchini. Your brother has told me that we shall go to the next ball under the Marchese's direction, and you can imagine how greatly I rejoice when I think that I shall be spending a whole night with you; but one thing troubles me. I am afraid the masquerade will not go off as well as mine did."

"Never fear; he is very intelligent and he loves my sister[10] as he does his own honor. He is certain we shall not be recognized."

"I hope not. He insists on paying for everything, even the supper."

"He is right."

At nightfall on the day of the ball I went to the pastry cook's, where I found the Marchese well pleased that everything was as he wished to have it. The room containing the clothes was shut. I asked him if he was satisfied with Zenobia, and he replied that he was, but only with her work, for he had asked no more of her.

"I believe you," I said, "but I fear that Signorina
F . . . may harbor some doubts on the subject."

"No. She knows that I can love none but her."

The rest of the company arriving, the Marchese tells
us that the masquerade is such that we shall enjoy it
more if we dress before supper instead of after. We
assent. So he takes us into the room, where we see two
rather bulky packages on a large table.

"This one," he said, "is for us, and that one, Signorine, for you. So stay here and let the maid help you
to dress, while we go to do the same in the other room."

He takes the larger package, we follow him, he locks
the door, he opens the package, which contained three
smaller ones. He hands me mine, gives the Lieutenant
his, keeps the third for himself, and says:

"Let us dress."

We could not but laugh heartily when we each found
a complete woman's costume even to the shoes. The
frocks were of fine, pure white linen. There were wom-
en's shifts, and I noticed some very gay garters. There
were nightcaps, to save us the trouble of having our
hair done up, but they were trimmed with Venetian
point lace.[11] There were also stockings, which we did
not need, for we could keep on our own; but there were
buckles, because ours could reveal who we were. I was
surprised to find that the women's shoes fitted me well;
but I learned that my shoemaker was also his. Corset,
petticoat, underskirt, dress, fichu, fan, workbag, rouge
box, full masks—he had forgotten nothing. We dressed,
helping one another only when it came to putting our
hair under the ample nightcaps. The Lieutenant really
looked like a very pretty, rather tall girl; but the Marchese and I were something surprising. Two girls five feet
ten inches in height were really too unusual a phenomenon. The amusing thing is that, without saying
anything to one another, we none of us put on underdrawers. I told the Marchese that the gay garters had

seemed to indicate that underdrawers were not to be worn.

"The trouble is," he replied, "that no one will try to find it out."

All three of us had large women's reticules, into which we put whatever we needed.

The young ladies were already dressed. We open the door, and we see the three beauties, with their backs to the fireplace, looking a little nonplussed at being costumed as they were, though they tried to make us believe they felt at their ease. We approached them with feminine curtsies and with the modest reserve appropriate to the part we were playing. This made them think they must imitate the manners of men; but their costume was not one in which they could show due respect to women. They were dressed as couriers, all in fine linen as we were; tight breeches, close fitting waistcoats, very short jackets, small caps with conventional arms of gilded and silvered cardboard. However, their shirts were trimmed with long ruffles of fine lace. Dressed in this fashion, the three girls could not fail to awaken inordinate desires in us, but we loved them too much to frighten them. All of us speaking out of our roles until we were served, the cousins and the Lieutenant's mistress assured us that they had never in their lives dressed as men, and confessed their fear of the risk they ran in daring to go to the ball dressed in that fashion if by ill luck anyone should succeed in recognizing them. They were right; nevertheless, we employed all our eloquence to reassure them.

We sat down at table, each gentleman beside his lady, and, contrary to my expectation, the first to enliven the occasion was the Lieutenant's mistress, who thought that the part of a man demanded that she be bold; the Lieutenant defended himself, slapping her hands, but that did not stop her from grappling with him. The two cousins, ashamed to show less spirit than she, began treating us no less brazenly. Zenobia, who was waiting on us at table, could not keep from laughing when my adorable Q . . . , reproaching her with having made my dress too tight in the bosom, reached out, and I responded by giving her a light slap, whereupon she asked me to forgive her and kissed my hand. The Marchese having said that he felt cold, his pretended cavalier asked him if "she" had on underdrawers, and felt for them; but she quickly withdrew her hand in dismay, which made us laugh; however, she recovered her composure and played the role of lover very well. The supper had been as choice as mine. We were heated with love and Bacchus. We had been at table for two hours. We rose, and we saw the cousins downcast. They could not prevail upon themselves to go to the ball dressed as they were. Both the Marchese and I saw that they were right and admitted that their reluctance was perfectly reasonable.

"But we must decide on something," said the Lieutenant. "Either to go to the ball or to go home."

"Neither," said the Marchese; "let us dance here."

"Where are the violins?" asked his mistress.

"You couldn't get any tonight for love or money."

"Well then," I said, "let us drink some punch and sing. We will play children's games, and when we are tired we will sleep. We have three beds."

"Two are enough," said the Marchese's mistress.

"Very true, Signorina, but the more there are, the more comfortable we shall be."

Zenobia having gone to sup with the pastry cook's wife, I had told her not to come up again until she was called. After two hours of harmless amusement, the Lieutenant's mistress had gone to lie down on a bed in a room above the one in which the young ladies' dresses were, and the Lieutenant had followed her. Signorina Q . . . said to me that, having drunk a little too much punch, she would be glad to lie down, and I showed her to a room into which she could even lock herself and offered her the privilege. She replied that she did not think she need fear anyone. So we left the Marchese alone with her cousin in the room where we had danced, in which there was a bed in an alcove.

La Q . . . , after spending a few minutes in the dressing room, asked me, as she came out, to go for her frock, and when I brought it to her she returned to the dressing room; coming out again after putting it on, she said that she could breathe again, for the breeches were too tight and had hurt her. She lay down on the bed.

"Where did the breeches hurt you, my beautiful angel?" I said, clasping her in my arms and then lying down beside her, neither of us speaking another word for a good quarter of an hour. I left her only to go to the dressing room, for one must never neglect what is owed to decency. When I came out I found her under the covers. She said she had undressed to go to sleep, and at once pretended to do so. I quickly got rid of all my women's trappings and lay down beside her, where I received every recompense due to my love and my chivalry. She let me spread all her beauties before me. She said that she wished for this moment, and that if we were sensible we would in future go to no balls but only wherever we could be happy and satisfied. I bestowed countless kisses on the beautiful mouth which so clearly foretold my happiness, and by my transports I more than convinced her that no man on earth had ever loved her more than I did. I had no difficulty in keeping her from sleeping, for sleep never visited her eyelids. On my side, her charms, her sweetness, and her fond transports made me insatiable. We did not stop until we saw the dawn.

There was no need for us to hide anything from the others, for we had all enjoyed what was ours to enjoy. A mutual modesty prevented us from congratulating one another. By this silence we did not deny that we had satisfied our desires, but we did not admit it either.

As soon as we were dressed I thanked the Marchese and invited him to supper in the same place, without any pretense at masking, on the night of the next ball, if the young ladies would accept. The Lieutenant said yes for them, and his mistress kissed him ardently, reproaching him with having slept all night. The Marchese and I said together that we had done exactly the same, and the cousins praised our chivalry. We left as we had done the first time, and the Marchese remained alone with Zenobia.

I went home to bed and slept until three o'clock, when, there being no one in the house, I went to eat at my apartment at the pastry cook's, where I found Zenobia with her husband, who had come to enjoy the remains of the supper. Her husband said that I had made his fortune, for his wife had received twenty-four zecchini and his woman's dress from the Marchese, just as I had given her mine. After eating something I went to see La Q . . . , whom I loved more than ever since the blissful night I had spent with her. I could not wait to find out what effect she would have on me after having made me so thoroughly happy. I found her more beautiful; she received me as a lover over whom she had gained rights. She told me she had been sure I would come to see her, and she exchanged ardent kisses with me even in her cousin's presence. I spent five hours with her which passed like five minutes, doing nothing but talk of love in terms of ourselves. In such cases self-esteem makes the subject inexhaustible. This five-hour visit on the day after our nuptials showed me that I was really in love with La Q . . . and convinced her that I was worthy of her affection.

I had had a note from the Countess asking me to sup with herself, her husband, and the Marchese Triulzi, who had invited all the friends of the house. For this reason I did not go to see Carcano, who, since my victory in the guise of Pierrot, had already won a thousand zecchini from me two or three hundred at a time. I knew

Auricular Confession

Young Lady Undressing

he was saying he was sure he would break me. At Triulzi's supper the Countess took me to task: I slept out, they seldom saw me; and she did her utmost to wrest the secrets of my successful amours from me. It was known that I supped at Teresa's[12] with Greppi, and everyone laughed at Greppi, who said that I was of no consequence. I replied that he was right, and that there could not be a happier life than the one I was leading.

The next day Barbaro, with the honesty of all sharpers who correct the mistakes of Fortune, came to bring me my two hundred zecchini, and more than two hundred from my half share in the bank because, having quarreled with La Q . . .'s brother, he declined to deal any longer. I thanked him for everything, and above all for having introduced me to his sister, who had chained my heart and whose severity I hoped to conquer. He laughed, and he praised my discretion. That afternoon at three o'clock I went to her house, and I stayed there until nine, as on the day before. There being no play, the porter had been ordered to tell all callers that no one was at home. Since I had become the declared lover of La Q . . . her cousin treated me as a friend; she begged me to stay in Milan as long as I could, for, aside from making her cousin happy by staying, I made her happy too, for without me she could not spend hours with the Marchese F . . . , who could not see her freely so long as his father lived; but she said she was sure that on his father's death he would marry her. Her hope was vain; the Marchese soon afterward fell into bad habits which ruined him.

The next evening the agreeable company of five, instead of going to the ball, came to supper at my apartment, where, after a delicious repast, we simply went off to bed. A charming night, during which, however, our joy was often interrupted by the sadly true thought that the Carnival would very soon be over.

On the next day but one before the Carnival ended, there being no opera, I sat down to play, and, never getting three winning cards in succession, I lost all the gold I had, and I should have left as usual if a woman masker in men's clothes had not given me a card, urging me in pantomime to stake on it. I put it in front of the banker for a hundred zecchini on my word. I lost, and, to win back the hundred, I lost a thousand, which I sent him the next morning. Wanting to leave to go to La Q . . .'s, I see the same ill-omened masker with a male companion, also masked, who comes up to me, shakes my hand, and tells me in a whisper to go to the "Three Kings" at ten o'clock to such-and-such a room if the honor of an old friend is dear to me.

"What friend?"

"I myself."

"Who are you?"

"I cannot say."

"I will not come, for if you are my friend nothing can prevent you from telling me your name."

I go out, he follows, asking me to go beyond the arcade we saw, where he would take off his mask. I go there, he unmasks, and I see Croce,[13] whom my reader may remember. I knew that he was banished from Milan, I was surprised to see him there, and, understanding why he had not wanted to tell me his name, I was very glad indeed to have refused him the favor of going to his inn.

"I am surprised," I said, "to see you here."

"I came, under cover of this season when masking is permitted, to force my relatives to give me the money they owe me, and they keep putting me off in order to give me nothing, being certain that, for fear of being recognized, I shall have to leave in Lent."

"And do you intend to leave in Lent, even if you get no money?"

"I shall have to; but since you are unwilling to come to see me, save me by giving me only twenty zecchini, which will enable me to leave for certain on Sunday, even if my cousin who owes me ten thousand lire refuses the thousand for which I have asked him; but before I leave I will kill him.''

''I haven't a soldo, and your masker there has cost me a thousand zecchini.''

''I know it. I am an unlucky wretch who brings bad luck to all my friends. It was I who told her to give you a card.''

''Is she Milanese?''

''No. She is from Marseilles, whence I carried her off. She is the daughter of a rich agent; I fell in love with her, I seduced her, and she ran away with me. I had plenty of money; but, unlucky as I am, I lost it all in Genoa, I sold everything I had, and I came here; I have been here a week. Make me sure that I can escape, ask someone for twenty zecchini.''

Moved to pity, I retraced my steps to ask Carcano for them; I gave them to him, telling him to write to me, and I left him. I went to La Q . . .'s, I spent the evening and arranged that we should sup together the next day for the last time in Carnival. We made the occasion as happy a one as we had the others. I spent the first day of Lent in bed, and very early on Monday Clairmont gave me a letter which a hire valet had delivered to him. I read it, and, seeing no name signed to it, I find: ''Alas, Monsieur, take pity on the most unhappy creature on earth. Monsieur de la Croix[14] has certainly gone away in despair. He has abandoned me in this inn, he paid for nothing, what will become of me? Come to give me at least your advice.''

I did not hesitate for a moment. It was neither love nor profligacy which impelled me to help the poor girl, but compassion, virtue. I quickly put on a redingote; I hurry to the ''Three Kings,'' to the same room where Irene had been; and I see a girl with a face worthy to interest anyone. I believe I see wronged innocence and candor. She rises and sadly begs me to excuse her for having inconvenienced me, asking me at the same time to speak in Italian to a woman who was there and tell her to go away.

"She has been troubling me," she said, "for an hour; I do not know her language, but I gathered that she wants to be of use to me. I do not feel inclined to beg for her help—"

"Who told you," I said to the woman, "to come to the Signorina's room?"

"A hire valet told me yesterday that a foreign girl had been left here alone and that she was to be pitied. I came, in the goodness of my heart, to see if I could be of any use to her. I leave very glad to be rid of the matter at no cost beyond my kind intentions. I leave her in good hands, and I congratulate her."

This language so clearly marked her a bawd [15] that I laughed.

The forsaken girl then told me in a few words what I already knew, and she added that her lover, having immediately lost the twenty zecchini I had given him, had taken her to the inn in despair and had spent all of the next day there, not daring to go out by daylight. He had gone out masked toward evening, and toward daybreak he had come in, put on a hooded greatcoat, saying that if he did not come back he would communicate with her through me. He had left her my address.

"If you have not seen him," she said, "I am sure he set out on foot and without a copper. The innkeeper will demand payment, and I have enough if I sell everything; but what am I to do after that?"

"Would you dare go home?"

"Certainly I should. My father will forgive me when I tell him, with tears in my eyes, that I am ready to enter a convent."

"I will take you to Marseilles myself, and in the meanwhile I will find you a room in the house of respectable people here. Until I find it for you, lock yourself in your room and admit no one."

I summon the innkeeper and tell him to bring his bill,

which came to very little; I pay it, and I leave her beside herself with surprise at what I had done and what I had said to her. I think it best to confide her to Zenobia, if she can lodge her, and I go there. I tell her the state of the case in her husband's presence, and he says that he will give up his place to her if she is willing to sleep with his wife, and that he will rent a small room near his house for himself and will stay there as long as the young lady remains.

"For her meals," he said, "she may do as she chooses."

I thought it an excellent arrangement; I wrote the forsaken girl a note, and I instructed Zenobia to take it to her and to do everything necessary. In my note I told her that the bearer of it had orders from me to take care of all her needs. I saw her the next day at Zenobia's, poorly lodged but content, and as pretty as possible. I was on my good behavior; but I sighed to think how impossible it would be for me to maintain it during the journey.

I had nothing more to do in Milan; but I had promised the Count that I would spend two weeks with him at Sant'Angelo. It was an estate belonging to his family, fifteen miles from Milan, of which he talked with enthusiasm. I should have mortified him too greatly if I had left without giving him the satisfaction of going there. He had a married brother who lived there, and who could not but be delighted, he said, to make my acquaintance. When we came back from the estate he would be perfectly content to wish me a good journey. So, having made up my mind to satisfy him, on the fourth day in Lent I took leave of Teresa, of Greppi, and of the fond Q . . . for two weeks. The Countess did not care to make the journey; she much preferred to remain in Milan, where the Marchese Triulzi let her want for nothing We left Milan at nine o'clock, and at noon arrived at Sant'Angelo, where we were expected for dinner.

CHAPTER IX

Ancient castle. Clementina. The Beautiful Penitent. Lodi. Declaration of mutual love, without fear of consequences.

THE SEIGNORIAL castle of the little town of S. A.[1] was enormous, at least eight centuries old, and without architecture of any sort, for neither outside nor inside did it exhibit even a trace of regularity. Vast rooms, all on one floor, and small ones on the ground floor and in the attic. The thick walls were full of cracks, the stone staircases lacked a step here and there, the floors of the rooms were of brick and far from level, the windows were open because they lacked panes, and not one of them had blinds; the beamed ceilings were full of the nests of various species of night-flying and domestic birds.

In this Gothic[2] palace, a monument to the ancient nobility of the Counts A. B., which was dearer to them than some very fine palace in Milan which they might have bought with their money, there were, however, in three of its corners, suites of four or five rooms. These were the apartments of the lords of the castle. In addition to his married brother, who always lived there, my dear Count had another brother,[3] who was serving in Spain with the Walloon Guards.[4] It was the apartment of this absent brother which was bestowed upon me. But let us turn to the reception I was given.

Count Ambrosio,[5] for he was called by his baptismal name, received me at the door of the castle, a door which could not be shut, for half of it was missing. Cap in hand, a respectable but unkempt figure, perhaps forty years of age, he told me in a tone of lofty politeness that his brother had been ill-advised to persuade me to come to see their insufficiencies, that I should find none of the comforts of life in their house, but, to make up for that, "the Milanese heart." This is an expression which they are forever using, and rightly. The Milanese are in general kindly and honest; the frankness of their character seems to condemn the Piedmontese and the Genoese, whom they have at an equal distance on the two opposite borders of their beautiful country.

Count Ambrosio presented me to the Countess[6] his wife and her two sisters, one of whom was of the most delicate beauty, with an air of intelligence, though a little ill at ease. The other was neither beautiful nor ugly. The Countess's very sweet countenance bore the imprint of dignity and candor; it was only two years since the Count had married her at Lodi, her native city. The three sisters were all very young, very highly born, but without fortunes. Toward the end of dinner the Count told me that he had married her more for the sake of her character than of her birth, that she made him happy, and that, though she had brought him nothing, he felt that she had made him richer, for she had taught him to reckon as superfluous whatever he did not possess.

At that the Countess, smiling with delight at the praise which her husband had just bestowed on her, took into her arms a pretty infant of six months[7] which

an old woman brought to her, and stopped eating to
unlace her corset and put between the baby's lips a
nipple which marked the center of a perfectly chiseled
breast as white as snow. Such is the privilege of every
nursing mother. She has learned, without being told,
that in this respect she is excused from all modesty.
Her bosom, become the sacred spring of life, is supposed
to awaken in the beholder no feeling but that of respect.

The dinner which Count Ambrosio gave us would
have been excellent had it not been for the ragouts,
since the good soup, the boiled beef, the salt pork, the
sausages, the mortadella, the fresh cheeses, the vegetables,
the game, the greens, and the mascarpone cheese[8] were
exquisite; but warned by his brother that I set up for
an epicure and loved to eat, he had insisted on having
made dishes, than which one could not imagine anything
worse. Politeness compelling me to taste them, my stomach was turned against the natural and solid viands;
but I quickly righted things, having it out with my
friend after dinner. I convinced him that the menu
would be excellent and appetizing with ten simple dishes
and not one ragout, and he easily persuaded his brother
to listen to reason. During all the time I spent there I
enjoyed delicious fare.

We were six at table, all in high spirits and talkative,
except the prettier and younger Countess, named Clementina,[9] who had already struck me; she spoke only
when she was obliged to answer, but always with a
blush. Having no way to see her eyes except by addressing her, I asked her questions, and she replied; but,
her blushing leading me to suppose I was making her
uncomfortable, I thought it best to leave her alone and
to wait for an opportunity to become better acquainted
with her.

After dinner I was shown to my apartment and left
there; I saw, as in the room in which we had dined,
glazed windows and curtains; but Clairmont said he

did not dare to unpack my trunks, since there were keys neither to the doors of the room nor to the chests of drawers, unless I would absolve him of all responsibility. He was right; I go to consult my friend; he replies that there is not a key anywhere in the castle except to the cellar, despite which everything was perfectly safe.

"There are no thieves in S. A." he said, "and if there are, they do not dare to enter our house."

"I believe you; but you must understand that it is my duty to assume they are everywhere, that my valet himself might seize the opportunity to steal from me without my being able to convict him of it, and that I should have to say nothing if it happened that I was robbed."

"I understand all that. Tomorrow morning a locksmith will put locks on your doors. You will be the only person in the house who thinks of taking precautions against thieves."

I could have answered him with Juvenal, *cantat vacuus coram latrone viator* ("the traveler with an empty purse sings when he meets a robber"),[10] but it would have mortified him. I told my valet to wait until the next day to open my boxes. We went out with his two sisters-in-law to take a walk through the town; Count Ambrosio stayed at home with the Countess, who never left her precious son. She was twenty-two years of age; her sister Clementina was eighteen, and she took my arm; my friend gave his to the Countess Eleonora.[11]

"We shall see," he said, "the Beautiful Penitent. She is a prostitute who lived for two years in Milan with such a reputation for beauty that people came from the nearby towns on purpose to see her. Her house door opened and shut a hundred times a day to satisfy all those who were drawn by her rare beauty; but an end was put to the charming spectacle a year ago. Count Firmian,[12] a man of learning and intelligence, was obliged, on his return from Vienna, to have the unfortunate beauty shut up in the convent to which we are going, in consequence of an absolute order given him by the august Maria Teresa, who could never in her life forgive mercenary beauty.

"The girl was seized, she was shut up, she was told that she was guilty, it was adjudged that she should make a general confession and be sentenced to lifelong penitence. She received absolution from her sins from Cardinal Pozzobonelli,[13] the grand pontiff of the Ambrosian rite,[14] who, bestowing the sacrament of confirmation on her, changed the name of Teresa, which she had received at the baptismal font, to Maria Maddalena,[15] intending thereby to set her on the sure road to eternal salvation by imitating the penitence of her new patron saint, whose life she had led until then. She was shut up in the Convent of the Penitents in this city, of which our family holds the right of patronage. It is an inaccessible convent, where the nuns live in community under the direction of a mother superior whose mildness of character in some measure offsets the sufferings they must endure in passing from the delights of this world to the greatest privations. They can only work and pray to God, and they see no man but the priest, their confessor, whose mass they hear every day. We are the only persons to whom the Mother Superior cannot refuse entrance to this holy prison; and it would not occur to her to exclude those who are in our company."

Poor Maria Maddalena! Oh, what barbarians! The story had made me go pale. As soon as the Count was announced the Mother Superior herself came to receive him at the portal. We enter a great room, where I was easily able to distinguish the celebrated young woman among five or six others, all of them Penitents but who could not have much to repent of, for I thought them ugly. They rose, stopping their sewing or knitting. Only Maria Maddalena, despite the austere woolen habit in

which she was garbed, surprised me. I saw beauty and
majesty in distress, and, with my profane eyes, instead
of seeing dread and hideous sin, I thought I saw holy
innocence; she kept her beautiful eyes turned toward
the floor. But what was not my surprise when, having
raised them and fixed them on my face, she cried out:

"God, what do I see! Holy Virgin, come to my aid!
Go, evil sinner, though you deserve more than I do to
be here."

I did not feel any desire to laugh. The Mother
Superior immediately told me that the poor creature
had gone mad, unless she had recognized me.

"No, Signora, for she can never have seen me."

"I believe it, but she is mad."

The fact is that in her outburst I was more inclined
to see indignant good sense than madness. She touched
me, I could hardly hold back my tears. I begged the
Count not to laugh; but a moment later Maria Maddalena went further, and with that I saw the symptoms
of a rage on the verge of insanity. She begged the
Mother Superior to make me leave, saying that I had
come there only to damn her. That lady, after gently
chiding her, sent her away, saying that she was mistaken
and that those who came to see her could wish only to
contribute to her eternal salvation. She had the stern-
ness to tell her that no one on earth had been a greater
sinner than she. The poor creature left us, shedding tears
in torrents and rending my soul with her sobs.

For my part, had I been the commanding general
of a victorious army in that city, it is more than certain
that in such a situation I would have taken Maria Maddalena by the hand and led her away with me, raining
blows from my cane on the honey-tongued Abbess if
she had tried to oppose my will. She told us that the
girl had angelic qualities, and that she would certainly
become a saint if she did not first go mad. She said that
she had asked her to remove two paintings from the

oratory, one representing St. Louis Gonzaga and the other St. Anthony, because their holy images irresistibly distracted her, and that she had thought it best to satisfy her wish, despite their confessor, who would not listen to reason in the matter.

The priest was an oaf, and the Mother Superior was intelligent. We left that inhuman house, all four of us saddened by having seen victims of tyranny. If in the truth of our holy religion the soul of the great Maria Teresa is destined to have a place in what is called eternity, or the other life, she must inevitably be damned, unless she has repented, even if she did no wrong but the one she did in countless different ways by persecuting poor girls who trafficked in their charms. Poor Maria Maddalena went mad and suffered the pains of hell in this world because nature, the God of all, had favored her with the most precious of all gifts. It may be that she had abused it; but for that crime, which is incontestably the least of crimes, was it necessary to inflict the greatest of punishments on her?

On our way back to the castle the Countess Clementina, to whom I had offered my arm, gave little bursts of laughter from time to time. It pleased me.

"Dare I ask you, beautiful Countess, why you keep laughing to yourself?"

"Pray forgive me. I am not laughing at her having recognized you, for she must have been mistaken; I am laughing at the surprise you showed when she told you you deserved to be shut up far more than she did."

"And perhaps you think so too?"

"I? God forbid! But tell me why it was that the madwoman did not attack my brother-in-law."

"Apparently she thought that I looked more of a sinner."

"It can be the only reason; and that is why one must never pay attention to what mad people say."

"Beautiful Countess, you are pleased to speak ironically; but I take it in good part. I am perhaps a great sinner, as I appear to be; but consider that beauty should be indulgent to me, for I am not often led astray by anything else.''

''I cannot understand why the Empress does not amuse herself locking up men too.''

''Because she hopes to see them at her feet when they can find no more girls.''

''Oh, you are joking! Say, rather, that it is because she is unwilling to forgive her sex the lack of that virtue which she possesses in the highest degree and which, furthermore, is so easy to practice.''

''I have no doubt, Signorina, of the Empress's virtue, but with your permission, and speaking generally, I very much doubt that the virtue called continence is as easy to practice as you suppose.''

''Everyone speaks and thinks in accordance with the ideas which he discovers by examining himself. Sobriety is often taken to be a virtue in one in whom it is no merit. You may find difficult what to me seems very easy, and *vice versa*. We may both be right.''

At that, the girl seemed to me a second Q . . . , with the difference that the latter was proud of her reasoning, whereas Clementina set forth her doctrine with the nonchalance of complete indifference. She stopped my mouth. What an example of sound intelligence! I felt mortified that I had judged her wrongly at table. Her silence, and the rapidity with which her blood rose to her face when she had to answer, had made me suppose that her mind harbored a confusion of complicated ideas which did little honor to her good sense. Excessive shyness is often only stupidity. The Marchesa Q . . . , more experienced than Clementina, if for no other reason than her age, was perhaps a better dialectician; but Clementina had twice eluded my questioning, which is the supreme accomplishment of that graceful parrying which becomes a well-educated girl of rank, whose duty it is not to reveal her treasures to one who may not be worthy to know them.

Back at the castle, we found a lady with her son and daughter and an abate, a relative of the Count's, who displeased me from the beginning. A merciless talker, who, saying that he had seen me in Milan, bored me to death with the most tiresome praise, he also kept looking at Clementina, and I was sure that I did not want this chatterer either as a companion or as a rival. I told him shortly that I did not remember having seen him, and this answer, calculated to abash, abashed him not at all. He sat down beside Clementina and, taking her hand and paying her stale compliments, urged her to conquer me; it was flat, and, since she could only laugh at it, she laughed; but her laughter displeased me. I thought she should have answered him at least by some impertinence. He whispered something into her ear, and, she having replied, I almost lost countenance; I thought it horrible. Some opinion was advanced, everyone made his comment, and the Abate contributed his, urging me to support him; but, angry with him as I was, I told him caustically that he was talking nonsense, hoping that he would hold his tongue; but he was tough-skinned; he appealed to Clementina, who supported him, blushing, and at that the conceited fool kissed her hand. Unable to bear more, I got up and went to a window. A window enables a man at the end of his patience to turn his back on a bore without laying himself open to a direct accusation of rudeness; but everyone sees what he is about. I pretended to contemplate the horizon. I could not bear the Abate, and I was wrong, for, far from having treated me offensively, he had tried to please me.

This irritability in cases of the kind was a characteristic of mine all my life, and it is too late today for me to try to cure myself of it. I even think I no longer need to do so, for those who listen to me relegate me politely, though silently, to a former age forty years ago.

Clementina had undone me, and to make so devastating an impression on me had taken her only seven hours. Feeling that I was wholly hers, I thought I must employ every means to make her wholly mine. I had no doubt that I should succeed, and in my conviction there was certainly some fatuousness; but there was also a becoming modesty, for, believing that I should have to overcome all possible difficulties in order to touch her heart, I thought that the slightest obstacle would suffice to defeat me. Now, the tonsured fool seemed to me a wasp whom I must crush. Cold jealousy also entered in, to wrong the object which had already captivated me; I imagined that Clementina was, if not in love, at least indulgent to the monkey, and this idea filled me with a thirst for a revenge of which she could not but be the object. Love is the god of nature; but what is nature if its god is a spoiled child? We know him for what he is, and yet we adore him.

My friend the Count interrupted my train of thought by coming to ask me if I needed anything. I replied that I would go to my room to write some letters until suppertime. He begs me not to leave, and he calls Clementina, charging her to keep me from going off to write. She shyly replies that if I have business to attend to it would be impolite to detain me. The Abate comes up and tells me in so many words that, instead of going to write, I should make them a bank at faro. A general "yes" insists that I give in. I consent.

Cards are brought, together with small baskets filled with counters in different colors, and I sit down, putting twenty or thirty zecchini before me. It was a large bank for the company, who only wanted to amuse themselves; losing fifteen counters amounted to losing no more than a zecchini. Everyone sat down. The Countess Ambrosio took the place on my right, and the Abate saw fit to take that on my left. It was Clementina who made way for him. Considering his action insolent, I said that I never dealt except between two ladies, whereupon Clementina resumed her seat. After three hours supper was served, and I stopped. Everyone had won except the Abate, who had lost twenty zecchini in counters. What a pleasure! As a relative, he stayed for supper; the lady took her leave with her son and daughter; no one could persuade her to stay.

Pleased enough with my evening, for I think the Abate is in despair, I am in a humor to be amused; I cajole the beauty beside me into talking by saying things to her which force her to defend herself. She shines, and she is grateful to me. Seeing the Abate in full defeat, I take it into my head to ease his discomfiture; I ask his opinion on a question; he replies that he has not been listening and that he hopes I will give him his revenge after supper.

"After supper, Signor Abate, I shall go to bed; but I promise you your revenge tomorrow, delighted that this little game amuses my kind hostess and her sisters; luck is against you today; tomorrow it will favor you."

After supper he left in great gloom. The Count saw me to my room and, wishing me good night, said that I need have no fear if there were no keys to my doors, since his sisters-in-law, whose room adjoined mine, had none either.

Greatly astonished by a hospitality so lavish, I tell Clairmont to put my hair in curl papers quickly, for I badly needed sleep; but halfway through the proceeding in comes Clementina and surprises me by saying that there is not a chambermaid in the castle to take care of my linen, so she begs my permission to perform the office for me without further ado.

"You, Countess?"

"I, and pray do not object. It will be a pleasure for me; and, what is more, I am sure that you will be satisfied. Have your man give me the shirt you will wear tomorrow; and say no more about it.''

I at once have Clairmont help me drag my trunk of linens into her room, and I tell her that I need a shirt, a waistcoat, a collar, underdrawers, and two handkerchiefs every day, and that I leave the choice to her. I am more fortunate than Jupiter. Farewell. Good night, charming Hebe.[16]

Her sister Eleonora, who was already in bed, outdid herself asking me to excuse her. I immediately ordered Clairmont to go and inform the Count that I no longer wanted him to have locks put on my doors. I felt ashamed. Was I to fear for my rags, when these living treasures did not fear my cupidity?

Having found my bed excellent, I slept very well. Clairmont was dressing my hair when I saw my Hebe come in carrying a basket. With great dignity she said she was sure I would be satisfied. On her beautiful countenance I see not the slightest trace of self-consciousness, of an unbecoming shame arising from the mistaken idea that to do me this service has detracted from her nobility. She had blushed, but without making any effort to hide it from me, for what had brought the blush to her cheeks was a satisfaction which bore witness to the beauty of her soul, unfettered as it was by the vulgar prejudices of narrow minds. Never had a shirt so greatly pleased me as the one I saw.

Just then my friend the Count arrives. He thanks Clementina for the kindness she has shown me, and he embraces her; I thought the embrace unnecessary. Oh, she is his sister-in-law, he is her brother-in-law, whatever you please; but if I am roused to jealousy, that suffices; nature, who knows more than you do, tells me that I am in the right. It is impossible not to be jealous of what one loves dearly and has not yet conquered; for one must always fear that what one wants to conquer may be carried off by another.

The Count asked me to read a note which he took from his pocket. The Abate, his cousin, asked him to tender me his apologies for not being able to pay me the twenty zecchini he had lost, within the time prescribed by the gamester's code. He would, he told him, pay his debt before the end of the week.

"Very good," I said. "But tell him not to punt at my bank this evening, for I will not carry him."

"You are right, but he can play for cash."

"Not that either, for he would be playing against me with my money. He may do what he pleases after he has paid me. You may even tell him to take all the time he wants, and assure him that I will never press him to pay me this insignificant sum."

"He will be mortified."

"So much the better," said Clementina; "why does he presume to lose on his word what he is not sure he can pay today?"

"Charming Countess," I said when I was left alone with her, "tell me frankly if the rather harsh treatment I accord this Abate pains you, and I will this moment give you twenty zecchini you can send to him, which he can pay me this evening, and so cut a good figure. I promise you that no one shall hear a word of it."

"I thank you, but no; I am not concerned enough for his honor to accept your offer. Let him feel the shame of his wrongdoing and learn how to live."

"You will see that he will not come this evening."

"That may well be; but do you think I should be sorry?"

"I might have supposed so."

"What! Because he confined his silly attentions to me? He is a scatterbrain on whom I set no value."

"He is as unfortunate as a man whom you value is fortunate."

"That man has perhaps not yet been born."

"What! You have not yet met a mortal worthy of your attention?"

"Many worthy of attention; but valuing is something more. I could value only someone whom I loved."

"Then you have never loved? Your heart is empty."

"Your word 'empty' makes me laugh. Is it fortunate or unfortunate? If it is fortunate, I congratulate myself; if it is unfortunate, I do not care, for I am not aware of it."

"It is none the less a misfortune, and you will know it when you love."

"But if, when I love, I am unhappy, I will know that my empty heart was my good fortune."

"That is true, but it seems to me impossible that you should be unhappy in love."

"It is only too possible. Love requires a mutual harmony which is difficult, and it is even more difficult to make it last."

"I agree; but God put us on earth to take the risk."

"A man may need to do that, and find it amusing; but a girl is bound by other laws."

Just then we were interrupted by the reappearance of the Count, who was surprised to find us still there. He said that he would like to see us in love with each other, and she replied that in that case he wished to see us unhappy—she because she would love an inconstant man, and I because my soul would feel the pangs of remorse. After delivering this dictum, she fled.

I was left as if turned to stone; but the Count, who had never had a thought in his life, said with a laugh that his sister-in-law Clementina was inclined to be romantic. We went to the Countess's apartment, finding her with her baby at her breast.

"The Cavaliere," he said, "is in love with your sister, and she with him."

"I should be glad," she replied, "if a good marriage made us relatives."

The word "marriage" serves only to mask the most flattering of all ideas. Her reply pleased me so greatly that I responded to it only with a bow.

We went out to take the air and to call on the lady who had declined to stay for supper, where we found a Canon Regular[17] who, after saying some gracious things to me and praising my native country, which he thought he knew because he had read its history, asked me what order of knighthood was indicated by the cross which I wore hanging from my neck on a red ribbon. I could not but reply, modestly proud, that it was a sign of the good will with which Our Most Holy Father the Pope honored me when, of his own motion, he had made me a Knight of San Giovanni in Laterano[18] and an Apostolic Prothonotary.

The monk had not traveled. If he had acquired the manners of good society he would not have asked me what my order was; but he innocently thought he flattered me by his inquiry, for at the same time that he did his best to convince me that he found me interesting he gave me leave to make a show of my dignities.

There are a great many questions which do not seem indiscreet among well-meaning people untouched by the corruption of manners, but which nevertheless are so. The order known as the Golden Spur was so little esteemed that it greatly annoyed me when I was questioned about my cross. I should have been pleased, no doubt, if I could have answered simply, "It is the Fleece," [19] but, after I had told the truth, my self-esteem demanded that I add a commentary, which at bottom was a gloss in justification; it was a burden; in short, my cross embarrassed me, it was truly a cross; but since it was a magnificent decoration and impressed fools, whose number is immense, I wore it even when I was not in full dress. The order of Christ,[20] which is the order of Portugal, is in the same situation, because the Pope shares with His Most Faithful Majesty[21] the privilege of conferring it. The order of the Red Eagle[22] has been held in estimation only since the King of Prussia became its Grand Master; thirty years ago a gentleman refused it because the Margrave of Bayreuth allowed it to be sold. The blue ribbon of St. Michael [23] is honorable today because it is now conferred by the Elector of Bavaria; no one wanted it because the Elector of Cologne conferred it broadcast. I saw a knight of the order at Prague five years ago; but asking him from whom he received it would have been a mistake. The madness for stars increases daily, and now no one can claim, when he sees the devices, that he recognizes them, for, aside from the symbols of a quantity of obscure chapters, there are the fanciful devices of private associations of hunters, academicians, musicians, bigots, lovers, into the nature of which it could even be dangerous to inquire, for they might be those of conspirators. As for women, common sense is enough to make any intelligent man refrain from asking the significance of a concealed medallion, or an aigrette worn in an odd way, or a portrait in a bracelet or a ring. Let us love them and not seek to penetrate their mysteries, the more so since more often than not the thing turns out to be some bauble or grotesque which they wear only to get themselves looked at and to arouse curiosity.

Things have come to such a point in good society that, if you want to be polite, you can no longer ask a man from what country he comes, for if he is a Norman or a Calabrian he has, when he tells you so, to beg your pardon, or, if he is from the Pays de Vaud,[24] to say that he is Swiss. Nor will you ask a nobleman what his arms are, for if he does not know the jargon of heraldry you will embarrass him. You must not compliment a gentleman on his fine hair, for if it is a wig he may think you are mocking him, nor praise a man or a woman for their fine teeth, for they may be false. I was set down as impolite in France fifty years ago because I asked

Countesses and Marquises their baptismal names. They
did not know them.[25] And a dandy who had the misfortune to be named Jean replied to my indiscreet
curiosity, but at the same time offered to fight me.

The height of bad manners in London is to ask someone what his religion is, and so too in Germany, for if
he is a Herrnhuter[26] or an Anabaptist[27] he will not
want to admit it. In short, if one wants to be liked the
safest thing is to ask nobody anything, not even if he
has change for a louis.

At table Clementina answered all my remarks with
wit and grace, but no one realized it. In some companies
intelligence is overwhelmed by stupidity.

Clementina filling my glass too often, I treated her
to reproaches which occasioned a brief dialogue which
gave me the finishing stroke. I rose from the table
mortally in love. Here is the dialogue:

"You have no right," she said, "to complain, for it
is Hebe's duty always to keep her lord's glass full."

"But you know that Jupiter dismissed her."

"Yes, but I know why. I shall never fall so awkwardly.[28] That will never be the reason for some Ganymede[29] to supplant me."

"That is very sensible. Jupiter was in the wrong; and
I now assume the name of Hercules.[30] Does that please
you, beautiful Hebe?"

"No, because he didn't marry me until after he was
dead."

"You are right about that, too. I can only be Iolaus,[31]
for—"

"Say no more. Iolaus was old."

"That is true; I was old yesterday; but I am so no
longer; you have given me youth."

"I am very glad of that, dear Iolaus; but do you remember what I did to him when he left me?"

"For pity's sake, what was it? I don't remember."

"That I do not believe."

"Believe it."

"I took away the gift I had made him."

It was at these last words that the conflagration broke out in the charming girl's face; I should have been afraid I would scorch my hand if I had dared to touch her forehead; but the blazing sparks which visibly shot from her eyes darted through my heart and froze me. Be not angry, you modern physicists who read me, for I do not present this phenomenon to you as a miracle; yes, they froze me. A great love which raises a man above his being is a most powerful fire which can only begin with its exact contrary, a cold of the same power, such as I felt at that moment and which would have killed me if it had lasted more than a minute. The superior ingenuity with which she had applied the fable of Hebe had not only shown me a Clementina versed in mythology but had given me a sample of a sound and deep intelligence. It had done more: it had convinced me that I had interested her, that she had thought about me, that she had wanted to surprise and please me. All these ideas need no more than a minute to spring up in the soul of a man already predisposed. They are incendiary. I had no more doubt. "Clementina," I said to myself, "loves me, and she has made me sure of it. We shall be happy."

She had run away, which gave me time to come out of my stupor.

"Tell me, Signora," I said to the Countess, "where and by whom that charming girl was brought up."

"In the country, by always being present at the lessons which Sardini[32] gave my brother, though he devoted his whole attention to him. Clementina was the one who profited by it, my brother was bored. She made our mother laugh, and she amazed the old tutor."

"We have poems of Sardini's which no one reads because he is too learned in mythology."

"Quite so. I will tell you that she has a manuscript of

his containing a quantity of pagan fables. Persuade her to show you her books and the verse she composes and lets nobody see."

I was beside myself. She comes back, I pay her compliments; I tell her that I am fond of poetry and belles-lettres, and that I should count it a favor if she would show me her books and especially her verses.

"I'd be ashamed. I had to stop studying two years ago when, our sister having married, we had to come here, where we see only good people who, thinking of nothing but the harvest, are interested in nothing but the weather. You are the first who, by calling me Hebe, led me to conclude that you are fond of letters. If Sardini had come here I could have continued to study; and he was willing to come, but my sister did not want it."

"But my dear Clementina," her sister replied, "what use, I ask you, could my husband make of an octogenarian who can do nothing but compose verses and weigh air?"

"All very well," said Count Ambrosio, "if he could have taken a hand in managing the estate; but he is an honest old man who refuses to think anyone a scoundrel. He is both learned and stupid."

"Good heavens!" Clementina cried, "Sardini stupid? It is true that he is easy to deceive; but he would not be deceived if he were less upright and less intelligent. I like it in a man that he is easy to deceive for those reasons. But everyone says I am silly."

"No, my dear sister," said the Countess. "On the contrary, everything you say bears the stamp of wisdom, but a wisdom outside your sphere, for letters and philosophy are not what is needed to manage a house, and when the time comes for you to marry your taste for the sciences will perhaps prevent you from making a good match."

"I expect so, and I am already prepared to die an old maid; but it does not speak well for men."

What a tumult of passion in my poor soul at this cruel dialogue! I was in despair. Had I been noble and rich, I would have given her a hundred thousand scudi then and there, and have become engaged to her before I rose from the table. She told me that Sardini was in Milan, sickly from old age, and when I asked her if she had paid him a visit she answered that she had never seen Milan, any more than had any of her sisters. Yet by carriage and at a fast trot one could go there in two hours.

I begged her so insistently that, after coffee, she took me to a study next to her room to show me her books. She had no more than thirty, all good, but all the sort of reading one would find in the library of a young man who had just finished his studies in rhetoric.[33] Her books could teach my angel neither history nor any of those parts of physical science which could raise her out of her ignorance of essentials and be the joy of her life.

"Are you aware, my dear Hebe, that certain books you should have are lacking in your collection?"

"I suspect it, my dear Iolaus."

"Be sure of it, and leave the rest to me."

After spending an hour looking over Sardini's works I asked her to show me her own.

"No, they are too faulty."

"I expect that; but the good I shall find in them will outweigh it. I will forgive the diction, the style, the absurd ideas, the lack of method, and even your unscannable verses."

"That is a little too much, for I do not believe I need so plenary an indulgence. Here, Signore. These are all my scribblings."

Delighted to have succeeded by my trick, I began by

reading her an Anacreontic song,[34] very slowly, bringing
out all its beauties by the tones of my voice and reveling
in the joy which flooded her soul and shone in her eyes
and in her whole face when she heard herself at such
a pitch of beauty. When I read her a verse which I had
made more touching by changing some syllables, she was
aware of it, for she was looking on while I read; but far
from feeling humiliated by the correction, she was grateful to me for it. She felt that my touches with the brush
did not keep the painting from being hers, and she was
in raptures, being aware that the pleasure I took in
reading her was far greater than that which made her
happy at the moment. Our mutual enjoyment continued
for three hours, an enjoyment of our souls already in
love, than which it is impossible to imagine a pleasure
either more pure or more voluptuous. Happy, and more
than happy, for us if we had known enough and had
strength enough to stop there; but Love is a traitor and
a deceiver, and laughs at all those who think they can
trifle with him and not fall into his snares.

It was the Countess Ambrosio who came to tell us to
forsake letters and join the company for a time. Clementina put everything back in place, thanking me, and, in
token of her gratitude, offering me her blood, the flame
of which I saw in her captivating face. In this state,
followed by myself and the Countess, she appeared before the company, only to be asked if she had been doing
battle.

The table had been made ready for faro; but before
sitting down I took Clairmont aside and ordered him to
make sure that at dawn the next day I should have four
horses harnessed to my carriage to take me to Lodi[35] and
bring me back in time for dinner.

The whole company punted, as on the day before, and
I was very glad not to see the Abate. I saw the Canon,
who was punting at ducati, with a pile of them before
him. At that I increased the bank, and at the end of

play I had the pleasure of seeing the whole family content. Only the Canon had lost some thirty zecchini; but the loss made him none the less gay at table.

The next day I went to Lodi, without telling anyone I was going. I bought all the books which I thought suitable for the Countess Clementina, who understood only Italian. I bought translations which I was surprised to find in the town of Lodi, which until then I had thought notable only for its excellent cheese, which the whole of Europe ungratefully calls Parmesan.[36] It does not come from Parma but from Lodi, and I did not fail that very day to add a comment to the article "Parmesan" in the dictionary of cheeses which I had begun and which I later abandoned, finding it beyond my powers, as J. J.[37] found a dictionary of botany beyond his. At that time he had taken the name of "Renaud the Botanist." *Quisque histrioniam exercet* ("Everyone plays a part"). But the eloquent Rousseau had neither the temperament to laugh nor the divine talent of calling forth laughter.

At the best inn in Lodi I ordered a dinner for twelve persons for the next day but one, giving a deposit and taking a receipt. I ordered whatever would serve to make my expenditure as large as possible.

Back at S. A., I took the bag filled with books to the Countess Clementina's room, and at the sight of the present she lost the power of speech. There were more than a hundred books, all poets, historians, geographers, physicists, and some romances translated from the Spanish or the French, for, with the exception of thirty or forty poems, we have not a single good romance in prose in Italian. To make up for it we have the supreme masterpiece of the human mind in the *Orlando furioso*,[38] which cannot be translated into any language. So, if that poem is made only for the Italian language, it seems that the Italian language is made only for it. The European author who has produced the truest, the most beautiful, and the simplest eulogy of Ariosto was Voltaire,[39]

at the age of sixty years. If he had not sung that palinode,[40] posterity would have raised an insurmountable
barrier which would have prevented him from ever
reaching the temple of immortality. I told him so, thirty-
six years ago, and the great genius believed me and took
fright; and nothing can prevent his apotheosis, unless
it be a great curtain which he should have refrained
from drawing.[41] Voltaire saw very well, but he foresaw
as badly as possible.

Clementina turned her eyes from the books to me and
from me to the books, seeming to doubt if they belonged
to her. Suddenly serious, she said that I had come to
S. A. to make her happy. Such a moment transforms a
man into a god. *Homo homini Deus* ("Man is a god to
man").[42] At such a moment the person who receives the
benefit inevitably determines to do everything possible to
make the person happy who has so easily conferred
happiness.

The pleasure one feels when one sees the divine handwriting of gratitude on a countenance with which one
has fallen in love is supreme. If it does not interest you
as much as it does me, my dear reader, I do not want
you to read me; you can be only a miser or a blundering
clown, in which case you are unworthy to be loved.
Clementina, after dining without appetite, spent the
rest of the day in her room with me, arranging her books.
She first ordered a carpenter to make her a bookcase
with a grille and a lock, which would be her constant
delight after I had gone. She was lucky at faro and in
high spirits at supper, during the course of which I
invited the whole company to dine at Lodi on the next
day but one. My dinner being for twelve, Countess
Ambrosio undertook to find two guests to make up the
number at Lodi, and the Canon promised to bring his
lady with her daughter and her son.

I spent the next day without leaving the castle, occupied with giving my Hebe some notion of the sphere

and setting her on the way to enjoying Wolff.[43] I made her a present of my case of mathematical instruments, which she considered an inestimable gift.

I burned for her; but would her taste for literature have made me fall in love with her if I had not first thought her pretty? Alas, no. I like a ragout, and I am a great eater; but if it does not look attractive I think it bad. The first thing which interests me is the outside, is the seat of beauty; examination of the form and what is within comes afterward, and if that enchants it kindles; the man who disregards it is superficial. And that, in the realm of ethics, is synonymous with "reprehensible." The new thing which I found in myself as I went to bed was that, in my conversations with Hebe, when we were alone together for three or four hours, her beauty did not distract me in the least. Yet what so constrained me was neither respect nor virtue nor so-called duty. What was it? I did not care to guess. I only knew that this Platonism could not last long, and, to tell the truth, the realization mortified me; the mortification arose from virtue, but from a virtue at its last gasp. The beautiful things we read interested us so strongly that feelings of love, rendered accessory or secondary, could not but remain silent. In the presence of the mind the heart loses its imperial power, reason triumphs, but the struggle is bound to be short. Our victories misled us; we thought we were sure of ourselves, but it was on a foundation of clay; we knew that we loved, but we did not know that we were loved.

This equally dangerous and modest confidence led me to enter her room to tell her something about the excursion to Lodi, the carriages being already waiting. She was asleep; she started awake, and it did not even occur to me to excuse myself. It was she who excused herself, saying that Tasso's *Aminta*[44] had interested her so greatly when she had gone to bed that she could not put it down until she had read it through. She had it on her bedside table. I told her that the *Pastor fido*[45] would delight her even more.

"Is it more beautiful?"

"No."

"Then why do you say it will delight me more?"

"Because it has a charm which acts on the heart. It softens, it seduces, and we love to be seduced."

"Then it is a seducer?"

"No, it is seductive, as you are."

"A fundamental distinction! I will read it this evening. I shall be dressed in a moment."

She dressed, forgetting that I was a man, but with modesty. Even so, I saw that she would have been more modest if she had been sure I was in love with her. I glimpsed, when she drew a shift over her buttocks, when she laced her corset, when she put on her petticoat, and when, getting out of bed, she put on her stockings and fastened her garters above the knee, I glimpsed—I say —beauties which drove me to distraction, made me answer her at random, and forced me to leave the room in order to save my carnality from too shameful a defeat.

I took a place on the folding seat of my carriage, holding the Countess's son on a big pillow in my lap. She laughed till she had no breath left, as did Clementina. Halfway through the journey the infant began crying; it wanted milk; its mother quickly uncovers a rose-pink spigot, which she does not mind my admiring, and I hold the baby out to her, while it smiles because it is going to eat and drink at the same time. I longed to possess the noble picture, my delight was visible. The pretty baby, satisfied, lets go; I see the white liquid still running.

"Ah, Signora! It is a crime; allow my lips to gather this nectar which will put me among the gods, and do not fear that I will bite you."

In those days I had teeth.

I suckled on my knees, looking at the Countess-mother and her sister, who, both laughing, seemed to pity me;

it is a kind of laugh which no painter has ever succeeded in imitating, except the great painter Homer, where he depicts Andromache with Astyanax in her arms when Hector leaves her to return to the army.[46]

With my insatiable desire to raise a laugh, I asked Clementina if she had the courage to grant me the same favor.

"Why not, if I had milk?"

"You need only have the source of it. I will imagine the rest."

But at that she blushed so intensely that I was almost sorry I had said it. Still in high spirits, we reached the inn at Lodi without having been aware of the time the short journey had taken us. The Countess at once sent her lackey to ask a lady who was a friend of hers to come to dine with her together with her sister. I seized the opportunity to send Clairmont to buy me an ample supply of paper, sealing wax, pens, ink, an inkstand, and a fine portfolio with a lock, for my beautiful Hebe, who was never to forget me. When she had it all in front of her before dinner, she did not know how to express her gratitude except with her beautiful eyes. There is not a woman on earth, whose heart is true and uncorrupted, whom a man cannot be sure of conquering by making her grateful. It is the infallible method and the shortest road to success, but one must know how to go about it.

The lady from Lodi came with her sister, who could challenge her whole sex for the prize of beauty; but at that time Venus herself could not have torn me from Clementina. The matrons and the young ladies embraced one another repeatedly, expressing their delight at meeting again. I was introduced, I was described, I was praised to the skies; I played the fool to put an end to the compliments.

My dinner was good and handsomely served; it being Lent, the scrupulous found various sorts of fish which kept them from regretting the fowl and the game. The excellent sturgeon was to everyone's taste.

After dinner the lady's husband came with her sister's lover, so the gaiety increased. I acceded to the request of the whole charming company by making them a bank; and after three hours I stopped, delighted to have lost thirty or forty zecchini; otherwise I should not have been proclaimed the finest player in Europe.

The beauty's lover was named Vegio, so I asked him if he was descended from the author of the thirteenth book of Vergil's *Aeneid*;[47] he replied that he was, and that he had translated it into Italian stanzas.[48] In response to my show of interest he promised to bring it to me at S. A. on the next day but one. I congratulated him on his ancient nobility, for Maffeo Vegio flourished at the beginning of the fifteenth century.

At nightfall we set out, and in less than two hours we were back at S. A. The moon, which shone on my every movement, helped me to resist the temptation inspired in me by one of Clementina's legs, for, the better to hold her nephew on her lap, she had put one foot on the folding seat. The mother, arrived home, paid me a thousand compliments on the good company I had been to her. None of us wanting to sup, we retired, but Clementina confided to me that she was in despair because she had not the least notion of the *Aeneid*. Signor Vegio was to come to S. A. with his thirteenth book, and she was plunged in gloom because she would be unable to judge it. I comforted her.

"Tonight," I said, "we will read the splendid translation of the poem by Annibale Caro.[49] You have it, and you also have the translation of Ovid's *Metamorphoses* by Dell'Anguillara,[50] and Marchetti's[51] of Lucretius."

"I wanted to read the *Pastor fido*."

"We will read it some other time."

So we spent the night reading that magnificent poem in Italian blank verse. But the reading was interrupted again and again by the witty laughter of my charming pupil. She laughed heartily over the chance which pro-

Meeting at the Park Gate

The Abbé X

vided Aeneas with an opportunity, though a very inconvenient one, to give Dido convincing proof of his love,[52] but even more when Dido, complaining of the Trojan's perfidy, says that she could still forgive him if, before forsaking her, he had given her a little Aeneas whom she would have had the pleasure to see playing about her court. Clementina was justified in laughing; but why is it that one does not laugh when one reads it in Latin? *Si quis mihi parvulus aula luderet Aeneas.*[53] It is only the beauty of the language which gives an air of dignity to this comical complaint.

We did not end our reading until the night ended.

"What a night, my dear friend!" she said. "I have spent it with you in the joy of my soul. But you?"

"With the utmost pleasure, seeing yours."

"And if you had not seen mine?"

"I should have enjoyed it two thirds less. I love your mind to the highest degree, but tell me, please, if you think it possible to love someone's mind without loving the case which contains it."

"No, for without the case it would evaporate."

"Then it follows that I must love you, and that I cannot possibly spend six hours alone with you and not die of my longing to give you countless kisses."

"You are right; and I believe we resist that desire only because we have duties, and because we should feel humiliated if we disregarded them."

"That is true; but if your nature is like mine, this constraint must cause you great pain."

"As much, perhaps, as you yourself feel; but I will tell you that I believe that resisting certain desires is hard only at the beginning. Little by little people grow used to loving each other without any risk. Our outsides, in which we now delight, will cease to concern us, and then we can spend hours and days together without any unwonted desire coming to trouble us."

"Good-by, beautiful Hebe. Sleep well."

"Good-by, Iolaus."

CHAPTER X

*Excursion. My sad parting with Clementina.
I leave Milan with Croce's mistress. My arrival in Genoa.*

I AT once went to bed, ordering Clairmont not to wait
up for me in future. I laughed at Clementina's plan,
based, as it was, on her belief that the way to take away
someone's appetite was to set before him the dishes he
liked, only telling him that he was forbidden to touch
them. She knew no more than I did about it; but when
she had said to me that if one resists desire one does
not feel humiliated after one satisfies it, her words had
been full of sense. The humiliation which she dreaded
arose from the attachment and respect she felt for her
duties, and she honored me in assuming that I thought
as she did. I must let her go on believing it. I fell asleep,
determined never to undertake anything which could
make her lose her confidence in me.

The next morning I rang very late. She came to wish
me good morning, carrying the *Pastor fido*.

"I read the first act," she said, "and I have never

read anything so sweet. Get up. We will read the second act before dinner.''

''Dare I get up in your presence?''

''Why not? A man need go to very little trouble to observe modesty.''

''Then be so kind as to give me that shirt.''

Smiling, she drew it over my head, and, thanking her, I said that I would do her the same service at the first opportunity.

''From you to me,'' she said, blushing, *''there is less distance than from me to you.''*

''This time, my divine Hebe, you have answered me like a true oracle, even as you did when you were worshiped in Corinth.''

''Did Hebe have a temple in Corinth?[1] Sardini doesn't say so.''

''But Apollodoros[2] does. It was even a place of asylum. But please do not dodge the issue. What you said is contrary to geometry. The distance from you to me must be the same as the distance from me to you.''

''What I said was stupid.''

''No, no. You had an idea; whether it was right or not, I want to hear it.''

''Very well. The two distances differ in direction, as to up and down. Isn't it true that a body simply released will descend without having to be propelled? Isn't it also true that without propulsion there is no ascent? If this is true, admit that I, who am shorter than you, cannot reach you except by ascending, which is difficult; whereas for you to come to me you need only let yourself go, which is very easy. Hence you risk nothing when you allow me to change your shirt; but I should risk a great deal if I let you perform the same office. Your too rapid descent on me might crush me. Are you convinced?''

''Convinced? I am beside myself. Never has a paradox

been more wittily justified. I could cavil; but I would rather be still, admire, and adore you."

"Thank you, but don't think of sparing me. How could you cavil?"

"On your cleverness in making my height one of your factors, whereas you would not let me change your shift even if I were a dwarf."

"Very good, my dear Iolaus; we cannot deceive each other. I should be happy if God had destined such a man as you to be my husband."

"Alas, why am I not worthy of it!"

The Countess-mother came to summon us to dinner, at the same time saying she was happy that we loved each other.

"Madly," said Clementina; "but we keep our heads."

"If you keep your heads, you do not love each other madly."

We dined, we played cards, and after supper we finished the *Pastor fido*. She asked me if Signor Vegio's thirteenth book of the *Aeneid* was beautiful.

"My dear Countess, it is worthless, and I praised it only to flatter a descendant of its author, who, however, composed a poem on the shrewd tricks of peasants[3] which is not without merit. But you are sleepy, and I am keeping you from undressing."

"Not at all."

After undressing without granting anything to the cupidity of my eyes, she got into bed, but sat up in it; I sat at her feet, and her sister turned her back to us. The *Pastor fido* being on her night table, I took it and opened it by chance to the place where Mirtillo speaks of the sweetness of the kiss he received from Amarilli.[4] Seeing Clementina apparently as touched as I felt that I was ardent, I pressed my lips to hers, and observing no sign of alarm, I was about to clasp her to me when, with the utmost sweetness, she put out one arm and drew away, begging me to spare her. At that I asked her to forgive me, bestowing countless kisses on the beautiful hand which she had surrendered to me.

"You are trembling," she said.

"Yes, my dear Countess; and I can assure you it is from fear that I have offended you. Good-by. I leave, wishing that I loved you less."

"No indeed, for such a desire can only be the beginning of hatred. Do as I do: I desire that the love you have inspired in me shall increase every day in precisely equal measure with the strength which I need to resist it."

I went off to bed very ill pleased with myself. I could not decide whether I had done too much or too little; in either case, I repented of it. I thought Clementina a creature as perfectly deserving of respect as of love, and I could not imagine myself able to go on loving her without the reward which love owes to love. If she loved me she could not refuse it to me; but it was my part to ask for it, I must even urge it upon her, in order to justify her defeat. The duty of a lover is to force the object of his love to surrender, and love can never adjudge him insolent. So Clementina could resist me to the point of denial only if she did not love me; I must put her to the test, and the more so because, if I found her unconquerable, I felt sure that would cure me. There was no doubt of it. But no sooner had I decided to follow this course than I considered it and found it abhorrent. The idea that I should stop loving Clementina was like poison. I loathed such a cure worse than death, for she deserved to be adored.

I slept badly. I rose very early and entered her room, she was still asleep, and the Countess Eleonora was getting dressed.

"My sister," she said, "read until three o'clock in the morning. Now that she has all these books she will go

mad. Let's play a trick on her. Get into the bed on this
side of her. We'll see how surprised she'll be when,
waking, she turns and sees you.''

"Do you think she will take it as a joke?"

"How can she help it? You are dressed."

I do as she tells me. In dressing gown and nightcap I
take the place which Eleonora has just left, pulling the
covers up to my chin; she laughed, while my heart
pounded, for my mind would not believe that I could
give the trick the air of comedy which alone could color
its grossness with innocence. I hoped she would be long
in waking, to give me time to assume a facetious expression.

At last Clementina wakes. She turns and, with her
eyes still closed, puts out her free arm and, thinking it
is her sister she is holding, gives me the kiss with which
she usually greets her, and lies there ready to go back
to sleep; but at the laughter which Eleonora cannot hold
back, Clementina opens her eyes and does not see me in
her arms until a second after she has seen her sister
standing there laughing.

"A pretty trick indeed," she says, without moving,
"and I admire you both."

At this beginning my faculties resume their functions;
my confidence returns, and I feel that I am sufficiently
in control of myself to play a part.

"And so it is," I say, "that I have received a kiss
from my beautiful Hebe."

"I thought I was giving it to my sister; it is the kiss
which Amarilli gave Mirtillo."

"That makes no difference. It produced the effect it
was bound to produce, and Iolaus is rejuvenated."

"My dear sister, what you let my dear Iolaus do is
too much, for we love each other and I was dreaming of
him."

"It is not too much," Eleonora replied, "for he is
dressed. See!"

So saying, she uncovers me to convince her; but in trying to show me to her sister, she spreads before me all the beauties which the bedclothes have kept me from seeing. Clementina quickly hides them; but I had already seen the cornice and the frieze of the altar of love, on which I longed to die. She covers herself, and Eleonora goes, leaving me leaning on one elbow with my head bent toward the treasure of which some occult power prevented me from taking possession.

"My dear Hebe," I said, "you are certainly more beautiful than the goddess. I saw what the gods saw when she fell; if I had been Jupiter, I would not have done as he did."

"Sardini says that he dismissed her; and to avenge Hebe I ought now to dismiss Jupiter."

"But remember that I am Iolaus. I am your handiwork. I love you, and I labor to stifle desires which torture me."

"You planned this trick with Eleonora."

"There was no planning. It was all pure chance. I came in, she was dressing, you were asleep, she told me to take her place so that we could laugh at your surprise, and I cannot but be grateful to her. The beauties I have seen surpass the idea I had conceived of them. My Hebe is charming. May I hope for a generous pardon?"

"It is strange that when one feels too tenderly fond of somebody one cannot help being curious about his whole person!"

"It is natural, my divine philosopher. Love itself could be considered a very powerful curiosity, if curiosity could be counted among the passions; but are you not curious about me?"

"No. I might find you pleasing; and I do not want to take that risk, for I love you, and I am delighted with the feelings I have which speak in your favor."

"That is quite possible, I see, and hence I must be very careful to keep my advantage."

"Then you are satisfied with me?"

"More than satisfied, for I am something of an architect. I find a regularity in you which is divine."

"I am glad of that, my dear Iolaus, but refrain from
touching it. Let your having seen it suffice for you to
judge it."

"Alas, grant something to the sense of touch, which
alone can judge the resistance and smoothness of these
marbles which Nature has so perfectly polished. Let me
kiss these two springs of life. I prefer them to Cybele's[5]
hundred, and I am not jealous of Attis." [6]

"You are mistaken. Sardini says that it was Diana of
Ephesus[7] who had a hundred breasts."

How could I keep from laughing when, at such a moment, I heard mythological erudition proceeding from
Clementina's lips? Can love expect such a thing? Can it
fear it? Foresee it? No. But, far from finding it cruel,
I saw that it could only be favorable to me. I told her
she was right, asking her to excuse me, and a feeling of
literary gratitude so restrained her that she did not
prevent my lips from descending on a pink bud of which
the only visible indication was its color.

"You suck in vain. It is sterile. Go to my sister. Are
you swallowing?"

"Yes. The quintessence of my own kiss."

"Perhaps a little of my substance, too, for you have
made me feel pleasure. That was a long kiss; but it seems
to me that the kiss which is discharged into the mouth
should be preferable."

"You are right. In that case the reciprocity is real."

"Precept and example! Cruel teacher! Let us stop.
There is too much pleasure in it. Love looks at us and
laughs at our temerity."

"Why, my sweet friend, do we put off allowing him a
victory which can only make us happy?"

"Love's happiness is uncertain. No. I beg you. Keep

your arms here. If kisses can kill us, let us kill ourselves; but let us use no other weapons.''

After a long skirmish as sweet as it was cruel, it was she who called a halt, and who, with her eyes darting fiery sparks, asked me to go to my room.

In the violence of my condition, my love had dissolved into tears, lamenting the constraint which a prejudice foreign to its nature had put upon it. After abating my fire by a toilet which I had never so greatly needed, I dressed and went back to her room. She was writing.

''I feel inspired,'' she said, ''by an exaltation which in all my past life I have never felt. I want to celebrate our victory over ourselves in verse.''

''Sad victory, hostile to human nature, source of death, which Love must abhor because it vilifies him.''

''That is poetry already. Let us both write as our Muses dictate, I praising the victory, you assailing it. But you look sad.''

''I am suffering, and, in your ignorance of a man's constitution, you cannot know why.''

Clementina did not reply; but I saw that she was touched. I was suffering a dull and torturing pain in the place where tyrannical prejudice had kept me garroted when love wanted me to be free. Only bed and sleep could restore the region to equilibrium. I dined gloomily enough, having paid scarcely any attention to the reading of the translation which Signor Vegio had brought me. I asked my friend the Count to deal for me, and I was allowed to go off to bed. No one could guess what my illness was; only Clementina could have some suspicion of it.

After sleeping three or four hours I set myself to writing, in *terza rima*,[8] like Dante, the story of the illness to which I had succumbed in consequence of that sad victory. It was Clementina herself who brought me supper, saying that the bank had won and that her brother-in-law would tell me about it the next day.

After watching me sup with a good appetite, she withdrew to put the same story into verse. I finished mine and made a fair copy of it before going back to sleep, and very early in the morning I saw Clementina at my bedside, holding her little poem, which I read with pleasure. The pleasure she felt when she heard me praise her ideas was far greater than mine.

But mine was greater still when, reading her what I had written, I saw that she was touched and often on the verge of tears. I also had the pleasure of hearing her say that if she had known the part of physiology which instructs the student in that subject she would have acted differently.

After taking a cup of chocolate with her I asked her to lie down beside me, dressed as she was, and to treat me as I had treated her the day before and so learn what sort of torture it was; and, after smiling, she yielded to my urging, but on condition that I would make no attempt on her.

So I had to let her do what she would; but in the end I had no reason to complain. Since she was mistress of the field, I enjoyed the despotism she exercised upon me, at the same time that I knew what pain she must suffer from my not exercising it on her and from her condemning her eyes not to see that of which her hands were in possession; I vainly urged her to satisfy herself in whatever way she might wish; but she would never admit that she wanted anything more than what she was doing.

"At this moment," I said, "it is impossible that your pleasure is equal to mine."

And she replied that in that case I had no reason to complain.

When she left me she said, all on fire with blushes, that she had convinced herself that in love one must do everything or nothing.

We spent the day reading, at table, strolling, playing,

laughing over countless things, without making the prog-
ress in love which the samples I had received promised
me. She wanted to dominate me, and she did not want
me to dominate her; I gently complained of it, and she
could not object.

Two or three days later about midnight I proposed
to her, her sister being present and in bed beside her,
the expedient one proposes to a nun, a widow, a nubile
girl who refuses love because of the consequences she
fears. I took from my pocket a packet of fine English
coveralls, explaining how they could be used and letting
her examine the shape and mechanism of the little bags
at her leisure. After laughing at them heartily, she declared, with her sister agreeing, that they were hideous,
disgusting, and scandalous. In addition she maintained
that they were not to be relied on, for they could easily
be torn. I vainly denied her "easily." I had to put them
back in my pocket when she said that the mere sight of
them horrified her.

I decided that Clementina could put up such a resistance only because she was not in love enough, and,
with this idea in mind, I saw that it was my part to
make her so by the infallible means of providing her
with new pleasures, regardless of expense. I thought of
giving her a fine dinner in Milan at the pastry cook's,
whose apartment was still at my disposition. I had to
take the whole family, but without telling them where
we were to go, for my friend the Count might have felt
obliged to inform his wife and to introduce his sisters to
her. That would have spoiled all my pleasure. The excursion could not but be attractive to the three sisters,
for none of them had ever seen Milan. Little by little I
found myself so taken with the idea I had conceived that
I determined to carry it out in magnificent style.

I wrote to Zenobia to go at once to buy three ready-
made dresses for three ladies of station, of the very
prettiest Lyons fabrics she could find; I sent her the

measurements, specifying the trimmings I wanted. The most expensive trimming, which was to be of stiffened Valenciennes lace, I intended for a dress of pearl-gray satin, which was to be the shortest and which would be for the Countess Ambrosio. I sent her a letter for Signor Greppi, who would give her a man to pay for whatever she bought. I ordered her to take the three dresses to the pastry cook's and to lay them out on my bed. I sent her a letter for the pastry cook in which I ordered him to prepare a dinner for eight persons on such-and-such a day, with both fish and meat, sparing no expense. I instructed Zenobia that everything must be ready in twice twenty-four hours, and that she must be waiting at the pastry cook's for me when I arrived with the three ladies for whom the three dresses were intended. I sent her my letter by Clairmont, telling no one where I was sending it.

Upon Clairmont's return, when I was sure that my orders would be carried out to the letter, I said at table to the Countess-mother that I begged the honor of giving her another dinner like that which I had given her in Lodi; but on two conditions: first, that no one in the family was to know where I was taking them until we were in our carriages; second, that no one was to leave the house in which I would give the dinner except to get back into the carriages, which would take us home to S. A. the same day.

The Countess, as politeness demanded, looked at her husband, who instantly said that he was ready and willing, as indeed he would be if I had proposed to carry off his entire family. I told him that we would leave the next day at eight o'clock in the morning, and that they need not concern themselves about the carriages. I did not exclude the good Canon from the party, both because he danced attendance on the Countess Ambrosio and because he had begun playing heavily and lost every day. Indeed, that very day he was cleaned out. He lost three hundred zecchini on his word, and at supper he said he must ask me to let him have three days to await the return of a man whom he would send to Milan early the next morning. I replied that all my money was at his service.

When we retired I as always accompanied my charming Hebe to her room. We had begun Fontenelle's[9] *Plurality of Worlds*. She said that, having to rise early, she wanted to go to bed, and, replying that she was right, I took Ariosto and, while she was getting into bed, read her the story of Fiordispina, Princess of Spain, who had fallen in love with Bradamante.[10] At the end of the charming tale I expected to see Clementina on fire; but not a bit of it, she was as downcast as her sister Eleonora.

"What is the matter, divine Hebe? Perhaps you did not like Ricciardetto?"

"I liked Ricciardetto very much, and in the Princess's place I would have done what she did; but we shall not sleep tonight, and it is your fault."

"I? What have I done?"

"Alas, nothing! But you could make us happy by giving us a great proof of your friendship."

"Speak. My life, all I possess, my will itself—all is yours. You shall sleep."

"Let us into the secret of where we are going tomorrow."

"Didn't I tell you you would learn that when we set out?"

"But we shall not have slept; and we will be in the dumps all day long."

"I should be very sorry for that."

"Do you doubt our discretion? In any case, it can't be a very weighty secret."

"And it is not. It is a made-to-order secret; but I will reveal it to you. I should be wronging you if I hesitated. I shall give you dinner tomorrow at my apartment in Milan."

"In Milan?"

"In Milan?" asked her sister.

They both get up, just as they are, they fall on me, they devour me, then they leave me to embrace each other, then they come back and sit on my knees, and they talk to me. They have never seen Milan, they have longed for nothing more than to see that magnificent city; when they had to admit that they had never seen it, they felt ashamed; but at the very moment when they learned that they were to have that joy the idea that they must return to S. A. the same night filled them with despair, and the condition I had made that they must not leave the house to which I would take them seemed to them harsh and inhuman.

"Can one travel the fifteen miles to Milan," said Clementina, "just to dine there, and travel them again just to get home?"

"Can we go there," said Eleonora, "without seeing at least our sister-in-law?"

"I foresaw all your objections, my dear children, and that was the reason for my secrecy; but that is how the excursion has been arranged. Perhaps you do not like it. I am at your orders."

"Not like it?" said Clementina. "The excursion is only the more charming just as you thought it up."

So saying, intoxicated with joy and gratitude, she did not think of defending herself from love. She was in my arms, as I was in hers; Eleonora had gone back to bed. Clementina surrendered to all my desires and shared my ecstasies, mingling her smiles with tears which arose from her amorous and blissful soul.

Two hours later I left her and went to bed, full of my happiness and impatient to renew it on the morrow all the more perfectly because my blood would have cooled.

The next morning at eight we all breakfasted; but despite my usual ability to do so, I could not enliven my companions. Clementina and her sister concealed their joy; but the others, in their impatience to know where I would take them, were a trifle somber.

Clairmont had carried out my orders well, and, the carriages being all ready in the courtyard, we go down and I put the Countess Ambrosio in my carriage with Clementina, who held the baby on her lap; after that I go to the other carriage and announce to the company, who are dying of curiosity:

"*We are going to Milan.* Whip up, postilion. To Milan: to the Piazza Cordusio, to the pastry cook's."

I at once leave them and get into my carriage, saying the same thing to my postilion. Clairmont mounts, and we set off. Clementina pretended astonishment, and the Countess Ambrosio looked as one does when one has had a surprise which, though pleasant, gives occasion for thought. We had plenty of time to discuss it and to reach a pitch of gaiety before we came to a village where we get out because, having gone at full speed, the horses had to be unbridled for a quarter of an hour.

I found my companions in good spirits, like people who have decided to make the best of something.

"What will my wife say?" said my friend the Count.

"She will learn nothing about it, and in any case I am the only guilty one. You will dine at my apartment, where I live incognito."

"You have been thinking about taking me to Milan for two years now," said the Countess Ambrosio to her husband, "and our friend thought about it for only a quarter of an hour."

"True," he replied; "but I wished to have us spend a month there."

At that I told him that if he wished to spend a month there, I would see to everything, and he thanked me, saying that I was an extraordinary man. I said I was a man who did not find easy things difficult.

"Admit that you are happy," the Countess Ambrosio said to me as soon as we were back in the carriage; and I admitted it:

"But it is the company which makes me happy. Banish me from your presence, and I shall be wretched."

I made them laugh till the tears came by putting the baby to my breast, where it sucked in vain until disappointment set it to crying. The loving mother soothed it, enjoying my praise of the beautiful picture she presented. She was only less of a beauty than her sister Clementina, who was also three inches taller. We laughed all through the journey, chiefly at the Canon, who had asked the Countess's intercession to gain him my permission to absent himself for half an hour to make a call. She had replied that he must abide by the same condition as all the others. He wanted to call on a lady who, if she learned that he had been in Milan without going to her house, would never have forgiven him.

We arrived in Milan as the clock was striking noon and got out at the pastry cook's door, his wife at once taking the sole offspring of the noble A. B. family in her arms; she begged the Countess to entrust him to her, exhibiting a bosom which proved her competence to make the offer. This scene of mammary hospitality took place at the foot of the stairs, and the Countess accepted the kind offices of the pastry cook's wife with a dignity which enchanted me. I felt that I was the author of all the little beauties which chance sent to embellish the play which my genius had brought forth. I was the happiest of all my actors, and I felt it.

She took my arm, and we entered my apartment, than which nothing could have been neater. I am surprised to see Zenobia with Croce's forsaken mistress, who strikes me as ravishingly pretty. I very nearly failed to recognize her. She was very well dressed, and her face, freed from the expression of sadness it had worn when I had entrusted her to Zenobia, had become enchanting.

"There are two charming young pullets," said the Milanese Countess. "Who are you, Signorine?"

"We are," replied Zenobia, "the Cavaliere's very humble servants, and we are here only to have the honor of serving you."

Zenobia had taken it upon herself to bring the other, who was already beginning to speak Italian, and who looked at me uncertainly, fearing that I might disapprove. But I quickly reassured her, telling her that she had done well to keep Zenobia company. Her brow cleared. The girl could not be unfortunate for long, because no one could look at her without becoming interested in her. A letter of credit displayed on a face is not liable to bankruptcy. Whoever has eyes pays it at sight.

So my "very humble servants" relieve the ladies of their mantles and show them to my bedroom, where they see the three dresses spread out on the large table. I knew only the one of pearl-colored satin trimmed with lace, for I had ordered it. It was the Countess Ambrosio who noticed it before she did the two others.

"What a charming dress!" she said. "You must know to whom it belongs."

"Of course I do. It belongs to your husband, who will do as he pleases with it. I hope that, if he gives it to you, you will not offend him by refusing it. There, Count, the dress is yours. I will kill myself if you will not do me the honor to accept it."

"We are too fond of you to let you kill yourself. The jest is as magnanimous as it is novel. I accept the dress with this hand, and with the other I give it to my dear wife."

"What, my dear! This dress, this charming dress, is mine? Whom shall I thank? Both of you. I insist upon wearing it at dinner."

The two other dresses were not as rich; but they were more striking, and I rejoiced, seeing my angel's eyes

fixed on the longer one, and Eleonora looking only at
the one she was sure I intended for her. The first was of
rose-colored satin with apple-green stripes, trimmed with
tufts of down; the other was sky-blue, variegated with
bunches of flowers in five or six colors and trimmed with
mignonette lace in large knots, which made the prettiest
effect. It was Zenobia who unhesitatingly told Clementina that the striped dress was hers.

"How do you know?"

"Because it is the longest of the three."

"Then it is mine?" she asked me.

"If I may dare to hope so."

"I will put it on."

Countess Eleonora declared that hers had a style which
made it superior to the two others. We left them to
themselves.

I went into the next room with the two Counts and
the Canon, who were thoughtful. They must have been
reflecting on the prodigality of gamesters, to whom
money cost nothing; but I saw that, even so, they were
astonished, and arousing astonishment was my passion.
It was an intense feeling of self-esteem which made me
superior to those who were around me; it was enough
that I believed it. I would have scorned anyone who had
dared to tell me that I was being laughed at, yet it is
possible that he would have been telling me the truth.

My contentment putting me in high spirits, I infected
my guests with my gaiety. I warmly embraced Count
Ambrosio, asking him to forgive me for the presents I
had given his family, and I thanked his brother again
and again for having made me acquainted with him.

The beautiful Countesses came in, shining like stars,
all three saying they were sure I had taken their measurements, but they did not know how. Countess Ambrosio
remarked that I had had her dress made in such a way
that it could be let out when she was with child; and
she admired the trimming, saying that it must have cost

four times as much as the dress. Clementina could not tear herself away from the looking glass; she supposed that in the rose and green colors I had wanted to give her Hebe's attributes.[11] As for Countess Eleonora, she continued to maintain that her dress was the prettiest.

Delighted with my beauties' satisfaction, I summoned the company to table, all of us being very hungry. At the dinner we were served every imaginable delicacy in the way of both fish and flesh, as well as oysters from the Arsenal [12] of Venice, which the pastry cook had managed to wheedle from the Duke of Modena's maître d'hôtel, and which we found delicious. We ate three hundred of them, and we emptied twenty bottles of champagne. We spent three hours at the table, drinking and singing, served by the beautiful girls whose charms rivaled those of the ladies who admired them.

Toward the end of the meal the pastry cook's wife came in with the Countess's baby at her breast. It was a striking tableau: the joy of the devoted mother, who exclaimed with delight when she saw him, and the pastry cook's wife, who seemed proud to have taken the Countess's place for four whole hours.

We spent another hour drinking punch and laughing, after which the Countesses went to undress. Zenobia saw to putting the three dresses into my carriage in a basket; and when I said that it was time to set out I saw everyone sad. Croce's forsaken mistress found an opportunity to tell me that she was very happy with Zenobia and to ask me when we should leave. I promised her that she should be in Marseilles two weeks after Easter at the latest.

Questioned privately, Zenobia assured me that she was a girl of excellent character, very well behaved, and such that she would be most sorry to see her leave. In my heartfelt satisfaction over the beautiful dresses she had bought, I gave her twelve zecchini. She said that I would find the mercer's receipts in the hands of Signor

Greppi's clerk. Content with everything, I paid the
worthy pastry cook whatever he asked. I loved, I was
loved, my health was good, I had a great deal of money,
and I spent it, I was happy and I confessed it to myself,
laughing at the stupid moralists who say that there is
no true happiness on earth. It is their "on earth" which
makes me laugh, as if one could look for it anywhere
else. *Mors ultima linea rerum est* ("Death is the final
boundary line of all things").[13] There is a happiness
which is perfect and real as long as it continues; it
passes, but its end does not mean that it has not existed
and that he who has enjoyed it cannot have been aware
of it. The men who do not deserve happiness are those
who, having it, hide it from themselves, or those who,
having the means to obtain it, neglect it. *Carpe diem
quam minimum credula postero* ("Seize the day, trusting
as little as possible to the day to come"),[14] and in another
place: *Prudens futuri temporis exitum caliginosa nocte
premit Deus ridetque si mortalis ultra fas trepidat.
Quod adest memento componere aequus: caetera fluminis
ritu feruntur* ("Wisely does the god conceal in dark
night what the future is to bring, and laughs if a mortal
feels concern beyond what is lawful. Remember to deal
calmly with what now presses upon you: the rest is borne
along like a river").[15]

We left the pastry cook's house at seven o'clock, we
arrived at S. A. about midnight; and we at once went
to bed; but I did not leave Clementina until I had spent
with her some of those hours which make a man happy
and which come back to make him happy every time
that, well in body and mind, he recalls them.

"Do you suppose," she asked me, "that I can be
happy after you leave?"

"During the first days we shall both be unhappy; but
little by little our fire will be quenched under the ashes
of philosophy."

"But admit that you will easily console yourself with

your young ladies; but do not suppose that I am jealous of them, for I should loathe myself if I thought I could be capable of receiving the kind of consolation you will certainly seek.''

''Do not imagine that, I beg you. The girls whom you saw are not of a kind to take your place, and they cannot fill my heart and mind. The taller of them is the wife of a tailor, and the other is a respectable girl whom I shall take back to Marseilles, her native city, from which a wretch carried her off after seducing her. In future and until the day of my death you alone shall reign over my soul, and if it ever happens that, led astray by my senses, I clasp in my arms some object which has tempted me, hideous repentance, my dear friend, will follow fast to avenge you and to make me unhappy.''

''I am sure that I shall never be unhappy for that reason. But I do not understand how, loving me as you love me and holding me in your arms, you can believe in the possibility of becoming unfaithful to me.''

''I do not believe it, I assume it.''

''That seems to me to be the same thing.''

What was I to answer? She was right, even though she was wrong; but what set her wrong was love; mine did not show a strength equal to that with which hers forbade her to foresee. I reasoned more correctly only because I loved less. The man who, in the arms of his mistress, is convinced of that can answer only by sighs and kisses mingled with tears.

''Take me with you,'' she said, ''I am willing. I shall be happy. You must, if you love me, be delighted with your own happiness. Let us make each other happy, dear friend.''

''I cannot dishonor your family.''

''Do you consider me unworthy to become your wife?''

''You are worthy of a monarch. It is I who am unworthy to possess such a girl as you. Consider that I have nothing in the world but the Goddess Fortune, who may forsake me tomorrow. Also, I do not fear her reverses, but I would kill myself if I saw you involved in my misfortunes.''

''Why does it seem to me that you can never meet with misfortune, and why do I feel certain that you cannot be happy except with me? Your love is not like mine if you do not trust in it as I do.''

''More than you can have done, my angel, I have had a cruel experience of life, which, making me tremble for the future, affrights love. Love affrighted [16] loses in strength what it gains in reasonableness.''

''Cruel reasonableness! Then we must subscribe to our separation?''

''My heart will remain with you; I shall leave adoring you, and if Fortune is kind to me in England you shall see me here next year. I will buy an estate wherever you choose, and I will make you a present of it, sure that you will bring it to me as your dowry, and our children will be our delight.''

''Oh, what a charming future! It is a dream. Would that I could fall asleep and make it last until I die! But what shall I do if you leave me with a child?''

''Ah, my divine Hebe! That will not be. Have you not noticed that I spared you?''

''Spared? I know nothing about it; but I can imagine. I am grateful to you. Alas! You were not born to bring me troubles. No! Never can I repent of having surrendered to love in your arms. Everyone in this household says that you are fortunate and that you deserve your good fortune. What praise! My dear friend, you cannot imagine how my heart leaps for joy when I hear that said in your absence. When I am told that I love you I reply that I adore you, and you know it is no lie.''

It was with these dialogues that we occupied the intervals between our amorous ecstasies during the five or six last nights which we spent together. Her sister, in bed beside us, slept or pretended to sleep. When I left, I went to bed, I rose late, then I spent the whole day with her, either alone or in company with the family.

What a life! Is it possible that a man who is his own master can bring himself to leave it? Fortune had ordained that I should win from the Canon all the money I had let the family win from me by never watching how they played. Clementina alone would never profit by my inattentiveness; but on the last two days I made her go halves with me in my bank, and, the Canon still being unlucky, she won about a hundred zecchini. The worthy monk lost a thousand zecchini, of which seven hundred remained in the house.

The last night, the whole of which I spent with my angel, was very sad; we should have died of grief if love had not come to our aid from time to time. When, the last half hour having come, we appeared at the table to breakfast with the entire family, both Clementina and I looked as if we were at death's door; but our state was respected. They saw me gloomy for once, and no one asked me the reason. I promised to send them news of me and to return the following year; and I wrote to them; but I stopped when the misfortunes which overwhelmed me in London made me lose hope of seeing them again. I did not see them again; but I could never forget Clementina. Six years later, on my return from Spain, I learned, and I wept for joy, that she was living happily, Marchesa di . . . ,[17] in the city of . . . , three years married and the mother of two male children, the younger of whom, now twenty-seven years of age, is today a captain in the Austrian army. How I should like to meet him! When on my return from Spain I learned of Clementina's excellent situation I was in wretched circumstances. Having traveled through Lombardy, I was on my way to Leghorn to better my fortunes. I found myself four miles from an estate where she might be with her husband; but I did not have the courage to go to see her. Perhaps I did well.

Having to go downstairs to leave, and seeing the whole family about to accompany me to my carriage and not seeing Clementina, I pretended to go for something I had forgotten, in order to bid her a last farewell. I found her dissolved in tears, her throat swollen, and unable to say a single word to me. Mingling my tears with hers, I took a last kiss from her trembling lips, and I left her there. After thanking and embracing the entire company, I set off with my dear Count, and in less than three hours, during which we slept, we arrived at his house in Milan, where we found the Countess, who did not expect us, with the Marchese Triulzi. After laughing heartily that amiable man sent to his house for dinner for four. They were able to tell us that we had been in Milan, and the Countess complained that we had not let her know of it; but the Marchese soothed her, saying that she would have had to give us dinner.

At the table I told them that I should leave for Genoa on the fourth day, and, unluckily for me, the Marchese Triulzi promised me a letter to Signora Isolabella,[18] a celebrated coquette, and the Countess promised me one for the Bishop of Tortona,[19] who was a relative of hers.

I reached Milan in time to wish my dear Teresa, who was going to Palermo, a good journey. I talked to her about our son Don Cesarino's bent,[20] trying to persuade her to abet him in it. She replied that she was leaving him in Milan, that she now knew what had given rise to his passion, and that she would never consent to it. She said that she hoped to find him changed when she returned; but he did not change. The reader will hear more of him fifteen years hence.

I settled my accounts with Greppi, who gave me bills of exchange on Marseilles and a letter of credit for ten thousand francs on Genoa, where I did not expect to need much cash. Despite my luck at play, I left Milan poorer by a thousand zecchini. I had spent money fast and furiously.

I passed every afternoon at the Marchesa Q.'s, sometimes alone and sometimes with her sister present. With Clementina's image constantly before the eyes of my soul, she did not seem to me the same woman.

Having no reason to keep it from Count A. B. that I was taking a young lady with me, I sent Clairmont to fetch her small trunk, after paying Zenobia all that she had disbursed for her, and at eight o'clock on the morning of my departure she came to my apartment, very nicely dressed.

After kissing the hand of the Countess who had made an attempt on my life, and after thanking my dear Count, I left Milan on the 20th of March in the year 1763, and I have never returned there.

The young lady, whom out of respect for herself and her family I shall call Crosin,[21] was charming and had an air of breeding which was above her station and a reserved manner which bespoke her excellent upbringing. Seeing her beside me, I congratulated myself on feeling in no danger of falling in love with her; but I was mistaken. I told Clairmont that I intended to present her as my niece, and I ordered him to treat her with due respect.

Having never talked seriously with her, I first took care to gauge her intelligence and, though I had no intention of making love to her, to inspire friendship and confidence in her. The wound which Clementina had made in my heart could not heal. I congratulated myself on being in a position to restore her to the bosom of her family without harrowing myself and in the certainty that I should leave her there without regret. I enjoyed my noble deed in advance, and I was proud of my ability to spend many days with a very pretty girl from no other motive than the heroic one of saving her from the disgrace she might have suffered if she had made the journey alone. She felt this.

"Indeed," she said, "I am sure that Monsieur de la

Croix would never have forsaken me if he had not found you in Milan.''

''You amaze me. Believe me, he acted basely, for, despite all your merits, he could not count on me as certainly as all that. I will not say that he deliberately scorned you, for his circumstances may have been desperate, but you ought to be convinced that he no longer loved you.''

''I am certain of the contrary. Finding himself without resources, he had either to leave me or to kill himself.''

''Neither. His duty was to sell everything you had and take you back to Marseilles. When one is in Genoa one can go there by water for very little. La Croix counted on the interest your pretty face inspires, and he was not mistaken; but you see what a risk he took. A man who loves, believe me, cannot bear such an idea. Permit me to tell you that, if you had not made a strong impression on me, my concern for you would have been very slight. But I am making a mistake in condemning La Croix, for I see plainly that you are still in love with him.''

''That is true; I pity him, and I complain of nothing but my cruel destiny. I shall not see him again; but I shall not love again. I will retire to a convent. My father has a kind heart; he will forgive me. I was the victim of love; my will was not free. When I reflect on what I have done, I cannot repent.''

''You would have left Milan with him, even on foot, if he had told you to?''

''Can you doubt it? But he loved me too much to expose me to weariness and poverty.''

''I am sure that if we find him in Marseilles you will go back to him.''

''No. My soul is already beginning to recover its freedom. The day will come when I shall thank God that I have utterly forgotten him.''

The girl's sincerity pleased me. Knowing the power

of love, I pitied her. She spent two hours telling me all the details of her unfortunate passion.

Having reached Tortona[22] at nightfall, I decided to spend the night there, leaving it to Clairmont to order me a good supper. But at supper my pretended niece showed me a cast of mind which I did not expect. In addition, she kept up with me in enjoying the excellent made dishes, glass in hand. I found her amusing, lively within the limits prescribed by good society, and not uttering another word about her wretched lover. To something I said when we had risen from table, she replied with a witticism which, after setting me laughing heartily, gave me a decided liking for her. I embraced her in the joy of my heart, and, having found on her beautiful lips a kiss as ardent as mine, I began to be tempted by the idea of love. I asked her if she would take it in good part if we shared a bed.

At this invitation she shows surprise and, in a serious tone and with a submissive air, than which nothing could have been better calculated to displease me, she replies:

"Alas, it is for you to command."

"Command? It is not a matter of obedience, or even of obligingness. You have inspired love in me; but if you do not share it I can stifle it in its infancy. As you see, there are two beds here."

"Then I will sleep in the other one. If that should make you less kind to me, I shall consider myself unfortunate."

"No, no, my angel; you will not find me deserving of your scorn. Go to bed. I shall find a way to win your esteem."

She drew out a screen, and she went to bed after undressing completely, as she told me herself at Genoa several days later.

The next morning very early I sent the Bishop of Tortona the letter from Countess A. B. An hour later, just as I was breakfasting with my niece, an old priest came to invite me to dinner at the episcopal palace with the young lady who was with me. The Countess's letter had said nothing of a young lady who might be with me; but the polite Spanish prelate saw that, unable to leave her alone, I should not have accepted his invitation; he forced me to accept by inviting me with her. He had apparently learned from the innkeeper's register that the lady was my niece. I told the priest I would go.

My niece, apparently in the best of humors, treated me as if I could feel no resentment at her having preferred her bed to mine. This pleased me. My blood having cooled, I saw that she would have degraded herself if she had acted otherwise. I did not even feel hurt. Self-esteem tells an intelligent woman not to yield to a lover's desires until he can suppose that she has been won by his attentions. I had invited her to share my bed as if it were expected of me. I had drunk too much. I saw that she felt flattered when I told her I would take her with me to dinner at the Bishop's. She attired herself with elegance and modesty. At midday Monsignore sent us a carriage.

I saw a prelate two inches taller than myself, eighty years of age, but active, serious, and affable. When my niece tried to kiss his hand he withdrew it, offering her the golden cross which hung from his neck. She kissed it saying:

"This is what I love." [23]

She then looked at me, and the ingenious jest rather surprised me. At table I found the Bishop learned. We were a company of nine or ten; in addition to four priests, he had invited two young noblemen, who treated my niece with every possible attention, which she received in a manner to convince me that she was accustomed to it. I noticed that the Bishop never fixed his eyes on her pretty face, even when he spoke to her. I determined to win the love of this girl by my assiduities.

I left Tortona at four o'clock and traveled to Novi,[24]

where I stopped for the night. At supper I turned the conversation to religion, and, finding her a good Christian, I asked her how she could have joked when she was kissing the cross of Our Lord. She said that the pun had come to her by pure chance, and that if she had thought about it such a jest would never have left her lips. I pretended to believe her. She was witty. The desires she inspired in me became stronger by the moment, but my self-esteem forced me to hold them in check. I refrained from embracing her when she went to bed; but, there being no screen, she did not undress until she thought I was asleep. The next morning we set out at six o'clock, and at noon we were in Genoa.

I went to lodge in a townsman's house of which Pogomas[25] had sent me the address in Milan. He had rented an apartment of four very well-furnished rooms for me, with which I was thoroughly pleased. I sent him word that I had arrived, and I ordered dinner.

VOLUME 8 • NOTES

CHAPTER I

1. As stated in the Introduction (Vol. 1, p. 19), Chapters I-IV of Volume 8 are missing from the manuscript. They must, however, have been available to Laforgue when he prepared his edition of 1826-1838 (*ibid.*). In the absence of C.'s holograph, Laforgue's version is the only available text of these four chapters. As such, it is printed in the Brockhaus-Plon edition of 1960-1962; and, as such, it has been translated in the present English edition. The translator has made a deliberate attempt in these four chapters to represent Laforgue's leisurely and interfering manner (see Vol. 1, pp. 11-17) in contrast to C.'s haste and vividness. To indicate that they do not represent C.'s own text, the four chapters are typographically distinguished by being printed in italics.

2. *Querilinte:* Obviously a name coined by C. (Laforgue makes the first *e* an *é*; but C. in his part of the ms. writes *e*.)

3. *Stormont:* David Murray, Viscount Stormont (1727-1796), English diplomat (cf. Vol. 7, Chap. XIII).

4. *To go to Lisbon:* In more than one passage in his memoirs C. refers to his projected journey to Lisbon but nowhere reports that he actually made it. Presumably he was there once, perhaps in 1767, before his lengthy stay in Spain; but even this is conjecture.

5. *Surrender . . . King's name:* Cf. Vol. 6, Chap. I.

6. *Charming girl . . . instigation:* Anne Roman-Coupier. See Vol. 7, Chap. II.

7. *The Duchess of Lauraguais:* Diane Adélaïde, Duchesse de Lauraguais (ca. 1713-1769). C. writes "l'Ouraguais."

8. *A son . . . wonderful things:* Anne Roman-Coupier's son, Louis Aimé, known as the Abbé de Bourbon, died of small-pox in Naples in 1787, aged 25.

9. *Madrid:* Château built by François I in 1528 on the northern edge of the Bois de Boulogne and named to commemorate his term of not very strict imprisonment in Madrid after his

defeat at Pavia (1525). The château was razed to the ground during the French Revolution.

10. *Horosmadis:* Presumably a coinage of C.'s from "Ormesius," the name of a legendary figure of Rosicrucianism. The doctrines of the sect were said to have been brought to the West by Ormesius, an Egyptian priest of Serapis, after the loss of Palestine in 1188; he was supposed to have made an amalgam of Egyptian and Christian teaching. King Frederick William II of Prussia (1744-1797) took the name "Ormesus" as a Rosicrucian.

11. *Iriasis:* Madame d'Urfé had lost her daughter Agnès Marie in 1756 (not in 1751, as her account seems to imply), but the girl was born before 1734, the year in which Madame d'Urfé's husband died. Since, according to the account, Iriasis was born in 1743, but, so far as is known, Madame d'Urfé did not bear another child after her husband's death, Iriasis must be a creation of her imagination.

12. *Anael:* According to cabalistic doctrine the Angel Anael governed Friday under the rule of Venus; he acted as her messenger.

13. *Genius of Mercury:* According to cabalistic doctrine Mercury is the planet governed by Ariel, the Prince of Hell.

14. *My brother . . . Porte Saint-Denis:* In 1762 Francesco Casanova was living in the Carré de la Porte Saint-Denis (2nd Arrondissement). However, C. cannot have met his wife in 1761, the year of which he is writing, for their marriage did not take place until June 26, 1762. Probably, then, when C. saw Francesco in 1761 he was still a bachelor, and the meeting with his wife did not occur until C.'s later stay in Paris in 1763.

15. *Impotent:* Francesco Casanova's second wife, Jeanne Catherine Delachaux, gave him 3 children. However, there is reason to believe that she was anything but faithful to him.

16. *Five or six years later:* Jeanne Casanova, née Jolivet, did not die until 1773. C. has obviously confused his several stays in Paris in 1761, 1762, 1763, and 1767. His brother married for the second time in 1775.

17. *Madame du Rumain:* Constance Simone Flore Gabrielle du Rumain, née Rouault de Gamaches (1725-1781), married

to Count du Rumain in 1746 (cf. especially Vol. 5, Chaps. IX and X).

18. *Halifax:* George Montagu Dunk, 2nd Earl Halifax (1716-1771), English Secretary of State from 1757.

19. *The Queen being dead:* A strange error, for Maria Le-szczynska, wife of Louis XV, did not die until 1768.

20. *Opera:* Opera was performed at the time in the theater in the Palais-Royal.

21. *Madame Vanloo:* Anne Marie Christine Vanloo (also van Loo), née Somis (1704-1783), singer, born in Turin, married to the then celebrated painter Charles André Vanloo (1705-1765) in 1733.

22. *Comédie Italienne:* The troupe of Italian actors then played in the Hôtel de Bourgogne, Rue Mauconseil (1st Arrondissement).

23. *Saincy:* Louis Pierre Sébastien, Maréchal de Saincy, held the office of *"économe général du clergé"* from 1750 to 1762.

24. *Nesle:* Contemporary records mention more than one Marquis de Nesle; it is impossible to determine to which of them C. here refers.

25. *Baby:* Manon Blondel, née Balletti, did not bear her first child until Nov. 19, 1761; it died the next day. Her second child, Jean Baptiste, was not born until 1765. C. is here again confusing his several stays in Paris.

26. *Louvre . . . Rue Neuve-des-Petits-Champs:* The Rue des Petits-Champs is in the 1st Arrondissement. Documents show that in 1761 Blondel was living with his wife in the Rue de la Harpe (5th Arrondissement). It was not until 1767 that, as an architect and a member of the Academy, Blondel was granted the use of an apartment in the Louvre; after his death in 1774 Manon had to vacate it.

27. *Coëtanfao . . . five or six years later:* Constance Gabrielle Bonne du Rumain, Marquise de Coëtanfao (1747-1783), married Marie Louis Alexandre, Marquis de Polignac (died 1768), in 1767.

28. *The beautiful stocking-seller:* Madame Baret, daughter of the Comptroller Gilbert, lived in the Rue des Prouvaires (1st Arrondissement) after her marriage; she became the mistress of a Councillor of the Parlement whom C. calls

Monsieur de Langlade and whose name she is said to have
assumed later. She became an actress in St. Petersburg and
died there in 1765 (cf. Vol. 5, Chap. XI).

29. *Langlade:* Like Gilbert and Baret, Langlade is obviously
a fictitious name.

30. *Camilla:* Giacoma Antonia Veronese, called Camilla (1735-
1768), Italian dancer and actress with the Comédie Italienne
in Paris (cf. especially Vol. 3, Chap. XI, and Vol. 5, Chap.
V).

31. *Corallina:* Anna Maria Veronese, called Corallina (1730-
1782), Marquise de Silly from ca. 1761; Italian actress in
Paris (cf. especially Vol. 3, Chap. IX).

32. *La Marche:* Louis François Joseph, Prince of Bourbon-
Conti (1734-1814), until 1776 Count de la Marche.

33. *Montréal:* C. is in error. Corallina's son received the title
Chevalier de Vauréal (1761-1785).

34. *My old friend Balletti:* Antonio Stefano Balletti (1724-
1789) was a friend of C.'s, an actor and ballet master; his
father, Mario Balletti, did not die until 1762; his wife may
have been a Mademoiselle Dumalgé or a Jeanne Marie Le
François Piedumont.

35. *Comédie Française:* It was then in the Rue des Fossés
Saint-Germain, now Rue de l'Ancienne Comédie (6th Arrondissement). Its later home in the Palais-Royal was not built
until 1786.

36. *Lord Lismore:* See Vol. 7, Chap. XI, n. 22.

37. *Milady:* See Vol. 7, Chap. XI, n. 23.

38. *Apollo:* The Greek god of poetry.

39. *Pactolus:* The River Pactolus, in Lydia, was famous for the
grains of gold found in its waters.

40. *Le Cercle:* Poinsinet's comedy *Le Cercle ou la soirée à la
mode* was first produced on Sept. 17, 1764, at the Comédie
Française.

41. *The physician Herrenschwandt:* Johann Friedrich Herrenschwandt (1715-1798), of Swiss descent, physician to the
Duke of Orléans from 1750 to 1755.

42. *Saint-Albin:* See Vol. 7, Chap. XI, n. 24.

43. *Hippocrene:* A spring on Mount Helicon, sacred to the
Muses.

44. *Morellet:* André Morellet (1727-1819), French writer and

contributor to the *Encyclopédie*; he was imprisoned in the Bastille on June 11, 1760, for publishing a controversial preface; he was released on July 30th of the same year.

45. *Order . . . conferred on me:* The Order of the Golden Spur (cf. Vol. 7, Chap. IX).

46. *La Dazenoncourt:* Ballet girl with the Paris Opéra, notorious from 1747 for her loose living. C. writes "Dangenancour."

47. *Choisy:* Choisy-sur-Seine, now Choisy-le-Roi, on the Seine south of Paris; then a well-known resort. Louis XV had a château there, in which Madame de Pompadour often stayed.

48. *Pont Royal:* Built under Louis XIV in 1685 from plans by Mansart, it still bridges the Seine between the Tuileries and the 7th Arrondissement.

49. *Santis:* Giuseppe Santis (born in Spoleto ca. 1724), professional gambler and adventurer; held a position in the administration of the École Militaire lottery under the brothers Calzabigi (cf. Vol. 5, Chap. II).

50. *Place Maubert:* In the 5th Arrondissement.

51. *Hôtel du Saint-Esprit:* See Vol. 7, Chap. XIII, n. 22.

52. *Desarmoises:* See Vol. 7, Chap. I, n. 6.

53. *Brühl:* Heinrich, Count Brühl (1700-1763), Prime Minister of Saxony under King Augustus III.

54. *La Renaud:* Catherine Renaud. She appears from 1753 as "Marianne Reneaud" in the roster of the ballet dancers of the Dresden opera; she returned to Paris in 1757, married the French Court jeweler August Böhmer (see note 73 to this chapter) in 1768; her second husband, whom she married in 1796, was Paul Bassenge, who had been his partner in business.

55. *Receives none of her pension:* C.'s mother Zanetta had fled to Prague on account of the Seven Years' War, the Court of Saxony having taken refuge in Poland. During these years Zanetta did not receive the pension which had been promised her.

56. *"Three Moors":* Still a well-known hotel in the Maximilianstrasse, Augsburg. Originally a house of business belonging to the Fugger family, it became an inn in 1731; it was rebuilt in 1945.

57. *French Envoy:* France had appointed two envoys to the

expected Congress at Augsburg. They were César Gabriel, Count Choiseul-Chevigny, Duke of Praslin (1712-1785), French Ambassador in Vienna from 1758 to 1761, and his predecessor, Henri Joseph Bouchard d'Esparbès de Lussan, Marquis d'Aubeterre (1714-1788). The French delegation arrived in Augsburg in June 1761.

58. *Carli:* Tommaso Carli, of Tremezzo on Lake Como, moved to Augsburg in 1727 and there founded a foreign exchange office which soon became a well-known bank.

59. *"Stag":* The "Golden Stag" inn ("Zum Goldenen Hirschen") was located at 18 Theatinerstrasse from 1728 to 1861.

60. *Almada:* See Vol. 7, Chap. VIII, nn. 1 and 4.

61. *Stormont, the English Ambassador . . . Bavaria:* There was no English Ambassador to Bavaria from 1758 to 1766. David Murray, Viscount Stormont (1727-1796; cf. Vol. 7, Chap. XIII, n. 8), was the English Envoy Extraordinary in Warsaw from 1756 to 1763 and was sent to Augsburg as Plenipotentiary.

62. *Folard:* Hubert, Chevalier de Folard (1709-1799), French diplomat, from 1755 French Envoy Extraordinary in Munich.

63. *The Elector:* Maximilian III Joseph von Wittelsbach (1727-1777), Elector of Bavaria from 1745.

64. *Dowager Electress of Saxony:* Maria Antonia Walpurgis (1724-1780), daughter of the Emperor Charles VII; in 1747 she married Friedrich Christian, Hereditary Prince of Saxony, who was Elector for only some 10 weeks (Oct. to Dec. 1763). She could not have the title "Dowager Electress" until after the death of her husband in 1763. In 1760 she and her husband had fled from the Prussian advance on Dresden, first to Prague and then to Munich.

65. *My brother-in-law:* The musician Peter August (died 1787), who was married to C.'s sister Maria Maddalena Antonia Stella (1732-1800).

66. *Rousseau:* Jean Jacques Rousseau (1712-1778); the first 6 books of his *Confessions* appeared in 1782, the complete text (in 12 books) in 1789.

67. *Afflisio:* Giuseppe Afflisio (Affligio), alias Count Afflisio, Don Bepe il Cadetto, or Don Giuseppe Marcati (died 1787),

adventurer, professional gambler, and impresario; he was sentenced to the galleys at Leghorn in 1779.

68. *Zweibrücken:* Friedrich Michael, Duke of Zweibrücken (1724-1767), Palatine, Field Marshal in the French army, father of Maximilian Joseph, first King of Bavaria.

69. *Kephalides:* Salomon Ambrosius Kephalides, physician in the Collegium Medicum of Augsburg; his name appears in municipal documents in 1757, 1761, and 1762.

70. *Faget:* Jean Faget (ca. 1700-1762), well-known Parisian physician (C. writes "Fayet").

71. *Algardi:* Francesco Antonio Algardi (died 1789), Bolognese physician, from 1761 physician-in-ordinary to the Prince-Bishop of Augsburg.

72. *Manna:* The exudate of the European flowering ash (*Fraxinus ornus*) and several related species; now known in pharmacy only as a mild laxative.

73. *Böhmer:* Karl August Böhmer (died 1794), Court jeweler to the King of France until 1789.

74. *Rohan . . . necklace:* Louis René Édouard, Prince of Rohan-Guémenée (1734-1803), French Ambassador in Vienna (1772-1774), Grand Almoner of France (1772-1786), Cardinal from 1778. The notorious "affair of the diamond necklace" was a scandal into which both Cardinal de Rohan and Queen Marie Antoinette herself were drawn and by which the already impaired status of the monarchy and the Court in the public estimation was still further undermined. In 1785 Rohan, who had fallen out of favor with the Queen, was persuaded by two dubious advisers (Countess Lamothe and the adventurer Cagliostro) to present her with a diamond necklace worth 1.6 million francs. Countess Lamothe, who was to act as intermediary, took the necklace to England and there sold it. The jewelers Böhmer and Bassenge, after waiting vainly for payment, laid a complaint before the Queen. Rohan, Countess Lamothe, and Cagliostro were imprisoned in August 1785. Rohan was released.

75. *Annemirl:* C. writes "Anna-Midel," doubtless to represent the Bavarian "Annemirl," contraction for "Annemarie."

76. *Rue du Bac:* In the 7th Arrondissement; named for a ferry (*bac*) over the Seine, which was replaced by a bridge in 1632.

77. *René of Savoy:* Renato di Savoia, Count of Tenda (ca. 1473-1525), General in the service of Louis XII and François I of France; grandfather of the Renée of Savoy who married Jacques d'Urfé in 1554.

78. *Great Work:* In alchemy, the secret of transforming baser metals into gold.

79. *Bicêtre:* Name of a castle in a former village south of Paris on the road to Fontainebleau; under Louis XIV it became a hospital and a prison; now an insane asylum.

80. *Lamberg:* Maximilian Joseph, Count Lamberg (1729-1792).

81. *His wife:* Maria Josepha, née Reichsfreiin von Dachsberg (born 1746), did not become Count Lamberg's second wife until 1763 (his first wife, Maria Theresia, née von Trautsmannsdorf, died in 1755). Hence C. cannot have known Maria Josepha and her 2 daughters until his later stay in Augsburg in 1767.

82. *Sellentin:* C. first met him in Augsburg in 1767, not in 1761. They met again in Dresden in 1797.

83. *Drew me . . . literary genius:* C. had already met Lamberg in Paris in 1757, but this is the first mention of him in the memoirs. Their correspondence (edited by G. Gugitz, Vienna, 1935) is one of the most important sources for C.'s biography. Lamberg's best-known publications were *Mémorial d'un mondain* (1774) and *Lettres critiques, morales et politiques* (1786).

84. *Daughters . . . excellent marriages:* Maria Josepha (born 1766) married Franz, Baron von Hofmüller; Maria Walburga (born 1767) married Clemens, Count von Nyss.

CHAPTER II

1. *The troupe:* The municipal archives of Augsburg make no mention of this company of actors.

2. *San Cipriano:* The Somaschian Seminary of San Cipriano was on the island of Murano, north of Venice; in 1817 it was transferred to Santa Maria della Salute in Venice proper (cf. Vol. 1, Chap. VI).

3. *Bassi:* Domenico Bassi (ca. 1724-1774), studied for the

priesthood but then turned to the theater, becoming an actor and the manager of a company.

4. *His wife:* Giacinta Bassi, actress (dates not known).

5. *His daughter:* Marianna Bassi (1749-1769), actress, singer, and dancer.

6. *Cosmopolitan charlatan:* So Laforgue; Schütz gives "*den berühmten* Scharlatan Cosmopolito." There was in fact an 18th-century Italian adventurer and charlatan who used the name Cosmopolita.

7. *Going to Venice:* Bassi did, in fact, later become the successful director of the Teatro San Cassiano in Venice.

8. *Theriaca:* The "Electuarium Theriaca Andromachi" was a sort of panacea, originally compounded from some 70 ingredients. Legend attributed its invention to Andromachus, physician to the Emperor Nero. Until the 18th century the Venetian theriaca, like that of other European countries, was compounded only in the presence of magistrates.

9. *Groschen:* German coin worth 1/24th of a taler or 1/20th of a florin.

10. *Margravate:* A district between the bend of the Rhine near Basel and the Breisgau, famous for its wines.

11. *Girl from Strassburg:* Probably a certain Teresa, a well-known *serva* (soubrette), who married the Arlecchino Nicola Menichelli (died after 1782) about 1761.

12. *Ducat:* Dukat, an Imperial coin minted from 1559 to 1857 and worth about 2 2/3 talers.

13. *Bolo:* Andrea de Bollo, diplomat in the service of the Republic of Genoa; from 1766 Polish representative in Genoa.

14. *A woman in disguise:* Probably the adventuress who used the name Countess of Tanis (Thanis) and who was unmasked in 1763.

15. *Dulcinea:* Name of Don Quixote's lady-love; used generically for "sweetheart."

16. *The burgomaster on duty:* In Augsburg there were always 2 such officials, called Stadtpfleger, one for Catholics, one for Protestants. If C.'s account refers to the year 1761, the official would be Franz Joseph Ingnaz Rembold (Stadtpfleger from 1761 to 1774); his colleague was Max Christoph Koch von Gailenbach (1751-1768).

17. *Latin . . . universities:* Instead of the elaborately Cicero-

nian Latin cultivated by the Italian Humanists, their German counterparts used a more colloquial and efficient style, which, to an Italian ear, might have sounded uncouth.

18. *Half a dozen names:* Personal names still tend to be longer in Spain and Portugal than in the rest of Europe.

19. *My second visit to Augsburg:* In 1767 (cf. Vol. 10, Chap. X).

20. *Compromising me before the magistrate in Augsburg:* Nothing has been found in the court records of Augsburg to throw light on this episode.

21. *The most expensive inn:* "The Three Kings" (Zu den Drei Königen) was opened in 1610. From 1739 to 1765 its proprietor was Johann Christoph Imhof.

22. *A sensitive soul:* The distinction between sensitive soul and intelligent soul goes back to Aristotle, from whom Scholasticism adopted it.

23. *Magistery:* Alchemical and cabalistic term, meaning "transmuting principle"; here probably used by C. for "occult doctrine."

24. *Fouquet:* René François de Fouquet, Intendant of Metz from 1759.

25. *Intendant:* Title of the plenipotentiary representatives of the central government in the various provinces of France under the Old Régime.

26. *Lastic:* Marquis (not Count) François de Lastic, French Field Marshal from 1748 (cf. Vol. 6, Chap. II).

27. *Lewenhaupt:* Adam, Count of Lewenhaupt (died 1775), of Swedish extraction, served in the French army from 1713, appointed Field Marshal in 1762; personal friend of Louis XV.

28. *Anhalt-Zerbst:* Johanna Elisabeth, Princess of Anhalt-Zerbst (1712-1760), mother of the later Czarina Catherine II, had lived in Paris from 1758 under the name of Countess of Oldenburg.

29. *The theater:* A theater was opened in Metz in 1752 on the present Place de la Comédie.

30. *Raton:* The names of all the actresses and singers who performed in Metz in 1762 are known. Raton was obviously Italian: probably she was a young Italian actress named Baulo, who acted and danced at Metz in 1762; her aunt

(or perhaps mother), also named Baulo, played character parts or second soubrettes at the same period.

31. *Vittorina:* Cf. Vol. 7, Chap. XII.

32. *Fleece, not of gold:* Allusion to the Greek legend of the Golden Fleece, which was carried off by Jason and the Argonauts with the help of Medea.

CHAPTER III

1. *Count N . . . :* Probably the well-known patron of the theater in Prague, Franz Anton, Count Nostitz-Rieneck (1725-1795), Austrian statesman.

2. *Lascaris:* A Byzantine family, documented from the end of the 12th century. In 1554 Jacques I d'Urfé (1534-1574) married Renée of Savoy, granddaughter of René of Savoy and Anne de Lascaris, Countess of Tenda. From then on the d'Urfé family often used the name Lascaris d'Urfé. Madame d'Urfé had earlier been taken in by a swindler who called himself Jean Paul Lascaris.

3. *Pont-Carré:* Near Tournan (Seine-et-Marne); after the French Revolution it was sold to Fouché, Duke of Otranto, as "national property," but it is now demolished.

4. *Civil wars:* C. refers either to the religious wars in France during the second half of the 16th century or, less probably, to the troubles during the period of the Fronde (beginning of the 17th century).

5. *Lyons:* A letter from Louis de Muralt, dated July 3, 1763, yields the information that D'Aranda was a pupil of Professor Daniel, or of Jean Bernoulli, in Basel in 1762 and 1763. However, he might have spent some time in Lyons before his stay in Basel.

6. *Rochebaron:* François La Rochefoucauld, Marquis de Rochebaron (1677-1766), was Commandant of Lyons at the time.

7. *Brougnole:* C. spells the name differently in different places: Brongnole, Brougnole, Brognole; it appears to have been an invention of his own. In her will Madame d'Urfé left a legacy to her favorite maid Marguerite Regnaud-Sainte-Brune; C. may refer to her. But the text at this point is ambiguous, leaving it in doubt whether the maid was Madame d'Urfé's favorite or La Corticelli's.

8. *At Aix:* The list of foreigners visiting Aix (Aachen) for May 21, 1762, contains the notation, "Monsieur le Chevalier de Seingalt avec sa femme," among the names of the guests registered at the "St. Corneille" inn.

9. *Two Princesses of Mecklenburg:* Probably Louisa Friederika, Duchess of Mecklenburg (1722-1791), née Princess of Württemberg, and Charlotte Sophia, Princess of Mecklenburg (1731-1810), née Princess of Saxe-Coburg-Saalfeld.

10. *Bayreuth:* Friedrich, Margrave of Bayreuth (1711-1763).

11. *The Duchess of Württemberg:* Elisabeth Friederike Sophie (1732-1780), daughter of the Margrave of Bayreuth; she married Duke Karl Eugen of Württemberg in 1748 but was separated from him in 1754 (cf. Vol. 6, Chap. III).

12. *D'Aché:* A name obviously coined by C., to conceal the identity of the mother and daughter. The officer so denominated may be the Captain of the Imperial Piedmontese Regiment, Alexandre Théodore Lambertz, who was dismissed from the service in Aix on May 11, 1762.

13. *Schmit:* Nothing is known of this person.

14. *Pienne:* A Chevalier de Pienne (C. writes Pyène) is mentioned as a professional gambler in a police report of 1760.

15. *Pythia . . . Delphi:* The Pythia was the priestess of Apollo at Delphi; she delivered her oracles seated on a tripod over a crevice in the earth from which vapors arose which put her into ecstasy.

16. *Write to the moon:* The moon played an important role in cabalism and magic; it was credited with power to foresee the future and to answer questions concerning it. As a cabalist, Madame d'Urfé would see nothing absurd in her being ordered to write to the moon.

17. *Monsieur D. O.:* Probably the banker Thomas Hope (1704-1779), of Amsterdam (cf. especially Vol. 5, Chaps. VI and VII, and Vol. 6, Chap. I).

18. *Selenis:* Name doubtless coined by C., after Selene, the Greek goddess of the moon.

19. *An English club:* There was no "English Club" in Aix until 1785; however, there was such a club in Spa. C. very likely confuses the two places. There were 2 coffeehouses in Aix at the period where billiards were played and card games and dicing were allowed.

20. *Militerni:* A Neapolitan Marchese di Militerni (C. writes Maliterni) (died 1776), an officer in the French army, was promoted to the rank of Field Marshal in 1768, but later served in the Neapolitan army.

21. *D'Estrées:* Louis Charles César Le Tellier, Duke of Estrées (1697-1771), from 1757 Marshal of France.

22. *Married:* Militerni married a certain Marquise de Puissieux as his second wife in 1744. Nothing is known of a later marriage with a Neapolitan heiress.

23. *A garden outside the city:* Probably in Burtscheid, whose baths then had the reputation of making childbirth easier for stout women. The inns there permitted couples to bathe together.

24. *Malingan:* Flemish or French officer (died ca. 1764); he introduced C. to La Charpillon in London (cf. Vol. 9, Chaps. X-XII).

25. *The beautiful Stuard . . . Vaucluse:* See Vol. 7, Chap. III, *passim,* and *ibid.,* n. 5.

26. *Grimaldi:* See Vol. 7, Chap. III, *passim,* and *ibid.,* n. 25.

27. *Ardennes:* Wooded plateau region in northern France, western Luxembourg, and southeastern Belgium; Shakespeare's "Forest of Arden" (in Warwickshire, England) was named after it. It was the scene of many knightly adventures in the Old French epics and later in Ariosto's *Orlando furioso.*

28. *Bayard:* Rinaldo's steed, in Ariosto's *Orlando furioso.*

29. *Bouillon:* The small city, dominated by the ruins of its ancient castle, is picturesquely situated in the narrow valley of the River Semois; it is on the border between France and Belgium (some 12 miles from Sedan).

30. *Duke of Bouillon:* Charles Godefroy de la Tour d'Auvergne, Duke of Bouillon (1706-1772).

31. *Sulzbach:* The village of Sulzbach, now Soultzbach-les-Bains, near Colmar in Alsace, enjoyed a certain reputation as a watering place in the 18th century because of its mineral springs.

32. *Schaumbourg:* The Lotharingian family of Schaumbourg had several branches, so it is impossible to identify the person to whom C. refers.

33. *Woman . . . by the name of Salzmann:* Possibly a member of the well-known Strassburg family of Salzmann. However,

since the original ms. of this chapter has not been preserved, it is not known if C. actually wrote "Salzmann." Schütz gives her name only as "Madame S."; and Laforgue, who here calls her "Salzmann," calls her "Madame Saxe" in the following chapter.

CHAPTER IV

1. *Piquet:* Card game for 2 players, played with 32 cards.
2. *D'Entragues:* Possibly a certain Pierre Louis d'Entraigues du Pin (born 1740), whose name appears in the police records of Paris for the year 1772.
3. *Noon . . . at eleven o'clock:* For this anomaly, which was ordered to be corrected toward the end of the 18th century but which lingered on into the 19th, see Vol. 6, Chap. X, especially n. 58.
4. *Porrentruy:* Georg Joseph Wilhelm Aloys, Freiherr Rink von Baldenstein (1704-1762), Prince-Bishop of Basel from 1744; bore the title "Prince de Porrentruy" from the town of Porrentruy in the Swiss Jura.
5. *Madness . . . home again:* This alleged characteristic is mentioned by no other contemporary source.
6. *Count B.:* Not identified.
7. *St. Lawrence:* According to tradition, St. Lawrence suffered martyrdom in Rome in 258 by being roasted to death on a hot griddle. The church in which he was buried, San Lorenzo fuori le mura, is one of the 7 principal churches of Rome.
8. *D'Aranda:* See this volume, Chap. III, n. 5. D'Aranda was clearly not yet in Basel at this time. Madame d'Urfé owned a house on the Place Bellecour in Lyons.
9. *Franche-Comté:* One of the provinces of France under the Old Régime; its capital was Besançon.
10. *Vetturino:* In the 18th century, travel was cheaper than by post if one engaged the services of a *vetturino,* who supplied the coach and saw to the hiring of the horses, obtained food and lodging for the travelers, and so on. He was paid according to the terms of a contract made beforehand.
11. *Raiberti:* See Vol. 7, Chap. XII, n. 30.
12. *Syndic:* See Vol. 6, Chap. X.
13. *House . . . Ferney:* From 1760 Voltaire resided at Ferney,

some 5 miles north of Geneva. He let the Duke of Villars have his house "Les Délices" in Geneva in the winter of 1762-63.

14. *I do not intend to visit him:* C. bore Voltaire a grudge because the latter had pronounced C.'s translation of his comedy *Le Café ou l'Écossaise* bad (cf. Vol. 7, Chap. V, *passim*, and *ibid.*, n. 21).

15. *Madame Lebel:* C.'s housekeeper in Soleure, Madame Dubois, was married in 1760 to Monsieur Lebel, major-domo to the French Ambassador in Soleure (cf. especially Vol. 6, Chaps. VI and VII). The names "Lebel" and "Dubois" are both fictitious.

16. *Pogomas . . . Passano:* See Vol. 7, Chap. VII, n. 6.

17. *M. F.:* See Vol. 7, Chap. VII, n. 11.

18. *The beautiful theologian:* Cf. Vol. 6, Chap. IX. Here C. gives her the obviously fictitious name Hedwig; she was probably Anne Marie May (born 1731), who later married a certain Gabriel von Wattenwyl.

19. *Agnes:* C. later gives her name as Helena; he uses Agnes here generically in allusion to St. Agnes, the martyred virgin the symbol of whose innocence is a lamb.

20. *My cousin, the pastor's niece:* I.e., Hedwig, "the beautiful theologian" (cf. n. 18, above).

21. *Helena:* The name is doubtless fictitious. She has not been identified.

22. *D'Harcourt:* Perhaps François Henri d'Harcourt (1726-1794).

23. *Ximénès:* The Marquis Augustin Louis de Ximénès (1726-1817), of Spanish descent but born in Paris; he was Voltaire's secretary for a time.

24. Cf. Matthew 24:36.

25. *Futurity:* Text, "*futurité*," a word which does not exist in French.

26. Horace, *Satires*, I, 9, 70-71. Properly, "I am without scruples"; but D'Harcourt seems to quote it, and Hedwig to take it, as a reference to religion.

27. *Amphidromia:* Ancient Attic festival at which, on the 5th, 7th, or 10th day after its birth, the infant was adopted into its family by being carried around the hearth, and was commended to the care of the gods and named.

28. *Chavigny:* See Vol. 7, Chap. VIII, n. 12.

29. *Madame de . . . :* Probably the Baroness Marie Anne Louise Roll von Emmenholtz (cf. Vol. 6, Chap. IV, nn. 21 and 22, and *ibid.*, Chaps. V-VII).

30. *My ring . . . her wedding ring:* See Vol. 6, Chap. IX.

31. *Twenty-one years hence:* C. died before reaching that date in his memoirs.

32. *Tronchin's . . . house:* Probably a small château in Louis XV style on the Lake of Geneva, which in 1762 belonged to Tronchin's intimate friend J. L. Labat. Now named "Mon Repos," it is owned by the city of Geneva, which has turned it into a small museum.

33. *Naiads:* The water nymphs of Greek mythology.

34. *The word:* Allusion to the opening sentence of St. John's Gospel: "In the beginning was the word. . . ." C. has previously used "word" in this sense in Vol. 5, Chap. V.

35. *The passage:* See Genesis 2:17 ff.

36. *Hobbes:* Thomas Hobbes (1588-1679), English philosopher.

37. *Neuchâtel:* Town in western Switzerland, on the lake of the same name, the shores of which produce excellent grapes.

38. *At Cologne on a like occasion:* Cf. Vol. 6, Chap. II.

39. *Rosa . . . Orio:* Marco Niccolò Rosa (born 1687), Venetian advocate, married the widow Caterina Orio, née Bianchi, at some date after 1741. C. refers to events recounted in Vol. 1, Chap. V.

40. *Signora Orio's nieces:* The Countesses Nanetta and Marta (Marton) Savorgnan (cf. Vol. 1, Chap. V).

41. *Clement of Alexandria:* Titus Flavius Clemens (2nd-3rd century), Father of the Church; his dictum on modesty, which he discusses in Books II and III of his *Paidagogos*, was cited once before by C. (cf. Vol. 6, Chap. X).

42. *Medicean Venus:* The statue is now in the Uffizi in Florence.

43. *The Aretine's postures:* Pietro Aretino (1492-1556), celebrated satirist of the Italian Renaissance. The by-name Aretino comes from his birthplace Arezzo. His 35 "Sonetti lussuriosi" were composed for engravings by Raimondi after drawings by Giulio Romano.

44. *They did not have to wait so long:* C. apparently did re-

turn to Geneva late in 1762, but he does not recount his stay there in the memoirs.

45. *Bresse:* District of France northeast of Lyons.

46. *Gualdo:* Federico Gualdo resided in Venice as a Rosicrucian about 1680; he is said to have vanished from that city in 1688 at the age of 90. He was probably of German origin and named Friedrich Walter.

47. *Madame Pernon:* Her husband was a prominent textile manufacturer in Lyons. Seven letters from him to C. were found at Dux.

48. *Bono:* Giuseppe Bono (died 1780), resided in Lyons from 1756 as a silk merchant and banker.

49. *Sacco:* Nothing further is known of him.

50. *Her young boarder:* See Vol. 7, Chap. XIII.

51. *The beginning of December:* There is documentary evidence that C. arrived in Turin by the middle of Sept. 1762, perhaps even earlier, and remained there until his expulsion in Nov. of that year.

52. *Rivoli:* A small town, then belonging to the Kingdom of Sardinia, a few miles north of Turin on the road to the Mont Cenis and France.

CHAPTER V

1. *Chapter V:* The hiatus in C.'s manuscript described in note 1 to Chap. I of this volume, together with the consequent substitution of Laforgue's text, ends at this point.

2. *D'Aglié:* Vicario (Police Prefect) of Turin; see Vol. 7, Chap. XIII, n. 7.

3. *Pacienza:* Not identified; the name can be either a surname or a given name.

4. *Dupré:* Probably Jean Denis Dupré (1706-1782), who appeared as a dancer at the opera in Turin until 1754 and may well have been employed by the Teatro Carignano afterward.

5. *Vicario:* See note 2, above.

6. *Ossorio:* See Vol. 7, Chap. XIII, n. 6.

7. *Passano:* See Vol. 7, Chap. VII, n. 6.

8. *Vittorina:* Girl in the employ of the milliner R.; see Vol. 7, Chap. XII.

9. *La R.:* Milliner; see Vol. 7, Chap. XII.

10. *Nostitz:* See note 1 to Chap. III of this volume.

11. *Martin:* Pierre Henri Martin, banker in Turin; about 1758 he married a woman much younger than himself.

12. *Moses:* See Vol. 7, Chap. XII, *passim*, and *ibid.*, n. 20.

13. *Caton:* C. does not mention her name in his account of his previous stay in Turin (cf. Vol. 7, Chap. XII).

14. *La Pérouse:* See Vol. 7, Chap. XII, n. 40.

15. *La Mazzoli:* See Vol. 7, Chap. XII, n. 29.

16. *Order of the White Eagle:* Said to have been founded in 1321 by King Vladislav V of Poland, it was reinstituted in 1713 by King Augustus II, transferred to Russia in 1815, and conferred until 1917.

17. *Borromeo:* Count Federico Borromeo (1703-1779), son of Carlo, Viceroy of Naples (1657-1734). He was given the Order of the White Eagle in 1736, probably on the ground that his father had shown hospitality to the King of Poland.

18. *A. B.:* Giuseppe, Count Attendolo-Bolognini (died 1776), member of an impoverished noble family of Lombardy.

19. *Borromean Islands:* The Borromean Islands, in Lake Maggiore, belonged to the Viceroy of Naples, Carlo Borromeo. The island now called "Isola Bella" was formerly called "Isola Isabella," after the wife of a Count Borromeo; its celebrated palace and gardens were built in 1637.

20. *Looking her up and down:* The text has simply: *"Toutes les danseuses mésuraient,"* which seems to require some complement; the most likely one is furnished by La Corticelli.

21. *Agata:* Obviously C.'s invented name for a dancer in Turin, probably the one who later married the advocate Aniello Orcivolo, of Naples.

22. *Teatro Carignano:* The theater was built in 1752 by the uncle of the famous dramatist Benedetto Alfieri and was several times altered; it still exists. In C.'s day it chiefly housed French companies.

23. *Redegonda:* See Vol. 7, Chap. VII, n. 8.

24. *Chauvelin:* François Claude, Marquis de Chauvelin (1716-1773), French commander, Ambassador in Genoa from 1747 to 1753 and in Turin from 1754 to 1765; friend of Louis XV

and Voltaire. For C.'s earlier acquaintance with him, see Vol. 6, especially Chap. VI.

25. *His charming wife:* Chauvelin had married Agnès Thérèse Mazade in 1758.

26. *Imberti:* Giuseppe Imberti, Secretary of the Venetian Senate in 1754 and Venetian Resident in Turin from 1762 to 1765.

27. *No children:* Count Attendolo-Bolognini was married to Countess Teresa Zuazo y Ovalla Zamorra (ca. 1738-1826). Twins (Matilda and Raimondo) were born to the couple in 1762, but must have died before 1763.

28. *In Milan:* There is documentary evidence that C. visited Geneva and then Turin in 1762, being expelled from the latter city in Nov. of that year. He then visited Geneva and Chambéry again, but in Jan. 1763 returned to Turin and thence traveled directly to Milan. He obviously confuses his numerous stays in these various cities.

29. *Alençon point:* The laces from Alençon (Normandy) and Valenciennes were the most highly esteemed and the most expensive at the time.

30. *Girandoles:* A kind of earring with small stones grouped about a larger one.

31. *Pernon:* See note 48 to Chap. IV of this volume.

32. *Lord Percy:* Hugh, Baron Warkworth (1742-1817), from 1766 Earl Percy, from 1786 Duke of Northumberland; English statesman. His mother was Elizabeth, Countess Percy (ca. 1716-1776), from 1766 Duchess of Northumberland.

33. *Marquise de Prié:* Gabriella Turinetti, Marquise de Prié (1739-1780), married in 1761 to Giovanni Antonio II Turinetti, Marquis de Prié (Priero) et Pancalieri (1717-1781), celebrated adventurer and gambler. For C.'s earlier acquaintance with him, see Vols. 6 and 7.

34. *Villa Faletta:* Cavaliere Faletti di Villa Faletta, brother of the Marquise de Prié.

35. *Twelfth Night:* As his correspondence shows, C. was in Turin in Jan. 1763.

36. *Saint-Gilles:* Caterina Maria Teresa, Countess Vignati di San Gillio, known as "Madame de Saint-Gilles" (ca. 1715-1800). Her salon in Turin was celebrated in C.'s time. For her husband, see Vol. 7, Chap. XII, n. 35.

37. *In manuscript:* No such manuscript has been found.

38. Ariosto, *Orlando furioso,* XXVI, 70, 5-8.

CHAPTER VI

1. *Two . . . Marchese Q.:* The original gives *"Les deux belles Marquises Q.";* in the course of the chapter, however, it appears that there is only one Marchesa Q., her cousin being the Marchesa F.

2. *Alessandria:* Piedmontese town, some 60 miles east of Turin. In 1763 it had only one theater, in the palace of the Marchese Filippo Guasco Gallarati di Solero, on whom the town had conferred the monopoly of theatrical performances. The Teatro Municipale was not built until 1772-1775.

3. *Zecchino:* Here the Piedmontese zecchino, first coined under Charles Emmanuel III, King of Sardinia, in the mint (Italian, *zecca*) at Turin.

4. *A written engagement:* C. coins the neologism *"scripturer,"* after Italian *"scripturare"* ("to engage in writing").

5. *Peace having been made:* The preliminary negotiations toward ending the Seven Years' War began on Nov. 3, 1762, in Fontainebleau. The Peace of Paris between France, Spain, and England was signed on Feb. 10, 1763, the Peace of Hubertusburg between Austria, Prussia, and Saxony on Feb. 15th of the same year.

6. *His mother the Duchess:* See note 32 to the preceding chapter.

7. *A. B.:* Giuseppe, Count Attendolo-Bolognini; see note 18 to the preceding chapter.

8. *Greppi:* Antonio Greppi (died 1799), man of affairs in the service of Archduke Ferdinand of Austria and later of Duke Francesco III of Modena; farmer-general in Milan; in 1778 he was ennobled as a count.

9. *Valet . . . Franche-Comté:* See Chap. IV of this volume, and *ibid.,* n. 9.

10. *Rosignano:* Doubtless a brother of the Marchese Grissella di Rosignano (cf. note 13 to this chapter).

11. *Casale:* Casale Monferrato, Piedmontese town, some 40 miles east of Turin. The direct road from Turin to Milan runs through Novara.

12. *Beware . . . only one book:* C. has already quoted this proverb (on that occasion in Italian) in Vol. 4, Chap. XIII.

13. *Grissella:* The Marchese (not Count) Grissella (Grisela) di Rosignano was the Sardinian Ambassador in Berlin from 1775 to 1778.

14. *Marchesa Corti:* She was the mother of the Marchese Cesare Corti (1740-1792), an officer in the Austrian service; in 1790 he was made a Major-General.

15. *Here . . . 1786:* In 1786 C. had recently arrived at Dux, where he began to write his memoirs about 1789.

16. Horace, *Odes,* I, 4, 15, where the text has *"spem . . . longam"* instead of C.'s *"spes . . . longas."*

17. *Belcredi:* This may be (1) the Marchese Carlo Belcredi (ca. 1706-1768), of Milan; or (2) the Marchese Francesco Belcredi (1696-1786), his brother; or (3) the Marchese Francesco Belcredi, a jurist in Pavia.

18. *Basili:* Nothing more is known of this officer.

19. *Carthusian monastery:* The celebrated Certosa di Pavia, some miles north of the city on the road to Milan; founded in 1396 by Galeazzo Visconti, it was one of the most important monasteries in Italy; the façade of its church makes it an outstanding example of Italian Renaissance ecclesiastical architecture.

20. *San Giovanni in Conca:* Carmelite church and monastery in the Piazza Missori. Legend attributed its foundation to St. Castriziano, Archbishop of Milan, early in the 2nd century; it was secularized at the beginning of the 19th century, and later was taken over as a church by the Waldenses.

21. *Milanese lire:* The lira Milanese was a silver coin minted from 1474 to 1778; value, 20 soldi of 12 denari.

22. *Gros de Tours:* A heavy silk fabric, originally woven in Tours but in the 18th century also produced in Turin, Florence, and Lyons, these several cities specializing in particular patterns and colors. Red silks came almost exclusively from Lyons.

23. *Agata:* In the ms. a name, crossed out so heavily as to be illegible, is replaced by "Agata," which would seem to show that C. used the latter to conceal the dancer's real name.

24. *Triulzi:* Probably the Marchese Carlo Triulzi, or Trivulzi (ca. 1719-1789), Abate, antiquarian, and well-known art col-

lector. There was also a Marchese Giorgio Teodoro Triulzi
(1728-1802), but he was not in orders. In an extant letter
the Countess Attendolo-Bolognini addresses the Marchese as
"Monsignore," a title reserved for high ecclesiastical digni-
taries.

25. *Prince Triulzi:* Probably an adventurer who used the name.

26. *The opera:* Opera was performed in the Regio Ducal
Teatro (Teatro Ducale), which was built in 1717 as part of
the ducal palace but was destroyed by fire in 1776. The first
performances of some of Gluck's and Mozart's operas were
given there. The celebrated Milanese opera house, the Teatro
della Scala, was not opened until 1778. In C.'s day there was
a well-known gaming room in the Teatro Ducale.

27. *Teresa Palesi:* See Vol. 7, Chap. VII, nn. 22 and 25, and
ibid., Chap. III.

28. *Zenobia:* Nothing is known of her except what C. relates.

29. *Greppi:* He was ennobled in 1778 (cf. note 8 to this chapter).

30. *Barbaro:* Marco Barbaro (born after 1719), son of the
Venetian patrician and Senator Bernardo Barbaro by his
second marriage; since his mother, Andriana Biasciutti, was
not of patrician birth, the names of Marco and his brother
Angelo are not included in the registers of patricians. Marco
Barbaro had incurred the disfavor of the State Inquisitors
and was living in Milan, but was pardoned in 1768. He was
Cornelia Gritti's half-brother, not her brother. C. does not
mention him in his account of the year preceding his imprisonment (Vols. 3 and 4).

31. *Signora Gritti:* Cornelia Gritti, née Barbaro (ca. 1719-
1808), Venetian poetess, friend of Goldoni, Metastasio, and
Algarotti, member of the Arcadian Academy under the name
"Aurisbe Tarsense." Married to Zuan Antonio Gritti in 1736.

32. *Gritti Sgombro:* Zuan Antonio (called "Sgombro") Gritti
(1702-1768), Venetian patrician; he was banished to Cattaro
and died there.

33. *Cattaro:* Cattaro was an important port on the Dalmatian
coast; from the 15th century to 1797 it belonged to the Republic of Venice, which fortified it. It is now Kotor, in Yugo-
slavia.

34. Cf. Vol. 4, Chap. I.

35. *Duke of Modena:* Duke Francesco III Maria d'Este; from 1753, as Duke of Modena, he had the title "Imperial and Royal Administrator of the Government and Captaincy-General of Austrian Lombardy."

36. *Carcano:* Probably Count Francesco Carcano (1733-1794), well-known gambler and poet, member of the Arcadian Academy under the name of "Floreno Corcirense."

37. *Prince Palatine of Russia:* Prince August Aleksander Czartoryski (1697-1782). See Vol. 7, Chap. IX, n. 49.

38. *Ruined it . . . make it greater:* After the death of King Augustus III (1763), Prince Czartoryski sent Count Stanislas Poniatowski to St. Petersburg to bring him back the Polish crown. However, Poniatowski very soon became the favorite of the Czarina Catherine II and made himself King of Poland, as Stanislas II Augustus in 1764. But in 1795, after being forced to take part in the partitions of Poland in 1772, 1793, and 1795, he had to abdicate.

39. *"Bankruptcy":* Text, *"banque route."* No game by this name is known.

CHAPTER VII

1. *Chapter VII:* At the top of the corresponding page in his ms., C. made the notation, "Ch. 3, ch. 4, ch. 5 *antecedentibus sublatis*" ("The former chaps. 3, 4, 5 have been suppressed"). As before, however (cf. Vol. 7, Chap. XII, n. 1, and Chap. XIII, n. 1), there is no discernible break in the narrative.

2. *Menafoglio:* The Marchesa Cristina Menafoglio, née Marchesina Ghilini, of Alessandria, married to the Marchese Antonio Menafoglio ca. 1762.

3. *Cascina dei Pomi:* Name of a group of old houses some miles from Milan in the village of Greco Milanese; now part of the city of Milan. In C.'s time it was a favorite place for excursions, as well as a resort of beggars and criminals. *Cascina* means cheese-dairy or dairy farm. Cf. Vol 2, Chap. X, n. 24.

4. *Quadruple:* Another name for the doblon, a Spanish gold coin worth 4 pistoles. It circulated in Milan, since Lombardy

was a dependency of the Spanish Crown. C. here uses it interchangeably with doblon de a ocho (for which see Vol. 7, Chap. II, n. 31).

5. *Venetian zecchini:* The Venetian zecchino was a gold coin worth 22 lire. There were also Milanese, Florentine, Roman, and Genoese zecchini.

6. *Deceased Elector of Cologne:* Clemens August, Elector of Cologne, died in 1761. For his gift to C. of his portrait, see Vol. 6, Chap. II.

7. *Messer Grande:* Title of the Venetian Prefect of Police; allusion to C.'s arrest and imprisonment in the Leads.

8. *Furlana:* A lively dance, originally from the Venetian province of Friuli.

9. *"Three Kings":* Well-known inn at the time, in the street of the same name (Via dei Tre Re), later Via di Tre Alberghi.

10. *"Extinguisher" position:* One of the so-called "thirty-nine positions" for sexual intercourse.

11. *Gossip:* C.'s sponsorship of the marriage of Zenobia and the tailor had established the spiritual relationship of "gossip" (*compere, comere*) among them.

12. *Countess Rinaldi:* Wife of Count Rinaldi, for whom see note 17, below. For C.'s earlier encounter with them, see Vol. 2, Chap. VIII.

13. *Zawoiski:* Count Gaetan Zawoiski (1725-1788), career officer, from 1765 court marshal to Clemens Wenzeslaus of Saxony, Elector of Trier, from ca. 1772 his envoy in Dresden (cf. Vol. 2, Chap. VIII).

14. *Castelletto:* Il Castelletto was the name of a group of houses in the parish of San Matteo in the Rialto quarter of Venice; the inn (*locanda*) to which C. refers was named after it (cf. Vol. 2, Chap. VIII, n. 8).

15. *Bragadin . . . cards:* See Vol. 2, Chap. VIII.

16. *Irene:* Irene Rinaldi (died after 1790), probably Irene Balzali, though Balzali may be not her maiden but her married name; Italian actress who is known to have appeared in Padua in 1779 and in Vienna in 1790.

17. *Count Rinaldi:* Died before 1774, adventurer and professional gambler; both the name and the title are probably assumed.

18. *Pinchbeck:* An alloy of copper and zinc, used to imitate

gold; named from its English inventor, Christopher Pinchbeck (died 1732).

19. *Austrian uniform:* The Duchy of Milan, from 1540 under
the rule of the Spanish Hapsburgs, became an Austrian
possession at the end of the War of the Spanish Succession
in 1713 and, except during 2 brief periods, remained so until
1859. Italy did not become an independent nation until 1860.

20. *All Counts:* Cf. Vol. 3, Chap. XVI, n. 17.

21. *A dancer . . . Mantua:* The reference is to the episode
with Marina, recounted in Vol. 2, Chap. X.

22. *O'Neilan:* Baron Franz O'Neilan (1729-1757), officer in the
Austrian army (cf. especially Vol. 2, Chap. X).

23. *English lace:* Bobbin lace made in England after Flemish
patterns and considered inferior in the 18th century.

24. *Sant'Angelo:* Now Sant'Angelo Lodigiano, southeast of
Milan.

25. *Sharpers:* C. uses "Grec" ("Greek"), in its slang meaning
of "cardsharper" (cf. Vol. 2, Chap. II, n. 12).

26. *La Bontemps:* Jeanne Marguerite Deshayes, née Leblanc,
known as "La Bontemps," celebrated fortuneteller at the
period; among her patrons were Madame de Pompadour and
the Abbé de Bernis.

27. *Priapus:* Antique fertility god, probably of Near Eastern
origin; during the 3rd century B.C. his cult spread from the
vicinity of the Hellespont through the Greek and Roman
worlds. He was represented with an enormous phallus.

28. *Zecchini:* C. writes "ducats," though he has previously
given the sum as 12 zecchini; the two coins were of approximately equal value.

CHAPTER VIII

1. *In the city:* Here C. first wrote *"dans toute la noblesse"*
("in the entire nobility"), then crossed it out and substituted
"dans cette ville."

2. *Pierrot:* French adaptation of one of the typical figures of
the Italian *commedia dell'arte.* He wore a loose white upper
garment and loose white trousers and daubed his face with

flour. To a certain extent he resembled the traditional circus clown.

3. *Ten years earlier . . . Pierrot:* The reference is to the Carnival ball in the convent visiting room, which C. gave for M. M. and C. C. (see Vol. 4, Chap. V).

4. *Teresa:* C. first wrote a name beginning with "Cal" (the following letters are illegible), then crossed it out and substituted "Thérèse" (cf. note 12 to this chapter).

5. *Piazza Cordusio:* It still exists, by the same name, between the Piazza del Duomo and the Largo Cairoli; in other words, between the cathedral and the castle of the Sforzas.

6. *Ambo:* In the Italian type of lottery, or Lotto Genovese, betting that 2 particular numbers would be drawn out of 90.

7. *Spinola:* Carlo Spinola, Count of Ronco (died after 1783), of Genoa; he was for a time Genoese Ambassador in Vienna, later in London.

8. *Four days longer . . . Christendom:* In Milan the Carnival did not end on Ash Wednesday but on the Saturday of Carnival week.

9. Already quoted by C. in Vol. 5, Chap. IX.

10. *My sister:* Up to this point C. has represented the 2 Marchese as being cousins. Their appearance in this passage as sisters can perhaps be attributed to his tendency to preserve the anonymity of his sweethearts.

11. *Venetian point lace:* The first European point lace was made in Venice, whence its patterns spread to France.

12. *Teresa's:* Here again C. first wrote a name beginning with "Ca" and ending with "i" (the 2 or 3 intervening letters are illegible), crossed it out, and substituted "Thérèse" (cf. note 4 to this chapter).

13. *Croce:* Antonio Croce, an adventurer, who also appears under the name Della Croce, De la Croix, Marchese di Santa Croce, and Crosin or Crozin. C. first wrote a now illegible name, which was perhaps Crosin or Crozin, crossed it out, and substituted "Croce." For C.'s earlier relations with him, see Vol. 3, Chaps. XV and XVI.

14. *De la Croix:* The French girl, writing to C. in French (for, as later appears, she does not know Italian), naturally uses the French form of Croce's name.

15. *Bawd:* C. writes *"maq. . . . . . ."* (for *"maquerelle"*).

CHAPTER IX

1. *S. A.:* Sant'Angelo; though he wrote the name in full in the preceding chapter, C. here and in the sequel uses only its initial letters. The "Castel Sant'Angelo sul Lombra," in the present town of Sant'Angelo Lodigiano, was famous for having figured in the Battle of Pavia (1525) between the Emperor Charles V and François I of France; it was destroyed by fire in 1911.

2. *Gothic:* C., like his contemporaries, uses the word not to designate the Gothic style of architecture but as the equivalent of "non-classical," hence "barbaric."

3. *Another brother:* Count Sforza Attendolo-Bolognini (died 1774), officer in the Spanish service, married to the Spanish noblewoman Doña Antonia Fons de Prado Hortado y Mendoza (born 1712), who is said to have died in Sant'Angelo at the age of 110 years.

4. *Walloon Guards:* In the 18th century the Spanish army consisted of some 40 regiments, a quarter of which were foreign troops, among them three Walloon regiments known as the *"petits wallons"* in distinction from the *"gardes wallons,"* an élite corps in the service of the King.

5. *Count Ambrosio:* Paolo, Count Attendolo-Bolognini, known as Count Ambrosio (1723-1792).

6. *The Countess:* Onorata, Countess Attendolo-Bolognini, daughter of the patrician Fabrizio Gandini, of Lodi, married to Count Ambrosio in 1757.

7. *Infant of six months:* Two sons, Luigi and Matteo, are documented, but they were not born until 1769 and 1770; the couple also had a daughter named Vittoria, who died in 1803. C. may be referring to her, or to a child who died early.

8. *Mascarpone cheese:* This cheese is a specialty of Lombardy.

9. *Clementina:* Angela Gandini, daughter of the patrician Fabrizio Gandini, of Lodi; she married Count Bassano Nipoti after 1763.

10. Altered from Juvenal, *Satires*, X, 22 (where the text has *"cantabit"*).

11. *The Countess Eleonora:* Fulvia Gandini, sister of Angela (see note 9, above); she became a nun after 1763.

12. *Firmian:* Karl Gotthold, Count Firmian (1716-1782), Austrian diplomat; from 1759 Governor of Milan.

13. *Pozzobonelli:* Giuseppe Pozzobonelli (1696-1783), of the family of the Marchesi di Arluno, Archbishop of Milan; Cardinal from 1743.

14. *The Ambrosian rite:* The Ambrosian rite of liturgy goes back, as its name indicates, to St. Ambrose, who died in Milan in 397. It differs from the Roman liturgy in its responses and anthems, which may be regarded as precursors of the Gregorian chant. It is still used in the Archdiocese of Milan.

15. *Maria Maddalena:* This nun has not been identified.

16. *Hebe:* In Greek mythology Hebe, daughter of Zeus and Hera, was the goddess of eternal youth and the cupbearer of the gods, for whom she poured nectar. She lost her office by falling and dropping a cup. After the death of Hercules, who was given a place among the gods, she became his wife.

17. *Canon Regular:* Designation of a member of certain Roman Catholic orders, for example the Augustinians.

18. *Knight . . . Laterano:* Persons decorated with the order of the Golden Spur had the title "Comites Palatini Lateranenses" (see Vol. 7, Chap. IX, nn. 43 and 47).

19. *"The Fleece":* The order of the Golden Fleece was founded by Duke Philip the Good of Burgundy in 1429; it survived in Austria-Hungary until 1918, in Spain until 1931.

20. *The order of Christ:* It was founded in 1318 by King Dionysius of Portugal and took the place of the order of the Temple, dissolved in 1312. The Pope, who confirmed the new order in 1319, reserved the right to name new knights to it. It was secularized in 1797.

21. *Most Faithful Majesty:* See Vol. 7, Chap. VIII, n. 3.

22. *Order of the Red Eagle:* Founded by Georg Wilhelm, Hereditary Prince of Bayreuth, in 1705, but taken over by Prussia in 1792.

23. *St. Michael:* The order of St. Michael was founded in 1693 by Joseph Clemens, Elector of Cologne and Duke of Bavaria; in 1777 it passed to Bavaria.

24. *Pays de Vaud:* Now the Canton of Vaud, in western Switzerland.

25. *Did not know them:* Since members of the nobility were given a great many Christian names at baptism and were usually addressed in society by the particle of nobility and the name of their estate, C.'s statement is perhaps no exaggeration.

26. *Herrnhuter:* A Protestant sect which derived from the Moravian Brotherhood (cf. Vol. 6, Chap. II, n. 5).

27. *Anabaptist:* A member of a Protestant sect which originated in Zurich ca. 1523. It suffered severe persecution.

28. *Fall so awkwardly:* See note 16 to this chapter.

29. *Ganymede:* A beautiful youth who was translated to Olympus to succeed Hebe as cupbearer of the gods.

30. *Hercules:* After his death Hercules (Heracles), the son of Zeus and Alcmena, wife of King Amphytrion, was made a god and lived on Olympus with Hebe as his wife; she bore him 2 sons.

31. *Iolaus:* Hercules' nephew and his charioteer; Iolaus helped him to overcome the Lernean Hydra. At Hercules' request Hebe gave him eternal youth. Like most authors of the period, C. uses a mixture of the Greek and Roman names of the gods (Hercules for Heracles, Jupiter for Zeus).

32. *Sardini:* No poet by this name is known.

33. *Studies in rhetoric:* Education in the 18th century was still based on the medieval division of disciplines. The basic studies were grammar, rhetoric, and dialectics.

34. *An Anacreontic song:* Lyrics in praise of love, wine, the dance, and social festivities were so designated, after the Greek poet Anacreon (6th-5th century B.C.), though many of the poems attributed to him in C.'s time were not by Anacreon himself but by his many imitators.

35. *Lodi:* Some 8 miles from Sant'Angelo Lodigiano.

36. *Parmesan:* Parmesan cheese, named after the city of Parma, is the best-known northern Italian hard cheese. It was and still is made not only in the vicinity of Parma but also around Lodi and, at the present day, in a considerable part of the Po valley. The cheese from Parma (*cacio parmigiano*) is softer and has a greater fat content than that from Lodi (*cacio lodigiano*).

37. *J. J.:* Abbreviation of Jean Jacques (Rousseau). C. here confuses two facts. In 1771 and 1772 Rousseau worked on a "Dictionnaire de Botanique" which he left unfinished; it was published in 1781, under Rousseau's name. Renaud le Botaniste is obviously a certain Regnault, who published an introduction to botany from 1769 to 1774. Rousseau criticized this work severely in marginal notes, which, however, were not published until the beginning of the 19th century. It is possible that C. had learned of the existence of Rousseau's marginal notes.

38. *Orlando furioso:* Epic poem in 46 books by Lodovico Ariosto, published in its final form in 1532 and one of the masterpieces of European Renaissance literature.

39. *Eulogy . . . Voltaire:* In his essay on epic poetry (*Essai sur la poésie épique*), published in 1726, Voltaire had ranked Tasso far above Ariosto. The praise to which C. refers is principally expressed in the article "Épopée" in Voltaire's *Dictionnaire philosophique* (1764).

40. *Palinode:* A song or ode in which the poet recants or retracts something he had said in an earlier one.

41. *A great curtain . . . refrained from drawing:* The reference, which C. seems purposely to have left obscure, is probably to Voltaire's attacks on "superstition," for which C. takes him to task in Vol. 6, Chap. X (see especially pp. 244-245 of the present translation, where "cursed" [p. 245, l. 2] is a typographical error for "crushed"); what Voltaire failed to "foresee" is the French Revolution.

42. C. may here be citing one of the surviving fragments of the comic playwright Statius Caecilius (fl. 200 B.C.), or possibly he is parodying the famous Plautine *Lupus homo homi-nis* ("Man is a wolf to man") (*Asinaria*, II, 4, 88).

43. *Wolff:* Christian, Freiherr von Wolff (1679-1754), German philosopher, propounder of a rationalistic system.

44. *Tasso's Aminta:* Drama by Torquato Tasso (1544-1595), first performed at Ferrara in 1573, and one of the greatest masterpieces of the pastoral genre in European literature. Its hero is named Aminta.

45. The *Pastor fido:* Pastoral drama ("The Faithful Shepherd") by Giovanni Battista Guarini (1538-1612), written in emulation of Tasso's *Aminta* and first performed in 1585.

It long challenged the supremacy of the *Aminta* and served as the libretto for several operas in the 18th century; modern taste, however, awards the palm to Tasso's play.

46. *Homer . . . Andromache . . . Hector . . . army:* C. refers to Homer, *Iliad*, VI, 466 ff.

47. *Thirteenth book of Vergil's Aeneid:* Maffeo Vegio (1406-1458), of Lodi, Italian humanist, author of an essay on education, also composed a continuation of Vergil's *Aeneid* (*Supplementum Aeneidos*, 1485).

48. *Italian stanzas:* That is, the Italian stanza par excellence, the *ottava rima*, consisting of 8 hendecasyllables rhyming abababcc. Nothing is known of the translation referred to.

49. *Translation . . . by . . . Caro:* Annibale Caro (1507-1566) published his celebrated blank-verse translation of the *Aeneid* (*L'Eneide di Virgilio recata in versi italiani*) in 1581; he was also famous as a poet in his own right.

50. *Dell'Anguillara:* Giovanni Andrea Dell'Anguillara (1517-1572), Italian man of letters; in addition to his translation of Ovid's *Metamorphoses* (1561), he published one of the first two books of the *Aeneid*.

51. *Marchetti:* Alessandro Marchetti (1633-1714) composed a celebrated Italian translation of Lucretius's *De rerum natura*; it was published posthumously (London, 1717).

52. Cf. Vergil, *Aeneid*, IV, 165-172.

53. Vergil, *Aeneid*, IV, 328-329.

CHAPTER X

1. *Hebe . . . Corinth:* Nothing is known of a temple of Hebe at Corinth.

2. *Apollodoros:* Apollodoros of Athens, Greek polygrapher (2nd century B.C.). Since only fragments of his work remain, C. probably refers to the pseudo-Apollodorian *Bibliotheke* ("Library") of the 2nd century; however, a temple of Hebe at Corinth is not mentioned in that work.

3. *Poem . . . peasants:* No such work by Vegio is known.

4. *Mirtillo . . . Amarilli:* Mirtillo, the "faithful shepherd," is in love with Amarilli. The reference is to Act II, Scene 1.

5. *Cybele:* Phrygian fertility goddess, whose cult spread to

Greece; she was sometimes represented with a hundred breasts.

6. *Attis:* Or Atys, Cybele's divine lover.

7. *Diana of Ephesus:* In Asia Minor the cult of Cybele was partly combined with that of Artemis (Latin, Diana). The many-breasted statues of the Ephesian goddess are represented by a Roman copy in the National Museum, Naples, known as the "Diana of Ephesus."

8. *Terza rima:* Italian verse form used in continuous narration and consisting of tercets of hendecasyllables rhyming aba, bcb, cdc, and so on indefinitely, the final stanza having the pattern yzyy. It is the verse form of Dante's *Commedia*.

9. *Fontenelle:* Bernard Le Bovier de Fontenelle (1657-1757), celebrated writer and precursor of the Enlightenment. His *Entretiens sur la pluralité des mondes* (Paris, 1686) was the first attempt in modern times to put scientific material into literary form and so make it accessible to a general audience.

10. *Fiordispina . . . Bradamante:* See Ariosto, *Orlando furioso*, XXV, 27-70. Fiordispina has fallen in love with the beautiful Princess Bradamante, who is disguised as a knight errant. To escape her misdirected love, Bradamante flees. Bradamante's brother, Ricciardetto, returns to Fiordispina wearing Bradamante's armor and wins her love.

11. *Hebe's attributes:* Though mythologically unsubstantiated as attributes of Hebe, rose and green, as the colors of spring buds and leaves, seem appropriate to a goddess of youth.

12. *Arsenal:* The name was extended to the adjacent fishing port. Oysters from the Lagoon were highly esteemed. C. mentions them on several occasions as being served at choice repasts (e.g., Vol. 4, Chap. VII).

13. Horace, *Epistles*, I, 16, 79. C. quotes the passage several times.

14. Horace, *Odes*, I, 11, 8.

15. Horace, *Odes*, III, 29, 29–34.

16. *Love affrighted:* The Brockhaus-Plon edition here (Vol. 8, p. 273, line 18) gives *"L'amour charmé,"* which makes no sense in the context. On the assumption, supported by the occurrence of the word *"alarmé"* in the previous sentence, that an "al" in the ms. has been misread as "ch," the present

translator had emended to *"alarmé"* and translated accordingly. Again, it will be interesting to see what the very conditionally announced facsimile will show, if it ever appears.

17. *Marchesa di . . . . :* As the daughter of a patrician, Angela Gandini married Count Bassano Nipoti at some date after 1763.

18. *Signora Isolabella:* Member of a wealthy Genoese mercantile family.

19. *Bishop of Tortona:* Giuseppe Luigi Andujar (died 1783), Bishop of Tortona from 1743. The name "Andujar" is Spanish.

20. *Don Cesarino's bent:* He wanted to go to sea (cf. Chap. VII of this volume).

21. *Crosin:* The adventurer Croce used the name Crosin, among others.

22. *Tortona:* Some 60 miles south of Milan on the road to Genoa.

23. *"This is what I love":* "This" = the cross (of Christ) = French *la croix* = La Croix (the name of her lover), together making a blasphemous pun at which C. himself professed to be "rather surprised."

24. *Novi:* Novi Lighure, some 13 miles south of Tortona.

25. *Pogomas:* See Vol. 7, Chap. VII, n. 6, and this volume, Chap. VI, near the beginning.